The AMA Handbook of Supervisory Management

The AMA Handbook of Supervisory Management

Florence M. Stone, Editor

amacom

American Management Association

This book is available at a special
discount when ordered in bulk quantities.
For information, contact Special Sales Department,
AMACOM, a division of American Management Association,
135 West 50th Street, New York, NY 10020.

This publication is designed to provide accurate and authoritative information in regard to the subject matter covered. It is sold with the understanding that the publisher is not engaged in rendering legal, accounting, or other professional service. If legal advice or other expert assistance is required, the services of a competent professional person should be sought.

Library of Congress Cataloging-in-Publication Data

The AMA handbook of supervisory management /
Florence M. Stone, editor.
    p.   cm.
   Includes index.
   ISBN 0-8144-5972-2
   1. Supervision of employees. 2. Personnel management.
I. Stone, Florence M. II. American Management Association.
HF5549.A58   1989
658.3'02—dc20   89-45457
                                        CIP

Printing number

10 9 8 7 6 5 4 3 2 1

Contents

Preface

If you've opened this book, you're probably a manager who wants to become more effective at overseeing the work of others. It doesn't matter whether you work for a small or a large organization, whether it's a public organization or a private business, whether you're on the lowest rung of the management ladder or the highest. You recognize how complex work procedures and processes are becoming today and how important your ability as a supervisor is to succeeding in today's workplace. It doesn't matter how experienced you are. You know your ability to get work done through others can always be improved on.

That's the purpose of this book. The articles here appeared originally in *Supervisory Management,* a monthly publication of the American Management Association. They represent "the best of the best"—chosen for this collection through surveys of first-line supervisors, the people to whom they report, even the very top managers in organizations. These are the articles successful supervisors read and companies are encouraging their supervisors to study as they tie supervisory training to organizational strategy, mission, and values.

If you think of it, supervision isn't just one skill but a compendium of skills. This book is divided into 14 parts, each representing one of these skill areas. Together, they form a framework for supervisory success.

For example, planning, taken alone, is useless. One must organize and implement those plans and develop control systems to measure performance against plans and ensure their implementation. That means delegation skills. Which could also require training—or retraining—your staff.

Even before that, the right people must be hired *and* retained. Then comes communication, evaluating performance, coaching and counseling when problems arise, problem solving when a project runs into trouble, and teambuilding to ensure that everyone is pulling in the same direction. Conflicts may need to be resolved. Discipline may be called for. Time management becomes critical. And, of course, there's the need for leadership, perhaps the touchstone of the superior manager. Each of these skill areas is interrelated and must be mastered for you to succeed.

Developing a supervisory approach that is successful and comfortable for you is vital to your personal bottom line—your career. Companies are demanding so much more of their supervisors, and supervisors are becoming so much more visible. As a supervisor in today's workplace, you must operate with optimum effectiveness and efficiency.

We hope *The AMA Handbook of Supervisory Management* will help you do just that.

F.M.S.

Part I

CAREER MANAGEMENT

Gaining Acceptance as a New Supervisor

ANTHONY M. MICOLO

Moving from the rank and file to a supervisory position can be a difficult transition to make. Corporate philosophies, new responsibilities, different ideas, and changing attitudes inevitably come into play. Here are some ways to ease the move into management while building up respect for yourself in your new position as supervisor.

Relating to Subordinates

Always be receptive to your subordinates. Be quick to listen to your workers' problems, comments, feelings, and criticisms and weigh them accordingly. They may see situations in a different light than you do in your supervisory role. Besides, if you ignore the feedback from your subordinates, you will find that it will dwindle and, eventually, disappear.

Set a good example. Get to work on time, preferably a half hour early. It will help you to get a head start on your day. Do not take long lunches. If you do, why shouldn't your subordinates? Avoid gossip and rumors; they are unprofessional. Give credit where credit is due—your workers expect it, deserve it, and will appreciate it. Criticize only for just cause and only in a one-on-one setting; also criticize with the intent to educate and foster change, not with the intent to demean. In short, be the kind of worker that

Reprinted from *Supervisory Management,* June 1985

you expect your subordinates to be. Only then can you recommend changes or improvements in their behaviors, attitudes, and work performances. Simply stated: Practice what you preach to them.

Good Management Skills

Make yourself available to other supervisors. The more you can help your peers fulfill their needs, the more valuable you make yourself. Remember that you may need a favor or some help from them at some future point in time. Prepare for this contingency by helping whomever you can right now.

Strive to keep the promises that you make. If you promise a project's completion by a certain date, make sure it is done by then. If you promise a worker a raise at the beginning of the year, be sure that it goes through. The most important promises to keep are those that are meaningful to others: timely reports, fair performance appraisals, accurate production data, up-to-date turnover rates, and the like.

Keep track of what you are trying to accomplish. Maintain a weekly diary of top priorities: meetings to attend, people to contact, and projects that must be started or followed up. Always know where you are in terms of your responsibilities and accountabilities.

Inspire confidence in your abilities. Go out of your way to do your job as comprehensively as possible. Every extra hour after work, each lunch hour, and all the Saturdays you devote to your job will help you gain the reputation of being a hard worker. Few supervisors who do not put in extra time, effort, and energy ever advance beyond their present position. Do not build a career plateau for yourself by being a nine-to-five worker.

Never communicate without accurate backup data. When you are a part of a committee, or if you must submit a report, be sure to have foolproof backup material: statistics, surveys, experts' opinions, and/or research data. Your contribution will count for much more if you can prove that what you say is true. Facts are rarely disputed; however, opinions and feelings are easily discounted or overruled.

When you are wrong, do not try to pass the buck. Nothing will irk a boss more than pointing out to you an error you made and getting a feeble excuse in return. Accept the responsibility for your actions and learn from your mistakes. Few new supervisors will readily admit that they goofed. By doing so, you might make yourself vulnerable, but you will definitely gain respect from those people who count.

Accept accountability for your subordinates. There will be times when your subordinates will make a mistake that is going to reflect negatively on you and your department. Ducking responsibility and claiming that it is not your fault is not good enough. Go to your superior and accept the responsibility for the mistake, even if you did not do it. Remember: As a supervisor, you are accountable not only for your actions but also for the actions of your subordinates. By the same token, if one of your workers is falsely accused of an error, be sure to come to that worker's defense. You expect your subordinates to work for you and with you; be aware that they also expect your loyalty and support.

Allegiance to Your Superior

As you begin your new position as a supervisor, you will find that in addition to being accountable for the work of your subordinates, you are responsible to the manager or director to whom you report. Gaining respect from your immediate superior is a crucial factor in your success or failure as a new supervisor.

Be loyal to your boss. It is imperative that you realize that the responsibilities and duties of your superior invariably filter down to you and become yours. If you can do your job and make your superior look good in the process, then you will reap great benefits. You will find that, in a pinch, your boss will back you up when you need it. A smart superior is well aware that the valuable subordinate is the one who looks out for his or her boss and their department. There is no substitute for true loyalty.

Cultivate honest communication with your boss. Of prime importance in the superior-subordinate relationship is honesty. Open lines of communication foster a team-oriented environment. Firsthand knowledge and information, whether it is good or bad, helps your boss infinitely more than second-hand knowledge obtained from his or her peers or third-hand information from the grapevine.

Go to your superior if you need help. If you need more time or help to complete a project, or if unforeseen circumstances arise, do not be afraid to seek your boss's help. If you do not ask for help, then be ready to answer your superior's question, "Why didn't you come to me about this?"

This is not an all-inclusive list of the things that will make you a good supervisor, but it is a beginning—and you have to start somewhere.

Managing Your Career

BRIAN H. KLEINER

Do you want a job or a career? These days, more and more people feel that they should be getting more from their work than monetary compensation. They want to receive emotional satisfaction from their jobs, not just salary increases—they want promotions and recognition. You probably feel the same. How can you achieve all this? By hard work.

But even outstanding performance in your job will not guarantee your success. The following strategies detail most of the bases you should try to cover in order to get ahead. But remember, there are no simple formulas, as all management literature asserts. The results depend on your ability to become the type of person that others will expect and help to succeed.

1. *Develop and maintain basic career competencies.* All careers, including yours, have a basic set of technical skills that need to be mastered before an employer will have confidence in the employee. Know what they are in your career and master them. If these skills are in an area that is rapidly changing, such as engineering, try to stay abreast of new developments so you do not become technically obsolete. Read trade magazines, or take a course at a local college.

Equally important to advancing in an organization's hierarchy are the skills of management. Learn both general management and the management of people. Without these skills, your chances of promotion will be slim, even if you are the best performer in your department.

2. *Know the formal criteria by which you will be judged.* Soon after you report to your unit, find out the specific form your organization will use to evaluate your performance and study it. Remember that outstanding performance is not always rewarded. Rather, what is rewarded is outstanding performance as measured by this document. And, depending on whether you are measured on the basis of certain key personality traits, solely by performance results, or something in between, gear your work behavior accordingly.

As you work toward these standards, keep a record of your performance that illustrates and supports your excellence in the specific criteria that will be evaluated during the formal performance review sessions. Then, you can substantiate to your boss why you are deserving of excellent ratings if there is a difference of opinion. Don't be afraid to defend yourself if you know that you are right.

3. *Know the informal criteria by which you will be judged.* Every boss doing a performance evaluation has a personal set of biases and values that may distort his or her perception. Find out what they are and then take what action on your part is appropriate. For instance, if the word is out that your boss values

Reprinted from *Supervisory Management*, March 1980

punctuality and sharp appearance even though they are not the specific measures of productivity formally evaluated in your unit, keep these additional criteria in mind in your day-to-day functioning.

4. *Develop alliances.* One excellent way of getting to know your boss's idiosyncrasies, not to mention getting support when you might need it, is to develop alliances with others in your organization. My experience has been that it is usually more effective first to develop a good working relationship with your subordinates, and then to become an accepted member at the peer-group level, before trying to score points or develop alliances with the people "upstairs." If you try to develop alliances with upper management before really establishing your base of support at the peer-group level, you may pick up a reputation as an "apple polisher"—and jealous peers can easily find ways of undercutting your performance and reputation if they desire.

5. *Be a top-notch performer.* Once both the formal and informal criteria for evaluation are known to you, make up your mind to be an excellent performer. Don't think that because you did well in school you will automatically succeed on the job. Success in the academic world does not guarantee success in the world of business. In fact, the most recent statistics show that the typical "C" student is more successful than the typical "B" student and the "B" student is more successful than the "A" student. This phenomenon has been attributed to the fact that "C" students tend to develop broader social and emotional skills than "A" students, who tend to be very conformity oriented and, typically, not very creative. "A" students also seem to be more easily disillusioned with the realities of the real world of business than "C" students.

How can you show that you're promotable? Even after a short time working, you know that while a good grade or high grade-point average is helpful in getting your initial job after graduation, it's results that count the most toward future promotions.

6. *Get an interim feedback report.* Knowing what the important performance criteria are, then making up your mind to meet them, is still not always enough to assure success. Because it's difficult to see one's own performance objectively, you need informal feedback from your boss. This information will help you correct your performance and ensure that, when the formal review period comes around, you are soundly "in port."

It may seem surprising to many subordinates that giving criticism is actually such an uncomfortable act for many managers that they choose to ignore it except during the formal review period. But asking your superior for further ways to improve your job performance makes the process much easier for him or her and goes a long way in building a sound boss-subordinate relationship.

7. *Become crucial to a boss who's clearly a "star on the rise."* If you are fortunate enough to have a manager who clearly has star potential, make every effort to be as invaluable as possible. In that way, as your boss rapidly ascends the ladder, he or she will be more likely to want to take you along. On the other hand, if your superior has reached, according to the Peter principle, his or her highest level of incompetence and won't be going higher in the company, it might be best to consider transferring somewhere else where opportunities for upward mobility are better.

8. *Look for ways to stand out from the pack.* In most organizations the number of upward vacancies that need to be filled is generally much fewer than the number of people who desire to fill them. For that reason it is important to distinguish yourself from all the other candidates. One way of doing this is to practice self-nomination, particularly on special projects that powerful figures in the company will be watching closely. Successful accomplishment on these projects is a sure means of getting favorable attention and increasing visibility. However, remember that there is an element of risk involved in this strategy. If you "drop the ball" in front of everybody, your security within the organization is likely to be threatened to a much greater degree. Proceed, but with caution.

9. *Train your replacement early.* One of the less pleasant but still true facts of organizational life is that many otherwise excellent bosses may not give you the promotion you deserve because of the boss's own fear that he or she cannot manage well without you if you leave. For that reason, let your superior know that should the opportunity for promotion be available to you, you will not leave him or her "holding the bag." Rather, you will train another highly competent person to take your place.

10. *Keep your options open as much as possible.* One excellently managed company that I know

makes a practice of putting its newly hired people in highly specialized jobs where for the next couple of years they learn to do a few critical tasks strictly in the company manner. Why? If after a couple of years the employees begin to think they might do better elsewhere, they soon realize that what they have learned has little transferability to another company. Hence, they would have to start all over. Needless to say, this inhibits their desire for leaving, and the company has a lower employee-initiated turnover rate than many other companies. From the company's point of view, this is a sound practice. However, from the point of view of its employees, it's lousy. To keep yourself from falling into such a trap, seek jobs that provide you with skills that could be transferred to a wide array of other jobs in other companies. The job of auditor for a C.P.A. firm is an example. Many chief accountants for private organizations are hired directly from C.P.A. firms.

A second idea for keeping your options open is to be willing to travel out of state. Once a promotion or even a transfer out of state that upper management views as essential in your career development is turned down, advancement opportunities are likely to be fewer in the future.

A final bit of advice pertaining to keeping your options open is to have in mind always another organization you could probably join if you were terminated in your present place of employment. Frequently, the next best job is very similar in terms of pay and psychological benefits to your present one. This awareness is reassuring, enabling you to define the limits of what you'll put up with if you find your relationship with your present company souring.

11. *Periodically reassess your career.* You and your career are continually in a process of change. Frequently, a fit that was good several years ago is no longer very satisfying. If this is the case, accept the fact and intelligently plan your next best move. Getting help from professionals in the area of career counseling can be useful here. Most universities have such trained professionals. One of many things that they would probably stress is the importance of planning your own career and that of your spouse collaboratively.

12. *Leave the company at your convenience and on a good note.* If your company lost an important government contract and you know there will be a lot of pink slips coming in the next few months (and you'll probably get one of them through no fault of your own), the time to find a job is *now* while you enjoy the status of being fully employed. It's amazing how much lower your market value can become once the other company knows you have been terminated by your last employer. It's not fair, because you have the same skills, but that's frequently the way it is. If the new company asks you why you are looking for another job while you are presently employed, just truthfully tell them that you are seeking to work for a company that will provide you with better prospects for advancement.

One final note: Whatever the reason that you leave, leave on a good note. I know of many people whose greatest source of job satisfaction came during the last day of employment when they told their particularly displeasing bosses in very articulate language exactly what they thought about them. And I do not find it surprising that years later when these same bosses were asked to complete letters of recommendation for these employees, they remembered that last day much more clearly than all the preceding days of employment, which may well have been characterized by fine performance.

It Takes Effort

The above are strategies for persons who are strongly motivated to advance in their careers. Needless to say, to practice them will involve a considerable amount of time and energy that others might like to channel into their family and recreational lives. This is a decision you must make. Each of us is free to choose how to budget his or her time and energy. But for those interested in "how to succeed in business by *really* trying," these strategies should be quite useful.

How to Avoid Professional Obsolescence

JACK J. PHILLIPS

Preoccupied with the constant day-to-day concerns of a job, we sometimes forget to take a good look at ourselves to see if we are better now than we were before. Periodically we need to review our professional development because to be any good at a job we have to keep learning. That's certainly true of us supervisors.

It is every supervisor's job to keep up with what other people are doing in his or her field. This requires a conscious program of self-development through activity that increases supervisory effectiveness and contributes to success.

Why improve? The answer to that should be obvious. In our society, processes, technology, and people are constantly changing; the supervisor has to change with them just to keep even. Most companies require their management personnel to continually update themselves, whether it is a formal rule or simply understood. In terms of career growth, the best opportunities go to the best qualified individuals. But perhaps the most important reason to improve oneself is to gain self-respect and the satisfaction of accomplishment.

Somehow for all the obvious benefits of self-development, we often do not spend the time we should on it. Here are some common reasons:

- *We lack the requisite discipline.* No one watches to see if we enrich the skills we already have. It requires sacrifice and a motivation that is internal.

- *We lack direction.* A program of self-development has to be planned with goals in mind. When we know what we want, we tackle each task with more purpose.

- *We lack the capacity for change.* Learning involves a change in behavior, and human nature tends to resist such change. When we recognize this, we can analyze the forces within ourselves that block our capacity for change. If we become dissatisfied enough with our performance to want to change, we will take honest steps in that direction.

- *We lack the necessary cash.* Self-development costs money. College courses, for example, are more expensive now than they have ever been. However, most companies offer tuition-aid programs that help reduce the cost of self-development, and many local schools or colleges offer community education programs at little cost.

- *We lack the time.* The process of self-development requires an investment of time—most of it personal time.

Reprinted from *Supervisory Management*, November 1980

Supervising Your Own Time

Of these obstacles, perhaps the most difficult to overcome is our shortage of time. Most of us feel there just aren't enough hours in the day to do all we'd like, making it especially important to plan the good use of what time we have.

Misspent time starts a vicious cycle because the less time we have, the less we can plan. The less we can plan, the more time it takes to do a job, so we run out of time. This goes on and on until finally we are swamped with work. We don't make a very efficient job of what work we get to, and important tasks are overlooked.

A good way to work toward better use of time is to analyze where it goes. Try listing your daily activities over a period of one to three weeks and cataloging activity by five- and ten-minute segments. Analyze the information while keeping these four questions in mind:

1. *What is the nature of the activities?* Most supervisors find they spend the better share of their time doing something other than managing. Often their time is spent on tasks that could be done by their employees or by someone in another capacity in the organization.

2. *Where does the work come from?* Most of the activities originate with one of five sources: the boss; subordinates; the organization's procedures; outside sources like professional or community activities; and the person himself or herself.

If you do this analysis, you will most likely find that self-initiated activities occupy the least amount of your time. Yet these are the activities that have the greatest value to your self-development. Unfortunately, since no one makes you follow through on these activities or imposes a deadline, they are easily put aside.

3. *What are the results of the activities?* Each should be analyzed in terms of the time used and the results obtained. One major company estimated that its managers ought to be spending 65 percent of their time on their major duties, 20 percent of their time on their next most important duties, and just 15 percent on duties that were least important. Analysis showed that the reverse was true among their supervisors, who spent only 15 percent of their time on their most important tasks.

4. *Do you delegate authority?* Examine whether or not each activity can be delegated to an employee or passed along to a more appropriate area of the organization.

A Road Map for Development

In mapping out a program for self-development for yourself, the first thing you need to do is identify the areas for improvement. Examine yourself and determine your weaknesses, then concentrate on improving those particular areas. There are a number of ways to do this:

Outline the areas in which you lack knowledge, or the skills you would like to learn.
Ask an associate in what area he or she thinks you could stand improvement.
Ask the boss to discuss some aspect of your ability that needs strengthening.
Ask a professional for advice—like the company psychologist, for example.
Rate yourself against the checklist in Figure 1.

When you have located where you are and where you would like to be, take steps to acquire the skills you need to get there. These steps should be measurable so that you can evaluate your progress. Compare the progress you're making with the progress you'd like to be making. If your particular approach is not working, try another; be flexible and make positive changes where necessary.

Each individual is different. Set a course that suits you best.

Figure 1

Self-Development Checklist

In the past year: **Yes**   **No**

1. Did you volunteer to take a formal training program to further your progress?
2. Did you read any management books?
3. Did you take a self-study course or listen to cassettes to improve your skills?
4. Did you increase your participation in company activities?
5. Did you volunteer for any special assignments or projects not normally within your job?
6. Were you involved in community activities, civic associations, or church groups?
7. Did you analyze your past activities to determine which should be increased or which should be discontinued?
8. Did you have fewer emotional flare-ups?
9. Did you observe others whom you consider to be successful to find out their secrets of success?
10. Did you devote more time to studying human behavior?
11. Did you learn more about other functions and activities in the company outside your own job?
12. Did you devote more time to helping others solve their problems?
13. Did you increase your knowledge of economics and the free enterprise system?
14. Did you keep up with the state of the art in your specialty?
15. Did you make more independent decisions?
16. Did you write an article, give a talk, or take some other step to improve your communication skills?
17. Did you show a willingness to expose yourself to new experiences?
18. Did you get involved in political issues that affect your company and community?
19. Did you make it a point to find out more about your company and the problems it faces?
20. Did you find out more about your business or industry?

The Sources of Development

There are innumerable ways for you as a supervisor to develop your untapped skills. One of the best ways is to watch others who get a lot of work done in the same amount of time. Study their behavior and their methods of organizing themselves and their jobs. Try to figure out what makes them so productive— and so successful.

Build your vocabulary. You cannot hide an inability to use language. The importance of a strong vocabulary to a career was shown in a survey done by a large university many years ago. The university tested the vocabulary skills of the members of one graduating class and then kept tabs on their careers over the next 20 years. Without exception, those who had scored highest on the vocabulary test were in the top income group, while those who scored lowest held a corresponding position in terms of income.

Read as much as you can. Start collecting books and articles relevant to your field. Books are not an expense item—they are an investment that pays a dividend out of all proportion to their cost.

When attending a formal training program, try to get the most out of it. You can't learn skills unless you are open to new knowledge and eager to learn. Regardless of where the training is conducted, it is up to you to learn what is going on. Look on each training session as an opportunity to develop your skills. Take advantage of every such opportunity you get.

Pursue your professional education part-time in college, vocational, technical, or special adult-education courses. Some schools offer degree programs and nondegree programs for credit and noncredit. Your training department can probably give you guidance on which courses to take.

Get involved in volunteer organizations. Communities are well-blessed with civic groups, and these are an ideal way to develop your leadership skills and gain experience in working with people.

Company-sponsored activities also offer an excellent chance for a person to develop leadership skills. In addition, the contacts you make may be valuable to you later in your career.

Self-development should be a continual process. That means that you should be constantly assessing yourself as a supervisor and as a person. True self-development calls for a certain amount of dissatisfaction with yourself at the start. For it is when you are too satisfied with yourself that growth stops.

The Risk Management Approach To Career Planning

BRUCE E. McEWAN

Many U.S. organizations have decided to take a positive approach to dealing with the risks they face in doing business and are adapting the Risk Management Process (RMP) used in insurance buying to analyze business-risk exposure. But individuals can also profit from personal use of the RMP. Since the process helps to identify risks that can affect one's ultimate success, it can be used in career planning to plot out the future and deal with the risks (problems) that one is likely to encounter. The same five steps that help businesses to make positive, conscious decisions relating to business-risk exposure can help us to assess the problems we might face as we try to achieve our career goals.

The five steps are quite simple:

1. Risk identification
2. Risk evaluation
3. Identification of alternative methods of handling risk
4. Implementation of alternative methods
5. Monitoring of the RMP

Risk Identification

The first step in career planning using the RMP is to focus on what we want to do with our lives. Where do we want to wind up? It could be as president or chairman of our present organization or any other company or as an independent consultant, a university professor, or a government bureaucrat. At this stage, no realistic goal is unattainable.

Basically, we have to consider our current position and attempt to plot our career plan by identifying where we want to be at significant stages. At the same time we have to identify those things that could prevent us from reaching each plateau. Specifically, risk assessment, the first step in the RMP, involves assessing the career problems we might face within the next ten years. To identify these, we can use a questionnaire like the one in Figure 1.

Reprinted from *Supervisory Management,* January 1984

Figure 1

Career Risk and Opportunity Questionnaire

1. What is my present position?
2. How long have I been in my present position?
3. When should my next promotion come?
4. How do I get along with my superiors?
5. How do I get along with my peers?
6. How do I get along with my subordinates?
7. At present, I see myself working for my present organization for _____years.
8. If I decide to retire from my present organization, I would like to retire as _____.
9. My greatest accomplishments in the last three to five years have been:
   a.
   b.
   c.
10. Does my superior realize my abilities? Potential?
11. What are my major assets?
    a.
    b.
    c.
12. What are my major liabilities?
    a.
    b.
    c.
13. Has my career progressed as I thought it would? Why? Why not?
14. Who are my major competitors for promotion?
15. Have I made my career ambitions known to my superior?
16. Do I know what chances for advancement lie ahead in this organization?
17. What have I done recently to better myself in my career?
18. What should I do tomorrow to help me move closer to my next career goal?
19. I feel I can be reasonably comfortable in projecting my career out for the next _____years.
20. Why do I think my career will be successful?

In assessing the risks facing us, we should try to be as realistic as possible. This step in the process requires a great deal of honesty on the part of the career planner and as objective an assessment of the current career position as possible.

To illustrate how this process works, let's consider Bob W., a 35-year-old assistant vice-president. Bob wants to be head of his own company by age 45. He has assessed his present situation and has identified the following as "risks" he might face in the next ten years: loss of present position, no promotion to vice-president, no assignment to projects where he could get necessary experience, no recognition for his efforts, no further education, lack of industry recognition, and lack of necessary capital.

Risk Evaluation

After Bob has identified the risks he faces, he has to estimate the probability of an adverse outcome due to the risk. This is the next step in the RMP. For instance, Bob has identified loss of present position as a risk, but the chances of that occurring are unlikely based on the evaluations he has received. Let's look at the other risks identified and Bob's assessment of their impact on his career plans:

- Competition for the vice-presidency is stiff, but Bob reasons that he has a 75 percent chance of receiving the promotion.
- There are two colleagues who are also interested in heading up the projects important to Bob's career plans, but he feels that he has a better than average chance of getting the assignments.
- Bob needs to receive recognition for his efforts but his present boss likes to take credit for the success of projects. Here, he has only a 40 percent chance of getting the credit he deserves.
- Bob feels that he will need to broaden his knowledge in light of his career plans. The company may not pay for the courses he needs or may require some kind of career commitment if it does.
- To get industry recognition, Bob needs to be published in a number of trade journals. Given his writing skills, this is possible.
- He may be able to qualify for a small business loan from the Small Business Administration, but he's not sure he would meet all the requirements.

Opportunity Identification

Besides examining potential risk situations, the risk management process can be used to identify and evaluate potential opportunities. In the case of Bob W., this opportunity identification and evaluation might look like this:

- Chance to head up the department reorganization task force—40 to 60 percent chance of being picked
- Join the professional society—can meet requirements in about two years
- Be hired by a competitor—no desire to pursue this option at this time

The Alternatives

The next step is to develop techniques for handling those risks and opportunities identified. The traditional risk-management methods are avoidance, retention, loss prevention-loss control, and risk transfer.

Avoidance. This method is used when the negative impact of the risk is so great or the loss of opportunity will have such a detrimental effect on the future that it is better to avoid the risk situation or forgo the opportunity. The decision to do this is consciously made.

Retention. When you feel that you are in control of the situation and the rewards for taking the risk or accepting the opportunity far outweigh any negatives, then this is the technique to use. Retention can take place because a risk is not recognized as such, but it is implicit in the procedures that retention be associated with a conscious decision being made.

Loss prevention-loss control. These methods are geared to eliminating or reducing the negative impact of a risk or the chance of missing an opportunity.

Risk transfer. This method deals with the intervention of another party to alleviate a risk or to help secure an opportunity.

In risk management, it is rare that only one alternative is used in a risk situation. Indeed, there is more likelihood that a combination of methods will be applied to the situation. Going back to Bob W., let's see how he might put the alternative methods of handling risks and opportunities into practice:

Risk #1—loss of present position—retention as method. Based on Bob's present situation and the good evaluations he has received, there seems to be little doubt that he will retain his position. Thus the risk here is minimal.

Risk #2—failure to become a vice-president—loss prevention as method. This is a major goal, and

Bob wants to be sure that he attains it. He can help by taking extra care with his work and making sure that he is visible to those who will influence his promotion.

Risk #3—may not be put in charge of the projects he wants—loss control as method. With two other people vying for the same projects, Bob cannot expect to be put in charge every time. But by doing a superior job those times when he is in charge, he can reduce the chance of getting passed over or at least not getting his fair share of projects.

Risk #4—lack of proper recognition—transfer as technique. Bob must show a superior what his talents are. This person will bring about his recognition. Based on his evaluation of this risk, he will have to transfer the recognition responsibility to someone other than his immediate boss.

Risk #5—need further education—loss control as alternative. Bob should be prepared to pay for some of his own education expenses in those instances where the company may not pay.

Risk #6—need for industry recognition—loss control and transfer as approaches here. Bob will need to set aside some time to write a number of articles for publication in trade journals. He should prepare to send these to several sources. Only after he acquires a reputation as an author will he start to get requests for articles.

Risk #7—need for capital—retention, loss control, and transfer as methods. Bob should seek assistance from an accountant who can advise him on this matter. For the most part, he will be on his own to develop the resources he will need. But by planning ahead and getting started early, he can decrease the chances of not having the resources he needs to start up his own business.

Opportunity #1—head up the department reorganization task force—loss prevention and transfer. Bob needs to do a superior job in order to show that he is more capable than others to head up the task force. He also needs to see that an influential superior is in his corner when it comes time to make a selection.

Opportunity #2—join the professional society—retention as alternative. Bob knows that he can qualify; it is just a matter of planning so he can meet all the requirements.

Opportunity #3—work for the competition—avoidance as technique. Since Bob has no desire to change companies and has a number of good plans going for him in his present job, Bob should avoid pursuing a move to a competitor.

Implementation

Once action steps are decided on, the career planner should be in control. Timing is always an important factor and one that should be given due consideration. Bob W., for instance, will have to review each of his risks and opportunities to decide which ones to give immediate attention. Some will naturally follow after others. Some will be long range. Bob will have to consciously think about each and plan its implementation.

Monitoring

Since situations can change, and a decision made based on today's facts may not hold up tomorrow, one must try to keep on top of events as far as career risks and opportunities are concerned.

If one has an idea as to the time frame in which one expects to be influenced by any risks or opportunities, one can schedule a monitoring review. In the case of Bob W., he decided that risk #2 would be affecting him in three years. At the end of each year, he would assess his progress to see if his alternative course had been successful. Risk #3 required more frequent monitoring because project assignments came up more often.

In terms of opportunities, opportunity #1 would be coming up within the next six months, so Bob

Figure 2

Career Path Planning Worksheet

Name: _____

Age: _____

Present Position: _____ Duties: _____

Career Path Planning Period: _____ years.

Career risks I see in the next _____ years:
1.
2.
3.
4.
5.

Career opportunities I see in the next _____ years:
1.
2.
3.
4.
5.

Evaluations of risks/opportunities:

	Risks		*Opportunities*
	1.		1.
	2.		2.
	3.		3.
	4.		4.
	5.		5.

Alternative methods I would use for each risk/opportunity:

Risks: *Comments*
1.
2.
3.
4.
5.

Opportunities: *Comments*

1.
2.
3.
4.
5.

Figure 2 (*continued*)

Implementation dates and monitoring schedule:

        Risks:

1. Implement   Monitor
2.
3.
4.
5.

       Opportunities:

1. Implement   Monitor
2.
3.
4.
5.

would have to monitor his progress almost on a weekly basis. Opportunity #2 could be reviewed annually or semi-annually.

Once a monitoring process has been set up, it must be adhered to. Recognition of a need for change requires immediate action. Old risks and opportunities may need to be re-evaluated and new ones identified and studied. Alternatives will need to be changed when the existing plan loses its effectiveness.

To help the reader get started in risk-management career planning, a sample worksheet of the type that one might use is included in Figure 2.

Interviewing for the Next Rung Up

MARY F. COOK

If it is your plan to be at a higher level in your organization a year from now, you need to begin planning your future actions now. That should include preparing for the job interview. Some people plan only for the obvious—developing the skills they need—overlooking what they see as a less important aspect of getting the next job. They fail to realize that their future could be tied to the success or failure of their next job interview. You can do all the goal setting and career planning you want; but if you fail the interview, your time will have been wasted. More importantly, a poor showing in this area could put a damper on your future in the company.

Preparing Before the Interview

Let us say you have identified the next job on the ladder, and you are aiming at that job right now. There are three things you should do right from the start:

1. Identify the key skills your boss will be looking for when the job is ready to be filled. Have you got these skills, or do you need additional education, experience, or mentoring in some areas?

2. Asses your competition for the job. If you have competition, try to identify their skills and abilities. Then take paper and pencil and plan an interview strategy that highlights your strengths and minimizes your weaknesses, especially in the areas where you believe your competition is likely to be strong.

3. Review the realities of your situation. Recognize immediately the differences between your perceptions of yourself and the perceptions that others, particularly your boss, have of you. Get these perceptions down on paper. You need a good hold on the realities of your prospects before the interview.

In addition to these key issues, identify what abilities you have that your boss needs to improve the reputation of the department. Sometimes we get so swept up in our desire for promotion that we forget the most important item of all—the fact that we must have the ability to make the person who will hire us look good.

Success Characteristics

There are certain dimensions and characteristics that a manager in any organization looks for in interviewing a job candidate. These are the characteristics of successful people.

Reprinted from *Supervisory Management,* November 1980

Impact. The ability to create a good first impression—to command attention and respect—is essential. The way you act and the impression you make have more of an influence on your promotability quotient than you may realize.

Communication skills. The ability to be persuasive, to make a clear presentation of the facts, and to be effective in your written communications is critical to your success.

Judgment. Your capacity to reach a logical conclusion and to show good judgment in the affairs of your department is extremely important. Your judgment is revealed by your ability to respond effectively to everyday situations that affect you and your group.

Planning and organization. Organizations look for people who are effective in organizing and controlling a function.

Initiative. You must be the kind of person who initiates action rather than sits passively waiting for someone to tell him or her what to do.

Sensitivity. Organizations look for people who are skilled in reacting sensitively to the needs of others. Questions in an interview may be aimed at identifying this trait in handling human resource problems.

Leadership. If the next job up the ladder is a managerial job, management will be appraising your leadership effectiveness—do you have the ability to get your ideas accepted, to guide a group, and to create a team atmosphere?

Creativity and problem solving. Management will be looking at your problem-solving abilities to see if you can come up with imaginative solutions to your work problems.

Interpersonal skills. Many people fail in their jobs because they have poor interpersonal skills; very few fail because they lack the technical ability to do their job. It is important to understand the styles of others and to be able to deal with a variety of people. One way to come to terms with styles of behavior is to develop a familiarity with transactional analysis.

Three Interview Stages

Just as there are stages of interviewing for personnel professionals who interview prospective employees, so there are key elements of a job interview for the person being interviewed. The more you prepare before an interview, the better your chance of success.

Stage 1: The preinterview. Preparation for the interview is almost as important as the interview itself. When the job is in the same company, and the interview with the management people in your department, you have a slight edge.

In the preinterview stage, it is important to plan your strategies for developing a rapport with your interviewer. The interview requires you to successfully articulate your thoughts and establish a good relationship with the interviewer. One way to establish this rapport immediately is to start the interview with a conversational style and to ask some open-ended questions that get the conversation going.

Stage 2: The interview. After a few minutes of conversation, you should begin your sales presentation. It's important that early in the interview you discuss what your boss is looking for in the way of particular skills. If you've done your homework, you know them ahead of time and have prepared your answers accordingly. Think of yourself as a salesperson—you are selling your skills, your abilities, your commitment, and your energy to do the job.

People tend to evaluate other's ability to get a job done by their "can-do" qualities. These qualities are frequently judged by a person's education, training, experiences, aptitudes, and so forth, and you want to stress these in the interview. You also want to make the interviewer aware of your "will-do" characteristics—your drive, determination, stability, commitment, enthusiasm, and creativity. These characteristics are taken as signs that a person will put basic abilities to good use.

When interviewing for the next job on your career ladder, it's important to stress these "will-do" qualities.

A boss is interested in promoting an achiever—a person who gets the work done and gets it done through others with a minimum of disruption. What the person will do in the future is best determined by what he or she has done in the past. Therefore, a certain emphasis must be put on your past and current achievements.

There are some questions that almost every person asks in a job interview. It is possible to anticipate these and to prepare answers that will impress the interviewer. Some standard interview questions are:

- *"Why do you want this job?"* One answer to that question is, "Because I feel I have a great deal to contribute. I'm excited about the company's future, and I want to be a part of it." It's a mistake to say that you're aiming at your boss's job. Don't be so aggressive that the interviewer feels threatened.
- *"What are your long-range goals?"* Be sure you know your goals and can communicate them. This question is nearly always asked, because it elicits a lot of information from the person being interviewed. Your answer tells the interviewer whether you have the maturity it takes to make a long-range career plan, whether you are realistic about your career goals, and whether you are committed to the company. When you reply, tell the interviewer what your career goals are and have in mind a job or two that you feel you could fill now, three years from now, and five years from now.
- *"What do you see as your greatest strength?"* This is a question that gives you the opportunity to sell your strengths. Select one of the key qualities you possess that is in demand on the job. If you've done your homework, you will know what is needed. State the quality, review your past achievements, and show how you will help the company attain its goals by using this personal strength.
- *"What is your greatest weakness?"* This one is a killer, but it's probably going to be asked, and it's best to face up to it immediately. You should have no problem, since you have identified your weaknesses in the preinterview strategy session you had with yourself and, hopefully, also identified what you are going to do to improve yourself in these areas. If you have a weakness, mention it and state what you are doing to improve it. Don't dwell on the subject. You will be hired because of your strengths, not your weaknesses. Get the interviewer back on the subject of your strengths.
- *"What is important to you on a job?"* A good reply might be that you get a personal feeling of accomplishment from doing a good job and from seeing that your contribution positively affects the company's business plans. Some people make the mistake of replying that they want more money, higher position, and prestige. Those things have their place, but not the first time around in a job interview.

As you progress through the job interview, remember that it is better to respond to questions than to merely react. Responding is less emotional, more logical. When you respond, you take control of the situation; when you react, someone else is in control.

Stage 3: Closing the interview. Don't let the interview drag on if you can help it. It is important to end on a high note, to express enthusiasm about the job and about the prospect of working with the person who is interviewing you. At the end of the interview restate your credentials for the job. Leave the interviewer with the feeling that you are a person with whom he or she may establish a productive working relationship.

A Perspective

We have all experienced some rejection in our work lives. If you don't get the job, it may be for the simple reason that somebody else was better qualified. On the other hand, perhaps you were just as qualified as your competition but didn't market yourself as well. A recent study by an executive recruiting firm found that 234 candidates for 16 top corporate jobs were not chosen for the following reasons: inability to project a special competence, appearing to be emotional or subjective, overaggressiveness and verbosity, lack of clarity in expressing views, overcriticism, poor dress or grooming, and frequent job moves without marked advancement.

Finally, being successful in an interview and climbing that next rung on your career ladder are certainly important goals, but they aren't everything. Learn early in your career not to take yourself or your career so seriously that it affects your personality or your health. Top management will soon spot the person who is so intent on achieving a career goal that the goal becomes obsessive. A career should be a pursuit of successively more challenging experiences—not an ultimate position, but an experimental journey of progressive achievements.

When Moving up the Ladder Means Moving out of Town

D. W. PRAH

You've just been offered a promotion by the vice-president. But to take the job, you'll have to relocate. This transfer could be the chance you've been waiting for, just the right step. You've been given time to think over the offer but told not to take too long. The corporation needs your answer soon.

How do you tell your family? Your first impulse may be to rush home and announce the good news. Don't. This approach assumes that the whole family will gladly sever present ties and commitments and be delighted at the thought of moving.

Deciding Together

The decision to accept a transfer will affect the entire family, so all need to be involved in making the decision. Break the news of the potential transfer by reviewing the discussion between you and the vice-president. Let the family know why this is good news for you and then find out how the news affects each member.

Everyone's interests have to be considered in deciding to accept the transfer because the family is the support system you will be bringing to the new location. When the family agrees to move, even with varying degrees of acceptance, then you can work together rather than against one another after the move.

Considerations

The financial, professional, educational, and personal impacts must be considered by all affected.

First, be sure the family understands the new job responsibilities, career potential, and fringe benefits offered. Review the corporate relocation policy. Some research and calculations will show if the proposed raise will meet any increased living and housing costs. The family must also consider how the new position and location will alter its current lifestyle.

If you are a two-career family, you and your spouse probably already mesh career plans. You are accustomed to conversations concerning travel schedules, professional meetings, and overtime commit-

Reprinted from *Supervisory Management*, July 1983

ments. The possibility of a transfer may even have been discussed. You and your spouse struggle daily to balance the mutually accepted need for each of you to advance professionally and keep your personal partnership intact. A decision about transferring will not be easy to make, but at least you both are accustomed to interacting and projecting in terms of your careers.

If you are a one-career/two-paycheck family or a one-career/one-paycheck family, the decision is trickier. When your spouse's job is considered secondary or your spouse provides a full-time support system at home, the considerations for transferring may weigh unequally. A balance must be carefully established. The importance of career advancement and monetary rewards can overshadow consideration of the relocation's impact on other family members. A large financial increase can easily clutter up an open mind to other family members' educational and personal considerations. It is important that all affected by the relocation be involved in some part of the decision-making process.

Schools, recreational facilities, community lifestyle, and neighborhoods should all be major considerations when deciding if the transfer is right for the family.

Questions about schooling generally involve the children in the family. A change may result in different teaching styles, textbook series, and philosophical styles in education. Special programs offered in one area of the country may not be available in another. The possible changes need to be discussed and understood by both parent and child. An introduction to the new school system by a personal visit or through correspondence can help ease a child's apprehensions.

Children's friendships are very special. Leaving special friends can be difficult. These experiences need parental understanding and support not only at the time of leaving but in the months that follow while new friendships develop.

Educational impacts need not be limited to children. You or your spouse may be pursuing further education. Job training, when interrupted by a move, can result in major career setbacks. Certification and graduation requirements often differ from state to state, and only a limited amount of credits may be transferred. Discovering this fact after a move is discouraging at best.

Considering personal impacts of a transfer often involve family ties and proximity of relatives, particularly aging parents. Many people favor a particular region of the country for family, recreational, or health reasons. Personal reasons may also include the need to settle down in one place without looking for a home with resale in mind.

The Answer Is "Yes"

When you and your family decide a transfer will be beneficial, you can tell the vice-president that you accept the offer. You have some assurance that this career opportunity will also provide opportunities for your family. You have done the groundwork that should keep your family support system intact.

The following is a list of considerations to discuss during the relocation process. It focuses on some of the stresses of relocation and provides practical ways to involve all affected by the relocation process. When you, your family, and your corporation work together, the chances are even better for a smoother relocation.

1. Develop a sensitivity to the transition process of relocation. The relocation process can extend from the time of the offer to transfer to at least a year after the actual move.

Moving is a major life-change experience. Stress can come from changes in responsibility levels, economic status, schools, job, church, friends, and services. Stress can also come from grief, loneliness, and the loss of identity associated with leaving friends and relatives, loss of the old job, and the disappointment regarding overly high or unrealistic expectations about the transfer.

Involving all family members in some part of the decision-making process before relocation can give family members a sense of control during the relocation and can help reduce the stress during the transitional period. When family members have been a part of the decision, it is easier for them to support the results of that decision.

2. Consider the career potential and job possibilities for your spouse. Providing your spouse with

career and employment services will help meet the financial and career goals of your family. Your corporation may make this available. Ask. Some businesses provide information on college, university, and vocational schools, as well as state licensing requirements.

If the transfer alters your spouse's career goals, employment and career services are even more necessary.

3. List the advantages and disadvantages of the new community. Assemble information about child care programs, private and public schools, professional and vocational facilities, medical services and facilities, shopping areas, vehicle and driver registration rules, and recreational opportunities. If you are unable to do this personally, ask for help in obtaining the information that you will need.

4. Involve family members in the housing search. The sooner your family is all together under one roof the better. Knowing where home will be and what it will be like can have a stabilizing effect. If it is unreasonable for the whole family to participate in the housing search, at least consider the requests of family members. Parents have their own parameters for housing, but children's requests may be as simple as a basketball hoop in the backyard or a functional doorbell. Being part of the decision, if even indirectly, will make the choice easier to support after the move.

5. Take time off during the household move. Moving is exhausting not only physically but also emotionally. When your spouse alone supervises the physical aspects of a move, the transfer may be interpreted to be one spouse's work and the other's profit. Bad feelings generated on the homefront may make it impossible for you to concentrate at the workplace.

6. Develop an outline of corporate jargon, titles, and names. Such an introduction will help your spouse understand what you are talking about.

7. Review your travel schedule immediately after the move. Long periods of separation can make the transition period following relocation tougher. If you can delay a stepped-up travel schedule, do so. It will provide the time and opportunity for your family to cope with the transition together. If travel cannot be avoided, communication with your family should be encouraged. Frequent telephone conversations, complete travel itineraries, and a back-up person in the new community for emergencies are some ways of providing a foundation for transition support.

8. Encourage the family to visit your place of work. A brief visit to the office can help bring the spheres of home and work closer together.

9. Find seminar opportunities on the effects of relocation on the employee and family. Many communities offer seminars that include opportunities to assess a potential transfer, develop decision-making and communication skills, and frankly discuss the personal issues of relocation. These programs can be focused on the family or on individual members. If these are not available locally, inquire if the corporation would consider providing them.

10. Allow yourself and your family time to feel at home. Each family member struggles with similar stresses from relocation. Everyone works through saying goodbye to old friends and a familiar lifestyle while at the same time carving out a new lifestyle with new friends. This must be done while keeping self-confidence intact. Some days this is difficult. Each family member has his or her own coping strategies and timetable for this transition process. You find yourself facing the responsibilities of a new job and the equally pressing needs you alone can fill for your family. Give yourself and your family time to work through this major life-change experience. You can make this career opportunity an opportunity as well to get closer to your family.

The Fear of Failure—
The Supervisor's Greatest Enemy

JAMES H. COREY, JR.

When you think about what characterizes a successful supervisor, what qualities immediately come to mind? Some more familiar ones are aggressiveness, decisiveness, and self-confidence. The last thing you would probably associate with a supervisor is fear. Yet to ignore the existence of fear is both naive and potentially dangerous to the success of the organization.

As a manager you have, at least once in your career, experienced fear—probably when you first assumed your new role as a member of management. You have also seen one of your subordinates become fearful when you have promoted him or her to a supervisory level or given that person greater responsibility. Fear is a presence in the business environment, like it or not, and therefore it is vital that you take the necessary steps to counteract its negative effect on your lower-level supervisors' performance and on organizational productivity.

Why Supervisors Fail

Failure is a direct result of the excessive fear and insecurity present in individuals who fill new and more responsible roles in the organization. There are several reasons why this is true. First of all, an individual assuming a new organizational role is no more or no less secure than in any other new role he or she plays in society. As a result, when such an individual is faced with an unfamiliar situation, insecurity, induced by fear of the unknown, sets in, and because of this fear the individual does his or her job not so much for the purpose of accomplishing its goals and objectives but to reduce the stress and anxiety that accompanies the fear of failure. In turn, this goal displacement leads to a "Catch 22" situation in which fear-induced stress and anxiety lead to poor decision making. This results in the very failure that the individual was trying to avoid.

Each successive failure leads to increased stress, fear, and poor decision making, until the relationship is finally terminated.

Before any solution to the problem is possible, the organization must recognize the fact that fear of failure exists in every person, and that the level of fear in an individual varies based on his or her level of self-confidence and what he or she perceives to be the failure potential in a certain job. However, recog-

Reprinted from *Supervisory Management,* December 1979

nizing that fear of failure exists is not enough. The organization not only must accept this type of fear as a normal part of every individual's makeup, it also must make its subordinates aware that the organization will not view them as abnormal if they experience fear or exhibit its symptoms. In fact, the organization should encourage fear of failure at a tolerable level so that employees will maintain desirable productivity standards. Only when fear adversely affects the decision-making process does it become a dangerous organizational problem.

Fear—The Outward Signs

During your subordinate's transition phase from his or her present job into the management level, you should be on guard for signs that he or she may be experiencing excessive fear-related anxieties and insecurity, and take immediate and decisive action. The symptoms you should look out for include the following:

- _Confusion._ Individuals suffering from excessive fear are unable to handle the input they receive from different organizational levels. Whereas they were previously able to deal with a multitude of data, they are now unable to assimilate any information at a rapid pace.

- _Illogical decision making._ An individual who previously made decisions consistent with input and who suddenly changes to a decision-making process that is inconsistent with the input received is usually exhibiting the effects of fear.

- _Failure to make decisions._ One of the classic symptoms of supervisors suffering from excessive fear is an increasing inability to make even the most routine decisions. What begins as procrastination may reach a point when the only decision the supervisor can make is to make no decision at all.

- _Deteriorating morale and increased turnover in the work group._ When your department or division suffers from reduced morale and increased turnover, there is a good chance that your newly promoted subordinate may be alienating his or her former co-workers.

- _Any unexplained personality changes._ Any time an individual changes jobs, he or she will change as well, but usually within the limits established by others who have previously filled that spot. When personality changes are more dramatic or longer lasting than usual, there is trouble ahead.

- _Excess overtime._ Long hours are a definite part of the management scene, especially with new supervisors who feel that they must prove themselves hard workers from the beginning. However, continuous and excessive overtime may be a symptom of the individual's fear of failure. It is often used to camouflage the real problem—that is, the individual's inability to cope with the job. As his or her superior, you should look at your subordinate's output rather than at how many hours he or she spends in the office.

- _Overconcern with success or failure._ Every employee has a normal amount of concern over his or her performance. However, indications that excessive concern exists mean that your subordinate is worried about the job. Don't confuse this for extreme dedication to the job. Take it for what it really is—an extreme fear of failure.

- _Interpersonal conflict with peers, subordinates, and/or superiors._ Employees who are fearful of failure ventilate their tensions by attacking those around them at the slightest provocation. Certainly, some conflict is inevitable in an organization; but when a subordinate is constantly at odds with others, it is an indication that deeper-rooted problems exist in that individual.

- _Nostalgia._ Reminiscing about the "good old days" is a pleasant pastime for all of us. However, when a new supervisor constantly refers to the past, what the person might be really saying is that he or she is uncomfortable in the new role and would like to return to the old job in which success was a way of life and fear of failure nonexistent.

- _Excessive absenteeism._ Absenteeism is a form of escape from an unpleasant situation—one in which people suffering from fear and anxiety often indulge. If a subordinate begins to absent himself or herself for unexplained or dubious reasons, it may be a sign that he or she is unable to cope with the job.

- *Covering up mistakes.* Supervisors who are afraid of failing often go to great lengths to hide their mistakes from their immediate superior.
- *"Passing the buck."* Confident and successful supervisors usually accept the consequences of their actions even when things go wrong. If your subordinate is constantly looking for a scapegoat, it is a sure sign of fear and insecurity.
- *Resistance to change.* One of the consequences of a job-related fear is the tendency on the part of the individual to resist change. In many cases, the person may reach a state of total rigidity in his or her adherence to a course of action, no matter how self-destructive it may appear to an outsider. In its extreme, resistance to change is an indication that the individual finds the situation he or she is in to be fear-provoking. A self-perceived helplessness in handling work-related problems may cause an increasing level of fear that, in turn, may lead to additional rigidity in the face of future change.

Eliminating Fear

Once the symptoms of fear of failure are familiar to you, the next step is to take remedial action. The following suggestions can help you eliminate the debilitating fear of failure in your newly promoted supervisor.

- One reason why new supervisors are fearful is because they feel they are not, or are not in fact, adequately trained. Only those employees who have participated in a well-developed supervisory training program should be promoted. Individuals who were promoted beyond their competence level because of organizational needs should receive intensive on-the-job training until they are competent to perform their duties.
- Perhaps your supervisor doesn't know the performance standards by which he or she will be judged. Each supervisory job should have clearly defined objectives, and its relationship to the rest of the management hierarchy should be specified as well.
- It is imperative that you develop a supportive environment for your subordinate during his or her transitional phase. This is a crucial time for both of you. You should be on the lookout for signs of fear of failure, insecurity, and anxiety. You should let the individual know that he or she can do the job well, and that if problems arise, you will be available for consultation. Encourage him or her to come to you with problems before they develop into major crises. Positive reinforcement is one method you should use to bolster your subordinate's confidence and self-esteem.
- You should instill in your subordinate the fact that making mistakes is an unavoidable part of the learning process and that both you and the organization are aware of this. Termination should be the last resort, and then only after possible avenues have been explored to improve his or her performance.
- Develop decision-making skills in your supervisor so that he or she can achieve an optimum level of risk taking. A "win all-lose all" philosophy should be discouraged.
- You should assure your supervisor that all channels of communication in the organization will and must be kept open. The individual should be kept abreast of (1) how well or poorly he or she is performing; (2) how the organization is performing; (3) what plans the organization has for the future; and (4) where he or she fits into those plans.

Followup Is Essential

Even if excessive fear of failure is eliminated in your new supervisor, it does not mean that he or she will never experience it again. Many individuals perform successfully for years only to have an isolated incident create the insecurity needed to produce this fear. Some events that contribute to a resurgence of fear are:

- Changes in personal life, such as divorce, death of a spouse, and so on.

▪ Lack of growth opportunities in the organization. When an individual sees co-workers being promoted while he or she remains in the same job, that person will begin to question his or her competence.

▪ Change in a reporting relationship that removes the supportive environment the individual has grown used to.

▪ Organizational change, such as acquisition by a larger company, expansion, economic crunch, and so on.

You should continually monitor your long-time supervisors for any signs of fear. It is as important to help these people overcome the damaging effects of fear as it is to help the first-time supervisor.

The manager's most important function, and perhaps his or her greatest challenge, is to develop subordinates for future positions in the management hierarchy. This does not only mean developing their technical skills; it means helping them to grow emotionally and psychologically in the job. The manager who realizes that fear of failure is the greatest barrier to supervisory success and takes the necessary steps to help subordinates overcome this fear is performing a vital service for his or her organization.

Preparing for a Move to Middle Management

ROBERT R. BELL and J. BERNARD KEYS

Many first-line supervisors, like many other managers, plan to move eventually into higher levels of management. To be ready for this move, these supervisors must *plan ahead*. In addition to performing effectively in their current position, they must also prepare themselves for the future. The next job for most supervisors will be as *middle* managers. Some of the changes involved in such a move, and some guidelines to help prepare for it, will be presented here.

What Will Change

As one moves from first-level supervision to middle management, several rather basic changes take place. Let's look at these.

The functions performed differ in emphasis. All managers perform the same basic functions; however, the time and effort spent in each function vary with the level of the manager. Middle managers tend to spend more time *planning* than do entry-level managers. Supervisors tend to focus more on *direction* and *personal control*. A typical eight-hour day for both a supervisor and a middle manager is shown in Figure 1.

The time-orientation will change. As managers move up, they have to extend their time outlook. Supervisors spend most of their time on daily or weekly activities; middle managers will require less of a daily focus. Higher-level managers must focus on planning for the future. Instead of working to keep weekly inventory levels balanced, for example, the middle manager may be working on a revision of the unit's entire inventory planning system.

New challenges must be met. The move to middle management poses new challenges. The first of these is a leadership challenge. Instead of working directly with the operating employees, the middle manager is now one or more layers away from the production line. Workers no longer report to the middle manager, *other managers* do. These other managers may even be supervisors as the middle manager once was. The new middle manager may, in fact, manage persons who were fellow supervisors a short time ago.

Figure 2 graphically shows the changed managerial role. As a supervisor, manager X may have been

Reprinted from *Supervisory Management,* September 1978

Figure 1

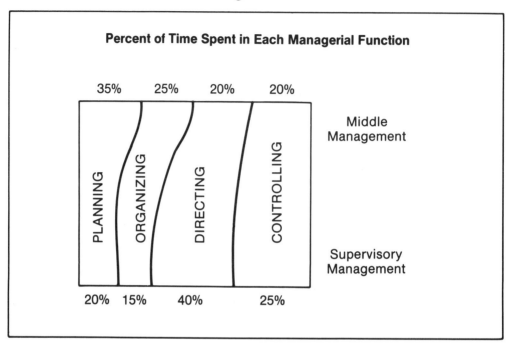

Percent of Time Spent in Each Managerial Function

35%   25%   20%   20%

Middle Management

PLANNING   ORGANIZING   DIRECTING   CONTROLLING

Supervisory Management

20%   15%   40%   25%

Figure 2
Organizational Relationships

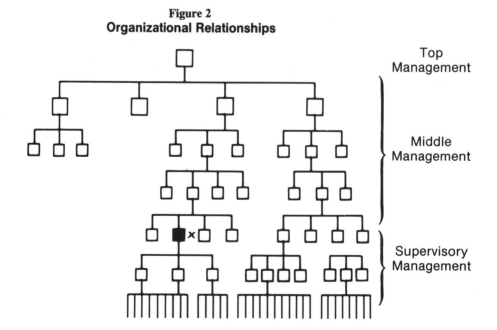

Top Management

Middle Management

Supervisory Management

responsible for the work of five subordinates. Now as middle manager, X is responsible for three subordinate managers and for the work performed by their 14 subordinates. Where he or she once supervised only production people, the middle manager may now be responsible for several entire administrative units.

The second challenge is one of coordination. The middle manager is literally the person in the middle, responsible to top management for the efforts of the workforce. So, the middle manager must be able to appreciate the long-term goals and objectives of top management. He or she must know enough about management systems to convert goals and policies into operating plans that will be carried out by that individual's work group.

A lot of time is spent moving back and forth between superiors and subordinate managers, trying to interpret and clarify goals and adjusting the goals and objectives to fit the people involved, or persuading the people to adjust to the goals as presented. For this reason, middle managers need to be "bilingual"— they must be able to speak the "language" of higher managers, and must be able to translate their longer-range, goal-oriented communications into the day-to-day operating language of subordinates.

The challenge of coaching and development is also different at the middle management level. The supervisor works on developing more effective skills and habits in employees, which typically center around a machine or procedure. The middle manager, on the other hand, tries to develop more effective managerial skills in subordinates.

Parenthetically, middle managers tend to relate more to higher managers than do first-level supervisors. Middle managers are usually required to spend more time with their superiors, which causes them to develop a stronger upward orientation than the first-level supervisor. In fact, several studies have shown that the leadership style of a subordinate manager is most influenced by his superior's style.

The "political system" will change. The higher one goes in the organization, the more political the job becomes. Middle managers often must deal with persons making conflicting demands on them. Norman Bonner, for example, had responsibility over three production departments. The supervisors in these departments had recently complained that they were pushed to the limit. Their people just couldn't stand more pressure for production and overtime. Yet Norm's boss had called him this morning to say that the Acme Company, a long-valued customer, had asked them to speed up its order. Norm knew the company had a policy to bend over backwards when Acme asked for help. Managers in middle ranks must walk a thin tightrope, making the proper moves both to satisfy higher-level managers and work with subordinate managers.

Another major difference in the political role of middle and supervisory management relates to the coordination required with other departments. Most middle managers recognize that a great deal of outside cooperation and assistance is needed to meet departmental objectives. The horizontal relationships in business are highly political, and subtle influence has to be built. Figure 3 shows some of the relationships that make the politician's role part of the middle manager's job.

How Do I Prepare?

The first step in preparing for a move to middle management is development of a career plan.

Don Arthur kept getting passed over for promotions, and he couldn't understand why. During a coffee break from a scheduling meeting, he confided to a higher manager that he was disappointed with his progress. "I never knew you were interested in a promotion, Don. What do you want to do?" the manager asked. "I don't really know which position I'd like—I'm flexible," Don replied.

Don here made several mistakes. Perhaps the first was not making higher-level managers *aware* earlier that he was interested in more responsibility. Second, he had no clearly defined career or promotion goal, and he didn't know where he wanted to go. Without a clear target, it was impossible for him to do the necessary preparation to reach the goal. Lewis Carroll's *Alice in Wonderland* has important advice for managers: "If you don't know where you want to go, it doesn't matter how you get there!"

Figure 3

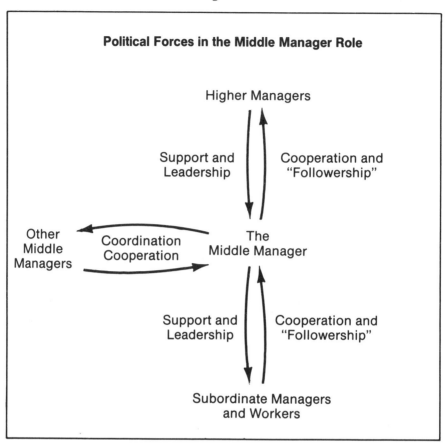

Political Forces in the Middle Manager Role

Higher Managers

Support and Leadership   Cooperation and "Followership"

Other Middle Managers   Coordination Cooperation   The Middle Manager

Support and Leadership   Cooperation and "Followership"

Subordinate Managers and Workers

Don hadn't asked himself some obvious but important questions: Where do I want to be in five years? What position, ultimately, do I want to hold in my life? What will the job require? What do I have to do, between *now* and *then,* to reach my goals?

Let's look at these questions in terms of a position in middle management.

What will the middle management job require? If middle management is the next step in the career ladder, Don has to examine the specific skill, aptitude, and leadership requirements of the jobs in his company. He may find that some of the characteristics described earlier in this article are important considerations for his career move. He may also find that the position in which he's interested has certain training requirements or stipulates certain types of experience.

The secret in career planning is to define the career goal, not just in terms of position, but in terms of accomplishments, competencies, and experience needed to attain the goal.

What skills and aptitudes do I now possess? After defining where he wants to go, Don needs to define where he stands now. He needs to develop an *inventory* of the skills, experience, and aptitudes he currently has. In dealing with leadership, Don needs to do a thorough evaluation of *who he is* as a manager. An interesting analytic device for this evaluation is the Johari Window shown in Figure 4.

The Johari Window provides four perspectives with which to view our leadership and managerial personalities. In Quadrant 1 ("open" window), Don would place the characteristics that are obvious to himself and to other people with whom he works. Quadrant 2 ("blind" window) emphasizes that other

Figure 4

The Johari Window

	Known to Me	**Unknown to Me**
Known to Others	Open	Blind
Unknown to Others	Hidden	Unknown

people may perceive some traits in us (good or bad) that we do not perceive. Don must ask, "How do others see me as a manager? Do they see the same person I see?"

Quadrant 3 ("hidden" window) categorizes those traits that *we know* we possess but that are hidden from others. Here Don must question whether higher positions will cause some of the traits or skills to become publicly known. Don may know, for example, that he doesn't understand materials requirements planning (MRP). On his present job, this lack of understanding is not important and not obvious to others. A move to middle management, however, may cause this deficiency to become known and may in fact hinder his performance. Obviously, this situation would indicate to Don that he needs to learn MRP.

Finally, Quadrant 4 ("unknown" window) reminds us that we all have certain leadership skills or aptitudes that are not recognized by ourselves or by other people. Some people blossom in a new position, and people wonder why they didn't recognize that hidden potential previously.

The Johari Window gives us a simple tool for building a profile of our managerial strengths and weaknesses. Once we have the profile, we must match it to the requirements of the position we seek and find ways to develop the skills and characteristics required for the job.

What skills and aptitudes must I develop? Don may find that the inventory and job requirements analysis has helped him eliminate some types of jobs from his career plan. He certainly will learn more about the company's requirements and the effort he'll have to make to accomplish his goals. If Don doesn't have a college degree, and if he finds that a certain middle management job will require a bachelor's degree in business, he knows he has six or more years going to school part-time before he can compete for the job. He has defined a long-term plan, together with the activities necessary to accomplish the plan.

How do I proceed? After the analysis, he now needs to develop a *plan of action* for accomplishing his objectives. This should be put in writing, specify each career goal, and define milestones and priorities for achieving the goal. Plans must be action-oriented; they must specify what Don will do, when he will do it, and why. Don should set specific times when he will be eligible for promotion. After promotion, he then must meet the challenge of becoming an effective middle manager.

Resiliency in the Face of Stress

DONALD G. ZAUDERER and JOSEPH M. FOX

The stresses and strains of corporate life in the executive suite are enormous. Many cannot endure it for long, and consequently they move on to less demanding careers. Those who do endure develop a personal strategy to manage the stress. The effective executive is resilient—able to bounce back and recover strength time and time again.

Stressful Thoughts

One $100,000 a year executive told us, "When I get called in to see the boss, the president, I never know whether he is going to fire me, demote me, or promote me. I've worked for him for two years, and that is the way he plays the game. I'm sure if I work for him for another five years, it will be the same. It's really frustrating."

This executive never anticipated this form of stress, but life in the executive suite often carries this and much more. An executive on the way to work might worry over:

The v.p. of X—our biggest client—was scowling a lot in yesterday's meeting, and he didn't say goodby to me. I wonder if our competitor is there. . . . I snapped at our newest manager in the morning meeting. I wonder if he's going to make it. . . . I haven't spent a decent hour with my 16-year-old daughter in months—I've got to get the orders in the next 90 days or I might be out. . . . I can't get that new product announced because the company is a stultifying bureaucracy. It takes 59 signatures to do anything, and the boss will hammer me to a pulp if I try to shortcut the approval chain. . . . My right hand man quit to go a competitor. His raise was a month away, but he made the emotional decision and wouldn't listen. . . . That new engineer is good. A promising executive—what can I do to develop him? . . .

Such concerns consume the life of the average manager. Managers who cannot endure the high level of stress will not survive long in the executive suite. The chart in Figure 1 lists frequent stressors that challenge the resiliency of every manager.

Reprinted from *Management Solutions*, November 1987

Figure 1

Daily Stressors

Stressor	*Example*
Role confusion	Unclear job responsibilities, causing others to resist.
Shifting roles	Serving as leader in one moment, a follower in the next.
Unclear expectations	Nobody knows what the boss expects.
Dry spells	Competitors win out for a period of time.
Bureaucratic decision making	Fifty-nine people have to review, comment, and sign a proposal.
Unrealistic expectations	The boss wants to look good and asks the manager to do the impossible.
Retention of talent	The boss expects the manager to keep the high-performing employee but doesn't give the manager the resources to do so.
Making hard decisions	It's hard to keep the loyalty of peers/subordinates when one has to make decisions that will have a negative impact.
Antagonism	People are out to get the manager.
Failure	Expected results don't appear.
Failure of subordinates	Employees let the manager down.
Unfair decisions	"Cronyism" gets peer X the promotion.
Organizational infighting	The battle of egos takes precedence over organizational needs.
Overload	Managing three crises at one time.
Direction reversed	Just when one gets the system going, the boss shifts direction.
Diminished influence	A manager makes one mistake and is moved out of the inner circle.

Living With Stress

An understanding of the stressors is the first step in your building resilience. But if you are to be a successful manager, you have to know strategies for reducing the impact of these.

Passionate beliefs intelligently applied are a hallmark of leadership, but passion without some detachment can lead to self-destruction. With that in mind, here are some strategies to follow to build resilience.

Keep a measure of emotional detachment. "We can't always control events, but we can control our reaction to these events." Resilient managers recognize this. When things go wrong, they do not blame themselves inappropriately. They recognize that they are neither the first nor the last ones to be in such a mess and that there are other jobs, companies, other deals. They can only do their best. They give it their best shot, assess what they could have done differently (learn from it), and move on to the next challenge.

Every manager is going to have setbacks, face humiliation, lose some deals, and be outmaneuvered by other corporate politicians. However, resilient managers play the game hard while maintaining a measure of emotional detachment. Their entire emotional psyche is not tied to each play in the game. They give each situation the emotional intensity it deserves and no more.

There is even a positive role for failure: It teaches. One cannot learn important lessons unless one takes risks, and some failure is inevitable in every achieving person's life. The founder of IBM said that he judged people by their failures. If they had never failed, they hadn't tried enough difficult things.

Building a support network. A support network can help you through difficult episodes. Such people can provide you with a sense of closeness, warmth, and acceptance. Honest communications with them can strengthen you when under emotional or physical stress. Julius Segal, in his book *Winning Life's Toughest Battles,* contends, "It is a healing experience simply to put our feelings into words." It is especially helpful to talk to people who have faced the same challenges. In Segal's words, "Communication helps us to recognize that others who face similar problems manage to survive."

Preserving security and independence. Executives who live modestly and save money are secure in the knowledge that there will be no crisis if they leave, get fired, or decide to return to a less challenging job, even at lower pay. Because such individuals feel more independent, they are less fearful of negative outcomes, knowing that their standard of living will not collapse. The existence of a financial nest egg is a key factor in maintaining resilience.

Plan your retreat. Resilient managers generally have made plans in the event all goes badly at work. They have a fallback position that is acceptable and have kept contacts open and healthy with others in their field. They know who is hiring and what organizations can use their skills. Toward implementing this strategy yourself, constantly work to build your competence. Knowing that you can change your job should reduce the stress and emotional burden of any setbacks. The sense of being in control, of having choices, should strengthen your ability to endure harsh episodes and enable you to bounce back.

Exercise. Resilient managers find ways to unwind, to back away and gain some distance from work problems. Exercise and recreation help to renew body and soul, and to build the capacity to withstand the inevitable pressures of high risk/high reward jobs.

Anticipate what's next. Many resilient managers play out possible scenarios in their mind. They foresee and are ready to accept the worst in any situation. They anticipate consequences in the most realistic terms and rehearse their reactions to them, thereby retaining a measure of control.

Stay flexible. In the song "The Gambler," Kenny Rogers sings, "You got to know when to hold 'em, know when to fold 'em, know when to walk away, and know when to run." The gambler recognizes when the forces are overwhelming and is willing to yield when necessary. Likewise, on the job, there are times when the boss cannot be convinced and we are obliged to follow orders. Resilient managers accept the fact that they will not always get their way in the organizational hierarchy.

Emotional Maturity—
An Important Executive Quality

JOSEPH M. FOX and DONALD G. ZAUDERER

Bill Johnson was a very bright and very energetic manager and had every reason to believe that his advancement would continue. His knowledge of systems design was respected throughout the organization. His new job was to supervise 12 engineers and scientists in the design of a computer package to control a new radar system. The design had to be completed in six months.

However, Bill's future in the company was bleak. He constantly engaged in arguments with his employees. Whether the issue was highly important or routine, Bill could be counted on to try to prove that he was right, or smarter, or more knowledgeable. It wasn't long before his employees said little at meetings; they waited to be told what to do. In time, many were asking for a change of assignments; several had left the company. Bill was soon shifted to a purely technical job with no supervisory responsibility. His dream of moving up the corporate ladder was shattered.

Unfortunately, Bill is not a rare case. Many talented professionals are stuck at their level because they exhibit emotionally immature behavior. Many aren't aware that these behaviors are placing limits on their effectiveness and mobilty. In Bill's case, his need to be right and dominate others proved disastrous.

Emotional maturity is expected of executives. Keeping one's balance when all hell is breaking loose, letting go of the need to look superb at all times, stifling vindictive impulses—these are all difficult. Yet the price is high for those who cannot curb these excesses.

Organizations aren't set up to provide much help, either. Such personality characteristics are generally not discussed in feedback and performance appraisal sessions. Bill's immaturity was displayed in a multitude of ways, each one so small that to mention it in an interview would have made the reviewer seem to be nitpicking. Consequently, Bill remained unaware of his problem, and the organization looked elsewhere for its managerial talent.

Bill is the classic dominator. But, as the following suggests, there are many other forms of immature behavior—each with the potential to derail an executive.

Are you or any of your superiors or subordinates on this list?

Dominator—grabs control; must do it his or her way.
Robin Hood—maintains battle with organizational authority.
Saboteur—stifles projects; sets others up to fail.

Reprinted from *Management Solutions*, September 1987

Prima donna—expects royal treatment at all times.
Attila the Hun—rants and raves, shouts others down.
Pleaser—compliant; tells boss what he or she wants to hear; follows orders without question.
Chicken Little—cynic, believes the sky is always falling.
Braggart—tells everyone every minute how wonderful he or she is doing.
Blamer—attributes failures to others.

Let's look more closely at these personality types.

Robin Hood

Robin Hoods are effective and diligent, and their followers—both subordinates and customers—love them. But they subvert the authority of their superiors and the organizational staff who administer corporate policy and monitor control mechanisms. Because of this, they are "targeted for annihilation" by the heads of such departments as finance, personnel, security, administration, and law.

Robin Hoods detest authority. They infuriate the heads of staff, insult their bosses, and demean their peers. It is only a matter of time before Robin Hoods are sent to the dungeon.

Saboteur

Saboteurs work in many ways. They may delay action on a project, put the wrong person on it, leak negative information to influential people, and send discouraging reports. Their motive may be to make a boss look bad, to prove that their initial opposition was justified, or just to defeat authority figures wherever they can be found.

Saboteurs are subtle and skillful and cover their tracks well. But they eventually are discovered, and trust never again comes their way as a result.

Saboteurs may, on occasion, provide a helpful service to the organization. But the organization knows that it cannot thrive without the "good faith" execution of orders. From a career viewpoint, the boomerang ultimately comes around for saboteurs.

Prima Donna

Prima donnas believe that their accomplishments warrant a strong demonstration of respect from everyone. They will not tolerate the oversight of any detail that might detract from their importance. Those who comply with these expectations are rewarded. Others who are more informal or democratic in nature are shunted aside. Prima donnas may thrive in the Metropolitan Opera; in most other organizations, they fail.

The prima donna doesn't seem to understand that these symbols of recognition come at the expense of others. They will be seen as insecure, stuffed shirts, and egomaniacs. They aren't particularly likeable, and management will question whether they could garner a following in the organization or are just fast trackers with a limited future.

Attila the Hun

Attila the Hun rants and raves at the slightest provocation. He or she carries a short fuse that goes off regularly. The good news in this kind of situation is that people go out of their way to try to do their best to avoid an explosion. The bad news is that people will be scared to take risks, will sugarcoat bad news when communicating with the boss, or take flight from the organization.

Some Attilas reach the top with this style. Most, though, are seen as too volatile to be trusted with power.

The Pleaser

The pleaser curries favor by telling the boss what he or she wants to hear. Loyalty is demonstrated by making snide remarks about people that the boss doesn't like. The pleaser wants the boss to know that "we're in this together," and he or she will distort the reporting of events to satisfy the boss's needs, values, and biases. Unfortunately, the pleaser's need to be accepted and valued overrides his or her obligation to provide reliable information.

When the boss moves on or out, the pleaser may also have to find a new job. Others in the organization could never count on the pleaser to carry the true message, and they don't want to perpetuate this situation.

Chicken Little

One successful businessman told us, "I can't visualize myself failing." His sense of confidence was infectious, and soon the whole organization was exuding a sense of confidence. It sustained people during periods of uncertainty, and before long the success prophesy became a reality.

One cannot be motivated by a prophesy of doom and gloom. There are always threats to the growth or survival of an organization. Those who become fixated on the negative communicate this fear and anxiety. The easiest way to fail is to believe that one can't meet the challenge. Chicken Little may not even make it to first-level supervision.

The Braggart

Bragging is excessive marketing of oneself.

Our society rewards people who project an image of self-confidence. They produce quality work, and don't need constant emotional reinforcement. But the braggart never stops talking about his or her accomplishments. The effect is boredom for listeners. But more importantly, the individual is projecting an image of excessive ego. Our culture rewards people who have strong egos, but resists those who overwhelm others with their achievements.

The Blamer

Every organization experiences its share of successes and failures. When things go wrong, however, many individuals subtly point to others as responsible. They point to what others could have done to change the situation. They rarely think of what they might have done differently or accept any responsibility.

Those in management observe this behavior, and conclude that these persons cannot be trusted. They are seen as climbers who will sacrifice others to preserve their own reputation. When there is mistrust in the fabric of relationships, it is very difficult to create a high performance team. A blamer will top out at middle management at best.

Summing Up

When a manager exhibits emotionally mature behavior, it is hardly noticed. But immature behavior stands out and reduces a person's influence and opportunity for career growth. We all have moments when we act childishly. The problem arises when it is frequent and we are not aware of it or its effect on our customers, peers, employees, and supervisors.

The first step in turning the situation around and professional growth is awareness.

Avoiding Political Pitfalls

H. B. KARP

In business and social organizations, politics is almost universally seen as an evil and corrupting force, something that should be eliminated. But the reality is that politics is an integral part of every organization and has to be realized and reckoned with, since it is definitely here to stay.

The trick is to see politics for what it is—a *neutral* force—and then to make it work for you.

Endless time could be spent recounting war stories about bad political experiences in organizations; however, progress can only be made if these are acknowledged and let go. To be a successful supervisor, the realities of organizational life have to be accepted.

Politics can be defined as "how influence is distributed in an organization." The "politician," therefore, is the one who sets, attempts to set, or strongly influences the policies by which the organization will run.

The Productive/Political Continuum

With this definition in mind, we can use the concept of a productive/political continuum to represent the ability to get things done in an organization. What this continuum suggests is that there are two polar and opposite ways to make positive impact in and on the organization. One is by being *productive*. Productivity refers to those acts that support the organization's objectives; that is, producing quality results, being creative, meeting deadlines, and working efficiently.

The other polarity is *political*. This refers to the ability to make personal impact, to get the support that is needed from others, and to influence others in ways that will benefit you and the system.

If supervisors have no capacity on the *productive* side of the continuum, they will not contribute to the organization and will not survive in it for very long. On the other hand, if they have no capacity on the *political* side of the continuum, they will not make the impact necessary to be productive. That is, some of the best ideas never reach fruition because the individual whose idea it was did not know whom to present it to, had made unnecessary enemies, or was totally unaware of the spheres of influence in the organization.

Reprinted from *Management Solutions*, October 1988

Political Dos and Don'ts

The following guidelines are not intended to help you gain more influence; however, they may help you avoid some of the larger and uglier pitfalls that could sap your ability to be more effective as a supervisor.

1. *Never embarrass your boss.* There is a managerial axiom that states, "Your number one job is to make your boss look good." Some days you'll make him look good, and on other days you'll make him look better. The one thing that you may *never, never* do is to make him look bad.

2. *If you lie, you die.* There is also a French proverb that states, "Speak truth to power." The message here is that in the employee position you're always vulnerable to some degree. As a last resort, you can always refuse to answer, and you may get away with this under the right circumstances. But if you get caught in a lie, you're finished.

3. *Don't brag to strangers.* When you're successful, your real friends are going to be happy for you. Everybody else either won't care or, worse, will resent your success because they may not be as successful at the moment or, if they are, your success may tend to diminish theirs.

Of course, never complain to strangers either! This is even more dangerous than bragging. You never know who knows whom in an organization or who has social connections to people you know.

4. *Be aware of your alliances.* It's impossible to live and work in a system and not form alliances with others. Knowing this, you must be aware that you're responsible for whom you select as allies.

5. *Never let your boss be surprised.* The last thing your boss needs is to be uninformed about matters that are of critical concern to the unit. This is certainly obvious when it comes to bad surprises. Put yourself in your boss's shoes for a moment. Suppose, at a staff meeting, your boss is confronted by his own manager who says, "I understand that you just lost the Digby account! What happened?" This is the first time your boss has heard about it. Not only does he have to absorb the blow, he has to defend immediately a position that he just found out about 30 seconds ago. It is going to be difficult for him to come out of this not looking incompetent.

Good surprises aren't much better and should also be avoided at all costs. Take the same scenario but this time your boss's boss says, "Congratulations! I just heard you landed the Digby account." In this case, unless your boss can really fake it well, it is going to be difficult for him not to come out looking out of touch with his people.

6. *Don't challenge authority unless you really mean it.* Organizational effectiveness and personal growth are, to a large extent, based on the premise of clear, productive confrontation among group members. The key here is to confront the issue at hand, *not* the authority of the other person. Think, for example, about one of your employees or kids saying to you, "You don't have the right to . . . ," compared to them saying, "I don't understand how come you want. . . ."

7. *Right or wrong, the boss is the boss.* When you're at odds with your boss over a specific issue, you need to be as clear and forthright as possible about your views. This is important until a decision has been made and declared irreversible. Once this happens, *say no more.* Remember, you're responsible for your views, but you're not responsible, nor are you accountable, for the decisions of your boss. Keep in mind, too, that your boss's perspective may be different because of his position in the system.

8. *Don't corner your opponent.* There is another old saying that goes, "Be nice to the people you meet on the way up because you are going to see them again on the way down." Like all old sayings, this one, too, has a grain of truth in it. Many political horror shows have occurred simply because someone lost face and felt compelled to get even. If you're victorious in a conflict, do whatever you can to safeguard the dignity of your vanquished opponent.

9. *Spot the small points.* One of the definitions of politics is "the art of compromise." Yet compromise is rarely an effective *strategy* for managing conflict, since both parties usually end up with less than each wants. On the other hand, it does have a place as a *tactic* on the political side of the spectrum.

When involved in conflict, it's sometimes wise to concede a small point in order to gain a larger one. If the smaller issue is of little or no importance to you, conceding to your adversary has three advantages! It not only allows you to save time for things that are more important to you; it also keeps your adversary willing to stay engaged with you, and it assures you that your adversary will come out of the conflict with something of value. This helps assure a positive on-going work relationship.

10. *Collect chips, but not too many.* A chip is what somebody ends up with when they do someone else a favor. Chips may never be called in directly, since no deal was made; that is, a favor is a favor. But while there is no direct debt or obligation on the part of the receiver of the favor, there is definitely an implied one. After all, how many times can you say to somebody, "Thanks, I owe you one," and not feel indebted?

Holding some chips is generally advantageous in that you're in a position to get some help and support when you need it; and it makes you look like a "good guy," when in fact you are. Holding too many chips can be dangerous, though, because you risk being strongly resented, rather than highly appreciated.

11. *Acknowledge others.* It is generally very astute politically to acknowledge others' contributions whenever possible. By doing so, you make them look good at no cost to yourself. Not only that, but you develop a reputation as an "acknowledger of good work." No matter how much you do this, as long as it is authentic, you still get the credit for getting the job done and your employees get the credit for doing their job.

12. *Avoid the rumor mill.* Organizational gossip is sometimes fun and harmless; however, in most cases it is tremendously damaging to careers and personal reputations. When you hear a rumor, or a choice bit of gossip, you're put in a position of either sitting on it or passing it along. If you sit on it, you may feel you're going to "explode." But if you choose to pass it along, you're as accountable for the effects of the rumor as if you had originated it.

13. *Your opinion is yours.* Are you aware that just because somebody asks you for your opinion, you're under no obligation to give it? Even more importantly, you never have to volunteer your opinion. Whether accepted or rejected, whether supportive or corrective, your opinion is almost always of value, if for no other reason than it presents one more viable alternative to consider. Remember, however, that there is a tremendous difference between a *considered opinion* and a *blunted value judgment.* The latter, if negative, is almost always going to get you in trouble.

14. *Avoid end runs.* An end run occurs when a supervisor can't get the support needed from his boss and then goes directly to his boss's manager for redress. When you're at loggerheads with your boss and the issue is important, attempt every means at your disposal to work it through with him. If an acceptable solution is still not available and you're positive you're right, let your boss know if you decide to take it to higher authority. You might even invite her to join you if the issue has not degenerated to personalities. To do less than this is to commit political suicide; after the situation is resolved, you and your boss are still stuck with each other, and only one of you can survive this.

Summing Up

While it's up to you to determine how much you want to get involved in the politics of your organization, it's important that, at the minimum, you don't run afoul of it. Politics, just like any other organizational force, is neither good nor bad in itself. It's simply one more organizational variable that exists and can be used to support the system as well as subvert it.

Part II

COACHING AND COUNSELING

Ten Basic Counseling Skills

RICHARD J. WALSH

Most managers in today's business world are faced with a wide range of "people problems," some of which are directly related to the job, while others are more personal in nature. But whether the people-problems are work-related or personal in nature, the manager sees their effects firsthand: Employees who are having difficulties not only slack off in their own work performance, but they also tend to drag down the performance of their fellow employees. When work performance drops off, the employee's problem necessarily becomes a concern of the manager as well.

Let me illustrate this point with a story I heard recently: A salesman—I'll call him Wally Jarvis—had been performing admirably for his company for more than five years. Then for no apparent reason, his sales record began to decline considerably. He became abrasive with both clients and other corporate personnel. When his boss consulted with him on a large potential contract, he accused his boss of second-guessing him. While Wally Jarvis in the past had been a consistently cooperative individual, he now seemed unpredictable, and no one could forecast how well he would work with other staff members on any given day. Unable to understand or help Wally in his time of need, the company made a hard choice. It decided not to give Wally another chance and fired him.

The Manager as Counselor

Every manager has faced at some time the problem that Wally Jarvis's sales manager faced. No company wants to lose good young talent like Wally, but too often managers and supervisors are ill-

Reprinted from *Supervisory Management*, July 1977

equipped to handle the personal problems of employees. The company that has managers with effective counseling skills will certainly have a "leg up" on the competition, which will undoubtedly lose many of its Wally Jarvises.

Managers cannot avoid having to deal with people-problems. In fact, managers are in positions where they must deal with these problems on an almost daily basis. Since they are often forced to make decisions and give advice that will affect the people-problems of their subordinates, it makes good sense that they be as informed as possible both in the methods of acquiring information and in the techniques of effectively guiding subordinates. When a manager acquires information from people and helps solve problems, he is engaging in "counseling." While this type of counseling may not be the same as an industrial psychologist or professional counselor renders, it does have the basic ingredients of a professional counseling relationship. The purpose of this article is to describe the basic counseling process and how it applies to managers as they help solve people-problems.

Counseling can be simply defined as the process whereby a manager tries to understand someone else's personal problem and then assists him in solving this problem. Obviously there are different levels of counseling, and the manager who is supporting and assisting another is counseling at a different level than the professional counselor. But this difference is primarily a matter of degree. The manager who has a basic understanding of the counseling process can be very effective in helping a subordinate. Furthermore, the manager who understands the counseling process will be better able to determine when he should turn to the personnel department or to other professionals for more intensive assistance.

Counseling Skills

Although most are not aware of it, many managers already use a number of basic counseling skills in their everyday activities. And a lot of jobs in organizations require counseling-related skills for successful performance of responsibilities. Consider a salesman, for example. Salesmen who are particularly effective convey a sense of personal concern to the client or customer. These salesmen exhibit strong skills in listening, attending, making appropriate responses, and problem solving, which are the same skills necessary to become a good counselor or "people-problem solver."

Of these skills there are ten that managers can use most effectively in dealing with subordinates' problems.

Four of these skills relate to establishing rapport with the employee and to acquiring information. These are the attending-behavior, listening-behavior, support-responding, and proper-questioning skills.

Getting into another person's frame of reference, or seeing situations from another's perspective, is also crucial in the counseling setting. Skills five and six—the reflection-of-feeling skill and the reflection-of-content skill—allow this empathy to be evoked.

Assisting the employee in the identification of his problem is also important. While many counseling skills aid in this process, skills seven and eight—the summarizing-feeling-and-content and interpretation-responding skills—are critical to succeeding in this area.

Finally, meaningful solutions to the employee's problems must eventually be arrived at. Skills nine and ten—that is, skill in rendering advice to an employee and skill in gaining an employee's commitment to change—facilitate the evolution of such solutions.

The Counseling Process

The first step in counseling subordinates involves the establishment of rapport between manager (or supervisor) and employee. This means conveying the fact that the manager is concerned about the employee's situation and is committed to helping him find a solution.

Skill #1: Attending behavior. By using appropriate attending behavior with the employee, a manager can begin to set the concerned, respectful tone of the counseling discussions. Since such an atmosphere is possible only in a setting conducive to putting both participants at ease, the manager and his subordinate should meet in private, preferably away from the areas where they usually work.

Although the employee may be somewhat nervous—especially during the first few counseling sessions—the manager should be physically relaxed and seated comfortably. This will enable him to attend to the employee's emotional situation in a more natural manner. Maintaining good eye contact with the subordinate is another key to effective attending behavior. Eye contact helps to communicate to the employee that the manager is "with" him as he expresses the reasons behind his problems. And a manager's use of comments that the subordinate himself uses is another sign that the manager is "with" him in the discussion.

Skill #2: Active listening. A second skill related to establishing rapport and displaying respect and caring is active listening. Though it may seem to be an easy task, it actually requires a good deal of concentration. For one thing, listening attentively requires us to slow down our thinking process; this is due to the fact that the average person speaks at a rate of about 125 words per minute but can think much faster. Consequently, the manager must fight the natural tendency to complete the employee's thoughts for him or to become distracted. Instead, he must focus totally on the subordinate's own words and problems.

A key aspect of active listening is to intermittently paraphrase or "sum up" what your employee is saying. An example of this would be the following exchange. Employee: "It seems that everything I touch turns sour." Manager: "You're saying that things aren't going well for you right now." By giving back to the subordinate what he has just said, the manager will be indicating that he is "on the employee's wavelength." The manager must constantly keep in mind that to be effective in solving people-problems, he must first listen to the employee's explanation of what the problem is.

Skill 3: Support responding. Many verbal and nonverbal responses by a manager can convey a tone of support to a subordinate and facilitate the building of rapport. A manager's nonverbal responses—such as head-nodding—communicate to an employee that his words are being understood. Verbal promptings are another means of supporting a subordinate; such comments as "Tell me more," "Go on," and "I see" show support to a person and encourage him to keep on speaking.

Skill 4: Proper questioning. Asking the right kinds of questions is very helpful early in the interview in establishing rapport and acquiring information. The use of the open-ended question is particularly effective in providing an opportunity for the employee to express his real thoughts and feelings. Closed questions do not provide the same opportunity for self-expression and often receive only a *yes* or *no* response; an example of this is the question, "Is the project going well?" To such a query the subordinate can only answer *yes* or *no* and usually will not elaborate. But an open-ended question such as, "How do you feel the project is progressing?" will encourage a subordinate to talk expansively about the project and hopefully use this opportunity to touch on his more personal concerns.

To make this counseling effort a success, it is critical that the superior get into the frame of reference of his subordinate. In other words, the manager needs to look at the situation from his subordinate's perspective rather than from his own; he must attempt to see the problem through the employee's own eyes, considering both his thoughts and feelings.

Skill 5: Reflection of feelings. When a manager makes a comment about another's feelings, he is beginning to see a situation from the other person's viewpoint. When focusing on the feelings of another and responding to these feelings, the manager is not only acquiring a better insight into the subordinate's situation but is also helping the subordinate become more aware of his feelings.

Reflection-of-feeling responses most often begin with "You feel . . ." For example, when a production worker complains, "Those guys in sales constantly undersell our products, and I'm fed up with it," the counselor-manager should reflect this feeling with, "You feel angry about this situation." In this example, the subordinate's basic feeling was one of anger, and the manager correctly reflected this in his response. In summary, the reflection-of-feeling response both increases the understanding of the manager and clarifies the feelings of the subordinate.

Skill 6: Reflection of content or meaning. While the reflection-of-feeling response is primarily concerned with the emotional aspect of a subordinate's statements, the reflection-of-meaning response emphasizes the cognitive side of the subordinate's communication. Through his response the manager helps the subordinate gain a clearer understanding of what he is actually stating. For example, a production employee might say, "I can't count on Jim. One thing he'll do is outstanding, while the next will be just shoddy." In response to this comment, the manager correctly reflects, "You're saying Jim is not always reliable in regard to finishing projects." Thus the manager focuses on the meaning or content aspect of his employee's communication. Both content and feeling reflections are necessary for clarifying the employee's problem and providing an avenue to a real solution.

As in most other problem-solving situations, counseling becomes more effective if the person can correctly identify his own problem. It should be the goal of the manager to assist his subordinate in this identification process. While the six skills already mentioned can aid in this process, a periodic summarizing of a subordinate's communications—along with a limited interpretation of these communications by the manager—can be instrumental in bringing about a new awareness in the employee.

Skill 7: Summarizing feeling and content. The purpose of periodically summarizing the feeling and content of what has been said in the interview is to give a certain objectivity to what has transpired. When condensing and clarifying what has been said, the manager is focusing attention on the basic theme of the employee's remarks; he is pulling together and clarifying the seemingly diverse important feelings and elements of the conversation, which encourages more in-depth concentration on sometimes revealing inconsistencies in the feelings expressed.

Skill 8: Interpretation responding. While the previously given skills are geared to view activities from the subordinate's perspective, the interpretation response is an observation made from the viewpoint or frame of reference of the manager. The manager presents a new, more functional perspective through which the employee can look at his problem.

In the interpretation response, the manager is giving his answer as to why the employee feels or acts a certain way. For example, consider the salesman who has had a series of setbacks and just can't seem to close contracts. After the salesman has related his problems, an interpretation response by his sales manager might be, "You're frustrated and upset with yourself because you're not closing business contracts. This, in turn, is due to the fact that you're not making enough calls and attempting enough trial closes."

At this point in the counseling, it is important for the manager to begin assisting his subordinate in coming up with solutions to the problem. Until now, the manager has been concerned with exploring the problem of his subordinate; from here on, he should steer the conversation toward the goal of providing concrete answers to the employee's questions and problems. This change in tactics will lead the manager directly into skills nine and ten.

Skill 9: Rendering advice. When a manager is seriously trying to help find answers to a problem situation, he should be very careful to avoid the tendency to come up with hasty solutions before he and his subordinate have thoroughly diagnosed what the problem is. It is critical that the manager fully satisfy the guidelines of the first eight counseling skills before concentrating on finding an appropriate solution to the subordinate's problem.

It is also important for managers to help subordinates ultimately solve their own problems, assisting the subordinates in coming up with the final solution. An established counseling principle states that it is much more effective for a person to arrive at his own solution to a problem than it is to have the answers spelled out for him. The person who makes a real personal investment in finding a solution—with, of course, the guidance of his manager—will have a greater recognition that the solution chosen is the right solution.

When rendering advice, it should be the goal of every manager to present the information in such a way that his subordinate can shape and utilize this in the most effective and meaningful way. What the manager-counselor should really be doing is assisting his subordinate in answering his own question, "What can I do about this problem?"

Skill 10: Gaining a commitment to change. The final question concerning the subordinate in a counseling situation is, "Will I follow through on implementing this solution?" Unless the manager receives a definite commitment to execute the solution, the employee may tend to aimlessly continue as before, even though he has identified both his problem and a real solution to his problem. Again the challenge facing the manager is to tactfully guide the subordinate through the solution-finding phase and then to carefully use questions and comments to lead the subordinate into making a real commitment to the new goal or solution already arrived at. In short the manager isn't "telling" the subordinate but is listening, asking questions, and tactfully guiding.

Summary

Personnel specialists have found that if managers can learn and use this ten-skill counseling process, they are well on their way to becoming effective "people-problem solvers." Too often management types are at a loss for techniques to use in really dealing with subordinates' problems. In order to retain and effectively motivate subordinates, it is critical that every manager be able to communicate with and counsel his subordinates.

Let's Talk: Solving Employee Problems

EDWARD L. LEVINE

One of the most important supervisory responsibilities is the handling of employee problems. A manager who is able to satisfy workers' needs by successfully handling their day-to-day problems will develop a group that works harder and better. Other benefits of solving employee problems are increased loyalty and heightened job satisfaction among workers.

Failure to handle day-to-day employee problems may lead to dissatisfaction, alienation, frustration, and anger. These negative emotional states can in turn contribute to turnover, accidents, and absenteeism.

What is the current state of the supervisory art? Are supervisors adequately handling employee problems? Although it appears that many problems are capably handled, improvement is needed. Indeed, the most consistent sore spot among employees as shown in *Work in America,* a report compiled by the U.S. Department of Health, Education and Welfare, was the failure of bosses to listen to workers who wanted to propose better ways of doing their jobs. Workers often feel that bosses demonstrate little respect for their employees' intelligence and creativity. Managers, too, complain that they often cannot get their ideas up channels effectively. Many in both groups also believe that their organization will not do anything about their individual problems. This can lead to a feeling that nobody cares.

How can a particular organization tell if its own supervisors are handling problems adequately or not? One way to find out is to survey managers and employees. A less direct but still sure sign that supervisors are *not* doing a good job of handling day-to-day employee problems is the extensive use of the formal grievance procedure. When supervisors are handling problems successfully, employees will rarely resort to filing a formal grievance.

Another sure sign is the overly frequent use of the organization's suggestion box for improvements that could easily be put into practice by a supervisor. Inadequate communication between a supervisor and subordinate contributes to the overly frequent use of this impersonal way for an employee's ideas to receive the attention they deserve.

Many factors are involved in the effective handling of an employee's problems. A supervisor must know how to weigh facts and make decisions, either independently or cooperatively with the affected employee. A supervisor must also be able to handle conflicts, particularly where solving one employee's problem creates another problem for a different employee.

Effective decision making and conflict resolution depend heavily on communication between the supervisor and the employee. Through communication, problems are defined, facts and opinions gathered,

The helpful suggestions of Jeffrey Jones, University of South Florida, are gratefully acknowledged.

Reprinted from *Supervisory Management,* November 1980

and decisions presented for consideration and acceptance by the affected employees and managers. Communication is important not only because of its role in effective decision making and conflict resolution but also because communication *alone* may be both the *source of* and the *remedy for* many employee problems.

Before illustrating my point, let me briefly define what I mean by an employee problem. An employee problem is an obstacle or barrier that stands in the way of achievement of the employee's goal or his or her need satisfaction. The employee perceives that he or she cannot remove the obstacle without help from the supervisor. And so, the employee initiates a one-to-one meeting to seek the supervisor's assistance.

A Tale of Two Supervisors

The Fictional Fixture Corporation, a manufacturer of fine lighting for businesses and residences, has just closed up shop for the day. Two of the company's supervisors have gotten into their automobiles for the commute home. As they drive, their thoughts wander back to the events of the day.

Wanda Solvem, the supervisor of chandelier assembly, is thinking, "Gripe! Gripe! Gripe! It seems that all my workers are constantly complaining about one thing or another. Well, on second thought, perhaps I am exaggerating. Anyway, I did handle four employee problems today. They really tire me out. That one on maternity leave was a real stickler. I had to research the fine print in the company manual to see that female employees can work up to the day of delivery at their own discretion. As steamed as Susie was about the issue, I guess I headed off a possible grievance or even a class action lawsuit on the matter.

"Two of the other problems came up because of the rickety old machinery we have to put up with. Everybody knows that the new machinery will be installed within a few months' time, but it sure can get frustrating to try to meet production standards when the machinery keeps breaking down. Those two meetings I had with Marv and Sal just served to let them blow off some steam. It got a little hot and heavy at times. They said some nasty things about top management, and I even came in for some choice words. But everybody knows I won't let what is said in emotional outbursts leak out, or affect my decisions. They both seemed to feel a lot better afterwards, and they went back to patch the old machines as best they could.

"That other problem I handled today might have cost us our new employee. Payroll didn't get his name into the computer in time, so his first check wasn't issued today. He was rather upset because his rent is due, and he was expecting his first paycheck to cover it. It took a little doing, but I was able to get payroll to issue him a special check for Monday. I also lent him ten dollars until Monday to tide him over.

"It's a wonder that we're able to get our work done with all these problems coming up. But when all is said and done, I guess one of my primary functions is to solve employee problems. We usually manage to meet or exceed our production standards, and my people seem to be satisfied all around. In fact, I guess I've got the lowest rate of turnover and the highest rate of production in the company. Tomorrow I'm going to tear into that paperwork that I couldn't get done today."

As Orville Orderly, supervisor of table lamp production, drives out of the parking lot, he is also thinking, "Things seemed to go pretty smoothly today. I was able to finish all my paperwork, and the machines only gave out twice. One thing is puzzling, though: Nobody seems to be complaining or griping. I know people have work problems, but they seem to bypass me to solve them. I can't understand it. Just last week I instituted a policy where everybody should send all problems to me in writing.

"In the policy memo I sent, I reminded everyone that personal problems must not interfere with our getting the work out. Also, I wrote that they should be sure that a problem was important enough before getting me involved. Most of the time their problems are too trivial for me to bother with. Each employee must read the company manual first. What the manual says goes. Production and paperwork have to come first. Imagine if I started spending too much time dealing with silly problems when I have to get out there and patch up the machinery that breaks down or solve the really important problems.

"Still, even though things appear smooth on the surface, I do have to respond to quite a few formal grievances. Also a lot of my workers seem to want to transfer to Wanda's unit, although there's no difference in pay and working conditions between the two. Another thing is that I keep losing people at a fairly high rate. Maybe that idea I read about last week will do some good—the idea was to leave my office door open during the day."

During the next few months Wanda is picked over Orville and several others for a promotion to production manager. Orville leaves his door open, but few of his employees come in to see him. He continues to experience an overly high turnover rate and a substantial number of formal grievances.

The Moral

What accounted for the difference in performance and turnover between Wanda's and Orville's units? Which of these two supervisors are you most like? The key difference between Wanda and Orville is in their approach to communication. Wanda is obviously approachable and open-minded. Her employees have learned that she can be counted on to lend an ear when they have a gripe. She can also be counted on to listen to a problem fully so that she understands exactly what it is. If it is just a matter of clearing the air, or releasing frustration, Wanda can be trusted to keep things confidential. She has a great deal of credibility with her employees, too, because she won't jump to conclusions or make a decision without researching all the facts. Nor will she make promises to do things that really are not under her control. She treats her employees fairly and with dignity and moves as quickly as possible to get a resolution. In many instances, she will work with employees to come to a decision or a solution of a problem. Perhaps most important of all, Wanda is willing and able to deal openly with feelings, including anger, anxiety, and depression.

By contrast, Orville has communicated to his unit that, despite his open door, he is really not interested in dealing with employee problems. Orville is more concerned with paperwork than people. He also is too ready to go by the book in making decisions and solving problems. Since his employees cannot communicate with Orville directly about the problems they have, they often turn to the grievance system. This has created a clear separation between Orville, who is now identified with impersonal management, and his employees. The gulf that separates Orville and his employees would take a strong effort, and perhaps even the assistance of a communication expert, to bridge.

Two Key Elements of Effective Communication

If I had to choose the two most important aspects of effective communication in resolving employee problems, they would be credibility and the history of the relationship between supervisor and subordinate. Credibility involves trust—trust that a supervisor will treat complaints with all due importance, that feelings and opinions can be freely expressed in confidence, and that the supervisor will not use an employee's problems to hurt the employee in any way.

The history of the relationship refers to an early and continuing establishment of the approachability of the supervisor. The supervisor must establish a *solid record* of treating problems in confidence, striving to understand employees' problems from the perspective of the employees, and even-handedly attempting to resolve problems in a way that the employees can understand and agree with.

A supervisor cannot expect to build a solid history merely by leaving his or her office door open. Instead, the supervisor must actively work to foster good relationships. If employees do not come in through the open door, the supervisor must use the open door to go out and get them.

The Nature of Employee Problems

What are some of the more common kinds of employee problems that a supervisor will find?

First, there are the problems that focus on the *employee's own shortcomings*. These might be exemplified by such statements as, "I just don't have the proper training on the new machinery to be able to do my job," or "I just seem to have difficulty closing a sale."

Another major set of problems arises from *company policies and procedures*. For example, employees may feel that they have been unfairly treated or poorly reviewed during a promotional competition. Or employees may complain about the length of time it takes to secure new equipment and supplies.

Still another major category revolves around *social relations*. Bickering and conflict among co-workers, soured relationships with clients, and even difficulties between the employee and supervisor are examples.

Yet another set of problems that leads to employee gripes focuses on *the work itself*. Tasks may be seen as boring or not challenging enough. Employees may feel that they are prevented from doing things better. The job may be too big for an employee, which leads to a constant feeling of stress and failure.

Often the most difficult problems to deal with are the *personal difficulties* that interfere with an employee's capacity to do the job. A spouse's illness, financial problems, transportation difficulties, addiction to alcohol or drug abuse, and house-hunting problems are all part and parcel of this type of difficulty.

To conclude my obviously incomplete list are those problems having to do with the *work setting* and *working conditions*. Drab, dirty, unsafe, and uncomfortable climatic working conditions underlie many employee gripes.

Dealing with this wide range of problems certainly requires diplomacy, tact, and in many instances a sense of humor. But effective communication is the foremost requirement of a supervisor, even if the problem goes beyond his or her ability to solve it. To demonstrate how critical it is, let's look at one employee problem and its successful resolution in order to see those elements of communication important to its solution and indeed to the resolution of most employee problems.

"My Daughter's Getting Married"

Presented below is a meeting between a supervisor and her subordinate. At critical points in the dialogue comments will be interjected that can serve as a list of dos and don'ts for employee problem-solving meetings. Although the meeting is fictitious, it is not too far from the kind of meeting most supervisors have had with their employees.

To set the scene, Al, the subordinate, has presented himself at the doorway of his supervisor's office. He looks concerned, troubled, and anxious. Mary, his supervisor, is working on a report.

Supervisor: (looking up attentively and smiling) Hi, Al! Hey, you seem to have something on your mind. I'm in the midst of this report, but it can wait a few minutes if you really need to see me right away.

Subordinate: Yes, Mary, I really do have something on my mind that I'd like to discuss with you right away.

Supervisor: Come on in and sit down.

Subordinate: Thanks, I'm really glad you'll be able to spend a few minutes with me. I'll try not to take up too much of your time.

Supervisor: Oh, no problem, Al. You hardly ever make demands on my time anyway. Let me buzz my secretary and tell her to hold all calls and visitors for a while.

[*Author's comments:*   The opening statements here are critical. They demonstrate that Mary was quite sensitive to Al's troubled look. She is obviously approachable. She did not put him off or simply refuse to see him. She paid him a compliment, which helped establish rapport very quickly, by telling him that he rarely bothers her or takes up her time unduly. If Mary were truly under deadline pressure, she could have asked Al whether the matter could hold until she finished off the report or at least came to a convenient stopping place in her work. An unacceptable response would have been to keep her eyes mostly on her paperwork while telling Al that she could not see him until she was done. This would have given Al the impression that he was not important enough to warrant a bit of attention from his supervisor. His emotional state, under the circumstances, might have caused him to take rash and foolhardy action.]

Supervisor: Gee, Al, you really look concerned. What's on your mind?

Subordinate: Well, Mary, as you know, I've got to have this presentation to top management ready by Thursday of next week, and my daughter's getting married next Wednesday night. I don't see how I'll have the time to complete the presentation when I've got to take Tuesday and Wednesday off to make final arrangements for the wedding. I'm feeling so pulled in both directions that I just haven't been able to think clearly and make much progress on the presentation.

Supervisor: Gee, that is a tough one. Are you saying that the stress is preventing you from getting the report ready? Or is it that you simply don't have enough time?

Subordinate: I guess it's probably a combination, but I really do need to have those two days to finish the presentation and get it up to snuff.

Supervisor: You don't think the problem is just that you may be feeling a little threatened by making a presentation to top management? It may be that that's holding you back.

Subordinate: (after a bit of silence) No . . . I don't think so; I've been in this business too long to let that bother me. No, I think it's a time bind, and, as the time gets closer, my stress level is growing to the point where I can't come up with any alternatives. That's where I hope you can help me.

[*Author's comments:*   Mary has shown the openness necessary to ensure full communication. She has invited Al to express his feelings, and she has helped him to define his problem clearly through the expert use of probes, or questions about specifics. She has also gotten sufficient information so that she understands the problem herself and is in a position to help. Moreover, she has not shown any resistance to treating a conflict between personal concerns and business concerns. An obviously inappropriate response to Al's statement of the problem would have been, "Well, Al, you know we can't allow off-the-job concerns to interfere with our business obligations. Get back to your office and work it out." The threat contained in this statement is a sure way to clog communication channels, since an employee will become aware of possible punishment if he or she is open about his or her problems.]

Supervisor: Well, Al, this is a toughy. To get us started on thinking up some ways to solve the problem, let me suggest that we see if we can get the presentation postponed until the following week. What do you think about that?

Subordinate: Well, they did seem to put a high priority on this presentation.

Supervisor: Uh huh (silence).

Subordinate: (fidgeting a bit uncomfortably in his chair) Postponement is an alternative. I guess I'm feeling uncomfortable because it really isn't my place to ask for a postponement.

Supervisor: Yes, I guess you're right. Why don't I go ahead and check out this possibility (silence).

Subordinate: Say, I have a thought! I could possibly shake loose from my personal business for a few hours on Tuesday and Wednesday, and I could delegate a lot of the leg work to one of my people. During the time I have available, I could make suggestions and outline any additional material that has to be covered.

Supervisor: Sounds like a pretty reasonable approach to me.

Subordinate: The only problem is that none of my people has all the information or expertise to carry it off. If . . . well, okay, I'll say it . . . if we can get one of the other unit managers to give the person on my staff who gets the task a bit of time, I think it can be done.

Supervisor: I can understand why you're a bit hesitant. This is a busy time, and everybody is pressed. But if you offer one of the managers some of your time later on, maybe you can get him to cooperate with you on this.

Subordinate: Sounds like we have some good alternatives. Why don't I see if I can line things up on my end.

Supervisor: Great! And I'll check on whether the presentation can be postponed. I'll just ask our plant superintendent casually. If the answer is no, and we can work things out at your end, why we can swing right into your plan.

Subordinate: (energetically) I'll get right on it!

Supervisor: Since we're working on a tight time schedule here, let's get the necessary information we need and meet early this afternoon, say about 1:30, to make a decision. Okay?

Subordinate: All right! Say, thanks a million, Mary. You've sure been a help!

[*Author's comments:*   In kicking off a discussion of possible solutions with a suggestion of her own, Mary has used some excellent psychology. Mary sensed that Al's dilemma had unleashed a flood of mental energy that was actually paralyzing his thought process. Through the use of a suggestion and a request for Al to evaluate it, she was able to direct the energy constructively. Once his thought processes were moving, Al was able to come up with some reasonable approaches to solving the problem. The bit of discussion between Mary and Al on solutions also illustrated the effective use of silence to bring out more feelings and thoughts. Mary was able to find out that Al had thought of a postponement but felt that she, rather than he, should ask for the postponement.

Another positive aspect of this meeting was that Mary used goal setting to ensure that the problem would be solved on a timely basis. Though many management specialists and social scientists speak glowingly of goal setting for achieving high performance, few have pointed out that goal setting has an important place in employee problem solving as well. The use of goal setting can ensure that sufficient information will be gathered and a substantial number of feasible alternatives will be considered in overcoming employee problems. Goal setting with respect to time can prevent an otherwise simple problem from becoming much more complicated just because it was not handled quickly. Reasonably short deadlines for delivering solutions to problems represent yet another way to communicate to your employees that their problems are important enough for quick action.]

Early That Afternoon

Supervisor: Hi, Al, come on in and sit down! I've been expecting you.

Subordinate: Thanks. Can the presentation be postponed?

Supervisor: No, unfortunately, it can't be. They need the information for a stockholders meeting that will take place over the weekend. So we're going to have to come up with the presentation.

Subordinate: Well, I've checked on the other possibility that we talked about, and I have it worked out. Nancy will take responsibility for the report. She'll coordinate with me next Tuesday and Wednesday. Also, Dick was nice enough to offer several hours, which I will make up to him the week after next.

Supervisor: Do you think that we can really get a top-quality presentation out this way?

Subordinate: Nancy can handle the assignment, particularly with Dick pitching in and me critiquing the presentation.

Supervisor: Okay, I'll be counting on you to do a good job! Say, while you're here, perhaps I can ask you something that I'm a little bit puzzled about. This is the second or third time over the past month or two that you have had trouble with deadlines. This isn't like you, and I'm a little bit concerned.

Subordinate: (looking down at his hands and blushing) Well, I guess you're right. It's a little hard for me to talk about.

Supervisor: I can see that. But you and I have worked together for quite some time now. You know you can count on me to keep things to myself.

Subordinate: I'm really grateful that you're concerned enough about me to notice these things. And I know I can trust you. Yes, I have had some difficulties recently. Marital problems. This is our youngest child who is getting married. The fact that we no longer will have children living at home with us has created a strain between Margaret and me. However, we have been seeing a marriage counselor, and I think we have it all straightened out.

Supervisor: I'm really pleased to hear that.

Subordinate: Yes, I think you'll see my problems with deadlines disappearing in the future.

Supervisor: I'm really glad about that. Oh, Al, please feel free to call on me anytime if I can be of any assistance. At any rate, for helping you out with this problem, I'll expect to have a seat of honor at your daughter's wedding.

Subordinate: (laughing) I'll see to that. Thanks again!

[*Author's comments:*   Mary again demonstrated the skills of an excellent communicator and problem solver. She was successfully able to go beyond the "symptom" and ferret out the real cause of Al's problem with the deadline. If Al had not resolved the problem, she would have been in an excellent position to help him with it. Mary used silence and supportiveness to garner the information she was seeking. She also closed the meeting with a very positive invitation to Al to seek her assistance in the future. She even demonstrated a sense of humor at the end of the meeting.]

Putting It All Together

Solving your employee's problems will be a lot easier if your one-to-one communication is effective. As a supervisor you must be sensitive to the status differences that exist between you and your subordinate, and strive to overcome them through your openness, approachability, and nonjudgmental attitude. Establishing rapport, asking the right questions, and using other sound interviewing techniques will facilitate your problem-solving meetings. Hopefully, studying the meeting between Mary and Al will make many of the big problems you face smaller and more manageable.

Why Won't They Accept Help From Supervisors?

H. KENT BAKER and RONALD H. GORMAN

Among the many roles a supervisor must fill, one of the most critical is his or her responsibility to aid subordinates in solving their work-related and developmental problems. But although a supervisor may have the technical qualifications to assist subordinates in these areas, this assistance is frequently offered inadequately. Thus the subordinate fails to receive the real help that a supervisor effective in counseling— and aware of the need for counseling—could provide.

This failure of a supervisor to be a good "helper" can often be attributed to inadequate training. There are, however, several guidelines that, if followed consistently, can enhance a supervisor's ability to provide genuine assistance to subordinates—and thereby meet his or her responsibilities more fully.

Recognizing Cries for Help

One problem a supervisor has in trying to help his subordinates is that he is often unaware they need help, many times because they are reluctant to ask for it. Consequently, a supervisor must stay alert to signs of employee need. A subordinate's performance appraisal is one obvious potential indicator that the employee may require assistance. If an employee's performance has declined or if an individual has failed to reach reasonable expectations, this could be because the subordinate has not received the assistance or training that his supervisor could provide. The supervisor should attempt to determine the underlying causes of such an inability to perform and work with the subordinate to overcome whatever problems are uncovered.

There are, of course, other indicators that may signal that a subordinate needs help. Such signs include indications of frustration or anxiety, defensive behavior, and absenteeism. An astute supervisor may also sense nonverbal clues that suggest the subordinate wants help but is unwilling to ask for it. For example, a supervisor may ask an employee if he or she needs help and, although the verbal answer may be no, other signs such as uneven intonation of voice, wringing of hands, poor body posture, or failure to make eye contact may signify otherwise.

A supervisor's helping relationships are especially important when major changes take place within

Reprinted from *Supervisory Management*, March 1978

the organization or within a person's job. For instance, an individual who has received a promotion or additional job responsibilities may be reluctant to ask for help because he may feel that such requests diminish the confidence his supervisor has in his ability. Furthermore, the subordinate may feel that asking for help is a sign of weakness or an indication of unworthiness to hold such a position.

To try to contain the effects of such reactions before they diffuse, a supervisor should establish clear role expectations for a subordinate in his or her new job. He should emphasize that new responsibilities require attitudinal changes and additional learning—both of which take time. By showing the subordinate that asking for and providing help are natural aspects of the subordinate-supervisor relationship, the supervisor has signified that such actions are not only "O.K.," but are actually to be encouraged. In other words, better that the subordinate ask one too many questions than make one too many mistakes. Thus a supervisor must be attuned to subordinates' silent cries for help and must establish an environment in which asking for help is viewed as perfectly acceptable behavior.

Help Wanted?

Reviewing the circumstances surrounding a subordinate's refusal to seek help with problems, an interesting irony emerges: When asked about their reluctance to seek help, usually they indicate that they would rather accomplish the task by themselves, feeling that a request for help is an admission of failure. Yet when asked if there is anything wrong with asking for assistance, they almost invariably answer no. Hence, in these situations, an apparent conflict exists between people's reported feelings and their subsequent actions. How has such an inconsistency come about? Let's probe the issue in greater depth and try to answer this question.

The disparity between the nominal attitudes of subordinates and their actual on-the-job activities suggests that they have learned from past experiences to second-guess their basic, forthright desire for assistance. In other words, the manner in which a supervisor has responded to previous requests for help plays a major role in determining whether a subordinate will now seek help. Such negative or positive experiences can have a major influence on a subordinate's future behavior.

To illustrate this hypothesis, let's imagine a situation in which an individual having problems with a particular task asks his supervisor for help. If the supervisor responds by simply taking over and doing the task himself, then this could prove to be a very unpleasant and disheartening experience for the subordinate. The person requesting help may feel "put down," and his self-image may be severely injured.

In this and other ways, a supervisor can inadvertently be patronizing or condescending toward the person requesting help. Although such help is offered without malice, the hurt to the subordinate is nonetheless felt deeply enough to dampen further requests for assistance. In psychological terms, the experience has been negatively reinforcing. Behavioral scientists report that activities viewed as distasteful or unpleasant will be avoided if possible in the future.

It is probably true that many people in any organization have just such an attitude toward asking for help. They deny their needs rather than be placed in a situation in which they are made to feel they have failed. Thus supervisors may wonder why a certain subordinate is so obstinate in refusing help when, in fact, such help is needed. Most likely, the subordinate's behavior emanates from previous times in which this or another supervisor "helped" in a negative way.

The "Please Help Me" Trap

A completely different, yet just as detrimental, supervisor-subordinate relationship can develop when the person seeking help is aware that the supervisor is only too happy to take over and handle the subordinate's task. In such instances, the subordinate may use his plea of "please help me" as a means to "reverse delegate" the work onto the shoulders of the supervisor. Unfortunately, this kind of situation tends to perpetuate itself because the helper feels useful, needed, and competent and therefore is quite willing to do the work. The subordinate then may use his helplessness as a ploy to avoid doing his fair share of work. Provided the ploy is not used too frequently or too blatantly, the supervisor may not even be aware of the real motive behind the subordinate's requests for help. But in effect "please help me" can become another type of game playing that, if allowed to continue, can prove detrimental to the functioning of the organization.

A supervisor should, of course, parry such attempts at reverse delegation because they do not help the subordinate grow and become more competent on the job. Instead of "accepting the monkey" by agreeing to do the task, the supervisor should make it clear that it is not his problem but that of the person being helped. By demarcating responsibility areas, the supervisor can help the subordinate understand what is expected of him and possibly reduce future attempts at reverse delegation.

On the other hand, although the supervisor must be firm, he must also take care not to handle the situation in a curt or demeaning manner. After all, the supervisor could be wrong in his reading of the subordinate's intentions. It is critical, however, that the person who has the problem accept his responsibility for solving it. This should be handled in a positive way by the supervisor.

Helping Guidelines

In order to make the helping relationship a positive experience, a supervisor should follow several guidelines. These guidelines will enable him to be firm and at the same time build rapport with his subordinates, thereby helping the subordinate while getting the job done:

1. *Demonstrate empathy.* In improving helping relationships, it is important for a supervisor to attempt to understand the opinions and feelings of his subordinates. This "feeling with" approach is called empathy and differs from sympathy (feeling sorry for) and apathy (having no feeling for). By being aware of another's feelings and emotional responses toward the issue of being helped, it is unlikely that a supervisor will intentionally do damage to a subordinate's self-image or take a course of action that would basically hinder the helping relationship. Thus if a subordinate feels that asking for help is a sign of weakness, the supervisor can make it clear that the person seeking help is not stupid, weak, or unusual. Indeed, a supervisor should make the point that requesting assistance is a normal circumstance in healthy organizations.

2. *Provide alternatives, not answers.* One of the major reasons subordinates become "turned off" when asking supervisors for help is that the supervisor often actually does the task instead of *helping* the subordinate do it. Instead of providing the answer or doing the job, the supervisor should only *help* the subordinate identify several alternative ways of resolving the problem or performing the task. The subordinate is then given the freedom to select what he feels is the most viable solution.

In this way, the subordinate is making the decision and will be more likely to accept responsibility for the outcome. If, on the other hand, the supervisor says, "Do it this way," and the suggested solution fails, the blame can be shifted to the supervisor because the subordinate felt he was simply carrying out orders. By enabling the subordinate to make the decision and accept its consequences, the supervisor is in effect saying, "I have confidence in you and in your ability to make the right choice."

3. *Instill a feeling of achievement.* Providing a sense of achievement for a subordinate is critical, because it can be the first step in a series of successes, hopefully leading to the habit of winning. Therefore, the problem that is currently being faced must be resolved by the person with the problem; in other words, the person wins by solving the problem himself. By encouraging such initiative, the supervisor says to the subordinate, "You have a problem. This doesn't say anything bad about you, but you'll feel really good when you solve it yourself."

A supervisor-helper may guide the process of achievement by asking questions, leading the discussion toward defining potential alternatives, and assisting the person to see things more clearly. Normally this is achieved through a questioning process. The helper must be careful not to offer so much guidance that the achievement directly results from his assistance. The questions should lead the person with the problem into thinking things through more carefully and ultimately toward problem resolution.

4. *Practice listening.* As previously indicated, before a supervisor can begin to offer meaningful assistance, he must first understand the subordinate's point of view regarding the helping relationship and the problem at hand. This, of course, requires that the supervisor be a good listener. And although the supervisor should guide the discussion at times by asking probing questions or by clarifying issues, most of the talking should be left to the subordinate.

Being an effective listener is a tough job and requires effort and practice. The supervisor must resist the temptation of giving a lecture on how to perform the task or resolve the problem, thereby monopolizing the conversation. As a helpful reminder, the supervisor may recall the old adage that a person is given two ears and one mouth and hence should listen twice as much as he talks. When trying to foster helping relationships, this is very sound advice.

5. *Assume a positive attitude.* One of the reasons subordinates do not ask for help is because they sense that their supervisors will not respond in a positive manner to their requests. Thus if they sense that a helping experience will not be reinforcing or will somehow be threatening, subordinates will usually avoid it. People have very precise sensing instruments and can readily pick up cues from another's behavior. As a consequence, supervisors should set the stage by conveying the attitude, "You're O.K. if you ask for help, and I'm O.K. if I provide it." This positive attitude should clarify the supervisor's position toward helping. The supervisor should also indicate that he expects employees to grapple with their problems and try to resolve them before coming for help. If they do this, then he will gladly provide whatever assistance he can.

Potential Pitfalls

Behavioral scientists point out that people will more likely repeat activities that have provided positive, rather than negative, feelings or reinforcement. Because the helping relationship can be a very positive experience for the subordinate—due to a great extent because of the attention he receives—the temptation exists for subordinates to become chronic help-seekers and to use the helping relationship as a crutch.

Such situations can pose problems for both the supervisor and the subordinate because, first, excessive reliance upon supervisory assistance can make subordinates dependent on their supervisors for all problem resolutions. As we noted before, such dependence can retard both personal growth and job satisfaction. Second, providing too much time for helping relationships can reduce the effectiveness of the supervisor when it causes him to ignore other aspects of his job. And third, knowing that help is always immediately available can diminish the sense of achievement motivation and initiative among subordinates.

The supervisor-helper should aid the subordinate by giving him the needed motivation to solve the problem and by helping him see possible courses of action. Often the person with a problem is too quick to seek assistance because he lacks sufficient motivation to struggle through the problem. Subordinates should be encouraged to develop a personal need to succeed and to become accustomed to a habit of winning. The supervisor can aid this development by reinforcing independent, original behavior that he wants to see continued and by providing timely and meaningful feedback on the individual's performance. The supervisor can also establish the precedent that his help will be provided *only* after the subordinate has made an honest effort to resolve the difficulty.

Since he is being reinforced for attempting to solve a problem with the supervisor's words of encouragement and praise, the subordinate is more likely to exert a substantial effort before seeking help because he has already been recognized for his efforts. Also, having been provided with the appropriate role expectations, the subordinate knows what is expected of him and when help can legitimately be sought.

Although serving in the capacity of helper is a vital role for any supervisor, fulfilling this task requires sustained, consistent effort. To be effective in dealing with subordinates, a supervisor must be aware that helping relationships are a natural part of the job. However, a balance should be struck between how often help is sought and how much help is provided. How fair this balance is and how it is achieved will contribute to the success of both the supervisor and his subordinates. Finally, although the helping guidelines provided above are not a panacea, they do serve as another useful means for helping the supervisor become more effective on the job and in his or her difficult role of trying to help—but not too much.

Improving Productivity:
Ways to Get People Started

CURTIS E. DOBBS

In the press for increased productivity, the attendant fanfare over quotas, indexes, and slogans sometimes diverts attention from the one really essential element of productivity: people. It is people, after all, who make plans work or fail. To get people back into the limelight when productivity plans are being made, managers may need to refocus on a few things. How do people affect productivity? What about people cost in productivity? What about the responsibility of supervisors for people and productivity?

First, let's look at the meaning of productivity. Productivity measures what is produced in relation to what is consumed in order to produce it. What kinds of things are consumed? Money, for one, and materials and wear and tear on plant and equipment and—of course—the time and effort of people. But people affect productivity not only in terms of their time and effort (which has a dollar cost measured in salary and benefits), but also in terms of the problems they create (which can also be measured in dollars, though much less precisely). Later, we'll take a look at the kinds of people problems that affect productivity.

To improve productivity, an organization must get more out of what it has—get more output from its consumption or input of resources and expenditures—*or* change the kinds or amounts of inputs involved to get relatively greater output. Can a department produce more reports, for example, by purchasing new equipment? Or can it produce the same number of reports with fewer people doing the work? In these examples, resources are changed to improve the productivity measure. But management may also be able to improve productivity simply by improving techniques to increase output (by using form paragraphs in reports, for example) without altering resources.

Potential Effects on Employees

In thinking about new programs and techniques for improving productivity, management needs to be aware of the potential effects on employees—because negative effects may stimulate employees to create problems. Although this is only common sense, it is often overlooked—especially when times are bad

Reprinted from *Supervisory Management,* March 1976

and an organization's financial position is shaky. Particularly important are the effects on production employees, clerical employees, and supervisors. These people do the day-to-day work, so most productivity programs are logically aimed at them. But such programs are fruitless if employees resist improvement efforts—and they have been known to do so strenuously enough to reduce productivity.

Let's look at two potential effects commonly occurring. An important one is the triggering of resistance to change. Many employees do tend to resist change—even those who claim to accept it readily. There are many reasons for this, but let's look at just one: fear.

Yes, the prospect of change often scares people. They may naturally fear:

- Job loss—"Maybe this change will eliminate my job."
- A speed-up—"They want me to do my job faster, but I can't!"
- Relocation—"Hey, could this new program cause me to transfer to a new department?"
- The unknown—"Hold it! I don't understand! What about my friends? Will I get a new boss? New responsibilities? I just don't know what might happen!"

Another effect is typified by the question, "What's in it for me?" The point is perhaps debatable—and has been debated—but it does seem that most people do not work for the pleasure of working. Most of us, and most of our subordinates, work to provide for our needs and obligations and those of our families. It's natural that an employee faced with new approaches like productivity programs will begin to think (consciously or subconsciously) about "What's in it for me?" Can he or she expect problems or "good things" like more pay or better working conditions?

The People Costs Involved

Now let's take a brief look at people costs as they affect productivity. The obvious ones are salary and benefits and an obvious way to decrease these is to reduce the number of employees. As we mentioned, however, there are other people costs to be taken into consideration—and although they are not so obvious, reducing them can improve productivity.

Turnover and absenteeism, for example, create many problems—especially for the manager or supervisor trying to increase productivity. Although the costs involved are hard to measure precisely, they take the form of late work, duplicated work, mistakes, additional administrative effort, lost time, and so forth. Management often places too little emphasis on the costing and control of these factors.

It is not too difficult to identify such turnover costs as those for recruiting, selection, placement, and training. Almost any organization can calculate the cost of recruiters, recruiting material, employment tests, medical examinations, and employee orientation programs; indeed, many organizations have formalized training budgets. But there are additional factors such as lowered morale and decreased company loyalty that lead to increased production costs, errors, and lower productivity. The dollar cost of turnover is difficult to assess in any organization, but may range from $300 for a production worker to $7,000 and more for a manager. These are significant costs.

Putting dollar figures on employee absence is more difficult. A key cost factor here is that of lost production. Even if management institutes cross-training programs to offset production loss during employee absences, there is an added training cost. And, of course, there is also the cost of various sick-pay programs, as well as other intangible costs.

The point is that the people cost—as a key factor in calculating productivity—is made up from more than simply salaries and benefits. The rate of turnover, absenteeism, tardiness, and the like can increase or decrease people cost and thus increase or decrease productivity. Managers who address themselves to these costs—that is, concern themselves with their people—have a significant opportunity to affect productivity.

Some Useful Approaches

Following are some approaches that can help increase productivity through concentration on the people who do the producing. These are not all new ideas—some, in fact, are a little old-fashioned—but they point up the availability of a variety of ways to increase productivity through people. (Note that an organization doesn't have to have a fancy or even formal program to get a better job done. Many of the following steps can be taken by individual managers in their own departments.)

1. *Make a diagnosis of on-the-job problems.* This should be a careful examination of what is going on in the work place, not an intuitive assessment. Don't let an abundance of problems pressure you into unplanned solutions. Set priorities for solving them and proceed accordingly.

One tool that can be used in both diagnosis and priority setting is a series of candid interviews with each hourly employee and any subordinate supervisor involved. These interviews often yield much information—some useful and some not—but by putting it all together, management can establish a meaningful pattern of concerns and problems. Upon analyzing such interview responses, managers have been surprised to see how well employees know the problems, can define them, and can set priorities.

When this diagnostic approach is part of a broad management undertaking, assistance may be required from outside the department. However, an individual manager or supervisor can make his own diagnosis if he is willing to be objective. To increase his or her objectivity, the manager can discuss the situation with another manager or get assistance from the personnel department.

2. *Don't forget training.* Sound, well-thought-out, formal (at least outlined in writing) training is a productive investment. Many companies have training budgets and full-time training directors. The meaningful content of this training, however, must come from first-line supervision and middle management. If your organization has formal training programs, make sure the content is good. If it is not, suggest changes. If there is no formal training, you might outline one or two basic programs and recommend them to the appropriate superiors.

3. *Involve your subordinates.* Supervisors should not forget that subordinates have knowledge about their work that can help. Let employees have input to productivity programs. Inform them of problems and goals. Anticipate with them the results of the new programs.

The need for effective communication and employee involvement cannot be overemphasized in productivity improvement programs. Meetings provide an excellent way to accomplish this. Depending on the scope and structure of the program, the meetings may be organizational, departmental, team (one team may consist of all managerial staff, another of all employees at a certain level, and so forth), or one-to-one. To be useful, however, any meeting must be specifically planned to facilitate the exchange of information on productivity plans and progress among all team members.

Attitude or opinion surveys and suggestion systems are considered by some to be old-fashioned, but they are nevertheless useful. When designed to elicit the proper response, they can open up communication on problems that block progress, establish management's credibility, and involve employees. A word of warning, however: Don't ask for ideas or suggestions unless you plan to respond to them. Inaction will destroy management's credibility in short order.

Many organizations use newsletters effectively to communicate with employees. Effective ones are not simply propaganda sheets, but include information meaningful to employees in terms of what they do, what they care about, and what affects them.

4. *Make use of performance appraisals and objectives.* Performance appraisal *is* important to the employee. He or she really does want to know "How am I doing?" Day-to-day compliments and constructive advice are most important—but the annual or semi-annual written appraisal is quite significant. A written appraisal lets the employee know his boss is willing to stand by his comments by putting them in writing. Giving the employee a copy of the appraisal will assure him that there are no secrets concerning appraisal of his performance. More and more organizations are building objectives into such appraisals. These objectives can be set jointly with employees and then measured and reset at each formal appraisal session. It is still true that if employees know what is expected of them, they usually perform better and more productively.

5. *Don't overlook training for subordinate supervisors—or for yourself.* Remember that you and any subordinate supervisors you have may also stand in need of further training and education to keep abreast of change. More and more supervisors are taking advantage of training sessions offered by management organizations and colleges on such supervisory techniques as performance appraisal, employee relations, communication, and the like. Training is important both for new supervisors and for "old pros."

All the ideas discussed are people-oriented approaches to productivity improvement. Remember that the people doing the work are the hourly people—not management. Don't forget that they know the work and have ideas about how it can be accomplished more efficiently. Managers who want to improve productivity will use these ideas, establish credibility by acting on them, and get meaningful participation from employees.

Teaching Responsibility to Poor Performers

JERRY CONRATH

Of your employees, which ones make you truly crazy? If you're like most managers, it's probably the externalizers—that is, those employees on your staff who see life as outside their personal control. When they do well, they attribute it to luck. When they do poorly, again it is luck. All their school years, possibly even work years, they have been lectured to by well-intentioned persons about "making something of themselves," "taking control of their lives," "accepting responsibility," but these lectures have fallen on deaf ears. Because these workers don't recognize a cause and effect relationship between job behavior and success, they aren't easily motivated to change the way they behave.

Now they are your responsibility. What can you do about them?

It will be tough for you to understand the externalizers on your payroll because, as a manager, you are probably an internalizer, seeing life well within your control. You realize the relationship between work behavior and performance and therefore take personal responsibility for your department's and organization's performance. But if you are to do something about these externalizers' performance, you have to understand reality from their perspective. Once you do that, you can begin to teach them to accept responsibility for what goes on at work. Admittedly, it will be a time-consuming process, but it is the only solution. None of the more traditional approaches to performance improvement is likely to work:

Threatening discipline. Threats, like the lectures, are likely to fall on deaf ears. All you would be doing would be releasing feelings of guilt in the employee. These feelings would exist for awhile, then move on. And in the future, the externalizer would just avoid the situations contributing to the feelings of guilt. For example, if the externalizer called in late to work and got chewed out, next time he wouldn't call in. If she asked for extra time off and was met with anger—however reasonable—she just wouldn't ask in the future; she'd just take the time off.

Putting the externalizer into a sink-or-swim situation. You would likely try this if all else had failed. But an externalizer, put into a sink-or-swim situation, is likely to sink. When one believes life is outside one's control, swimming is incomprehensible.

Using external rewards to produce desired behavior. This may have a short-term payoff, but it does little to change the viewpoint of the externalizer. Indeed, it's likely to reinforce it, causing him or her to attribute external causes to failure to earn a desired reward.

Reprinted from *Management Solutions*, October 1988

Reasoning with the employee. Unfortunately, it doesn't pay to talk about past mistakes and encourage externalizers to relate past experiences to future tasks. Such logic just won't work with them. Externalizers learn little from their mistakes because they believe they had little personally to do with the mistakes; they just happened.

You shouldn't give up hope, however. There are ways you can get those low-esteem, externalizing workers in your department to assume responsibility. You do this by:

Insisting externalizers take personal responsibility for their success, not only their mistakes. Of course, it won't be easy to get these employees to acknowledge their accomplishments. You'll have to point them out and talk to these workers about their successes until they truly see them. It will take patience.

Helping externalizers understand that all achievement is a product of effort, skills, and luck. You shouldn't ignore the impact of luck when it plays a role, but you should stress the importance of effort. To develop a sense of responsibility in a worker, you first have to build self-pride in the individual. If the externalizer is young enough, you can make great strides by pointing out frequently what the employee should be proud of. At first, the employee will look dazed; but the words will eventually sink in. One bit of advice in doing this: Remember the externalizer's self-pride is more important than your own pride in the employee's growth. Start with, "You should be proud of . . . " before talking about what in the employee's behavior you're proud of. You should also only praise real effort and achievement.

Assigning the externalizer tasks for which he or she is qualified. Externalizers do not think effort pays off in achievement. Telling them so will not change their viewpoint. Only experience will. They need to see that they can be successful.

Emphasizing skills over "smarts." Indeed, the word "smarts" should be eliminated from your vocabulary. Externalizers think "smarts" is a genetic quality and therefore totally outside their control. They don't realize that "smarts" translates into skills, and that skills can be learned through individual effort and effective training.

Emphasizing behavior over "attitude." Attitude is a fuzzy concept at the best of times, but over the years externalizers have probably been told time and time again they were "born with a bad attitude." Besides, it's a lot easier to talk about behavior. And behavior, like skills, can be talked about in terms of internal responsibility.

Reinforcing the message you want heard and internalized. To make sure the message gets through, communicate it verbally, not in writing. Written performance reviews are too impersonal. Also, since the more removed feedback is from an event, the more it seems to the externalizer that success "just happened," give positive feedback as soon after it has been earned as possible. You have to make clear to the externalizer that his or her good performance was due to skill. If the employee tries to attribute it to luck, you have to cut him or her short, insisting that it was effort on the employee's part that was responsible.

Obviously, none of this will be easy. Nor will your externalizers turn over a new leaf overnight. But over time you should see a real change in those employees who for so long have driven you crazy.

Managing the Troubled Employee

ROBERTA ROYAL and GEORGE W. AYERS

At one time or another, each of your employees will experience some sort of personal problem that hinders work performance. Often the problem won't be too serious: The worker will get over it, and his or her performance will return to normal. The problem for you, of course, is in knowing how to distinguish between such a minor problem and a more serious and longer-lasting one so that your employee gets any professional assistance he or she may need.

Toward that, the Effective Management Response (EMR) Technique consists of four steps:

1. Recognition that the problem exists and is affecting performance on the job
2. Response in an effective manner
3. Referral, offering concrete assistance
4. Review, setting objectives and monitoring the effectiveness of the intervention

Recognition

Effective use of this technique depends on your ability to recognize a decline in work performance and to identify those employees who could benefit from assistance through the Employee Assistance Program (EAP).

General performance signs include tardiness, excessive absenteeism (even if within approved sick-leave policy), pattern absenteeism (that is, Fridays, Mondays, and/or before or after holidays), changes in work relationships, a decrease in quality of work, a decrease in quantity of work, excessive work breaks, and defensiveness.

Of course, one of these signs alone does not indicate that an employee needs or could benefit from an EAP. In combination, however, these signs can alert you to look for more specific signs associated with emotional, stress, or substance abuse problems.

Depression. Depression is a common problem affecting approximately 20 percent of all Americans. The performance and behavioral signs associated with depression include sleep disturbance (that is, inadequate sleep or rest); weight gain or loss; tearfulness; depressed mood; withdrawal from social situations; irritability; change in working relationships; and suicidal thoughts or actions.

Reprinted from *Management Solutions,* October 1988

Manic illness. Manic illness typifies the opposite of depression in many ways. Everything the employee does is exaggerated and accelerated. Specific signs usually associated with manic illness include agitation; grandiose thinking; disconnected thoughts; rapid and pressured speech; and behavior that is often self-destructive in some manner.

Thought disorders. Thought disorders are some of the more common yet most severe forms of emotional illness. The severity of the signs is quite exaggerated and usually will be exhibited without warning. That the person has performed successfully for a period of time without exhibiting these signs is usually meaningless. There may be, for example, a previous history of a thought disorder that has been in remission and has suddenly exhibited itself in acute stage. The signs associated with thought disorders are delusions; hallucinations; flight of ideas; isolation from others; withdrawal from others or social situations; disturbances of expression; and strange behavior.

Personal or family problems. Personal or family problems can include marital separation, divorce, marital conflicts, death of a loved one, and problems with children. Performance and behavioral signs often associated with personal or family problems include tardiness; absenteeism; tearfulness; longer-than-usual work hours; irritability; withdrawal from co-workers; defensiveness; and excessive sharing of personal problems with co-workers.

Chemical dependency. Chemical dependency, whether drugs or alcohol, presents a set of signs somewhat different from those of emotional illness but equally as disabling. These signs include problem denial; tardiness; excessive absenteeism; pattern absenteeism; actual use of the drug on the job; excessive work breaks; and changes in working relationships.

Response

The second step of the EMR Technique is management response to these signs. The key here is to focus on the employee's actual job performance problems—and not to "diagnose" or identify his or her emotional, personal, or substance abuse problem.

In responding to an employee's performance problems, you must avoid compounding the problem by responding inappropriately. Examples of inappropriate/ineffective response include:

Avoiding or ignoring the problem. A major temptation for managers is to avoid or ignore the specific problem being identified—particularly if the employee has proven to be an effective, dependable, and conscientious employee in the past.

Reassigning work responsibilities. At times, a manager may recognize that an employee is experiencing emotional or personal problems and will attempt to "help" by reassigning some of the employee's work to co-workers. But, again, this approach will not result in the employee receiving help and may cause morale problems or frustration within the employee group.

Advice-giving. Often, managers will try to help the employee "solve" his or her problem by providing suggestions or advice. But managers should recognize when advice is not enough.

Responding with firm discipline. Generally, this approach is used after the manager has tried to support the employee, reassigning work responsibilities and taking other steps designed to help. But when performance problems continue, the manager may become frustrated and assume a firmer approach with the employee. The problem, again, is that the employee has not received the needed assistance.

The EMR Technique overcomes these approaches' short-comings. In a manager-employee conference, the manager describes the specific problems *and* offers the employee the assistance he or she needs. The purpose of the conference is not to discipline the employee. If disciplinary actions are necessary, they are taken in a separate meeting.

To ensure an effective manager-employee conference, follow these steps before and during the conference:

Gathering the facts. Prior to the conference, collect the facts about the employee's specific performance problems, including dates, times, place (if applicable), and specific behavior or performance that did not meet job expectations.

Selecting the setting for the conference. As with any meeting with an employee, the site must guarantee no interruptions and provide confidentiality.

Establishing immediate control. At the beginning of the meeting, you must establish immediate control—preventing unrelated, tangential issues from being discussed.

Showing concern. During the first few minutes, say to the employee, "I am concerned." This statement serves two purposes. First, it shows your concern and caring for the employee and leads toward the offer of assistance later on. Second, it tells the employee there is a serious reason for the meeting.

Encouraging the employee's response to the problems. You should try to get the employee to share his or her feelings once all the performance problems have been described. Doing so will help you gather additional information either reinforcing the need for an EAP or indicating such assistance is not needed.

Recommending professional assistance. Often, participation in an EAP is not mandatory for an employee, but studies show it can be beneficial to the employee who chooses to participate. You should offer the EAP, even offer assistance in scheduling the employee's first EAP appointment. If the employee accepts the EAP referral, you should call to schedule the appointment during the meeting. If the employee refuses the EAP referral, accept the decision but emphasize that in your opinion assistance may help the employee correct his or her performance problems.

Emphasizing improved work performance. Whether or not the employee agrees to accept the EAP referral, you should emphasize that work performance must improve. Set specific objectives and specific time periods for performance improvement. In the end, the employee should leave the conference with three messages: You are concerned and eager to help; you have identified problems with his or her work performance; and work performance must improve or further disciplinary actions will be taken.

Referral

The timeliness of the referral is extremely important. But remember, an offer to help that is not accepted will not solve the problem.

Review

Review, the final step of the EMR Technique, consists primarily of watching to see if the employee improves his or her job performance. Once performance objectives have been set, you need to monitor the employee's performance. If the problems continue or the employee is unable to meet the objectives, you should take disciplinary actions. Keep in mind, too, that during the review period you're responsible for providing the employee with feedback about the progress made toward meeting the established objectives.

The First Steps in Solving People Problems

PEG SNYDER

Turnover in one firm's marketing department far exceeds the industry average. In another firm, members of an interdepartmental project team aren't talking to one another. And the employees of two recently merged departments are clashing daily over unfamiliar work procedures, policies, and values.

If left unchecked, such people problems will ultimately affect the organization's performance, productivity, and profit-making ability. Yet these relatively easy-to-spot problems aren't so easily solved. One reason is that solutions are too often based on false assumptions about the *underlying* causes. In such cases, symptoms typically reappear soon after the intended remedy has been implemented.

By trading assumptions for more objective, diagnostic methods, managers can accurately identify the actual cause of most human resource problems in their departments and implement effective, long-term solutions. To understand the value of such objective diagnosis, let's look at two real-life situations.

Case 1: The Problem Was Not Conflicting Attitudes

Two regional-level managers of a Fortune 500 financial services institution complained that their respective departments were in a state of high conflict. This was a serious problem for the organization because periodically various members of both departments had to form project teams to collaboratively market a new financial service. Such collaboration was becoming increasingly difficult due to increasing hostility between the two departments. Neither respected the other, and the members of both blamed the other for declining quality and output of project team efforts.

The two managers assumed that the differing attitudes, perspectives, and work values held by the two departments were causing the conflict. They further assumed that recently increased pressures on the institution, caused by industry deregulation, had exacerbated and magnified those differences.

Discussion of the problem with the managers was followed by a three-step diagnostic approach in which key members of both departments were interviewed, a structured survey was conducted about their methods for working together in project teams, and meetings of the project teams were observed.

The open-ended, private interviews confirmed the managers' assumptions. Interviewees frequently made "we vs. they" statements, which underscored the competitive nature of the relationship, and they openly made disparaging remarks about "that other" department.

The specific questions asked during the interview, and tabulated results of the survey, however,

Reprinted from *Management Solutions,* November 1987

revealed that there were few established policies or procedures to guide the collaborative efforts of the two departments. Gross ambiguities existed about project team goals and neither department had any substantive knowledge about the other, about how to identify or gain access to resources in the other department. Furthermore, there was at best an *ad hoc* communication system in place to keep members of both departments informed about the activities of the other.

During observation sessions of the project-team work, it was also evident that no efforts were being made to clarify at the outset respective roles, responsibilities, or priorities.

By using these diverse methods to analyze why the departments clashed—and failed to meet organizational expectations—we were thus able to focus intergroup team-building activities on a specific action step: the development of clear policies, procedures, and methods for working more effectively together. Of equal importance to increasing mutual respect and effecting a more cohesive project team was the fact that while the tasks were being accomplished, the very process of working together gave the two departments common goals and objectives to aim for.

Case 2: Human Behavior Can Cause Human Resource Problems

The second case illustrates the tempting, but sometimes misguided ease with which managers can blame inefficient work procedures for declining performance. The case involved a regional manager of customer service in an east coast telephone company. She and her 13 supervisors felt that there should be ways to improve productivity.

Of special significance to this case is the fact that the company had recently diversified and was facing strong threats from its competition. As a result, the customer service department was required to add marketing responsibilities to its traditional customer service function.

The staff was required to log all transactions of both types into a computer system. The data were irrefutable: Performance was declining in both areas of responsibility.

By using diagnostic methods similar to those employed in the first case, however, it was found that the actual cause of the problem was the manager herself. In her relationships with her supervisors, the manager exhibited behaviors commonly associated with resistance to organizational change: reluctance to trust or delegate responsibilities to others, increased "watchdogging," and failure to share needed information with those required to achieve specific departmental objectives.

It came as no surprise to learn, through observation, that the supervisors who had expressed frustration with such management behaviors were replicating the same behaviors as they managed their respective staffs. The result: Lack of incentive, anxiety, escalating morale problems—and the resulting decline in productivity—permeated the entire department.

Although procedural or structural changes had been recommended to resolve what were felt to be behavioral problems in the first case, this case indicates that the reverse is sometimes necessary. Revising work procedures would have been fruitless. Instead, structured activities were conducted to help the manager and supervisors become more aware of the contradictions between their expressed goals and actual behaviors; to help them confront their resistance to the changes wrought by recent diversification; and to improve their ability to manage those changes.

Summary

While the actual problems described here differed in each case, both reflect the significance of using multiple approaches to analyzing the actual, underlying cause of work-group problems before prescribing or implementing a remedy. To assure a return on any investment made to resolve identified problems, it is critical to identify and treat the cause—not the symptom—of the problem.

Just as critical—to both the diagnosis and the success of the solution—is involving all members of the group in the process of identifying and solving the problem. No single individual holds full responsibility for group problems; none should hold sole responsibility for repair.

When Family Stress Affects Worker Productivity

JOHN K. ROSS and THEODORE J. HALATIN

Bob has just been called into his supervisor's office. Although normally a good employee, Bob's work quantity and quality have fallen off in recent weeks and his attitude has been poor. As Bob enters his supervisor's office, the supervisor has the secretary hold incoming calls and begins a counseling interview.

After a few words of casual conversation, the supervisor tells Bob, "Your work hasn't been up to your regular high standards. Can you tell me what the problem is and what I can do to help?" Bob replies, "I don't know. I've really been under pressure from home lately. The kids are driving me and my wife crazy. They stay out all night, and I think Jim, our oldest, is taking drugs. Every night we have a knock-down, drag-out fight. I can't sleep, and when I'm at work I can't concentrate on what I am doing. I just don't know. . . ."

Bob's supervisor sits back in his chair, pictures the situation, and recognizes that family stress is affecting Bob's performance on the job. Yet he thinks back to a discussion he recently had with another employee who is also facing family problems but seems to be leaving his problems at home and is actually performing better on the job.

Non-job Factors and Productivity

A supervisor's concern for productivity often involves a similar concern for the well-being of the employee. When productivity and performance decline, the concerned supervisor may inquire about and discuss non-job related factors that may be affecting the employee.

A reasonable assumption for the supervisor to make when family stress is the problem is that stress can result in decreased productivity. Such an assumption appears to be quite reasonable when one considers that the stressed employee may carry various physical, psychological, and emotional aspects of the stress on to the job.

But a recent study that examined family stress and productivity found that a *positive* relationship existed between these two factors. Employees who reported stressful family situations were also reported to be *more* productive. These research findings served to disprove the assumption of decreased productivity due to family stress and suggest the existence of several possible relationships, which are shown in Figure 1.

Reprinted from *Supervisory Management*, July 1982

Figure 1

Model of Family Stress and Job Productivity

High Productivity 2 Low Stress	High Productivity 3 High Stress
Low Productivity 1 Low Stress	Low Productivity 4 High Stress

(vertical axis label: Job Productivity)

Family Stress

The Model

Along the base line of the square we find family stress ranging from low on the left to high on the right. The vertical line presents a scale of productivity ranging from low at the bottom to high at the top. The model shows four different types of situations.

In the lower left quadrant of the model (area 1) is the person who reports low levels of family stress and relatively low levels of productivity. This person is generally not productive, and it appears that a personal marital situation is not a cause of his or her performance problems. In such cases the supervisor need not be concerned about domestic problems as a factor causing low productivity.

The upper left quadrant of the model (area 2) describes a person who reports low family stress and high productivity. The person without a great number of domestic problems may be free from the on-the-job distractions that such problems can cause. Such a person may find that the satisfying marriage and family life have actually motivated him or her to do a good job.

In the upper right quadrant of the model (area 3) is the person who reports a high level of family stress and who shows high levels of productivity. In some cases this person is actually using the job as an escape from the stressful domestic situation.

In this area we also find the career-minded person who places career above marriage and family. For such an individual, the job may actually be an outlet and a way to be removed from the stress of the family. Productivity and job performance may become a source of satisfaction.

The lower right quadrant of the model (area 4) is used to describe the person who reports high levels of family stress and low levels of productivity. This employee's emotional state and thoughts in the aftermath of a domestic argument or conflict may detract from quality performance. Anger not released during an argument or feelings of depression and guilt may be carried on to the job.

This model is an important tool for helping supervisors to understand the different relationships between family stress and productivity. Locating various employees on the model can be instrumental in determining how best to supervise each. The supervisor can use this information for making assignments, scheduling, and deciding where to focus extra attention. The model can also be used for career counseling for employees who are experiencing severe domestic problems and are starting to show lower levels of productivity and performance.

Pattern of Development

The value of the model can be further increased by considering the pattern of the relationships as they develop. Based on the research and writings of R.H. Meglino and others, the way in which stress affects productivity can be described as an inverted U. (See Figure 2.)

Productivity increases when stress is at the lower end of the scale. This increase continues to a certain point that is represented by the top of the U. Beyond that point, any increase in stress causes reduced productivity and increased dysfunctional behaviors.

One of the difficulties and limitations in working with the inverted U is defining the peak. Because of the differing perceptions and values held by individuals, this critical peak for one person may not be the same as for another. Also, the rate at which a person arrives at that critical peak and the factors that contribute significantly to approaching the peak are very personal and individual. Still, a supervisor can gain by understanding the relationship and what can happen as stress does increase.

Suggestions for Supervisory Action

Even with an understanding of family-related stress, the supervisor is still left with the problem of what to do about employees experiencing it at high levels. If the employee's job performance is not being affected, the supervisor should do nothing unless specifically approached by the employee. It is important to remember that an employee's personal life is just that—personal—and not to be questioned lightly.

In those instances where poor performance has become a problem, the following actions are suggested.

Figure 2
Total Stress and Job Productivity

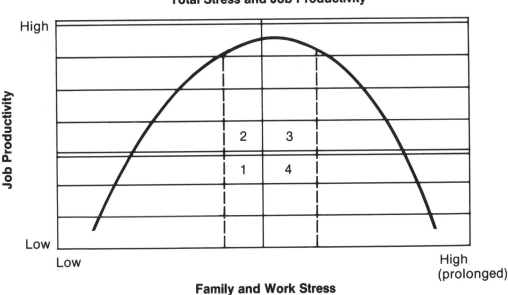

Family and Work Stress

1. Be understanding of the employee's problem, even though you may never have experienced it, but realize that the problem may be affecting the employee's performance and productivity.
2. Be aware of your qualifications for giving advice. Some domestic problems are minor and temporary, whereas others are quite complex and long term. Giving advice on family problems may not fall within your realm of skills and abilities, for most supervisors are not trained family counselors.
3. Be available to the highly stressed employee. Your willingness to meet with the person in confidence can be enough to help the individual through a temporarily difficult period. The employee may appreciate your support to the extent of staying to the left side of the peak in Figure 2. This could mean that the employee will use the job as a source of satisfaction during this temporary period of family turmoil rather than as a source of additional stress and conflict.
4. Use the techniques of active listening to gain information and help the employee. Active listening involves rephrasing in a nonjudgmental manner the statements made by the employee and trying to clarify in the employee's mind the actual nature and extent of the problem. Through active listening, the employee may be able to identify factors that may lead to a solution of the problem.
5. Stick to the agenda at meetings with the employees. The agenda should focus on productivity and the factors that are causing the lowered performance level. Do not become involved in monopolizing meetings by sharing personal past experiences that seem to play down the importance of the employee's current problems and result in the game of one-upmanship to see who has or has had the worst problems.
6. Monitor the time spent meeting with the employee. There is not only the time spent counseling the employee but also the time spent analyzing the results of the poor performance, planning to offset the poor performance, and the length of time expected for improvement to take place.
7. Present information. Examples of work, samples of techniques used to measure productivity, and reports should be gathered for discussions with the employee. The presentation of such information can be very threatening to a person who is already belabored by personal problems at home. Thus you must use discretion in presenting such documentation to the individual. At the same time, the employee may be unaware of the extent and magnitude of the problems being created on the job by the problems experienced at home. This documentation can serve a useful purpose in pointing out to such employees that the performance is being affected and something needs to be done.
8. Prepare documentation. Keep a written record of your observations, evaluations, and discussions with the troubled employee. Be sure to record the times and dates. This documentation may be very valuable if it becomes necessary to terminate, discipline, or formally evaluate the employee. It can also help to ease your mind when you recall your efforts to help this troubled person.

Family stress and its impact on job performance must be recognized. Supervisors who understand and are prepared to deal realistically with employee reactions to family stress will have the advantage of maintaining productivity and preserving their employees' careers.

Prevention and Cures of Absenteeism

HARVEY H. SHORE

Most studies show that on a given workday somewhere between 3 percent and 7 percent of the labor force is absent. Or, put another way, the "average" American employee is absent from work 7 to 12 times a year. This represents a cost of about 15 to 20 billion dollars per year, just in wages paid for days when employees were absent. First, let's look at preventive measures for absenteeism that can be taken before a person becomes a regular member of the staff:

1. In selecting personnel, try to avoid hiring people whose previous work record or whose state of health shows them to be absence-prone or otherwise unlikely to work at the required level. Requiring physical examinations and thorough reference-checking is helpful.
2. Don't place people in positions that will either bore them or overwhelm them.
3. Impress upon new employees that unwarranted absences are regarded as a serious matter. Be particularly firm in following up on this policy during an employee's probationary period. If, for instance, a new hire has two occurrences of unexcused absence during the first 60 days of employment, warn him or her or take other disciplinary action. If the employee shows no improvement during a set period of time thereafter, dismissal is in order.

You should try not only to prevent the development of absenteeism problems, but also to "cure" the tough cases that don't seem to go away. In thinking about cures for such problems, it is useful to distinguish between approaches intended only partly to reduce absenteeism and those that are, for all practical purposes, intended exclusively to reduce it and its associated costs. Let's consider these two categories in turn, referring to the first as "alleviative cures" and to the second as "specific cures."

Alleviative Cures

Alleviative cures for absenteeism include a wide range of management programs and practices—including:

1. The four-day workweek
2. Flextime

Reprinted from *Supervisory Management*, October 1975

3. Flexible compensation programs—also referred to as "the compensation cafeteria"
4. Job enrichment
5. Regular medical examinations for all employees
6. Programs of education and treatment for alcoholics and drug abusers
7. Building of teamwork among work groups
8. Encouragement of good two-way communication practices

Let's consider more closely how these programs and practices bear upon absenteeism.

1. *The four-day workweek.* According to its proponents, conversion to the four-day week has the happy effect of reducing absenteeism. It is true that in firms that have switched from a five-day week to a four-day week, each unexcused absence costs the employee 25 percent instead of 20 percent of his or her weekly earnings. This factor may well lead to some reduction in absenteeism. But the evidence seems to suggest that much of this reduction will last only for the *short* run. In other words, so long as the four-day week is perceived as a novelty by individual members of a company's workforce, absenteeism may indeed decline from previous levels. But it seems that much of this effect wears off fairly quickly. Significant reductions in absenteeism are not likely to be sustained very long merely by maintaining a four-day workweek (while ignoring other alleviative and specific cures).

This seems to hold true for each of the "cures." That is, except in rather unusual circumstances, no single cure—whether alleviative or specific—will significantly and lastingly reduce absenteeism. (Since the causes of absenteeism are multiple, the cures are usually multiple.) In general, it's only by applying several of these cures in combination—or in different combinations at different times—that significant, lasting reductions in absenteeism will be achieved. Exactly which combination of cures is suitable for a particular firm or department at a particular time is, of course, something that must be determined through diagnosis of each situation.

2. *Flextime.* Also aimed partly at curing absenteeism woes, flextime allows employees a certain degree of flexibility in choosing their own working hours. Originating in West Germany, the flextime approach is now used at a number of firms in this country; the New York offices of Nestlé and of Lufthansa were pioneers in using flextime here in the States. In practice, at least two kinds of flextime arrangements have been used. The first, called "gliding work time," stipulates that each employee must be on the job for certain fixed hours each workday (say, from 10:00 A.M. to 12:00 noon and from 2:00 P.M. to 4:00 P.M.), with the employee's other working hours to be a matter of personal choice (usually within the confines of, say, an 8:00 A.M. to 6:00 P.M. workday). The other type of flextime, called "individual working time," allows each employee to select at the start of each month, from among several specified work schedules, schedules in which the total number of hours of employment may vary. Since flextime does give employees more freedom in arranging their medical appointments and other personal matters, it's understandable that employers who adopt flextime typically experience a drop in absenteeism. Unfortunately, this drop, too, is likely to be only temporary.

3. *Flexible compensation programs—also referred to as "the compensation cafeteria."* Flexible (or cafeteria) compensation involves giving each employee some voice in the form and timing of at least part of his or her compensation. The primary advantage of this approach lies in providing extra motivation at no extra expense, since each worker's compensation package is tailored somewhat to his or her specific needs and preferences. Clearly, needs and preferences vary widely among people, or even for the same individual over a period of time. Given his choice, for instance, John Smith might well exhibit the following pattern of behavior during his work career:

John Smith's Circumstances	*Items That John Smith Might Emphasize in Choosing His Compensation Package*
Age 25, single	Time off from work
Age 35, married, father of 2 young children	Medical and dental insurance

Age 45   Cash to be able to afford college for his
                                                    children

Age 55   Retirement benefits

Under a typical flexible compensation program, each employee is allowed (within limits) to select his or her own compensation package annually. And the employer can protect each worker by requiring that he or she take at least minimal amounts of life and health insurance, at least minimal amounts of vacation time, and so forth. The motivational aspects of such a program could lead to an appreciable (if temporary) drop in *unexcused* absences. But if employees are given wide latitude in choosing their compensation, some may elect to take more days off from work than they were taking before the flexible compensation program was instituted. It is true that if employee X chooses, as part of his annual compensation package, to take 20 days off from work, management would at least have the advantage of knowing the employee's intentions ahead of time so that arrangements could be made to cope with any problems that might arise. In the absence of a flexible compensation program, an employee's decision simply to take 20 days off from work could wreak havoc in his department.

4. *Job enrichment.* Here, the attempt is to redesign job structures and conditions so as to make routine jobs less boring. It is argued (no doubt with some merit) that some employees stay away from work because they can't bear the prospect of another dull day on their dull jobs. Thus, enriched jobs may give jobholders enough incentive to go to work more regularly (and to show more interest in their work) than they did before. Again, though, job enrichment is not a panacea. Neither it nor any other approach will cure absenteeism once and for all. Many workers—in many different occupations and industries—don't want their jobs "enriched." These employees prefer to have relatively fragmented jobs that they can perform with a minimum of personal adjustment and with a minimum of on-the-job learning. Such workers want little direct responsibility (so that few demands will be made upon them) and little in the way of job variety or complexity (since either of these would be personally troubling). Enriching the jobs of such workers may actually increase their absenteeism.

5. *Regular medical examinations for all employees.* A program of providing all employees with regular medical and dental examinations on company premises (and perhaps on company time at company expense) may also cut absenteeism rates, at least for the short run. Such a program should reduce the number of absences necessitated by medical appointments. This number, of course, will not be very large. Regular medical exams for all employees have the added advantage of revealing and/or preventing illness.

6. *Programs of education and treatment for alcoholics and drug abusers.* Success with drug prevention and treatment programs (including alcohol) can yield significant and lasting reductions in absenteeism among addicted employees. (Since addiction is usually limited to 5 or 10 percent of a company's work force, success with these programs obviously won't solve a general absenteeism problem—but, for the employees affected, these programs can certainly be helpful.) The main elements of an effective program to prevent and treat drug abuse are to:

- Educate employees to the fact that alcoholism and drug abuse are *medical* problems requiring treatment (unions can help greatly in this education effort).
- Give employees periodic physicals (liver or pancreas ailments may signal the abuse of alcohol or other drugs).
- Alert supervisors to other symptoms that might help them identify alcoholics and other drug abusers.
- Counsel and offer psychological support to any employee known to be an alcoholic.
- Insist (perhaps with the aid of employees who have kicked the habit) that the alcoholic "take the cure" as a condition of staying on the payroll.

7. *Building of teamwork among the groups.* There are a variety of ways in which management may try to build teamwork among groups of employees. Some that have been successful include:

- Group incentive programs (in which each group member's compensation depends exclusively or at least primarily on the output of the entire group)
- Work-group activities off the job (bowling or softball teams, for example)
- Training exercises aimed at "team building." These exercises could involve attempts to instill in each employee: (1) feelings of responsibility toward the performance of his or her job, and (2) an understanding both of the importance of that job and of where it fits in (technically and in terms of the schedule) with the work of other employees.

Almost by definition, teamwork in a work group gives each member extra incentive to avoid letting other group members down. Whether this incentive will be consistently directed toward avoiding unnecessary absences is uncertain. Something as fragile as a spirit of teamwork may also prove difficult to sustain (for long). This is particularly true where turnover rate within the group is high.

8. *Encouragement of good two-way communication practices.* These practices include:

- Keeping employees well informed, particularly on the kind of performance expected of them and how well they are doing in meeting these expectations
- Praising or giving other kinds of recognition to employees who do their work well
- Inviting employees to participate in decision making whenever possible; also, being accessible to employees with questions and complaints (so that specific dissatisfiers can be rooted out)

The sort of work climate that these practices help create should to some degree discourage employee absences. But again, by itself, good communication will generally not be effective enough to squelch absenteeism for long.

Some of the alleviative cures may be adopted because they have a beneficial effect on problems other than absenteeism. If these cures help reduce absenteeism also, that's fine—but specific cures are generally preferable to alleviative ones. With alleviative cures, there's usually a greater danger of treating only one symptom rather than the ailment itself. Let's look at some specific cures.

Specific Cures

1. *Developing an employee attendance policy.* If absenteeism is a recognized problem, the logical place for management to begin is to devise an employee attendance policy. Amazingly, studies indicate that many companies have no written policy and/or procedure for controlling absenteeism. Establishing a clearly worded policy statement and then periodically reminding employees about it will certainly diminish the number of absences caused by ignorance or misunderstanding of standards.

"Progressive discipline," whereby the penalties imposed upon an employee absent without excuse become more and more severe as the number of such absences increases, is the underlying principle behind attendance policies. Employees are forewarned that unexcused absences incur increasingly severe penalties. A usually responsible employee will hesitate to play hooky if he knows the costs involved. The penalties might range from oral warnings, to written warnings, to forfeiting of pay or chance for promotion, to suspension, to dismissal. Actually, the use of suspension as a penalty has come under fire on the grounds that suspending an employee (for three days, for example) is a strange way of trying to convince him or her that regular attendance is important. But whatever form of discipline is used, it should be administered as promptly as possible after the unexcused absence.

All managerial personnel should be (or become) familiar with these concepts of discipline and their potential value in controlling absenteeism. Line managers in particular have a vital role in carrying out the company's attendance policy. Managers and supervisors need to realize that they can benefit directly from absence-control efforts. It also makes sense to enlist the aid of the union (if there is one) in educating employees in the importance of regular attendance. By increasing costs and lowering productivity, high rates of absenteeism jeopardize the company's competitive position and ultimately employees' jobs (and the union's security). In unionized firms, management's absenteeism policy may be included in the labor contract.

2. *Helping employees comply with the attendance policy.* Management can do several things to make it easier for employees to comply with stated attendance policy. One simple possibility is to help employees organize car pools—making a special effort to include chronic absentees. Or it may be feasible to offer interesting lunch-time programs (informal clubs, occasional speakers, and so forth). Some firms use a telephone-answering service or device to make it easier for an employee to call in the night before he or she will be absent. Messages received in this way are retrieved by a secretary first thing in the morning. He or she promptly transcribes the message and notifies the appropriate supervisors of who will be absent that day.

3. *Checking up on absentees.* Some firms "check up" on each employee who is absent but has not notified the company of the absence. Either the employee's immediate supervisor or someone from the personnel department or medical staff calls or even visits the employee's residence. Such personal attention may discourage some employees from being absent for frivolous reasons—but, on the other hand, it is an expensive approach and one that risks arousing employee resentment toward the company.

4. *Tailoring the approach to the individual.* This a particularly good practice when the absentee in question is not a chronic offender. Suppose, for example, that a usually reliable employee has just returned to work after an unexcused absence. The employee's supervisor might try to be understanding about his absence, but could also stress that he has been missed and that his absence has put the department or work group in something of a bind. The employee might be given a few extra "catch up" tasks to reinforce the idea that absences do matter. Consistent and honest use of this sort of approach should serve to discourage the occasional absentee from staying away from work for frivolous reasons.

5. *Counseling chronic absentees.* Whenever an employee's attendance record is tending toward a chronic condition, his immediate supervisor should confer with him, ask about the absence problem, and then counsel the employee that:

- His or her attendance record is becoming unsatisfactory or unacceptable.
- This situation is not to be taken lightly, because good attendance by each employee is basic to efficient operation.
- Good attendance is important to each employee in terms of his or her performance appraisal; that is, job security, pay raises, and promotability depend partly on attendance record. Then, of course, the employee's attendance should be discussed during appraisal interviews. If it is not discussed, the importance you have placed on attendance loses validity.
- Since regular attendance is ultimately the employee's responsibility, another absence will result in some specified disciplinary action, and this action will become increasingly severe if the employee's absenteeism persists.

6. *Taking a firm stand.* Managers should take a firm stand with out-and-out absentees. Tell them as clearly and emphatically as possible that their attendance records are not up to standard and that serious disciplinary action will be taken against them. (Tolerating chronic absenteeism encourages a continuation of such behavior.) Under certain circumstances, even an enlightened manager has to take a heavy-handed approach.

Management is well advised to take such an approach in dealing with employees who engage in "dirty tricks." Examples include:

- The chronic absentee who seems to be forging a doctor's name on notes that explain his or her failure to report to work

- The chronic absentee who keeps changing physicians. It may be that he or she does this whenever the previous physician refuses to give a medical excuse for an absence.
- The employee who was in an accident and is suing an insurance company but seems to be delaying recovery for longer than usual. The longer such an employee stays out of work, the more serious he or she can claim the injury to be.

To cope with the first two situations, management should simply refuse to approve the employee's claim for sick-leave benefits unless an M.D. of the company's choice says that such approval is warranted. In the third situation, management can simply stop paying accident benefits unless an M.D. of its choice says that the employee is still entitled to receive them.

7. *Avoiding a moralistic approach.* It is important to know when drastic measures are needed and when they are not. Far too often, managers see all absenteeism as a moral issue and, accordingly, view nearly all absentees as moral degenerates—lazy, shiftless, no good. But such a viewpoint is distorted, and managers who act upon it can do much harm. Moralistic criticism of *every* employee absence lowers employee morale because it lumps together employees whose attitudes and circumstances are significantly different.

8. *Using positive reinforcement.* It is important not only to give negative reinforcement for poor attendance, but also to offer positive reinforcement to employees with excellent attendance records. In many firms, instituting the practice of offering a bonus (in cash or some other form) for excellent attendance has been closely followed by appreciable decline in absenteeism. Critics have argued that these bonuses simply reward employees who would be regular attenders in any event. And, admittedly, bonus plans are not likely to do much good where chronic absentees are concerned. Nevertheless, in firms with a bonus for excellent attendance, the good attender is likely to become even better. Suppose that on a particular day an employee is a trifle under the weather but realizes that he or she is eligible for an attendance bonus. The bonus is likely to make the difference between whether he goes to work or stays home.

9. *Adhering to a broad-based program.* Because absenteeism problems differ considerably in nature and severity, effective programs are based on: (1) a good understanding of the leading causes of absences; (2) careful, ongoing analysis of the firm's and each department's actual absence records; (3) regular and clear communication to workers of the company's attendance policy, including disciplinary procedures to be invoked against violators; (4) proper—that is, knowledgeable, impartial, and consistent—implementation of this policy by all line managers and staff assistants; and (5) imaginative use of a flexible combination of alleviative and specific cures for absenteeism.

No one will ever develop a vaccine to eradicate absenteeism problems totally and for all time. Success in keeping absenteeism under control will always require sustained efforts. But almost any manager (in almost any set of circumstances) can exercise such control by continually trying to improve the combination of alleviative and specific cures in use.

Part III

COMMUNICATION

Crummy Communication Climate (And How to Create It)

CORWIN P. KING

"Communication climate" refers to the degree to which an organization permits but preferably promotes a free and open exchange of ideas and information among its members. A good communication climate gives people the information they need to do their jobs well and also builds morale and encourages creativity. A bad communication climate, on the other hand, creates doubt and confusion, demotivating people and leading to cynicism.

Obviously, a good climate makes working easier and more productive than a bad one does. But if you're the type who likes to do things the hard way, here are some tips on how to create a poor communication climate in your department or division.

1. Communicate with your peers and subordinates as little as possible. Be secretive. Mysterious. Make them guess what you're thinking and what you're likely to do. Communicate only when pressured and, then, preferably do so a little bit too late to do anybody any good. That way, no one can challenge your decisions because matters will already be beyond control.

2. When and if you do communicate, be vague and obscure. Speak in generalities, or smother people with irrelevant details so that they think they're getting more information than they really are. Don't hesitate even to be deceptive. Feel free also to be inconsistent or contradictory without explanation. After all, everyone has the right to change his or her mind, and people will admire your flexibility.

Reprinted from *Management Solutions,* July 1986

3. Don't communicate with just anyone. Give information to only a chosen few, and let everyone else find out about it through the grapevine. Take advantage of office cliques. Feed the rumor mill. Not everyone needs to know everything anyway, and what people don't know won't hurt them.

4. To insure selectivity, make it hard for people to have access to you. Surround yourself with assistants. Hire a good secretary who will screen your calls and turn away the "unworthy." Create "front men" who will speak for you and who will seem to have control over the information people need, while you sit in the background pulling the strings.

5. Remember that information is power; don't give it away for free. Communicate only when you have an advantage, or when there's something in it for you. Cooperating with others is fine, but competing is better—especially when people *think* you're cooperating. If there are rewards to be gained from having information, why share the wealth?

6. Above all, ignore information communicated to you, particularly if it's in the form of "bright ideas" from employees. Be careful, however, to make it *look* as though you're listening. Accept ideas (those few that happen to get through your defenses) graciously and enthusiastically. Promise to take action on them, then appoint a committee to study them. This gets you off the hook ("I can't make a decision, you know, until the reports are in"), and it will probably take so much time that people will forget about their ideas. In fact, if you do this often enough, they'll soon forget about *any* ideas and just "follow the leader."

In the unlikely event that the above procedures don't work, and there is still a glimmer of optimism among your employees, don't despair! Be patient. A crummy communication climate, like a good one, takes time to develop. Trust, confidence, achievement, motivation, and all of the other products of a good communication climate will not last long if you are genuinely devoted to killing them.

Words: A Supervisor's Guide To Communications

DON CARUTH

If you're a typical supervisor, you spend some 70 to 80 percent of your work day communicating in some fashion: making job assignments, listening to progress reports, conducting staff meetings, and the like. Obviously, many factors influence the effectiveness of a supervisor's interpersonal communications, but perhaps none so directly does as the words he or she uses to convey thoughts, feelings, attitudes, opinions, or facts.

Words can be "turn-ons" that enhance employee motivation, or they can be "turn-offs" that bruise a person's ego. The selection of words, then, can increase or decrease communication effectiveness.

To illustrate the impact of words, let's take a brief look at words that are ineffective and words that are effective in communicating with others.

Here are the least effective words a supervisor can use in conversations with employees:

The ten least effective words: "Don't give me any excuses, just get the job done."
The nine least effective words: "I'm the boss and don't you ever forget it."
The eight least effective words: "Either get with it or hit the road."
The seven least effective words: "I do not care what you think."
The six least effective words: "We've always done it that way."
The five least effective words: "You're not paid to think."
The four least effective words: "Because I said so."
The three least effective words: "It's company policy."
The two least effective words: "That's stupid."
The one least effective word: "Never."

Now let's look at the most effective words a supervisor can use in communicating with his or her employees.

The one most effective word: "We."
The two most effective words: "Thank you."
The three most effective words: "I don't know."
The four most effective words: "I made a mistake."
The five most effective words: "Your idea's better than mine."

Reprinted from *Management Solutions*, June 1986

The six most effective words: "Let's work together to do it."
The seven most effective words: "What do you think should be done?"
The eight most effective words: "I trust and respect you as a person."
The nine most effective words: "You know more about the job than I do."
The ten most effective words: "What can I do to help you fulfill your needs?"

Words—they can stimulate, inspire, and encourage but they also can deflate, discourage, and damage. So choose your words carefully to make certain that you make the positive impact you desire.

Building a Professional Image: Using "Feeling-Level" Communication

H. KENT BAKER and PHILIP I. MORGAN

Picture the following exchange between Joe Henson and his supervisor. Joe has just been handed a new assignment when he suddenly blurts out, "I am sick and tired of this company. I've worked late for the last two weeks to meet the new deadline and what thanks do I get? None! Instead, I get another rush job. I tell you, I'm about ready to quit!" Joe's supervisor just as suddenly responds, "Now, Joe, calm down. That's no way to talk. This company has been good to you. Don't get upset. Snap out of it, man. Let's discuss this rationally, in an adult manner, without getting emotional about it."

What do you think about the way the supervisor handled Joe's outburst? If you were Joe's supervisor, how would you have handled this situation?

Many supervisors react in a manner similar to that of Joe's supervisor in an emotionally charged situation. They let instinct override better judgment, become defensive, reprimand the individual, and cut off any further expression of feelings or monopolize the conversation. Such responses are ineffective because they deny the legitimacy of the employee's feelings by telling the employee how he or she ought to feel. This only increases the worker's sense of frustration.

The manager's image also suffers because of his or her inability to defuse the situation and to deal effectively with the employee's concerns.

Emotionally charged situations by their nature seem difficult and often unpleasant to handle but they don't have to be. Knowing how to deal with anger, fear, frustration, or whatever level at which a person is communicating just takes skill in "feeling-level communication."

A supervisor needs to be able to recognize the level at which a person is communicating and respond to that level. This requires not only being tuned into what is being said and how it is being expressed but also being able to interpret the message correctly and respond to it on the proper wavelength. If a supervisor is on the wrong channel, the communication is distorted and may degenerate into an exchange of words without either person hearing or understanding what the other really means.

A person sending a message at the feeling level should receive a message directed at the feeling level, just as a person communicating at the rational level should receive a response from the rational level.

How can you keep the communication lines open and operating effectively? Whenever you are faced with highly charged emotional statements, you should use the following steps to improve the communication flow:

Reprinted from *Supervisory Management,* January 1986

1. Recognize the feelings.
2. Encourage others to express their feelings.
3. Check the correctness of your perceptions.
4. Verbalize your own feelings.

Recognize the Feelings

The first step is to recognize whether the message primarily involves a feeling statement or a factual statement. For example, Joe expressed his feelings loud and clear, but his supervisor ignored them. Joe felt slighted that his extra efforts in meeting the deadline weren't recognized. Perhaps he might also have felt that he was being taken for granted. Instead of recognizing these feelings, his supervisor reprimanded him for stating them and told him that his behavior was childlike. These responses clearly missed the mark and revealed insensitivity to Joe's feelings.

To identify whether or not a feeling statement is involved, you need to recognize their characteristics. The following should help you do this:

- *Feelings are subjective.* They tell you more about the person making the statement in terms of his or her values, needs, and emotions than they tell you about an actual state of affairs.
- *Feelings are neither right or wrong*; they simply *are.*
- *Feelings represent a system of absolute truth* for the individual. The person is literally saying, "I feel it; therefore, it is so." No further evidence is necessary.
- *Feelings are usually disguised as factual statements.* For example, when a person says, "It's cold in the office," they are really saying, "I feel cold in the office."

Besides recognizing that a feeling-level message is involved, you need to ascertain the specific feelings involved. Is the person angry, frustrated, hurt, or disappointed?

Recognizing a person's true feelings is not always easy but the likelihood of doing so can be increased by letting the person freely express them.

Encourage Others to Express Feelings

Trying at first to get an emotionally upset person to discuss an issue in a calm, rational manner often fails. The reason is that the person is not yet ready to do so. For example, simply asking Joe to act rationally would probably not have brought about rational behavior. Some action must first have taken place to prepare him for communication at the rational level.

The following analogy may help illustrate this point. Imagine trying to grasp a balloon out of your reach. The task would be easier if some air leaked out of the balloon, thereby bringing it closer to you. The same is true of a person who is in a highly emotional state and allowed to ventilate feelings. If the individual airs his or her feelings and lets off steam, his or her emotions will subside. This allows the person to come down to earth. When this is done, it is possible to communicate with him or her rationally.

Therefore, as a supervisor, when faced with an angry person you should encourage the individual to ventilate his or her feelings. This can be done in several ways. One way is simply to ask the person to express his or her feelings. You might say, "Joe, I'd like to hear more about how you are feeling right now." After saying this, you should be quiet. Your silence should stimulate Joe to talk because the silence will be psychologically uncomfortable to him. And you will still be in control despite the fact that Joe is doing most of the talking at this point. In such instances, don't monopolize the conversation. After all, you are trying to let Joe get his feelings off his chest.

You might want to provide emotional support by saying, "Yes, I see," or "Go on." Nodding will indicate you are listening, and maintaining eye contact will show interest.

You can also rephrase the other's words as a question. Asking Joe, "You give up?" allows him to elaborate his statement. You can also summarize his statement of feelings—saying, "Joe, I sense by your comments that you don't feel that you were recognized for your efforts." Such statements give Joe feedback about his communication and serve as further cues for him to talk.

Still another approach is to put the issue before an employee. You might say to Joe, "I'm not exactly sure what's bothering you. Is it work scheduling, lack of recognition, or something else?" The question should be one the employee cannot answer with a simple "yes" or "no." Either/or questions should also be avoided because they put the person on the spot. For example, a question should not be phrased, "I gather your major complaint has to do with either work scheduling or lack of recognition. Which is it?" Joe is being asked to select a single response that may not truly represent his major concern.

Sometimes impasses occur. The employee may remain silent, and communication may break down. If this occurs, try "linking." This involves connecting one idea or feeling that the person has expressed to another. You might say to Joe, "How does your feeling of giving up relate to receiving another rush job?" When asking this type of question, avoid sounding punitive or suggesting the employee is a poor communicator. Remember, you are trying to convey to the employee that you want to gain a better understanding of the situation and his or her feelings about it. Allow for "face-saving" in case the employee really doesn't mean what you understand him or her to be saying.

Impasses can also be handled by using a story-telling approach. This involves sharing an experience or feeling similar to the one expressed by the subordinate. For example, you might say, "I remember a time when I had a similar experience in which I felt. . . ." By sharing experiences and feelings, you should be providing the emotional support that fosters further discussion and sharing of feelings. However, avoid sounding patronizing when using this technique.

In encouraging ventilation of feelings, try to use a quiet, soothing tone of voice. This is especially appropriate when a person is angry and raises his or her voice. Emotions are contagious and responding in a similar manner may lead to a shouting match, resulting in further wounded feelings. Speaking in a quiet manner often has a calming influence.

Check the Correctness of Your Perceptions

During emotionally charged situations, avoid mindreading or assuming that you know how the other person feels. You may be wrong. Besides, a supervisor can be left speechless if she says to a subordinate, "I know exactly how you feel," and the other replies, "Oh, no you don't. How can you?" If such exchanges occur frequently, you may be viewed as a supervisor who jumps to conclusions.

You can check the correctness of your perceptions simply by stating how you think the other person feels and asking for feedback. For example, you might say to Joe, "You seem to be pretty upset," or "You feel that you are not being appreciated for your efforts." Such responses to emotional statements allow you to retain control over the conversation, prevent your defense mechanisms from dominating your behavior, and allow you to receive additional feedback from the employee.

What happens if Joe indicates that your perceptions are wrong? No harm is done because you can simply ask Joe to help you understand the true nature of the situation and how he feels. For example, you might say, "I guess I'm off base. Perhaps you can help me understand what it is that's upsetting you." This shows that you are genuinely interested in gaining a better grasp of the situation.

Verbalize Your Feelings

So far, the communication has focused on others' feelings. You may also wish to express your feelings. One way to verbalize your feelings is to use an "I" message.

"I" messages generally contain three parts: your perception of the other person's behavior or feelings, your feelings about the behavior, and the reasons for your feelings if appropriate. For example, in response to Joe's comment, "I really feel like giving up," you might say, "I really feel concerned because you are one of the most productive people in the office."

An "I" message has many uses. First it is a good means of defusing stressful and emotionally charged situations. It provides a feeling response to another's feeling statement, and mutual sharing of feelings introduces a positive dimension into the communication process by getting feelings out. Second, using an "I" message enables you as a supervisor to tune into the other's feelings. Employees generally respond favorably to a supervisor who recognizes and tries to understand their concerns. Third, an "I" message gives you a chance to share your feelings about another's behavior without being judgmental. And, finally, an "I" message allows you to check the accuracy of your preceptions of others' feelings.

The use of "I" messages isn't limited to subordinates. They are applicable in many situations. For example, your boss calls you into her office and habitually keeps you waiting. You are becoming increasingly irritated because waiting wastes your time. Although some risk is involved, you could use an "I" message to make your boss aware of your feelings the next time this situation occurs. You might say, "When you keep me waiting for 30 minutes for a scheduled appointment, I get upset because it reduces the time I can spend on my work." Your boss might be offended, but this is unlikely if a good working relationship exists.

One warning: "I" messages should be asked to clarify feelings, not hide your true feelings about another person or situation. Be yourself. Otherwise, a person may feel manipulated, and mutual trust and respect—a basic condition for true communication—will be destroyed. The "I" message isn't a gimmick but a legitimate means of expressing your feelings in a nonthreatening way.

In conclusion, when dealing with feeling-level communication:

- Learn to accept feelings as feelings. Don't argue with the person by telling the individual what he or she *ought* to do or *should* feel.
- Encourage a full expression of feelings. Ventilation of feelings provides a catharsis for the individual.
- Identify the personal referent. Ask yourself, What is the person really telling me about his or her needs, values, and the like?
- Show that you accept the person's right to feel the way he or she does. This helps to legitimize feelings.
- Don't get caught up in the other's emotions.
- Learn to express feelings as feelings. Don't disguise them as facts.

The successful use of feeling communication requires a special sensitivity and attitude on your part. But its effective use enables you to be a better communicator and supervisor.

Why Managers Use Criticism Instead of Praise

CHARLES J. HOBSON, ROBERT B. HOBSON, and JOHN J. HOBSON

"I never hear from my boss until I do something wrong, and then I catch it!"

How many times have you heard someone say that? At some point, you may have said it yourself. We have all been victimized in this manner, and we are all guilty to varying degrees of the same abuse of our own subordinates. It is a widespread and serious problem confronting all organizations today. Managers at all levels demonstrate an over-reliance on criticism and negative feedback. They are quick to spot and react to substandard performance but frequently overlook or ignore good performance. We term this phenomenon the *captious complex,* a tendency to be excessively and exclusively fault-finding and overly critical.

The Consequences of the Captious Complex

The manager who exhibits the captious complex can expect a number of very negative, dysfunctional consequences to follow from his or her emphasis on criticism and negative feedback. Most of the people affected by such behavior are subordinates, although peers, customers, supervisors, and others can also be victimized.

First, from a motivational perspective, it is counterproductive to focus exclusively on poor subordinate performance while allowing instances of good performance to go unnoticed and unrewarded. Genuine positive feedback and praise for a job well done are excellent mechanisms for motivating continued good performance. Behavioral science research has confirmed the devastating problems and pitfalls associated with motivational techniques based upon intimidation, fear, and a single-minded emphasis on instances of substandard performance.

Certainly, instances of poor performance cannot go unnoticed or not be commented upon. This would tend to encourage the continuation of the substandard performance. But the optimal approach to subordinate motivation involves a blend or combination of both positive feedback following good performance and negative feedback following poor performance.

A second important area adversely affected by the captious-complex manager is subordinate job satisfaction, a major determinant of which is the quality of the supervisor-subordinate interpersonal rela-

Reprinted from *Supervisory Management,* March 1985

tionship. The behavior of the captious-complex manager alienates and offends subordinates, often leading to chronic job dissatisfaction and associated problems with loyalty and commitment.

Nearly everyone likes to be complimented for a job well done and appreciated for his or her efforts. In addition to being very satisfying, positive feedback can foster higher levels of loyalty and commitment and lead to improved attendance and job performance. Unfortunately, the many positive outcomes associated with satisfied subordinates are lost to the captious-complex manager in his or her single-minded focus on poor performance.

Closely related to the first two problems is the third major dysfunctional consequence of the captious complex—low levels of performance. The captious-complex manager who, through the exclusive use of criticism and negative feedback, fails to motivate subordinates cannot expect consistently high levels of performance. Instead, subordinates will tend to perform only at the level required to avoid the criticism and negative comments. Thus, in terms of the bottom-line of job performance and productivity, the captious-complex manager again falls short.

A fourth and final problem resulting from the captious complex is a general inability to interact socially in a positive manner and relate well to others. Interpersonally, an exclusive focus on criticism and instances of poor performance communicates a general negativism and pessimism that are unappealing and offensive to most people. The captious-complex manager will unfortunately find it extremely difficult to form positive social relationships and interact well with others, and this could substantially impair his/her overall effectiveness as a manager. After all, good people skills are a prerequisite for success.

Causes of the Captious Complex

At this point in time, the captious complex is in the initial stages of investigation. Therefore, in addressing the potential causes of the captious complex, informed speculation forms the basis of our discussion. While in all likelihood the origins of the captious complex are numerous and interrelated, we will attempt only to identify what we consider to be the most important probable causes of this phenomenon.

When discussing potential causes, a fundamental issue is whether or not the captious complex is an innate or learned behavior pattern. In other words, are some managers naturally more captious as part of their personality, or does one learn to become captious? The answer is probably a combination of both, so it is worthwhile to consider the captious complex from both perspectives.

Innate and personality factors. Looking at innate or personality factors as potential causes of the captious complex, we can begin to develop a profile of the typical captious-complex manager. Such a person can probably be characterized by a low need for affiliation, an insensitivity to the feelings and needs of others, an inability to empathize, and a low level of affectivity in relating to others.

Interestingly, in these four factors, females, in general, differ significantly from males. They tend to have a stronger need for affiliation, to be more sensitive to the needs and feelings of others, to be able to empathize more easily, and to have a higher level of affectivity. Thus a major, though as yet untested, hypothesis in this area is that more men than women exhibit the captious complex as managers. Viewed in this manner, the fact that women are increasingly entering managerial ranks indicates one major positive byproduct of the "feminization of management"—that is, an anticipated reduction in captious-complex behavior.

Another personality variable that warrants greater attention as a potential contributing factor to the development of the captious complex is an individual's level of self-esteem. In many instances, managers with little sense of self-worth or self-respect find it difficult to compliment or praise others. Upgrading the stature of another person is viewed as further detracting from their own self-worth by comparison. Such people often attempt to enhance their own limited self-esteem by criticizing and belittling those around them. Thus, an individual with chronically low self-esteem is a prime candidate for the captious complex.

Finally, there is preliminary research suggesting that many managers experience general inhibition when called on to give positive feedback face to face. These managers find it difficult to directly communicate compliments or praise to their employees. The precise reasons are not known at this time, but research on general communication apprehension as a trait-based impediment to effective interactions could provide clues.

Learning and socialization factors. Although innate personality traits represent likely causes of the captious complex, perhaps more important are factors inherent in the learning and socialization process that managers routinely go through—the ways in which they learn about and become socialized to the role of manager. Typically, the managerial role dictates a strong degree of responsibility and accountability for the performance of subordinates. Role theorists have long recognized that one of the most compelling and frequently occurring reasons for supervisor-subordinate interaction is below-normal subordinate performance. In such a situation, managerial role prescriptions exert strong pressures to provide some type of feedback, typically in the form of criticism. This is the old "squeaky wheel phenomenon"—when something goes wrong or someone performs poorly, attention and action from the supervisor are demanded.

Unfortunately, the typical managerial role does not include similarly strong prescriptions requiring feedback when a subordinate does a good job. Managers often argue that the good performer doesn't need feedback, and that it is best to leave well enough alone. Thus, in terms of the commonly defined managerial role, it seems that positive feedback and praise following an instance of good subordinate performance are discretionary in nature while negative feedback and criticism are nearly mandatory after poor performance.

Looking at the managerial role from a slightly different perspective, we see multiple tasks, duties, and responsibilities for which the typical manager has limited time and energy. To assist managers in the allocation of their time and effort, one of the basic tenets of management—the exception principle—was developed. This principle suggests that a manager should devote time and attention only to significant deviations from expected performance. Responding to any and all minor deviations is not considered an efficient utilization of one's time.

While the exception principle has much to recommend it from a theoretical perspective, in practice we find too frequently that "exceptions" are defined primarily in negative terms. In other words, managers tend to pay attention to below-expected or -normal performance while ignoring positive deviations above the norm. Thus, when subordinates perform at substandard levels, they are far more likely to hear about it from the boss than when their performance is above-average.

Finally, in searching for potential learning-based causes of the captious complex, one cannot overlook the powerful impact of managerial stereotypes. In our society, we have some very strong, pervasive, and explicit stereotypes of the "successful manager." The image of the tough, aggressive, intimidating, hard-to-please manager for whom criticism and argument are the standard modes of interaction has been embellished and aspired to by many seeking success in the business world. Being pleasant, friendly, and providing frequent compliments and praise are just not often associated with the stereotype of the successful manager. In fact, those exhibiting such behaviors are considered too easy or too soft to be really successful.

Interestingly, some preliminary behavioral science research suggests that managers adopt a behavioral style largely in response to the expectations and reactions of their own subordinates, peers, and supervisor. Thus, not wishing to be perceived as soft or easy, managers may shun use of praise and positive feedback and instead rely solely on criticism and negative feedback.

It is also instructive to note that many of the characteristics associated with the successful manager are masculine as opposed to feminine in nature. Women entering management have often adopted these behaviors as a means of furthering their careers and enhancing their image as tough-minded, aggressive executives. Unfortunately, many of these "desirable" behaviors are major contributing factors to the development of the captious complex.

Perhaps it is time that both women and men in management exhibit the resolve and courage necessary to break down these misguided stereotypes and provide frequent praise and positive feedback to subordinates without fear of being perceived as soft or easy. It is time that we put an end to the traditional adversarial role that often exists between supervisor and subordinates and turn instead to a more cooperative, helping mode of interaction in which praise and positive feedback are freely given.

Solutions to the Captious Complex

The captious complex represents a very serious problem confronting management, for which a number of potentially useful solutions are available. One is based on a training approach, the other deals with the use of a performance appraisal system.

Training. Just as managers, to a large extent, learn captious-complex behaviors, so it is also possible for them to "unlearn" these behaviors and replace them with more appropriate approaches to dealing with others.

A basic first step is developing a sensitivity to the problem and an awareness of its devastating consequences. In order to stimulate behavioral changes, one must first clearly understand exactly what the inappropriate behaviors consist of. The serious negative consequences of such behaviors must then be explicitly delineated. The purpose of this initial stage is to make managers aware of their own inappropriate behavior and how it adversely affects those with whom they interact.

Next, accepted alternatives to captious-complex behaviors should be introduced and demonstrated, using appropriate role models, along with a forceful discussion of the anticipated benefits: increased subordinate motivation, satisfaction, commitment, loyalty, and performance; and improved interpersonal relations with others. Managers should be shown how to compliment and praise others in a genuine manner and encouraged to actively seek out situations in which they can provide positive feedback to subordinates.

A word of caution is necessary at this point. Managers must be discouraged from providing praise or positive feedback in an artificial or a mechanical manner. For it to work, subordinates must believe that the praise is genuine and given in a thoughtful manner.

After presenting role models displaying appropriate behaviors, managers should be given the opportunity to practice these frequently new behaviors and receive objective feedback concerning their effectiveness. An excellent mechanism for accomplishing this is role-playing with the exercises followed by a group critique. Managers need to practice giving compliments and praise in a genuine, realistic manner, and to receive feedback about their behavior.

In all likelihood, many managers will find it difficult to praise or compliment others after years of captious-complex behavior. But if a concerted effort is made to use praise and positive feedback more frequently and reduce the reliance on criticism, the new behaviors will over time become self-sustaining as a result of their positive consequences. We believe that the payoff in terms of improved subordinate motivation, satisfaction, and performance, coupled with more positive interpersonal relations, will certainly justify abandoning the captious complex in favor of more frequent praise and positive feedback. In other words, if one genuinely tries to give up the captious complex and adopt the new behaviors, for most managers enhanced effectiveness will result.

Any training-based approach to reducing the captious complex must realistically encourage increased use of praise and positive feedback in the work environment. One common excuse offered to explain the low frequency of these behaviors by managers is the time and energy involved in actually providing positive feedback. Managers, it is argued, are very busy people and will not efficiently be using their time if they spend it seeking out and providing positive feedback to subordinates.

While it is theoretically possible to spend too much time praising subordinates, we would assert that this rarely, if ever, occurs. Certainly, managers are extremely busy and effective time management is essential for their success, but it is crucial not to overlook good subordinate performance.

An innovative midwestern health services firm has resolved this dilemma by providing all of its managers with preprinted blank Thank-You-Grams or T-Grams for use with subordinates, co-workers, customers, or anyone else deserving a compliment. Top management actively promotes and encourages the use of T-Grams as a way to compel managers to pay attention to the positive aspects in the performance of others. The convenience and efficiency of T-Grams have much to recommend them as a realistic method of encouraging more frequent positive feedback.

Performance appraisal approach. If an organization were convinced that it was desirable to reduce captious-complex behavior and promote more frequent positive feedback, one straightforward method of "putting teeth" into its conviction would be to include these factors as part of every manager's performance appraisal. Thus, in order to discourage captious-complex behavior and encourage positive feedback, these behaviors would be measured in the performance appraisal process and organizational rewards (raises, promotions, and the like) distributed accordingly. While there are many ways to do this, one potential method would involve the collection of anonymous evaluations of all managers by their subordinates and peers specifically addressing the frequency of positive and negative feedback.

Subordinates and co-workers are the best sources of information concerning a manager's feedback and thus should be included in the performance appraisal process.

Managers persisting in their use of captious-complex behaviors could be easily identified and dealt with. Old dogs not wishing to learn new tricks could be reassigned to positions requiring minimal human interaction or terminated. In this manner an organization could clearly communicate the importance of reducing captious-complex behaviors and increasing positive feedback.

Probably an optimal strategy would involve the combination of these two approaches: first, training managers to minimize captious-complex behavior and increase positive feedback, then measuring their behavior using the performance appraisal system and providing corresponding rewards.

Clearly, for any approach to work, top management must be fully committed to the eradication of captious-complex behavior and actively support strategies to accomplish this goal. Equally important, top management must provide appropriate role models for the rest of the organization, minimizing its own captious-complex behavior and maximizing the use of praise and positive feedback.

Implications for Management

The implications of the captious complex for management are numerous, straightforward, and important. First, managers must be sensitive to the existence of this pervasive problem (what it is and how it develops) and recognize that most of us are guilty of exhibiting captious-complex behaviors, albeit to varying degrees.

Second, managers must be aware of the very serious and dysfunctional consequences associated with the captious complex. The negative impact on subordinate motivation, satisfaction, and performance cannot be overlooked, nor can the associated difficulties in interpersonal relations. All of these work to substantially impair a manager's overall effectiveness.

Finally, managers must take forceful action to overcome the captious complex, not only in themselves, but in their subordinates as well. We must all make a conscious and concerted effort not to allow good performance to go unnoticed and unrewarded.

The Nature of the Organizational Grapevine

DONALD B. SIMMONS

The grapevine or informal communication network is an inherent part of any organization. The network helps employees make sense of the world around them and consequently provides a release from emotional stress. The grapevine also draws employees together because of their common interests and shared beliefs.

If left unguarded, the grapevine can become an organization's worst enemy. But if properly managed, it can significantly increase employees' productivity and job satisfaction. Therefore, it's important for managers to understand its nature and dynamics.

The following statements, drawn from a wide variety of research, give a broad overview of the subject.

Participants in the Grapevine

Employees fall into one of three categories in terms of the way they relate to the grapevine. Liaison or key communicators receive and pass information to other people and are primarily responsible for the success of the grapevine. Research shows that 10 percent of an organization's employees will be highly active grapevine participants because they are friendly and have positions that allow them to cross department lines. Dead enders hear the information but neglect to tell others or tell only one or two additional people. Isolates do not hear or transmit information.

Anyone can be part of the gossip mill given the situation and circumstances. For example, an ideal setting for the grapevine is the carpool. A person can be in the know if his or her car contains the CEO's secretary, the mail clerk, the controller, and a personnel employee. Another breeding ground for the grapevine is the clique structure. Communiqués are spread to friends and alliances while nonmembers are isolated as valuable information is kept from them.

Staffers spread the most rumors because they are constantly moving through various departments and know what is going on in each. Further, people are active on the grapevine when their friends and colleagues are involved. And a person on the edge of a group or one who has relatively low status will be inclined to spread sensational stories to attract attention.

Reprinted from *Supervisory Management,* November 1985

Characteristics of the Grapevine

The grapevine doesn't carry information that everyone knows is patently false, but it relies primarily on rumors. About 80 percent of its communications pertain to business-related politics rather than personal, vicious gossip. And interestingly about 70 to 90 percent of a message's details are accurate. According to Keith Davis, writing in *Human Relations at Work: The Dynamics of Organizational Behavior,* "People tend to think the grapevine is less accurate than it really is because its errors are more dramatic and consequently more impressed on memory than its day-to-day routine accuracy. Moreover, the inaccurate parts are often more important."

There are three kinds of rumors. The wish-fulfillment or pipe-dream variety expresses the wishes and hopes of those who circulate them. It is the most positive type of rumor. The second kind is the bogie rumor, which grows out of employees' fears and anxieties. It makes dire and specific predictions that reflect a general uneasiness among employees, as during a budget crunch. The third type of rumor is the wedge-driving or aggressive rumor, which is motivated by aggression or hatred. It is used to divide groups of workers or departments and destroy loyalties.

Rumors serve several purposes. For instance, during a period of retrenchment, workers may feel anxious about their job or status; but because their fear is unspecified, they cannot relate it to a particular event or decision. Rumors provide structure by focusing workers' anxieties on a specific decision.

Rumors also help make sense of a situation. Because people want a unified picture of a happening, they will use rumor to fill information gaps and to help clarify managerial decisions.

Some people use rumors to organize a strategic posture—that is, to protect their decisions or influence others and to organize people into supporting factions.

Finally, rumors are used to signal status or power. The explicit content of a rumor is its facts—the what, when, and where of a rumor. The implicit content is the relationship between the rumor source and receiver—"I can make you in the know." Information is power.

How the Grapevine Works

Rumors originate, grow, and spread along the grapevine in direct proportion to their importance to workers and the lack of news on a subject from official channels. The grapevine fills a basic human need to send or receive information on such concerns as who is up for the big promotion, who is going to be transferred, and what new jobs are available.

Employees tend to be more active on the grapevine during periods of change, excitement, anxiety, and sagging economic conditions. False rumors at this point can harm an organization's productivity and morale, which contributes to high accident rates.

Good rumors, in contrast, raise morale, and official confirmation of them boosts morale further. Good rumors can help build teamwork, motivate personnel, and create a positive corporate identity.

The sooner employees know about an event after it happens, the more likely they are to tell others. In fact, the informal network, which moves by word of mouth free of organizational restrictions, often reaches people before formal communications do. Only a firm's public address system can get information out faster than the grapevine.

Once a rumor's central theme is accepted, there is a tendency to reorganize and distort events to make them consistent with the central theme. As a result, a message becomes more twisted and garbled as it spreads. What begins as speculation can end up in general organizational havoc.

Two differences exist between formal and informal communication networks. First, the informal network has no official standing. Therefore its leaders cannot be held responsible for harmful behavior or officially rewarded for positive contributions. Second, the informal organization is less permanent and less stable because its leaders and patterns of action change readily.

As rumors decrease in number, their diffusion may increase. And the more a rumored statement is transmitted, the more valid it becomes to those hearing it.

Controlling the Grapevine

Managers can control the grapevine—that is, limit the range and impact of rumors—by:

- Accepting the grapevine's existence and paying heed to rumors
- Acting promptly to determine how far a rumor has spread by contacting customers, vendors, and the like
- Preventing false rumors by keeping employees well informed. That means using the formal communication system (including the bulletin board and flyers) to provide information.
- Developing employees' faith in the credibility of management's communications
- Making themselves available to answer employees' questions
- Guarding against employee idleness and boredom. Rumors breed in such situations.
- Determining the cause of a rumor to better understand employee complaints and misconceptions
- Informing key communicators of important organizational decisions and changes as soon as possible. They should even talk to informal leaders of important groups in their company to get their attitudes and opinions about prospective changes in procedure, personnel, or work methods.
- Clarifying their intentions to prevent individual inference making. If a decision hurts several people, management should be sure everyone understands why the decision was made. If it hurts only a few, management should explain why to them privately before telling the group.
- Presenting negative information honestly, not sugar-coating the facts
- Remembering that rumor cannot be stopped by silencing the key communicators; the grapevine will continue to flourish because someone else will take their place. After all, the grapevine is more a product of the situation than the people.

Managers are continually faced with the challenge of learning to live in harmony with the grapevine. Those who understand the rumor mill—the power it wields, its structure, and its goals—can better meet the information needs of their employees.

Recognizing—and Overcoming—Defensive Communication

ROBERT F. DeGISE

No matter how hard we try to communicate effectively, good interpersonal relations are often diminished or destroyed by "defensiveness." This term encompasses a variety of attitudes that can have significant negative effects on the communicative process. Perhaps you are already aware of these attitudes; anyone who has put a great deal of effort into communicating something to a person—only to find that person has a "closed mind" and doesn't understand what you're trying to get across—has experienced "defensiveness." But we can all become more aware of the dynamics that make up the successful communicative process. At stake is our continuing ability to communicate in meaningful terms our ideas, values, and goals.

Let's begin with a few basic questions: How do you relate to other people? How aware are you of the image you project? Do people "turn off" just when you're trying hardest to "turn them on"?

It's appropriate to do some introspecting on these questions. Look into your own mind and feelings, and you may conclude, as I have, that we base our relationships with others *not* on the traits they possess—conscientious, dependable, logical, punctual, level-headed—but on the kind of person they "come through" as being. It is not so much *what we do* as *how we are seen* by others that determines our ability to communicate successfully.

Thus, it is obvious that an important step in improving our relationships is to "see ourselves as others see us." Unfortunately, this is a very difficult thing to do, for most people have a tendency to see their own behavior differently from the behavior of others. A pertinent example of this comes to mind: Among my acquaintances is a man who does not "enter" others' conversations—he "barges" into them abruptly, rudely, uncouthly. Yet when this same tactic is used on him, he's the first to take offense and quickly condemns his own foible in others.

A Rush to Reciprocate

Another aspect of the relationships we have with our bosses, wives, children, parents, and in-laws is that the behavior we show these people will usually bring forth similar behavior from them in a "rush to reciprocate." In other words, anger is met with anger, argument with argument, trust with trust, humor

Reprinted from *Supervisory Management*, March 1977

with humor, and indifference with indifference. These two characteristics of behavior—the lack of self-awareness and the rush to reciprocate—are major elements in defensiveness, one of the most destructive factors in interpersonal relationships and organizational communications. In fact, defensiveness lies at the core of most of our communication problems.

Being aware of this threat can help us cope with it. Therefore, we need to learn as much as possible about the way people communicate and relate to each other at work and in the everyday world.

One fundamental result of defensive behavior is our inability to acknowledge differences between how we see things and how they *really* are and also differences between how *we* see things and how *others* see the same things. Since these differences reflect our own diverse backgrounds, experiences, and motivations, we can never finally reconcile them, but we can at least recognize that they do exist. This is the indispensable first step that all meaningful communicative efforts must take, but it is not an easy thing to do.

Most of us assume, "The world is as I see it." Consequently, we find life continually threatening because there are many others who think the world is as *they* see it. We are often compelled to defend or protect our personal world and to attack or deny the other person's.

Defending or protecting our world erects a barrier between free, open, interpersonal communication. And this behavior we aptly label "defensiveness." What are we defending against? Perceived threats against our self-concepts.

Real vs. Imagined

Let me explain this another way: Imagine a picture of yourself. This picture represents who you *think* you are—your self-concept. But when others conceive a picture of you, that picture is closer to who you *really* are—your real self.

The self-concept is a composite of the things we know about ourselves, including the past (both good and bad parts), present status on and off the job, roles played in various environments, sense of values, hopes and plans for the future, and relationships with others. In more concrete terms, we express our self-concepts in simple statements: "I eat too much," "I'm a good mixer," "I pay my debts promptly," "I am lousy at mathematics," "I'll never be rich," "I always finish what I start," "I have less money than my friends, but I'm smarter," and "I believe in always playing fair."

So a person's self-concept is a nice, neat, well-organized package of perceptions—self-opinions about ourselves. We feel these self-opinions make perfect sense and have some semblance of internal organization and integrity, even if to others our self-opinions make no sense at all. The fact that we are organized is enormously important in understanding behavior; it means that it is difficult for us to change any aspect of our beliefs or attitudes without having to rearrange our entire internal organization.

Someone once noted an unfortunate fact about human behavior: Those who most need to change are the least likely to know it. But it is also true that those of us who do recognize shortcomings in ourselves are often unwilling or unable to do anything about our problems. In some cases, the bad habit or peculiar behavior apparently cannot be overcome, even when it threatens to disrupt our interpersonal relations. Why? Because our self-concepts are "on the line," so to speak, and change would represent a very real threat to those self-concepts. We are especially sensitive to such threatening comments of others as, "You're not the same person I married," "My mother told me it would be like this," "If I knew then what I know now," "Let me give you some advice," "I've been watching you," and "For your own good, why don't you?"

Self-Concept Preservation

Although most of us have long accepted Charles Darwin's premise that self-preservation is the first law of nature, one authority on human behavior has stated that "the chief mode of human behavior is not self-preservation but preservation of the self-concept." In other words, the concept of self-preservation falls short; it fails to take into account the wide range of human motivations. For example, self-preservation has little to do with:

- The businessman who gets stomach ulcers in his climb to the top of his field
- The romantic girl who buys her own diamond engagement ring because her boyfriend isn't able to afford one
- The daredevil motorcyclist who risks his life catapulting himself over 25 cars
- The fishing enthusiast who spends $100 or more a year on equipment to catch $9.75 worth of fish

These are examples of human behavior in which actions are dictated by self-concepts. The strength of these self-concepts forces us to modify our view of self-preservation: "The fundamental motive of human behavior—after self-preservation—is preservation of the self-concept. The basic purpose and goal of much of our behavior is to protect, maintain, and enhance our self-concept."

No doubt there have been incidents in all of our lives when we have used perceptual defenses or distortions to protect our self-concepts. Whether the threat is real or not, we are all susceptible to and practice this mode of behavior when we are confronted with facts that contradict our preconceptions. So we deliberately distort the facts to eliminate the contradiction. By perceiving inaccurately, we defend ourselves against having to change our preconceived ideas.

Body Language

Similarly, we often use "body language" to communicate our rejection of threatening information or ideas. So let us add to our previous statements: "Nonverbal defensiveness is communicated by what we *do,* not by what we *say.*" Crossed arms, for instance, are a universal sign of defense. Youngsters cross their arms when defying their parents, and the elderly do the same when they are defending their rights. With arms crossed, a protection is erected against anticipated attack.

Crossed arms are the most understandable—yet least recognized—of nonverbal indicators. If you notice such an indicator and sense that you have caused a defensive attitude in another person, communication is virtually impossible until you reduce his or her defensiveness. One way is to change your approach: Draw out the other person's feelings by listening to him and finding out what his needs are.

So when you observe someone with his arms crossed—or eyes narrowed or body hunched backward—perhaps you should reconsider what you are doing or saying to that individual. He may be emphatically communicating that he has withdrawn from the conversation. If you could read his mind, he might be thinking, "My mind is closed. No matter what you say, I'm not listening. We can't communicate." Failing to recognize early signs of disagreement, discomfort, or discontent usually leads to a more complicated situation where agreement on any issue is almost impossible.

If there is a question about whether an individual is being defensive or merely trying to be comfortable, notice other signs of defensiveness. For example, are his hands relaxed or clenched into fists? Or are his fingers wrapped around his arm in a "I'd like to strangle somebody" grip?

Verbally or nonverbally, defensive behavior can clearly disrupt the communication process. But we can do a lot to help foster a nondefensive attitude through openness; this is our willingness to receive from others cues that we can use to evaluate, modify, and verify our own self-concepts. For some, unrealistic and erroneous self-concepts are preserved because it is too threatening for them to accept contrary cues from other people.

Not only are we vulnerable to defensiveness as individuals off the job but also as members of the organizations we are a part of. Consider, for example, the implications of defensive behavior in our interaction with others in a business environment. As we become more or less defensive, two distinct climates are identifiable in terms of perceived behaviors: *defensive (threatening)* and *supportive (nonthreatening)*. Let's look at two situations that illustrate these climates.

Situation (Threatening)

Bill Johnson, a supervisor, has seen that several of his letters and memos must be retyped because of misspellings and typographical errors. He takes them back to his secretary, Mary Smith, and merely points out the errors and tells her to correct them as soon as possible. Then the following conversation takes place:

Bill: Mary, your work is below standard. You're going to have to improve your performance, or I'll be forced to take drastic action.

Mary: My workload is brutal, Mr. Johnson. Why can't some of the other gals help out? It doesn't seem fair that I should have to be under so much pressure. And I've been upset about my mother's recent illness.

Bill: You're taking a very negative view of this. You shouldn't let your personal feelings interfere with your job performance. I'm not concerned with your mother's illness or the other girls. Keep your mind on what you're doing from now on. After all, you're being paid to do accurate work.

Analysis

This interaction is fraught with implied threats for Mary: She is being harshly evaluated by her boss; he is demanding a change in her behavior and also disregarding her personal welfare; he is not interested in helping solve her problems but insists on an immediate improvement without any consideration for the special circumstances involved. This is an extremely threatening situation for Mary. An invisible barrier of defensiveness goes up in front of her that precludes a cooperative and participative climate. Bill is at an impasse in trying to communicate with her.

How can Bill transform this defensive climate into a nonthreatening situation? One way is to encourage openness and to show an honest desire to solve the problem together. Let's look in on Bill and Mary again:

Bill: How's your mother doing, Mary?

Mary: Not too well, Mr. Johnson. She's been having a lot of pain lately. The doctor is giving her some new medication and thinks it will ease her discomfort.

Bill: Sure hope so. If there's anything I can do, let me know. I know your mother's illness certainly makes things more difficult for you, but I hope we can work together in trying to eliminate the errors in our memos and letters. Do you have any suggestions?

Mary: I think if I typed a rough draft first and you looked at it before the final typing, we could catch a lot of them.

Bill: Yes, I think that would help, Mary. And I know my writing is not too clear at times. I need to be more careful in spelling names, too. Maybe I could even print them.

Mary: That would help, Mr. Johnson.

Bill: Let's see if we can work together to eliminate these errors. It would make both our jobs a little easier. How about it?

Mary: Sounds fine. I'll do everything I can to make it work.

Bill: Thanks, Mary, and keep me posted on your mother's progress.

This is a sincere request for help from the boss. The problem is identified by Mary and Bill, who then collaborate openly and freely in order to reach a common objective. There is no critical assessment made of Mary's performance. Instead, Bill shows empathy for Mary's home situation and elicits her positive response. The results are a sincere relationship and a climate that generates a willingness to rectify the problem.

Situation (Threatening)

Steve Wilson, forecasting analyst, is in charge of a project requiring sales statistics for a specific product. The data he needs is relatively small in quantity but is critical for his assignment. Although computer time within the company is at a premium and the data processing group has a heavy workload, Steve feels his project merits special attention. Tom Scott, systems programmer, does not share this view:

Steve: What I need, Tom, is pretty small in quantity, and the time involved would be minimal. I'd like you to work up a program to pull my data out of the computer so I can complete my project as soon as possible. I'll even write a memo to your leader about how cooperative you are.

Tom: Just like that, huh? Instant service. What makes you think your program is so special? Everything that comes in here is super-hot. All I need is a 30-hour day, and I could work you in.

Steve: Hey, wait a minute, Scott, don't get your back up. I need a small program. That shouldn't put a big strain on you. You're a service group. How else do you justify your existence?

Tom: That's what they all say. Every program is small, and everyone needs his data *yesterday.* Look, we're not made of rubber here. We can only do a given amount of work in a given block of time. There's no way we can stretch our capacity.

Analysis

Obviously, both men are in the attack-defend mode. Each is trying to control the other. There are strong self-serving motivations on both sides, and even some manipulation is involved. Steve and Tom are unsharing and unwilling to enter into a problem-solving relationship.

Steve's dogmatic, know-it-all approach is perceived as a threat by Tom. No productive communication can or will exist in this climate. There is a need here for problem-oriented, objective viewpoints. Instead of trying to diminish the other's role, Steve would be better off recognizing the difficulty of the situation and not attempting to impose a preconceived solution.

What kind of language would foster a nonthreatening climate? There should be an effort by Steve—and Tom too—to convey a nonjudgmental attitude and to seek a solution that is mutually satisfactory, with no hidden attempt to establish a superior position. Let's try the scenario again.

Steve: Tom, every time I come in here this place is going full blast. I bet the last thing you could use is another program.

Tom: You know it, Steve. Would you believe we've already exceeded our projected output for this quarter three times? And when that new plant comes on-stream, this place may cave in.

Steve: That's enough to turn me away, Tom. But I'll try anyway. What I need is a program to pull out some sales statistics for a project I'm working on. It seems like a small program, but I'm not the best judge of that. Small to me may be big to you.

Tom: Yeah, right, we're loaded. And all our programs are small to our clients. But our programming man-hours sure tell a different story.

Steve: If I simplified my data requirements, would it be possible to get some computer time within the next two weeks?

Tom: There's a good chance we could write a program in that time and come up with your data. In fact, one of our programs may be cancelled next week. We could do yours then.

Steve: I'd sure appreciate it, Tom. If there's anything I can do to help, let me know. I sure don't want to make your job more complicated than it is already.

The result of lowered defensiveness is that Steve has empathy for Tom and his problems. There is a spontaneity in their conversation that fosters respect. No attempt is made to force Tom to do something he doesn't want to do or can't do. Because of this permissive climate, Tom is amenable to exploring possibilities for solutions rather than taking a stand against Steve's request for a program. The two men meet in a climate of equality and identify an approach that is acceptable to both.

Clearly, a supportive climate permits the most effective communication. The more supportive the climate, the less likely we are to distort our communicating with personal feelings, interests, and values. Similarly, we perceive more accurately as we become less defensive. And as the element of threat diminishes, so does the need to defend ourselves. Finally, as defensiveness subsides, we can better focus on what is being said and what the intended meaning of the message is. In a nondefensive mode we are not compelled to attack or counterattack, so we can develop a supportive relationship with others.

Summary

Although the defensive and supportive climates appear to exist independently, they are in fact interactive. For example: *Evaluative* behavior generates defensiveness, as we've seen. But if a listener *feels* the speaker regards him with *empathy* and is also being *spontaneous,* the evaluativeness of the message can be neutralized or not even perceived by the listener. Thus, one of the most significant factors in all human communication is:

The perceptions of the receiver rather than the intentions of the deliverer determine how defensive or supportive the communication climate will be.

In other words, it's not what you *mean* but what is *understood* that counts. Think about this factor. Because if you fail to consider this in all your communicating, you should anticipate "anything that can be misunderstood will be misunderstood." Inherent in all communication is the unavoidable fact that failure doesn't result from what is *not* said, but from what *is* said and misunderstood.

As you ponder the viewpoints just presented, consider what kind of return you can expect on your investment in time. I would hope that the result of using these guidelines would be an enlarged awareness of the potential distortion of meaning that comes from defensiveness. This awareness means that we do not insist on proving how right we are and how wrong the other person is, but we understand that effective communication thrives in an environment where defensiveness is disallowed as a dominant influence. And this happens only when we *make* it happen and only when we constantly strive to see ourselves as others see us.

Leadership Strategies for Successful Meetings

WILLIAM KIRKWOOD and JANICE WILSON

Consider for a moment the last few meetings you have attended as a participant or leader. Were you less than satisfied with their overall success? Certainly most people will agree that many of the meetings they attend leave much to be desired. Indeed, the meeting that effectively accomplishes its goals with efficient use of members' time and talents seems more the exception than the rule in many organizations. This is unfortunate, since careful planning of the meeting and the application of group leadership skills during the session itself can overcome the ineffectiveness that too often plagues meetings.

The efforts of a leader before and during a meeting can either foster or limit its effectiveness. The checklist in Figure 1 should help you assess some of your own group-leadership skills. Further exploration of these areas will enable you to develop the means to more productive meetings. Perhaps the most essential consideration is the realization that effective meetings result from careful preliminary planning and skillful orchestration of the group session itself.

Preliminary Planning

When meetings are less than successful, there is a tendency to assume that some unforeseeable situation arose during the session itself. But often the chaos, boredom, frustration, or lack of direction characteristic of ineffective meetings can be averted by adequate preparation. By asking several basic questions, you can clarify the nature of the meeting, the roles of group members, and the specific tasks you must accomplish to be an effective leader. Attention to such questions is the first step to the conduct of successful meetings.

1. *What do I hope to see achieved as a result of this meeting?* While you may have a general idea of what must be accomplished, unless you can clearly state your objectives, team performance may be less than satisfactory. Establishing specific, measurable, realistic goals is essential to success and to helping group members feel satisfaction when they do succeed, and to reassessing their efforts when they don't.

2. *Is each member attending the meeting really necessary for its success?* Often members are included more as a matter of courtesy than of efficacy. If your major concern is that some individuals don't feel left out, then a solid reason has not been established for their presence. Because too many people in

Reprinted from *Supervisory Management*, October 1981

Figure 1

Checklist for Meeting Leadership Skills

In preparing for meetings, do you:	*Yes*	*No*	*Sometimes*
1. Write out your goals and objectives in advance of the meeting?	_____	_____	_____
2. Evaluate the meeting and members in attendance for cost effectiveness?	_____	_____	_____
3. Determine the number of topics that can be discussed productively within the time limit?	_____	_____	_____
4. Send those who will attend a clear, descriptive agenda prior to the meeting?	_____	_____	_____
5. Review possible procedures for conducting the meeting (for example, brainstorming or buzz groups) and then select the most appropriate?	_____	_____	_____

In conducting meetings, do you:			
1. Temper your own role in the meeting so that others feel free to fully contribute?	_____	_____	_____
2. Employ effective listening skills?	_____	_____	_____
3. Match your leadership and decision-making style to the needs of the particular situation?	_____	_____	_____
4. Recognize the strengths in what others are saying as well as the weaknesses?	_____	_____	_____
5. Help group members to voice their criticisms in an open, constructive manner?	_____	_____	_____
6. Feel equipped to handle the problem roles of such members as monopolizers, aggressors, quiet types, and chronic complainers?	_____	_____	_____

the session will hinder the overall effectiveness of the group, be diplomatic, but include only the necessary personnel.

3. *What do I need from each person to accomplish the goals of the meeting?* Know in advance the skills, expertise, and knowledge of each person attending the meeting. Ask yourself how these various people may contribute to its success. You should also consider whether some who will attend the meeting may impede the group's effectiveness. For instance, consider the hidden commitments, loyalties, alliances, and animosities members will be bringing to the session. And don't overlook the history of the group you're leading. How will the past experiences of this group influence its ability to perform its present tasks?

4. *What is the most effective format for conducting the meeting?* The traditional committee format, utilizing some variation of parliamentary procedure, is not always the best way to proceed. In fact, by answering the questions already mentioned here you may determine that there is no real need for a group session at all. Also, analysis of your goals, available personnel, and time constraints may reveal that a "huddle"—an informal conversation between two or more persons—is a better approach than a more formal session.

5. *Have I provided group members with a descriptive agenda memo in advance?* In most cases, the more explicit you are about the nature of the business to be worked out, the greater the opportunity for members to consider in advance possible ideas and solutions. For example, if the group is to discuss new guidelines for grievance procedures, instead of merely identifying the topic, also include the major issues to be resolved in this area.

Conducting the Meeting

While much attention has been given to helping managers evaluate and improve their personal style of leadership, studies have shown that the most successful leaders adapt their leadership methods to the particular needs of each task they encounter. In other words, it is less important to try to refine one prescribed style of leadership than to develop the skills needed to meet the demands of a variety of situations. Among the most useful group leadership practices are the following.

1. *Be an attentive listener.* Poor listening isn't just bad manners—it is a real hindrance to the effectiveness of a meeting. Half-hearted listening can become a twofold problem for you. First, when your attention strays from others' comments, you lose valuable information. Second, when you don't listen, people aren't fooled. As a leader you'll give the impression that ideas other than your own aren't important. Others will likely follow your example. In sum, poor listening equals poor decision building as well as poor decision making. The meeting characterized by less than attentive listening fails to make full use of the time and efforts of all of its members. In so doing it may create an apathetic climate that also threatens future team efforts.

To develop effective listening skills, you may want to try this approach. Try summarizing in a sentence or two the major idea just presented by a group member. This practice will have two benefits: (1) You will become a more attentive listener, better able to understand what others in the group are trying to communicate, and (2) your example will encourage others to strive to appreciate the ideas presented in the meeting. You may also want to ask other group members to summarize a speaker's idea before it is further discussed by the group. The small effort of paraphrasing another's idea can increase communication efficiency by ensuring that members really understand it before they evaluate or act on it.

2. *Increase motivation by responding constructively to ideas.* Everyone acknowledges that this is a good idea, but how do you do it? William Gordon and George Prince, founders of Synectics, Inc., have suggested a way to respond constructively in a variety of situations. Called the spectrum approach, this method is based on the observation that ideas expressed in meetings can range from the positively brilliant to the utterly worthless. However, most ideas fall somewhere within these extremes: They contain the germ of a usable contribution as well as certain obvious weaknesses. Groups may not maximize their usefulness because they wait for the perfect, flawless idea, which never comes (perhaps because it doesn't

exist). Many contributions that may provide adequate or even creative solutions once modified are abandoned prematurely because of their obvious drawbacks. Eventually, with time running out and frustration running high among participants, group members accept a mediocre solution uncritically simply to be done with the task at hand.

The Prince and Gordon spectrum approach is designed to help group members build on the contributions of their colleagues by identifying and correcting noticeable weaknesses in ideas in a positive, constructive manner. To use this method, you do the following after an idea has been expressed:

1. State what you like about the idea—its strengths.
2. State what you feel are its weaknesses.
3. For each shortcoming identified, suggest a specific correction.

Always follow these steps in this order.

When discussion during meetings is guided by the spectrum policy, several benefits can result. First, this process highlights the strengths of ideas that may otherwise be overlooked. Second, the practice builds motivation and a supportive climate within the group because participants know every contribution will receive positive acknowledgement. Further, because members must offer a means of correcting each weakness they see in an idea, criticism is truly a way to improve available ideas instead of chronic complaining. And by providing members with a structured and acceptable format for responding to ideas, the spectrum approach can encourage members to express reservations that they would otherwise keep to themselves. Since avoiding disagreement and criticism can lower the productivity of a group just as much as hypercritical or defensive talk, this too is a real advantage.

3. *Match your decision-making style to the needs of each situation.* Which do you believe is better: to make decisions for your group or with it? While some leaders strongly prefer one approach to the other, studies of successful leaders show that they make use of both options, depending upon the situation or task at hand.

Obviously, if a satisfactory decision requires input from other group members, making decisions with the group is appropriate. However, if you possess adequate information to make a decision or if you doubt the group's ability to reach an unavoidable but unpopular conclusion, you may elect to resolve an issue for the group. In either case, don't overlook the need for group members' support for the decision. Act to get members behind your decision.

However you choose to make a particular decision in a meeting, be open and straightforward in your methods. Your own experience as a participant should remind you that people know when there is bogus participation in decision making. It is bad enough to sit in a meeting when you feel you aren't needed. It's even worse to be asked to make decisions that you sense have already been made.

4. *Use all the group's resources.* After you have carefully determined who should be present at a meeting, remember that the group does not benefit unless each person participates. The effective leader is constantly alert to silence and dominance.

First, you should not allow people's shyness to prevent them from sharing their insights and skills in the group. Develop an ability to draw out and deal with the silent or reticent person.

Second, avoid at all costs allowing some members to dominate while others aren't given time to express their views. If a meeting is set up for a 20-minute time slot and 15 minutes are taken up by one or two individuals, that leaves only five minutes for the remaining participants to present their ideas. This clearly does not permit full use of the entire group's talents. In dealing with dominant persons, be decisive. When they begin to monopolize a meeting, tell them you appreciate their contributions but others must also voice their opinions. You may find it useful to quickly summarize the long-winded members' views to show that you have heard and acknowledged their contributions, then openly invite a different group member to speak.

Don't overlook, either, the possibility that you may be the one most guilty of hogging the group's discussion time as a platform for your own ideas. If you feel a need to do most of the talking, perhaps you did not need a group session in the first place. In such cases a memo announcing your decision would be a more suitable communication method. This approach is more cost-effective, and it avoids frustrating others by including them in discussions about decisions that have already been made.

In order to most effectively conduct a meeting, you may want to consider using a variety of techniques specially designed to gain information, solve problems, or stimulate creative thinking. These techniques can help you to structure and conduct meetings to make optimal use of the particular skills available in the group. Some of the more widely used group communication procedures are presented in the following books:

1. On synectics: *The Practice of Creativity* by George Prince
2. On nominal group process and delphi technique: *Group Techniques for Program Planning* by Andre Delbeqc and others
3. On brainstorming: *Applied Imagination* by Alex Osborn

Considering the number of meetings that you attend each month, efforts to improve your planning and communication skills should yield substantial payoffs for you and your associates. Increased efficiency and productivity, and feelings of satisfaction and enthusiasm—rather than frustration and irritation— should be the result.

Building a Professional Image:
When You're Asked to Make a Speech

PHILIP I. MORGAN and H. KENT BAKER

As a manager, you may have to speak in front of work groups, even make presentations before larger audiences. Your first reaction may be one of panic or fear, but with preparation and practice, you can become skilled enough at making presentations to enjoy doing so.

Few things enhance your image more than being able to speak confidently and comfortably in front of an audience. Whether you're selling an idea or just making a report, good presentation skills will get you noticed. Poor presentation skills can tarnish your professional image and thereby impede your advancement.

Effective presentations demand attention to both *preparation* and *delivery*. *Preparation* entails planning, organizing, writing, and practicing the presentation. Good *delivery* requires close attention to the mechanics of the presentation.

Preparation

Preparation begins with a clear statement of purpose, an audience analysis, and a design for your presentation.

Purpose. Begin by defining the purpose or goal of your presentation. This step is critical because it will help clarify what you want to communicate to the audience. There are generally three purposes of presentations: The first is to inform by imparting knowledge or information. The second is to persuade— that is, to change attitudes or behavior. The third and final purpose is to amuse or entertain. When defining your purpose, you should have a clear idea of the main point you want to make. It may help to ask yourself, "What do I want my audience to know or do at the end of my presentation?"

Analyze your audience. Understanding your audience enables you to tailor your presentation to it, and this is vital to a successful presentation. In analyzing your audience, be sure to answer the following questions: What do they know about the topic? What are they interested in hearing about it? What are their likely attitudes toward my topic and my position on it? Consider the composition of your audience— sex, ages, education, and backgrounds.

Reprinted from *Supervisory Management*, December 1985

Once you have a clear idea of your presentation's purpose and audience, you are ready to start planning and organizing your presentation.

Design. Like any good story, your presentation should have a beginning (introduction), a middle (body), and an end (summary).

Your introduction sets the stage for the rest of your talk. Therefore, try to establish rapport with the audience and motivate them to listen by indicating why your topic is important to them. Try to capture the essence of your message in a single sentence, then indicate how your talk will deal with this message or theme.

The body should be arranged according to some logical sequence. You might use time—perhaps tying your message to the history of the company—identify a problem, then solutions, or go from the general to the particular. You want to structure your presentation so that the people in your audience can easily understand your message.

Don't attempt to write out your speech. Instead, prepare an outline. Determine your key points; then, beneath each, list those items that will substantiate or illustrate it.

Your summary should restate your key points and main message. At this stage, you may also make conclusions and recommendations or ask your audience to take some specific action.

There are a number of questions repeatedly asked by managers about to make a presentation. Let's examine these one at a time.

■ Should I use visual aids? As the old saw has it, "A picture is worth a thousand words." So, if appropriate, use handouts, overhead projections, flipcharts, or a chalkboard to help clarify your points or save time. But remember to keep your visuals simple and be thoroughly familiar with the working of any equipment involved in their use.

■ Should I use humor? Humor can be an excellent means of establishing rapport with your listeners, relaxing them and positively disposing them to what you have to say. However, unless done properly, it can easily backfire. For example, using humor inappropriate to your audience can work against you.

■ What should I do about stage fright? Remember "stage fright" or "butterflies" in the stomach are normal, not fatal. In fact, being a little nervous helps set you up for the occasion. Even experienced speakers feel this way.

The best way to avoid "stage fright" is preparation and practice. The better prepared you are, the less nervous you'll be when you make your presentation. Practice everything, including the walk up to the podium if there is one. Check all AV equipment. Use a tape recorder and stand in front of a mirror to see the image you present.

How can I relax? Being prepared should help you feel more at ease. You can also prepare yourself psychologically by mentally visualizing yourself as a success. If you feel "panicked," though, try deep breathing. Slowly inhale, hold it, then exhale fully. Repeat this process until you feel more relaxed.

The replaced oxygen in your lungs should help not only to relax you but also to energize you.

■ What should be my general attitude toward my audience? Your general demeanor should be poised and relaxed. As you walk up to the speaker's platform, do so with determination. Starting this way will help you throughout the presentation.

Your attitude toward your listeners should be one of friendly geniality. To encourage this, converse with them informally if possible before the presentation. If you do, you'll find this goodwill will carry over into your presentation and make your job that much easier.

To win acceptance of your ideas, you need to demonstrate sincerity, competence, trustworthiness, confidence, enthusiasm, and rapport with your audience. All these characteristics are important to projecting a possible self-image.

Let's examine each separately.

For *sincerity* to be communicated, your presentation needs to be substantive and clear, and your delivery should demonstrate interest in the ideas stemming from an understanding of the subject.

An image of *competence* largely stems from having prepared and practiced your presentation.

Trust is a belief in the honesty, integrity, and reliability of another person. It comes when you fit your words to your actions—that is, you don't say something contrary to what you do. During your presentation, you can also increase your credibility by recognizing that legitimate positions other than your own exist. Presenting the other side of the picture will increase your stature in the eyes of others by giving the impression that you have considered the big picture.

Confidence and conviction are often shown by the level of *enthusiasm* of your presentation.

Audience rapport comes from developing a common ground between you and your audience. Talking in terms of common interests, experiences, and beliefs helps build audience rapport. Similarly, using "we," "us," and "you," rather than "I," during your speech makes the audience feel you are considering its interests rather than your own.

Delivery

Having planned and practiced your presentation, the "moment of truth" is upon you. You are now ready to make your presentation.

The following will be important to the delivery of your speech: eye contact, body posture, gestures, and voice.

Eye contact. The importance of eye contact cannot be overstated. Speakers who avoid eye contact with their audience make the audience feel ill at ease and are perceived as untrustworthy. This doesn't mean you should stare at anyone. Instead, pick out several people in different sections of the audience and shift your gaze from one to another to give the impression you are attending to the whole room. Select people who look friendly and appear to be enjoying your speech.

Body posture and stance. To help you project the right image, stance is extremely important. Standing solidly on both feet, shoulders back and squared, with hands by your sides or resting lightly on the lectern, can help convey this image.

Gestures. Gestures should be used to emphasize the points you want to make, not made randomly. Gestures should also be suited to the size of the audience—large gestures generally work best for large audiences. Inappropriate gestures not only are distracting but also may be embarrassing.

Speaking voice. Don't think you have to put on a special voice for public speaking. This is unnecessary. Just use a normal voice and speak in a conversational tone but loud enough to be heard.

Pacing is also important. Don't speak too fast or too slow. The former can make your audience uneasy, the latter turn your audience off. Instead, learn to speak at a comfortable speed for your audience and to pause for emphasis and for ideas to sink in.

There are also speaking habits to avoid. To keep from saying, "ah," "uh," "OK," and "you know," learn to speak in thoughts, not words. And stay away from colloquialisms unless they serve to build audience rapport. The same is true of technical jargon, acronyms, or abbreviations. Always keep your audience in mind when speaking.

In making your points, it will help if you are concise, to the point, and as specific as possible. Provide examples. Don't ramble when you come to the end of your speech. Instead, stay within your time allotment. When you've finished your presentation, do so crisply so that the audience is left with little doubt that it is over. Don't just fade out and go blank.

As you're talking, try to be aware of visual cues like facial expressions or people yawning or checking their watches. Rather than getting mad at your audience, learn to adapt to their moods. For example, if they look puzzled after you've made some point, explain it in another way, by example or analogy, until you see the nods of comprehension. See their apathy as a challenge that you must overcome.

Finally, don't be guilty of overkill. This doesn't mean you shouldn't go out of your way to provide as much information as possible. Rather, it means that you should provide as much information as your audience can handle. You should leave them wanting to know more. If they need further information, the question-and-answer period afterwards should provide this opportunity.

Handling Questions

A presentation should generally include a question-and-answer period. Learning how to handle this is almost as important as making the presentation itself. The main purposes of the question-and-answer session are to reinforce the main presentation, increase the audience's knowledge, and provide valuable feedback.

To accomplish this, aim for a lively, intelligent exchange at the end that leaves the audience with a warm afterglow. To ensure this:

Get it started smoothly and keep it moving. If questions are slow in coming, the chairperson may start the ball rolling if you prepare him or her beforehand. Recognize subsequent questioners with alacrity.

Say, "I don't know." Admit it when asked a question outside your expertise. Don't try to bluff your way through. No one's an expert in everything.

Think before replying. Divide up multiple questions by saying. "Let me deal with your last question first. . . ." Learn to spot "loaded" questions and dismiss irrelevant questions politely and adroitly.

Handle statements disguised as questions. We are all familiar with the member of the audience whose opening gambit is, "Is it not true that. . . ." Some speakers wait for an opening and then say, "O.K., but what's your question?" This may help you feel good but it may cost you points with your audience. Remember you want to leave them with a sense of goodwill toward you. A better approach is to say, "Thank you. Are there any other questions?" This approach doesn't embarrass anyone.

Handle hostile questions. If a questioner is obviously hostile, either you can agree in principle with the statement of his or her feelings on the subject, or you can tell the questioner you feel the question requires a fuller answer and agree to meet with him or her after the session to address the issue.

Above all, don't drag the session out. Instead, end the session while you're ahead. Be prepared to summarize the question-and-answer period and then sit down.

Evaluation

Although you may breathe a sigh of relief after your presentation, all is not finished. Now is the time to evaluate your talk. This will help you do a better job the next time.

You may find taping yourself for further self-analysis and evaluation a rewarding experience. If you have video equipment, this is even better since you'll not only be able to hear yourself but be able to see how you come across to an audience.

Let's Talk:
Tools for Spotting and
Correcting Communication Problems

EDWARD L. LEVINE

Effective communication—no organization or manager can function well without it. In terms of one-to-one, face-to-face communication, effective communication is measured by the quality of the communication process itself and the consequences of the communication encounter for work productivity and job satisfaction.

Of these two measurements, the last would seem to be the easiest to determine. By then, though, it might be too late; any damage that might result from faulty communication would already have occurred. Fortunately, you don't need to wait that long. There are three tools that you can use to identify whether the communication process is going smoothly or poorly. These will also give you immediate information as to why the process is effective or not so that you can take action to improve the situation. And when you are able to enhance the quality of the communication process, you will dramatically increase the chances of positive consequences following the communication exchange.

Factors Affecting Interactive Chemistry

You can probably recall any number of times when you got together with your supervisor or subordinate to discuss important matters, but the discussion never really got off the ground. You had the sense that the two of you were not really communicating. I use the term "interactive chemistry" to describe the degree to which information and energy are exchanged and *accepted* by each party in a one-to-one communication encounter. When your discussion does not get off the ground, the chemical reaction is poor or lacking.

Successful interactive chemistry is related to a number of factors, including communicator credibility, the similarity between the two people, the message's quality or content, and the history of the relationship. These are factors that lie *under the surface*. Two other factors—whether the parties are listening to each other and the form and quality of the interaction process—are *observables* or *symptoms* of the

The author wishes to acknowledge the helpful suggestions of Jeffrey Jones, University of South Florida.

Reprinted from *Supervisory Management*, July 1980

interactive chemistry. As such, they may be watched as the communication encounter takes place, and action may be taken to enhance the chemical reaction.

The communication process can be improved by working on the symptoms themselves or by working on the subsurface factors. For now, I will concentrate on the symptoms, but it should be apparent that both symptoms and subsurface factors are not completely independent of each other. In other words, as we work to improve the form and quality of the interaction and the listening process, improvements will be made in the subsurface factors as well.

Let's consider an example. You and your subordinate have gotten together to talk about the subordinate's career development. During the course of the meeting, your subordinate senses you are not really listening to his or her statement of career needs. Rather, you are merely repeating company policies about career development from the company manual. The communication encounter is marred by embarrassing silences on your part because you have failed to listen, apprehend, and keep track of what your subordinate has been saying. Your face shows a bored expression, and you are yawning a good deal. You are looking at some papers on your desk, not at your communication partner. You offer few concrete suggestions on ways for the subordinate to attain career goals. You interrupt the subordinate several times and cut the meeting short by pointing out that you have another meeting to attend.

Your subordinate's reaction is predictable. A bored or annoyed expression creeps into his or her face. There is much staring at the clock on the wall. Your subordinate's contributions to the discussion wane, so you do most of the little talking that occurs. As the meeting proceeds, your subordinate thinks, "Gee, my own supervisor doesn't know much about career development in this company. Maybe that's true of other things that I must get assistance on to succeed here. Everybody knows that stuff in the company manual was obsolete months ago. Well, of course! Managers are different from us underlings; they've got it made. What do they care about us? I'm going to remember this for a long time to come."

You can readily see that your *credibility* has suffered. Your subordinate has drawn clear *lines of distinction* or *difference* between the two of you, and the quality of the messages exchanged is poor. One glaring incident has been added to the evolving *history of the relationship* between you and your subordinate. All these, of course, are subsurface factors.

Along with my main point about the relationship between the process and the subsurface factors in interaction chemistry, the example I just gave of poor communication also contains the aspects of the communication process that will concern us here. These are the nonverbal signs that have occurred during the meeting, the frequency and direction (manager to subordinate, or subordinate to manager) of the messages, and the form the messages take. The social sciences have developed over the years a number of techniques that enable us to take a reading of these three aspects in an objective, systematic way. There are three, in particular, worth noting. Before we explore these techniques, though, I must emphasize the need for proper preparation and practice. You cannot put these techniques to use immediately merely by reading about them. You need to try them out first, and get feedback where it is feasible. Perhaps you might enroll in a training course that uses role playing and subsequent feedback discussions to try these tools out.

Communication Tool #1: Reading the Nonverbal Messages of Others and Controlling Your Own

Can we read the nonverbal messages of others reliably? Yes, but only within rather narrow limits. Can we control our own nonverbal messages? Yes, but only if we work at it. In order to see more clearly what can and cannot be done with nonverbal messages, let's consider them in more detail.

There are two categories of nonverbal communication. One is *body language*. The other I call *speech-surplus*. *Body language* includes facial expressions; eye contact; body position or posture; body orientation; the space between our body and that of our communication partner; whether we touch our partner or not; and hand, arm, and body gestures.

Facial expressions may communicate a number of emotions or messages in such a way that others can recognize them with some degree of reliability, at least others who come from the same cultural background as we do. However, the number of facial expressions is much more limited than the number of emotions that we may experience. For example, the same facial expression may be used to express impatience and disgust or to express interest and puzzlement. You can probably look in the mirror and produce facial expressions that correspond to these and other emotions.

Eye contact is the extent to which we gaze directly at the face and eyes of our communication partner. Eye contact that is somewhat frequent and of some duration will generally convey the impression of interest and trustworthiness. On the other hand, overly frequent eye contact that lasts just a short period of time—in other words, when the eyes are darting to and from the face and eyes of our communication partner—may suggest anxiety and deception.

Body position or posture may indicate degree of interest in the subject of conversation and even indicate our feelings of status or power in comparison to our communication partner. At the extreme, if we turn our face from, and our back toward a person, we are communicating that the individual has little power, and his or her words are of no interest. An overly erect posture may suggest tension or low status. An expansive, slouching, foot-on-the-desk posture may suggest relaxation or high status.

The degree of liking one has for another may be conveyed by our body orientation. Communicators tend to lean toward those they like and away from those they dislike.

The amount of space we maintain between ourselves and others may suggest how much we like them. Moreover, we probably ought to move closer when we deliver good news, or further away when we deliver bad news, in order to maintain a positive relationship between ourselves and our communication partner.

Touching the other person on the arm or shoulder may be an effective way to indicate warmth and acceptance, if the context makes it appropriate. It may also help to persuade our communication partner to accept our message.

Hand, body, and arm gestures may complement facial expressions in communicating our emotions. They may also be used to illustrate a point we are trying to make. Gestures used to illustrate a point may consist of drawing a kind of picture in the air, stabbing with a finger, or tapping on the desk to highlight a word or phrase. Tremors, nail biting, picking or squeezing at one's body or face, drumming the fingers, and other such gestures are often associated with tension. Covering the eyes or ears with the hands may suggest fatigue or deception.

In contrast to body language, *speech surplus* refers to the tone of voice used, how loud or soft we talk, how quickly words are delivered, and the number and duration of silent pauses between our statements. A monotone may indicate fatigue or boredom. Speaking too loudly or too rapidly may suggest anxiety or deception. Too many silences may indicate unwillingness to discuss a matter or confusion. (Silence will come up again later in the discussion.)

You probably noticed the wishy-washy nature of the statements I have made about nonverbal communication—statements characterized by "*may* indicate" or "*may* suggest." This is because the state of our knowledge about nonverbal communication is far from complete. Moreover, the context of communication and the cultural background of the partners to the communication will affect the meaning attached to the nonverbal messages we send and receive. For example, in a particular encounter we may interpret lack of eye contact as indicative of anxiety or deception; but if our partner is a Mexican-American, it may be a sign of respect. For these reasons, our capacity to interpret the nonverbal messages of others and to control the nonverbal messages we send is quite limited.

How can we make practical use of nonverbal communication in light of the many kinds of nonverbal cues that exist and the difficulty of attaching fixed meanings to them? We should look at nonverbal cues only in the most basic ways. As suggested by Mehrabian, one of the foremost researchers in this area, we should consider nonverbal cues along three lines. First, nonverbal cues may bear on the *degree of liking* one person has toward another. Secondly, they may bear on the degree of *dominance or status* one person possesses compared to another. Third, the degree of *responsiveness* and *attentiveness* can be contained in nonverbal cues.

The most important advice I can give concerning the reading of others' nonverbal messages is to be alert to these three dimensions, and be wary of *overinterpreting* or drawing definite conclusions about nonverbal messages *without discussing them verbally*. This will help you pin down more exactly what they mean. Also, it will alert your communication partner to some unintended inferences you are drawing about the communication process.

It is especially critical to translate nonverbal cues into verbal messages when these nonverbal cues do not match the verbal messages being exchanged. Lying, or the masking of true opinions and emotions, may often be spotted in this way. For example, suppose your subordinate tells you that things are going really well but keeps his or her eyes to the floor. If this occurs, you should tell what you are seeing in the nonverbal behavior and probe for additional information.

Also, there may be instances when a nonverbal message strongly indicates dislike for you or what you are saying, or an overly submissive attitude or disinterest (you think). These are signs that must not be ignored. If they are discussed and handled properly, they can serve to enhance the interactive chemistry and cement a relationship. If left undiscussed, they may serve to sour a relationship and create substantial barriers to effective communication.

The key to being able to discuss these issues is the creation of a permissive, nonthreatening climate so that the subordinate feels comfortable in sharing his or feelings, beliefs, and opinions. Without full communication in these areas, nonverbal cues may never be fully understood, and continuing deterioration in communication effectiveness will take place.

To control the nonverbal messages you send and enhance communication, I would recommend the following:

1. Be attentive to eye contact. You should gaze at the face and eyes of your communication partner frequently and with some amount of duration. However, don't stare too long at your partner. This may create a feeling of competitiveness and discomfort.
2. Have your facial expression and posture reflect interest and acceptance, if not liking. This may be accomplished by arching the eyebrows, smiling, maintaining a fairly erect posture, and nodding as the other person speaks. Your facial expressions and posture may be practiced in the mirror.
3. Maintain a reasonable social distance—approximately four to six feet from your partner.
4. Lean forward and use gestures that are not too exaggerated to emphasize an important point. For example, tap lightly on your desk to "spice up" the conversation; don't smash it with your hand or fist.
5. Speak at a reasonable pace, not too slow to bore your communication partner and not too fast to be misunderstood. Modulate your voice in tone and amplitude: a monotone is obviously boring. Speech courses or toastmaster's groups can be helpful in achieving these objectives. Prior preparation for a meeting will likewise assist here.
6. Since lying or masking true opinions or feelings often come through nonverbally, they should be avoided. We are generally not very good at lying nonverbally.

Communication Tool #2: Flow Charting the Messages

The use of a flow chart is based on the notion that an effective one-to-one communication process is marked by a lot of talking on the part of *both* people. A high rate of activity and mutuality of communication generally lead to high productivity and high job satisfaction. The flow chart is a simple, systematic way to determine whether a high rate of activity and mutuality of interaction are present.

The procedure for flow charting is simple. But it can be made slightly more complex, if more information is desired. Figure 1 illustrates the procedure. The form allows you to tally (on the left side), merely by drawing a line, every time you direct a verbal message (suggestions, opinions, questions, and so forth) to your subordinate. A tally is made for each separate message you utter. You may likewise tally (on the right side) the frequency of communications directed from your partner to you.

Figure 1

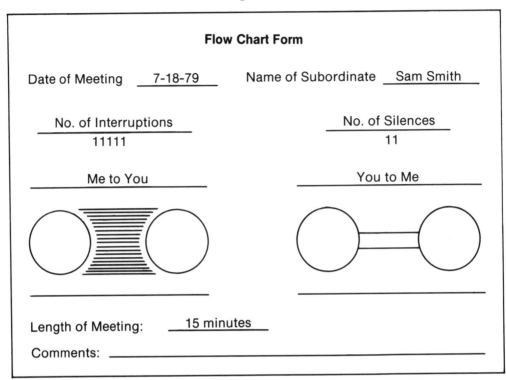

The tally pattern shown in Figure 1 reveals an extremely one-sided communication process. This will often suggest that a communication problem exists, one you may not even be aware of. You are dominating the conversation! For some situations this may be all right. For example, when you are training a subordinate in a new work method, this may be a typical flow pattern. However, in most other situations, more participation by your subordinate would usually be expected and desired.

The number of silent periods that last for more than five seconds may be tallied in the upper right portion of the form. One tally mark is registered for each five-to-ten second silent period. Figure 1 reveals that there were only two silent periods lasting ten seconds or less. Along with the large number of messages exchanged over the 15-minute period, this suggests a high rate of activity.

The number of times you interrupted or were interrupted by your subordinate may be entered in the upper left portion of the form. Interruptions are times when you started to speak or were in the middle of a statement but were cut off by statements of your partner, and vice versa. If the number of interruptions is high, this will often indicate a communication problem. From the form, it appears that your subordinate tried to speak on a number of occasions but was cut off by you. This is based on the fact that your subordinate only spoke twice, but there are five interruptions.

You should make the tallies on a form like this as the communication process is taking place. Once you have practiced a bit, you should be able to make these marks without detracting from the communication process at all.

Finally, the form in Figure 1 contains a section for you to write in comments for your own use. You can record your impressions or explanations of the process as you experienced it and use the comments for improving the process as you prepare for future meetings.

Perhaps the most worthwhile way to complicate this process is by keeping tallies for specific time segments of a meeting. Suppose you have prepared in advance for a fact-finding meeting with your subordinate. You have anticipated that you will spend the first five minutes in discussing the issues with your subordinate, then you will launch into a series of questions to gather facts and opinions. Finally you will conclude by thanking your subordinate and giving instructions for future action. You could make up a form like that shown in Figure 1 for each one of the meeting segments as you have planned. You might expect that the first and last segment will show more interactions from you to your subordinate than the second segment. Ideally, none of the meeting segments should show as one-sided a pattern as the form in Figure 1.

You can probably think of additional ways to modify the form to meet your needs. However, you should not make the procedure so complicated that its completion will, in and of itself, detract from the communication process.

Communication Tool #3: Charting the Form and Quality of the Communication

Knowing the rate and mutuality of interaction may give you a start in overcoming communication problems; but you may need even more information to diagnose and remedy communication problems. The tool I am about to describe will provide such information. The information should provide you with insight into the *form and quality of the communications* shared by you and your subordinate. However, the method requires a good deal of practice. It also requires a great deal of objectivity about your own communications, so it should only be used when other methods have not led to the solution of communication problems.

The tool is adapted from the work of the eminent social psychologist R. F. Bales, and is based on the idea that one-to-one communication in a work setting deals with two major issues—*task accomplishment* and *social-emotional issues*. Task accomplishment refers to those aspects of the communication process aimed at producing *outputs* from the meeting (solutions to problems, a new list of objectives to shoot for, new knowledge about work procedures, and so on). Further, task accomplishment involves the exchange of suggestions or decisions, opinions or evaluations, and information of a factual nature. People in one-to-one communication may either give or ask for any one of these three categories of communication (suggestions, opinions, or information). As a result that portion of the communication process devoted to task accomplishment may be divided into six categories, each of which is listed below with a few examples to help in its definition.

1. *Gives suggestion/decision.* "Let's proceed with the new product." "How about trying out Jim on the territory?" "We'll go with your idea about increasing morale."

2. *Gives opinion/evaluation.* "I think that there are other alternatives to consider." "That is an idea whose time has come." "In my judgment, it can't work."

3. *Gives information.* "It is 3:15 PM." "Our work needs to be completed by the end of the day."

4. *Asks for suggestion/decision.* "What do we do now?" "What shall our decision be?" "How can we hit our target for this month?"

5. *Asks for opinion/evaluation.* "What do you think of Jane's idea?" "What do you feel is the economic state of our test market site?" "What is this report on company communication problems really saying?"

6. *Asks for information.* "What time is it?" "When do we need to get the work out?"

The social-emotional aspect involves the "cement" that keeps you and your subordinate working together harmoniously and energetically. The portion of the communication process dealing with social-emotional issues may be categorized as either positive (binding) or negative (nonbinding, splintering). Positive social-emotional communications include indications of solidarity—(for example, the use of the pronoun "we" to refer to you and your subordinate and praise for the two of you, such as, "We really work well together")—occasional joking, sighing, side comments, personal stories to release pent-up tension, and agreement or acceptance of ideas, suggestions, and information. Negative social-emotional communications include exhibitions of aggression or hostility (for example, interrupting the other person or saying, "That's a dumb idea"); showing tension (evident from the use of "uh" and "er uh," the drumming of fingers, pulling at one's ear or gripping of a chair hard); disagreeing in a hostile way with suggestions, opinions, and information; and excessive release of tension to the extent that work tasks are not able to be handled (for example, 40 minutes of jokes and tall tales in a 45-minute meeting).

To chart the form and quality of communication you can set up a form like that shown in Figure 2.

As a one-to-one meeting proceeds, you would make tallies in the proper category, one tally for each type of message exchanged. You would place the tallies under the space for your communication or that of your subordinate depending on who initiated the message. Sometimes you may code a single message in two or more categories. An example might be when you ask, "How about both of us taking a long lunch break today so we can discuss this problem away from the office?" This could be coded by making a single tally in the categories Gives Suggestions, Asks Opinion (if you are really seeking an evaluation of this suggestion), and Positive Social-Emotional. One valuable lesson to be learned from this example, in addition to how to tally, is the idea that many of the messages we exchange *contain both task and social-emotional components mixed together.* At any rate, you can readily see that the tallying is more complicated than the tallying for the flow chart. So prior preparation and practice are musts.

With the addition of a place to tally the number of silences (five to ten seconds long) in the upper right-hand corner of the form, it should be clear that this tool pretty much duplicates the information in the flow chart. The total number of communications initiated by you as compared to those initiated by your subordinate may be determined by adding all the categories. Also, a space is provided for your comments.

How do we interpret the information provided by this tool? As with the flow chart, we could look at activity rates and mutuality in the process. Also, we could look at the differences between the number of "Gives" messages and the number of "Asks" messages. Also, we could look at the number of "Positive" versus "Negative Social-Emotional" messages. Generally, a productive one-to-one meeting will be characterized by a lot of "Gives," particularly "Gives Suggestions," few "Asks," a relatively equal number of communications initiated by you and your subordinate, a high rate of activity (few silent periods, many communications), and a relatively frequent occurrence of positive social-emotional communications.

When you have diagnosed a problem, if one exists, you can then take corrective action. For example, if there are a high number of "Asks" relative to "Gives," this may mean that you and your subordinate have not prepared adequately for the meeting. Or it could indicate that you need to call in an expert. Another problem that might arise is that there are too few positive social-emotional messages exchanged relative to task-based messages. This may mean that you are not delivering sufficient praise and indications of solidarity to cement the relationship between you and your subordinate.

Putting It All Together

We have discussed three communication tools to help you spot communication problems. The three tools—reading the nonverbal messages of others and controlling your own, flow charting the messages, and charting the form and quality of the communication—deal with the observables or symptoms of the interactive chemistry taking place between you and your subordinate. Perhaps I can anticipate a reaction from you sharp-eyed readers. You are probably saying, "But wait! The symptoms include whether the parties are listening to each other, as well as the communication process itself. The tools seem to deal only with the process." My response is that if you make use of the tools, you will *have to listen* more actively and attentively than you ever have before. And you will be able to spot and correct listening problems on the part of your partner.

Because they require a great deal of concentration, there is always the danger that the tools I have described here may detract from the effectiveness of one-to-one communication. This may happen if you are not fully prepared and well versed in their use. Or you may overly complicate the suggested procedures if you seek to record too much information during a meeting. Finally you may begin to lose sight of the

Figure 2

Charting the Form and Quality of Communication

Date of Meeting_____ Name of Subordinate_____
                                                                            No. of Silences

Subordinate's Interactions

Positive Social-Emotional	Gives			Asks			Negative Social-Emotional
	Suggestions	Opinions	Information	Suggestions	Opinions	Information	

My Interactions

Positive Social-Emotional	Gives			Asks			Negative Social-Emotional
	Suggestions	Opinions	Information	Suggestions	Opinions	Information	

Length of Meeting_____

Comments: _____

_____

real objectives of a one-to-one meeting because you have begun to concentrate so much on the process. For example, you may be focusing on communication flow and nonverbal signs when the purpose of the meeting is to plan work objectives. For these reasons, the tools discussed here are to be used only when you are having a specific problem, or when you think your overall communication effectiveness could stand substantial improvement.

Two more points before I end the discussion. One is that these tools are useful not only for one-to-one communication but for group meetings as well. Secondly, you may be faced with a communication problem that these tools cannot help you solve. In this situation the use of a third party in your office, or an expert from outside the organization, may be the answer.

Communication effectiveness is a key element in productivity and job satisfaction. No matter what strategy or tools you choose to overcome communication problems, they must be solved to allow for maximum achievement of your work goals.

Plugging the Communication Channel—How Managers Stop Upward Communication

PHYLLIS THOMAS

Open communication channels are obviously beneficial to a company. Ideas can be exchanged, and many problems can be resolved or avoided. Indeed, a supervisor who is a good listener can learn much about the attitudes, interests, and needs of his or her employees.

Most managers recognize this and invite their employees to discuss problems and ideas, and to offer suggestions for improving their jobs and the organization. But too often they do not receive communications from their subordinates as often as they would like. Frequently, the managers view communication channels as much more open than what is perceived by subordinates. Perhaps the managers committed strategic errors that are reducing or stopping the communications flowing from subordinates. Upward communications can be curtailed by identifying information sources, publicly confronting subordinates, discriminating against critics, making a promise that cannot be fulfilled, letting friendships influence judgments, and opening meetings in a way that discourages discussion.

Let's look at each inappropriate action in more detail.

Revealing Sources

An employee discussing a controversial subject with a superior generally believes that the discussion will be confidential. A manager who violates the employee's trust is unlikely to be trusted by that employee again.

Managers who disclose the identity of an individual revealing a problem or suggesting an unpopular solution inadvertently discourage upward communication.

Disclosure may occur in a variety of ways. In a discussion with another supervisor about a problem in his or her department, for example, a manager might disclose information that only a few employees could possibly know. In such a case, the details will have identified the information source. The manager may also disclose that the information came from a new and not an old employee or a female and not a male employee. The supervisor or employee may ask if it was John, and the manager may say nothing.

Certainly, confidence is lost in the system if a complaint made in confidence becomes public and the

Reprinted from *Supervisory Management*, April 1985

source of the information is named. So, if communication is to stay open, care must be exercised to avoid identifying an individual indirectly or by name.

Public Confrontation

Managers also plug the upward communication channel with public confrontations. "Dressings down" will leave the confronted employee annoyed, embarrassed, angry, or hurt. If the employee does not know how the manager knew he disagreed, the employee may feel threatened, betrayed, or suspicious of the people around him. In any case, given the threat of another public confrontation, the employee is unlikely to open up to either the supervisor or co-workers.

A public confrontation may also limit communication from other employees. These employees will be embarrassed, annoyed, and often fearful that the same thing may happen to them. They may be afraid to voice any complaints or suggest possible problems with a plan preferring to wait in meetings until their manager has taken a stand and then to agree with him or her. They may not make useful suggestions from fear that their ideas may seem to be a criticism of the manager.

Much is lost because of a public criticism of an employee. A manager would achieve better results if he or she met alone with the employee in his or her office. After all, the manager needs to find out first-hand what is what. The story being told may not be correct, important details of the story may not be correct, or important details of the story may have been left out.

Discrimination

Channels can become clogged if employees believe they will be discriminated against for voicing criticism or holding an opposing view. Many times the discrimination is not intentional. The manager is hurt, mad, or upset because of a complaint and treats that employee differently from other employees. The manager may change the employee's job, either making it too difficult or too boring. The manager may expect the employee to do a job that the employee has neither the ability nor the skill to do, or a promotion may be denied an employee who has voiced opposition to the manager's plans.

Even if the manager's actions are justified, the appearance of discrimination will still hurt the organization. Fellow employees will discuss the treatment of the person and reason that this action is the standard treatment for anyone who is not a "yes-person." This causes discontentment and lowers morale. When employees even say jokingly, "If you disagree with the boss, you'll end up like old Joe (or Jean)," there is damage to the organization.

A situation that contributes to the appearance of discrimination is a change in criteria for evaluation following a disagreement with an employee. Often the change in criteria is not the result of the disagreement but rather stems from changes made at a higher level in the organization or from a manager's incomplete understanding of the criteria for evaluation. In either case, damage is done if later the manager tells the employee(s) that different criteria are being used. At best, the conflicting signals will undermine the manager's authority and credibility with the employees. But often the changed criteria will be seen as a retaliatory act on the manager's part. And this undoubtedly will damage future communications.

Discrimination is hard to see in oneself, but managers should be on guard against it at all times. Clearly stated criteria and policies on how employees are assigned to tasks, promoted, or retained can help avoid feelings of discrimination. If there are written criteria, it is easier to justify the decisions of a manager and so avoid charges of discrimination.

False Promises

Another common communication block is the old "smile, agree with the suggestion/complaint, promise to work on the situation, and do nothing" strategy. Many managers believe that it's enough to allow an employee to "get something off his (or her) chest." In many cases this is true, but managers need to be careful in agreeing to do something that they either can't or don't intend to do.

Idle promises erode employee confidence in a manager. Soon employees begin to question, at least in their own minds, everything that their manager says. After a while, even when the manager does what he or she promises, the manager may not get praise or respect from the employees. They may say to one another, "Well, everyone has to follow through occasionally."

The idea of listening to employee problems is good. Listening helps employees to air problems. It is an unfulfilled promise to change the situation that blocks communication. A better approach to employee problems may be to explain why the situation is as it is. Many times an explanation helps employees to accept the situation and to go on with their work. A manager should try not to make promises that cannot be kept. Good intentions are not enough if time after time a manager fails to live up to his or her promises.

Clouded Judgments

When dealing with employee conflicts in which one of the employees is a personal friend, special care must be exercised. Communication problems arise when an employee is told that the person he or she is concerned about could not have acted in the fashion described. Where does an employee go with the problem if the manager will not try to see even the possibility of a problem? The employee will feel trapped. In many cases, the employee may discuss the situation with friends and co-workers. The problem may then grow as other employees become involved and take sides.

In dealing with any employee situation, personal friendship should be set aside in fairness to everyone. A supervisor should consider the situation objectively, ask for both sides of the story, and if possible have a meeting with all concerned. Many times, having both sides present will avoid exaggeration and buck passing.

Opening Meetings

Still another communication barrier is the way some employee meetings are started. Occasionally, managers start a meeting by telling their employees that they are just too busy and really don't have time for the session. The meeting then proceeds with whatever business is to be addressed. Employee ideas or problems are requested but nothing is brought up for discussion, which surprises the manager because the meeting had been requested by the employees to air their problems and ideas.

If real discussion is wanted, care needs to be taken in starting meetings to put employees at ease. Managers should avoid making employees feel that their managers' time is too valuable to be spent on them.

Summary

Communication is something that must be handled with care, skill, and thought, for broken or clogged communication channels are difficult to restore to good working order. A manager can improve the chances of having good communication by looking carefully at his or her attitude and reaction to communications from below. Confidentiality is important to keep communication flowing. Public confrontation and discrimination should be avoided. Idle or impossible promises should stop and explanations of situations should be substituted. Friendships should not be allowed to cloud one's judgment. Finally, when employee meetings are called, care should be taken not to stop communication before it starts. Employees should feel their communications are important. With some careful thought on a manager's part, employee communication can be maintained or started up the channel.

Building a Professional Image: Learning Assertiveness

PHILIP I. MORGAN and H. KENT BAKER

What would you do? You invite an old friend to dinner but your boss asks you at the last minute to work late on a "rush job." Your friend will be in town only one night. Would you typically:

- Say nothing about your important plans and simply agree to stay late to finish the work?
- In no uncertain terms tell your boss that you refuse to work late tonight, berating him for his lack of planning and foresight?
- Explain you won't be able to work late this evening because you have made special plans that cannot be changed but you would be willing to start work early the next day?

Here's another hypothetical case. Let's suppose one of your subordinates has made a serious job error. You feel that this error should be called to her attention. Would you typically:

- Apologize and act embarrassed at having to mention the error, even offering to fix it for her?
- Angrily reprimand the employee, telling her that you "can't believe anyone could make such a stupid blunder" and demanding that it be corrected immediately?
- Discuss the mistake with the employee, attempting to discover its cause and ways to avoid its recurrence?

These three responses characterize very different types of behavior. In both situations, the first response illustrates *passive* behavior, the second *aggressive* behavior, and the third *assertive* behavior.

An assertive response will generally help you achieve your goals while preserving the rights of others. To understand why, let's examine the three supervisory behaviors in detail.

Passive supervisors deny their own rights or concerns and permit others to control them. They often do this because of a lack of *self*-control. They accept all criticism as valid and feel guilty, even apologetic, when criticism is invalid. Further, they take the line of least resistance and say or do nothing, concealing their feelings or desires. When this happens, they experience a loss of self-esteem. As a result, they often feel exploited, helpless, angry, or resentful. This causes others to lose respect for them.

Aggressive supervisors, on the other hand, make their feelings known, often disregarding the rights

Reprinted from *Supervisory Management,* August 1985

of others in the process. They may be domineering and insensitive, and hence others feel resentful, angry, and "put down" by them.

Although subordinates may not openly defy an assertive supervisor, they are often uncooperative. Generally, aggressive behavior results in "win-lose" situations in the short run but "lose-lose" situations in the long run. Aggressive supervisors may win the battle but they ultimately lose the war.

Assertive supervisors also stand up for their rights but they do it in ways that don't violate others' rights. Assertive behavior is self-enhancing but not at the expense of others. In communicating with others, assertive supervisors are open, honest, and "up front," because they believe that all people have an equal right to express themselves honestly. This openness and honesty encourages respect and cooperation from subordinates.

Supervisory Assertiveness Rights

In short, being assertive will enable you as a supervisor to exercise your rights without denying the rights of others. If you are inhibited, and easily give in to others' wishes while holding your own desires in check or, conversely, if you must destroy others to have your own way, your self-esteem will probably be low. And a poor self-image can affect your work.

The purpose of developing a more assertive style is to increase your effectiveness in professional and social situations. It is based on the assumption that people are more likely to achieve their goals by letting others know what they feel, think, and want, and that fostering a climate of cooperation by respecting others' needs, feelings, and rights improves overall work effectiveness.

Assertiveness is also based on acceptance of certain fundamental human rights. For example, assertive supervisors implicitly believe that people have the right to be treated with respect, express feelings and opinions, defend themselves, be listened to and taken seriously, say "no" without feeling guilty, ask for what they want, make mistakes, and even choose not to assert themselves if they don't want to do so.

Techniques for Becoming Assertive

There are several techniques you can use to become less prone to manipulation by others. Among the techniques described by Manuel J. Smith in his book *When I Say No, I Feel Guilty* are "negative inquiry," "broken record," and "fogging."

Negative inquiry(ni) entails asking a question of someone in such a way as to get the person to examine his or her value system and to be more assertive (and consequently less manipulative) in the relationship. For example:

You: Jim, I was wondering why you didn't recommend me for the merit raise.
Your supervisor: You didn't deserve it.
You: I see. What did I do that was unmeritorious(ni)?
Your supervisor: Well, you're new at the job. You're not bad, just average.
You: What am I doing that makes me just average(ni)?
Your supervisor: You make all the typical mistakes a new supervisor makes.
You: What typical mistakes am I making specifically(ni)?
Your supervisor: Well, you're a bit slow in submitting your work.
You: I'm taking too much time(ni)?
Your supervisor: No, just average for the amount of time on the job.
You: I see. What else do I do that's just average(ni)?
Your supervisor: Well, you underestimated the number of people it would take to complete that last assignment.

You: I guess I should have asked someone more experienced how many people it would take to complete the job.

Your supervisor: No problem. You'll learn.

You: Well, if I correct all these problems you've mentioned, will I have a chance to receive a merit raise next year?

Your supervisor: Very probably.

In this example, by practicing negative inquiry, you were able to keep from becoming upset by criticism because the criticism was focused. And you know exactly what behavior is bothering your supervisor. Negative inquiry encourages others to say what it is they really want.

Let's look at another example of negative inquiry.

Fellow supervisor: Say, George, do you have any problem working in your office?

You: No, I don't find it a problem working in my office. Why do you ask(ni)?

Fellow supervisor: Well, I can't seem to get any work done in my office.

You: I don't understand what it is about your office that prevents you from working(ni).

Fellow supervisor: It's so stuffy and airless.

You: Well, why don't you put on the air conditioner?

Fellow supervisor: Well, that's only part of it. It's the light in my office that's the problem.

You: What is it about the light in your office that prevents you from working(ni)?

Fellow supervisor: It's artificial light.

You: What is it about artificial light that prevents you from working in your office(ni)?

Fellow supervisor: It hurts my eyes.

You: I see. What kind of light do you prefer(ni)?

Fellow supervisor: Daylight, of course.

You: I see. So if you had a window in your office that provided natural light, and that you could open to let fresh air in, you'd be better able to work?

Fellow supervisor: That's it exactly! (pause) Say, doesn't *your* office have a window?

In this example, you used negative inquiry to expose the fact that your fellow co-worker was trying to manipulate you into switching offices with him. Negative inquiry encouraged him to come right out and say what he wanted. You then could either say no, that you didn't want to switch offices, or you could comply with his wishes.

Broken record(br) is another technique for increasing assertiveness. It entails simply repeating over and over a word or phrase used by the other person without showing any signs of anger or irritation. It's particularly effective if you have trouble saying "no" to people. For example:

Salesman: You do want your salespeople to sell more, don't you?

You: I understand, but I'm not interested(br).

Salesman: But these materials have proven to help boost sales 40 percent!

You: I understand, but I'm not interested(br).

Salesman: You *don't* understand or you'd want to buy these. Let me ask you, who's your nearest competitor?

You: I understand, but I'm not interested(br).

Salesman: Can't you say anything besides "I understand, but I'm not interested"?

You: I understand, but I'm not interested(br).

Salesman: Say, do you think your competition would be interested in buying these materials?

You: I understand, but I'm not interested(br).

The salesperson usually would give up at this point.

The third technique—*fogging(f)*—also calls for persistence. The goal is to avoid the compulsive habit of responding to every statement or question put to us. Fogging involves agreeing in principle or agreeing with the truth of a statement without getting angry. This technique is especially useful in dealing with criticism from peers. For example:

Fellow supervisor: I see you've turned out your usual sloppy paperwork.
You: You're right. My paperwork could be a little neater (f).
Fellow supervisor: And another thing, I see you're dressed in your usual sloppy manner.
You: That's right, I'm dressed in my usual way (f).
Fellow supervisor: How do you expect to get promoted looking like that?
You: True. Sartorial elegance (or dress sense) isn't exactly my strong point (f).
Fellow supervisor: Strong points? I didn't know you had any.
You: I do have a lot of faults (f).

Your fellow supervisor will eventually give up.

Scripting, developed by James Waters of McGill University, creates an assertive response by using various combinations of standard responses. For example, an assertive response might include some or all of the following:

- *Describe* the situation or the behavior of people with whom you are dealing.
- *Express* feelings and/or explain what effect the other's behavior has on you.
- *Empathize* with the other person's position in the situation.
- *Specify* what changes you would like to see in the situation or in the other's behavior, and offer to
- *Negotiate* those changes with the other person.
- *Indicate* the possible consequences that will follow if change does not occur.

An example of a response that utilizes all of the script elements might be: "Bob, your work hasn't been up to par lately (describe). I'm annoyed (express), and it's having a negative effect on the other employees in the department (explain). I assume that you must have some extra demands on your time (empathize), but I would like your work to improve (specify). If that's not possible, perhaps we can work something else out, such as sharing the workload (negotiate). In any event, unless these problems are settled, we can't keep you in the department any longer (indicate)."

Developing an Assertive Image

Developing an assertive style isn't easy. Constant practice is necessary. Albert Emmons in *Your Perfect Right* recommends the following eight steps to help a manager develop a more positive, self-enhancing image:

1. *Examine your own behavior.* How are you behaving now? Are you being appropriately assertive? Are you satisfied with your personal effectiveness in interpersonal relationships? Are you too passive or too aggressive?
2. *Keep a record of your assertiveness.* Keep a diary for one week and record each day those situations in which you found yourself responding assertively, those in which you "blew it," and those you avoided altogether so that you would not have to face the need to act assertively.
3. *Reflect on a particular situation.* Take a few moments to review how you handled a specific situation—for example, having a subordinate come in late after speaking to him or her on numerous occasions.
4. *Review your responses.* Write down your behavior in step three, examining carefully its components to identify your strengths. Be aware as well of those components that represent passive or aggressive behavior.

5. *Consider alternative responses.* What are other ways the incident could have been handled? Could you have dealt with it more to your own advantage? Less offensively?

6. *Imagine yourself handling the situation in a new way.* Try out new responses to situations that you would like to change. Be assertive, but be as much your "natural self" as you can. At this point, it may be helpful to model yourself after someone who has handled a similar situation well.

7. *Do it.* Be aware of the feedback you receive, both verbal and nonverbal. Did you accomplish your goals? Were the other person's needs met?

8. *Continue to shape your behavior to achieve your desired interpersonal goals.* Review your behavior when necessary and be aware of feedback.

Other things you might do are:

Trust yourself and your feelings. Effective, results-oriented supervision requires that you be open and direct, that you be clear about your feelings and what you want and need. When this happens, you are comfortable with yourself, and others are less likely to be a threat or feel threatened. Openness begets trust and builds confidence.

Be clear and objective-oriented. Supervisors tend to get results when they unambiguously communicate their goals and objectives. Energy is often wasted defending and attacking when in reality goal-oriented behavior usually works best.

Confront issues. Don't accept "put-downs," verbal attacks, or exploitation. Confront the issues in a straightforward manner and encourage others to do the same. This helps to avoid manipulation by others and promotes a healthy self-respect while it enhances your image in others' eyes because they don't have to be devious to have their needs met.

By following the above guidelines and practicing techniques such as fogging, negative inquiry, broken record, and scripting, you should enhance your professional image by being better equipped to deal with manipulation in the workforce.

How Do You Rate as a Listener?

JEAN W. VINING and AUGUSTA C. YRLE

"I'm sorry that I didn't return your call. My secretary misunderstood your message."

"May I speak to Mr. Smith? I'm returning his call. What? There's no Mr. Smith there. Is this 123-2322? It is. Then I must have received the wrong message."

Do these conversations sound familiar? Perhaps they sound all too familiar, reflecting similar situations that frequently occur in your own department. Have you ever wondered why so many messages are incorrectly reported? Perhaps the personnel in your organization do not know how to listen effectively or do not recognize how important listening is if a message is to be transmitted correctly and appropriate follow-up action taken.

You, as supervisor, are well aware of the need for effective listening skills. Instructions on doing a job that are not clearly understood can lead to costly mistakes. And an incorrectly reported telephone message from a client or customer can mean the loss of that individual's business. But employees are not the only individuals with poor listening skills. On occasion, you, too, may be guilty of ineffective listening. That can be even more costly to your organization.

Ineffective listening skills are certainly not unique to your organization, this generation, or even to this century. They've been around at least from the time of Socrates who complained that the youths he tutored were generally poor listeners. Only recently, however, has the importance of receiving and transmitting verbal ideas clearly, concisely, and coherently been emphasized. Much of the research in the past in communication focused on written messages.

Why People Listen

Individuals listen for a number of reasons, including to receive a message; as a basis upon which to make a decision; to obtain needed information; and to enhance their ability to instruct, supervise, guide, manage, or counsel others. Any of these reasons for listening may be used repeatedly each day by an executive and his or her subordinates. In each instance, listening errors can occur. The message perceived by the listener and the resulting transmitted message may be entirely different from the sender's intended message.

Receiving and comprehending abilities vary with an individual's surroundings at the time that the message is received. They may also be influenced by previous listening experiences and by noises present

Reprinted from *Supervisory Management*, January 1980

at the time that the message is transmitted. Still another factor relates to the words used in the message. People are able to hear more accurately and to convey a message more correctly when familiar vocabulary is used. For your part, that means that a conscious effort should be made to use terminology that is easily understood by all personnel in your organization. To assist new employees in becoming operationally familiar with the terminology of their jobs, you might consider providing a list of terms relevant to the particular situation, department, or industry.

Improving Listening

As with many skills, practice in listening tends to improve one's ability to listen effectively. As a supervisor, you'll find that as your listening skills grow, your managerial effectiveness will increase because your decisions will be based on a clear understanding of the facts. Also, you will be perceived by your subordinates and your co-workers as a manager who listens before acting. Because of your new image as a listener, your decisions may be implemented more smoothly and more quickly by both your subordinates and fellow workers.

You can actively work to improve your own listening competency and that of your staff by practicing the following techniques and advocating that your people try them, too:

Figure 1

How Do You Measure Up as a Listener?

Directions: Read the questions listed below and rate yourself on each of the listening characteristics using the following scale:

Always	= 4 points
Almost always	= 3 points
Rarely	= 2 points
Never	= 1 point

Listening Characteristics	*Responses*			
1. Do I allow the speaker to express his or her complete thoughts without interrupting?	4	3	2	1
2. Do I listen between the lines, especially when conversing with individuals who frequently use hidden meanings?	4	3	2	1
3. Do I actively try to develop retention ability to remember important facts?	4	3	2	1
4. Do I write down the most important details of a message?	4	3	2	1
5. In recording a message, do I concentrate on writing the major facts and key phrases?	4	3	2	1
6. Do I read essential details back to the speaker before the conversation ends to insure correct understanding?	4	3	2	1
7. Do I refrain from turning off the speaker because the message is dull or boring, or because I do not personally know or like the speaker?	4	3	2	1
8. Do I avoid becoming hostile or excited when a speaker's views differ from my own?	4	3	2	1
9. Do I ignore distractions when listening?	4	3	2	1
10. Do I express a genuine interest in the other individual's conversation?	4	3	2	1

- Learn to let the speaker express his or her thoughts without interruption.
- Learn to listen between the lines because what the speaker actually says may not completely represent his or her intended meaning.
- Concentrate on developing retention ability. Do not take too many notes—make your memory work for you.
- Do not "tune out" your speaker if you find the subject or speaker to be boring.
- Do not become hostile or emotional just because the speaker's ideas differ from your own.
- Learn to ignore distractions.

You can identify your listening weaknesses and rate your listening effectiveness by using the quiz in Figure 1. It will help you to pinpoint specific areas that need improvement and evaluate your overall listening competency.

How did you rate as a listener? If you scored 32 or more points, you are an excellent listener—a positive receiver of ideas through listening. A score of 27 to 31 makes you a better-than-average listener. A score of 22 to 26 points suggests that you need to consciously practice listening. It is a signal that there are weaknesses that need to be eliminated. If you scored 21 points or less, many of the messages that you receive are probably garbled and are not likely to be transmitted effectively. By consciously working to eliminate the "never" and "rarely" responses, you should significantly improve day-to-day operations and your relations with subordinates, co-workers, and superiors.

Besides taking the listening quiz yourself, you should encourage your subordinates to take it. Encourage them to rate themselves and to refer to the quiz as they work to change their listening behavior. The listening evaluation quiz can help both you and your employees assess the department's listening competency and identify specific areas that need improvement. Consider how much your business and managerial abilities would improve if everyone in your organization listened effectively each day. When was the last time you really listened to those around you? Why not start listening today?

Inflation Hurts Business Language, Too

MARK S. BACON

Ever read a memo and wonder what the writer really meant?

"Some ballpark parameters have been established for the maximization of relevant input in terms of the present time frame. This should impact our position in the marketplace in a major way."

That sort of language borders on nonsense, but it's characteristic of business writing today. Our language has become clogged with redundancies, clichés, and all manner of unnecessary words. Letters, memos, reports, and policy manuals are being created with puffy and imprecise language. Some people confound readers because they're trying to sound impressive or more businesslike. Others abuse language through an almost studied carelessness.

People have become accustomed to the idea that more words are better and that bigger words and sentences are better still. This notion has created an inflated language. Most forms of business writing are getting almost unbearably long, wasting time, money, and copier machines. Deflating language and putting meaning back in business writing can be done. It requires simple, concise writing; close attention to organization; careful editing; and common sense.

Deflating Language

During a recession, improving writing skills can be an excellent way for organizations to save money, become more efficient, and improve rapport with employees and customers. Concise writing, however, does not appear on many business or marketing plans. It should. For example, it now costs more than $6 to produce and mail a single business letter. If that letter produces misunderstanding, it will require more letters or phone calls, just to explain what should have been clear in the first place.

Deflating language would reduce the time it takes employees to write letters, reports, memos; reduce reading time for internal communications; give customers a good feeling about an organization; cut down the cost of paper, typewriter ribbons, and printing. It would even reduce costs for staples and paperclips. One-page memos don't need them.

"What do you mean you didn't know we wanted you to follow the new personnel policy?" complained the manager on the phone. "We sent you three memos on it."

Three memos that don't communicate are as useless as one, but they cost three times as much. If one of the memos said, "Start the new policy," it probably would have been started. But if the memos said,

Reprinted from *Supervisory Management*, August 1982

"Adjust the internal policies to facilitate the implementation mode," the memos may well have been filed along with the rest of the routine correspondence from the head office.

One summer, a Los Angeles organization distributed a memo to its staff about energy conservation: "In accordance with energy conservation procedures . . . employees will be permitted to dress casually to minimize the discomfort because of higher air conditioning temperatures. Casual dress will consist of properly accepted business attire. . . ."

Results of fuzzy language can be unintentionally funny. The following appeared on Pacific Southwest Airlines (PSA) boarding passes: "If you terminate your flight in midjourney, please contact a PSA passenger service agent."

Puffy language is not limited to business. A recent report from a Southern California school district said that, in addition to swings and slides, a new playground would have "a body awareness structure with a visualization tower." It's not obvious, but the school officials meant a jungle gym.

While this type of poor communication may be common, when used in business, it can be costly. The purpose of writing is to communicate, and communication implies understanding. If your report or memo is not easily understood, it doesn't matter that your word processor and copier made 125 duplicates to be distributed to all departments. Creating understanding must be your first goal in writing.

Phrases With Little Meaning

Simple language usually gets results, but in the business world simple language is rare. The everyday language of business is impersonal, cluttered, and vague. It is clogged with thousands of inviting words and expressions that sound comfortably familiar but add little to understanding. The inflation of language has the same effect that printing money has on the economy. Monetary inflation reduces the value of the dollar, and language inflation reduces the value of individual words. You can put value and meaning back in words by using fewer of them. To do that you have to avoid the trite and the fuzzy. Here are some examples of inflation: *prior to the start of, at this point in time, due to the fact that, and relative to the matter of.* Each of these too-common expressions contains five words and each can be replaced by one word. Try these words instead: *before, now, because,* and *about.*

There are many other examples. Look at any interoffice memo, and you're likely to find some of these unnecessary words rather than the shorter versions: in a timely matter (*on time*), at which time (*when*), subsequent to (*after*), get the feeling of (*find out*), so as to (*to*).

In addition, there are inflationary phrases that mean nothing: *insofar as the subject is concerned, please be advised of the fact that, let us take the opportunity to tell you.*

Each of these phrases can be eliminated without altering the meaning of any sentence. For example, you could say, "Let me take the opportunity to tell you that the shipment will arrive in three days." Or you could cut the sentence in half and get the message across loud and clear.

Redundancies and Clichés

Redundancies are also clogging our language. Some are so common yet so ridiculous when you consider what they imply. You're often given the *true facts* about something. (That's supposed to be helpful in distinguishing them from false facts.) Then you're told something is green in color. (Can something be green in shape?) Some redundancies are easy to use. You'd never say a three-wheeled tricycle, but you'd be quick to laud a product as a *new innovation.* (Are there old innovations?)

Language is so inflated that it has become almost a requirement to use certain redundancies to get your point across. A piece of paper with no marks on it used to be called blank. Now, it's completely blank or totally blank. Advertising has fostered this type of redundancy with phrases such as *totally free, absolutely free* or—and this is a favorite—*free, at no cost to you.* Are such redundancies necessary?

A list of often-used redundancies could fill up several chapters of this book. Here are a few examples: exact opposites, many numerous, currently being, unexpected surprise, advance planning, jointly sharing, successfully passed, I myself personally, cancel out, and distribute around.

Clichés are another part of language inflation. Clichés start out as phrases used to add color. After they are used thousands of times, they become hackneyed. Rather than add color to language, they make it boring. The first time it was used, *reinventing the wheel* was a lively option to *duplicating efforts*. Now the phrase is anything but lively. Clichés have a place in language, but in business writing they're often just *excess baggage*. Here are some more examples: *a whole new ballgame, getting down to brass tacks, through thick and thin, nose to the grindstone,* and *get on the bandwagon.*

Using the Wrong Words

There's another group of unnecessaries that include fad words, jargon, misapplied computer lingo, and just plain wrong words. A few examples:

Hopefully. This word literally means, "with hope." Therefore to say, "Hopefully the regulations will change," implies that the regulations can have hope. It should be, *"I hope the regulations will change."*

Utilization. This word's frequent usage stems from the idea that longer words are inherently better. Shorter words like *use* take up less space, are quicker to read, and don't sound so ponderous.

Planning process. To begin the *planning process* is similar to beginning the eating process. Take away *the* and *process* and you've said the same thing.

Interface. Technically this represents the interconnection or interrelationship between computers. However, it's been used so long to mean everything from a business meeting to a phone conversation that anyone who objects to its many vague meanings is considered a dunderhead or an English teacher.

Thrust. A thrust is a sudden and forceful push, especially with a long, pointed weapon. Used to mean a main point, it's a cliché.

The Advantages of Simplicity

What's the answer to all this inflated mush? Simple, concise writing. Why use a big word when a small one says the same thing? Why use five sentences when one conveys the meaning? If you can say it in a few words, use a few words.

Simple does not mean unsophisticated. It does not mean undramatic. It means direct, concrete, uncomplicated and straightforward. Short sentences can be powerful. They attract attention. They're concise. You write for many purposes: to explain, praise, criticize, inspire, persuade, inform, apologize. You often write about technical subjects. Keep your language simple, and you'll be able to accomplish your purposes and write effectively about complex subjects.

Using simple, concise language has many business advantages. First, it will make you and your organization different from everyone else. Your organization will gain the respect of employees, customers, and stockholders. And you'll be perceived as a dynamic, clear-thinking decision maker.

Simple language can identify you as a clear thinker because you no longer hide decisions or opinions in a mass of words that can be interpreted differently. When you say, "We welcome your ideas," you've committed yourself, made a bold statement. Don't worry that simple language will force you to stick your neck out or make decisions unnecessarily. The statement, "I don't know," or "We haven't heard enough facts," is unique and dynamic itself.

Avoiding confusion among customers while creating a positive, friendly image is another advantage of concise language. For example, financial institutions have an impersonal, unfeeling image that's fre-

Figure 1

Dear_____

We were adjusted by our clearinghouse for a loan payment against your checking account.

The check was written for $____. Please check your records to see if you wrote a check for this amount around _____.

If so please send us a photo of the front and back of the cancelled check. . . .

---

quently reinforced by language. Figure 1 shows an excerpt from one form letter used by the largest bank in California.

What this letter means is that the bank received a check and has no idea to which account it should be posted. Bankers know what a clearinghouse adjustment is; sadly, most people who receive this letter do not.

Or try the example in Figure 2, also from the California bank. Sounds like a bank, doesn't it? You might have a different feeling about the institution if the letter had said, "Congratulations, your auto loan is paid off. The car is all yours! Here's your ownership certificate. . . ."

Removing the Stuffiness

The simple approach makes business writing more friendly and less formal. Depending on your background, making business writing a bit more casual may seem foreign. Authorities used to discourage any hint of informality and direct language. The slight stuffiness of business English was what separated it from ordinary, personal correspondence. If a more relaxed form does not sound businesslike to you, remember what you write is going to be read by people. Do you want those people to get the feeling of a legal document or a personal letter?

One often-suggested way to avoid stuffy language is to write the way you talk. That's fine if you speak in complete sentences. Most people do not. What's helpful about this advice is that it introduces a conversational tone in your writing.

Talking to someone instead of writing is the best way to help yourself when you can't seem to find the right words. Occasionally, in the middle of writing a report or letter, you become stumped. The best thing to do when you're at a loss for words it to tell someone what you're trying to write.

Figure 2

Dear Customer,

We have received the final payment on your loan contract and we thank you for this opportunity to serve you.

With this letter we enclose certain important papers (checked below). If the following are enclosed. . . .

When you write or dictate, you concentrate more on the structure of what you have to say than when you just talk. When you talk, you're less inhibited by grammar. You can usually find a way to explain something. Tell someone what you're trying to write, and 99 percent of the time, the words you need will come right out of your mouth. Listen to what you say and take notes. Then, all you have to do is put your spoken words into complete sentences. This device usually works even if you just talk aloud to yourself. If you normally dictate your letters, and find yourself fumbling for words, stop the formal dictation and just explain conversationally what you're trying to dictate.

A Matter of Form

The form, or the order in which that information is presented, is almost as important as the language. Again, simple form is the easiest to read and understand. An excellent guide or model for business letters and reports already exists. It's the newspaper news story.

The form of a news story is simple and well-suited to business writing. It's called the inverted pyramid, a term that every college journalism student learns. It means that the most important elements of a story are contained in first few paragraphs. Information in the rest of the story is arranged in descending order of importance. News stories are written this way so that you can read the first few paragraphs and have a fairly good idea of what the story is about. You don't have to read through the whole story to get the most important facts. Baseball stories have the score at the beginning. Election stories tell you, in the first sentence, who won. On the other hand, how many reports have you had to read all the way through to get the most important information?

This does not mean that memos and reports should be lists of facts. News stories aren't either. It may be important for a report to contain information in chronological order. A memo might contain information on several subjects. Regardless of the form or order in a memo or report, it still can begin with a summary.

Think how much time you could save if every report you had to read began with a summary of the most important information. Think of the effect it would have on those who read your reports or memos. Again, the simplicity could have startling results.

What are the most important facts? Journalists use the answers to six basic questions to determine the facts of a story. The questions are: Who? What? When? Where? Why? and How? If most of these questions are answered at the beginning of a report, you've probably summarized what your reader needs to know.

Keep your reader in mind when you decide what is important, especially when this journalistic form is applied to letters. If you have good news, use it first. "Congratulations, your loan was approved." "We completed the sale." "You have been promoted." "Acme was awarded the contract." You may feel it necessary to impress a customer with your organization's interest in him before you state your specific business. If you are interested in your customer, you won't burden him with ponderous paragraphs that begin, "Pursuant to our firm's long standing commitment to provide meaningful service. . . ." In routine and form letters, get to the point.

There are exceptions to the "just the facts, ma'am" form. You may want to entice the reader, feeding him or her bits of information along the way. However, if you save the best for last, understand the risks. People don't savor the last few pages of a report the way they do the ending of an Agatha Christie novel.

Writing and Thinking

There's a final and compelling argument for simple writing. Language has an effect on thinking. At least, language is a reflection of one's thinking. Having knowledge is useless if you can't communicate it. If someone's written or spoken language is vague and unclear, isn't it logical to assume that his or her thinking is equally clouded? What other means do we have to judge a person's thinking or intelligence?

The following statements were randomly selected from a recent business meeting. They seem to say something about the thinking of the speakers.

"The results indicate a major validation of the viability of this learning experience."

"We are physically in place as far as the facilities move is concerned."

"We're undertaking the development of some guide-chart profile process methodology parameters."

Making Report Writing Easier

As a supervisor/manager, you are called upon increasingly to write reports, whether their purpose is to discuss the progress of a productivity report, analyze a sales campaign's success, or recommend the purchase of additional PCs.

There are basically three types of reports you're likely to be writing: informational, interpretive, and recommendation reports. The type of report dictates, in part, how you will organize your information and the tone you will use. To help you do the best job you can, here are some model outlines you can follow.

Informational Reports

The first set deals with informational reports. These reports simply describe situations without providing any analysis. Examples include progress and narrative reports.

Progress reports. These document the status of a project or program. The focus is on what has happened to date and what will happen in the future. Your reader wants to know, "How is the work coming along?"

The timing of a progress report is very important. Your objective is to produce the report to meet a predetermined schedule or when the information is most meaningful to your reader. The more current and complete the information, the more it will probably help your reader make a decision.

Included in such a report would be:

1. Executive summary
2. Overview/background
3. Work completed to date
4. Work in progress/actions initiated
5. Work left to do and anticipated completion dates
6. Anticipated problems
7. Forecast for the next stage

Let's look at an example. A medium-sized wholesaler has outgrown the storage space in its warehouse. To increase storage capacity, a decision was made to build additional racks in an unused area of the warehouse. The construction started in January, with a projected completion date in April. The ware-

Reprinted with permission from "How to Write Effective Business Reports," by Quill Corporation
Reprinted from *Management Solutions*, January 1988

house manager has been asked to prepare a progress report on the work completed to date. Using our model, the report would cover the following:

Executive summary: Construction is on schedule and within budget, and completion should occur on the designated date.

Overview background: The reason for the rack construction is the lack of storage space, and the project was initiated by the president on January 1st.

Work completed to date: The plans were submitted to and approved by the fire department and city board, and all necessary materials were ordered and/or subcontractors hired.

Work in progress: The racks are under construction, the sprinkler system is being installed, and the alarm system wires are in place.

Work left to do and anticipated completion dates: The completion of the sprinkler and installation of the alarm by April 5th, the completion of the rack construction by April 12, and the movement of material to the new racks by April 15th.

Anticipated problems: None.

Forecast: The new racks will be completed and ready to stock on schedule by April 15th.

Narrative reports. The sequential format is usually a good choice for organizing narrative reports, such as meeting minutes and sales trip reports. A report on a meeting, for example, would include such information as attendees; date, time, and place of the meeting; the name of the person who called the meeting; purpose of the meeting; summary of what took place; actions to be taken and by whom before the next meeting; and the date, time, and place of the next meeting. Likewise, the sales trip report might cover the date of the trip, who went, the locations and people visited, why the trip was taken (its purpose), and the overall results.

Interpretive Reports

Interpretive reports make up the next category of reports. These not only describe but analyze situations. Sales marketing reports provide information on and analyze the performance, perhaps, of a particular product or service or a group of products and services for a given period of time. Financial analysis reports, also in this category, describe and analyze the financial condition of an organization or an individual. A scientific report, still another report in this category, usually examines and interprets the results of an experiment. A technical report, which is within this category too, might report on why a piece of equipment is malfunctioning.

As you can see, interpretive reports can cover a very broad range of topics.

Here's a possible model for these reports, using a modified form of the logical format:

1. Executive summary
2. Overview/background
3. Present situation
4. What's being done to pursue the opportunity or solve the problem, and the time schedule (optional)
5. Expected results (optional)

Let's assume a computer software manufacturer introduced a new product in the first quarter. It's now the end of the second quarter, and actual sales haven't come close to projected sales. The president of the company wants to know why. He has asked the sales manager to analyze the product's poor performance.

Executive summary: Sales of the new product are 50 percent below the projected level for two reasons—a major competitor introduced a similar product at a lower price shortly after the company's was released, and the salesforce was never adequately trained to sell the product. Given this situation, the sales manager is currently making changes in advertising and sales training, and in the cost and design of the product, to improve sales.

Overview background: The sales projection for the product was $100,000 per quarter. Actual sales were $70,000 for the first quarter and $30,000 for the second quarter. Sales began to decline at the same time the competitor introduced its comparable product.

Present situation: Sales show no sign of picking up, and the competitor continues to expand its market share.

What's being done to solve the problem, and the time schedule: The product is being upgraded with added features and better materials to distinguish it from the competitor's product. Advertising is being changed to reflect the higher quality of the product. A training program is being developed to educate the salesforce on the product's capabilities and benefits. And all of these actions should be completed within two months, by January 30th.

Expected results: Gradual increase in the sales of the product at first (February–March), then picking up as the programs are well under way (by April). Sales should reach the goal of $100,000 per quarter by the first quarter of next year.

Recommendation Reports

Recommendation reports might discuss the feasibility of some action; propose the purchase of some equipment, pursuit of some objective, or implementation of some program; or analyze and identify one of several options that provides the greatest benefits.

Feasibility reports. These usually require considerable research prior to writing them. Charts, tables, and illustrations are often included to explain the more complex data. Contents would include:

1. Executive summary with recommendations
2. Overview/background
3. Review of the problem and the issues involved
4. Criteria for the solution
5. Analysis of the option
6. Risks/solutions
7. Recommendation
8. Recap of the benefits of the recommendation

Comparison reports. These are similar in many respects to feasibility reports. But while feasibility reports look at just one option, comparison reports always look at more than one, measuring the advantages of each alternative. They conclude with a recommendation of the best option, the one with the fewest problems and risks and the greatest opportunity for success and/or payback.

In writing a comparison report, you should include the major points and recommendations in the executive summary. As you analyze each option, show its advantages first, followed by its disadvantages. In the final section, you make your argument for your recommendation. You can do this by clearly stating the benefits to be achieved and following them up with a plan of action. A comparison report contains:

1. Executive summary and recommendation
2. Overview/background
3. Criteria for analyzing the options
4. Options

5. Comparison and analysis of the options
6. Recommendation
7. Recap of the benefits of the recommendation

Proposals. The length and complexity of a proposal varies depending on the purpose. It may be as simple as a two-page proposal from the manufacturing manager to the president for the purchase of a new piece of machinery. Or it may be as involved as a 20-page document requesting senior management to approve funding for a major project.

Regardless of the length or complexity, a proposal is written to persuade the reader to take action. The entire report must focus on convincing the reader of the benefits resulting from a positive decision on his or her part. Therefore, you may not want to include an executive summary, which reveals your conclusions and/or recommendations up front before you've had a chance to present your case.

Here's a likely model to follow:

1. Cover letter (proposals are usually submitted with a cover letter briefly stating the proposal)
2. Problem or situation
3. Solution
4. Benefits of the solution
5. Cost
6. Implementation
   - Steps to be taken
   - People who will take action
   - Timetable
7. Conclusion
   - Restate the recommendation and its benefits

For example, a small medical supply company has a field salesforce of 30 representatives. Currently, there is no formal sales training program. What training does occur usually comes after a sales goal is missed. The sales manager believes that a formal training program is needed. He needs funds to develop and run this program, so he prepares a proposal for the president of the company.

Cover letter
Problem: Sales goals are not being met, and the company is losing sales that it should have because sales reps aren't as familiar as they should be with the product's features.
Solution: Find and hire an outside sales training consultant and design a sales training program.
Benefits of solution: Increase sales and profits, upgrade image, improve morale of the salesforce.
Cost: Outline of the budget, cost/benefit analysis.
Implementation: Outline of tasks and responsibilities.
Conclusion: By developing a training program, the company will increase sales and profits, improve its image, and improve the morale of the salesforce.

Summing Up

To determine which of these models is the best one for that report due next week, ask yourself these questions:

1. Why am I writing this report, and how will it be used?
2. Am I trying to persuade, inform, report, request, or analyze?
3. Do I want the reader to take action or simply to review my report?

Giving Feedback to Foreign-Born Employees

JAMES B. STULL

Tsu Pang Chiang works as an accountant for a large bank in San Francisco. He has been in the United States for two years. He was born in Hong Kong. One afternoon at a department meeting, Chiang's boss tells Chiang that he likes the way Chiang works and that he is doing "all right." Chiang doesn't respond outwardly to the comment and, in fact, remains aloof for a few weeks. His boss cannot understand Chiang's behavior.

Bernardo Chavez is a human resource administration trainee in a manufacturing plant in Texas. Bernardo was born in Mexico and has worked in the United States for only six months. At Bernardo's first performance review, his manager asks him to sit down and immediately begins to discuss Bernardo's past performance and future expectations. Bernardo becomes defensive and, from that day forward, responds to his boss's comments with an insincere smile.

Masoud Shahidi is a customer services representative for a high technology firm near Boston. Originally from Tehran, Masoud has worked in the United States for two years. At his first performance review, Masoud is told clearly by his supervisor how he can improve during the next quarter, and Masoud agrees to work on these areas. Two weeks later, Masoud is asked to sign his written performance review. Masoud becomes irritated, complaining that he does not understand why this written document has to go into his personal file.

Giving feedback to foreign-born employees often is a greater challenge to managers than the already difficult responsibility of giving feedback to employees in general. People from different cultures give and receive feedback in ways often very different from the ways most U.S.-born employees give and receive feedback.

For example, Chiang comes from Hong Kong where people show little or no emotion when paid a compliment. Indeed, it is commonplace to deny that one has done anything worthy of praise or not to respond at all. In many Asian cultures, employees do not wish to be singled out, as it may decrease group harmony. Some Asians, it has been found, may even regard compliments as a signal that something is actually wrong and that the feedback is a way of telling them that they are *not* doing a good job. After all, if they *were* doing a good job, they reason, they would be rewarded with something tangible. Of course, another explanation for Chiang's behavior could be that he misinterpreted the phrase "doing all right" as "doing mediocre work."

Reprinted from *Management Solutions,* July 1988

Chavez comes from a culture where it is appropriate to engage in "small talk" before discussing job-related matters. In terms of interpersonal skills, U.S. managers, compared to managers worldwide, tend to rank on the low side, while Mexican managers on the high side. U.S. managers tend to be more direct, getting down to business right away; after all, to them "time is money." In Mexico, one takes time to get to know another person and asks about the person's family; business will get done when the time is right.

Masoud is used to dealing more through the spoken word. In the Middle East, one's word is one's honor. Putting things in writing is not as important as it is in the United States. In fact, if one *did* write up a performance review after an appraisal interview, chances are that the written review would "glow," giving a more favorable report than actually occurred during the interview.

What are you, a U.S.-born and trained manager, to do? "Praise in public, scold in private" is often-heard advice in the United States. However, in cross-cultural situations, generalities notwithstanding, the following techniques may be more appropriate:

Tell a third party. Interpersonal networks are a main source of information for immigrant groups. So you should use existing informal networks, particularly when giving feedback to someone from a culture where singling out the individual might cause discomfort. Identify a leader from that culture—someone who is respected—and give the feedback to that person who, in turn, will relay it to the appropriate person. Another technique might be to give the feedback to a third person within earshot of the person for whom it is intended.

Tell the entire group. By directing feedback to the entire work group, managers will foster group harmony. The group will be reminded that their success was based on a group effort and further improvements will require a group effort. And for those from cultures emphasizing group harmony, the response will be more positive.

Ask for feedback. It is important for you to know that your employees understand your feedback. Toward that, ask your employees to explain to you what you have just asked them to do. You should get your employees to respond to you in ways that allow them to give open-ended feedback. If you ask questions that only require a "yes" or a "no," you run the risk of being misinformed about an employee's understanding of a situation. In many Asian cultures, too, the word "no" is avoided and questions are typically asked so that "yes" can be given. In Japan, one might ask (loosely translated), "Don't you understand?" This negative question allows the employee to answer "Yes," meaning "Yes, I don't understand." In the United States, if a Japanese employee were asked, "Do you understand?" and responded, "Yes," meaning "Yes, I don't understand," the U.S. manager would interpret the answer as "Yes, I understand." Allowing employees to explain your requests will clarify matters as well as increase their opportunities to speak English, thus improving their communication skills.

Modify your language. Your ability to communicate in any cross-cultural situation will require a certain amount of language modification. You should simplify, clarify, and specify. For example, choose a simple word or phrase whenever possible, and the more concrete, the better. Say "memos" rather than "internal communications," "pay" rather than "remuneration," and "at the same time" rather than "simultaneously." Use short sentences, and limit the ideas expressed in each sentence. By doing this, you won't overwhelm your employee with information, particularly if the employee is momentarily at a loss for the meaning.

Also, avoid long discourses; allow a conversation to go back and forth. Two-way communication increases understanding.

Needless to say, use standard English: Avoid slang and figures of speech. Expressions like "that rings a bell," "proof of the pudding," and "they'll eat that up" are difficult to grasp. Avoid jokes and sarcasm, too.

Speak slowly, making sure you separate your words. Do not drop word endings. Avoid compressed speech like "Whaddya' doin?" or "Whatcha' been up to?"

At the end of each phase of a discussion, recap the essential items with an interjection such as, "Let me review the points we've just discussed. . . ."

When your employee seems to pause momentarily or to grope for a way to express a thought, be patient. Do not let the conversation drift away from that person.

Finally, be specific and illustrate your points whenever you are able. Recall a previous incident; specify the behavior that you want from your employee; show the results you want; give examples. Use several media, including pictures. Use the correct names for things.

Put it in writing. If possible, provide in advance of a conversation or meeting a summary of ideas, proposals, or vocabulary the other party might find difficult to understand or discuss. People appreciate the chance for preparation.

Take notes on or record your meetings, too, and provide your foreign-born employees with a detailed report. This will assure them that they heard you correctly, and it will minimize misunderstandings about what transpired.

These suggestions on giving feedback to foreign-born employees can also be applied to those employees born in the United States. The sensitive manager applies those techniques that work best. Try different ones; see how they work. You'll be pleased with the results.

Part IV

CONFLICT RESOLUTION

Keeping Your Cool

JOHN M. STORMES

Keeping your temper under control, important as it is to a productive work environment, isn't a simple matter. The problem is that the urge to blow up often occurs when you are least prepared for it.

Put yourself in Joe Barnes' position, for instance. He came to work one morning feeling pretty good. He had completed an important report for his boss only the night before. He was eager to get back into the old routine, where things had gotten a little behind schedule.

Then, that morning, his boss found a glaring error in the report. At the same time, in another part of the plant, another executive was making an important presentation based on the same erroneous information! For a moment, Joe saw his career and his reputation for dependability in serious danger, all because of a little carelessness, a brief lapse of attention.

His anger rose quickly but subsided when his boss gave him more time to fix the report. Joe could do nothing about his embarrassment, of course, but he could easily reassemble his project staff and, with extra effort, make up for the lost time. It was frustrating and embarrassing, but not hopeless.

Then came more disappointments. The latest computer analysis of the project was misfiled, and Joe needed to catch up on his regular responsibilities. One member of his project team was absent for the morning, another was away from the office. Finally, he reached the remaining member of the team, Jane Wells, but she had already started on another assignment.

Reprinted from *Supervisory Management,* December 1980

Anger—The First Step to a Blowup

Joe Barnes is a character in National Educational Media's motion picture *The Fine Art of Keeping Your Cool.* In the film, he is seen facing a morning in which nothing goes right. He is, of course, upset when he learns of the errors in his report. He feels he has let himself down. He is disappointed that his plans for the day are interrupted. These feelings are symptoms of several anger-producing elements of the situation, elements you are probably familiar with from your own work experience:

- *Criticism.* His boss blames him for not producing up to expectations.
- *Threat to status.* Joe is the lead member of the report team, a responsibility he may not get again.
- *Another person's anger.* His boss is upset.
- *Pressure.* He has to fix the error within a short time.

Joe resolves to save face and meet the new deadline. This resolve is good; it provides an outlet for the energy buildup from anger, allowing the anger to subside.

Anger is emotional energy generated automatically in response to danger. Feelings of fear and anger are associated with a buildup of energy. When life was simpler than it is today, the energy meant physical survival, providing the strength either to run away from a hopeless situation (fear) or to fight (anger). Anger is neither good nor bad in itself. What we do with the emotional energy that it creates is the problem.

In today's industrial society, our lives are rarely threatened directly. We do, however, perceive threats to our livelihoods, our status, or our careers, as did Joe. They trigger the same emotional energies for self-defense as a physical attack would. In its initial stages, this energy may increase our alertness. If it rises too high, though, mental effectiveness is reduced. Attention seems to shift to "fight or flight" and away from problem solving.

Most of us have learned to control our expressions of fear or anger when we are at work. We know that an emotional display will only get us into more trouble. Many of us, however, have never learned what to do with that emotional energy. Often, we try to stuff it down inside, ignore it, and hope it will go away.

If we jam our anger down inside, it does not go away, however. Ignored, it affects some people physiologically. Others project their feelings of anger onto someone else, blaming the person for their troubles.

At first, Joe handled his anger pretty well, but then he encountered another common source of anger, a series of disappointments producing feelings of frustration. Because of the pressure to do something, he could not take time to deal with each irritating disappointment when it occurred. The feelings of frustration generated in this way are insidious. No single incident seems important enough to deal with immediately. Instead, we go on until the buildup reaches a point where one small irritant, irrelevant though it may be, can make us explode.

If we can sense the growing frustration and take positive steps to deal with them, we can avoid some possibly damaging consequences. In Joe's case, his resolve to overcome the basic problem was good, but he had to reach a point where he could see positive results. Sensing his increasing irritation, he needed to look for other ways to view his situation. Here are several things Joe might have done. How many of these four temporary solutions do you use to keep your cool?

1. Recognize that the irritations are upsetting but nothing can be done about them at the moment. Try to view them with a sense of humor.
2. Ignore the pressure and get away from the problem for awhile; some physical exercise is helpful.
3. Attack some part of the problem where less interpersonal involvement is required.
4. Sometimes just patience is all that is needed. Remembering that 90 percent of what might go wrong never does go wrong is all that is needed.

Joe did not sense what was going on inside him. He was too busy trying to get his job going. While anger under control is not bad, encountering a series of frustrations, as Joe Barnes did, and not dealing with the anger as it is created, can have serious consequences. It is as though one is being drawn into a trap unknowingly. The more difficult the situation becomes, the more emotions work against one. Let's see what happened to Joe.

The Blowup

Jane Wells criticized Joe for not checking the figures in the report more carefully. At this point, Joe blew up. He was responsible for the report, but he blamed Jane, standing now in front of him, because she had had something to do with gathering the erroneous information. There was no shred of proof that she had made an error; no pause to reflect that accusations, false or true, would only hinder reaching Joe's main objective of getting the job done right; no consideration for the future when he might need Jane Wells's assistance again. He just dumped all of his pent-up anger on her. Her anger rose, too. While she recognized that there was a problem, she thought he was overreacting. She tried to take the problem away from him to handle in her own way. This infuriated Joe further. He yelled at her, "If necessary, I'll do it alone. You've messed things up enough already. Just keep out of it!" As a result of the fight, things can never be the same between the two again.

The Damage

Such explosions of temper are not unusual. They happen at all levels of organizations. They are the ultimate response to the pressures and frustrations of modern-day business.

Psychologists say that anger is a response to the fear that one is not in control. Energy is built up to exert control, but at each new frustration, it is prevented from being released in a productive way. The realities of working with others in a disciplined environment tend to keep people from expressing their feelings. When their guard is down, or they have someone cornered and unable to fight back, they are strongly tempted to strike out and release that energy. And why not? The only alternative seems to be defeat, slinking away from the situation, and admitting failure.

Before looking at what can be done to prevent this primitive reaction to frustration and loss of control, let's go over some of the effects of expressing open hostility to subordinates, co-workers, or others.

1. Losing your temper shows a side of you people do not expect. Regardless of the image you have created—whether as an outgoing, affable person who wins cooperation from others or a firm-handed disciplinarian whom people may not love but will respect—a violent display of temper will tear away at that image. A note of uncertainty is injected into your relations with others, and they are a little less comfortable with you around. Once you have caused this shift in perception about yourself, you may have to work a long time to regain their confidence.
2. The frustration and fear thus created in others place them in the same emotional dilemma that caused your blowup: to either accept defeat or be hostile. In either case, what will that do to their productivity, their cooperation, or their sense of teamwork? To make matters worse, temper blow-ups are sometimes directed at people whose only mistake is to be an available target at the moment. The energy released is totally wasted.
3. Losing your temper can limit your ability to contribute. You are less likely to see other alternatives. You will not hear the concessions others are willing to make to solve the problem. Important issues lie buried under inconsequential ones in the heat of battle. And how can you regain control when you are not thinking clearly, anyway? Losing your temper shows the world what you really

do not want anybody to know—you are not in control of the situation; you are not even in control of yourself!

4. Losing your temper is not necessarily good for your health. It increases your physical and emotional stress. You lose your normal spontaneity and initiative. Lost tempers rarely help solve the problem, and they can become a subtle form of self-destruction.

Suppose you get your way by losing your temper. There is a danger of its becoming habit-forming. Take the case of an engineer who had a legitimate complaint that his boss was not adequately supervising others in the department. He blew up at the boss, and his boss took action to correct the situation. Personal frustrations in the engineer's life and other annoyances when his own plans did not work out engendered more anger. He would lose his temper for minor reasons. The quality of his own work was adversely affected, and his hopes for promotion and career advancement vanished, heaping more coals on the fires of anger. Ultimately he lost his job.

Controlling Temper

Controlling your temper involves four steps:

1. Recognize that you are angry.
2. Identify the cause of your anger.
3. Understand why the situation produced anger.
4. Deal with the anger realistically.

Let's look at each step in turn. The first one begins long before you are in danger of losing your temper. You must identify feelings that tell you something is upsetting you, and try to deal with them as we discussed earlier. By being in touch with your feelings, you will know you are about to lose your temper and can stop it. Do not do or say anything. Conventional wisdom—counting to ten—applies here.

The second step is to figure out what is causing your anger—the real cause. In Joe's case, it was not that Jane had made a mistake; it was the accumulation of incidental frustrations on top of his initial encounter with his boss.

The third step, determining why these things produce anger, means looking at the threats you may be feeling. Are they based on solid information or are they imagined? Are they threats to your personal feelings or to achieving your goals? Interestingly, threats that generate the most anger are those against self-esteem, status, and autonomy, not those that interfere with reaching a goal.

Fourth, after you have identified the emotional cause of your anger, you must try to deal with it realistically. If it is imagined, try to ignore it and focus on your main goal. If it is real, try to come to terms with the person threatening you. One way to help get your feelings in perspective is to share your feelings with someone you can trust. Joe, for example, could have taken Jane into his confidence and explained to her how he felt. By communicating his feelings, he might have gotten cooperation rather than hostility.

Sharing feelings is very difficult for many people, however. It can be more threatening than the original cause of the emotion. To open up to each other is particularly difficult for people at different levels in an organization.

So, what are your alternatives if you are not comfortable talking problems out with others, or you work in an organization with a high level of mistrust? One is to talk to yourself. Get away for a while. Take a walk or meditate. The idea is to give yourself time to examine the situation and your feelings more coolly.

Another option is to put the present situation aside temporarily and apply built-up energy to other tasks that need to be done. Not only will your emotional energy be consumed, but you should come back to the problem situation with a better frame of mind to deal with it. You may even have some new ideas and the resolve to overcome the problem without losing your temper.

What it all amounts to is focusing your energies on the central problem of regaining control over your own life. When things start to go out of control, start planning. Decide what *you* are going to do about it. Avoid the temptation of thinking such thoughts as, "It's got to get better; it can't get any worse," looking for someone else to take charge; or taking the blame. Those lead only to worse problems later.

Reacting to Loss of Temper

The effects of Joe's flareup did not end with Jane getting upset. She told Harry Charles, another member of Joe's team, about it. Harry became extremely upset and stormed into Joe's office. But Joe had learned a few things from his own blowup, and he just sat there listening to Harry's accusations. When Harry challenged him by saying, "What have you got to say for yourself?" Joe answered, "You're saying it pretty well, Harry. Go ahead." He was applying the first of five principles in dealing with another person's anger:

1. *Listen.* Try to discover why the person is angry, and what the nature of his or her anger is. Maybe the individual has a right to be upset.
2. *Don't argue.* Right or wrong, let the other person have his or her say. And, right or wrong, assure the individual that there is nothing wrong with feeling angry about the situation. Such an attitude breaks the anger cycle in which hostility breeds hostility. When no one is willing to take this step, the results can be unfortunate as was the case with Joe Barnes and Jane Wells.
3. *Explore what is upsetting the other person.* Ask open-ended questions, questions that cannot be answered with a simple "yes" or "no." Find out details. This process helps shift attention from the anger itself to underlying problems. It helps the person analyze his or her own position and limit future actions to more rational behavior.
4. *Empathize.* Show the other person that you really understand how he or she feels. Empathizing is putting yourself in the individual's place.
5. *Admit a mistake.* If you had something to do with causing the person's anger and were wrong, own up to it. Apologize. That may be hard to do, but it is important in establishing a better relationship. If you are the boss, admitting an error that you made lets the other person know you are only human, too.

Preventing Lost Tempers

The final question is, if we can prevent ourselves from losing our tempers and help others control theirs, is there any reason why members of an organization should ever lose their tempers? Probably not. There is the occasional employee who is emotionally unstable. He or she should be encouraged to seek professional advice. Otherwise, a temper flareup should occur rarely.

Members of management can play an important role in preventing the occurrence of blowups. You, as a manager, can set an example and influence many more people than can the example of the individual employee.

Controlling tempers in an organization depends on honest but tactful communications and awareness of people's emotions. Toward those ends:

- When you correct an employee, be sure you criticize performance, not the person.
- Whenever you must change an employee's status, prerogatives, or authority, avoid the appearance of reducing them unless you have had a frank discussion of the reasons with the individual in-

volved. Employees expect that as they gain experience with the organization, their status, prerogatives, and authority will naturally increase. If these things shrink without valid explanations, employees feel threatened.

- Don't blame anyone for making a mistake unless you have to do so. Then be 100 percent sure that you are blaming the right person.
- Encourage cheerful attitudes and light humor. People can harmlessly vent their feelings in such an environment. Channels for releasing emotional energy are needed, and humor is useful here.

Building a Professional Image: Handling Conflict

H. KENT BAKER and PHILIP I. MORGAN

When you think of the word "conflict," what comes to mind? Is it likely to be disagreement and fighting? Conflict is often viewed negatively, although it is neither good nor bad in itself. If properly handled, conflict can become a positive source of energy and creativity; if mishandled, it can become dysfunctional, draining energy and reducing both personal and organizational effectiveness.

Because conflict is unavoidable in life, the ability to successfully cope with it is one of the most important skills you can acquire. If you are like most supervisors, you will have acquired your conflict management skills without formal training or guidance, modeling them on a former supervisor's skills in this area. If your role model was good, you may have no problem with conflict. But role modeling is a hit-or-miss affair.

Fortunately, managing conflict successfully is a skill that can be learned. It requires understanding not only the nature of conflict but also gaining awareness of the various strategies available for managing it effectively. Recognizing alternative conflict management modes provides a wider choice of actions to use in a given situation.

Nature of Conflict

Conflict exists whenever incompatible activities or perceptions occur. For example, a supervisor has one idea about how to perform a job and an employee another. In this instance, the source of the conflict concerns the method of doing the job. Other potential sources of conflict include different beliefs, goals, and values.

Conflicts may be destructive or constructive depending on how one handles them.

The negative or dysfunctional conflict is all too familiar. For example, a supervisor's refusal to listen to differing views from employees may destroy initiative or creativity and even lead to hostile and disruptive behavior.

Another negative consequence of conflict is the development of a "me" or "us" versus "them" attitude. This divisiveness can destroy team spirit and the desire to work toward common goals. Each side becomes concerned with getting the most it can and ignores or discounts the ideas of the other. Deadlocks

Reprinted from *Supervisory Management*, September 1980

and stalemates result as members refuse to adjust their positions. Resolution of the conflict becomes almost impossible.

Even worse, destructive conflicts can escalate. The initial cause may be forgotten or become irrelevant as the conflict takes on a life of its own. Each party attempts to meet his or her own needs and concerns at the others' expense. A win-lose attitude develops that fosters distorted communication, suspicion, and hostility.

When handled properly, however, conflict can be healthy. It can be productive if participants are satisfied with the outcome and feel that they have gained as a result of the experience. These gains include a broadening of understanding about the problem, an increase in the number of possible alternatives, and stimulating interaction and involvement. For example, by exploring different viewpoints and combining ideas, both supervisor and employees may jointly develop more effective ways to perform a task. The conflict resolution process results not only in a better decision being made but also commitment to the decision by the employees.

Strategies for Management Conflict

There are five major conflict management strategies: avoidance, accommodation, competition, compromise, and collaboration. As managers deal with conflicts, they tend to become more comfortable with some strategies than with others and to develop certain preferred styles. This may be unwise, for no single strategy is best for all situations.

Let's examine each of the five conflict management strategies and how they could be applied. The example used is a conflict between a supervisor and an employee over the best method to be used in performing a particular job.

The first of these strategies is *avoidance*. It occurs when the parties choose not to address the conflict, diplomatically sidestepping the issue or postponing it to a better time. There is nothing wrong with this strategy if neither the issue nor its timing is critical or the damage of confronting the conflict outweighs the potential benefits. An avoidance strategy may also be appropriate if time is needed to cool down or gather more information. For example, if emotions are running high about the best method of performing a particular job, a supervisor might be wise to avoid confronting the issue until emotions have subsided.

Accommodation is another approach to conflict management and involves placing another's needs and concerns above one's own. Accommodation might take the form of yielding to another's point of view or obeying someone's instructions. This strategy might be used by you when the issue is much more important to the other person. Accommodation can also be used to help maintain a cooperative relationship and preserve harmony. In a way, an accommodating strategy can even help in the development of subordinates. By allowing them to make decisions, you can let them learn from their mistakes.

When a *competitive* conflict strategy is used, one person's needs and desires are achieved at the expense of another. This strategy is frequently based on position power. In many situations, a supervisor's position permits exerting power to resolve a conflict. The purpose may be to enforce a rule or to take disciplinary action. Supervisors may also adopt an assertive posture when they feel strongly about the issue or the issue is important to the company's welfare.

Although a competitive approach may result in compliance, it may do little to foster commitment to the decision. To illustrate, a supervisor could insist that an employee follow a prescribed method of doing a job because the employee's recommended method violates safety regulations. The employee may follow these orders and not be happy about doing so.

Compromise is a middle-ground position in which both parties give a little. Although compromise rarely results in full commitment by either party, it does have merit. Compromise may be justified when prolonging the conflict would be harmful. It may also be used to gain a temporary settlement when sufficient time is not available to work out a totally satisfactory solution. For example, a supervisor and an employee could compromise by agreeing to use a certain method until they have time to explore other options.

Finally, *collaboration* involves working with another to find some solution that fully satisfies the concerns of both parties. This strategy is appropriate when the issue is too important to be compromised. But this approach requires the integration of the insights from people with different perspectives in order to achieve the best solution. Considerable time and energy may be required, but collaboration often results in a consensual decision in which full commitment exists for the resolution of the conflict.

Guidelines for Constructive Conflict

Establish the "rules of the game." Just as a fair fight requires adherence to certain rules, so does constructive conflict. The primary purpose of having guidelines is not to eliminate conflicts but to help manage them when they develop. This is possible if guidelines set are clear and known to all.

Create a supportive environment. Constructive conflict requires that a variety of options be generated before choices are made. This means that people must feel comfortable about making suggestions that may be unpopular. For this to be the case, people must be cooperative toward one another and open to ideas other than their own.

Creating such a supportive environment for conflict has several positive aspects. It tends to energize people, foster creative thinking, and lead to better solutions. People also feel safer knowing that they can express their opinions openly. This tends to strengthen, rather than weaken relationships.

Stress noncombative conflict. Conflicts conducted as open warfare are generally unproductive in a work setting. When fighting erupts, people tend to blame others, engage in name-calling, become hostile, and withdraw from the conflict. Combatants often try to corner an opponent and strike a winning blow that results in further hostility and retaliation.

Noncombative conflict is intended to provide better understanding of and solutions to the problem at hand. It does not produce winners and losers.

Choose an appropriate time. Sometimes one person is angry and wants to confront another immediately. This does not mean that the other party is obliged to enter the conflict at that time. Engaging in a conflict when unprepared or uninterested usually leads to unnecessary defensiveness and resentment. However, postponing confrontation too long may cause the conflict to fester and worsen.

Focus on issues, not personalities. Some people have difficulty in separating the issue from the person making the comment about the issue, and consequently, the person making the comment becomes the object of attack. But personalities should be left out of a conflict and attention focused on the issues. Just because a person's views differ from one's own doesn't mean that the person is necessarily bad.

Foster communication. Conflict often causes people to stop listening and to begin preparing a defense. When this happens, communication stops. The communication channels should be kept open and that means communicating one's own interests *and* actively listening to understand another's perspective. Each person has a right to be heard and an obligation to understand what the other is saying.

Get perceptions up front. A common cause of conflict is differing perceptions. People see what they want to see, and their perceptions cloud their objectivity.

Each party in a conflict needs to clarify his or her own perceptions and to understand the perceptions of the other. This involves putting oneself in the other person's shoes. Understanding his or her perception of the conflict does not necessarily mean agreeing with it but it does open the way to further communication and eventually to a solution.

Emphasize mutual interests. Taking positions is not uncommon in conflicts. But people get entrenched in their position and don't want to budge, and stalemate then results.

Instead of defining a problem in terms of positions, a wise manager emphasizes each person's interests. Reconciling interests rather than positions works because there are often several possible positions that could satisfy every interest. Frequently, more interests are shared or compatible than opposed. For example, both a supervisor and a subordinate share a mutual interest in getting a job done but have different positions on how to perform the job. Identifying these mutual interests will serve as a building block for resolving their conflict.

Separate issues. Conflicts frequently involve multiple issues, and trying to resolve all of them at the same time can complicate the process. Separating issues into components also reduces the chances of having a single winner and loser. The issues that make up the conflict may vary in importance. If an issue is important to one party but unimportant to another, the disinterested party may be willing to accommodate the other on this point. Those issues which are important to both parties can then be confronted.

Avoid premature resolution. The desire to settle a conflict may lead to selecting a solution before all options have been examined. The danger in doing this is that the solution adopted may not be the best one for the long term. One party may still feel dissatisfied so the conflict is likely to surface again. If time is an important consideration, a better solution is for both parties to agree to a temporary solution that will be examined after an agreed upon time period.

Conclusion

Conflict is often misunderstood and unjustly maligned. It is frequently viewed negatively when in reality it can be a positive force if handled effectively. The guidelines presented can be used to convert potentially destructive conflicts into constructive ones. Being a skilled conflict manager requires effort but has the payoff of letting you control the conflict rather than letting it control you.

A Complaint Processing System That Will Work for Your Business

BARRY J. BARONI

Managers at both large and small firms are becoming increasingly aware of the need for efficient employee complaint processing procedures. While the more loose organization of smaller firms permits a less formal complaint processing system than that for larger firms, the grievance machinery for both kinds of firms has much in common. Part of the solution rests in training and part of it lies in the adoption of a workable complaint processing system that ensures employees are given fair treatment and the fullest opportunity to express themselves. This goal can usually be accomplished through the establishment of a series of appeal steps within the organization. The number of steps will vary among types and kinds of organizations, with smaller firms usually requiring no more than two or three levels of appeal.

Appeal Process

First step—the immediate supervisor. The supervisor should try to put the grievant at ease and encourage him or her to feel free to discuss anything openly and frankly. To accomplish this, a proper setting is required. The meeting should be kept on an informal basis and can be conducted either in the supervisor's office or in the grievant's office or work space, provided confidentiality is not jeopardized. The familiar surroundings of the employee's work area are especially conducive to creating an overall relaxed environment.

Informality at this stage is a good policy. If a grievant is made to feel that there is no need to file a formal grievance, the complaint may be settled while it is still fresh. The grievance should be investigated and the facts, as related by the grievant, should be documented as soon as possible after the initial meeting. Even if the grievance is settled, the facts of the complaint and its disposition should be put into writing at this stage. This documentation early in the game firmly protects against later changes or embellishments of the facts in the event that the grievant raises the issue again.

Second step—next management level or proprietor. In small business firms this appeal level usually suffices as the final one. In larger organizations the grievance can also be settled at this level if it has been properly processed. The presumption is that through additional review, sufficient light can be shed on the problem. An attempt should be made to emphasize management's fairness, while preserving the dignity

Reprinted from *Management Solutions*, July 1986

and authority of the immediate supervisor. The higher-level official reviews the case facts with the immediate supervisor and permits him or her to make the reversal and personally notify the grievant of the case's disposition.

Third step—additional appeal. The need for a third level depends on the complexity of the complaint and the size of the organization. Extended appeal can provide the grievant with additional access to higher authority and can, perhaps, also increase understanding and knowledge. Many smaller firms are sole proprietorships or closely held organizations and the second-line management level is also an ownership level. Consequently, they do not enjoy the luxury of this higher appeal level.

Processing Grievances

From a manager's viewpoint, employee grievances can best be processed through the use of the following four-step procedure:

Step 1. Get the facts.
Step 2. Weigh and decide.
Step 3. Take action.
Step 4. Monitor results.

Step 1. Get the Facts.

Perhaps the most important step is this first one. The manner in which the grievance is received may make the difference between whether the grievant accepts or rejects a supervisor's final decision. A good first impression will certainly ease the tension and perhaps even improve the grievant's own receptiveness. Toward this, a supervisor should:

Listen. The manager needs to give the grievant his or her full attention and listen to the grievant's entire story without interruption. Notes should be taken to see that the entire story as presented by the grievant is understood. If the employee displays anger, the manager shouldn't lose his or her temper.

Rephrase. The manager should review the story in his or her own words, picking out and highlighting important parts of the story, then ask the grievant if the facts as stated are correct.

Step 2. Weigh and Decide.

Once all of the facts have been related by the grievant, they need to be carefully reviewed before a decision is made. The facts need to be fitted together and the effect of each fact on the entire case and the effect of each individual fact on all of the other facts need to be considered. Should the manager detect discrepancies, he or she should attempt to determine which facts are valid. During this process, the manager has to keep in mind both the objective of the grievance and the effect that the decision will have upon others. Objectivity should be maintained and adherence to company policy should be strived for. If policy interpretations arise, the manager should seek advice from other supervisory personnel. This advice should be solicited from supervisors at the manager's own level or at a higher management level. The personnel department is also available for consultation. This type of request should not be considered buck-passing.

Step 3. Take Action.

The manager's answer or response should be in writing, be direct, and be to the point. If the grievant has been wronged, corrective steps that will be taken should be indicated.

If the manager decides that the grievance is without merit, he or she should announce the decision and pass the facts of the case on to his or her supervisor with emphasis on the part that was critical to the decision. Should he or she inquire, the grievant should be informed of the next step in the grievance procedure.

As part of this process, the decision should be documented, together with the entire facts of the case. Documentation serves to protect a manager's position and facilitate future processing of the grievance.

Step 4. Monitor Results.

Finally steps need to be taken to ensure that the decision is carried out.

Notice must be given to both the personnel department and the employee's first-line supervisor of the exact details of the decision. The notice should be in writing and delivered to the first-line supervisor in a personal conference arranged for that purpose. This type of deliberate and special treatment in the rendition of the decision will greatly enhance its enforceability. Subordinate supervisors tend to place more emphasis on clearly issued personal statements than they do on memoranda decisions. Followup, through interviews with the implementing supervisor, is also advisable.

After the decision is announced, employees should be observed to detect changes in attitudes. By doing so, a manager may be able to determine whether he or she has remedied the problem and prevented other grievances from occurring out of the same source of discontentment.

Case in Point

Let's look at a hypothetical grievance to see how the suggested practices and procedures found in this article should be implemented. In this case, company policy clearly stated that overtime would be assigned on the basis of seniority and ability to perform the job. Overtime was usually allotted on a voluntary basis. In assigning 15 hours of overtime needed one day, the two most senior employees who were working that day were consulted. The more senior of the two consulted, employee X, refused the hours, and employee Y accepted the overtime. The following morning, employee Z, who was off the previous day, inquired why he had not been offered the overtime. After all, he said, he was more senior than employee Y who performed the work. Z's immediate supervisor, who assigned the work to Y, replied that he was not at work the previous day and consequently was not considered for overtime. This explanation was not accepted by employee Z, and he filed a written grievance contending that he should have been called at home and offered the overtime.

Under the circumstances, the immediate supervisor should first attempt to settle the grievance at his level. The company policy must be reviewed to determine if presence at work on the day of the assignment is a condition for overtime eligibility. The personnel department and higher-level management should be given an opportunity to fully air the complaint, and the first-line supervisor should be patient and open-minded at the meeting with the employee. The manager should avoid argumentation, emotionalism, personality clashes, and temperament at the meeting. He should be prepared to freely and openly admit his mistake in the event that he misinterpreted company policy on the overtime eligibility question. If that is the case, the wronged employee should be offered the opportunity to perform the next available overtime assignment. The supervisor should provide the employee with a written response to his grievance, thus documenting his oral decision.

Employees must be made to feel that management is aware and concerned with their problems and that every effort will be made to deal with them. Only in a favorable human relations climate such as this can a firm survive and grow.

Resolving Conflict Through "Win-Win" Negotiating

PHILIP I. MORGAN

Recently, during a short stay in a hotel, a leak developed in the shower stall above my room causing water to drip from a hole in the ceiling. I immediately called the manager, and he quickly agreed to provide me with another room that same day when one became available. Afterwards, however, I reflected that it would be inconvenient for me to move since I was comfortably settled. Besides, the leak was more of an inconvenience than a real nuisance. The real source of my discomfort was the *price* I was being charged for the room! I then looked at the situation from the hotel manager's viewpoint and reflected that since the hotel was full, it would mean a loss of revenue to him since the room couldn't be rented while the ceiling was being repaired. Wasn't there a better solution, one that would meet both our needs? I called the manager back, explained my real problem with the room, and he quickly offered to substantially reduce the rental price for the room. Both of us were happy with this outcome.

Since people generally want different things and must compete for scarce resources, conflict is inevitable. Whether the conflict is over hotel room prices, wages, working conditions, layoffs, grievances, procedures, or budgets, it's important to learn to deal with it constructively. This usually means learning how to develop effective negotiating skills.

All managers negotiate; some are better at it than others. What determines whether an outcome is successful or not is the degree of skill of the negotiator.

Hard vs. Soft Negotiators

Not all negotiated agreements end so amicably as the one above. What typically happens is that the parties become locked into ways of thinking and operating predicated on a set of faulty value assumptions. These positions can be characterized on a continuum of "Hard" versus "Soft" negotiating styles (see Figure 1).

Being a hard negotiator is generally more certain to get someone what he or she wants, provided that person "hangs tough" and provided he or she is dealing with a soft negotiator. However, if the person meets with an equally hard adversary, the result is usually a refusal to negotiate and deadlock. Even if both sides get *some* of what they want, the relationship invariably deteriorates.

Reprinted from *Management Solutions,* August 1987

Figure 1

Hard vs. Soft Negotiators

Hard Negotiators	Soft Negotiators
Open with high demands.	Open with modest proposals.
Stick to their guns.	Are flexible, make many concessions.
Make a few trivial concessions and reduce even these as negotiations proceed.	Make large concessions.
Appear unconcerned about the threat of deadlock.	Are terrified of deadlock (and show it).
Emphasize winning.	Emphasize the relationship (that is, say "Let's be friends").
Make threats.	Make more concessions.

Hard negotiators will always win over soft negotiators where one emphasizes "winning" and the other the "relationship." What typically happens is "Soft" will make a concession to "Hard" to set an example, but the only response from "Hard" is to increase his or her demands. And every concession made by "Soft" unwittingly reinforces "Hard's" behavior by rewarding him for being hard.

Fortunately, there is an alternative.

The Integrative Solution

The reason the hotel situation was resolved so amicably was because the negotiated settlement followed certain guidelines common to all successful negotiations. Primarily, it was an example of an *integrative* solution. An integrative solution is one where both parties' needs are met. Obviously not all problems can be resolved in this way. Nevertheless, the integrative approach seems to offer a better alternative to the more common adversarial one practiced by most managers.

For an integrated solution to work, certain preconditions must exist. First, the parties must be motivated to collaborate rather than to compete. Both parties must perceive that they have a common stake in this situation and that there is more to be gained by negotiating than by *not* negotiating. One way to encourage such thinking is for each party to prepare by setting goals and objectives for himself or herself.

Once the negotiation process gets under way, superordinate goals can be emphasized; for example, that the company should make a profit or stay in business. Usually there's little argument here. It's only when deciding the means to these ends that there is disagreement. Therefore, generating many alternatives in a mutual problem solving, "brainstorming" process may be motivating and may facilitate the negotiating process. Once the problem is separated from the personalities involved, both parties can then become involved in *mutual goal setting and problem solving*.

Second, rather than downplaying the other party's needs and wants as unacceptable, each party must recognize the other's *legitimate* right to seek his or her own best interests.

Finally, a spirit of *mutual trust* should be developed between the parties. This is difficult to accomplish, but without it the integrative approach will fail. The absence of trust engenders defensiveness, withdrawal, and suspicion of the other's motives. To build trust, it's important to share information about oneself as openly as one judges appropriate. The parties must each state their needs and work at understanding by *listening* to the other's point of view and also clarifying issues. This doesn't mean being indiscriminately open and trusting. It does, however, mean that each should share his or her concerns with the other party and work toward a mutual agreement.

The following are a few further dos and don'ts to follow in seeking an integrative solution. Even when the integrative approach is not immediately apparent, the following guidelines should enable a manager to become a more skillful negotiator. They should also create a climate where an integrative solution can at least be considered.

Some Don'ts

First, some things to avoid:

Either/or—win/lose thinking. The major feature of hard vs. soft negotiating is that both parties become locked into an either/or style of thinking. The assumption is that one side must win and the other must lose. For example, "Hard" must say, "Look, this is my final offer; take it or leave it!" This usually induces in "Soft" a false sense that this is the only choice left. The way out of this faulty dilemma is to recognize that there are nearly always other alternatives and that an attempt should be made to search for the commonalities in the situation.

Bargaining based on positions. Typically in negotiation parties take *positions* on certain issues and attempt to bargain from this standpoint. Much time is wasted in posturing. People become ego-involved with their pet positions and are fearful of losing face if they are seen to have to give in to the other side's demands. As both sides tend to paint themselves into a corner from which there is little room to maneuver, the result is deadlock.

Selling short. Sometimes people will do this to avoid hassles. For example, they may say, "I just want to get it over," "I was glad to get *anything* at all," or "I gave in to get a quick settlement." There may be some legitimate reason for "giving in" under certain circumstances. However, when this behavior becomes habitual, a person may simply be taking the easiest way out.

Such behaviors come from the mistaken assumption that one alone is under pressure. We may forget that other people may be under even greater pressure and assuming they're not merely strengthens their hand and weakens our own.

Some Dos

Now here are a few things one should actively do:

Adequately prepare. Poor negotiators begin negotiating before objectives are set or adequate alternatives are considered. The attitude seems to be one of, "Let's see what the other side has to say for itself, then we'll develop our strategy as we go along." The problem with playing it by ear is that the initiative is lost and, at best, each side simply muddles along.

Consider alternatives. Roger Fisher and William Uhrey in *Getting to Yes* suggest that before one even begins to negotiate, one should develop what they call one's BATNA—"Best Alternative to a Negotiated Settlement." They suggest that it's important to know beforehand what one intends to do if one doesn't reach agreement. They believe that if someone knows what his or her best alternative is, every negotiation will be successful in the sense that the outcome will be better than the *best* alternative. Otherwise, it needn't be accepted.

One should also consider the other side's BATNA. What can they do if there is no negotiation?

Set objectives and establish criteria. Setting realistic objectives and establishing criteria are one and the same since objectives determine how successful or unsuccessful one has been in negotiating. However, one should be sure the objectives are realistic and measurable. "To get as much as we can for as little as we can give away" may be a nice ideal, but it won't take a manager very far since he or she has no way of measuring any settlement from the negotiation process.

In setting objectives, one should begin by making a list of *all* one's objectives; for example, to survive in business, to make a profit, and to avoid a price war. Next, one should divide the objectives into two lists, one titled "likes," the other "musts." "Likes" are things that would be *nice* to have but that could be done without. "Musts" are those items one absolutely must have for the negotiations to be successful. As negotiations progress, a manager may find himself or herself abandoning many of the "likes" since these items consist of the least important objectives. The "must" objectives are those he or she really *aims* to achieve and is willing to bargain for.

"Must" objectives are the manager's "bottom line"or limits. If he or she doesn't achieve these objectives, the manager is willing to forgo bargaining. Naturally, both kinds of objectives aren't as set in concrete as may be implied here. Circumstances may dictate that the objectives or their order changes. So a continuous review process is necessary.

Insist on objective standards. Negotiations should be based on a set of principles. For example, using fairness, the golden rule, equal treatment, or the going rate for a job makes it easier to reach agreement.

When selling a car, for example, one doesn't arbitrarily set a price for it. Instead, one generally decides on the price based on the "Blue Book" market rate for the particular car, year, and other comparables. Arguing from a set of principles makes it easier to reach agreement since reasoning is based on objective standards, not subjective ones.

Clarify interests and values. Is it money? Ethical principles? The working relationship with the other side? Job security? Next, one needs to determine what actions are likely to enhance or jeopardize these concerns. It is important, too, to decide what the other side really cares about. The tendency is to assume that the other side wants the exact opposite of what one wants. But that isn't always so.

Only by actively listening to the other side can both parties' interests and values be clarified.

Get closure on agreement. When the negotiation session ends, it's a good idea to obtain closure by summarizing what has been agreed on in writing. Many negotiations have gone wrong on just this final point because perception is such an individual thing. It's important that one state specifically just what it is to which one is agreeing. It may even be necessary to paraphrase what the other party says to the individual's satisfaction before leaving the bargaining table.

Mediating Between Disputing Employees

BRUCE E. McEWAN

Any situation involving interpersonal contacts can lead to disagreement and conflict. A manager knows that it is a rare instance where employees, working closely together, don't have an occasional tiff or problem with one another. When such a situation occurs, it is usually the manager who is asked to step in and preserve the harmony of the work environment.

In essence, the manager becomes a mediator between the two parties involved in the dispute. Actually, mediation is a skill that can be effectively utilized by managers to deal with the majority of personnel problems that arise between subordinates.

What Is Mediation?

As management is more an art than a science, so is mediation. It is a process whereby the parties to a dispute can come together to resolve it with the aid of a neutral third party, that is, a mediator. The primary role of the mediator is to facilitate communication between the people. Often the key problem— indeed, the cause of the dispute—is a broken channel of communication. The mediator assists both parties by helping to bridge the gap.

Because the mediator must be neutral, a manager who decides to use mediation to help his or her employees must be sure that he or she is seen by the disputing parties as impartial. If one employee feels that the manager is biased against his or her case, then mediation probably won't work.

The first step in mediation is establishing an atmosphere conducive to negotiation, one in which the parties will be willing to settle their dispute. Because conflict usually involves emotions, values, needs, or a combination of these, the manager/mediator has to keep the session as relaxed as possible.

The Mediation Process

In establishing the proper environment, the manager/mediator stresses that no one is there to judge guilt or innocence. The purpose of the mediation is to help the employees get to the root of the problem

Reprinted from *Supervisory Management,* May 1984

and devise an acceptable solution. In keeping with this, the manager/mediator should point out that the focus of the meeting will be on the future; the past is the past. Employees should concentrate on their future working relationship. Finally, the manager/mediator should stress the importance of flexible thinking and a willingness to compromise in any effort at mediation.

The goal of the mediation is a signed agreement between the two parties that give a basis upon which to both solve their problem and avoid future ones. Thus a benefit of mediation, not only to the disputing parties but the manager as well, is the potential of a long-term solution.

Although an informal process, mediation, to be successful, must follow some specific steps.

Opening statement. At the beginning of the meeting, the manager/mediator explains in detail the mediation process and answers questions that the disputing parties may have. At this point, also, the confidentiality of the mediation session is stressed and assurances are given that no outside parties will know what takes place.

Forum. Next, each employee is given an opportunity to speak. No one is allowed to interrupt as the employee tells his or her side of the issue. This phase can be emotional and time-consuming depending on the nature of the problem and its cause. But it is extremely important that the parties be allowed to vent their emotions. That way they will be more receptive to discussion later on.

Caucuses. After each person has stated his or her position, the mediator meets individually with them. Again, these are confidential sessions. There is no limit to the number of caucuses, as the mediator goes from one party to the other trying to reach an agreement. With the permission of the parties, information is transmitted by the mediator from one to the other and back again.

Problem-solving/joint session. When points of agreement begin to emerge, the mediator writes them down. If there appears to be a number of these, or further group discussion is needed, the manager/mediator brings both parties together. At this stage, the parties iron out any differences on the points agreed upon and continue discussion on those issues that still need to be resolved, if that is possible. At the end of this session, the points in agreement should be clear in everyone's mind. Any points where agreement is not possible should be separated out.

Written agreement. With the help of the parties, the manager/mediator writes out an agreement based on the problem-solving session. The agreement is reviewed and signed by everyone, including the mediator. This written agreement is a reminder of what each party has agreed to do in order to resolve the mutual problem.

Why Mediation?

The benefits of the mediation process are many. First, it boosts employee morale and helps employees work out their own problems and vent pent-up emotions. The organization benefits from the opportunity that mediation offers to show its commitment to employee welfare and to maintaining a healthy work environment as well as its support of employee participation. The manager/mediator has the chance to show employees that he or she cares about their welfare and respects their abilities to solve their own problems. But this is only the beginning of the benefits of the mediation process for the manager.

Mediation increases the manager's stature with his or her employees.

Since mediation requires strict impartiality, the mediation process provides an opportunity for the manager to show his or her objectivity and to exhibit his or her fairness to subordinates. Also, because the manager doesn't play a dominant role in the mediation, only serving as a facilitator, the process gives the individual the chance to interact with employees in other than a superior/subordinate relationship.

To be effective in the mediation process, the manager must be an active listener. He or she must concentrate on every word and be aware of the body language of the employees. This listening ability will stand the manager in good stead in future interactions with employees. The communication skills that the manager refines in the mediation process are also ones that the individual needs to be successful in whatever he or she does.

The maintenance of the confidentiality of the mediation supports the integrity of the manager and encourages employees trust in him or her.

As the manager helps others face their problems head on, he or she learns how to do the same. A manager can develop a whole new perspective on problem solving from the mediation experience.

The biggest hurdle in using mediation as a management tool, after getting management support, will be gaining employee confidence and trust in the process. It would be naive to think that the mediation will always be successful. But once there are some successes, more and more employees will want to use the process themselves.

Are You a Party
To a Personality Conflict?

MARCIA ANN PULICH

Every manager has at least one employee with whom he or she is always at odds. The manager and this employee seldom get along well. Yet this employee appears to fit in and get along with co-workers and can even be observed eating lunch and taking breaks with others.

Why is it that the only person this employee has trouble with is the supervisor? Whose fault is it? What can be done? The problem may be a personality conflict. This can be very stressful, and if not dealt with as soon as possible, the situation may lead to other, more severe problems in the work environment.

A Case in Point

Joe and Mary complain to each other that their supervisors do not understand them. Their supervisors are always on their backs and they cannot ever seem to do anything right. No one else in their departments is treated like this, and they guess their supervisors just do not like them.

Joe's and Mary's supervisors have been heard to say to each other that they do not know what the problem is with Joe and Mary. They never seem to get orders straight; they do not listen to directions; and they have to be constantly watched. In fact, life would be simpler if Joe and Mary had never been hired. While the question of termination has not yet been raised, it would appear that if things do not improve Joe and Mary may find themselves looking for new jobs.

What is the problem? Are all of these people right? Or wrong? Personality conflicts may be causing the performance problems. Then, again, the poor job performance may be due to other problems like lack of training or poor communication. In this day and age of protective legislation, an organization cannot easily terminate an employee simply because of a personality conflict between him or her and a supervisor. Termination must be based on a job-related performance problem, not just on the inability of a supervisor and an employee to get along with each other.

So the first step for a manager faced with a problem like Joe's or Mary's is to determine if it is due to a personality conflict or a job performance problem. Actually, the latter can be more readily solved, once discovered, than the former. What is the employee doing or not doing? Is he or she not following orders correctly? This may be the result of poor communication on the part of the supervisor. Is the

Reprinted from *Management Solutions*, July 1986

employee not carrying out his or her job duties properly? Perhaps the employee needs some on-the-job training.

A personality conflict occurs when an employee and a supervisor do not agree with each other. But it can also go further than this. Besides a difference of viewpoints, there may be a strained relationship and even destructive actions on the part of the employee. The staffer may do his or her job in an acceptable fashion but question the supervisor at every turn of events. He or she may not be insubordinate but approach insubordination. The employee in question may be sullen or unpleasant in speaking to the supervisor, ignore the supervisor as much as possible, even look through the supervisor as though he or she were not there. Supervisors in this type of situation have a very unpleasant time trying, in turn, to be civil and polite to these employees.

Once the manager has determined that a personality conflict does in fact exist, he or she needs to work to reduce or resolve the conflict. Here are some steps that can be taken to make the situation at least bearable for the supervisors and the employees involved.

Who's Really to Blame?

Be self-introspective. Supervisors should try to step outside of themselves and look at themselves from the viewpoint of others. Supervisors should ask themselves a very important question, "Do I contribute to a personality conflict situation?"

Sometimes the answer is not a welcome one. Human beings are very talented at practicing rationalization. It is easy to say that one is not involved in or contributing to an unpleasant situation and to place all the blame on another person. It is particularly easy to do this as a manager and to fall back on one's formal organizational authority, issuing orders to an employee that the employee must follow on pain of discipline. This, of course, is one way to supervise, but it's not the best way. Effective management is based on positive work relationships.

Supervisors are subject to errors just like anyone else, and they should learn to recognize these errors and keep them from contributing to a personality conflict. Good supervisors are aware of the impact that the halo effect, being short-tempered, or always being in a hurry can have. For example, a supervisor committing halo effect judges an employee's total work behavior by only one characteristic. An employee with an extremely untidy work station may be perceived as a poor worker whereas in reality this person may be a top performer. Another example: A manager who is always in a hurry may frustrate and even alienate an employee who needs time to question the manager about work assignments.

It sometimes requires a rigorous self-examination to discover that a supervisor may be unconsciously fueling a personality conflict. In order to successfully cope with a personality conflict, a manager must first make sure that he or she is not a contributing factor. Only then can the individual deal effectively with the employee.

No Socializing Called For

Concentrate on work only. A manager should not worry that he or she does not socialize with the employee in question with regard to nonwork matters. Where a supervisor knows that a personality conflict exists, it is foolish to pretend that everything is normal. It is better to leave the employee alone except when work is involved. The manager should not feel guilty about doing this. Assuming that there is no reason to fire that employee, the supervisor will have to deal with him or her. Dealing only with work-related issues makes it more probable that personal emotions and feelings are left alone and the personality conflict is held down to a manageable level. The two parties will be meeting on neutral ground and can even agree or disagree with one another without feeling that the difference in opinion is based on the personal antagonism.

Accentuate the positive. In a personality conflict, an employee who already dislikes a supervisor will dislike or even hate him or her more where the relationship is also overwhelmingly negative with regard to work. Therefore, it is important for a supervisor to deliberately look for evidence of positive performance and let the employee know when his or her work is fine, that such job performance is appreciated.

Formalize the Relationship

Be more formal. Some supervisors err in engaging in an overly informal interpersonal relationship with subordinates. These supervisors think they must be kept abreast of all events in their employees' lives. Questions are routinely asked about employees' vacation plans, health, marriage, spouse, friends, or new car. A supervisor may think he or she is being "friendly" and solicitous to an employee. The supervisor may feel that not asking questions of this nature indicates a lack of interest in the employee. What the supervisor does not realize is that questions of this sort may not be flattering to every employee. To employees with a personality conflict, questions delving into their personal life may cause a faltering work relationship to deteriorate even more.

Supervisors who have or suspect they have a personality conflict on their hands may want to be more formal with that employee. Being more formal does not mean shunning the individual. It means confining interest in this employee to work-related matters. It means recognizing that if employees wish to discuss non-work-related matters with their supervisors, they will do so of their own accord.

Communicate work matters. An employee with a personality conflict may already feel that the supervisor is "after" him or her. So it will be easy for that employee to see a communication oversight on the supervisor's part as a personal affront. An employee like this may be firmly convinced that any slip is deliberate and not inadvertent. For example, a supervisor gives new instructions to several employees but just plain forgets Employee X because Employee X is on his break. Employee X is later notified by the supervisor but this employee sees this as an attempt by that supervisor to somehow interfere with his work routine.

In order to avoid further harm to the work relationship, a supervisor should make sure that the lines of communication remain open. This means being sure to pass on the same messages, instructions, and comments to this employee as everyone else. No employee should hear of work changes from another employee, but this is especially true with personality-conflict employees. These employees will merely see this as more evidence that their supervisors simply do not like them.

Treat employees alike. A supervisor should not single out the personality-conflict employee for any better or worse treatment than other employees. Other employees are frequently aware of the personality conflict; it is usually no secret. The employee has most likely complained or griped to fellow employees about the supervisor. To single out the employee in any manner generally just calls more attention to the problem.

If the supervisor treats the employee better than other employees, it may appear that the supervisor is trying to bribe the employee to behave better, or that he or she is actually being rewarded for being a problem. Supervisors sometimes let matters slide instead of bringing them to the employee's attention. An employee may not be reprimanded when needed. Supervisors may even do things themselves rather than asking the employee to do it. The bottom line is that other employees may become aware of this and may adjust their behavior over a period of time. This is not what a supervisor wants.

Treating an employee more harshly than others may also cause unwanted problems. "Riding" an employee may cause the employee to behave even worse than usual. Unjust discipline may prompt unnecessary grievances. Unjust firings may result in lawsuits. At the very least, this type of treatment generally worsens the work relationship between the supervisor and employee. This is usually the opposite of what the supervisor is trying to achieve.

A Mature Approach

Talk with the employee. A frequently overlooked tactic is to talk to the employee in a mature fashion. It is possible to talk in a frank but non-threatening manner and achieve results. Perhaps an employee does not know his or her behavior bothers the supervisor. Perhaps something about the supervisor bothers the employee.

This type of discussion must be handled carefully. Both parties must remain calm and be prepared to listen to the other. The supervisor who decides to talk with an employee must be mentally prepared for the employee to say just about anything. The supervisor must not be offended by an employee's comments and should make it perfectly clear that there will be no repercussions for being candid. The idea is to clear the air.

After both parties have had an opportunity to speak, the focus should be placed on coming up with a mutually agreeable way to handle the situation. Perhaps it is nothing more than an agreement to stay out of each other's way except where necessary for work purposes. It may be that both parties recognize that additional meetings are needed to arrive at a solution.

A supervisor must realize that talking with an employee may accomplish nothing. An employee may remain firmly convinced that any problem is created solely by the supervisor or that there is no problem. If this is so, then the supervisor may only be able to remind the employee that he or she is expected to cooperate by carrying out the supervisor's work directions without being insubordinate, careless, or untimely. The most the two parties may be able to do is to agree that they disagree.

The Issue of Discipline

Take final measures. A final measure open to the supervisor is to discipline the employee. But to take such action the supervisor must be very sure that the personality conflict is causing problems in the employee's work performance.

Once this is determined, appropriate measures can be taken and might include oral warnings, written letters of warning, suspension, or termination. A supervisor should not ignore a problem simply because it is feared that the employee may become impolite or even verbally abusive. A supervisor should try to remain calm and concentrate only on the work-related problem. Any supervisor who uses a personality conflict as the basis for discipline may be accused of discrimination by the employee. A personality conflict that affects an employee's work performance usually shows up in some identifiable concrete manner. For example, an employee who dislikes the supervisor and is insubordinate may not obey a work directive immediately. The supervisor disciplines the employee, not for being insubordinate, but for not carrying out an order as directed.

Summing Up

Personality conflicts have always existed and will continue to exist. Supervisors and employees will not always get along together in an amiable fashion in a work relationship. However, there are things that a supervisor can do to lessen the tension in a personality conflict. These suggestions do not guarantee 100 percent that a supervisor will be fully successful in dealing with an employee in personality-conflict situations. But they may enable a supervisor and an employee to exist together in a more peaceful atmosphere.

Part V

DELEGATION AND FOLLOW-THROUGH

Key Factors in Positive Delegation

DON CARUTH and TREZZIE A. PRESSLEY

Positive delegation is the art of assigning additional duties, and commensurate authority, to employees in a manner so that the assigned work is completed effectively and the employees feel that their time and talents have been used wisely.

Traditional definitions of delegation emphasize the assignment of duties, the granting of authority, and the creation of accountability for performance as the three main aspects of delegation. Today, however, recognizing the increasingly necessary requirements of providing a psychologically stimulating work environment and personal fulfillment for employees, delegation must include an additional aspect: the engendering of feelings of achievement and satisfaction on the part of the employees. Delegation that fulfills the three traditional requirements as well as this new requisite is positive delegation.

Customarily, delegation has been viewed as a means of accomplishing work through other people. Its focus has been primarily on results; that is, getting a job done on time and within budget and quality specifications. Positive delegation still emphasizes results, but it also stresses the equally important factor of enhancing employee motivation.

Positive delegation does not simply happen by itself. It is a management technique that requires a thorough understanding of the principles involved, a commitment to its use as a motivational tool, and a willingness to perfect its application through thoughtful practice. It is a results-and-motivation-oriented

Reprinted from *Supervisory Management*, July 1984

approach to making work assignments that succeeds when managers understand and apply the key factors essential to its success.

Factor 1—Know What to Delegate

In practicing positive delegation, the starting point for a supervisor is to understand which aspects of his or her job can or should be delegated to others. Activities with a high potential for delegation include the following:

Paperwork. Filing change notices or procedure revisions, writing first drafts of production reports or memos, and updating schedules and charts are examples of administrative duties that can be readily delegated to subordinates. These are important tasks that must be performed but do not necessarily have to be done by a supervisor.

Routine. Closely related to paperwork are routine tasks—those activities that occur in a work unit on a regular or frequent basis. Such tasks generally have a high potential for delegation to subordinates. Verifying time cards, checking inventory levels, or ordering supplies are typical routine pieces of his or her job that a supervisor can assign to others.

Technical matters. Questions concerning machine settings, procedural steps, or other mechanical details of a department's operations are frequently best answered by a senior employee who is generally more knowledgeable about these things than the supervisor may be. If the work unit has such an employee, delegation of technical duties is a distinct possibility that a supervisor should consider.

Tasks with developmental potential. Any assignment that enables a subordinate to learn new things, to expand his or her horizons beyond the confines of the current position, to acquire additional skills, or to exercise creativity in the solution of a problem is an assignment with developmental possibilities. Examples include tasks that enable a subordinate to obtain the skills necessary to qualify for a higher-level position and assignments that provide a better understanding of general departmental or company operations.

Before making any assignments to others, it is important for a supervisor to recognize that delegation is not simply an opportunity to rid himself or herself of unpleasant or meaningless tasks. Assignments delegated to subordinates should have the potential for learning and personal development.

Factor 2—Know What Not to Delegate

There are some activities that cannot or should not be delegated, even though a supervisor may strongly desire to pass them along to someone else. Among these are:

Personnel matters. Hiring, firing, resolution of work group conflicts, counseling, grievances, and salary matters are managerial responsibilities that should never be delegated to subordinates.

Confidential activities. Where a need for secrecy exists, the possibility of delegation is nil. Fact gathering relative to a plant relocation, the addition of an extra shift, and possibly policy changes are matters too delicate or confidential in most instances.

Crises. In a crisis situation, there is normally no time to explain matters to a subordinate; action must be taken quickly. Thus, delegation is not a viable option. The supervisor must handle the situation himself or herself.

Tasks assigned personally. Any job assigned to a supervisor by his or her superior with a definite "I-want-you-to-do-this" imprinted on it is not something that can be delegated to an employee.

Factor 3—Select the Right Person

Obviously, all employees do not have the same capabilities, needs, and motivation. A task that is appropriate to delegate to one person may well be an entirely inappropriate assignment for another employee. A supervisor must match talent to task, aspiration to assignment, and willingness to work, if positive delegation is to be accomplished.

One of the first responsibilities of every supervisor is to develop to its fullest extent the potential that exists within each employee. Positive delegation, to the extent that it is used to assist subordinates to learn, achieve, and grow, is a means of accomplishing this. It is, therefore, imperative that a supervisor know as much as possible about each subordinate's skills, interests, and needs. This knowledge will enable a supervisor to make an assignment to the particular subordinate who is most likely to gain the greatest benefit from the task.

In many organizations, there are unfortunately many capable people who are frustrated because they are never given the opportunity to utilize their capabilities and develop to their fullest potential. Interestingly, until a supervisor delegates, he or she often does not recognize the true level of capabilities existing within subordinates.

Factor 4—Give Thorough Instructions

Positive delegation always includes information on what, when, why, where, who, and how. To complete an assignment effectively, a subordinate must clearly understand what results are expected, what his or her limits of authority are, why he or she was selected for the assignment, where the work is to be performed, who is involved in the task, and how the job is to be accomplished if following a prescribed procedure is important.

Failure to communicate thoroughly what needs to be done can result in lost time, ruined materials, missed schedules, or frustration on the part of the employee trying to accomplish the task.

Factor 5—Grant Sufficient Authority

Authority to obtain materials, use equipment, or instruct others must be commensurate with the job to be done. If this isn't the case, the task won't be completed.

Authority must be clearly spelled out and clearly granted. Each time a task is delegated, a supervisor should carefully think through the degree of authority that will be required to accomplish the job. That amount of authority—neither more, nor less—must be assigned along with the job. It is also important to let other employees know the scope of the delegation in order to assure their maximum cooperation and assistance.

Positive delegation can be further enhanced by delegating an entire action or function to a single individual rather than delegating small parts of a total job to several different people. A delegation of this nature not only results in increased feelings of responsibility, but also helps minimize gaps in responsibility and improves the ability of the delegator to coordinate and control the delegated assignment properly.

Factor 6—Maintain Feedback

Feedback, that most neglected element of communication, is absolutely essential to positive delegation. In delegation, instructions are the forward flow of communications; feedback is the reverse flow of questions, comments, and progress reports.

What is effective feedback is largely determined by the attitude of the supervisor—an attitude indicative of the supervisor's willingness to answer questions, listen to comments, respond to suggestions, and so forth. It is important for a supervisor to remember that the only "dumb question" is the one not asked, the only "stupid comment" the one not made.

Feedback is the vehicle for assuring that the subordinate is on the right track and that the assignment will be completed within the allotted parameters of time, cost, or quality specifications.

Wherever possible, it is advantageous to delegate in such a manner that the employee can measure his or her own performance. This enhances motivation and provides a means of self-feedback that does not require additional amounts of a supervisor's time and involvement.

Factor 7—Make Criticism Constructive

Delegation is a learning experience for the employee. Mistakes will be made. Whether the errors an employee makes are a positive or a negative experience depends largely on how the supervisor handles the situation. If the supervisor criticizes, chastises, and condemns unduly, an employee will almost assuredly refuse or seek to avoid additional delegated assignments. On the other hand, if the supervisor explains, encourages, and elaborates, an employee will most certainly welcome or seek out further assignments because he or she views them as psychologically rewarding developmental opportunities.

An important rule in addressing errors in work performance is to focus on the problem, not the person. If a supervisor says, "Wow? You really blew that one!" an employee is apt to suffer ego damage. But if a supervisor reacts to a mistake by saying, "Let's see what happened. Maybe I didn't explain this clearly," the employee's dignity and sense of worth are more likely to be preserved. Remember, positive delegation focuses not only on getting the job done, but also on enhancing employee motivation. Therefore, employee mistakes should be viewed as further opportunities for growth, training, and development.

Another point to keep in mind is that when mistakes are made, a supervisor, though sorely tempted, should not take back the delegated assignment. He or she should work with the employee, coaching, counseling, and communicating as necessary, to see that the job is done correctly. In this way, present as well as future results are more likely to be assured.

Factor 8—Show Trust

Control is always necessary to assure that a delegated assignment is done properly and on time. But the amount of control exercised by a supervisor does much to demonstrate the amount of trust he or she has in a subordinate. And a supervisor's trust or confidence in an employee is critical in positive delegation.

Control, for the purposes of positive delegation, may best be accomplished by building check-points into an assignment in the form of specified times for reporting progress or by making periodic spotchecks of work. Too much control deprives a subordinate of the opportunity to build self-confidence.

It is also helpful for a supervisor to focus on the goals to be achieved or the result to be accomplished, rather than on "how" a particular job is to be done—unless there is an overriding need to adhere to specific methods. Focusing on goals or results allows a subordinate to feel that he or she has the freedom to use his or her own judgment in completing the work. Moreover, it implies that the supervisor trusts the employee.

Work performance should improve with each delegated task if the employee experiences successful results in carrying out the delegated assignments. So a supervisor should delegate to a subordinate gradually, allowing the employee to build upon his or her successes. The supervisor should stretch the employee's capabilities through progressively more challenging assignments. Placing too much on the employee at one time—creating an overload condition—can negate or minimize the results of positive delegation.

Factor 9—Reward Performance

A pat on the back, a word of encouragement, a sincere "thank you" for a job well done—simple, but powerful rewards—all help to create a motivational atmosphere and increase the willingness of subordinates to take on additional assignments. A supervisor should always recognize a good job and call it to the attention of the person who has done it.

Promotions and merit increases are other kinds of rewards that a supervisor can use when an employee consistently demonstrates the willingness to take on assignments and the competence to carry them out successfully. When coupled with the psychological rewards of praise, they create a highly productive organizational climate.

Positive delegation increases employees' motivation in the workplace and enhances job satisfaction because it fulfills the intrinsic needs of employees to learn, to grow, to develop, and to be recognized as worthwhile contributing members of a work group. At the same time, positive delegation enables a supervisor to handle more important duties and responsibilities, to utilize talents more productively, and to focus personal attention on managerial tasks. Thus, positive delegation becomes a rewarding, highly motivating, and satisfying experience for both employees and supervisor.

Why Supervisors Don't Delegate and Employees Won't Accept Responsibility

A. T. HOLLINGSWORTH and ABDUL RAHMAN A. AL-JAFARY

Andrew Carnegie expressed his view of delegation in a single statement: "When a man realizes he can call others in to help him do a job better than he can do alone, he has taken a big step in his life." Thus Carnegie laid to rest two wrong assumptions about delegation. First, by delegating work, a supervisor is not showing himself or herself incompetent in doing it. Second, by delegating, the delegator is not avoiding responsibility. The fact is, the delegator does not have the time to do the job alone and do it well. Conferring authority from manager to subordinates does not reduce the manager's authority. Rather, the area of operations is extended.

The functions of a manager are planning, organizing, recruitment, administration, and control. Delegation is a part of the organizing function. The distribution of tasks, authority, and responsibility are part and parcel of this.

Why Is Delegation Important?

Delegation is needed because it gives a supervisor more time to do those things that are truly the responsibility of supervisors. When a supervisor doesn't delegate, for instance, he or she no longer has time to plan. This results in continuous firefighting.

Delegation also allows employees to develop. It helps them learn to accept responsibility and to utilize their talents in solving problems. That someone trusts them enough to delegate work and not keep looking over their shoulder can also be highly motivating.

Delegation can also be used as a reward. As employees learn new skills, their jobs can be expanded through delegation of choice assignments. Over time, by delegating work to talented subordinates, a supervisor can develop a replacement for himself or herself. This is important for the supervisor interested in advancement. Many organizations will not promote individuals unless a properly prepared replacement is available to fill the subsequent vacancy.

But most important, delegation makes fullest use of a department's personnel. Failure to delegate often results in missed deadlines and other evidence of poor performance due to the supervisor making all the decisions and trying to do all the work for the group.

Reprinted from *Supervisory Management,* April 1983

Why Don't Supervisors Delegate?

Supervisors don't delegate for a number of reasons. One is a *feeling of job insecurity.* Being busy makes many feel indispensable. They don't realize that not delegating work conveys the wrong impression to those who hire, fire, and promote. Instead of someone on top of his or her job, management sees someone constantly harried and a department out of control. Certainly that's not an impression likely to please management.

Some supervisors don't delegate because *they believe that only they are capable of doing the job.* Besides showing a lack of confidence in their subordinates, this attitude also suggests an unwillingness to develop subordinates.

There are also supervisors who don't delegate because *they are fearful of a mistake being made.* They don't want to take any risks and they try to minimize errors by keeping all work under their direct control. What they don't realize is that, while minimizing risk, they are also demonstrating to their boss that they are not promotable and to their subordinates that their supervisor has no faith in them. They don't realize that they can make a decision and see that it is carried out by others by setting up controls. It's not necessary for them to do the work.

Poor delegation is also caused by the *inability of the supervisor to communicate what needs to be done.* The supervisor begins to explain a job and then realizes that he or she doesn't really understand its requirements. At this point, the manager should admit that he or she is unable to continue until more information is available. Unfortunately, most supervisors are more likely to push on, ending up confusing rather than clarifying the job for their subordinates. They do this because they are afraid they might lose their subordinates' confidence if they admitted they didn't have all the answers. So, when the subordinates admit to being unsure, these supervisors blame them for being too thick-headed to understand and start doing the task for the confused employees.

Confusion concerning a supervisor's authority is often also a problem with delegation for a supervisor. When he or she isn't sure of either the tasks or the individuals to be assigned to these tasks, then difficulties in delegation are bound to occur. Consider what happened to Jean, manager of a small accounting office. She supervised five employees. Unfortunately neither Jean nor her employees had any idea what their responsibilities were. The office had grown quickly and with little direction, and the four accountants to whom Jean reported had never clarified the responsibilities of either the office manager or support staff. They also asked Jean's staff from time to time to help out and do small clerical tasks for them, often without checking with Jean. Work that Jean had delegated to an employee was frequently left undone while the person completed some small errand or task for one of the accountants. Often Jean had to stay late to complete work she had assigned to her staff. The accountants couldn't understand why the office wasn't running smoothly. In the end, Jean quit out of frustration.

In the above case, Jean wasn't clear as to her role or that of her subordinates or superiors. The lack of clarity hampered her ability to delegate and eventually prevented her from doing it.

In this case, the accountants should have met with Jean, outlined her responsibilities and authority and then explained this to the entire office. Jean as a supervisor, however, was not entirely blameless. She should have brought the situation to the attention of the accountants before office operations had deteriorated so badly.

Still another reason why supervisors don't delegate is that *they feel the controls or feedback mechanisms are too weak.* "If things go badly," they say to themselves, "I won't know in time to correct the situation." Again, this is a supervisory failure. Instead of worrying about the lack of controls, a supervisor should be putting into place the proper controls. Poor management is not a sufficient excuse for nondelegation.

Some supervisors would rather firefight than set up systems that enable them to manage. They don't like to sit and plan; they prefer handling details. Consequently they won't delegate. They argue that *they don't delegate because they can do the work faster* than their subordinates, but the reason that it takes their subordinates so long to complete the work is that they aren't accustomed to having jobs delegated to them. Likewise, the reason that the supervisor can do the work quickly is that he or she gets all the practice from never having trained subordinates to handle their jobs.

Finally, getting back to one of the assumptions that Carnegie tried to put to rest, many supervisors *feel that they shouldn't delegate anything they wouldn't or couldn't do themselves.* As Carnegie pointed out, this is ridiculous thinking. The reason that one hires subordinates is because they have the necessary skills to complete a job or a segment of a job. It is the responsibility of the supervisor to plan and assign work. By letting employees do their jobs, supervisors free themselves so they can manage.

Creating a Climate for Delegation

The influence of top management on delegation is well-established in management literature. Therefore, top management is not blameless for a nondelegating supervisor. Making the potential delegator feel secure, establishing a work climate free of fear and frustration, and assuring delegators that they will be rewarded rather than penalized for delegation are the responsibilities of top management.

But supervisors are also responsible for creating a climate that supports delegation. A supervisor can't delegate if he or she is in a constant state of crisis. No one can talk to someone who is rushing about putting out one fire after another. Besides, that person wouldn't listen anyway. This is not the kind of atmosphere that enhances delegation or any other management practice.

For delegation to work, it is preferable to have a relaxed work environment where jobs and duties can be discussed and clarified if need be. This kind of environment is only possible when the supervisor has set objectives, communicated them to subordinates, and planned how the department or workgroup will reach the objectives. A relaxed environment gives subordinates the feeling that they can ask questions and discuss their ideas without fear of being cut off, that they can have different opinions from their supervisor, and that they can try new techniques to achieve objectives.

Why Subordinates Resist Delegation

Even if top management supports delegation and the supervisor creates a climate conducive to delegation and wants to delegate, there is no guarantee that employees will assume responsibility and make decisions. There are a number of reasons why subordinates resist delegation. The most prevalent one is that *it's easier to let the supervisor make all the decisions.* Why change a good thing? It requires no effort on the subordinate's part and it also gives him or her a built-in excuse if something goes wrong: "I didn't make the decision; my supervisor did."

Bill is manager of a painting shop. He spends the majority of his time making decisions and giving instructions. Bill thinks that he's an effective supervisor. What he hasn't realized yet is that his employees don't get to work until he arrives and tells them what to do. Bill sees his workers busy and thinks that this is a sign of a good manager—keeping subordinates occupied. But Bill is failing to utilize the full potential of his workforce by limiting it to doing exactly what he tells individual members. What's more, the situation is unlikely to change. The workers aren't going to beg him to delegate responsibility to them.

Another reason that subordinates fail to accept delegation is that *they aren't sure of their own level of authority and even who their supervisor is.* This may sound silly, but all of us have seen at one time or another an individual receive different directions from those of their supervisor from someone one or more levels above the immediate supervisor. Even when the orders are not in conflict, they may well represent conflicting uses of time.

Then there are subordinates who play a game called "cover yourself." Since the supervisor levels criticism at every mistake the subordinate makes when being decisive, *the subordinate double-checks every decision he or she makes first with the supervisor before implementing it.* Only when mistakes are used as teaching devices will subordinates be willing to accept delegation and make decisions.

Some subordinates feel uneasy about being delegated jobs because *they feel that they haven't received the proper information to handle the work.* Moreover, they feel that obtaining the needed information is beyond their control. Some employees may have the information they need but they worry about getting the necessary equipment or help to fulfill the commitments that have been delegated to them.

Then there are those employees who feel that *they are not prepared to accept responsibility.* Perhaps in the past they were offered too much delegated work too soon, and now they worry about their ability to handle responsibility. They have to be psychologically prepared to take on the work. Their supervisor should first give responsibility for small increments of jobs. As the employees become more accustomed to the idea of delegation and their self-confidence grows, they can accept more responsibility.

Finally, *employees may not be convinced that they can gain anything by accepting responsibility.* They ask, "What's in it for me?" A supervisor has to be prepared to explain the importance of delegation to the subordinates' development. He or she may even have to face the fact that some subordinates are not willing to take responsibility for delegated authority. They are satisfied in their present position and do not want to make any changes. When this is the case, delegation is not going to be effective. Such subordinates must be either replaced or used on very specific types of jobs.

A Self-Analysis

Most supervisors think they do delegate. But some don't and others could do more. To find out how one stands, a supervisor should examine the following list of questions:

- Do you take yourself too seriously?
- Do you worry about postponed decisions that can't be made without you?
- Do you never get a day off?
- Do you never get to take vacations of a week or longer?
- Do you take work home every night and on weekends?
- Do you rarely read for self-development or recreation?
- Do you suffer frequent interruptions because people need your advice or consent?
- Do you work more than your employees?
- Do you keep very close control on all aspects of work within your department?
- Do you expect to know where your employees are at all times?
- Do you feel that no one can do the job as well as you can?
- Do you worry over every detail in your department?
- Do you constantly worry about the loss of your job?
- Do you get frequent calls at home regarding trivial details concerning your department?
- Do you rarely have time to discuss job details?

A "yes" answer to any of these questions suggests a problem with delegating. The supervisor is overburdening himself or herself with too much detail and consequently is under considerable stress.This will result in one or all of the following: the supervisor will become ill from trying to do too much, employees' growth and development will suffer, and/or the department will operate at less than maximum efficiency.

The Art of Exclusion

H. B. KARP

In stressing the need for employee growth and developing programs to achieve it, management has been creating a major dilemma for supervisors. That is: How can they foster employee development and involvement as an organizational value and deal with the reality that sometimes it is inappropriate? Or, more specifically: How do supervisors exclude an employee for the good of the organization when the employee wants to be included?

The Nature of Exclusion

Under the best of conditions, exclusion is difficult to deal with. There is probably nothing more damaging to the self-image than to be told, "You are not wanted here!" by a particular group or preferred individual. Also, most people will avoid gratuitously hurting someone else, which makes exclusion as painful a process for the excluder as it is for the person being excluded. It becomes doubly difficult when the exclusion occurs right in the midst of trying to get everyone involved.

To deal with exclusion constructively, three conditions have to exist. First, the specific task or responsibility that the individual is to be excluded from must be something that is clearly over and above the scope of his or her present job duties and responsibilities. Some examples might be promotion to lead hand, responsibility for training new employees, or special overtime assignments that require additional skills or talents not necessary for performing the regular job.

The second condition is that there is evidence to support the supervisor's view that the employee does not have the ability to perform the new task at this time. The third condition is that the exclusion is for this particular event: There is no implication that exclusion will occur again under different circumstances.

When the exclusion adheres to these three conditions, it provides several benefits to the individual and the organization.

The Advantages of Exclusion

1. Prevents failure experiences. Being excluded, for whatever reason, is almost always painful. If dealt with tactfully, however, the pain can be temporary and nondamaging. If, on the other hand, appro-

Reprinted from *Supervisory Management*, July 1985

priate exclusion is avoided, the pain will be chronic and damaging. Allowing an employee to take on a task or to shoulder a responsibility that is 80 percent destined for failure results in loss of self-confidence and ego damage for the employee, disappointment and a strained working relationship for the supervisor, and damaged reputations all around.

2. *Provides needed role clarification.* When a supervisor excludes an employee from a specific task, telling the subordinate, "I think that you are not ready to take on this new job," he or she is providing a boundary statement that clarifies for that employee the areas of his or her contribution. Anything that the supervisor does that results in his or her employees, individually, becoming clearer about how they fit into the organization and how their best contribution is made is going to result in better work, less confusion, and more stable working relationships.

3. *Provides a springboard for employee development.* By being forced to exclude an employee from a specific job or responsibility, the supervisor becomes aware of where the employee needs to grow. Rather than view exclusion only as a painful and humiliating experience, the employee can view it as an opportunity to become aware of where his or her development needs lie and the supervisor can view it as an opportunity to support the employee's development through training, coaching, or other forms of organizational support.

4. *Provides stronger, more effective supervisors.* I am sure you would agree that the supervisor who, as a matter of policy, makes a point of excluding employees from the opportunity for more responsibility and more challenging work would be considered an ineffective manager. The paradox is that the supervisor who makes a point of involving everyone, all the time, as a matter of policy, is no more effective. If a supervisor is to survive and prosper in the organization, he or she must involve everyone to his or her minimal level of capability. To do otherwise would be to invite a disastrously high failure rate, since everyone is not capable of doing everything he or she would like to do, all the time.

Excluding people appropriately also allows the supervisor to be a better support to the employee. For example, if I know that you, the supervisor, will exclude me when that is appropriate, I can more readily trust your judgment when you choose to include me.

Now that we've examined the issue of exclusion, let's look at how it can be carried out.

The Curative Approach to Exclusion

No matter how effective or well-intentioned the supervisor, occasionally there is going to be the situation where either the supervisor, the employee, or both have overestimated the employee's ability to handle the new task, or responsibility. That is, when employee involvement is running high, an occasional overestimation of employee ability comes with the territory. What frequently happens is that the employee and/or the supervisor only sees the challenge of the new assignment and not the roadblocks. Formal and successful programs in management by objectives, job enrichment, and goal setting will periodically incur this type of error as will supervisors who want to see employees grow and who therefore delegate or promote too quickly.

Once the supervisor sees the employee has failed in the new responsibility, it is relatively easy to get the employee out of the stressful situation. In fact, so long as the supervisor handles the situation supportively, the employee may even be thankful for the removal of the new assignment.

Although this attempt at increasing the employee's involvement failed, both parties are to be congratulated. They attempted something new and risky and now have the opportunity to learn from the experience so that the next attempt will have a much higher chance of success.

Is there another option?

The Preventative Approach to Exclusion

To manipulate an old bromide, I am going to suggest "A pound of prevention is worth an ounce of cure!" It is far more difficult to prevent these errors than to cure them; but certainly prevention is the better approach in terms of what is in the best interests of the employee, the supervisor, and the organization.

With prevention, the employee is excluded from the new job, duty, or responsibility. There is no testing, no challenge, no risk. It is simply a matter of the supervisor's judgment of those same abilities; and there is no basis for dealing with the issue beyond that.

By way of example, let me recount the incident that brought this whole issue into focus for me. I was recently doing some supervisory development work in a chemical plant with a group of foremen with whom I had been working over the past three years. The session was devoted to the supervisors' identifying a current problem they were experiencing, writing it up, then choosing a specific strategy to deal with it. One foreman, Mike, had a real stumper. Mike was in charge of shipping. A special order had come in from a foreign customer, and because of its size and complexity, Mike decided it would be handled on an overtime basis. The problem was that Mike's most senior employee did not, in Mike's estimation, have the ability to process the complex paperwork that this unique order required. Not only was this employee to be denied the opportunity for more challenging work but also he was to be singled out from his group and denied the opportunity for additional income. In handling the situation, Mike simply bypassed the employee in the first run of overtime, then told him just that morning that he would not be included in that assignment. The employee felt very dejected, left out, and most of all discriminated against. Mike felt guilty and somewhat helpless.

The most frustrating aspect of this problem was that nobody was at fault. It is not the employee's fault that he is not qualified to do more than his present job requires of him. Nor is it the supervisor's fault that a unique situation arose that called for a tough decision. If there is any fault at all in this, it has to rest with me, the consultant, who simply should have been, but was not, aware of this type of problem.

The Strategy

Whether the situation calls for a curative or preventative approach, there is a six-step strategy the supervisor can use.

Step 1. Indicate that a situation exists that will not include the employee. I recommend that as soon as the employee sits down, he or she be told directly that such and such is going to occur that will not include him or her. The sooner the employee knows exactly what the situation is, the better. If the supervisor attempts to soften the blow by being defensive, unclear, or apologetic, the situation is bound to get messy and difficult to control. If done quickly and cleanly, it may not need to be mentioned again.

I also strongly suggest that the supervisor take full responsibility for this decision and not sidestep it by spreading the blame to the situation, the boss, or the organization. By saying, "Charlie, *I* have decided not to include you in the Finster project," the supervisor is establishing his or her authority more clearly and setting the stage for increased communications as the meeting progresses.

Step 2. Explain the reasons for the exclusion in a friendly, supportive manner. Check for understanding. It is essential that the supervisor's decision be backed up by clear evidence. This is one of the very few times in organizational life where the supervisor is accountable to the employee. The employee has every right to know the reasons the supervisor chooses to exclude him or her.

The supervisor first has to be clear about the additional qualifications that the new task or responsibility demands. The supervisor then has to be just as clear in pointing out that the employee does not possess these qualifications at this time. By being able to present evidence to prove the employee does not have the necessary mathematical ability, experience, communications skills, or whatever, the supervisor sets the stage for a productive meeting in two ways.

First, the issue is depersonalized. The sole focus is on the requirements of the new assignment. This allows the employee to realize that there is no personal fault involved, so any risk of ego damage to the employee is greatly reduced if not completely eliminated. The second benefit to having all the data available is that once the situation is made clear to the employee, the supervisor can easily shift roles from excluder to supporter.

Step 3. Listen and respond empathetically. After the employee has been informed that he or she is to be excluded and understands why the decision was made, his or her reactions can go from apathy to dejection and from anger to self-recrimination. Regardless of the response, the supervisor can safely bet that it won't be a positive one.

It's at this stage that the supervisor should take control of the process by listening to what the employee is saying (or not saying) and responding empathetically. That means the supervisor should let the employee know he or she is hearing what is being said and that it is perfectly appropriate for the employee to be feeling whatever he or she is feeling at this point.

Just as it would be inappropriate for the supervisor to castigate or yell at the employee for feeling badly, so also would it be inappropriate to attempt to talk the employee out of this feeling. Statements like "You shouldn't feel that way," "It's not so bad," or "Things will look better tomorrow" will only prolong the bad feelings and convince the employee that the supervisor still isn't listening and really doesn't care. Even if the employee reacts with open anger, it is wise for the supervisor to keep in mind that the hostility is defensive: The employee is in the act of protecting himself or herself and is not attacking the supervisor. With this in mind, the supervisor should not take a defensive posture and/or counterattack.

On the other hand, empathetic statements such as "I can really see how this decision is hurting you," "In your position I'd be angry too," or "I can understand how you might be doubting your own capabilities at this point" will encourage the employee to state his or her feelings openly. This, in turn, will give the supervisor the opportunity to express genuine concern and support for the employee and to honor and alleviate the negative feelings as soon as possible. Furthermore, it will enable the supervisor to hear what the employee's primary concerns are—loss of income, loss of face, denied opportunity for growth or advancement, or feelings of inadequacy—so that the supervisor can help the employee do something about them.

Step 4. Recognize the employee's specific contributions on the job. At this point the supervisor should emphasize that the decision to exclude the employee from the new job or responsibility is no reflection on the employee's performance on the regular job. It is essential that the supervisor be able to cite specific instances of the employee's on-the-job effectiveness with specific times when they occurred. If the supervisor fails to deal in specifics, the attempt to bolster the employee's self-image will come across as nothing more than a half-hearted, insincere, human relations sop. At best, the supervisor will be ineffective and, at worst, he or she will lose a considerable amount of credibility.

The objective of step four is to reinforce the positive contributions of the employee so that, first, the employee's self-image is maintained and, second, the employee is aware that he or she is valued and why this is so.

Step 5. Identify and support actions that will improve the employee's abilities. It is well to note here that the employee has been excluded for lack of a specific ability. Since others in his or her job designation or unit are being involved, chances are that the employee does have the potential for this new responsibility. What is needed here is to use the exclusion event as an opportunity to begin to actualize this hidden potential.

For example, the supervisor could look into getting tuition aid for the employee so that the person could get needed training. Of if inexperience is the problem, the supervisor could look for ways to increase the employee's experience on the job. But whatever action is identified, it must be agreed to by both the supervisor and the employee; otherwise, little of value will emerge.

There is another issue that can be dealt with in this step that is unrelated to the employee's growth needs but is no less important. That is the issue of equity. No matter how clear and demonstrable the reasons for exclusion, in all probability the employee is going to have the feeling of being dealt with unfairly. While the supervisor has nothing for which to apologize, I personally find nothing wrong with the supervisor doing something for the employee that will restore some semblance of equity—if it is available and if it does not compromise the supervisor or the organization. For example, if the supervisor has found out the employee is primarily concerned about loss of extra income, the supervisor can promise him or her the first shot at the next overtime project that falls within the employee's competencies. Or if the employee has been excluded from a specific delegated assignment, perhaps there is something else that could be delegated at this time.

Step 6. End the meeting on a positive note. It is important that the employee leave this meeting feeling as good about himself or herself as the situation realistically allows. The closing step of the strategy is to end the meeting by summarizing the constructive and positive aspects of the situation and to express confidence in the employee's ability to succeed in the steps agreed upon. The supervisor should further express appreciation for the employee's cooperativeness during the meeting and for the overall good job that he or she is doing.

Giving Instructions That Get Followed

ERIC MATTHIESEN and JOHN HOLLWITZ

As managers quickly discover, it can be devilishly difficult to get even routine jobs done in a simple, direct manner. Discussions about work seem prone to misinterpretation, misunderstanding, and confusion, even those between experienced managers and employees who have the best intentions. Since such problems seem impossible to avoid, they frequently are summarized under the shadowy heading of "impaired productivity," which is what results, and dismissed with a resigned shrug of the corporate shoulders.

In reality, though, the situation may be more manageable than managers realize. Organizational exchanges always involve interpersonal contact, and interpersonal contact requires communication. So it may be possible to improve operations within companies by improving the communication styles with which personnel interact. Good communication should produce better relationships, and better relationships can affect both the quantity and quality of work.

The Problem

For most managers, issuing directives and seeing that they are accomplished seems largely a matter of routine. Yet the process of perceiving an organizational need and directing its solution is actually quite complicated: Many steps separate the perception from final implementation, and once a manager involves others in the solution process—once he or she delegates tasks to a subordinate for completion—a variety of difficulties may arise.

Consider a typical situation. Manager Smith has analyzed a departmental problem and has decided upon a solution. He consults with employee Jones, who is directed to implement that solution; Manager Smith will oversee Jones's operation at some point in the future to guarantee that the solution has indeed been implemented, that the job is done. The situation seems quite simple: Once the message has been transmitted from Smith to Jones, an understanding is born and a direction achieved. Yet three outcomes might result from this apparently simple transaction, and two of these outcomes are wasteful, expensive, and unproductive. Jones might follow the directive completely. On the other hand, he or she might ignore the directive or forget about it entirely. Worse yet, Jones might only *partially* follow the directive, leaving some things undone or others done incorrectly.

Consider how many dollars Smith might lose as a result of the misunderstanding, and in how many different ways these dollars might be wasted. If the worker doesn't follow the directive at all, missed

Reprinted from *Supervisory Management*, May 1983

deadlines and lost opportunities result. If Jones only partially completes the task, Smith will again face a missed deadline or a lost opportunity; in addition, the job will have to be redone, adding unnecessarily to its cost.

Combine the number of undesirable outcomes that can occur in such routine situations with the enormous number of directives that managers issue daily and we may legitimately suspect that the aggregate dollar loss is staggering.

Substantial dollar loss, of course, is the bad news. The good news is that the problem is treatable without personnel shifts, without added technology, without organizational upset. By following a relatively simple set of guidelines, managers can significantly reduce the number of dollars they waste through the inefficient assignment of tasks.

Communication occurs in several steps. It begins when we formulate an idea (stage one of the process); it occurs through the verbal and non-verbal mechanisms by which the idea is transmitted (stage two, the transmittal aspect of communication); and it concludes when a respondent hears the message, decodes it, and signals an understanding of it (stage three, the feedback aspect of communication). Each of these three components of the communication process applies in issuing directives, and each suggests relatively simple ways to improve the process as a whole.

Stage One: The Message

An efficient directive, one that guarantees economical compliance, begins with a bit of forethought. Five general guidelines can assist here.

1. Formulate a clear purpose. Actually issuing the directive should not be the beginning of the process. Before doing so, managers might ask themselves two questions: "What do I want this person to do?" and "Why am I asking him or her to do this?" As obvious as these questions might seem, they enable a manager to anticipate and avoid possible misinterpretation and misunderstanding. In addition, thinking through answers helps the supervisor to explain to subordinates how their compliance might benefit the organization.

2. Identify the items that the directives will cover. Directives commonly consist of three components. The first is the activity itself—the task that needs to be done (for example, "Bring the latest reports," "Read page six," or "File contracts in blue files"). The second consists of the interactions with respect to the task ("Keep Pat informed of developments," "Get Pat's ideas on the project," or "Call Jim for approval before we begin"). The third component, the most difficult to handle, involves sentiments—internal states of individuals with respect to job performance (reflected in statements such as, "I want you to work hard to accomplish these changes," and "This will be frustrating, but I want you to keep your cool").

Managers will find it worthwhile to analyze their directives to determine which of these components is emphasized, and to keep in mind that each focus requests different kinds of employee response. The more clearly a manager understands the differences, the more likely the employee will respond in an appropriate fashion.

3. Limit the number of directives given at any one time. The three items mentioned above constitute the different aspects of a particular task; they account for what specific actions an employee must take, for other people who might be contacted in the course of these actions, and for the personal feelings of the employee with regard to the directive. For maximum comprehension, managers should limit a discussion to one directive alone, so that each of the three items is fully covered. Of course, such a limitation is not always possible. In any event, the fewer the directives given, the more likely complete understanding.

4. Formulate a sequence for presenting the items that the directive will cover. Directives containing sensibly ordered items are easier to present and much easier to understand and remember. Consider the differences between casual comments on a political issue and a carefully argued, sensibly structured speech: The one will be remembered if at all as a random sequence of ideas, the other will be perceived as a persuasive, memorable message. The same is true for assigning tasks. No one organizational pattern is best for all situations, but *any* organization is better than none. In assigning most routine tasks, a supervisor might first cite a specific organizational goal that the directive addresses, then state the behaviors, interactions, and sentiments that the employee is expected to achieve, and conclude with a summary of how the requested activities, interactions, and sentiments meet the organization's goals. But any plan is better than none so long as it is plotted in advance and serves as a basis for the actual discussion with the employee.

5. Review the language that the directive will use. Managers should ask themselves three questions about their messages: "Do my subordinates and I disagree on the meanings of the terms that we are about to use?" "Does the directive use loaded terminology that might produce bad feelings (terms like "stupid," "level of incompetence," "human engineering")?" "Does the directive have racist or sexist implications?" A "yes" answer to any of these questions suggests that the directive might be better phrased when issued.

Stage Two: Transmittal

Delivery of the directive is as important as the message. Managers might consider the following in communicating instructions to an employee.

1. Select appropriate communication channels. Communication channels consist of routine social acts that connect interdependent individuals. Letters, memos, reports, conferences, staff meetings, and conversations at the drinking fountain are all examples of routine social acts. These acts are termed "routine" because people have formed expectations about them—expectations about what kinds of behaviors are acceptable or are obligatory, who should begin speaking and who respond, and when and in what order things should be done. These expectations help us coordinate our behavior with others.

Some channels are better than others for particular directives. For example, a directive that emphasizes an employee sentiment ("I want you to keep your cool while dealing with Jones") might better be communicated in a one-on-one situation, in private, than in a memo or at the water fountain. On the other hand, a directive that includes complicated detail might better be transmitted in a memo format to obtain a permanent record.

2. Include internal summaries in the directive. Regardless of the format, internal summaries in a directive offer the opportunity to review items just mentioned and to anticipate new material. At the same time, they reinforce the message that has just been given and serve as a transitional device in the message as a whole.

3. Avoid overqualifying. In their attempts to be specific, supervisors sometimes go too far, qualifying and requalifying their points. For example, a supervisor might say, "Don't overreact to complaints of others. It's O.K. to defend yourself, but don't express resentment or anger. Of course, if you are truly angry, you've got to express those feelings. Then again. . . ." Overqualifying stems from feelings of anxiety and apprehension. While qualifiers help managers formulate accurate statements, overqualifying can signal uncertainty and insecurity and reduce a manager's credibility.

Stage Three: Comprehension

Once the directive has been planned and delivered, compliance begins. But compliance will occur only if the employee has comprehended the message, and two further steps will guarantee that comprehension has occurred.

1. Allow for feedback. Often we automatically reply "sure" when asked if we understand something when in fact we *don't* understand or we understand incompletely. Subordinates do the same. Managers can test their employees' comprehension of a directive by phrasing questions about directives so that employees must reveal their exact level of understanding. For example, they should avoid asking, "Do you understand what I've said?" Instead, they should ask, "Can you summarize what I've said?"

2. *Monitor for compliance.* Employees need to know that their work will be monitored and that noncompliance with instructions will be noted and will affect their performance evaluations. Otherwise, it's unlikely that they will treat the directive as a priority and follow it.

It's not always easy to follow these guidelines. It's particularly tough for those managers who issue directives on the spot, under pressure, and in response to unanticipated events. But paradoxically, the unanticipated events that necessitate hastily formulated directives often occur as a result of having previously issued ineffective directives—a vicious circle. Managerial success may depend on breaking that circle.

How Effective Is Your Follow-Through?

ROBERT CHASNOFF and PETER MUNIZ

Follow-through is a key supervisory function. It is the means used to check the degree to which an employee is performing assigned tasks and achieving his or her job objectives.

Follow-through is important. Another job in the department may depend on the degree to which the employee finishes one of his or her jobs. Or a customer may be waiting. Then, again, you may just want to know when the employee's task is completed so you can assign him or her the next task.

Follow-through is also important because it's a way to assess a subordinate's competence to take on more complex assignments and to determine if the team you have assembled is a capable one.

Prerequisites

Successful follow-through depends on a clear understanding between you and your employee about your employee's job. That means you must agree on such factors as:

Responsibility. This includes tasks or activities that the individual is expected to perform and objectives he or she is to achieve.

Authority. This refers to the individual's power to make decisions influencing that person's and others' results.

Accountability. This is the obligation to discharge responsibility and exercise authority to achieve results. The accountability may be to oneself, a supervisor, a team, or a customer, and it may be connected to the company's reward system.

Project objectives. Sometimes employees are assigned projects that are not a part of their regular responsibilities. These projects and their objectives must be clearly defined and agreed to by you and your subordinates.

Project and other timetables. Every responsibility or project should have a due date assigned so that you and your employee understand when it must be completed. In addition, substeps or activities necessary to achieve the objectives should be assigned due dates.

Reprinted from *Supervisory Management,* November 1985

Other Considerations

You may think that if you take all these factors into consideration, you will be successful when following through with your employees. This is not necessarily so. There are personal and organizational factors as well that can influence the effectiveness of your follow-through. They range from your motives and objectives in following through to the needs of your employees, to the culture of your company.

The role of the supervisor. Asking yourself the following questions can help you understand how your personal objectives and approach to follow through can affect its success.

1. Why am I following through? Do I want to cover myself in case my boss wants to know what's happening? Do I want to play "I gotcha" with my subordinate? Do I merely want to keep tabs on what's happening in my unit? Is this project very important to the entire organization?
2. Have I made a clear, mutually acceptable agreement with my employee regarding the timing, type, and purpose of the follow-through?
3. What feedback have I received from my subordinate regarding my follow-through stance and behavior?
4. Was I successful in improving performance, and if so, why? If not, what did I do wrong?
5. Is my follow-through really necessary or would the work get done without it?
6. Is the leadership style I'm using appropriate to the employee? For example, does my frequency and type of follow-through conflict with the subordinate's need for freedom? Or am I giving too much leeway to a subordinate on a project where results have to be supervised more closely? Worse, am I avoiding the discomfort of having to deal with an employee who is unable to achieve expected results?

The role of the employee. As the last group of questions implies, you must consider the needs of your employees when planning your follow-through. Some employees require constant follow-through because they don't know the job well enough yet or they want the boss's approval. Others wish they were not bothered by having to report to anyone except, perhaps, to a customer and then only with the finished product. They believe they have the talent, ability, self-confidence, and feel for accountability to the appropriate parties to warrant little, if any, follow-through. When you do not adjust to the different follow-through needs of your employees and apply the same frequency and type of follow-through to all, you can alienate your employees. To understand how they might feel, concentrate for a moment on yourself and your peers and the follow-through system that your boss uses with each supervisor at your level. Is it tailored to each individual or is the same system applied to all? If your boss uses the same system for everyone, how does it make you feel?

The hierarchical nature of organization. Besides employee needs and your own motives and behaviors, you have to take into consideration the built-in dependency nature of the hierarchical relationship. You don't want your follow-through approaches to reinforce this dependency. Rather, you want them to encourage subordinate freedom.

How Much Follow-Through?

This issue brings to the fore the problem most supervisors have of deciding how much follow-through to give. If you give too much, then you are probably fostering counterproductive dependency relationships. But if you refuse to work toward the "just right" level of follow-through, then you will probably end up using too little or, worse yet, completely abdicating that part of your job as supervisor.

To understand how much follow-through is enough, let's look at two case studies.

Case #1: The situation. James has been on the job for one month. He performed exceptionally well on his previous job and was transferred to this one when the incumbent was promoted to overseeing the entire unit. James' supervisor, then, knows James' job very well. One of the agreements she made with

James was that she would help him learn the job as rapidly as he wanted and would be available when he needed her help or advice. James' supervisor is about to assign him a job that falls within his normal responsibilities but that he has never done before.

Planning the follow-through. James' recent arrival on the job and his lack of knowledge about the responsibility to be assigned dictate that his supervisor plan for frequent follow-through. If failure to meet the responsibility successfully could lead to serious repercussions, James may have to prepare daily or weekly progress reports or meet with the supervisor to report in person every two or three steps in the assignment. If, however, the assignment represents little risk, then James and the supervisor may decide on less frequent follow-through and allow James to cover several activities before reporting on their status. James' inexperience on the job is a major consideration in this case. Furthermore, although James' supervisor may want to give him greater freedom in determining the frequency and type of follow-through, James does not yet have the necessary job knowledge to influence such a decision.

Case #2: The situation. Nina has been on her current job for three years. She has consistently demonstrated that she is an excellent performer and needs very little guidance. Besides handling her day-to-day responsibilities, she always gets her special projects done on time, often before their due date. A few weeks ago, her supervisor became curious about Nina's progress on a particular project and asked for a quick update. She gave him a verbal report, as requested, but after he thanked her for the information, Nina asked: "What's wrong, don't you think I'll get this one in on time?" The supervisor was surprised at her reaction, but the only response that he could think of at the time was: "No, I trust you; I was just curious about where you were on the project. Also, I think you'll agree that I have every right to know where everyone in my unit is regarding his or her job." What was left unsaid was that the supervisor was planning to assign to Nina a high priority emergency project that would be monitored very closely by upper management.

Planning the follow-through. Nina is a very talented, responsible, high performer who needs very little guidance or control from her supervisor. In determining the frequency and type of follow-through for Nina on the emergency project, her supervisor must first decide how much risk he is willing to take on it. If, for example, he is very anxious about the fact that top management will be watching the project very closely, he may want to follow through more closely than on others he previously assigned her. He must also be willing to admit the anxiety that he feels about the project and even to tell Nina about it if he insists on closer follow-through than usual.

Nina will most likely understand the pressure her supervisor is feeling from upper management, but she will probably want to influence the frequency and type of follow-through that will be implemented. She might not agree to a day-to-day or week-to-week follow-through. That would appear to her as excessive or having the potential to interfere with the crucial work required to get the project done. Nina's boss, then, must be ready to negotiate a follow-through process that will satisfy pressure from above, his own need to be informed of progress, and Nina's need to continue experiencing the level of freedom she has earned.

Each case determines the degree of follow-through. As these examples illustrate, there are no easy answers. But if you will follow the suggestions in this article, you'll find yourself better able to make judgments and will increase your effectiveness in fulfilling this responsibility.

Reversing Reverse Delegation

WILLIAM G. CALLARMAN and WILLIAM W. McCARTNEY

Doing our subordinates' jobs can eat up a lot of our time as supervisors. And through reverse delegation, we often find ourselves doing our employees' work. Despite our best efforts, at one time or another we have all fallen prey to what is a simple three-step process:

The bait is a simple statement to a supervisor. That statement may be:

- "Boy, I have had a rough time today."
- "Boss, I need your help with a real toughie."
- "Boss, we've got a problem."

With any of these statements or one similar to them, the employee succeeds in getting a supervisor's attention.

The swallow, the second step in the process, occurs after the employee has the manager's attention. The natural tendency of the supervisor to say then is:

- "Tell me about it."
- "What kind of help do you need?"
- "What kind of problem is it?"

The supervisor has swallowed the bait, hook and all.

The catch occurs after the supervisor and the employee have discussed the problem and the help the employee needs. At the end of the discussion, after the manager and employee have identified a number of solutions, the supervisor says something like, "Thank you for making me aware of the problem. Let me think about it, and I'll get back to you."

The supervisor is now caught—the problem is no longer the employee's. The supervisor has accepted the reverse delegation, and the problem is now his or hers.

Sound familiar? Such situations occur often in the workplace and are generally due to one of six reasons (or some combination of them):

Reprinted from *Management Solutions*, July 1988

1. The employee wishes to avoid risk.
2. The employee is afraid of criticism.
3. The subordinate lacks confidence.
4. The employee lacks the necessary information and/or resources to do the job.
5. The manager wants to be "needed."
6. The manager is unable to say "no" to requests for help.

The employee wishes to avoid risk. It is easier for some employees to ask their manager what to do, how to do it, or even to get him or her to do a job than it is for them to accept the risks associated with doing it wrong. Getting the boss to do it is a way of sharing, if not shedding, responsibility. If an employee is successful in avoiding risk over a period of time, a habit of dependence results and the employee rarely acts in the future on his or her own.

The employee is afraid of criticism. Employees are like most of us in that they dislike criticism and will avoid placing themselves in positions that will generate it. And the easiest way to avoid criticism is to do nothing for which one will be criticized. Therefore, employees don't do a job when they can reverse delegate it to their manager so he or she cannot criticize when it is not done right.

The employee lacks confidence. When employees lack confidence in their abilities, they avoid doing things that will expose their incompetence. Thus they do only those things they know they can and leave the remainder to the supervisor to do.

The employee lacks the necessary information and/or resources to do the job. The employee may say something like, "Boss, I'd love to get this done, but I can't because I don't have the time or the report from the marketing department to get it done right." The boss may respond, "Well, let me contact the marketing department for that information, and I'll get it done." *Gotcha.*

The manager wants to be needed. Many supervisors believe that they must know everything that is going on. They think it is important to the successful completion of the group's goals, and that employees can't make decisions. Therefore, they make all employees' decisions to demonstrate their indispensability.

The boss is unable to say "no" to requests for help. Many managers encourage, even demand, their employees check with them before doing anything. Also, participative management encourages managers to provide support and assistance to employees whenever needed. The result is a dependency by employees on their manager.

Reversing the Pattern

Turning this pattern around—reversing reverse delegation—requires training, resource planning, communication, and just plain common-sense management.

Training. Employees wish to avoid risk-taking, are afraid of criticism, and lack confidence often because they are improperly trained to do their jobs—they simply don't know how to do them well. Training programs that properly equip employees with the skills to do the job go a long way toward instilling confidence. Employees can also be trained to understand that a certain amount of risk-taking is necessary for growth and development and to accept the challenges that risk brings. The most crucial element to any such training is that the employees realize that the purpose of training is to improve performance and that improved performance will be rewarded.

Resource planning. Part of delegating tasks is the careful identification of all the resources that will be necessary for their successful accomplishment—times, tools, skills, and authority. A close examination of a staff's jobs may indicate that some staffers have been delegated far too much and other staffers far too little; that the necessary information is not available, nor is the equipment or other tools; that the individual is ill-equipped to do the job at hand because of lack of training; or that the individual does not have authority commensurate with responsibility. Proper resource planning will overcome these kinds of problems.

Communication. We all work best when we know where we stand with our bosses and what our bosses think of our performance. We can gain this knowledge only through communication. Managers must clearly communicate expectations, how performance will be evaluated against those expectations, the evaluation itself, and what they will do to assist subordinates to overcome weaknesses and bolster strengths.

Common-sense management. The Golden Rule has a great deal of merit. None of us likes to be criticized openly, in front of others, or to have only our poor qualities pointed out. Managers must realize that criticism must be constructive and offered in private. Additionally, they might take a note from the book *The One-Minute Manager:* ". . . catch them doing something right." How different that is from the usual behavior of supervisors. Managers think they should find all the things that their subordinates do wrong, criticize them in front of their peers, and remind them of all the things that were done wrong during the annual performance appraisal. How different things might be if they focused instead on the things that were done right and rewarded employees for those.

Passing the Buck Down

When employees come to their supervisor with the bait, "Boss, we've got a problem," the manager must ask about the problem, but he or she should do it at his or her convenience, not the demand of the subordinates. For example, when an employee comes to a manager with a problem, the manager might say, "I am interested in your problem, but unless it is absolutely essential that we discuss it now, I'd like to see you at three this afternoon to discuss it."

With this response, the manager is saying that, yes, the problem should be discussed, but, no, not now. The manager might even add, "Why don't you think about the problem in the meantime and be prepared to discuss possible solutions."

When the discussion takes place, it should center around understanding the problem—separating symptoms from causes—and it should conclude with an examination of possible solutions.

The final statement in that discussion should be one from the manager saying not, "Thank you for making me aware of the problem; let me think about it, and I'll get back to you," but rather, "Thank you for making me aware of the problem. The next time I see you, make me aware of the solution, and let us get together tomorrow afternoon at two for that discussion."

This statement does a number of good things for the manager:

First, it makes clear that the manager thinks the employee can make decisions.

Second, it establishes that the manager expects the employee to make decisions.

Third, it establishes a timeframe in which a decision must be made.

Fourth, it is the first step in an evolutionary process that will reduce the amount of time the manager will spend in dealing with employee problems.

Evolutionary Process

Looking at this evolutionary process, the next step will be taken once the employee is relatively comfortable with his or her boss. Once that relative comfort is there, the employee will approach the manager and say, "Boss, we've got a problem; here's how I recommend that it be solved."

Over a period of time, with the manager and employee feeling good about the recommended solution, the next step in the evolutionary process is the statement: "Boss, yesterday we had a problem, and here's how I solved it."

Through this evolutionary process, employees will develop a "good feel" for what their supervisor wants; will gain confidence; will learn to take risks, but know the kind of risks the manager expects; and criticism should be minimized. Discussions with the manager in earlier stages of the process will enable both employee and manager to understand the information and other resources necessary to do the job and train the employee in how to gather the information and marshall the resources to solve problems.

By training, resource management, communication, and common-sense management, many of the problems associated with reverse delegation will be overcome—indeed, reverse delegation will be reversed.

Part VI

DISCIPLINE AND TERMINATION

Productive Progressive Discipline Procedures

ROGER B. MADSEN and BARBARA KNUDSON-FIELDS

Jerry Thompson was furious. When an ineffective employee quit several months ago, he was relieved. If the employee had not quit, Jerry probably would have had to fire him. When he chose to leave, Jerry considered himself fortunate. But then the employee filed for unemployment compensation. Now the company lawyer has handed Jerry a copy of a civil suit, which includes issues raised at the unemployment compensation hearing.

How can an employee who voluntarily quit be causing Jerry all these problems?

All too often a supervisor adopts the attitude of the proverbial ostrich, ignoring a performance problem in the hope it will go away. Worse, the manager will give pay raises, praise, and positive performance appraisals to these employees. The manager may believe that if the issue is confronted, it will only make the situation worse.

When the supervisor finally decides to be tough minded and confronts the employee, the situation may further deteriorate. The supervisor may find himself or herself with an angry and antagonistic employee who wants to get even, rather than an employee who is highly motivated to make behavioral changes.

Reprinted from *Management Solutions*, May 1987

The Need for Answers

Situations like this often happen when supervisors don't have clearly defined policies and procedures to assist them in resolving performance and discipline issues. Otherwise, they can result in grievances, litigation, or the unnecessary intervention of an external third party.

More than ever before, managers are having to defend their personnel actions in courts of law. Compensation claims and hearings can be utilized in Title VII and wrongful discharge cases. Anti-discrimination laws require that all personnel transactions be free of discriminatory treatment and impact.

Court decisions are made case by case, and no set of specific rules can provide absolute protection, but with the growing number of cases going to the courts, it is important for employers to have a discipline process as an integral part of their personnel policy and procedures. In addition, supervisors must be fully informed and trained to properly implement those procedures.

With the continued increase in the number of court cases, the inclination of supervisors may be to avoid addressing problems in the hopes of avoiding a lawsuit. But this defensive style of management can result in ineffective supervision, poor productivity, and low morale. Besides, a supervisor does not have to carry a big stick. Punishment should not be the goal. An employee's perception of the fairness and quality of the work environment is often found in the discipline program. Employees expect sound management, and they appreciate receiving information regarding their performance so long as the information is presented in a constructive and objective manner.

Employees need to know the job requirements and expectations of their supervisors. They need to have ongoing feedback about their performance and behavior. It is a shock for an employee to find out that he or she has been devoting too much time and effort to doing the wrong thing. An annual performance review or a termination meeting is not the time for the employee to hear that he or she has not been meeting expectations for the last six months. Many employees are hurt and angry. Unless handled in a timely manner, the situation is perceived as unfair and morale is debilitated.

Discipline Steps to Consider

Despite job clarification, there will be occasions where it is beneficial to confront employees about their performance or behavior. The progressive and productive discipline process provides for increasing penalities for repeated infractions. Assuming the offense is not so serious as to warrant immediate suspension or termination, such as assault and battery, destruction of company property, or theft, the process should begin with an informal conversation about the situation and the expectations. If the performance or behavior does not improve, a second meeting is held, and if necessary a third meeting, which may result in a a written warning. The discipline process should be positive but corrective; it should encourage and provide the employee with an opportunity to change. But if that does not happen, then there is the basis *and* documentation for termination for cause.

Problems that usually can be addressed in the progressive and productive discipline process include, but are not limited to, performance or behavior concerns (like quality of work, use of time, responsiveness to requests, and insubordination and attitude problems) and attendance concerns (tardiness, absenteeism and sick leave, coffee breaks, and lunch hour abuses).

Preparation. When a situation arises that requires the supervisor's intervention, the first step is to gather the facts in preparation for a meeting with the employee or employees. It is essential to define the problem. Supervisors should state their perception of what is happening and what they want to have happen; the difference is the problem. Who is involved? When and where is it happening or not happening? Why do they think this situation has occurred?

Timeliness is important, and the matter should be addressed as soon after the fact as possible. If a supervisor waits too long, the situation may no longer be relevant. Further, the employee may become angry if he or she was not informed that there was a problem, then is told that the problem has been ongoing for six months and somehow the employee should have guessed something was wrong.

It is usually wise to allow time for the parties involved to cool off if the situation has been an emotional one. This is especially true for the supervisor. An emotional confrontation by a supervisor often results in an extremely defensive and agitated employee. Facts cannot be properly discussed when people are excited.

Meeting. Once sufficient information has been gathered, the manager should meet with the employee to discuss the situation. The meeting should take place in a private office with no interruptions. A lot of initial small talk should be avoided—the employee will be anxious to know why he or she is there.

This initial meeting should be informal, positive, and supportive. The supervisor's goal is to motivate the employee to change. This is also a good opportunity to praise the individual for any work that is meeting or exceeding standards, and not just dwell on the negative.

State the problem. This can be done by identifying what is happening and what the supervisor wants to have happen: "Sally, I have noticed recently that the reports that are due at the end of each day have not been getting in until noon the next day."

The expectation or rule must be reasonable, the employee must have clear knowledge of the expectation or rule, and the employee should know the probable consequence of not meeting the expectation or breaking the rule.

Listen. The supervisor first states his or her concern, then he or she attempts to elicit information. "Sally, why are the reports not getting in on time?" The supervisor may believe that he has all the facts, but he still needs to hear what Sally believes are the issues.

In this example, the supervisor needs also to be certain that Sally knows the importance of having the reports in as requested and that she has the tools, skills, and information necessary to complete the task. Is anything interfering with getting them in? Have her job demands changed recently? Are personal problems interfering with her work performance?

A word of caution: Personal problems often interfere with work, but it is not a supervisor's responsibility to become involved in an employee's personal problems. A good rule is to refer personal problems to the personnel department or an outside professional resource. Supervisors can be empathetic and supportive, but they should remain focused on work-related concerns.

In this "listening" part of the process, it is important for the supervisor to ask "what" and "how" questions rather than "did" or "do" questions, which can be answered with a yes or a no. This should be considered a problem-solving process and the employee should be truly a part of this process. As such, he or she will have an investment in the solution working as well as be less likely to oppose the supervisor in court.

Most employees feel a need to tell their story, and they should be given this chance. This not only defuses their initial defensiveness but also elicits valuable information. Sometimes, the problem under discussion is only a symptom of a deeper problem. Going back to the previously mentioned problem, for example, Sally may say, "It is not my fault. I do not get the information from John until four o'clock, and I have too many things that have to be done at the last minute. Besides, you never use that information until the afternoon of the next day anyway."

The supervisor then has to ask himself if he really does need the information by quitting time. Let's assume he does need the information first thing—that he is required to phone in those reports early in the morning but that he then waits until afternoon to meet with staffers about the reports. He has to explain that to Sally. It shouldn't require a long explanation. In fact, supervisors frequently talk too much. A brief and to-the-point explanation is best.

Get agreement on the problem and explore options. Toward that end, the supervisor might say, "Sally, I do need those reports by quitting time so this is a real problem for me. I am relying on you to meet the deadlines. Let's see what we can figure out."

Sally may have a priority problem, or she may have too much work to do. Why is the information not getting to her in time? Can it be transmitted sooner, or does she have to live with those time frames? Are there any real obstacles that are in fact a part of this problem? The conversation should focus on the problem and the need to correct that problem.

Develop a plan. Sally should be asked for input. "What needs to happen to get those reports to me?"

The focus of responsibility should be on her efforts. "I can understand how not getting the information on time interferes with getting the reports to me, but how can you make that work since I do have to have them?" The emphasis has to be on the supervisor's expectations.

Summary and follow-up. After a satisfactory plan has been established, Sally should be asked to state her understanding of the problem and the conclusions reached. This reinforces her ownership of the problem. A time should be set to get together to check on the issue and, if resolved, reinforce Sally's efforts.

Documentation. Even with this informal conversation, there often needs to be some documentation, depending on the severity of the problem. This need usually can be handled with a handwritten note for the file. Employees will often ask if this incident will become a permanent part of their record. Unless there are extenuating circumstances, the answer is no. These conversations should be considered a part of the day-to-day coaching and feedback process. Only if the employee's performance or behavior does not change should the process take on a more formal note.

Should that be the case, another meeting should be held. The employee should be reminded of the previous conversation and the agreement reached. The employee should be aware that this second meeting is a verbal reminder and a part of the discipline process.

Of course, if the situation has changed in some way, the supervisor can opt to let this session be a coaching session. Personnel policy and procedures will serve as a guideline and should be written in such a manner to allow supervisory flexibility.

Documentation of this second meeting should include names, dates of incidents, the problem, expectations, the employee's explanation, and the meeting results. A follow-up date is again set. If no progress has been made by the employee by this date, the meeting process is repeated, but the result is now a written reminder, with a copy to the employee and to the supervisor's files. Depending on the nature of the problem or if in doubt, it may be appropriate to involve the personnel department at this stage of the problem-solving process.

As the supervisor moves from the coaching through the discipline process, the meetings become more frequent and formal. The employee should clearly understand that he or she is involved in a discipline process. The consequences of not meeting the expectations should be clear. Documentation in each subsequent step covers all pertinent information, including a summary of previous conversations.

Reinforcement

All too often, poor performance is rewarded and desired performance or behavior is ignored. In dealing with a problem performer, demotions, pay decreases, suspension, and probation are all possible consequences of continuation of the behavior in question. A judge will not easily understand why a supervisor gave a raise to an employee who is in the middle of the discipline process. And rarely does an undeserved promotion motivate an employee to change.

Discharge: The Final Step

If all else fails, the employee should be terminated. Before taking that final step, however, a manager should check his or her documentation and discuss the situation with the personnel department or company attorney. Did the employee have sufficient opportunity to change? Did the employee understand the expectations and the consequences of not meeting those expectations? Has the supervisor consistently and fairly applied the rules? Are there alternatives to consider, such as a transfer, demotion, or leave of absence?

The goal of this process is to improve productivity and enhance employee morale by coaching and encouraging, but some employees are just not in the right job or situation and changes must be made. If this proves to be the case and termination can be supported by documentation, then the termination meeting must be held.

Regardless of how one approaches the termination, it will be difficult for all parties. A meeting on Friday should be avoided. Early-in-the-week terminations allow the employee to start the job search process. The sermon itself should be brief and to the point. Once the employee has been told he or she is no longer working for the company, little else will be heard.

Another appointment should be set to review benefit or insurance procedures or an appointment made with personnel for the employee to review the situation.

Some employees will try to argue their supervisor out of the termination. The supervisor has to respond firmly but sensitively. For example, "I can understand, Sally, how you are upset by this decision, but we have previously outlined the consequences. The decision is firm."

All documentation becomes a part of the file, unless otherwise stated in company policy. If the manager has to appear before a commission or the courts to support his or her termination decision, the documentation may be useful.

Sometimes a situation arises in which the process, or at least a part of the process, is inappropriate. Fighting, stealing, sabotage, or whatever, requires more immediate action, but the facts still need to be gathered before a termination decision is made. Unless the facts are so indisputable at the moment that firing is justifiable, suspension, pending an investigation, may be the more appropriate action until all the facts are in.

Management has the right to have employees satisfactorily performing their jobs in a constructive and timely manner. In turn, employees have a right to expect fair and consistent treatment from the management. A progressive discipline process creates a well ordered and productive work environment with clear and understandable rules.

Discipline With a Clear Sense of Purpose

JOSEPH SELTZER

There are two primary goals of a disciplinary system. When an individual breaks a rule or behaves inappropriately or incorrectly, the first objective is to change that behavior by providing information to the employee about the offending behavior and what alternative behaviors would be acceptable. The psychological principle here is that behavior that is punished will be less likely to be repeated. The individual, recognizing that a particular behavior will lead to punishment and that an alternative behavior will not, should choose the latter in the future.

The second goal of the system relates to other employees. Information about disciplinary action travels rapidly through a company's grapevine. If other employees feel that a supervisor is unfair or weak, there is a tendency to lose respect for the rules—and for the supervisor.

If a supervisor doesn't handle one disciplinary situation well, he or she is likely to have lots of others.

In exercising discipline, it's important to remember, however, that not all discipline cases are the same. The goals may differ in relation to the particular employee and may be more than the two primary ones. The chart in Figure 1 identifies four general types of discipline situations. For each type, the goals of discipline are different.

Type I Employees

A Type I employee usually follows the rules. Where there is a violation, it is frequently because the employee didn't know or understand the rule. For example:

> Mary Smith worked as a clerk in the accounts receivable department of a large bank. She had a good record of performance and attendance in her four years, but last Monday she was late for work and didn't call in. When she arrived, she explained that her car wouldn't start. She is told that it is important to call the office if she will be late and is given a written warning (the first step in the formal discipline system).

Reprinted from *Management Solutions*, February 1987

Figure 1

Type		Primary Goal	Secondary Goal
Types of Problem Employees			
Type I	does not intentionally violate the rules, does so unintentionally and infrequently.	To correct the behavior, to inform and train.	To maintain the individual's motivation.
Type II	will violate the rules when he or she considers some treatment unfair; will occasionally violate the rules.	To correct the behavior *and* to avoid discipline problems with others.	To identify and deal with why the person feels treated unfairly. Otherwise, future problems will occur.
Type III	will violate the rules whenever he or she can get away with it, generally creates problems, and is often disciplined.	To avoid discipline problems with others.	To document the use of discipline (toward eventual termination).
Type IV	is not so much a problem employee as an employee with a problem.	To get help for the individual and to provide a reason to use that help.	To document if the individual is unwilling to seek help or the problem recurs.

In this example, we have a good employee who apparently doesn't understand the need to let her supervisor know that she will be late. The goal of discipline is to provide information and a reason to behave differently in the future (to avoid additional punishment). By dealing directly with this situation, the supervisor is less likely to have future problems with either Mary Smith or other employees.

Type II Employees

A Type II employee will often follow the rules if the person feels that he or she is being treated fairly. However, if something seems unfair or inequitable, then the Type II employee may change his or her behavior in an attempt to "get even." If that is the case, the employee may even violate the rules or in other ways become a discipline problem (such as giving less to the job). This is a more complex situation than that of a Type I employee, because the supervisor's actions have a direct impact on both the offending employee and his or her fellow workers. The supervisor must deal with the employee in a way that is seen as "fair" by others, or they too may become Type II problems. Further, the supervisor needs to learn what was perceived to be "unfair" and change it if possible. Otherwise the employee may continue to be a Type II discipline problem. For example:

Jack Anderson has worked in the maintenance department of a public transit company for 11 years. While there has always been a rule against bringing coffee into the work area, it has been ignored for many years, and some of the workers will carry coffee cups back from the morning break. Recently, Paul Jones was named supervisor, and he told his subordinates that a number of changes would be made in the department, including no coffee in the work area. A number of people complained, but all except Anderson stopped bringing coffee into the work area. For two days Jones ignored Anderson's violation of the new rule, but on the third day Jones called Anderson into his office and gave him a one-day suspension. At the end of the week, Jones was amazed that his department's productivity had dropped to an all-time low. Even people who had never drunk coffee were disgruntled.

Now, rather than a single discipline problem, Jones has a major morale problem. A better course of action would have been to call Anderson into the office on the first day and discuss the situation. At that time a warning could have been issued. Jones might have said, "If you bring coffee to your work station, you will be punished according to the company's policies." If the offense were repeated, Anderson then would have been punished. Jones might also have discussed his reason for the new rule with the other employees.

Type III Employees

A Type III employee is a habitual offender. He or she is often disciplined but with little change in behavior. For such an employee, the major goal of using the discipline system should be to avoid problems with others. If other employees see a Type III person treated "unfairly" (which could include ignoring the problem), then they are likely to change their behaviors (and become Type II problems). The supervisor must avoid widening the discipline problem by dealing directly with the Type III person according to the company's policies and procedures. The supervisor should do so even if it seems unlikely to change the Type III employee's behavior because it is important to document the use of discipline for the purpose of eventually terminating the employee. Here's an example of a Type III employee:

George Harris was recently transferred to Joe King's department. He is very stubborn and difficult to supervise. King assigned Harris to test the electrical systems being rebuilt by the department. He did about 90 percent of the job in a slow but satisfactory manner. However, when King attempted to get him to use a different procedure to test one of the new types of controls, he gave King a "hard time." Later when King checked, he was still doing it the same way as before. King reinstructed him, but Harris continued to use the incorrect method. King had the personnel department send him Harris' file and in it he found some interesting information. Some years ago, Harris had reached the top level in the organization's progressive discipline system. However, when he was terminated, Harris filed a grievance and was reinstated. Since that time, Harris had been disciplined for "insubordination" and "poor work performance" numerous times and had been transferred six times. It appeared that the past record was ignored with each transfer, and he started at the bottom of the discipline system again.

King should now begin to document the "poor work performance" to make sure that in the likely event of continued discipline the final termination will stick. If King does not deal with Harris, other employees will be encouraged to "do it their own way" and King's effectiveness as a supervisor will be diminished.

Type IV Employees

Finally, there is a Type IV employee. This is a person who has an addiction to alcohol or drugs or some other personal problem that interferes with his or her work performance. While the discipline system could be applied to this person, it is my belief that the company has a responsibility to get help for the individual. Only if the person is unwilling to be treated or helped should the discipline system be applied. A policy that allows a person to ask for help (and pays for it as a health benefit), and also states that if the person does not deal with the problem he or she will be subject to future disciplinary action, would be both effective and socially responsible.

For example:

> Anne Andrews works in a clerical department of a large organization. Generally a good worker, recently she has begun calling in "sick" most Mondays. Her supervisor has heard from some of her fellow workers that sometimes she goes on a "binge." The supervisor has no reason to believe that Anne ever has been intoxicated while at work, but she often looks as if she has a hangover. Because of her long service, Anne has accumulated a lot of sick days, but in the past year and a half she has used all of them up. The next time she is absent, the supervisor could choose to discipline her.

The most appropriate action would be for the supervisor to tell Anne that she must be at work. He should state that he doesn't care why her absences occurred but that the situation must change. He could then suggest the possiblity of a specific treatment program. Another alternative would be to send Anne to the company medical department or personnel department (or to a union representative if there is one who handles these sorts of referrals). Again, other employees are likely to be aware of the problem and expect the supervisor to respond in an appropriate manner.

Needless to say, discipline systems in organizations should be seen as only one of the managerial tools available to a supervisor. They should not be overused and make threats the only way to change behavior. On the other hand, a discipline system is important because it can bring about change. And if it is used well, it won't be necessary to use it very often. But to use it well a supervisor must recognize how all discipline situations are not the same and must have a clear understanding of his or her objectives.

How to Fire Without Getting Burned

L. MARSHALL STELLFOX

Increasing numbers of employees are taking to the courts, challenging the right of supervisors to fire them—and they're winning substantial awards. As a supervisor, it's important for you to understand why and what you can do about it.

Frequently, employee claims are based on alleged violations of EEOC regulations. While discrimination charges continue to involve race, color, and creed, the big surge in EEOC-based cases has been in the areas of age and sex bias—with awards often running in six and sometimes seven figures. To cite a few examples: A utility settled an age-discrimination suit for $3.2 million in back wages and extra pension benefits. An airline had to pay $18 million to pilots and engineers it dismissed at age 60. And a drug company paid several million in back wages to 107 white collar employees aged 40 to 65.

Employees are also taking to the courts for alleged violations of other agreements. Unfair firing suits in the case of union employees are expected to spread because of a recent federal appeals court decision in San Francisco stating that union workers are not barred from bringing such suits because they can use a formal grievance and arbitration process.

In fact, if you fire a union employee you will probably face a grievance—and it's a reasonably good bet that the matter will eventually reach arbitration, if not the courts. A recent survey indicated several reasons why companies lose such cases. These include inconsistent rule enforcement, unreasonable application of unreasonable rules, excessive penalties in terms of company policies, evidence that doesn't support the charge, and not telling employees which actions can bring penalties.

While these developments do not abrogate your right as a supervisor to terminate employees for legitimate business reasons, they emphasize that you must abide by the limitations placed on you by collective bargaining agreements, antidiscrimination legislation, civil service regulations, and employment contracts.

Precautionary Measures

To be on the safe side, before firing an employee ask yourself, Is he or she in the protected age group (over 40)? Is the employee being dismissed for cause? Is the employee to be replaced by someone younger? Many times an airtight case is found to have a slow leak, as when court-subpoenaed personnel records of an employee let go for not "cutting the mustard" are found to contain annual performance

Reprinted from *Supervisory Management*, February 1985

review and salary action forms rating the employee as doing a good, satisfactory, and often excellent job. This, needless to say, is difficult to explain to the hearing judge!

The way to avoid this pitfall is to present accurate data during performance reviews and evaluations. Don't give an employee a distorted evaluation to support a request for a pay increase or to avoid confrontation when discussing performance. Distortions of actual performance not only make defense against unfair charges difficult but weaken the merit-salary program, destroy the performance-review system, and deprive the employee of knowing about performance problems so they can be corrected.

Have explicit, clear procedures for terminating unsatisfactory employees. The worker should be told specifically how he or she is failing on the job and given a specific time by which he or she must demonstrate improvement. If the ax must finally fall, the worker should have been fairly and adequately warned.

Be certain all disciplinary action, warnings, and corrective comments are in writing and in the employee's file.

If evaluation reports and salary-increase recommendations have been inflated, or if there is nothing in the files to indicate that the employee has not been performing adequately or has been warned, it may be wise to delay the employee release for another six months so a factual record can be established to support discharge.

To fire from the hip without substantiation could make you personally liable as well as your company.

If a review of the records, files, and discharge circumstances indicate a green light without fear of court action, there is still a proper way to fire employees without causing unnecessary ill will, an adverse impact on the morale of remaining employees, and pain for you if you are doing the firing.

Telling people they no longer have a job is traumatic for both parties. In a recent Goodrich & Sherwood survey of top companies, over 90 percent of those polled stated that terminating employees was the most stressful part of their job. For this reason you should be aware of the apprehension and anxiety you will likely experience, and you should recognize that these reactions will sometimes trigger negative emotions in the employee being terminated. Your inappropriate remarks or handling of the situation may serve as the basis for a lawsuit or may so traumatize the terminee that the job search process is severely complicated. So often is this the case, in fact, that you are advised to involve a termination expert at this time.

If you choose to go it alone, the problems resulting from termination can be minimized by following these guidelines.

What You Should Do

- Within the first few minutes of the interview, notify the person that the termination decision has been made. This is not a social time; don't treat it as such. In most cases, the terminee will respond emotionally. Allow the person to express these feelings and ventilate. Empathize with the individual, but be firm. Listen to the employee's comments and jot down concerns and questions for future follow-up.

- Present the facts as they are. Don't gloss over the real problem or give a phony excuse for termination; you may have to support it later. Also, this is not the time for platitudes or conflicting stories that will in the long run complicate the situation, so don't be defensive or argue.

- Break the news in a way that will alleviate undue trauma. Discuss continuing benefits and severance pay to reduce the immediate shock. In many cases, when the employee has heard the statement, "You're being released" or "Your job has been eliminated," additional conversation will be turned off and tuned out. In many cases, the terminee hears only positive comments and is unable to address the problem. While allowing the individual to express feelings, don't encourage unrealistic hopes about a change of decision. Confirm that the decision is final and the subject is not open for debate or reprieve.

Companies have tended toward more liberal severance policies in the past few years in an attempt to soften the terminated employee's attitude toward unfair treatment and increased tendency toward litigation.

In addition to internal termination assistance at the time of firing, more companies are engaging the services of professional outplacement firms to help the employee in the job search. Over 60 percent of the major firms Goodrich & Sherwood recently surveyed use outplacement services to assist fired or laid-off employees. This represents a dramatic increase over the past two years when only 38 percent of the companies polled used this service.

To sum up, if you practice fire prevention, you need not get burned. Plan the termination of employees as carefully as you would any other major business project, and you will minimize the stress for all, short-circuit litigation, and end up with a clear conscience.

To Fire or Not to Fire?

STEVEN BUCKMAN

Sue Miller was upset. She had assigned Ed Alcott the responsibility of keeping the personnel records on benefits changes up to date and the recent in-house audit that was completed showed the company had been paying insurance dues for employees who had left months ago. What's more, several employees who had been with the company for four or five months had never been added to the insurance eligibility listings.

Sue now had the unpleasant task of reviewing these errors with the insurance company and, of course, her own supervisor. She knew she would have to have another talk with Ed. This would be the fourth time in the last six months she had discovered problem areas in Ed's work. As she prepared yet another counselling memo, she asked herself, "Where is this leading? I can't continue to give Ed counselling memos. What if he never improves?"

This situation is not unfamiliar to all managers.

Whither Discipline?

The system of progressive discipline implies that any disciplinary steps taken will "lead" or "progress" to a specific goal. That goal is resolution of the problem.

Often, in fact usually, the resolution of the problem occurs when the employee's poor performance or unsatisfactory conduct is brought to the employee's attention. For example, after Jane Smith had been late for work over a period of several days, her supervisor, Bill Greenburgh, mentioned it to her. When the latenesses still continued, Bill called Jane into his office, explained the importance of on-time attendance, and made it clear that continued lateness could result in termination. Once Jane understood the importance of the problem, she made efforts to correct it.

However, in some cases, the employee is either unable or unwilling to correct the problem. That is when the supervisor must make the decision either to retain the employee and continue to work with him or her or to fire the individual.

"Sack," "let go," "terminate," "fire," "make redundant," "dehire," "ask for resignation"—these words have different connotations but the effect is the same. It is not a decision that should be taken lightly. There are serious emotional, economic, and legal implications when a manager fires an employee.

The employee must deal with anger, disappointment, uncertainty, and anxiety from being fired.

Reprinted from *Supervisory Management*, February 1986

For the company, there is the significant loss of years of training and experience that will be difficult, if not impossible, to replace.

Many managers look for easy answers. "Should I fire someone after two writeups or after three?" "What absentee rate is grounds for dismissal?" "If I fired Joe last year for this, shouldn't I fire Susan for it today?" Any manager with more than a few years' experience understands that answers to the "to fire or not to fire" question are not easily found.

Each case is different. The manager must consider a host of issues, including the past performance of the individual.

Also to be considered are any special circumstances surrounding the person's employment, company policy, and employees' legal rights. The courts have put pressure on managers to have sufficient documentation to justify a termination decision.

The information below and the chart in Figure 1 will help managers think through the decision process. It is a hard decision—there is no way around it. But these questions should help a manager clarify his or her thoughts on the issue.

A Matter of Training

1. Has the employee received adequate training/information about the job? If the employee is in a new assignment, has he or she been given the opportunity to learn the job? Different people have different learning curves. Sometimes an extra week with a new employee will turn him or her into an asset.

A related question to ask if this is a new assignment is, "Did the employee understand the job going into it?" It is possible that the employee was "over-sold" on the job and has found it to be not what was promised. This can cause performance problems.

2. Does the employee understand the seriousness of the problem? Has the manager or supervisor explained to the employee the possibility of job loss if the problem is not corrected? No employee should be brought into a termination interview and be completely caught off guard.

Except in a few circumstances (for instance, theft or commission of a felony), employees should be given some written notice of the problem under discussion with language that makes it clear that the employee's job is in jeopardy.

Too many managers regard written counselling memos as a nuisance; however, a written memo records the details of the meeting as well as sends a strong message to the employee about the seriousness of the problem under discussion.

Protected Groups

3. Is the employee a member of a protected minority group? If so, has the manager allowed that fact to cloud his or her judgment? For example, has the manager placed unreasonable demands on an employee because she is a female in a traditionally male position? Or does the manager have a personal prejudice against an employee because he is a recovered drug or alcohol abuser? Or is the manager opposed to having older workers in jobs that have traditionally been held by younger workers?

If the employee is a member of a protected minority, it might be helpful to have someone in the personnel department review the decision to terminate before the decision is implemented.

Time to Improve

4. Has the manager given the employee adequate time to correct the problem? It may not be realistic for a manager to expect a long-term employee to correct performance problems in a matter of a week or two.

Figure 1
To Terminate – or to Counsel More

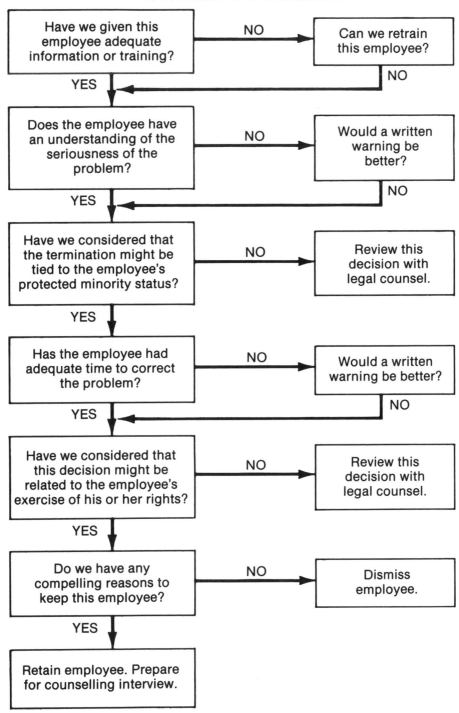

If the manager is counselling an employee with, say, an attendance problem, setting follow-up dates and then reviewing progress on those dates is important. If the employee has shown progress, he or she should be told so. If there has been no progress, that should be communicated as well.

If a manager isn't sure the employee has had adequate time to correct the problem, there is justification for keeping the employee on another few weeks to determine if progress is possible.

5. Is the termination of this employee related to his or her exercise of employment rights? For example, is the employee being fired *in part* because he or she filed a complaint with a state agency regarding the company? Terminations made because an employee exercises certain rights available under equal employment laws, the National Labor Relations Act, ERISA, and the like are illegal. Recently, the courts have been more willing to step in to protect an employee who has been dismissed if the employee can demonstrate that the dismissal was related to his or her participation in a protected activity.

A related consideration is, "Does this termination violate company policy?" Some companies require that supervisors follow very strictly defined procedures before dismissing an employee. In all instances, companies require their managers to show cause for the discharge.

6. Does the manager have a good reason to keep the employee? Obviously, the company cannot retain employees who are not productive. In spite of everything else you may read, managers are perfectly within their rights to dismiss employees for bona fide business reasons. The mere fact that an employee coincidentally falls into a protected class does not make that employee immune from dismissal. *If an employee does not meet the reasonable and consistent standards set by the employer, he or she should be discharged.*

In Conclusion

Managers are urged to carefully consider their decision to discharge an employee; however, managers have a responsibility to their other workers to set reasonable standards and then stick to them. Managers cannot allow one employee to regularly fall below the standards to which other employees are adhering.

Avoiding Wrongful Discharge Suits

LAURENCE P. CORBETT

Employment at will—an employer's right to discharge an employee for any reason or for no reason at all—is on the way out.

Lawful termination for cause is taking its place. More and more wrongful discharge cases are going to court, with unhappy results for many businesses. In California, for example, plaintiffs win 70 percent of the wrongful discharge cases that go before juries and awards range from $200,000 to $1,000,000.

In many cases, an employer has lost because an inexperienced first-line supervisor made a mistake that higher management could not correct.

Many employers have had long experience with just-cause termination cases under union contracts. Arbitrators Adolph Koven and Susan Smith, in their recent book *Just Cause: The Seven Tests,* have made an exhaustive study of discharge arbitrations and have used seven established tests for measuring whether just-cause exists. The tests are valuable tools for all levels of management, and not just union but nonunion situations as well. Using the seven tests can help avoid litigation or at least establish a good defense if a case does go to court. Some of the tests may not be applicable to a particular situation, but the remaining tests must be met for a successful defense of a just-cause lawsuit.

The Seven Tests

1. *Reasonable rule.* Employees are entitled to know what is expected of them. This calls for clear rules, tailored to the employer's needs, that govern the day-to-day conduct of employees. Such rules, to be effective and enforceable, must be (a) reasonable and (b) reasonably applied.

Example: A home health agency prohibited employees from wearing political campaign buttons on their uniforms. An arbitrator struck down the rule by concluding it was too broad. The arbitrator said it was reasonable to prohibit wearing political campaign buttons in patients' homes to avoid upsetting patients with controversial subject matter but unreasonable to enforce the rule in the agency's headquarters.

2. *Notice.* Employees are entitled to have advance notice of the employer's rules and to be forewarned of the consequences of violating them. Generally, this is accomplished by posting the rules in conspicuous places or using some other form of continuous communication. Rules also should be divided into two categories: (1) flagrant offenses, such as stealing, which call for immediate termination, and (2) lesser offenses, such as unexcused absenteeism or tardiness, which call for progressive discipline in the form of

Reprinted from *Management Solutions,* June 1986

written warnings, suspension, and eventually discharge. In a termination case, the employer must show that an employee knew about the rule and also knew that violation would result in discipline.

Example: A package delivery driver who was out of uniform on the job contended that he didn't know about the rule requiring that a full uniform be worn at all times while on duty. There were no posted rules, and he didn't remember any reference to the requirement in the company orientation. "Besides," he said, "even if I knew about the rule, I wouldn't expect discipline. I've seen all of the guys out of uniform at one time or another when they were on duty and nothing happened to them."

3. *Investigation.* The employer must investigate the cause for termination promptly to make sure that the employee did, in fact, violate a rule. If it appears to be a serious violation, management may wish to suspend the employee pending the outcome of the investigation. Someone other than the supervisor recommending termination, such as a personnel director, should make a careful, objective investigation. The investigator will be gathering specific *facts* and not *conclusions,* building a file of all relevant written material, recording information obtained orally in a memorandum, and reviewing company records to see how management has handled similar conduct by other employees.

In this, management should not neglect to interview the employee in question. Even if the employer does not believe the alleged violator, at least the employer will know what excuses to expect. There also is the chance the violator will change his or her story at a later date, damaging his or her credibility.

Example: An employee of a manufacturing plant was terminated a month after he allegedly violated a safety rule. At the arbitration hearing, the grievant produced the plant's former safety director who testified that the conduct did not violate the rule. "That's not what they fired me for," the grievant said. "The real reason is that they learned last week I'm organizing for the union."

4. *Fair investigation.* The employer must make a fair and objective investigation to ensure that the supervisor who recommended discharge is not prejudiced against the employee and that the discharge is not based upon either personal conclusions or emotions. Some form of due process should be available to the employee so that the supervisor is not both prosecutor and judge. Gone are the days when a company can afford to blindly support a supervisor, right or wrong.

Example: A college dean who recommended termination of a faculty member was on the review committee that approved the recommendation. He also presented the termination recommendation to the board of trustees in executive session. The faculty member successfully contended in a rehearing that he had been "framed."

5. *Proof.* The burden of proof rests with the employer in discharge cases. Management must see that a clearly stated charge is consistent with the evidence.

Example: A company terminated an employee, claiming the job was "abolished"; the real reason was the employee's poor performance. The company lost its "job abolished" claim in arbitration and was unable to claim poor performance because it lacked proof.

In another case, a department head discharged a medical laboratory technologist because he was "by far the worst technologist in the department." As a physician, the department head expected his opinion to carry great weight. The arbitrator held that the opinion was not supported by concrete evidence, such as records showing that the technologist made many more serious errors than other personnel, performed far fewer tests per shift, was not able to perform special procedures without supervision, or called upon fellow technologists for help much more frequently than others.

6. *Equal treatment.* The employer must apply rules even-handedly and consistently. A company may have met the other tests for discharge for cause only to find that it has allowed the same conduct by other employees to go unpunished.

Example: An office "troublemaker" was discharged for taking sick leave without submitting a doctor's certificate when she returned to work. At the hearing, she proved that the office manager had not required a certificate from his "friends" in the office.

7. *Penalty.* Disciplinary penalties must be reasonably related to both the seriousness of the proven offense and the record of the employee. In arbitration under union contracts, the arbitrator, by mutual agreement of the parties, generally has the authority to rule that discharge is too severe for the misconduct involved and reduce the penalty to suspension or warning. The courts do not reinstate wrongfully dis-

charged employees, but juries award damages depending upon the extent to which they believe the former employee was harmed.

Additional Considerations

For the employer faced with a jury trial over wrongful discharge, the seven tests are not enough. The employee will be seeking damages rather than reinstatement and may also be seeking compensation for negligence, slander, infliction of emotional distress, or implied contract. Some additional tests are in order for such cases.

1. *Implied contract.* The employer must not, in the hiring process and throughout employment, make direct or indirect assurances to employees that they have a job for life. Promises by an enthusiastic recruiter or by a corporate officer can be the basis for a lawsuit.

Example: A corporate president commended his general sales manager for outstanding performance over several years and said he hoped the manager would be around until retirement some five years hence. A year later, after a corporate reorganization, the new president fired the manager without cause and the manager recovered substantial damages.

2. *Documentation.* Documentation must be accurate and must be preserved. This includes copies of warning letters, evaluations, notes on counseling, correspondence, commendations, productivity reports, and attendance records.

Example: A head nurse was asked in court why she gave satisfactory ratings to a substandard employee over a three-year period. "I wanted to encourage her," she replied. A jury found no evidence that contradicted the employee's satisfactory ratings and ignored the head nurse's retraction.

3. *Manner of termination.* The employer must handle a discharge in a considerate but firm manner. Singling out a long-term employee for a barrage of written warnings followed by an abrupt termination could lead to charges of intentional infliction of emotional distress.

Example: Several years ago a radio station manager bombarded two marginal announcers of long service with warnings on their performance. Eventually they both resigned, unable to take such pressure any longer. There was no legal protest, but the situation occurred long before the era of wrongful discharge suits.

Part VII

INTERVIEWING, HIRING, AND RETENTION

Sharpening Your Job Interviewing Techniques

DARREL R. BROWN

Most supervisors dislike conducting an employment interview—and with cause. Many have been given little or no training in interviewing. Thus their knowledge of interviewing theory and of the legal issues surrounding that part of their job is limited. Furthermore, unless they interview frequently—and most supervisors don't—they have little opportunity to improve their interviewing skills.

How about you? How confident are you in your interviewing ability? How competent are you as an interviewer? If you suffer from either a lack of confidence or a lack of competence, you may find the following guidelines of help. If followed conscientiously, they will improve any supervisor's interviewing proficiency.

Preinterview Planning

1. *Identify interview objectives.* Most interview objectives for a given position remain the same each time a vacancy occurs. However, there are times when they will change—for example, when projects,

Reprinted from *Supervisory Management,* August 1985

workload, specific skill needs, organization policy, and other work factors change. For instance, for a particular vacancy, more emphasis may be placed on writing skill, working with a particular machine, or affirmative action considerations. So each time you have to interview to fill a job, you should consider what you will be looking for in a successful candidate. After all, if you don't know what your objectives are, you can't know whether you've achieved them.

2. *Use standardized, predesigned, job-related questions.* After reviewing the job description for the position, develop a few questions to open discussion on each major job requirement. The purpose is to elicit comparable information from each candidate.

Research into employment interviews has shown poor validity and reliability largely because comparable information was not secured from all interviewees. The use of predesigned questions can go a long way toward overcoming this problem. Using job requirements to formulate questions will also assure job-related questions, and this will not only help secure the information needed to select the best qualified candidate, but also keep you from hearing non-job-related information that could conceivably be used to discriminate. Keeping the entire interview focused on job-related issues can contribute to a feeling that the interviewer was unbiased and fair and be a good defense against a charge of discrimination should one be leveled against you.

The Interviewing Process

3. *Keep the interviewee talking while you listen.* Experts say interviewers should talk no more than 20 percent of the time. Toward this end, avoid closed questions that can be answered with a "yes" or "no." That means questions that begin: "Do you? . . ." "Are you? . . ." "Did? . . ." "Can you do? . . ." and "Have you done? . . ." All of these, if the applicant is so inclined, can be answered with a single word. Generally, it is much better to ask questions beginning with, "What do you know about? . . ." "How did? . . ." "Why did you? . . ." and "Tell me about. . . ." Questions phrased in such a way almost always require a long answer.

"Listening responses" can also encourage an applicant to talk and give relevant information. The responses say, either verbally or nonverbally, "Keep talking, I'm listening, go ahead." They are really just elements of good conversation that can also be effective in the interview setting. Such responses include the nod, the pause, casual remarks, the "echo," and the "mirror" or "reflection." The nod merely communicates the interviewer's attention and nonverbally says. "Continue, keep talking, I hear you." The pause not only allows the interviewee to collect his or her thoughts and resume talking but also may be perceived as slightly stressful and thus may compel the applicant to fill the silence with more information. Casual remarks like "I see," "Go on," and the like, also serve as encouragement for the interviewee to keep talking.

"Echoing" entails repeating the last word, or last few words, the applicant has said, possibly just before a pause, with a questioning inflection. This can lead to elaboration or more information. The "mirror," on the other hand, involves reflecting back the interviewer's interpretation of something the interviewee has said. For example, the interviewer might say, "Then you felt that . . . ?", "This was important to you . . . ?", or "The whole thing was a failure, then?" Mirroring allows the interviewer to check his or her understanding of what the applicant has said and lets the interviewee confirm, deny, correct, or elaborate on that interpretation.

4. *Probe* to get complete information, to be sure you really understand, and to enable proper evaluation of the candidate. Some applicants may respond fully, but most must be questioned further to secure complete information.

Some inexperienced interviewers either avoid or are apologetic about asking a candidate for details, to explain something more fully, or to substantiate their work experience or knowledge. But such an attitude won't give you the relevant information you need to make a well-founded decision. Don't hesitate to ask such questions (when appropriate) as:

- "Why do you want to leave your present position?"
- "What was the problem between you and your last manager?"
- "What kind of person do you least (or most) like to work with? Why?"
- "What areas of your work need improvement?"
- "Please explain that again—I didn't understand you."

As part of your probing, you might also want to ask technical questions, to learn whether or not a candidate really knows the business.

5. *Accept; don't prejudge, leap to conclusions, or decide prematurely.* Research shows the untrained interviewer tends to reach a decision about a candidate in the first five minutes of the interview then spends the remainder of the time going through the motions, hearing only information that substantiates the original decision. If you find yourself leaning to a premature decision, deliberately withhold judgment and concentrate on securing all the information you can get. Only then can you make a valid decision.

6. *Use hypothetical questions to assess the interviewee's knowledge and understanding* when questions about specific job experience aren't possible. This means asking how the interviewee would handle a realistic, though hypothetical, situation on the job.

Interviewer's Role

7. *Specify important job requirements or unusual features of the job*—for example, "During emergencies, every one must work overtime" or "Occasional overnight travel is required." Such requirements should be carefully communicated to avoid misunderstandings. For example, you should not say, "Would you be able to work overtime?" or "Would occasional overnight travel cause you any difficulty?" Such questions imply a flexibility that may not be there. It is much better to state, in no uncertain terms, what the interviewee will be required to do, if hired.

8. *Allow self-disqualification.* A realistic job preview should be conducted, one that covers the undesirable features of the job as well as the desirable ones. Then candidates should be asked if they have heard anything that leads them to withdraw from consideration. It is much better to have such candidates disqualify themselves before employment than to have them accept a job they can't handle or don't really want.

9. *Conclude the interview.* The last steps in the interview should be to answer the interviewees' questions, ascertain their interest in the job, and advise them what to expect regarding the selection decision.

Decision Making

10. *Review what you have learned about the candidate.* In considering the information from an interview to determine whether the candidate meets your objectives for the particular vacancy, ask yourself such things as:

- Is the level of technical knowledge and proficiency appropriate for the position?
- Are the person's interpersonal skills satisfactory for the job?
- Does the candidate appear willing to learn and to cooperate with others to the extent necessary?
- Does the candidate possess sufficient personal and technical flexibility?

In other words, keep your objectives for filling this vacancy firmly in mind in considering an applicant. Don't be influenced by a fine personality, by eagerness to learn, or even by a specific skill unless it fits the job requirements. Above all, don't be overly influenced by the candidate who has good interviewing skills or who communicates well orally, if the skill is not needed in the job you are trying to fill.

The Hiring Decision:
Assessing Fit Into the Workplace

ELIZABETH DICKERSON

One of the rewards of being a supervisor or manager is having the opportunity to build your own work team. However, this isn't as easy to do as it seems. According to the Bureau of National Affairs, in this country, there is a current new-hire attrition rate of 52 percent. In other words, one out of every two people you hire this year will leave before the first anniversary date! This high attrition rate should be of major concern to you.

The situation is far from hopeless, however. A manager or supervisor who is well versed in assessing employee motivation can markedly turn this statistic around. There are some very specific skills and techniques that can help you hire and retain productive and committed personnel.

Key Elements of the Hiring Decision

As employee potential is assessed, there are four key elements that are particularly important:

1. Work history
2. Education
3. Technical competence
4. Motivation

The first two of these are fairly easily assessed—references can be checked, educational background can be determined by contacting the educational institutions an individual has graduated from, and past employment history can be verified. Assessing a future employee's technical competence is a more difficult task. If the competency requirements of a certain job are low enough, an actual hands-on test in which the candidate performs a specific job function may be adequate to assess ability. The task of assessing technical background, however, becomes more difficult as the job for which you are hiring becomes less specific.

Work history, education, and technical competence are vital as predictors of job performance. However, total performance is only achieved when an employee is motivated.

Reprinted from *Management Solutions*, January 1987

Motivation

When supervisors and managers are hiring, they want to answer the question, "How can I tell if the potential employee is motivated?" But the fact of the matter is that the vast majority of all employees *are* motivated, given the proper working environment. In order for an employee to be productive, there must be a "fit" between the working environment and the employee's values. The reason most employees are not motivated is a reflection of an incompatibility between the working environment and the needs of the employees, not a reflection of the workers.

The crucial objective during interviewing then is to determine the values of the employee and whether or not these values are consistent with the working environment provided by the employer. Do you offer a highly structured, routine, steady kind of work? Generally, older, more security conscious employees are attracted to a structured, routine working environment. Or, on your work team, is there a value placed on participation and responsibility, with decisions being made at the lowest level possible by groups of individuals? If so, your work team or organization will be highly appealing to most baby-boomers. Thus, the big problem in the hiring process is not finding motivated individuals; it's placing the right individuals in the right jobs.

Assessing Cultural Compatibility

The corporate culture is a reflection of the working environment and is made up of the beliefs, assumptions, and patterns of behavior that govern *how* work gets done. Culture can be defined as the unwritten rules of the game, including how decisions are made (slowly or quickly, by individuals or by groups), leadership style (autocratic, participative, or somewhere in between), work pace, detail orientation, creativity, how information is shared, and problem-solving methods. Cultural compatibility occurs when the beliefs, assumptions, and patterns of behavior of the work environment match the beliefs, assumptions, and patterns of behavior of an employee.

The first step in determining cultural compatibility, and thereby determining if your work environment will be motivating to a potential employee, is to assess the culture of the work unit for which you are hiring. To do this, you may want to enlist the help of the entire work unit. Not only will good cultural audit results be obtained, but the work team members will likely find the experience productive.

During the audit, group members should be asked to list the actual norms that guide their behavior and attitudes. Some examples of norms people tend to list in a more structured traditional organization are:

Overtime is expected as part of the job.
The boss is being paid to make the decisions.
No one is allowed to rock the boat.
Disagreement with the boss is not tolerated.
Appearance counts.
You're required to ask before you do.
Proper channels must be followed.
Employees don't need to know what's not going to affect them.
The customer is always right.
The way we've been doing things is the best way to do them.

In a younger, less structured organization, some cultural norms might be:

Risk equals growth; failure is a learning experience.
The boss is *not* always right.
The person closest to the source of the problem is the best problem solver.
Women are first-class citizens.
Change equals growth.
Rules are made to be broken.

Employees have a right to information—not only what they need to know but what they want to know.

As long as the work gets done, who cares what hours you keep.

These are very brief examples, and organizational extremes at that. But they do illustrate cultural differences that are important to consider as part of the hiring process.

After doing a cultural audit, the next step in the process is to write a "person specification." This needs to include not only the technical skills the prospective employee is expected to have but also the personal traits that the candidate should have to fit into the culture of the organization or work team.

Looking at the first example, in a more traditional, structured organization, some person specifications might include: neat, clean appearance; appropriately dressed; detail oriented; steady and dependable; willing to work overtime; able to take direction from superiors; and sensitive to the needs and vagaries of the customer.

Examining the younger, less structured organization, some person specifications might include: risk taker, self-confident, willing and able to fail as part of the learning process, a decision maker, a challenger, not needing a lot of rules, and able to treat all people as equal.

The question, then, is, How do you determine if a job candidate meets the person specifications?

Stair-Step Interviewing

The stair-step approach to interviewing is a set of techniques an interviewer can use to obtain in-depth information about a job candidate, including cultural fit between the candidate and the job.

As an interviewer progresses up the steps, the interview process will tend to be more threatening to a job candidate. If you use this technique, it's important you understand the risks, particularly of using steps four and five of the interview ladder. There is a possibility that a candidate will be alienated by the interview process and refuse the position as a consequence.

Stair-Step Interviewing Process

1. & 2. *Past and present.* Steps one and two focus on the job candidate's past job history, educational background, and present job situation. Focusing on the past and present is usually nonthreatening to a job candidate. During these steps the interview process is relatively comfortable, but it's also fairly nonrevealing to the interviewer. Sometimes enough information will be gleaned in talking about the past and present to know whether a job candidate will be a productive, motivated employee. However, often the interviewer needs to probe deeper in order to determine whether an individual truly has the technical background for a specific position and to assess if there is a cultural fit between the job and the candidate. One way to do this is to develop critical incidents or hypothetical situations.

3. *Critical incidents.* The first step in developing critical incidents is to research the job by talking to anyone and everyone who can help with information about it. These people are asked to develop anecdotes, case studies, and situations that typically occur in the job, not routine events but occurrences that would make or break the success of the job if they weren't handled correctly. The interviewer writes up these incidents, having in mind "good" answers to how situations should be handled. When interviewing candidates, the interviewer describes these incidents, then asks each for his or her reactions to the situations. The job candidates' answers are then compared with the answers the interviewer has previously worked out.

4. *Role play.* There are times when asking a candidate how he or she might respond faced with a critical incident doesn't elicit the information the interviewer needs to assess cultural compatibility. The interviewer then needs to progress to the next interviewing step. This is to put the job candidate into a role playing situation. Usually, the candidate is asked to play the part of himself or herself in a typical but

challenging work situation, with the interviewer playing the part of either the job candidate's subordinate or co-worker. This gives the interviewer an opportunity to assess such traits as the candidate's leadership style, decision making skills, ability to give instructions, and ways of interacting with different kinds of individuals.

When people are asked to "act," they usually feel ill at ease and uncomfortable. An interviewer must determine if the risk of possibly alienating a good candidate is justified to get the kind of information needed to make a good hiring decision.

5. *Devil's advocate.* A devil's advocate is a person who upholds the wrong side, perversely or for argument's sake. In step five, the interviewer, as a devil's advocate, assumes the opposite view of the job candidate in order to assess such things as how a candidate responds to pressure, the confidence level of the individual, the candidate's ability to stick to a point of view, or the individual's verbal communication skills. An example might go something like this:

Interviewer (to candidate): "Tell me a little about where you see yourself professionally five years from now."
Candidate: "My goal is to be the manager of our local sales office within the next five years."
Interviewer: "It strikes me that your career goals are fairly modest."

In this example, the point is not whether the interviewer thinks the career goals of the candidate are realistic or ambitious enough. The intent is to challenge the candidate to bring out aspects of the candidate's personality that the interviewer might not otherwise have a chance to glimpse. Does the candidate immediately become defensive and antagonistic when challenged or is the candidate able to reasonably stand up for his or her viewpoint under pressure? Can the candidate effectively communicate under stress? Does the candidate exhibit self-confidence? These are just a few cultural traits an interviewer might be looking for when using the devil's advocate interviewing mode.

Since the devil's advocate posture can be extremely uncomfortable for a job candidate, it is recommended only when it is essential for the interviewer to have more information about the candidate.

Summary

The stair-step interviewing process is primarily used to determine work "fit": When faced with a critical incident, how does the job candidate make decisions? Does the person go through the channels or does he or she prefer to make autonomous decisions? When put in a role play situation, what kind of leadership style does the candidate exhibit? Is this leadership style in line with the norms of the group? When his or her opinions are challenged, does the candidate buckle under and submit to authority or does he or she stand up for the beliefs? In other words, using critical incidents, role plays, and devil's advocacy, you as the interviewer have at your disposal the cultural information you need to make the best hiring decision possible.

Assessing employee potential is not easy. It involves a lot of hard work and preparation before the interviewing process even begins. However, it's well worth it. The losses associated with attrition are both direct and indirect: hiring costs including recruitment, advertising, agency, and relocation costs; training expenses; reduced productivity; negative impact on employee morale; organizational instability; declining labor market reputation; and decreased management effectiveness.

The first step to retention is to establish a solid, objective hiring process. Finding the right person for the right job is never easy, but in the long run it's well worth the time and effort to do the job well.

Integrating Your New Employee Into the Organization

LINDA J. SEGALL

As a supervisor, you're responsible for making your new employee a member of the team in as short a time as possible. But that may not be easy, for a new employee will typically exhibit certain "newness" behaviors that will make you, the employee, and his or her co-workers feel uncomfortable and slow his or her integration into the organization. It's important, therefore, that you learn to recognize these behaviors and how to deal with these to speed the individual's acceptance into the organization.

"Newness" Behaviors

Typical "newness" behaviors include:

- *Recurrent use of "we/you."* "We" refers to the new employee's old employer, while "you" refers to the new company or department. For example, the new employee may say, "At Widget Company we always got our birthday as a holiday. Do you do that here?"
- *Frequent anecdotes about previous work.* When co-workers describe a work situation, the new employee may join in with his or her own story, saying, "Let's see . . . that reminds me of the time when I had to deal with a very stubborn sales manager. . . ." Or, "A funny thing happened with my secretary the day she got her word processor. . . ."
- *Direct or inferred comparisons of facilities, policies, and so on.* For example, "It sure would be nice if we could have some outdoor lunch tables like they have at Widget Company." Or, "Oh, you mean that you have to work here 15 years to get a three-week vacation!"
- *"I-can-do-it-ness!"* This is an overeagerness to jump into projects before the individual's credentials are fully accepted by anyone other than you, the supervisor. The new employee may say, "I've done that many times before at Widget's, so let me handle it for you."

Clearly, these behaviors are ways the new employee asserts his or her ability and desire to perform on the job. But they are also subtle manifestations of the individual's insecurity and are perceived by

Reprinted from *Supervisory Management,* February 1986

colleagues as coming on too strong. Consequently, they tend to discourage the new employee's acceptance instead of encouraging it.

Fitting In

How can you help the employee deal with these behaviors and otherwise speed the individual's integration into the organization?

The following guidelines should help.

1. Recognize the situation your new employee is in, watch for "newness" behaviors, then supportively tell the employee which behaviors inhibit colleagues' acceptance of him or her.

2. Clearly define your new employee's role and functions—not only for the individual but also for co-workers; direct reports of the individual, if any; and management. Do this in a manner that shows the employee you value him or her. For example, you might say, "George joins us as the new marketing manager. He'll not only do what his predecessor did but also be an internal resource for advertising."

3. Specify how often you want the person to check in with you, whether you want the individual to inform you about his or her activities before or after the fact, and what the person's authority level is.

4. Meet regularly and frequently with your new employee. Encourage independent decision making, but understand that the individual wants and needs positive reinforcement from you when things go well and encouragement and support when they don't.

5. Help your employee learn the nuances of the organization's politics, protocol, and procedures. For example, you might say, "In the production department, always go to the superintendent first and ask if it's all right to talk with the unit supervisors. But in marketing, it's all right to go to the analyst directly for consultation."

6. Include your new employee in meetings that will enhance the individual's role and help establish his or her credibility among those with whom the employee works. Advise the individual whether his or her role in these meetings is as an observer or as a participant. If it's as a participant, help the person along by directing questions to him or her. For example, you might say, "I think Dave can answer that better than I."

7. Create opportunities for your new employee to become known and accepted in his or her area of expertise. Even small things, like having the individual deliver a report to management in person, can go a long way toward establishing the employee as an integral and valued part of your department.

Obviously, newness goes away with time. But few organizations have the luxury to use time frivolously. So watch out for newness behaviors in your employees and help them become "old" as fast as possible.

Supervising Temporary Employees

CAROL HANNAH

While it may not be one of your everyday concerns, sooner or later you will find yourself in the position of hiring temporary help. If your first reaction is to reach for the yellow pages and point a wild finger, stop and think again. Temporary workers are an expense that should not be taken lightly. There are two points to be carefully considered: (1) what the temporary help service can and should do for you; and (2) what you can do to make both your job, and the temporary's, as easy and as productive as possible.

First of all, let's define what is reasonable to expect when you call for temporary help. Very simply, you have a right to expect someone with the skills that you have specified will be needed. And you have the right to expect someone who is reasonably interested in, and willing to perform, the work. In return, the temporary help service has a right to expect that you'll provide a safe work environment, make fair work requests, and give suitable directions concerning the work to the temporary employee.

With that agreed upon, let's look at exactly what you can do to receive competent temporary help. The key to consistently obtaining competent help begins before you call a temporary help service with the selection of a good temporary help service that conscientiously fulfills its employer responsibilities toward temporary employees. "Employer responsibilities" in this case is defined in the broad sense, including far more than the traditional "hire/fire" employer responsibilities.

Most personnel professionals would agree that it is the employer's responsibility to identify fairly and objectively each employee's work skills and abilities. It is both practical and responsible to, whenever possible, place employees in situations in which they can use their best skills and perform work they find interesting. In the case of temporary workers, this is not only an employer responsibility to the temporary employees, but a responsibility of the temporary help service to you and your company. If you are assigned temporary employees who cannot perform the work duties or are not interested in performing the work, the temporary help service is not meeting its obligation to you, the customer.

Step 1: Select a Temporary Help Service That Identifies Thoroughly Both Work Skills and Work Interests

For a number of years, the temporary help industry suffered an identity crisis, mimicking the procedures and personnel practices used in permanent placement. The industry now recognizes that the two functions—permanent placement and temporary help—not only are dissimilar but are contradictory.

When checking how a temporary help service identifies the work skills and interests of a temporary

Reprinted from *Supervisory Management,* February 1980

employee, check to see that permanent placement techniques are not used. A permanent placement agency matches a person to a job. A temporary help service should be matching work assignments to the person. The intake process for permanent placement involves working from a (usually well-defined) job description and, using the process of elimination, identifying the best person to fit the requirements of the job description. When temporary help used the permanent placement procedures, the practice was to have "job descriptions" such as, "typist: 55 words per minute with no more than four errors, six months' experience." Applicants for temporary work were slotted into a particular job description category by asking questions designed to eliminate those who did not fit the requirements of the job description category (such as, "Can you type 55 words per minute?").

Obviously, this "elimination process" isn't good enough. Since temporary employees can be expected to handle a variety of work duties on different work assignments, each with different working conditions and under different supervisors, it doesn't make sense for the temporary help service to identify a single job description into which a temporary employee would be assigned. Instead, the temporary help service must learn the full range of worker skills and experience, and the working conditions under which each worker best performs. Does, for example, the applicant prefer to work under pressure? What about the size of the work group? If you are assigned a worker who cannot stand working in a one-person office, and you have a one-person office, that worker's ability to type 85 words per minute with no errors isn't going to make much difference. The work will not be satisfactory. The match between the temporary employee and the work assignment was not good enough.

Step 2: Select a Temporary Help Service That Is Concerned That Every Temporary Employee Establishes a Successful Work Record

A responsible temporary help service maintains an active employer commitment to its temporary employees. Much of this commitment is centered on helping each temporary employee establish a successful work record. This isn't just pure altruism. If all temporary employees establish successful work records, then customers will be satisfied with the work and will likely call the temporary help service again when there is more work than workers.

For a temporary help service to help its employees establish successful records, it takes more than careful identification of work skills and interests and matching these skills and interests to work assignments. It takes follow-up, feedback on performance, and coaching. In other words, the temporary help service must actively supervise its employees.

The temporary help service must maintain a high profile for the temporary employee. Only in this way can the temporary worker get consistently the guidance and motivation needed to continue enthusiastically as a temporary employee. (Remember, it's not easy going from work assignment to work assignment, facing many "first day on the job" situations and adapting to a number of work environments.) This high profile includes a consistent system by which feedback on performance is gathered. Coaching must be offered for needed areas of improvement and praise and recognition given for excellent performance.

While many customers are concerned supervisors who give suggestions for performance improvement and who think to say "thank you" for a job well done, there are other supervisors who are less concerned. If the employer function of guiding, encouraging, and supporting workers is handed over (or defaulted) to the customer by the temporary help service, it is possible that you will have a temporary employee arrive at your doorstep who is already discouraged and demotivated.

Step 3: Select a Temporary Help Service Whose Service Representatives Can Act As Consultants in Helping You Solve Your Temporary Help Needs

For example, the most common mistake made in ordering temporary help, interestingly, is to overestimate the need. This includes identifying too long a period in which the temporary employee will be needed and identifying too high a skill level required for doing the work. Since temporary help services

Figure 1

Supervising Temporary Employees
Checklists of Actions

When Placing an Order With a Temporary Help Service: YES   NO

1. Have you identified all equipment (by make and model) to be used by the temporary employee?

2. Have you identified the primary skill required to do the work?

3. Have you identified all other skills required to do the work?

4. Have you considered what qualities in a temporary worker are most important to you in this assignment *and* communicated that to the temporary help service representative?

5. Have you carefully identified all job duties the temporary employee *might* be involved in?

6. Have you clearly given "smooth takeover" information to the service representative, including: travel directions, working hours, availability of nearby restaurants or onsite food service, and dress and other special requirements (such as a no-smoking policy)?

7. Have you told the temporary help service representative why temporary help is needed (for example, to replace someone on vacation or to meet a tight deadline on a special project)? This information helps the service representative identify the amount of pressure the temporary employee may experience on the job and to select a suitable worker.

8. Have you listened closely as the service representative recapped your requirements? The information you have given is used to select the best available temporary employee to do the work. Don't try to save time by giving too little information here. And make certain that you were clearly understood by the service representative.

Before the Temporary Employee Arrives: YES   NO

1. Have you informed others in your work area that a temporary employee is coming to help? Some co-workers of the temporary employee may feel threatened about "a stranger in the midst." Let them know someone is coming and why.

2. Have you informed the receptionist that a temporary employee is coming? The receptionist's warm greeting can help put a temporary employee at ease and pave the way to a productive work day.

3. Have you selected an appropriate work station for the temporary employee?

4. Have you checked that the equipment to be used is in working order? Many times equipment will be taken out of storage to be used by the temporary employee. When the temporary employee arrives is no time to discover the equipment isn't working properly.

5. Have you appointed a "second in command" who can answer questions and help with any work problems if you're not available throughout the assignment?

6. Have you estimated what you feel is a reasonable day's work and made sure that the day's work is organized and ready to be performed? (If for any reason the temporary employee does not complete what you feel is

a fair day's work, you can and should advise the temporary help service immediately. The temporary help service representative should work with you to identify the problem and solve it.)

7. Are supplies available and handy? YES NO

8. Have you gone over in your head the work instructions you plan to give the temporary employee? When doing so, check to make sure you aren't using "jargon" unique to your company or organization that the temporary employee may not understand.

When the Temporary Employee Arrives: YES NO

1. Have you given the temporary employee a brief tour of the facilities? It's important to identify where you can be found, where the restrooms and the cafeteria are located, and so on.

2. Have you communicated with the temporary employee:

   a. What work needs to be done? (Help the temporary employee understand the importance of the work being performed. People work harder when they feel there is a good reason for the work to be performed well.)

   b. What your work expectations include? (How much should the temporary employee be able to complete by noontime? Must the typing be camera-ready copy? Is the work confidential?)

   c. What are the work rules, including working hours, policy on answering telephones, and so on?

   d. Who will be available to answer questions and handle any work problems (and how that person can be located)?

3. Have you given instructions clearly and asked the temporary employee to repeat them to be sure that they have been heard and understood?

4. Have you provided samples of correspondence, invoices, or other work the temporary employee may be doing, so that he or she can use the samples as a guide?

5. Have you checked the work within the first two hours or so to make sure it is being done properly?

6. Have you said "thank you" for work well done?

charge an hourly rate, based on the skills specified as needed, it is wasteful to overestimate the skill need. Likewise, time can be overestimated. While temporary help users are charged only for the hours actually worked by a temporary employee, remember that work expands to meet the time allotted for it. Many temporary help users identify the need for a typist for, let's say, a two-week period. The typist is excellent and completes the work in a week and a half. The temporary employee is kept on the job performing routine filing duties for the last three days. The user is charged for a typist for two weeks. The user isn't happy about that. And neither is the temporary employee who identified his or her interests as typing and not filing.

A service representative, who comes to your work site, visits with you, the supervisor of the temporary workers, and asks detailed questions about the work to be performed and the working conditions under which the work will be performed, is in a position to advise you about the skill-level needed and the length of the assignment. This visit by the temporary help service's representative should not be confused with a sales call. It should be a call strictly designed to help the service representative work as a consultant with you, gathering information that will help the service send the people you need to get the work done.

If you identify a temporary help service that fairly and objectively identifies work skills and the interests of its temporary employees, that shows genuine concern for helping its employees establish successful records, and that has representatives who can help you identify when you do and when you don't need temporary help, you have accomplished the lion's share of the "supervisory requirements" for consistently and reliably getting temporary employees who can and will do the job that needs doing.

Figure 1 contains checklists of actions you can take when you need temporary help, after you have selected a good temporary help service.

As we have already stated, ensuring the success of temporary employees is a responsibility that lies with both you and the agency. It is up to you, however, to choose a service that carries its share of responsibility. If you go over the checklists in this article and can honestly check "yes" to each question, you can rest assured that you are carrying your share.

Reducing Turnover of New Hires

ANTHONY J. BUONOCORE

Mary Smith sat restlessly in a plush armchair in the employment office reception area, waiting for Ted Brown, the personnel manager, to call her in for her exit interview. She knew he'd be concerned about her leaving only eight months after being recruited from one of the top engineering schools in the country, and would want to know why. How could she explain that the main reason she was leaving was just that she had never felt comfortable here?

Across the pleasantly furnished reception area, Charles Murray also waited for the start of his exit interview. Murray had been an employee for a little over a year and was nervously trying to hide the anger he felt toward the company. It had promised him so much—challenging work, interesting assignments, and the opportunity to apply the research started in his dissertation activities at school. It had never materialized, and he couldn't shake the overpowering sense of having wasted a year.

Redirecting Attention

These two incidents reflect a tendency of many corporations to direct all their energies toward identifying and attracting new professional employees, then all but ignoring them in the first few critical months of their employment. The result is a new employee who feels abandoned, confused, often frightened, and terribly helpless—an employee who begins to second guess the decision to accept employment. For some of these people, the response is to resign.

Fortunately, many of these resignations can be avoided. These short-term terminations can be reduced through an employee assimilation system that addresses the needs and concerns of the new employees and helps them make the transition to the new workplace a comfortable, pleasant, and rewarding experience.

The basis of this assimilation is mentoring as it was originally conceived.

Although the concept of mentoring has been around for thousands of years (in Greek mythology, Mentor was Odysseus's counselor), today the original concept is misunderstood and, accordingly, misused. This misunderstanding results in the failure of most corporations to consider mentoring and reaping the significant cost savings from reduced new employee attrition.

In today's corporation, the term "mentor" is generally used to identify a powerful person who has, for whatever reason, singled out a fledgling and decided to provide the guidance and support needed to

Reprinted from *Management Solutions,* June 1987

ensure the fledgling's success. This concept works, particularly in succession planning, as the mentor not only grooms the recipient in his or her own image, but is available to ensure recognition and to smooth over mistakes that could be major obstacles and deterrents to the person who is struggling to make it in the organization.

It is this "godfather" connotation of mentoring that is most often referred to in the literature and given to the concept, and the corporations that resist mentoring are reacting to difficulties with the adaptation of such an approach. There is, however, another mentoring concept that is slowly gaining acceptance, though not wide usage, and it is more in line with the old Greek mythological concept, wherein a mentor did not have power but did have knowledge and, as a trusted and faithful friend of Odysseus, imparted this knowledge to Odysseus's son, Telemachus.

This "traditional" mentoring system, when applied to corporations, would have as its major objective the imparting of knowledge and guidance to all new employees, as opposed to the singling out of one or a few for grooming; and it is this early nurturing that has potential for significant bottom-line results.

Smoothing Assimilation

When new employees come to the corporation, whether fresh from college campuses or years with another company, they come with many questions and concerns. They wonder whether they will fit in, whether they will like it here; whether they will have the opportunity to learn and grow; whether they will be challenged; how they will perform and how their performance will be measured and communicated; and, finally, whether they will stay. During the early months, the answers to these questions begin to form, and it benefits the supervisor and the corporation to provide an environment of stimulation, guidance, feedback, and open communication to assure a smooth and comfortable assimilation.

From a corporate viewpoint, a smooth and comfortable transition into the corporation has a number of benefits:

- Quick group identification and a feeling of belonging will add to the cohesiveness and team potential of the group.
- Maximum productivity will be reached earlier.
- Loyalty and company commitment will be fostered.
- Identifiable communication channels will ease concerns and allow the channeling of energy to performance-related tasks.
- Understanding of performance criteria and regular feedback will ensure early job satisfaction.
- Open communication will facilitate quicker learning and growth.

The secret of such assimilation is the assignment, to each new employee, of a mentor who will perform the role of host, friend, confidant, and advisor for a period beginning prior to reporting to work and ending at a time when the assimilation has been completed. The phrase "prior to reporting to work" refers to the time between acceptance of the offer of employment and the first day of work and, in the case of a campus recruit, it could be as much as three or four months. The ending time will vary, depending on the nature of the job, the personality of the new employee, and the success of the early phases of the program.

Identifying Mentors

The success of a new employee mentoring system hangs heavily on the selection of the person who will fill the mentor role. Overwhelming data, gathered in interviews with over 100 new professionals in a *Fortune* 500 corporation, indicated that the selected person should be a peer, with similar academic and work backgrounds. In no case should a supervisor assume the role since the mentee will be reluctant to ask questions for fear of appearing ignorant.

In picking mentors from among staffers, supervisors should also look for employees with at least two years' experience at the work locations and physical placement with, or near, the new employee. Needless to say, the mentor should be a person who is recognized as a good performer, and who will present a good image of the corporation.

Should the mentor be of the same race and/or sex as the new employee? On this, opinion is mixed. Some women and minorities have found the climate insight obtainable from a same race/sex mentor invaluable, whereas others have preferred to assimilate into the majority as quickly as possible. To deal with this uncertainty, supervisors may want to develop a system in which a mentor can be changed after two weeks of employment. The initial mentor assignment, during which time the mentor's primary roles would be host and guide, would match race and sex, and would begin upon acceptance of the job and continue through the two-week period. At that time, the mentor and mentee would discuss the relationship and make a joint decision about the efficacy of the match from all perspectives. If the relationship is failing in any way, a new mentor assignment can be made for the remaining period, during which time the mentor's primary role will be helper and advisor.

The Mentoring Task

The responsibilities of the mentor can be looked at in terms of three distinct phases: before the new employee arrives, the first two weeks, and thereafter. In the first two phases, mentors are essentially hosts. As the employee's career with the company continues, the mentor's role changes to that primarily of advisor.

Before a new employee arrives, the mentor should:

1. Call a new employee and introduce himself or herself and explain the mentoring function, as well as the entire mentoring program.
2. If physically possible, arrange to meet the employee and determine from the new employee what it is that could be done, prior to the employee's first day at work, to ease the transition.
3. Ask the new employee if he or she would like any preliminary reading material as an introduction to the company or new job, but be clear that this is voluntary and should not interfere with completing school or current job responsibilities. If the employee would like such material, what would be appropriate should be provided.
4. Make the "mentoring" role clear to the new employee in words and spirit. (The mentor should not be overbearing or try to force the new employee to take help that he or she feels isn't needed. The role is to increase comfort levels and instill an early feeling of belonging to the corporation.)

At the new employee's arrival and for the first two weeks, the mentor should:

1. Help the new employee locate stockrooms, cafeteria, restrooms, and the like and familiarize him or her with general procedures (memoranda formats, clerical support, and so forth).
2. Provide initial educational or orientation material.
3. Answer questions and be observant of the new employee's assimilation.
4. If mentor change option is available, be mindful of the efficacy of the relationship and be prepared—and willing—to recommend a change if it seems appropriate.

The end of the initial two-week employment period marks a critical juncture in the assimilation process as the new employee goes from the "getting acquainted" stage to the "blending in" stage. At this point, the mentor's responsibilities begin to shift from those of a host to those of an advisor, and it is here that a mentor change can be made if it seems appropriate.

On an ongoing basis, the mentor should:

1. Remain available for questions while encouraging independence.
2. Take an active interest in the new employee's reading, work, and course work (if applicable) each day.
3. Volunteer information, particularly if the mentee seems reluctant to ask.
4. Introduce the new employee to "experts" in related work areas and encourage the new employee to interface with them.
5. Explain corporate "jargon" when used.
6. Try to expose the new employee to others in and outside the work group and to other new employees.
7. Keep the new employee informed about meetings he or she should attend and give pre-meeting and post-meeting analyses.
8. Make the new employee aware of social groups, such as softball, dance, golf, and chess.
9. Get the new employee physically out of the office periodically.
10. Be sure to maintain the helper and friend relationship and not be seen as a surrogate supervisor. This is best done by never giving the mentee the feeling that he or she is being "checked up" on.
11. Encourage the new employee when his or her spirits are down; provide the needed reassurance.
12. Monitor assimilation and be prepared to sever the "formal" mentoring relationship when appropriate.

The success of a new employee mentoring system can benefit from corporate support but it can be implemented by a concerned supervisor who will allow a committed mentor to take time away from the job and who will reward the mentor for his or her dedication. If the mentoring system is to work, the mentor position must be one that is sought, not one avoided by all.

Part VIII

LEADERSHIP AND MOTIVATION

Working on Your Leadership Skills

V. DALLAS MERRELL

While working with a troubled organization recently, I assessed the performance of its top officials. I was struck by my analysis of one particular executive who had been trained in one of the nation's finest graduate schools, spent nearly 20 years in senior positions carrying out complex technical functions, and commanded a substantial salary and fringe benefits. This man was a long-standing confidant of the chief executive and owner, yet was in trouble on many counts. Upon receiving a recent promotion, his newly designated subordinates had, in clear terms, rejected him. He lost the respect of the owner and was obviously under considerable personal stress. Though no particular event could be pinpointed to explain the present conditions, the diagnosis was unmistakable: In prior assignments he had perfected technical skills but had been insensitive to the leadership dimensions of his work.

Leadership has been studied for decades in scores of research projects. Assorted studies have focused on differentiating among leadership "styles" and each one's application in various settings, on differing social conditions and the rise of leadership, on the processes by which leadership functions are carried out, and on the leadership personality.

In my own work, I find that we already know enough about leadership to do something about it. I support the continued study of these phenomena and the advancement of knowledge about leadership, but I also see a considerable need for applying better what we know already.

Reprinted from *Supervisory Management,* June 1981

The Dimensions of Leadership

I focus on eight aspects of leadership. These are conceptual categories around which to organize the facets of leadership. At the top of the list is *power*.

To influence events and people, a leader must have power, which is a social and psychological leverage with people and institutions. The sources of power include professional and technical expertise, formal positions of authority, the legal rights of office, a knowledge of procedures, and the control of scarce resources and services.

Power is also effected by interpersonal skills—the ability to persuade, motivate, and organize. Access to influential people in an organization enhances power, as does access to vital information that would be helpful in carrying out organizational goals. The capacity to dominate and intimidate others when necessary and the ability to resist domination are also important.

The capacity to lead is one thing, but the courage to act decisively to make use of power is what finally counts. Power allows leaders to move the organization in a meaningful direction toward the achievement of key objectives.

Prominence brings power that is essential to being heard and getting results. Only rarely is visibility inadvisable for a leader.

Several things can build a person's prominence: status among associates, having one's name and face recognized, good standing with higher-ups, and visible expertise. Awards, honors, titles, status symbols, and formal education also build prominence. People pay attention to someone whom they know is marked for leadership, someone who is seen as a "comer," though this can also produce feelings of jealousy if not properly handled.

Respect and Awareness

Leadership is built not only on prominence but on *respect*. Gaining a favorable reputation with others gives legitimacy to a person's uses of power in leading others.

Respect comes, in part, from success in past assignments, popularity, trustworthiness, ethical standards, and strong convictions. With a concern for the rights and well-being of others and a tolerance for individual differences, more respect is gained. Dependability, conscientiousness, self-control, and self-confidence are other positive factors in the ability to exercise leadership.

Leaders must also be *aware* of what is going on around them and receptive to feedback—even disagreeable news or tough criticism. They must be attuned to informal sources of information and opinion. If one is serious about providing leadership, it is important to be awake, alert, and ready to respond.

Direction and Implementation

Almost by definition, leaders have to *know where they're going*. Developing specific objectives, working out a practical course of action, getting things moving, and keeping matters on track all contribute to leadership ability. Persuasiveness, constructive aggression, forward thinking, and a "can do" attitude contribute to providing direction for others.

But plans are not self-executing, nor does order impose itself. If left alone most things disintegrate or slide into disarray. Effective leaders *structure* activities.

In organizing work activities, it is important to let others know what is expected of them. Through leadership, roles are defined, responsibilities are delegated, and expectations are established. Building teamwork and scheduling activities are leadership functions that also should not be neglected.

Handling Conflict and Achievement

Leaders should be *prepared for conflict,* not surprised or disheartened by it. Short-fused crises come up and must be handled. It helps for leaders to be poised under stress while facing diverse situations in the organizational ruckus.

A *good record* for producing results is especially important for a leader. People like to be teamed with a winner, a doer. Personal drive and effort add to the luster of achievement. So persistence and endurance count.

Assessing Leadership

Now let me emphasize that these dimensions of leadership are not concocted from personal opinion, nor do they simply constitute a nice shopping list. They are derived from decades of research. The lack of any one will diminish the results sought through leadership efforts.

Most people—managers especially—have difficulty getting feedback concerning their leadership performance. Too many simply don't know how they stack up (or where they should improve). In part, this is an indictment of the performance appraisal practices of most employers. Failed supervisors are often unaware of their troubles and their consequences. But resources are available to make things better.

The simplest way to better understand one's personal skills is through self-assessment, though this has obvious limitations. Supervisors can, by being observant, pick up some self-evaluation ideas from magazines, news features, and other published materials but these smatterings of ideas and methods are limited by being fragmented. Still, they might be useful. It might be worthwhile here to suggest a start at self-assessment.

Compare yourself. To make your evaluation, first think of yourself in relation to the other people with whom you deal. This is important because no absolutes exist for measuring leadership. Your rating must be like those of athletes who don't know for sure how fast they must run to win—it depends on who else is running and how they all do in the race. So, keep in mind those with whom you work, or even those with whom you desire to work, and try to give yourself some evidence that would support any judgment you make. Don't ignore bad news and subtle warning signals about your performance. Think not of your potential on each dimension, but of your past record—successes and failures.

Consider each dimension. When considering your rating on each leadership dimension, think only of that dimension. Remember that you will probably be stronger in some areas than in others. Let your judgments reflect that.

Judgment of others. If it's not inappropriate or risky, you might wish to get independent reactions from others as you make your evaluation. Since your self-evaluation should reflect your performance in each category, anyone asked to make ratings should have observed you in action. Otherwise, you are only expanding fantasy, not dealing with reality.

Target improvement. Improvement will result from better use of existing strengths, from avoiding troublesome activities where your deficiencies undermine your effectiveness, and from working to correct deficiencies and perfect strengths. Depending on your targets, consider the resources that would be appropriate in carrying out your development objectives.

Position and technical ability alone don't make a success or guarantee leadership skills. Effectiveness grows through understanding of the essentials of leadership and recognizing strengths and deficiencies. Most people I've met are born followers, not leaders. Because of that, a lot of hard work is needed to ensure that those who seek or are thrust into leadership roles have the best chance to succeed and to contribute to the success of others.

How to Measure
Your Leadership Potential

OLIVER L. NIEHOUSE

In early times, leadership was equated with wealth and social position. This notion continued, to some extent, right into the twentieth century. It wasn't until the start of World War I, when the armed forces needed to identify leaders quickly and in large numbers, that leadership became associated with various traits.

The problem is that for every characteristic or trait of a leader that one can name, leaders without that attribute can be cited. Not only does this verify the diversity of the human species, it also suggests how truly difficult it is to find a good leader. That is why effective leaders are so highly sought after and valued by organizations.

Are you potentially such a treasure?

It is possible to answer that question even though there are no consistent characteristics or traits that one can point to and flatly state, "That's what makes an effective leader." Based on my long experience as a leadership trainer for many major organizations, public and private, I have developed a single device for measuring the extent to which one's thinking is or is not in line with what is known about effective leadership. Thinking and subsequent behavior can change, so this is by no means a test of one's leadership ability. Rather, it is an indicator of one's leadership potential at this moment in time.

To use Figure 1, simply read the statements carefully. After each statement, circle whether you would most likely agree or disagree with that statement. Do this for all 11 statements before you look at the answers.

Scoring Your Responses

A point value has been assigned to each statement relative to how you responded. Values will be briefly explained to facilitate understanding. To determine your score, simply total the values of your responses.

Now let's consider each of the statements again.

1. Good leaders are born, not made. *Agree (0), Disagree (1)*. Yes, some leaders are born. They have that special attribute "charisma." But for the most part, leadership is an acquired management skill.

2. I tend to treat my subordinates well so long as they do what I say. *Agree (0), Disagree (1)*. The

Reprinted from *Supervisory Management,* January 1983

Figure 1

Leadership Potential

1. Good leaders are born, not made.   Agree Disagree

2. I tend to treat my subordinates well so long as they do what I say.   Agree Disagree

3. Good leaders depend on their followers as much as they depend on themselves.
                                                                                 Agree Disagree

4. As a leader, I would always include the reasons why when asking a subordinate to perform a task.   Agree Disagree

5. A good leader will achieve his or her objectives at any costs.   Agree Disagree

6. As a group manager, I would never entrust a vital project to anyone but myself, even if that meant working overtime.   Agree Disagree

7. A key to good leadership is being consistent in how one leads.   Agree Disagree

8. If justified, I would recommend a subordinate for a promotion to a position equal to or even higher than my own position.   Agree Disagree

9. Some subordinates can participate in the decision-making process without threatening a leader's position.   Agree Disagree

10. If my group failed to achieve an objective because of a group member's failure, I would explain it as such to my superiors.   Agree Disagree

11. I consider myself indispensable to the company in my present position.   Agree Disagree

---

thinking expressed in this statement is similar to that in Machiavelli's concept of the benevolent dictator. Though such behavior can be useful, it tends not to be successful, a point that Machiavelli himself understood when he wrote *The Prince* and followed that with his *Discourses*.

3. Good leaders depend on their followers as much as they depend on themselves. *Agree (1), Disagree (0).* Mutual dependence is as important in an organization as it is on a battlefield. The best generals cannot win a battle singlehandedly.

4. As a leader, I would always include the reasons why when asking a subordinate to perform a task. *Agree (1), Disagree (0).* "Always" is the key word. Subordinates neither always need nor always should be given the reasons. An emergency in which there is no time for explanations is one kind of situation in which a leader would not give the reasons for taking action.

5. A good leader will achieve his or her objectives at any costs. *Agree (0), Disagree (1).* While achieving one's objectives are important, a supervisor should not try to do so at any costs. Sometimes, the real costs may outweigh the value of the goal. Also, a supervisor should not seek a goal at the expense of his or her subordinates. If that happened, it would be an invitation to subordinate revolt through malicious obedience. Most likely, it would lead to failure in achieving subsequent objectives.

6. As a group manager, I would never entrust a vital project to anyone but myself, even if that meant working overtime. *Agree (0), Disagree (1).* Difficult as it is, a good leader recognizes the need to delegate responsibility to subordinates who are capable of handling it. When justified, this should include responsibility for vital projects.

7. A key to good leadership is being consistent in how one leads. *Agree (0), Disagree (1).* The need for consistency is a leadership myth. There is no one way to lead that is appropriate for all subordinates, in all situations, at all times. An effective leader is a flexible leader—someone who can change his or her style of leadership relative to the needs of subordinates and the situation.

8. If justified, I would recommend a subordinate for a promotion to a position equal to or even higher

than my own position at the time. *Agree (1), Disagree (0)*. One measurement of leadership effectiveness is the ability to successfully promote qualified subordinates to any level.

Note that this is a result, not a characteristic, of effective leadership.

9. Some subordinates can participate in the decision making process without threatening a leader's position. *Agree (1), Disagree (0)*. Participative management is currently in vogue. Unfortunately, there appears to be little recognition of the fact that not all subordinates have the experience or the knowledge to meaningfully participate in the decision making process. Further, subordinates do not develop these skills simultaneously; some are more along in their development than others. So participative decision making is not for everyone. When subordinates do participate in the decision making process, however, the leader is still the leader.

10. If my group failed to achieve an objective because of a subordinate's failure, I would explain it as such to my superiors. *Agree (0), Disagree (1)*. An effective leader should always take responsibility for a subordinate's actions, whether those actions result in successes or failures. By comparison, an ineffective leader tends to blame everything and everyone else instead of his or her own leadership skills.

11. I consider myself indispensable to the company in my present position. *Agree (0), Disagree (1)*. Despite what you may want to believe, no one is or should be indispensable to an organization. To be so is to admit that you have not developed a successor from among your subordinates. This can "lock" you into your position. When that happens, neither you nor your subordinates can progress within an organization. What kind of leadership is that?

Assessing Your Potential

In assessing your score, bear in mind that this device is not a test but an indicator of your leadership potential. If your score was 11 to 9, you have excellent potential; indeed, your leadership ability is probably already self-evident. A score of 8 to 6 shows a good potential but that some thinking needs to be sharpened or changed. A score of 5 to 0 suggests that drastic changes are needed and now.

How did you do?

It is important to recognize that individuals can change over time. What you scored today is not necessarily what you will score tomorrow. It could be better, but it could also be worse. That's why you need to monitor periodically your thinking about leadership behavior.

There are three ways you can manage this monitoring process. First you can look at other supervisors and managers and decide which of them you would follow. Why would you follow them? Is their behavior consistent with the responses to the 11 statements I've discussed? Consider, too, those whom you would not allow and why. How does their behavior differ from those individuals whom you would follow? Answering these questions can provide a better understanding about your own leadership behavior because the type of leader you would follow is the type of leader you would most want to be.

Second, you should go back and review the statements that you missed. Do the explanations make sense to you? Could you successfully apply them to situations at work? If not, why not? In answering this last question, try to be as specific as possible. Listing all the negative reasons is a worthwhile exercise since these reasons likely reflect your own behavior.

Let's look at a specific example. Take your indispensability to your organization (statement 11). You read the explanation but have concluded that it isn't applicable to your work situation. You might list among your reasons that there is no one worth grooming as a successor and there is no where for you to go. Such negative thinking can easily be translated into negative actions—steps like hindering the progress of a worker who threatens your position or not trying as hard to succeed. Your own behavior might be perpetuating the negative situation. Knowing that, you would be in a position to consider actions that once implemented would reflect a change in your thinking and could convert the negatives into positives.

Leadership, itself, is a positive. It's a positive for your subordinates and your organization. But to be effective, leadership has to be monitored periodically by the one person it will most benefit—you.

Understanding Values—
Your Own and Theirs

GORDON P. MILLER

Values are at the base of every decision you make. They also determine the level of commitment you make to a task, impact on motivation, and are the most frequent cause of differences—even conflict—between you and your employees. In short, to be successful as a supervisor, your understanding of values is critical.

Using Values Effectively

Understanding values and using them effectively in manager-employee relationships is not easy. Values are learned, and also usually change from time to time, even from decision to decision. Consequently, you have to be aware of the changing values of employees to maintain effective working relationships.

Remember, however, that the starting point is with you, not your employees. Before you can deal with value differences, you must be fully aware of your own values. A value may be defined as a standard that helps you choose among courses of action or behaviors. Because one standard may be more or less important to different individuals, a sensitivity to these differences is vital. A new employee, for example, may be more preoccupied with acceptance by the team than with any promise of future growth on the job. Another team member may be concerned about how safe it is to disagree with the boss, and still another may prefer more time off—rather than a pay raise—as a reward for a job well done.

Of course, you may prefer a certain standard but your employees may not agree with it. These differences are to be expected, and fortunately, they can be resolved if you're clear about the values driving your decisions.

To get some insight about your standards, keep a log of your major work and non–work-related activities for seven days. Ask yourself, "Where do I spend most of my time and what does that tell me and others about what I value?" You might even go a step further and get some feedback from your employees. Ask them to tell you what they think are your three top priorities at work. It's not necessarily important that your employees agree with what you value, but it's certainly crucial that they trust you to pursue what you say is important to you.

Reprinted from *Supervisory Management,* April 1989

Since you can't force your values on others, it's necessary to identify the differences and to find some common ground so a win-win situation can develop. In this regard, these guidelines may prove useful:

Don't assume anything. You may think you know what is important to your employees, but the best way to avoid problems and conflicts is to ask.

Be prepared to give a little. Things will not get done if employees don't see some benefit—a value payoff. True, you may be able to prove what the best solution is, but unless it can be carried out, the "best" decision is useless. It's always worth compromising with employees when you can because it will raise their level of commitment.

Communicate frequently. Situations change and so do values. The more you talk to your employees, the more likely you are to be in touch with what drives or motivates them. This includes seeking input from employees when making decisions.

Encourage differences. A climate that permits differences of opinion fosters thinking, and that, in turn, leads to better decisions. This is where you have to be clear about what is important to you. By doing this, you'll be able to channel differences toward more productive and creative results.

Define. Definition is the key to any well-considered action, and it is a requisite for taking action and getting full commitment to that action. For instance, what do you mean by quality product, customer concern, employee loyalty, success, or poor performance? Before you're able to move ahead, you and your employees must be absolutely clear about the definition of what you're trying to attain or of what value judgment is driving your actions.

Revisit and clarify organizational values. Employees need to see consistency from the top to the bottom of the organization to feel secure and confident. Mixed signals of any kind will cause confusion and hurt productivity.

Should You Change Your Leadership Style?

LARS-ERIK WIBERG

Leadership comes in four basic styles and eight combinations of these. Is there a best style for a manager? Yes, it is at once none of them and all of them. In other words, organizational success comes from acceptance of this variety and recognition that each of us operates best from one of these 12 styles of leadership. There is something ungainly about leaders trying to adopt a style that doesn't fit their way of managing.

The Beginnings

What determines an individual's leadership style? Everybody has one, whatever the extent to which it may be used, but what is its foundation?

Evidence suggests that it is from among several, natural decision-making patterns, at least one of which we all possess. By decision making, I mean personal judgment in action. The underpinning of a person's natural leadership style is the manner by which judgment is expressed through decision making.

Patterns of Decision Making

Let's look at these four patterns, keeping in mind that the designations are arbitrary—the numbers are simply labels.

Decision-making Pattern I proceeds from concepts, theories, or principles. There has to be a fundamental notion of some sort from which conclusions can flow. It is almost like having a formula that can generate the correct answer, but it is not so simple because this decision maker will personally go to great pains to develop the concepts, theories, and principles necessary as the foundation for "good" decisions. Further, just as often as not, Pattern I will not necessarily accept another Pattern I's concept, so it isn't a question of swapping formulas. It is a matter of high-quality, analytical thinking combined with personal imagination.

Pattern II needs a background of systems, policies, procedures, rules, and regulations. A well-

Reprinted from *Management Solutions,* January 1988

crystallized structure is desired so that conclusions can be drawn according to agreed-upon practices. Only then can the conduct of affairs proceed in any orderly way.

The right kind of organization is most important as a proper decision-making framework, and it will usually be considered satisfactory if surprises are few and results can be anticipated with accuracy. Here high-quality analytical thinking combines with common sense.

Pattern III places a premium on precedent, tradition, and experience. It makes a big difference whether this or that approach worked before or whether it is working now somewhere and may be worth emulating. These decision makers refuse to discard any scrap of useful background that could have a bearing on a present problem; they see no reason to venture into the unknown without solid support based on accumulated, practical knowledge. Since they tend to be persuasive, they are more subject than the other patterns to personal persuasion.

Pattern IV depends on impulse, inspiration, and revelation. These are the hardest decision makers to "get a handle on" because they will go their own way, guided as they are from within. There is less centrality of result with Pattern IV. This means that where, in a given situation, others might come to similar conclusions in line with their respective patterns of decision making, Pattern IV will not. This does not mean that individuals with this pattern tend toward erratic decisions; as individuals, they are as consistent as anyone else. However, more than others, they depend on a unique, inner orientation as a personal guide to what they should do.

Four Leadership Styles

These four basic decision-making patterns lead in turn into some basic leadership styles. It is a natural order since one flows from the other. Where do you fit among these?

Leadership Style I—"Founding." Decision-making Pattern I produces leadership Style I, which is exercised, as you might expect, through theories, concepts, and principles. Decision making is characterized by rapid identification and integration of applicable data and information. Of special interest is the apparent ease with which such leaders can bring forth decisions and solutions when faced with complicated data and alternatives. Indeed, it is not always apparent that they are leading. But they are synthesizers; they see relationships among facts and phenomena that, on the surface, might appear to be unrelated. They have great skill at decision making in a scientific environment, but they can be burdened by "people problems," which are far more difficult for them to cope with.

Style I leaders are strategic by nature; their capacity to plan effectively well into the future is built in. When called upon to produce written plans, they may find it difficult to generate a good product because they are apt to leave out what is obvious to them; what they perceive as evident, others are likely to find obscure. Because of this, they may often need trusted associates to interpret for them. But they are the givers of models, many of which, once they have stood the test of common sense and experience, become the precedents and traditions for others to follow. They are pioneers and like to experiment, and have high tolerance for ambiguity, including deliberate duplication of effort.

Leadership Style II—"Managing." Whereas Style I has a "blue sky" quality, Style II is grounded in practicality. Here decision making typically involves analysis and testing of available data and information—all of it. This process depends heavily on thoroughness, on "touching all the bases," and judgment is reserved, decisions held back, until all the facts are in. It is noteworthy that this style of leadership has come to be called "management" with its emphasis on controls, rules, regulations, systems, policies, and procedures. Style II leaders have just as much trouble with "people problems" as do those of Style I, but whereas Style I leaders are likely to throw up their hands, Style II leaders will believe in others once they have proved themselves. They are "organization minded" and highly systematic, and their overall plan—they always have one—contains provisions for every pertinent activity. It is within these "slots" that subordinates prove themselves.

Style II leaders are bureaucratic and forensic by nature. They are also naturally tactical and have that strong sense of "what to do next." They are the givers of structure with which to face a given need. When that need changes, they will never hesitate to restructure. Their tolerance for ambiguity is extremely low, and they much prize efficiency and economy of effort.

Leadership Style III—"Developing." Style III leaders are motivated by personal feeling and desire. Issues of character and conviction dominate over those of analysis and testing. Problems are solved and decisions made within a framework of applicable precedent, and which precedent the leader believes to be applicable can be a matter of powerful, personal certitude. Such leaders customarily adopt principles and structure from among traditional models—those that have withstood the test of practical experience and are "tried and true"—and they are likely to stick with the models they adopt "through thick and thin." They are deft in their resolution of "people problems"; they believe that people are good until they prove themselves otherwise and will not only try subordinates in various "slots" in an effort to identify their best niches but even permit subordinates to build their own niches where "slots" can't be found. They are team builders, loyal up and down the line. They place a great deal of faith in teaching and coaching, tend to go the last mile with their people, and become visibly upset if "things don't work out." Style III leaders are neither strategic nor tactical themselves. They try to "do what's right" and get their supporting strategy and tactics from trusted associates.

Leadership Style IV—"Inspiring." Style IV leaders can experience great difficulty in following those who possess the other styles. They have a highly personal, internal guidance system, based on intuition and inspiration, which helps them to make decisions almost instantaneously, and their problem-solving skills appear to be equally rapid and often baffling to others because of their effectiveness in the absence of formal logic. They have the least trouble of all the styles in establishing their leadership credentials; it is almost as if they can't avoid leading. Such leaders have immense confidence in what others can accomplish if only they try, and it is to get them to try that Style IV leaders bend their efforts. They lead chiefly be example in a charismatic way.

Style IV leaders do not plan as such because they feel intimately involved in a larger plan that already exists and prefer to seek their place in that plan through intuitive means. Of all the leaders, their accessibility varies the most with prevailing mood; they are the least self-conscious, invariably idiosyncratic, often mysterious, and sometimes scary.

How do the various leadership styles relate to one another? Much depends on the specific nature of the tasks at hand since each style is suited to a particular environment. Nevertheless, there are interpersonal risks generated by certain reporting relationships. In general, Style I should report to another Style I or to Style IV, not to Styles II or III unless the leader is gifted. Styles II and III can report to any style. Style IV can report to Styles II and III for brief intervals, to a Style I leader who is older and wiser than the Style IV, or to another Style IV.

Co-existence

How do the various styles co-exist in one individual? The first axiom is that only neighboring styles can co-exist in one person. The second axiom is that they co-exist either by combination or by alternation. In other words, Styles I and III cannot be found in one person, nor can Styles II and IV; "neighbors" can occur in the same individual. By "combination," it is meant that the two styles actually blend so that each loses a part of its identity in the creation of a new style that is a sort of "hybrid." By "alternation," it is meant that each style retains its identity for independent, tandem use. Let's see what happens in actual practice.

Leadership Styles I & II. In combination, the main emphasis will be on impersonal evaluation—analytical thinking and logical processes. Some practicality and timeliness may be lost, and there won't be much room for hunch playing. This combination favors a lean staff in an austere working environment where both sophisticated strategies and tactics will be thoroughly explored, refined, adopted, and finally implemented.

In alternation, the swing will be between the theoretical and the practical in this highly perceptive pairing. Analysis will be subordinate to synthesis and common sense, but it will play a significant supporting role. This style of leadership has available a common touch that, along with the vision inherent in Style I, can make for an environment that is fresh and exciting, where new ideas can be freely "kicked around" but for adoption must fill a realistic need that is presently felt.

Leadership Styles II & III. In combination, this pairing of styles produces the utmost in practicality, an exceedingly realistic and down to earth approach to both people and problems. The emphasis is so focused on what to do now that planning, as well as adherence to existing systems and organizational protocol, can be disregarded in the heat of reaction to an immediate problem. Nevertheless, if it is a reliable response in a crisis that you need, this is where you will find it.

In alternation, practicality is ever present, though in a subordinate role. There is a swing between a systematic/analytic emphasis that is strong on tactics and a socially conscious outlook that can actually approximate benevolence. This leader will never lose sight of realistic goals and objectives but will approach them from opposite points of view that, as they alternate, can confuse an observer. On one hand, there is a highly intellectual and impersonal outlook; on the other, a most personal orientation full of warmth and feeling.

Leadership Styles III & IV. In combination this pair of styles produces unquestionably the most activist kind of leadership, not in terms of reaction to problems, though this is possible, but in original action toward a personal goal. There is emphasis on achieving something new and aesthetically satisfying; however, traditional values will not be lost and may be most important. In the eagerness to "get on with it," there may be some neglect of factors that should be taken into account, variables that the exercise of sharper perception would include.

In alternation, we find a reemphasis of perception with the activist influence subordinate though present. Thus is produced a more calm and considered leadership environment in which there is a swing between outgoing and effective communication of realistic and pertinent traditional values, and a sort of uncanny, even evangelical expression of what the future might bring.

Leadership Styles IV & I. In combination, vision and intuition are most prominent. This is a highly future-oriented brand of leadership, in which the present will be subordinated to the leader's perception of the future and what must be done to prepare for it. This leadership is not only prophetic but also theoretical, and of all the styles it is the most difficult to understand yet not hard to get along with because what others are doing and thinking is usually not the leader's main concern. It may take such leaders more time than most to "get moving" but when they do, it is with unique assurance. Their outlook is uncluttered by precedent.

In alternation, the influence of future-oriented perception is diminished as two startlingly different behavioral modes alternate. One is that of the aesthetically sensitive leader who actively pursues goals in which artistic beauty predominates. The other is the analytical experimenter who methodically pursues objectives that have an applied scientific or strategic business purpose. In either pursuit, invention is a likely outcome, one rich in feeling and character, the other in intellect and rationality.

Do you see yourself among these 12? With all the styles and variations available, there is no reason for anyone to attempt a style at odds with "what comes natural." Should you believe it a good idea to adopt an expedient pattern and consequently style, remember that it is always best to "stick to one's last," not to waste time and effort that could be put toward cultivation of a natural strength on self-improvement in an area of natural weakness.

If your forte is "developing," don't try to make yourself into a pioneer. The real pioneers will skin you alive as long as they aren't trying to give themselves a developmental veneer. If your great strength is "inspiring," make peace with your inefficiency. Try to make yourself systematic, and you will be about as effective as the "managing" production wizard who attempts to succeed as an epic poet. If it is at all possible, refrain from a style that is less than your best.

You have seen how, for example, "managing" is long on tactics, short on strategy, deficient in inspiration, strong in organization, and weak in development. "Founding" is adept in strategy, inept in development, weak in tactics, indifferent to precedent, unparalleled in pioneering. Tradition-rich "developing" is unexcelled in team building and conservation of useful experience, strong on communication, yet indifferent to theories and weak in planning. With "inspiring" you get charismatic personal example at the expense of efficiency and organization.

It is possible to have many leaders and not enough leadership; just gather an overabundance of the same style in support of the same effort. Think of the weaknesses that could show through. There has to be a leadership mix. One comes to the inescapable knowledge that a balance of leadership styles is essential for any enterprise that wishes to excel.

Targeting Your Audience for Strategic Supervision

THEODORE J. HALATIN

Success as a supervisor often involves more than just overseeing the work of others. In many organizations, supervisors are expected to provide the strategic leadership that directly supports the organization's mission, goals, and philosophy. The supervisor must communicate these to employees, but before he or she can do this, the supervisor must have a real understanding of the organization's target audience—who is to be served.

Every organization has such a target audience. This is the focal point for action and priorities. It is the basis for goals, objectives, procedures, and processes.

A supervisor must define the target audience before attempting to understand the mission, goals, objectives, and philosophy of the organization. It is the target audience that brings reality to the concepts of mission, goals, objectives, and philosophy.

Communicating the strategic mission, goals, objectives, and philosophy to others is also easier when done in terms of the target audience. The supervisor can use actual examples related to the specific target audience to help employees understand the teamwork needed in support of the organization's strategic plans.

Needless to say, daily leadership in support of the organization's mission, goals, objectives, and philosophy must be directed toward the audience that the organization is wanting to serve. The supervisor's daily efforts must prioritize and focus on the audience targeted by the organization.

TA 1-2-3-4

The target audience is not always easy to identify or prioritize. Profits are essential in business, yet throughout the years many profit-oriented businesses have selected or redefined their goals and objectives to include targets other than just profits. These organizations have not abandoned profits but have recognized the relationship and impact of additional goals and objectives on profits. This can cause confusion and problems in organizations that have not clearly identified and communicated the target audience to everyone in the organization.

Supervisors in profit-oriented businesses can gain a better understanding of the organization's mission, goals, objective, and philosophy from Figure 1. It presents, in a cumulative fashion, four different target audiences that may be at the focal point of their business's mission and philosophy. Although it

Reprinted from *Supervisory Management,* April 1989

Figure 1

Target Audience 1	Target Audience 2	Target Audience 3	Target Audience 4
Profits	Profits	Profits	Profits
	Customers	Customers	Customers
		Employees	Employees
			Society

may not cover all organizations or situations, it does provide a supervisor with insights into, and expressions for understanding and communicating, the target audience.

TA 1-2-3-4 expands, from left to right, the number of parts in the target audience. As new elements are introduced, each receives a relative degree of emphasis. Elements are not necessarily equal and their values may change over time. Yet each part should be recognized for its importance in the organization's mission, goals, objectives, and philosophy.

While TA-1 has a single element in the target audience, TA-2 has two elements. The relative emphasis for each element in TA-2 may differ among as well as within organizations. Daily events and situations may promote a change in emphasis. For example, the arrival of a new competitor may cause an existing business to change its strategy. The new strategy may *provide* additional customer services. Although costs for the additional services may reduce profits, the new strategy requires increased emphasis on customer satisfaction. Strategic supervision requires a supervisor to understand, communicate, and lead to support this specific target audience.

Each element in the target audience has an emphasis. Figure 2 provides an overview of the issues of importance to each element in the target audience.

TA-1: Profits

In some businesses, the emphasis is solely on profits. The concern is often for a product or service that meets immediate needs.

Effective supervision in such situations involves emphasis on productivity and bottom-line results. The concentration is on cash-flow, quantity production, and profits. Employees must direct all their efforts and energy toward these goals and objectives. Close supervision may be required to assure that valuable time and resources are not wasted on activities that detract from short-term profits.

TA-2: Profits and Customers

Many businesses emphasize customer satisfaction as the key to profits. In TA-2, the target audience includes both profitability and customers.

Figure 2

Audience	Issue of Importance
Employers	Profits
Customers	Customer Satisfaction
Employees	Quality of Work Life
Society	Social Responsibility

These businesses recognize that satisfied customers mean repeat sales. They realize that dissatisfied customers may return products, refuse to patronize the business, and damage the reputation of the business.

Customer satisfaction is important for businesses depending on a long-term relationship with current and prospective customers. A local restaurant must offer food, service, and prices that will create a repeat customer. A company building a national image must support its name and reputation with products and service that satisfy customers.

Providing customer satisfaction can be expensive and may detract from short-term profits. Yet if the philosophy and goals of the organization are to create satisfied customers while making a profit, all supervisors and employees must work toward these ends. Supervisors may have to train employees in customer relations. Supervisors themselves may have to develop human relations skills and be directly involved in satisfying customers while at the same time protecting profits.

TA-3: Profits, Customers, and Employees

Employees are a part of the target audience for many businesses. Such organizations recognize that employees are not expenses but valuable assets that satisfy customers and produce profits.

Employees who are satisfied, motivated, and trained to do their jobs are seen as more likely to produce high-quality results for the organization. They can work as team members to build a profitable business that will provide them with long-term employment in a company that they are proud to work for. But organizations that include employees as a target audience must be willing to devote resources for enhancing working conditions and the quality of work life.

Supervisors must be aware of employee concerns and needs. Supervisors must develop and use interactive skills that create a positive work environment for the employees. Although short-term profits may be reduced, the supervisor builds a team that works for long-term profits.

TA-4: Profits, Customers, Employees, and Society

Many businesses include society in their target audience. These businesses recognize that society provides the employees, customers, and the rules for making profits.

A business may be very profitable as it satisfies customers and provides an excellent quality of work life for employees, yet elements from society may object and challenge the business. The challenges may include bad publicity, protests, boycotts, new laws, court orders, financial penalties, or taxes.

The impact of special interest groups in society is quite evident and challenging for businesses. Special interest groups are making demands that affect business operations, customers, employees, and profits. These demands include smoking restrictions, parental leave, smokestack pollution, labels for hazardous materials, toxic material handling, combatting illiteracy, and substance abuse. On a local level, these demands may be for financial support, for community activities, or hiring programs for special groups.

The business may develop a philosophy and state certain goals and objectives that include society as a part of the target audience. The supervisor must be aware of these intentions. Employees must be informed about the goals and objectives, the possible effects on the employees and operations, and suggested methods for supporting the goals and objectives. Supervisors must be prepared to deal with disagreements among the workers, such as when smokers have to change their habits for the benefit of non-smokers. In addition, supervisors need to prepare statements that can support the organization's goals, objectives, and philosophy.

Interpreting Employee Needs: Assuming vs. Understanding

ANDREW K. HOH

As a supervisor, do you know what makes your employees tick? If you do (even if you don't and would rather not think about it), let me offer this challenge: Suppose for the moment that you were a production supervisor in a lumber company. How would you assess the job needs of workers who meet the following description?

Your group of about 50 employees is responsible for processing walnut logs into high quality lumber and gunstock; the process includes loading and unloading, stacking lumber, kilning, and sawing. All the positions except one (band-sawyer) are filled with semiskilled or unskilled labor. The workers in the sawmill are subject to considerable amounts of noise and dust. Those in the lumber yard do not have any weather protection throughout the year; the temperature ranges from 25°F in the winter to 105°F in the summer. Starting pay is the minimum wage.

The company personnel records show that your employees have the following demographic characteristics:

Sex: 96 percent, male; 4 percent female.

Age: 25 percent, under 20; 18 percent, 21 to 24; 40 percent, 25 to 29; and 17 percent, 30 or over.

Education: 10 percent completed elementary school; 15 percent completed junior high school; 52 percent completed senior high school; and 23 percent completed some college.

Tenure with the company: 50 percent, three months or less; 20 percent, one year or less, 20 percent, five years or less; and 10 percent, five years or more.

The above describes an actual situation that was found at a sawmill in the Midwest. Even with firsthand information, the six production supervisors who worked at the sawmill and were surveyed on worker attitudes had difficulty identifying their employees' likes and dislikes. Consider the survey results that follow and see if they square with assessments that you would have made.

What Was Asked

The supervisors were given a list of 16 job characteristics and asked to order them according to how their employees would value the items. (The 16 job factors were ones that Daniel Yankelovich found in

Reprinted from *Supervisory Management,* April 1980

his 1973 nationwide survey to be most demanded by young, noncollege-educated blue collar workers.) The rankings of the six supervisors were averaged, with the results shown in Figure 1.

The same supervisors were requested to select from the same 16-item list five characteristics that were most important to *themselves*. The five items that were most frequently mentioned were:

1. Participation in decisions regarding job
2. Chance to use my mind
3. Good pay
4. Interesting work
5. Chance to develop skills and abilities

The two rankings show a striking contrast in how the supervisors viewed themselves and their employees. More specifically, the supervisors' attitudes seem to indicate:

- "We want challenging work. They simply don't care about their work."
- "We are dedicated to our job. They are lazy. They avoid responsibilities."
- "We prefer intrinsic rewards. They just expect extrinsic rewards from their work."
- "We are achievement-motivated. They are money-motivated."

These contrasts indicate the supervisors' feelings of superiority over the employees, their rationalization for rather autocratic leadership behaviors.

How Accurate Were the Estimates?

To test how realistic was the supervisors' understanding of their employees, the same questionnaire was then administered to the employees. The questionnaire was slightly modified to measure their satisfaction with each item. For each characteristic they were asked to give three ratings:

Figure 1

Job Characteristics Ranked by Supervisors as Being Important to Employees

Rank	Job Characteristics
1.	Good pay
2.	Having a job that does not involve hard physical work
3.	Not too demanding a job
4.	Friendly co-workers
5.	Not expected to do things not paid for
6.	Recognition for a job well done
7.	Not being caught up in a big impersonal organization
8.	Participation in decisions regarding job
9.	Chance to use one's mind
10.	Good pension plan
11.	Interesting work
12.	Seeing the results of one's work
13.	Chance to make a lot of money later on
14.	Chance to develop skills and abilities
15.	Job in growing field/industry
16.	Socially useful work

Figure 2

Rank	Job Characteristics	Rating (1 to 7)	Satis- faction (−6 to 0)	Yankelo- vich Survey Ranking
	Sixteen Job Factors Rated by Employees According to Their Importance and Satisfaction			
1.	Pay	6.07	−2.05	3
2.	Chance to develop skills	5.98	−1.61	6
3.	Friendly co-workers	5.95	−.52	1
4.	Pension plan	5.93	−3.12	10
5.	Recognition for a job well done	5.85	−1.88	8
6.	Not being caught up in a big impersonal organization	5.78	−.70	13
7.	Chance to make a lot of money later on	5.77	−1.91	9
8.	Interesting work	5.44	−1.16	2
9.	Chance to use one's mind	5.42	−1.00	5
10.	Job in growing field/industry	5.19	−1.44	11
11.	Participation in decisions regarding job	5.09	−.93	7
12.	Not expected to do things not paid for	5.09	−.43	15
13.	Not too demanding a job	4.88	−.51	14
14.	Seeing the results of one's work	4.81	−.85	4
15.	Having a job that does not involve hard physical work	4.65	−.62	16
16.	Socially useful work	4.50	−.95	12

a. How much of the characteristic is there now connected with your job?

b. How much of the characteristic do you think should be connected with your job?

c. How important is this characteristic to you?

Each rating was on a scale ranging from 1 ("almost none") to 7 ("an exceptional amount"). The difference between ratings *a* and *b* was considered a measurement of the employees' satisfaction (or dissatisfaction) with that job characteristic. And their rating of *c* was used as an indication of the value (importance) they assigned to that characteristic. Figure 2 shows the ranking of the 16 items according to their importance, average ratings, level of satisfaction, and Yankelovich's survey (1973) result.

From Figure 2, we can see how wrong was the supervisors' understanding of their employees. What is worse, motivation and control programs were established on the basis of this misunderstanding, which resulted in employee resentment and poor production. This, in turn, reinforced the belief that employees "simply didn't care about their jobs." It was a vicious circle, a self-fulfilling prophecy.

What Do Workers Really Want?

The data indicate that the workers view themselves as follows:

- "We are not lazy by nature. We don't mind putting an extra effort in our work if the job is right."

- "The job is pleasant to us when it is interesting, requires the use of our minds, provides feedback, and helps us meet good people. Of course, we demand a fair day's wage for a fair day's work."

The employees seem to demand work that is challenging enough to require creativity and use of their talents—work that is of variety and complexity to develop new skills that will bring about opportunities for advancement and greater compensation.

The employees express their desire for friendship at work. They enjoy working with pleasant associates who provide assistance at work, share joy and sorrow, and provide recognition for a job well done.

An analysis of their satisfaction with each of the 16 items suggests a similar conclusion regarding their desires. The three most significant sources of their dissatisfaction appear to be: (1) inadequate compensation, (2) monotonous work, and (3) poor recognition.

What Could Be Done?

After study results were discussed and understood, the six production supervisors considered these questions: What could be done to make sawmill employees' work more pleasant so that both employees and the company benefited? What changes were needed to improve employees' job satisfaction and production as well?

Some of the ideas that were suggested by the supervisors during a brainstorming session are described below.

- *Rotating jobs within the same job classification or alternating jobs that can be easily taught.* Job rotation reduces monotony; helps workers meet different people; allows them to learn new skills; and helps them see the entire production picture and thus understand how their jobs fit together to make the whole.

- *Giving frequent and concrete production feedback.* This gives employees a feeling of accomplishment, becomes a sort of recognition, and gives them something to compete against the next day—a desire to surpass the record.

- *Allowing more frequent but shorter breaks.* This reduces the monotony, gives a chance to stretch backs from physically hard work, and facilitates development of friendship.

- *Willingness to accept some mistakes.* Without risk, there is no innovation. When a possible failure would not be very costly to the company, full delegation to employees can be considered. This is a way of developing employees' skills, reducing managers' workload, giving employees a feeling of greater control over their work, and increasing job satisfaction.

- *Asking for suggestions at small group meetings.* The workers live and breathe their work problems and probably have good ideas on how to improve work situations. Giving them an opportunity to voice their opinions is a recognition of their creativity and a sound path toward building team spirit. However, people are afraid of making public speeches, and, in addition, when two or more departments are gathered together, it is difficult to find some common interest. The spirit of free discussion without fear of ridicule can best be developed in small group settings.

- *Improving physical working conditions within budget and technological constraints.* Safer, quieter, and cleaner working conditions help reduce absenteeism, tardiness, and turnover. Further, employees can devote attention and energy to work activities rather than worrying about job hazards.

Insight Gained

The results of the study and brainstorming session were a shock to the six sawmill supervisors who felt they'd gained a new insight into the human elements of the company. The following remarks were made by the supervisors in summing up their views:

- "It is too dangerous to 'guess' or 'assume' what employees are satisfied and dissatisfied with."
- "It is imperative to maintain open and honest communication with employees to solicit their opinions and desires."
- "We need to gather more often to brainstorm new ideas, evaluate the costs and benefits of the ideas, and propose to upper management changes that can be justified."

A Baker's Dozen of Ways to Motivate People

ANDREW SHERWOOD

A question frequently asked by managers is, "What really motivates people?" Over the years, many answers have been given. Synthesizing all of these, you would probably come up with something like these 13 fundamental principles of motivation:

Giving Recognition

1. *Make sure that accomplishment is adequately recognized.* Most human beings need to be recognized, but individual accomplishment often seems to get lost, particularly in larger organizations.

2. *Provide people with flexibility and choice.* Whenever possible, permit employees to make decisions for themselves. People who are not given this opportunity tend to become passive and lethargic.

3. *Provide support when it is needed.* And make sure that employees do not hesitate to make use of it. Asking for help should never be considered a sign of weakness; it should be considered a sign of strength.

Delegating Responsibility

4. *Provide employees with responsibility, along with their accountability.* Nothing motivates people as much. The responsibility should be neither too high nor too low for the employee. Too often, employees are held accountable for tasks that are beyond their area of responsibility. This is unfair and can lead to frustration. Few people will reject accountability as long as the tasks in question are within their power.

5. *Make sure that employees are aware of how their tasks relate to personal and organizational goals.* A few extra minutes of explanation can prevent boredom over routine work and increase productivity.

6. *Encourage employees to set their own goals.* At least, they should participate actively in the goal-setting process. People tend to know their own capabilities and limitations better than anyone else. In addition, personal goal-setting results in a commitment to goal accomplishment.

Reprinted from *Management Solutions*, May 1987

The Right Mix

7. *Provide an appropriate mix of extrinsic rewards and intrinsic satisfaction.* Extrinsic rewards are rarely enough to motivate people on an on-going basis these days. Employees also need to obtain intrinsic satisfaction from their jobs. Intrinsic satisfaction results from tasks that are interesting, varied, relatively short, and challenging. In addition, you should realize that excessive use of extrinsic rewards, such as praise, can overwhelm intrinsic satisfaction. So be careful to provide an appropriate level of extrinsic rewards while permitting employees to experience the personal satisfaction that results from doing an appropriately challenging job well.

8. *Individualize your supervision.* Some people need closer supervision than others, and some people do not need supervision at all. Motivation can be increased through facilitative supervision, providing the minimum amount of supervision that is required by the individual for optimal performance.

9. *Provide immediate and relevant feedback that will help employees improve their performance in the future.* Feedback is most effective when it follows performance, is relevant to the task, and provides employees with clues on how they might improve their performance at the task. Never give negative evaluative feedback without providing informational feedback.

Self-Fulfilling Prophecy

10. *Exhibit confidence in employees.* There is a great deal of research to support the contention that people who are expected to achieve will do so more frequently than others.

11. *Increase the likelihood that employees will experience accomplishment.* The old saying "Nothing succeeds like success" is definitely true. So every employee should be provided with the opportunity to be successful or at least be a significant part of success. All employees who have contributed to a successful project, no matter how small their contribution might appear, should be given credit for the accomplishment.

12. *Establish a climate of trust and open communication.* Motivation is highest in organizations that encourage openness and trust. Threat is one of the great obstacles to individual motivation, and it should be eliminated.

13. *Demonstrate your own motivation through behavior and attitude.* Nothing turns people off faster than a manager who preaches motivation but does not practice what he or she preaches. The motivator must be motivated; this means animated, striving, realistic, and energetic. Modeling appropriate behavior is a very powerful tool indeed.

How do you rate on these 13 points? Of course, no manager could be expected to do everything that is outlined here on all occasions, nor probably would it be wise. There is always the possibility of motivational overkill. But understanding these 13 principles is requisite to establishing and maintaining effective work relationships—and that is essential to successful management.

Keeping Your High Achievers Motivated

J. ALAN OFNER

High potential/high achievers (HIs) probably represent less than five percent of the workforce, but they provide most of the energy that fuels corporate growth. Maximizing their talents is a challenge for management even in the best of times, but it is particularly difficult now.

Traditional opportunities for advancement have diminished. The number of available slots has shrunk. The wave of mergers and acquisitions created redundant positions, many of which have been eliminated. At the same time, the highly competitive business climate placed a premium on cost reduction and downsizing. More positions were lost in a trend that continues today.

In fact, smaller may be better—and more efficient—but this is small consolation to the high potential/high achievers whose careers are apparently stalled because their employers can't give them the chance to grow.

Under such circumstances, what can managers do to keep their high potential/high achievers (HIs) motivated?

Career Management

Actually, the process should begin even before HIs are in the workplace—during the hiring process. Managers should make it a point not to hire candidates who are clearly over-qualified. Candidates should be told the truth about a job opportunity and the immediate tasks to be performed.

Naturally, this advice applies to all candidates, but it's absolutely critical in the case of HIs. They get frustrated easily when they feel they are being unfairly held back or that they are not getting the opportunities promised to them.

Some organizations—J. C. Penney, Exxon, General Motors, General Electric, and Eli Lilly, for example—have created career management programs for their HIs. No two programs are exactly alike, but these programs have similar objectives—to:

- Identify *high potential*/high achievers, not just the top performers in the division.
- Involve line management actively in running the program, with corporate staff in a supportive role.

Reprinted from *Management Solutions,* July 1987

- Develop "doers" (not learners) who can be held accountable for results.
- Encourage line managers to make positions available for developmental moves.
- Provide special training, both internal and external, and funding if necessary.
- Make special task force positions available.
- Train the supervisors of high potential/high achievers.

Companies with career management programs for HIs have reaped the benefits. Unfortunately, they are in the distinct minority

Identifying

HIs are difficult to identify. Many companies mistakenly assume that they will reveal themselves through performance. This approach doesn't work well because it fails to take into account the bureaucratic variables in a large organization. For example, some supervisors may try to "hide" high achievers and keep them in their departments by giving them less than outstanding performance reviews. Others may proudly claim a large number, even if there are only one or two who truly meet the criteria.

Other companies make the mistake of forcing all employee appraisals into some variety of bell curve, which requires that a fixed number of people receive top grades. Inevitably, either some nondeserving employees will be pushed into the highest grade or deserving executives will be forced beneath it. In any event, this system does not guarantee that those in the top tank will be the HIs one wants to find.

Management must take an active role in identifying HIs. Administrative profiles are often a good departure point: Individuals rated "exceptional" in performance and "highly promotable with potential" are likely candidates for the fast track.

Interviews with department heads will provide further definition for individuals who meet the administrative criteria. Comments to look for include "goal oriented," "risk taker," "good interpersonal skills," and "a leader." They describe HI candidates for career management.

Providing Feedback

HIs seek constant feedback in a variety of ways, and they get frustrated when promotions, assignments, or even access to higher management doesn't happen according to their timetables. The same holds true if the tasks involved in their jobs don't measure up to their expectations.

To prevent frustrations, supervisors must assess and communicate the realities of the work situation to the HIs. In this active counseling role, they can:

- Advise about the hazards of the track that is "too fast."
- Point out the performance and behavior characteristics that lead to true success in the organization.
- Help define the next milestones in an HI's career path.

The last is critical because it is the thread that ties the individual to the organization.

Job Enrichment

Still, today's leaner corporate structure cannot always support the promotions or new assignments that meet the expectations of many HIs. How then can we maintain their enthusiasm and productivity?

One solution is to make an HI's current assignment more challenging. With the greater challenge necessarily comes increased responsibility. This approach may require a change in managing values in the organization. Managers must look at each position as an opportunity for people to grow—as well as to perform tasks.

Proponents of work redesign and job enrichment believe that both individual and corporate needs are met by this approach. Skills improve along with knowledge of the organization. It is a particularly appropriate vehicle for HIs, whose high degree of motivation can carry them to success in challenging assignments that could daunt or overwhelm a marginal performer or plateaued worker.

Job Rotation

Historically, job rotation has been another approach to stimulating and satisfying high potential/high achievers. It is not nearly as viable an option in large companies today due to organizational realities like downsizing and cost cutting. In small firms, few opportunities ever existed.

When job rotation is possible, managers must take care to provide suitable opportunities within the organization while avoiding the mistake of pushing impatient HIs up the corporate ladder too quickly. Some promising employees have been moved so fast, so often, that they haven't had time to polish their skills, gain the experience, or develop the behavior that leads to long-term success.

The solution lies in an approach similar to what Eli Lilly & Co. terms "quality movement." Management must determine what the employee should learn from a particular assignment and make sure that the term of the assignment is long enough for the employee to do so. Lateral movement within the company is fine—a marketing person can certainly benefit from a stint in manufacturing—as long as the employee can develop a broad range of experience.

A caveat: Some HIs practice job rotation between different companies. If a prospective employee has a résumé with a number of different positions in different organizations, the manager may be at risk in hiring, no matter how attractive the candidate.

Special Assignments and Training

Even though cost cutting companies have eliminated many management development programs, there are other initiatives that can be used to energize HIs. A developmental assignment, tailored to the needs of the individual, is one good example. Such an assignment would place an HI on a corporate task force or committee dealing with a special project or issue. For instance, assignment to a task force evaluating corporate expansion opportunities could help improve a person's solving, influencing, and negotiating skills.

Companies that are developing new products and/or markets—or even buying new businesses—may provide HIs with opportunities that meet their needs. For example, some can be satisfied by assignment to the team charged with responsibility for the new venture. As a rule, senior managers should give serious consideration to HIs when the question of staffing these operations arises.

Assignments outside the organization should also be considered. "On loan" support to a local government, for example, can provide experience not available in the working environment and also help strengthen a company's relationship with the community.

Supervisors may discover that HIs need specific training. For some, it may be in areas related to self-awareness, such as training in sensitivity, interactive skills, or team building. Others may benefit from job-related training, such as instruction in problem solving or computer-assisted decision making.

Finally, having a senior executive act as a mentor is another strategy that has been used to help HIs adapt to an organization and grow with it. To make this form of behavior modelling work best, there must be a good personal chemistry between the mentor and the HI from the outset.

Monitoring the Program

Once the program is in progress, monitoring its effect on the HI and the organization is crucial. For example, has the individualized attention given to the HI caused resentment among co-workers? Is the fast-track individual becoming a learner rather than a doer?

There is no established, uniform way to maximize development or high potential/high achievers. Managers must tailor their strategies to the needs and characteristics of the individual. They must carefully weigh their organization's culture, climate, and values, because the HI program must relate to the company's interpersonal style and business traditions.

Any program for HIs must be based on an acute understanding and acceptance of the individual and commitment to his or her development. Supervisors should realize that HIs must be observed more closely than their colleagues and take the time to do so.

Some Final Observations

Development must be a "real" experience for high potential/high achievers, preferably relating to operations. Managers should avoid assigning people to artificially created jobs or token projects that create a learning experience at the expense of a "doing" experience.

Overcoming Resistance to Change

WALDRON BERRY

Managers issue directives to subordinates almost daily and are frequently disappointed when they are not carried out well. This is usually attributed to the employees' inability to understand instructions, low motivation, or poor training. Sometimes the manager simply blames it on his or her subordinates' tendency to resist change. But the real problem too often may be the manager's inability to manage change effectively. After all, most directives represent a need for change by one or more employees.

To manage change effectively, a manager must realize that directives and requests for seemingly unimportant changes in work routine represent sometimes significant changes to subordinates, understand that employees do not automatically resist change, and be aware of how his or her subordinates view a request to accomplish a task or behave in a particular manner.

The Employee Response Model

It is fairly obvious that important organizational changes such as the implementation of a new performance evaluation procedure, a new company compensation system, or the establishment of MBO in the company will concern an employee. Such changes will affect the employee very directly and importantly. It is not so obvious to most managers that the subordinate will have an opinion one way or the other regarding small, seemingly unimportant requests. Actually, the employee probably goes through the same thought process each time a directive or a request is received, regardless of its nature.

The first thing that the employee does is consider the effect of the request or directive on himself or herself. There can be an infinite number of conclusions but generally he or she will evaluate it as very negative and harmful, neither negative nor positive, or very positive and helpful. After making this judgment, the employee will respond accordingly. The response could be active or passive opposition, acceptance, or commitment and positive action. This process is shown in Figure 1.

Several factors can affect an employee's response to change:

Economic. Any change that negatively affects employees in economic ways—such as lower pay, longer hours with no increase in pay, fewer promotions, or procedural changes that make the current job obsolete and require employee retraining—will be met with strong resistance.

Sociological changes. Changes that influence work relationships are thought by some experts to

Reprinted from *Supervisory Management,* February 1983

Figure 1

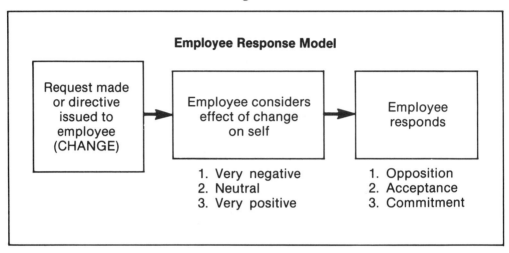

cause greater resistance to change than any other factors. The change might be in the organizational structure so that employees will be with different people or in management so employees have to report to a new supervisor. Changes initiated by outsiders—particularly staff or technical personnel—are strongly resisted by line employees.

Personal and/or psychological. Individuals respond to a request for change differently. The reasons for opposition to a directive vary. For instance, some employees are frightened by the unknown and will resist any action for which they do not know the reasons. The manager may believe that the logic of a directive or request should be apparent to subordinates, so he or she may offer no explanation. But logic has nothing to do with these employees' responses. They resist out of fear. Providing complete information to these employees could make the difference between opposition and commitment, and it doesn't take much time—just some planning.

Sometimes opposition is based on an individual's past experiences. Take John. He has had bad experiences with his supervisor and the organization in terms of job changes in the past. The supervisor had previously made two or three offers that Jon accepted and all had adverse effects on his career. The organization also changed the performance evaluation procedures twice in the past three years, and both changes have turned out badly for John. After these experiences, it's not surprising that John opposes any change.

Some supervisors are surprised when a talented subordinate turns down a promotion. They forget that people can perceive such an opportunity differently. When Jane, for instance, was offered a promotion, it was to a position in which she had had little experience. After considering the offer, she concluded that she would not do well initially and could be demoted or lose her job. Her boss thought that she would see this as a wonderful learning experience and consequently he was surprised when she turned the offer down. It never occurred to him to mention to Jane that management had confidence in her ability to learn the job and that there were several well-qualified employees in the new office who would provide assistance until she had gained experience.

In considering Jane for the new position, her boss made one mistake: He thought that she would react to the offer as he might have reacted 20 years earlier. Instead, he should have considered how she would react. This requires that he learn as much as possible about Jane and her needs and wants.

What Should a Manager Do?

Before issuing any directive that requires a positive response from employees, a manager should:

1. Determine the response needed from the employee to accomplish the task effectively.
2. Estimate the expected response if the directive is simply published or orally passed to the employee (as many are).
3. If there is a variance between the needed response and estimated response, determine how the two can be brought together.

Opposition is never an acceptable response. Even if employees do as requested, the request or directive will usually not be carried out satisfactorily under such conditions. However, on some occasions acceptance is all that is possible, and perhaps all that is required. If the manager wants routine purchasing procedures changed, it is unlikely that an employee will become highly motivated toward such a change regardless of how it is presented. The employee who simply accepts the change and is not necessarily committed will probably accomplish the task in a satisfactory manner. If the employee were highly committed and positively motivated, it is doubtful that there would be much difference in the end result. All that is necessary is satisfactory accomplishment of the various steps in the purchasing procedure. If a machine is to be used and a checklist is required to be followed before its use, all that is required is that the items on the checklist be accomplished satisfactorily, not that the checks be made eagerly or in a highly motivated fashion. On the other hand, if the manager were attempting to establish an MBO system in the department, a high degree of commitment from all department employees would be required. Certainly the results of an employee who merely accepts the request to start implementing MBO and one who tackles the job in a highly motivated manner will be different.

Achieving the Needed Response

If the manager issues an unclear written directive to change the purchasing procedure with no explanation of the reason for change, a response of opposition or resistance is likely. A clearly written directive accompanied by a face-to-face explanation should result in at least acceptance. Little extra effort would be required in such a case.

Past unsuccessful attempts to install MBO have shown clearly that commitment is the necessary response. Many reasons have been given for the failure of MBO; they include inadequate training, lack of knowledge of the system, not enough active participation of top management, and too much paperwork. This probably indicates lack of participation and lack of information and understanding of the system—the employee does not know what is going to happen. Although implementing MBO is not easy, managers could do a much better job if they prepared their employees more than they do. This would increase employee commitment.

Once employees respond to the directive, the manager must check to see that the response received is the one needed to accomplish the task effectively. If there is a difference between the required and the forecast response, what does the manager do to bring the two together?

If there is an opposition response, the manager can apply pressure to accomplish the results required—possibly even change the opposition to acceptance at least for the short term. Applying pressure, however, cannot change an opposition response to one of commitment and may not even change it to acceptance. And once an employee has been put under this type of pressure, it will be more difficult for the manager to gain commitment from that employee in the future.

The manager may also be able to gain acceptance by offering desirable rewards such as better pay or better working conditions. Even with these extrinsic rewards, though, it is questionable whether real commitment can be achieved.

Employee participation in planned changes may be more useful in gaining an acceptance response. Although it may not be feasible to follow all of the suggestions received, it may be possible and even desirable to follow many. Certainly acceptance can be achieved by inviting employee participation. A commitment response may even be forthcoming if employees perceive their participation as a sincere desire to receive employee suggestions and it represents normal company practice.

Needless to say, along with the invited participation must go a willingness to adjust original directives and requests.

The *only* way that the manager can consistently gain commitment from an employee is to convince him or her that accomplishing the task will help the employee as much or more than it will help the organization. The answer to the employee's question, "How will this affect me?" must be "very favorably" if commitment is to be achieved.

Why You Can't Motivate Everyone

WILLIAM H. FRANKLIN, JR.

Take 60 seconds and write down your definition of motivation.

As you have defined it, what is motivation? Is it the way someone acts? Or an attitude, maybe? If it's an attitude, who is responsible for creating that attitude? These are all important questions because there is probably no supervisory process more widely misunderstood than this thing we call motivation. Consider: Who is primarily responsible for the attitudes *you* have toward *your* job? You, of course. And, if you are primarily responsible for your job attitudes, doesn't the same apply to everyone else? Yet much is being taught and written to convince you and others that you are responsible not only for your own disposition on the job but also for your employees' attitudes as well!

The Motivation Process

Motivation is essentially the state of mind with which a person views a particular task or goal. It is spontaneous, uniquely personal, and often colored by a person's life experiences. Both the intellect and the emotions contribute to this mind state or attitude, and at least four preconditions must exist before a person is motivated to action:

1. *A recognizable need.* It's obvious that a totally satisfied person has no incentive to do anything. And one fact of life in a country as prosperous as ours is that most people do not want for the essential things in life. With the growing body of social legislation, company benefits, and the influence of labor unions, adequate pay and security are increasingly taken for granted and are no longer basic motives for work. Yet for a person to be motivated to action, there must first be a clear and present need, an internal shortfall that demands attention.

We shouldn't confuse wishes for needs. Needs are worth sacrifices to satisfy them, but wishes never mobilize effort. One person needs an education and is willing to work a full-time job and go to school at night to get it.

2. *A goal.* The other side of a need is a goal. As was true for needs, it should be obvious that a person cannot become motivated unless there exists some goal structure. Goals channel and focus effort; they are targets that eliminate needs.

3. *Drive.* Drive acts like a tension spring, connecting needs to goals. This tension or drive may be strong or weak depending upon two uniquely personal factors that can best be described by example.

Reprinted from *Supervisory Management*, April 1980

A worker has a need to excel in his company and, therefore, determines that his goal will be a promotion to higher rank within a particular time. If he were asked, "To what level would you prefer to be promoted?" the answer would likely be, "To become president and, if not that, a vice-president and, if not that, the department manager" and so on. In other words, the employee can establish within the framework of his own values a definite *ordering* of *preferences* from the highest to the lowest. However, if this person were further asked to assign a weight to each of his preferences reflecting his *expectation* of success in achieving them within the given time, he might find his highest preference had no expectation of success. Thus his drive in achieving that goal would be zero.

Drive is the result of a mental computation in which desire is modified by reality as reality is perceived by the individual. We may want something very much; but seeing little chance of getting it, our drive is low. Similarly, we may have a high expectation of success but low desire for a particular objective, so that drive is again low. On the other hand, if our desire to achieve some end is high, and our belief in success is also high, then our drive is strong.

4. *A payoff.* No one does anything "for free." There must be some intrinsic reward or payoff in its accomplishment. Even an act of benevolence pays off in terms of self-satisfaction.

Also, it's important to recognize that there is no absolute worth in a particular reward or payoff, rather, an individual's own value structure assigns what a reward is worth to him or her personally. It should be apparent, for example, that $100 in added income would be assigned different values by a person making $400 and another making $2,000, or by a person already working 40 hours per week and another working 60 hours. This value judgment also compares a person's evaluation of the reward's worth to the effort required to receive it.

The Motivation Myth

The relationship between needs, goals, drive, and payoff in the motivational process is shown in Figure 1. In its usual version, the motivation myth assumes that an outside agent, a supervisor perhaps, can set goals for subordinates and dangle an enticing reward, and suddenly the subordinate needs to achieve that goal because he or she is driven to receive the reward. Let's examine this myth from a realistic perspective.

First, remember, a person's needs are quite personal, and, as much as we may "need" a person to be something other than he or she now is, nothing happens until that person needs it. Similarly, it is inconceivable that one human being could truly set goals for another, unless one of them is really a robot. Unfortunately, though, supervisors are sometimes tricked into thinking they can set goals that employees will pursue with the same zeal as if they had set them. An employee may be indifferent to the point that he or she is willing to play along with this deception for the present, but otherwise remains uncommitted. Or an ambitious employee may decide he or she can achieve real aims by appearing to go along with the boss's aims for him or her much like a trained dog jumps through a hoop. Sooner or later, however, the indifferent employee becomes bored and doesn't want to continue the game, and the ambitious person either achieves his or her real ends or matures and becomes independent enough to withstand having someone else set the goals to be accomplished.

Figure 1

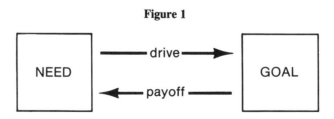

Next, it is important to understand that goal-directed drive is a complex interaction between an individual's desire to achieve a particular goal and his or her notion of the likelihood that the efforts will be successful. Both are powerful factors reflecting one's own personality and inclination toward risk taking. In a normal adult, it seems quite unlikely that either factor is susceptible to external manipulation.

The final element in the motivational process—the reward or payoff—is also something that involves a valuation in uniquely personal terms. A reward is a reward only if an individual sees it as a reward. The reward or payoff condition must be needed by the individual, and it must be reasonably related to the effort required to receive it.

This latter point may explain why organizational inducements such as pay, promotion, and praise fail. Too often these are standardized in keeping with organizational policy.

So, needs, goals, drive, and the value of the payoff condition are all bounded by an individual's own psychology. As such, they cannot be directly controlled by anyone other than the individual, meaning that one person cannot "motivate" another person. To be able to motivate another person suggests an ability to transplant something in someone that is not naturally and spontaneously at home there. While the function of parenting might approximate this ability during the period in which a child is forming values, it's doubtful that it can be accomplished between responsible adults. Regrettably, what often is taken as an example of successful motivation of one person by another is really nothing more than a disguised form of mutual seduction wherein each party has something the other wants or of fear instilled in one person by another. One could hardly be considered motivated with a gun in his or her back. Peter the Great seemed to recognize this in his acknowledgement that he could own a man's body but never his heart— as the well-worn adage says, "You can lead a horse to water but you can't make him drink."

What Can a Supervisor Do?

Admitting that a supervisor cannot motivate his or her subordinates does not mean that the manager is helpless, only that supervisory input is limited and at best bears indirectly on the performance of others.

The motivational process, as we have said, involves a succession of individual value judgments and choices. So whatever a supervisor can do is limited to creating or modifying the environment in which these judgments and choices are made. This is an important distinction. *Environmental modification is not synonymous with motivation.* Suppose, for example, a prisoner has a desire to escape and does so. Upon recapture, the warden can place him in solitary confinement and inflict hard labor upon him. However, if freedom is worth the risk of escaping and the consequences upon recapture, the prisoner will undoubtedly try to escape again—a scenario upon which the motion picture *Papillon* was based. The warden cannot prevent escape, he can only establish the cost of an attempt that fails. Possibly the warden can make the cost of escaping so expensive that the prisoner will no longer attempt it, but that is a judgment only the prisoner must make. The warden can only indirectly influence it.

In the same way, a supervisor can establish the climate in which an employee makes choices, but he or she can't control the choices made. Hopefully, by understanding this, the supervisor can focus energies where they belong and avoid dissipating them on attempts to achieve the impossible.

What can a supervisor do to create an environment in which positive behavior rather than negative behavior is more likely to occur? Here are several suggestions.

1. *Make expectations abundantly clear.* Can you imagine a supervisor having any basis to complain about an employee's performance when that employee did not know what was expected of him or her? Hardly. Yet, in a well-known research study of superior and subordinate communications conducted by the American Management Association, it was found that the supervisor and employee could correctly describe the subordinate's job in only 23 percent of the cases surveyed. Almost unbelievably, in more than seven out of ten working relationships, the employee does not know what is expected of him or her. A supervisor who fails to create a clear climate of job performance expectations is actually interfering with an employee's ability to make competent choices regarding his or her own performance. What otherwise

might appear to the supervisor to be an uninspired performance may be in fact that manager's own failure to provide clear direction.

The more important a particular outcome is to a supervisor, the more clearly it should be communicated to the employee. A secretary, for example, who has a boss with a strong inclination for promptness in completing work and neatness in typing should certainly share those expectations, with specific emphasis on what *he* or *she* considers promptness and neatness. While this won't guarantee these results, it does give guidance if they are to be forthcoming from the employee. Remember, again, research has shown that no job performance can be assumed to be so obvious that a clear statement of expectations can be ignored by a supervisor.

2. *Specify performances that earn special rewards.* A mistake of long standing in industry and government is that people are not told how the reward game is played—that is, what kind of performance they need to put in to get a raise or promotion. This is the case despite the fact that people make decisions allocating effort based on what's in it for them.

For an employee to make a decision to pursue a particular reward, he or she must know the performance level that produces that reward. But such information is infrequently communicated, probably because most supervisors don't have a clear idea themselves of which job outcomes are worthy of special reward. Instead, using some vague criteria, they decide what a special effort is worth *after the fact,* when it obviously has no influence on the employee's decision to put forth that effort. This is an arrangement that can lead to frustration for both supervisors and their subordinates.

Research, for example, has shown that people invariably place a higher value on their own work and effort than do others, a finding that should not be surprising. In the absence of a specific advance agreement as to what performance earns rewards, a supervisor is left wide open to an employee who, relying on his or her own standard of what constitutes rewardable performance, feels defrauded when the supervisor's evaluation doesn't agree. On the other hand, it takes a great leap of faith by even the most ambitious employee to be willing to perform "above and beyond" in an ambiguous reward system that relies on the supervisor's sense of justice to determine the fair reward *post facto.*

Certainly, some outcomes are easier to quantify than others; it's easier, for example, to measure a decrease in a drill press operator's reject rate than to measure the company image that a PBX operator projects on incoming calls. However it is accomplished, though, rewardable outcomes must be established in advance if they are to have any influence on the choices employees make concerning their efforts.

3. *Don't promise what you can't personally deliver.* In all but the smallest organizations a supervisor exercises limited influence outside of his or her work group. That's why that individual must be careful not to make commitments to employees for which he or she cannot virtually guarantee delivery and protection from subsequent withdrawal. To illustrate what happens when this is forgotten, consider what happened at one plant where an assembly line was producing about half of what it should have been producing. Its young supervisor negotiated an understanding with the assembly line workers that, if they met the standard hourly output, they could have any remaining time in the hour for a break. Shortly thereafter the workers were meeting the standard in 35 minutes and taking a 25-minute break each hour. Both the workers and the supervisor realized this arrangement could not last, so they agreed to raise their hourly standard to 30 percent above the company standard, again with the understanding that time left over in each hour after meeting the standard rate belonged to the workers. In time this rate was met and still allowed an hourly ten-minute break. The arrangement worked fine until a divisional vice-president, impressed with the spectacular improvement, dropped by to see how it had been done. Unfortunately, his visit occurred in the middle of a ten-minute break. In no uncertain terms, the executive let it be known that the workers were being paid for eight hours of work, and work eight hours they would. His action had the expected effect—production returned to its original substandard level as the line returned to the original work arrangement.

Regardless of the vice-president's shortsightedness, the fact remains that the line's young (and now considerably more experienced) supervisor learned a bitter lesson—don't promise a reward that you might have to depend on someone else to deliver or to keep from being later withdrawn.

Closely related to this principle is another: Don't promise rewards that are contingent on events outside of your control and that may not happen (for example, bonuses based on company profit goals being realized). Invariably, the promises are remembered and the contingencies aren't.

4. *Give personal attention to all work.* Probably no supervisory act has as great an impact on the climate of the workplace as the supervisor giving *personal* attention to the work produced by his or her subordinates.

If the supervisor is not careful, he or she can very easily find time dissipated by paperwork, personnel actions, and meetings, leaving little chance to get out of the office and personally see what is going on. This can create the impression among employees of the manager being "too busy" or of having other things more important to do.

A supervisor has to demonstrate interest in the work done by the department by asking questions, commenting on results, and correcting poor performance. The benefits of this exercise should be obvious. When the members of an organization realize that it makes a difference how their work is performed, and that their supervisor is willing to take pains to assure it is being accomplished properly, they are more likely to adopt his or her standards as their own.

5. *Be a good model.* Besides giving personal attention to the work, a supervisor should personify what he or she expects of others. This means more than conveying a "I wouldn't ask my people to do anything I wouldn't do" attitude. In every organization there exists a multitude of unwritten rules and norms having to do with everything from getting to work on time to how many minutes are really in a ten-minute break, and many of these norms grow up around the boss's behavior. In one manufacturing company, for example, a department manager began to go into his office on Saturdays to catch up on work without the usual interruptions that occurred during the week. Before long many of the department members were also coming to the office on Saturday, although most had no real need to be there and would simply put in an appearance, then duck out the back door. Despite the fact that they had not been asked to work on Saturday, they felt considerable resentment that their manager's example more or less compelled them to be there.

More than he or she may realize, a supervisor is a powerful behavior model. A manager can do more to affect the performance of his or her employees through example than could ever be accomplished by rule of organization. The supervisor's break ritual, for instance, will most likely be duplicated by members of the department; if it is the individual's tendency to remain an extra five minutes, then the inclination of his or her subordinates will be to do likewise. On the other hand, if the manager returns to work promptly, those reporting to that individual are not likely to remain behind. In essence, the supervisor shows by example what he or she considers to be important.

On Balance

As supervisors, we've all been frustrated by the fact that we couldn't "turn on" some people. When this occurs, the real danger is taking personal responsibility for the supposed motivational failure and turning the frustration inward. It is tempting, then, for us to redouble the effort that most certainly will be resisted even more by the employee. As supervisors, we would be well advised instead to concentrate our efforts on what we can do and to do that well. You cannot be responsible for your employees; you are responsible to them.

Being responsible for someone implies that you can essentially be that person, make choices for him, and motivate him to achieve goals that have been selected for him. If we could succeed at this, we could make a person over in our own image. But it isn't possible. There is an old adage that says, "You can't make a silk purse out of a sow's ear." It's true. Some people are sow's ears because they wouldn't have it otherwise.

On the other hand, to be responsible to someone implies making available every opportunity for that person to be whatever *he* or *she* chooses to be and to create a work climate that clarifies as much as possible expectations and the opportunities and consequences of choices that that individual might make. This is clearly something that a supervisor can do. Admittedly, this response is limited, but it is not ineffective. And accepting the fact that a worker is responsible for his or her own performance will leave a supervisor less frustrated at the end of the day. Needless to say, if that performance is outside of what can be tolerated, then the employee should be disciplined or dismissed. Don't continue to throw good supervisory time after bad. And, by all means, don't take responsibility for that person's choices!

Job Satisfaction:
It's the Little Things That Count

R. BRUCE McAFEE and MYRON GLASSMAN

John Timmons, sales rep, is on his way to work at Rustic Kitchen Company. John has been with the company for three years, makes $25,000 per year, and should get a promotion to manager within two more years. As John pulls into the company parking lot, he sees that he will have to get his feet wet again. "Darn it, when is someone going to unclog the water drain? It's been clogged for weeks!"

As he walks into the office, John notices that he has only five minutes to get together the papers he needs for the upcoming meeting. "Let me see, I will need ten copies of this outline," he mumbles to himself as he heads down to the copying machine. Looking down, he reads the sign, "Out of Order." "Oh, no, not again! How am I ever going to make my presentation without copies of the outline?" Heading back to the office, he asks the department secretary, "Is there any coffee?" She replies, "No, we ran out of filters yesterday. We should get some in a few days."

"Hey, John, do you have a minute?" asks Chris, one of John's co-workers. "Did you see this memo from the boss? It says he wants to meet with the department tomorrow at 4:00."

"You must be kidding!" exclaims John. "Why couldn't he have given us more warning? I've an appointment tomorrow at 4:00."

"The memo also says that he wants sales reps to fill out a new form documenting sales calls," responds Chris.

"But we already do that. It makes no sense to duplicate what we already do," retorts John.

As John walks back to his desk, he starts to think about his job. "Why is it that the company doesn't improve the parking lot or duplicating machine or get filters for the coffee maker? Why is every meeting an emergency? Why do we fill out needless forms? These types of things have been going on ever since I joined this company. I've just about had enough of this nonsense."

John is so frustrated over these little things that he is right now receptive to a job offer from a competitive firm.

For years, managers have been told that it is the big things that determine employee job satisfaction. They have been told that the key to high satisfaction is to provide employees with high pay, plush offices, good promotional opportunities, interesting and challenging work, and friendly and competent co-workers. But is it only these major factors that count? John wasn't upset with any of them. Rather, it was a series of small items that antagonized him and brought him dissatisfaction.

Reprinted from *Management Solutions,* August 1988

Why "Little Things" Are Important

Job satisfaction can be thought of as the difference between what an employee wants, expects, or needs from a job and what he or she actually receives. The closer the two are aligned, the greater the job satisfaction.

When employees interview for a job, they bring these wants, expectations, and needs with them. During the interview, they check to see what the firm offers in terms of the "big things" such as good pay and fringe benefits, pleasant working conditions, and nice co-workers. If the firm is unable to meet their wants, expectations, and needs in terms of these "big things," they will not accept employment. Admittedly, some will take the job out of desperation but most will not, particularly the top performers. Thus, most employees start work knowing that the "big things" will meet their wants, expectations, and needs. This is a given. But so is the expectation that the firm will attend to the "little things" as well.

When employees suddenly recognize that it does nothing to remove the "little things" that they find annoying, it is no wonder that these things have a significant negative effect on their job satisfaction. They find the firm's or manager's lack of concern appalling, and they feel they have been betrayed. They felt certain when they joined the firm that it would address these issues. They wonder why a firm willing and able to address the "big things" does not address the little ones.

Effects of Irritants

The illustration in Figure 1 depicts the effects of an accumulation of "little things" (irritants) on employee job satisfaction. It shows that there is a direct relationship between the two variables, that is, the greater the number and severity of irritants, the lower an employee's job satisfaction level. It also

Figure 1

Effects of "Little Things" on Job Satisfaction

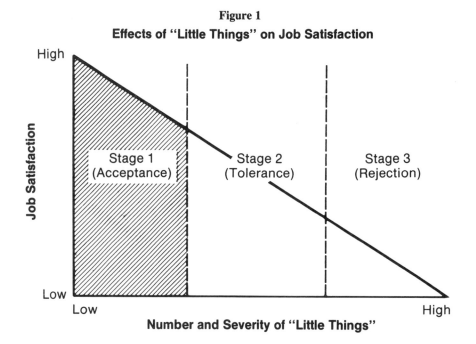

shows that employees pass through three stages in response to these irritants: the acceptance stage, the tolerance stage, and the rejection stage. Each stage has its own set of characteristics, attitudes, and behavior.

Acceptance stage. In this stage, employees are faced with only a few irritants and nuisances. There are few "little things" that bother them. To be sure, the firm may occasionally run out of supplies or the duplicating machine may not always work, but when these things do occur they are viewed as normal, not the result of incompetent or uncaring management. Employees realize that no organization is perfect, that even the most effective ones aren't problem-free.

Employee attitudes toward management and their job are very favorable during the acceptance stage. Workers view management as supportive and on their side. They feel that their manager will act on the "little things" that need changing. They view him or her as proactive rather than active to these problems. Further, they believe that the only step they need to take to get the irritants resolved is to inform their manager of them.

Tolerance stage. As the number and severity of irritants increase, however, employees' job satisfaction deteriorates. Their attitudes toward management shift, and they begin to question the administration's competence, sincerity, and willingness to address and resolve problems. Employee behavior also changes, and workers become more argumentative. They may petition or file a grievance requesting that one or more of the little things be looked into. More noticeably, they may start to complain and joke with each other about the problems that exist and management's slowness in responding to them.

Rejection stage. As the number and severity of irritants continue to rise, employees eventually reach the rejection stage. At this point, employee job satisfaction is minimal. Workers feel that no one in management cares about the fact that needed equipment is broken, the parking lot is flooded, or offices are in desperate need of painting. They conclude that management is incompetent, uncaring, or both.

Employees' behavior patterns change also. They spend considerable time and energy complaining among themselves and to their manager about the "little things" that the company could but for some reason won't address. Some employees may start demanding that management make changes. They may encourage workers to sign petitions, pass resolutions, work to the contract, even sabotage management's actions. They may call for particular bosses to be fired. Other employees may choose a "flight" rather than a "fight" response. A few of these will seek employment elsewhere. Others may develop a "who gives a darn" attitude and do a minimum amount of work. They will psychologically retire or quit the firm and look for satisfaction outside their jobs.

What can managers do to improve employee job satisfaction? In short, managers first need to determine the employees' present job satisfaction level (whether they are at the acceptance, tolerance, or rejection stage) and, second, they need to develop and implement a strategy for improving job satisfaction.

Measuring Employee Attitudes

Traditionally, firms have measured employee job satisfaction via specific questionnaires such as the Minnesota Job Satisfaction Questionnaire or the Job Descriptive Index. These instruments are designed to measure all the "big things" that affect job satisfaction. They also may provide clues to the "little things" since employees angered by a barrage of irritants will vent their frustrations on these questionnaires.

While one could use these, perhaps a better approach is to talk with employees directly about their job frustrations. What are the "little things" that are aggravating them? How severe are these? How do they feel about management and the firm as a result?

Yet a third approach is to examine employee behaviors. Are they complaining about the work environment and, if so, what form does it take (requests, demands, and/or threats)? Are they engaged in flight or fight responses? Are they performing their jobs well and with a high commitment or not? In sum, a manager needs to examine both employee *attitudes* and *behaviors* to determine whether they are in the acceptance, tolerance, or rejection state.

Improving Employee Attitudes

The particular techniques a manager uses to enhance employee satisfaction need to be tailored to the three job satisfaction stages. No one approach is appropriate for all stages.

Acceptance stage. If a manager finds that employees as a group generally are in the acceptance stage, the appropriate action is clear: Keep up the good work! Obviously, employee needs are being met, and there are few "little things" bothering them. The major challenge here is for the manager to clearly identify those actions being taken that are creating these positive results. It is important that these actions be brought to a conscious level of awareness. Otherwise, they may be neglected, lost in the shuffle, or forgotten.

Tolerance stage. If employees have reached the tolerance stage, a different approach is required. Managers cannot simply continue following their present course of action because employee satisfaction has deteriorated, and they are questioning management's competency, credibility, and concern for them.

A manager's objective must be to restore this credibility and to reassure employees the organization is responsive to their needs. This can be done by identifying those "little things" bothering employees and correcting them. For example, employees in one firm were complaining that they were having trouble opening and shutting doors on bookcases. The firm removed the doors and complaints ceased.

In another firm, employees complained that the parking lot was not sufficiently large to accommodate all the cars. The firm painted lines showing where cars were to park and the problem was solved.

In still another firm, employees were bothered by the fact that their telephone was ringing on all incoming calls. The firm changed its system so that all incoming calls rang in only two offices, thereby eliminating the problem.

Note that many of these "little things" are inexpensive to correct. In the above situations, for example, the firms' costs were minimal. Yet the payoff was significant.

Rejection stage. If employees have reached the rejection stage, managers must approach the problem entirely differently. At this stage, employees have concluded that management is incompetent and unconcerned about their well being.

The thrust of a manager's response here must be to demonstrate via deeds, not just words, that he or she will and is addressing employee concerns. At this stage, "actions speak louder than words." Toward that, the manager may want to hold meetings with his or her employees to develop a list of irritants and a mechanism for dealing with them. Employees could also be assigned to work on finding solutions to these problems. For example, employees at one insurance firm were having difficulty communicating with the main office. The manager assigned the problem to one employee who developed a solution for it—buying car telephones for those who spend considerable time in their cars.

Even if management makes drastic changes in these "little things," there may be some employees whose attitudes won't become favorable. These employees are beyond the point of no return. Regardless of what the manager does, they will not trust him or her or believe that management cares. In this situation, the employees must be counseled, transferred, or perhaps terminated.

New Motivational Strategies to Pursue

GARY SCHUMAN

In the good old days, a pat on the back, the promise of a promotion, and more cash in the pay envelope were sufficient elements of a motivational strategy. But today, the workplace has changed and the old strategies just don't have the same effect anymore.

Much of the change is attributable to the movement of the post-World War II babyboomers into the work force. This has created two serious problems. The first is logistical. There is a people bottleneck in many organizations. The pool of available talent has increased at the same time organizations are trying to downsize and streamline their workforces. This creates a compression effect that seriously reduces promotional opportunities for employees.

The second issue is generational. The babyboomers have grown up during the greatest period of affluence in American history. They have more formal education than any generation before them. And perhaps the most dramatic impact the generation has had is the new roles that women play in the workplace.

These factors have created a new set of values about the meaning of work.

Intrinsic Values

Today's workers place a much higher value on intrinsic rewards such as achievement, personal growth, challenge, satisfaction, and quality of work life than on extrinsic factors such as pay and promotion. They are more interested in defining career success in relation to fulfilling their own personal goals and objectives than in climbing the corporate ladder.

This situation creates a critical problem for the world of work. Pay and promotion have traditionally been the motivational "currencies" of work. They are particularly convenient because they are tangible and concrete rewards.

Intrinsic motivators are softer currencies. They are more troublesome to identify, see, understand, and most importantly dispense.

The situation is also complicated by the fact that many managers are still paying by the old currencies. Pay and promotion worked to motivate their generation, they think, so why shouldn't these currencies work now? So you have the people dispensing payoffs in currencies they believe in, while the people receiving these payoffs would prefer different currencies. To use an economic example, it is as if a

Reprinted from *Management Solutions*, January 1987

Canadian came to Chicago and tried to use Canadian currency. A store might accept the currency, but the individual is going to get less for his or her money than in Canada. The same is true at work. Money or promotions just don't buy as much as they once did.

To effectively deal with this situation, managers must take clear steps that incorporate the new intrinsic currencies into their motivational efforts. A recent Gallup poll provides help defining some of the intrinsic motivators. When a cross section of 1,200 workers were asked to rank a list of 46 motivation factors (including money), the top ten selections were: working with people who respect me, interesting work, recognition for good work, chance to develop skills and abilities, opportunity to be creative, work with people who listen if you have an idea on how to make things better, seeing an end result for your effort, working for an effective manager, a job that isn't too easy, and having a mentor.

A Change in Strategy

These motivational factors can easily be built into present organizational systems without overhauling the way people perform their work. The specific approaches that will make a difference will vary from employee to employee. However, here are ten basic strategies that have proved to be effective.

Assignment of a mentor. A less experienced employee can work with and be coached by a more experienced "pro." This can have a motivating effect on both partners in the relationship.

Rotational assignments. An employee can be given a temporary assignment in a different job or department to broaden his or her skill base.

Cross training. Training employees to perform each other's functional duties allows for substitution of tasks and assignments when someone is missing and provides an opportunity, again, for employees to broaden their skill base.

Stretch projects. Employees can be assigned a task or activity that meets a department objective and also stretches their capabilities.

Team approach. An employee can work as part of a team, to broaden his or her contacts and ability to deal with others.

Special assignment. An employee can be given an opportunity to serve on a task force or committee, or work on a special project, as a way to enrich his or her current work experience.

An opportunity to create. Employees can have the chance to come up with a creative or innovative approach for handling an assignment.

Plum responsibility. An employee can be given a responsibility that is interesting or has high visibility.

Learning opportunity. A training or other learning opportunity can be used as a strategic way to expand an employee's abilities. The skills to be learned can be pinpointed when the employee asks to find the appropriate learning experience.

The lunch strategy. Over lunch, the employee can be given some specific feedback about his or her current performance. The employee can also be asked for some input into how he or she feels things are going and what kinds of assignments would be interesting.

None of these are magical formulas. But they do require a serious commitment on a manager's part to define new motivational opportunities. Management will have to do a significant amount of rethinking of its current motivational systems, mixed with a liberal dose of visionary thinking and a great deal of strategic planning.

Part IX

ORGANIZATION AND TEAM BUILDING

Gauging Organizational Climate

JAMES L. NAVE

Organizational climate has become the subject of a great deal of attention recently. A number of articles and books have been published that describe organizational cultures and offer suggestions on what supervisors can do to improve the climate in their organizations. But none of these has presented an instrument for accurately gauging the organizational climate and for identifying specific conditions affecting the climate. The Organizational Climate index described here and shown in Figure 1 can satisfy that need.

The Organizational Climate Index Survey (OCIS) is a quick and easy way to get an accurate reading of the climate within the organization. It can be used effectively in all types and sizes of organizations and can be used either for entire organizations or for individual departments.

The survey document is divided into four sections that relate to the four major components of organizational climate: job, communication, management, and motivation morale. The first section allows respondents to express their feelings about their job responsibilities and the environment in which they work. Section two measures the organization's attitude toward communication. The pattern of communication within the organization is identified by the survey, as are both the quality and quantity of information conveyed. Managerial practices that affect the climate are assessed in section three of the survey.

Reprinted from *Management Solutions,* June 1986

Figure 1

Organizational Climate Index

The following survey will be used to determine the state of our organizational climate. Rate each item on the basis of the following ;

90–100	Excellent
80–89	Good
70–79	Fair
60–69	Poor
0–59	Very Poor

Your thoughtful, accurate responses will help make our organization stronger and a better place to work. If you have questions about the survey, please ask your supervisor. If you do not have sufficient information to answer a question or have no opinion on a topic, do not answer that question. Place your complete unsigned survey in the box located at _____
                                                                                          (location)

by _____ _____
     (date)   (time)

Section I: Job

1. Our organization provides adequate training for new employees. _____
2. Our organization provides adequate training for new employees to develop new skills. _____
3. Job expectations are realistic and clearly stated. _____
4. Our facilities are clean, safe, and functional. _____
5. Information, materials, and equipment necessary to do my job are provided. _____
6. My job is challenging and contains enough variety to be interesting. _____
7. The quantity of work associated with my job is not too much or too little. _____

                                                                         Subtotal _____

Section II: Communication

1. Our organization has clear, well-written policies, procedures, and guidelines.
2. There is an adequate amount of communication within our organization. _____
3. Methods of communication within our organization are varied (individual contact, group meetings, memos/letters, newsletters, etc.). _____
4. Communication within our organization is timely, accurate, and complete. _____
5. Two-way communication is encouraged and present in our organization. _____
6. There is regular direct person to person contact and opportunity for communication between supervisors and staff. _____

                                                                         Subtotal _____

Section III: Management

1. Effective planning is characteristic of our organization. _____
2. Decision making is timely and effective. _____
3. People are given an opportunity to participate in decisions that affect them. _____
4. Evaluations are handled in a fair and professional manner. _____
5. Disciplinary action is taken only when justified and actions taken are appropriate. _____
6. Grievence situations are handled in a fair and unbiased manner. _____
7. Authority is adequately delegated in our organization. _____
8. Our organization is receptive to innovation and change. _____

                                                                         Subtotal _____

Section IV: Motivation and morale

1. Salaries are fair in relation to job requirements, experience, and quality of work. _____
2. Benefits are adequate. _____
3. Working relationships with co-workers are positive and enjoyable. _____
4. Working relationships with supervisors are positive and enjoyable. _____
5. There is tolerance for individual differences and dissent within our organization. _____
6. Good work brings appreciation and recognition. _____
7. A spirit of cooperation and respect for others exists in our organization. _____
8. Employees take pride in their work and our organization. _____

Subtotal _____
Organizational Climate Index _____

Section four evaluates several of the factors that affect motivation and morale. Rather than rating broad general topics, participants are asked to grade the organization on the basis of detailed statements. In addition to measuring the organizational climate, this technique identifies specific problems that deserve attention.

Once a decision has been made by a manager to use the OCIS, it should be announced two to three weeks in advance of its administration. This will increase employee interest and understanding and create an atmosphere of participation. It is also helpful if the manager distributes the survey. This gives him or her an opportunity to emphasize the importance of the survey and to answer questions concerning it. If this is not possible, well written comments and directions accompanying the survey form will suffice. Subsequent survey forms can be distributed with pay checks, placed in mailboxes, or even mailed to employees' homes.

When administering the survey, particularly the first one, it is important to let the participants know that their honest responses can have a favorable impact on their working environment, review the rating scale, emphasize that each question should be answered separately rather than letting either a high or low score on one item influence the responses to other survey items, and assure that respondents will remain anonymous. Participants should be given plenty of time to complete the survey, distributing the forms and collecting them 30 minutes later is counterproductive. A week to complete the survey allows ample time for considered responses. Employees should be encouraged to work on the survey when they have sufficient time, whether at work or at home.

Survey respondents rate items on a scale of 0–100. This scale was chosen because everyone is familiar with it. The scale also provides a wide span of scores within each rating category and allows for more precise assessment. Improvement or deterioration identified by subsequent surveys will also be more readily apparent when using this scale.

Evaluation of survey results offers a variety of information. The overall climate score comes from the average of the total scores of all the survey sections. Individual items may be evaluated by averaging the scores from those specific questions. Scores can also be obtained for each of the four survey categories. In addition to measuring the temperature of the organizational climate, these scores show management where to direct efforts to improve the internal state of the organization. This allows resources to be used more effectively.

Comparing the scores of management and staffers on individual items and total scores can also be revealing. A wide variation in management and staff scores would be an indication of potentially serious problems within the organization. Other comparisons can be made between classifications of employees, different departments, or various locations.

The benefits of the survey can be increased by administering it on more than one occasion. It is best to conduct the survey no less than two times per year. The survey should not be conducted more than three or four times per year because if it is administered too frequently not enough time will have elapsed for changes to occur in the climate between assessments. Multiple assessments allow management both to monitor positive or negative changes in the climate over a period of time and to judge the effectiveness of its efforts to improve the climate of the organization.

Fine-Tuning Team Spirit

BRUCE D. SANDERS

The right amount of team spirit energizes a work group, whether that group is a football squad, a production unit, or a board of directors. To understand why, consider how you feel when you're a member of a team. Generally you view your tasks in terms of the group's objectives rather than in terms of an individual agenda, and you feel a responsibility to your teammates to give your best to the effort. Further, you praise other members of your team when they do well, and you compensate with your own skills for the weaknesses you see in others. In short, being a member of a team is a very satisfying experience for the employee and, because of the high productivity that results, a very effective way to manage.

Destructive Forces

There are forces on the job operating against teamwork. A major one is specialization. As the tasks to be done become more complex, the tendency is to subdivide the task, assign each component to a different individual or group, and then appoint one overall coordinator. That coordinator may have some sense of a team working under him or her, but the workers themselves can feel quite isolated.

Even when the workers are satisfied in their isolation, they still need an awareness of the overall team objective. Without that, much time and effort can be wasted. Consider the case of Carole Black.

A supervising clerk, Carole provided reports summarizing vendor usage to the purchasing agent. Because she felt that it would help in making buying decisions, she included in her reports an analysis of each vendor. These were based on records on vendor performance carefully kept by her clerks. Unfortunately, besides giving Carole an inner sense of satisfaction, these analyses were of little use. The purchasing agent, unbeknownst to Carole, made his decisions solely on the basis of the bids submitted by prospective suppliers. So, Carole continued to waste her time and that of her clerks in needless record-keeping.

The other major factor on the job operating against teamwork is competition. From early in our lives, we are taught that the only way to win is to make somebody lose. Think what can happen to a group when that kind of thinking prevails and its members start competing among themselves. Supervisors encourage this destructive tendency when they pit one employee against another. Sometimes interpersonal conflict is unavoidable, as when two candidates vie for one job opening. But supervisors who think interpersonal competition is necessary for increased performance are using the wrong type of motivator. In trying to

Reprinted from *Supervisory Management*, June 1980

exceed sales quotas, the enemy is the quota, not other members of the sales force. In coming up with good ideas to solve a production problem, the competition should be with the problem, not with the ideas of others.

The Need to Belong

Specialization and competition are powerful forces, but they can be overcome by an equally powerful characteristic of human nature—the yearning to belong. To be part of the group, don't we put up with some pretty outrageous things from time to time? Consider, for example, those boring staff meetings that we attend, knowing all too well that little will come from them. Why do we go? For the status of being invited and the sense of belonging.

Perhaps for the same reasons, a staff meeting—a good one rather than an outrageously boring one— is the best place to develop team spirit. It is one of the few times all the members of a work unit can see themselves physically as a unit. Each can see who else is working alongside him or her to achieve the same organizational goals.

The staff meeting is where new employees in the unit can become a part of the team by presenting their qualifications and background to the others and explaining the role they will be filling. The meeting is where you, as the supervisor, can set for the work group new challenges that will tend to unify it. The meeting is also where you can spot conflicts between specific employees that might be getting in the way of team spirit. And, finally, the meeting is where you can take steps to keep team spirit from getting out of hand.

The Other Side of the Story

Team spirit is a powerful medicine; and like any strong medicine, it can have undesirable side effects. Let's look at some of these.

Secrecy. When a work group views itself as a team, the members view those not on the team as outsiders. Sometimes a competitive spirit develops that focuses on keeping these outsiders from doing well. That can lead to denying outsiders the commodity most valuable in competing effectively—information. If the team is the entire organization, there's nothing wrong with this. After all, trade secrets are an honorable part of many successful enterprises. But most often teams are units within an organization that have little business keeping secrets from each other, especially when the result of that secrecy can harm the company.

The "them" syndrome. When you isolate yourself from others with whom you're competing, it's easy to believe the worst you hear about them. Eventually you believe that all that's wrong with the company is the fault of "them." Such thinking leads to a discounting of any suggestions from those outside the team. "We can't trust what they're saying. Why would they want to help us out? And, anyway, their bad advice is what's keeping this organization from moving ahead."

Drop in critical judgment. Without a free exchange of information with those outside the team, the quality of group decisions drops. But that's only one of the reasons for the poor decisions made. The second is the team spirit. As the team spirit reaches its peak, the group believes it can do no wrong. It feels so good to be working as an effective unit that it avoids doing anything to disturb the unity. At this point a member wouldn't call attention to a flaw in another group member, even if he or she saw it. More importantly, the individual is not likely to see it because he or she is not looking for it. Bad decisions pass for creative team output.

As it happens, team spirit helps even bad decisions work, encouraging a high energy investment from each member to maintain the team's success. But the decisions aren't as good as they could be with some critical judgment. What's worse, they are often out of joint with what the rest of the organization is doing.

Illegal behavior. As team spirit grows, the lack of critical judgment can lead to decisions that not only are bad but also are illegal. It's like the spirited football squad that believes if some action moves the ball forward, that action by definition is good. Those players let the referees be their conscience. Similarly, the work group, isolated and lacking critical judgment, uses only one criterion in decision making. Will it increase team success? The team takes no responsibility for playing fair and fails to see the implications of its actions for the organization as a whole. The result: trouble.

Infighting. Fortunately, the stage with high possibility for illegal behavior passes. What usually follows is a slow disintegration of the work team. After a team has been successful for a time, even if that success is only in the nonobjective view of its members, some "all-starring" begins. "I wonder how well this team could do without me. Let me hold back a bit; then they'll appreciate me more." Or, more likely, "This is too easy. I can do it without the rest of the team." Out of dislike for the all-stars or out of a quest for places where they think their skills will be more appreciated, members leave the team. What was once an effective working unit destroys itself.

The Wrong Answers

The perceptive work group can use its regular staff meetings to spot these bad effects of high team spirit. "Do we often leave significant information out of the meeting minutes that we distribute to other units in the organization?" "Do we insist on knowing who originated an idea before we're willing to judge its merits?" "Are we taking actions that would prove embarrassing to the organization if they were widely known?" "Are we starting to spend more time struggling with each other than we spend struggling with the challenges facing the overall organization?"

If the answer is yes to any of these questions, it's time for quick action. Unfortunately, too many supervisors at this point take action that is destructive, transferring individuals to other units, believing the team is getting cocky. But this is as foolish as disbanding a winning football team if it openly disagrees with the team owner. Winning may not count for everything, but it does count for something.

Another destructive technique is to encourage individual achievement at the expense of the team. A supervisor might assign an exciting task to one team member and tell that individual that he or she should keep it secret. But this tactic only speeds up the infighting and hastens the loss of team spirit.

Still another wrong approach is to set up impossible goals with unrealistic deadlines that guarantee failure with the thought that the team needs a little humbling. "Let's give those hotshots a really tough task," the supervisor thinks. The team members are likely to be humbled all right, but they are also likely to be angered, frustrated, and saddened. And what wise supervisor wants to have subordinates who are angry, frustrated, and sad, or even just humble?

Some Solutions

Although each of the methods above is destructive, there is a set of parallel methods that are constructive and applicable at staff meetings.

Invite outsiders. Rather than transfer team members out, invite outsiders in to join a staff meeting. The group will temporarily be made larger, which can delay decision making. But the presence and participation of new group members, especially those who represent the stereotyped "them," can dissolve group isolation and remind the team of its obligations to the organization as a whole.

Recognize individual achievements. We all want recognition for what we do as individuals, even when we enjoy being on the team. During the staff meeting, praise the group as a whole, but don't miss the opportunity also to praise a deserving individual in front of his or her peers. Assign tasks to the team, and then assign some tasks to specific individuals. When done from the start of the team's existence, these techniques can curb the destructive all-starring.

Set tougher challenges. A successful team eats up realistic challenges and thrives. It's when the challenges are too hard or too easy that group spirit plummets or infighting starts. Help the team to plan realistically and to earn rewards for its successes. Set deadlines and points where progress will be checked, first because time limits make the task more challenging and second because checkpoints allow a group to celebrate if it has been successful and make corrections if it has erred.

When you're the work unit supervisor, you've the power to set tougher challenges for your people, recognize their individual achievements, and invite outsiders to your staff meetings. You're also able to develop team spirit when it's too low by, for instance, involving all members in important unit decisions and helping to integrate individual objectives with unit objectives. So with a variety of techniques, you can increase the quantity and quality of work unit output. It's a matter of fine-tuning team spirit.

Total Teamwork: How to Be a Leader, How to Be a Member

MARY WALSH MOSSOP

Donald Petersen, chairman of Ford Motor Corporation, says he finds himself having to come to terms with issues not covered in his graduate school curricula. "I'm coming to grips with teamwork and trust and respect—how to treat people and inspire their very best efforts," he says.

This is exactly what you will have to do if management asks you to lead a project team in your department.

When that happens, here are some guidelines that can help you structure and lead the team for optimum effectiveness.

Defining Purpose

Be crystal clear on the team's mission. Call your team together and spend the first meeting or two fine-tuning your goals. Defining the mission isn't going to come easy. But this dialogue allows you to set the tone for the team, establishing a climate where people can voice feelings, ideas, and opinions.

Even if the purpose comes from top management, the members should still discuss it in order to arrive at a shared understanding and to build commitment to the team's purpose.

The team's mission statement should include the reasons for its existence and the limits of its authority. A clear mission statement leaves people clear within and outside the team about the team's purpose. Remember, the team's subsequent success will be measured against it.

Share your mission statement with senior management, too, to ensure its agreement and commitment.

Write up the mission statement and hang it in a spot where it is a constant reminder, keeping the team on track and providing a yardstick against which all team plans and actions can be assessed.

Carve out your success criteria. Start by having the team visualize success in reaching its purpose. This will make it easier for members to spot when they are off course, and it will help to highlight potential problems before committing to action.

The definition of success begins with the customer. Target who your external and internal customers are; if you have more than one customer group, make sure you recognize this in defining team success.

Reprinted from *Management Solutions*, August 1988

The team needs to know what the needs and expectations of the customers are, and in turn, you need to be absolutely clear what you need from the team so that you both are able to reach the finishing line as winners.

Encourage customers to be as explicit as possible about their needs. If necessary, provide them with information, suggestions, models, or other concrete representations of your anticipated products or services. Consider using innovative problem-solving techniques (like brainstorming and visual analogies) to help them fully explore alternatives.

Follow this up by having the team do a little introspection on its strengths and weaknesses and resources; this includes identifying the talents, skills, and experience of team members. You need to know what you can and can't deliver. Share your verdict with the customer. Try to avoid the temptation of making promises you can't keep.

Targeting Responsibilities

Be action-centered. From the mission come the goals and targets broken down into clear objectives. Precede this by having team members give their views on how best they can contribute to the team's goals. Where possible, try to match tasks to the team member's strengths and interests.

Try to mutually arrive at decisions on what specific objectives each team member must achieve, including how much will be achieved, how well, in what time frame, and with what resources. You need to be tolerant of the team's widely varying abilities. The very able and motivated should be allowed considerable freedom and discretion with periodic support from you. Conversely, those less able and motivated require considerable direction and more frequent progress reviews. Team members who are really not suited to teamwork can be called upon for their knowledge and expertise. They can be an important resource to the team without being active participants.

Let people know beforehand how their performance will be judged and what help they can expect from you. Performance standards should be regularly monitored and adjusted in light of changing circumstances. Right now, your job may be to review members' performance, but remember, team members are beginning to have an input into team appraisals, including appraisals of the team's leaders, and you may want to consider trying this practice out.

You should consider getting some hands-on experience so you can fully understand the practical difficulties your team's members face. Remember, though, you will probably have to fit this in with your regular duties.

Structuring Meetings

Establish a teamwork pattern. You need to reach agreement on how you will work as a team. For example, in your group meetings, try for agreement on each of the following:

- Only calling meetings when there is a purpose
- Having people well-briefed for meetings so they come fully prepared
- Allocating time for each agenda item
- Encouraging brevity
- Having a good minutetaker or recorder
- Splitting into subgroups for multifaceted problems. This saves time, keeps energy levels up, and makes for quicker progress.
- Keeping out disturbances during meetings
- Allowing time for "mind stretches" as people tire
- Finishing each item before moving onto the next
- Trying to set aside a little time for chitchat

During meetings, also ask questions and summarize important points. Make sure all team members understand the points being made and their implications in terms of the team's goals. Clarify commonly shared definitions of important problems, especially where you have experts and non-experts. As group leader, try to blend with the group as much as possible. Show you are prepared to change your own preconceived ideas on the basis of facts presented by team members. This acts as a model for others, encouraging open expression of ideas and more innovative solutions.

Get agreement on managing conflict. It can be a trigger to searching for new alternatives. Use conflict, or important data may get overlooked. Conflict can enhance group decisionmaking by ensuring that all views are heard, but it also can get in the way of progress. The preferred approach is to combine confrontation with mutual problem-solving. Rather than engage in win-lose battles, try to find the next best strategy or an alternative acceptable to everyone.

Periodically allow time to review how you are working together as a team. If relationships are hampering progress, examine how the team is working together. You can learn group processes in time, but sometimes you need to practice teamwork on already solved problems or smaller issues. It is often easier to analyze how you are working as a team when not dealing with pressing problems. Consider doing your own needs-analysis. Don't rush for help from outsiders; they may prescribe behaviors and point out errors when it is not necessary.

Within one to two days of each meeting, publish action plans and responsibilities on the team's bulletin board.

Encourage team members, too, to periodically provide each other with short, catchy updates on progress.

You should also put out brief summaries on the team's overall progress.

Sharing Information

Manage the outside. Unless told to keep plans within the group, let others in the department know what the team is up to, and invite their expertise and feedback where applicable.

Give senior management regular progress reports. If you don't manage people's perceptions of the team, they will form their own, some of which may be less than flattering to the team.

Keep the communication gates open to those who will be impacted by your decisions and those whose commitment the team needs to get information and support to implement solutions.

Building Team Unity

Cultivate a team identity. Try to acquire a special team room. Have slogans. Have a chart showing where the team fits in with the rest of the organization. Encourage the occasional social get-together and have some fun.

Invite members of senior management to a team meeting when there has been a success or a difficult goal has been achieved. They can congratulate the team and reaffirm the important work the group is doing.

Cultivating an *esprit de corps* doesn't preclude individuality. In fact, the more the members become a team, the more individuality is permitted. Differences of opinion are respected and people agree to disagree.

Being a Team Member

Sometimes, rather than being a leader, you may be asked to join a project team as a member. Here are a few pointers on being a team member.

Gain entry. Try to get acquainted quickly. This is helped by sharing information about yourself. Let the team know about your previous experience as a team member, what your main strengths are, what your likely contributions will be, what particular skills you bring to the team. But let the team know that you are open to negotiation. If, however, you are assigned tasks you feel ill-equipped for, ask for some training or exchange assignments with the leader's permission.

Be clear on your team assignment. Before you get into action, be clear on your role in the team, the objectives you have to achieve, the time frame for achieving them, your resources, and the parameters of your decision-making powers. Don't feel foolish about asking questions; you will look twice as foolish if you subsequently make mistakes because you did not know where you were going. Let others know the help you may need from them. Let them know what you expect from them, and be clear on what they expect from you. Deliver on promises. If your work assignments impact on other members of the team, arrange get-togethers with them, and keep the communication flowing freely between you. Share your team assignments with your regular boss. Don't leave him in the cold; besides, you may need to have your regular work reassessed in light of your team assignment. But be prepared for an extra workload during these times. On the positive side, challenging work assignments offer the probability for growth and diversity. If work pressures are too much, speak to the team leader; don't bury your head in the sand.

Be well-prepared. Participate at team meetings. Stick to relevant comments and keep in mind time constraints when giving presentations. Ask yourself, Is my contribution moving the group forward, adding values to the team goal? Be open to others' ideas; try to build on them, and be willing to explore options. If you want to be critical of others' ideas and work, present the advantages of their ideas first and then phrase your critique in the form of concerns or possible limitations.

Also, try to avoid competing with other team members for attention and influence. Your ideas and opinions, though different, should be raised, but also allow time for others to express their ideas.

Show commitment by being willing to share ideas and information; don't withhold information that will impede the team's progress. When changes or events occur, ask about their possible impact not only on you but on other members of the team, and share this with them. Be willing to tell bad news, and to admit failure or setbacks. Periodically ask yourself what you could do better—how you could help the group more—and discuss this with the team leader and other members. Avoid the tendency to be satisfied just because things appear to be going well for the moment.

Approach problems and setbacks not with complaints but in a problem-solving mode; ask, "How can we solve this? How can we prevent its recurrence?"

When the Team Is Apart

Stay in touch. A team's work is carried out even when members are apart, working alone on their specific assignments. Try to do your part by meeting with other team members informally and keeping up frequent interaction and by doing your share of preparing short memos to team colleagues to keep them up to date with any important information in your area.

Above all, keep the core mission in mind. Clarify what you are doing to aid the team in meeting its goals and to help other members with their tasks.

Stepping Up to Supervision: Building an Effective Work Group

H. KENT BAKER and STEVAN R. HOLMBERG

Don North, a new supervisor, had experienced some difficulties motivating his subordinates until he tailored his management style and approach to the individual needs and preferences of those he supervised. As Don sought to further improve his efforts to motivate his employees, he found that the task was increasingly difficult because individual goals and work assignments were interdependent and interrelated with those of others.

Because group productivity had declined, Don sought advice from Matt Thompson, an experienced supervisor, who pointed out that some team building efforts were needed. Don and Matt examined the various approaches that could be taken to revitalize Don's complacent staff, and they developed a plan for building an effective work team.

Why Are Groups Necessary?

As Matt Thompson explained, understanding how to manage groups effectively is essential to Don's success with his department. Matt suggested that three major ideas are critical to the understanding of the process of managing groups. The first is tied to why groups are necessary. Through groups made up of different individuals, each with expertise in different skill areas, it is possible to achieve overall objectives. Most objectives in business require not a single skill but a set of multiple skills. The many individual skills needed can be brought together in a work group or team, and one of the major responsibilities and challenges of a newly appointed supervisor is to identify the necessary individual skills in order to build an effective group or team.

Supervisors also need to realize that informal groups with their unique set of social relationships emerge from formal groups. New supervisors are not often fully aware of the development and importance of informal groups. But in determining initially job objectives and workflow (for example, the step-by-step process that leads to achievement of objectives), the supervisor strongly influences the membership in and the basic characteristics of the informal groups that are to develop.

Third, as Matt Thompson explained, groups are necessary because they can satisfy some very significant human needs. First, groups provide an individual's social or affiliation need. This need for social

Reprinted from *Supervisory Management,* February 1982

contact and interaction exists as much in the work environment as it does in nonwork settings. Formal and informal groups also provide members with a sense of identification that becomes an integral part of their self-concept and their communications of their work role to others outside of work. The strength of group identification is another important element in the building of group cohesion. Groups can offer individuals emotional support that can help them deal with the stress elements in their job and nonwork environments. In addition, groups can provide advice and assistance in meeting job objectives to employees who may be hesitant to ask their supervisor for help. Finally, groups can offer individuals a sense of protection from threatening individuals or situations outside the group. If a new supervisor is viewed as a threat to group members, they will likely react by protecting the threatened members.

Determining Performance and Social Expectations

As Matt Thompson told Don North, groups perform a wide variety of necessary and essential task and nontask functions that can either facilitate or inhibit the successful accomplishment of a department's objectives. The newly appointed supervisor should be aware not only of the general need for groups but also of their more specific roles in determining performance and social expectations.

Don, as a newly appointed supervisor, had operated under the assumption that he alone as supervisor gave directions and individual employees and the employees collectively as a work group carried them out. Hence, Don was implicitly assuming that he, the supervisor, was the essential, and perhaps sole, determiner of both individual and group expectations. This is not the case.

Groups themselves play a large role in establishing and maintaining both group and individual expectations. The newly appointed supervisor certainly *influences* those expectations, but he or she does not *control* either individual or group expectations. Job-related expectations or roles are defined by the relevant group and exist in terms of behavioral expectations identified for each position. As such, they almost become an informal job description that then combines with the formal job description.

A new employee in Don's department very quickly learns the set of formal and informal expectations related to his or her position. The people who interact frequently with the new employee informally serve as the communicators of the group's expectations. The group's expectations in turn condition the new employee's actual behavior. He or she senses that, besides formal expectations, there are expectations or norms about what constitutes acceptable group behavior. These group norms or expectations define how members of the group "ought" to behave and range all the way from acceptable dress to the amount and quality of work performed. Group members enforce these group norms and are tolerant of deviations from established group norms but only up to some limit.

Major Group-Related Dimensions

There are a number of group dimensions that need to be carefully evaluated by the newly appointed supervisor. These dimensions first come into play when the supervisor considers the appropriate structure of the work groups in his or her department. The initial structuring of work groups is critical as this decision influences the formal and informal communications, interactions, and the degree to which task and social objectives are likely to be achieved.

The first major group dimension is size. Don had structured his department into two identifiable work groups whose tasks were interrelated in a variety of ways. While these work groups were large, with over 35 individuals in each, Don thought it might be better to keep things relatively simple. But grouping employees into very large work groups had created several problems. Expectations as to what needed to be done were fuzzy, at best. Communications within and between each of the two groups were not as timely or as complete as desirable. Organizing his department into eight to ten work teams of from seven to nine individuals each would have enhanced both task and social goals.

The second consideration is the allocation or assignment of work to the work groups and associated individuals. The systematic identification of the major events and activities for each work activity helps in arriving at a decision concerning rational number and size of work teams and leads to an intelligent structuring of workflow throughout the entire department.

A third group dimension relates to the group process—the way the group itself works. With this, the new supervisor needs to identify the behaviors that have resulted from the established set of group norms or expectations. The level and nature of participation, cooperation, and communication can offer some important clues to the nature of the group process.

The complex set of interpersonal relations is a fourth major group-related dimension that the new supervisor must identify and evaluate. These interpersonal relations are strongly influenced by the way work is assigned, the selection of work groups, and the resulting geographical proximity of people. The simple positioning of offices, desks, and other work stations has a significant influence on the sets of interpersonal relationships that result.

A fifth group dimension relates to the responsibility, authority, and accountability assigned to the group and the individual members therein. This becomes even more important as the interdependencies and interrelationships of individual work activities increase. To achieve work goals, the efforts and skills of many group members are essential. In addition, contributions from other work teams within the same department or from other departments may be required. Group and individual member performance and satisfaction will be conditioned by the provision of sufficient authority and resources to achieve the tasks for which they are responsible and, in turn, for which they will be held accountable.

A sixth group dimension is the reward and recognition structure. Within a given group or work team, individual rewards or other recognition should be clearly and closely related to achieving performance goals. To the extent that different performance and skill requirements exist within the work group, there need to be different rewards and recognition given. Providing rewards and recognition that reflect both performance and skill requirements encourages striving to achieve performance-related goals and enhances employee satisfaction. Besides individual recognition for individual performance, consideration should be given to group rewards and recognition. Work team rewards can build a strong sense of team spirit and cohesion that will further enhance task and social goal accomplishment.

Finally, the new supervisor can help to enhance his or her effectiveness in dealing with work groups by working with and through the group leader(s). A typical assumption is that there is only one leader in a work group—the individual granted the position and responsibility for accomplishing the formal task objectives. However, in many instances groups will have more leaders. To some extent these leaders perform different roles for the group. One may be a group leader in accomplishing work/task objectives, while another person may emerge as the social leader of the group. There may well be other leaders related to more specific aspects within the overall task and social group dimensions.

As Matt Thompson explained, consideration of these major group dimensions is extremely helpful to the newly appointed supervisor in developing an effective work group. Then Matt offered some additional suggestions on how to develop an effective work group.

Developing an Effective Work Group

The effectiveness of a work group, is determined by the size of the group, the reward/recognition system, group expectations, the role of the leader, and the communication between the supervisor and the group.

Matt suggested, as an initial step, that Don restructure his work teams. He should begin by analyzing the objectives and associated workflow with an emphasis on the sequencing and interdependencies of the work activities. Work teams could then be structured to most effectively accomplish the necessary work. The size of these work teams would depend on a number of factors, but the single most important factor should be the nature of the task to be accomplished. If a job involves tasks that are highly complementary, the larger the group but also the more difficult the tasks of motivation, coordination, and communication for the supervisor. For Don, eight to ten teams composed of from seven to nine individuals was a more appropriate setup than two teams of 35 individuals each.

Developing an appropriate reward/recognition system both for the individuals and the work teams is an essential ingredient in developing effective work groups. Rewards and recognition should be clearly based on agreed-upon performance goals.

Consideration of group expectations is essential to developing effective work groups. Don's work with individual employees and especially with the task, social, and other group leaders can influence the group's expectations.

As the department supervisor, Don can also try to establish a positive work climate.

Don, as a new supervisor, had been engaging largely in one-way communication. He believed that if the proper information were communicated to his employees, they would understand and cooperate. His employees, however, were not always sure they were being told the "full story" and in some cases thought there might be a better way to achieve objectives. Good two-way communication will enhance employee understanding and sense of participation. If individual goals can be merged with or strongly identified with group goals, group cohesion or togetherness will also be strengthened. In turn, cohesive work teams with positive group expectations concerning productivity and other task objectives will provide a powerful incentive for individual performance.

As a result of his talk with Matt, Don developed an increased sensitivity to the need for a clear link between performance results and a reward/recognition system for individual employees as well as the work teams. He had changed his "across-the-board" raise policy and, working with his employees, had begun to establish precise performance targets for individuals and work teams. The reward system was developed in a similar way with rewards based solely on performance by the individual and with a separate, but related, reward system for the entire work team. Awards were established for excellence in several performance categories.

Don had read about Japan's use of quality control circles and had asked Matt if the ideas they had been discussing were related to the Japanese concepts. Matt replied that the concept of quality control circles could be used to implement many of the ideas they had discussed to increase the effectiveness of Don's work group. Quality control circles are voluntary groups and all QC programs have three common elements. First is the emphasis on worker participation. No one knows better the problems and potential solutions than those actually engaged in the work. Workers meet frequently with management to discuss problems or any other matters of concern. Second is that performance incentives are tied to specific performance standards, such as rate of output or quality, for both the work team and the individual. The third element common to quality control circles is the employee security they provide. Qualified workers are not fired even if the job position is eliminated. Instead, they are transferred to another job.

Don North is now convinced that by taking a number of the specific steps discussed with Matt, he can build a more effective work group.

Tapping Into the Power of
Informal Groups

H. KENT BAKER

Mike Knowles was at his wits' end. As a newly appointed production manager, he had tried virtually everything to get his work group to come up to production standard. The equipment was operating properly, and the group had the training and experience to meet expectations, yet it was not performing well. What was wrong? And what could he do to correct the situation?

Supervisors frequently face such a dilemma—standards that should be met but aren't for what seems like no apparent reason. What Mike Knowles and other supervisors sometimes fail to realize is that within every organization there are often informal group pressures that influence and regulate individual behavior. Informal groups formulate an implicit code of ethics or an unspoken set of standards establishing acceptable behavior. In Mike's department, the informal group may have established a norm below that set by the company, subtly exercising control over its mentors regarding the amount of output.

The Power of Informal Groups

Informal groups almost always arise if opportunities exist. Often, these groups serve a counterorganizational function, attempting to counteract the coercive tendencies in an organization. If management prescribes production norms that the group considers unfair, for instance, the group's recourse is to adopt less demanding norms and to use its ingenuity to discover ways in which it can sabotage management's imposed standards. Informal groups have a powerful influence on the effectiveness of an organization, and can even subvert its formal goals.

But the informal group's role is not limited to resistance. The impact of the informal group upon the larger formal group depends on the norms that the informal group sets. So the informal group can make the formal organization more effective, too.

A norm is an implied agreement among the group's membership regarding how members in the group should behave. From the perspective of the formal group, norms generally fall into three categories—positive, negative, and neutral. In other words, norms either support, obstruct, or have no effect on the aims of the larger organization.

For example, if the informal group in Mike's shop set a norm supporting high output, that norm

Reprinted from *Supervisory Management*, February 1981

would have been more potent than any attempt by Mike to coerce compliance with the standard. The reason is simple, yet profound. The norm is of the group members' own making, and is not one imposed upon them. There is a big motivational difference between being told what to do and being anxious to do it.

If Mike had been aware of group dynamics, he might have realized that informal groups can be either his best friend or his worst enemy. He should have been sensitive to the informal groups within his area and he should have cultivated their goodwill and cooperation and made use of the informal group leadership. That is, he should have wooed the leadership of the informal group and enlisted the support of its membership to achieve the formal organization's aims. The final effect of his actions might have been positive or negative, depending upon the agreement or lack of it between the informal group and himself.

Harnessing the power of informal groups is no easy task. The requirements include an understanding of group dynamics and an ability to bring about changes in informal group norms that positively reinforce the formal organization's goals. As a starting point, supervisors should at least be aware of the reasons behind informal group formation and the properties and characteristics of these groups.

The Formation of Informal Groups

Individuals are employed by an organization to perform specific functions. Although the whole person joins an organization, attention is usually focused on the partial person, the part of the individual doing the job. Because people have needs that extend beyond the work itself, informal groups develop to fill certain emotional, social, and psychological needs. The degree to which a group satisfies its members' needs determines the limits within which individual members of the group will allow their behavior to be controlled by the group.

Several major functions are served by informal groups. For example, the group serves as a means of satisfying the *affiliation* needs of its members for friendship and support. People need to belong, to be liked, to feel a part of something. Because the informal group can withhold this attractive reward, it has a tool of its own to coerce compliance with its norms.

Groups also provide a means of developing, enhancing, and confirming a person's sense of *identity* and *self-esteem*. Although many organizations attempt to recognize these higher needs, the nature of some jobs—their technology and environment—precludes this from happening. The long assembly line or endless rows of desks reinforce a feeling of depersonalization.

Another function of groups is to serve as an agent for establishing and testing social reality. For instance, several individuals may share the feeling that their supervisor is a slave driver or that their working conditions are inadequate. By developing a consensus about these feelings, group members are able to reduce the anxiety associated with their jobs.

Finally, the informal group serves as a *defense mechanism* against forces that group members could not resist on their own. Joining forces in a small group makes the members feel stronger, less anxious, and less insecure in the face of a perceived threat.

As long as needs exist that are not served by the formal organization, informal groups will form to fill the gap. Since the group fills many important needs for its members, it influences member behavior.

Informal Leadership

Informal groups possess certain characteristics that, if understood, can be used to advantage. While many of these characteristics are similar to those of formal organizations, others are unique.

One attribute of informal groups is *rotational leadership*. The informal leader emerges as the individual possessing qualities that the other members perceive as critical to the satisfaction of their specific needs at the moment; as the needs change so does the leader. Only rarely does a single individual possess all of the leadership characteristics needed to fill the various needs of the group.

Unlike the formally appointed leader who has a defined position from which to influence others, the informal leader does not possess formal power. If the informal leader fails to meet the group's expectations, he or she is deposed and replaced by another. The informal group's judgment of its leaders tends to be quicker and more coldblooded than that of most formal groups.

The supervisor can use several strategies to affect the leadership and harness the power of informal groups. One quick and sure method of changing a group is to cause the leader to change one or more of his or her characteristics. Another is to replace the leader with another person. One common ploy is to systematically rotate out of the group its leaders and its key members. Considering the rotational nature of leadership, a leader may emerge who has aims similar to the formal goals of the organization. There are problems with this approach, however. Besides the practical difficulties of this, this strategy is blunted by the fact that group norms often persist long after the leader has left the group.

A less Machiavellian approach is for the supervisor to be alert to leaders sympathetic to the supervisor's objectives and to use them toward the betterment of the formal group's effectiveness. Still another method is to attempt to "co-opt" informal leaders by absorbing them into the leadership or the decision-making structure of the formal group. Co-opting the informal leader often serves as a means of averting threats to the stability of the formal organization. Remember, though, a leader may lose favor with the group because of this association with management, and group members will most likely select another leader.

The Grapevine

Another characteristic of the informal group is its *communications network*. The informal group has communications processes that are smoother and less cumbersome than those of the formal organization. Thus its procedures are easily changed to meet the communication needs of the group. In the informal group, a person who possesses information vital to the group's functioning or well-being is frequently afforded leadership status by its members. Also, the centrally located person in the group is in the best position to facilitate the smooth flow of information among group members.

Knowing about informal group communication, the supervisor can provide a strategically placed individual with information needed by the group. This not only enhances the stature of this individual, perhaps elevating him or her to a leadership position, but also provides an efficient means of distributing information. Providing relevant information to the group will also help foster harmony between the supervisor and the informal group. By winning the cooperation of informal group leaders, the supervisor will most likely experience fewer grievances and better relationships.

Hanging Together

A third characteristic of informal groups is *group cohesiveness*—the force that holds a group together. Group cohesiveness varies widely based on numerous factors—including the size of the group, dependence of members upon the group, achievement of goals, status of the group, and management demands and pressures. For example, group cohesiveness increases strongly whenever the membership perceives a threat from the outside. This threat produces the high anxiety that strong group cohesiveness can help reduce.

If the supervisor presses the group to conform to a new organizational norm that is viewed as a threat to the security of group members, the group will become more unified in order to withstand the perceived threat. Thus management can limit its own effectiveness by helping to increase the group's cohesiveness.

With the passing of the threat, the group tends to lose its cohesiveness. Perhaps paradoxically, the most dangerous time for group cohesion is when things are going well.

Supervisors can use the factors that affect group cohesiveness to increase their own effectiveness. For instance, a supervisor can involve the informal group members in the decision-making process. Input from group members will not only reduce their feeling of alienation but also improve communication between the supervisor and subordinates, thereby reducing potential conflict. Where group participation in decision making is not practical, the supervisor should carefully explain the reason to play down what might be seen as a threat to the group.

In some cases, the supervisor may want to increase the group's cohesiveness, deliberately devising situations that put one group into competition with another. If this gambit is carefully controlled, the solidarity that results may bring a higher level of performance. The danger of this strategy is that the supervisor may be unable to control the reaction of the group. The ploy could backfire, bringing competition and dissension *within* the group.

Unspoken Rules

The final characteristic of informal groups is their establishment of *norms*. As we discussed earlier, norms keep a group functioning as a system instead of a collection of individuals. Norms are of great importance to the informal group in controlling behavior and measuring the performance of members. Because norm violations threaten a group's existence, departures from the norm usually carry severe sanctions. The members must either conform or sever their group affiliation. The latter action is unlikely, especially if the individual values group membership to satisfy certain needs.

Several points are important to note about the norms of informal groups. First, where both formal and informal norms exist, the informal norms transcend the formal. At moments when norms conflict with organizational objectives, organizational effectiveness suffers.

Second, members of an informal group may be unaware that the norms of the group influence their behavior. Norms are particularly potent because without knowing it members would not even think of acting otherwise—norms are that ingrained into their behavior pattern.

Changing Group Norms

A supervisor should attempt to encourage norms that positively affect the formal organization's goals, and to alter those that are negative. If this is accomplished, the informal group will direct its energies toward desired goals.

How can a supervisor bring about a positive change in a group's norms?

Once a group has developed its norms, they are strictly enforced until changed. But norms change frequently because the group must be responsive to changes in its environment for self-protection. When a perceived change occurs in the environment that affects the group, it tightens, eases, or changes it norms.

There are three stages to fostering group norms that are congenial to the organization. The first stage involves determining what the group norms are, and then getting group members to recognize their existence and influence. This can often be accomplished by observing the behavior patterns of the group, interviewing group members, or asking the group to identify its own norms.

As we noted, people frequently respect and follow norms unconsciously. Helping define norms is useful because it assists the group in clarifying its thinking and frees members from behavior patterns that they may not really wish to follow in the first place. When group members actually become aware of negative norms, they commonly reject them and seek alternative modes of behavior. And the supervisor can't begin to change negative norms to positive ones until group members first become aware of their existence.

Figure 1

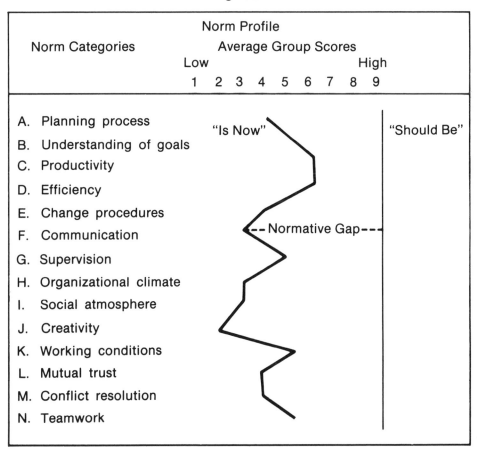

Once the group's norms are identified, the next stage is to measure the norms and establish a norm profile. Various norm categories should be established that relate to organizational and group effectiveness. Each group member should then be asked to rate the norm's intensity from low to high. A nine-point scale may be used in which nine represents where the group should realistically be. As shown in Figure 1, the responses can be averaged and plotted in order to obtain a norm profile. The difference between where the group is and where it should be represents a normative "gap." These gaps provide a starting point for determining where changes should occur.

The final stage is to bring about normative change. A systematic change process consists of six steps:

1. Demonstrate the importance of norms in achieving organizational and group effectiveness.
2. Create positive norm goals through cooperative effort.
3. Establish normative change priorities.
4. Determine a plan of action to bring about change.
5. Implement and monitor the change strategy.
6. Review the effectiveness of the strategy periodically and modify where necessary.

This process emphasizes the creation of positive norms through cooperative effort that benefits both the supervisor and the group. Positive group norms increase the effectiveness of the supervisor while providing an environment in which group members can satisfy their own needs. The process also improves communications and trust, reducing the anxiety sometimes created by perceived threats from management.

If the informal group's norms are negative, they can negate the interests of an organization many times the group's size. The process of change is a tool by which a supervisor can deal with the informal group stresses that exist within the organization and that tend to demotivate employees. By fostering positive group norms, a supervisor can harness the power of informal groups and release the energies of the group to achieve desired goals.

Learning How to Influence Others

MARVIN R. WEISBORD and C. JAMES MASELKO

While it is possible for organizations to have too many levels of management, or too many goals and objectives, we have never met a manager or supervisor who believed their organization suffered an excess of interpersonal skills. Indeed, the number-one frustration reported by managers is finding ways to influence the behavior of people they work with or for.

Those who do this easily or naturally are said to have "good interpersonal skills." Those who don't are frequently packed off to workshops and seminars.

In this article we want to suggest a do-it-yourself approach to interpersonal skill development that any manager can experiment with on the job without announcing to the world that some changes are about to be made. Over many years and dozens of workshops we have reduced the basic skills required to just two—"supporting" and "confronting."

Supporting is something you do for the *other* person. To do it well requires that you separate your judgments about what somebody else is saying from the feelings that that person is expressing. Confronting, on the other hand, is something you do for yourself. It requires that you accept others' wants as legitimate and speak up directly for your own.

Support—the ability to hear, understand, and act upon what others are saying—shows up prominently on the list of characteristics of high-performing managers studied by Rensis Likert. At the same time, P. R. Lawrence and J. W. Lorsch in their widely-quoted differentiation-integration research show that confronting differences openly is the preferred method for conflict resolution in productive organizations.

In his classic case for managerial teamwork, the late Douglas McGregor graphically described what "a really good top management team" does in meetings. "The members listen to each other!" he wrote. "Every idea is given a hearing . . . even if it seems fairly extreme." At the same time, "there is disagreement. The group is comfortable with this and shows no signs of having to avoid conflict. . . ." In short, the members support and confront one another.

Self-Diagnosis

Improving supporting and confronting skills requires a bit of self-diagnosis. Some people are better at one skill than the other, and some have trouble with both. Take a minute to rate yourself on the scale

Reprinted from *Supervisory Management*, May 1981

in Figure 1. Which skill do you use least now? That is the one to start practicing immediately, and learn to use together with the skill that's better developed.

You don't need to go to workshops to practice. Instead, try the behavior we will recommend with bosses, subordinates, and peers. We're talking about using the innate abilities most people are born with: the ability to hear and be heard. Unfortunately, many of us lost these abilities on the education treadmill and must relearn them later in life as "interpersonal skills."

Think about a relationship you want to improve, a task you want to accomplish, an unsolved problem you want solved. Think about the person you must speak with, what you want him or her to do, and what your discussions with that person have been like until now. Then, consider the relationship in light of your own ability to support and confront.

An Emphasis on Resolution

In working with managers we often ask what the word "support" conjures up in their minds. Responses are surprisingly consistent: trust, help, assistance, back-up, aid, and agreement. This list is notable in two ways. First, the words are loaded with positive feelings. Second, the words always imply that the supporter *agrees* with the person being supported.

At first, it seems contradictory to managers that it is possible (and productive) to support people they

Figure 1

Self-Diagnosis

(Circle the number that fits best for you right now.)

Receiving support from others for me is:

Embarrassing/difficult   Pleasant/easy

                               1   2   3   4   5   6   7

Offering support to others for me is:

Unnatural/rare event   Easy/frequent event

                               1   2   3   4   5   6   7

Confronting others for me is:

Clumsy/awkward/usually avoided   Natural/smooth/useful

                               1   2   3   4   5   6   7

Being confronted by others for me is:

Uncomfortable/scary/avoided   Welcome chance for dialog

                               1   2   3   4   5   6   7

What have you concluded about yourself? Check below:

_____ I'm satisfied with my skills as they are.
_____ I need to support more.
_____ I need to confront more.
_____ I need more of both skills.

don't see eye to eye with. It seems somehow dishonest to support someone with whom we disagree. But that would be to hear only the *facts* in another's statements and to miss the *feelings* behind the facts.

Consider this recent situation, for example, where the parties could not hear the feelings for the facts. The scene was a meeting among physicians and administrators of a hospital to work out a new practice plan.

Administrator #1: The plan we want you to accept is fair, reasonable, and essential to the survival of this hospital.

Physician #1: I think it's a threat to our practice. We won't have control over the management of our patients.

Administrator #1: No, it's not a threat. That's ridiculous. It's hardly any change at all from. . . .

Physician #2: There's no way we can buy this plan.

Administrator #2: Well, if that's an example of your cooperativeness, we're in serious trouble. The government is insisting. . . .

Trustee: We have to have this issue resolved. I want you to sit down together and work out a plan for the survival of this hospital.

Physician #1: We're sitting down now!

Trustee: Yes, but we're not getting anywhere.

Administrator #1: Well, if the physicians would just cooperate and try to see this thing in its true perspective. . . .

Physician #1: Who's uncooperative? We didn't dream up this plan.

Both physicians and administrators are blaming each other and digging in their heels for a long battle. Neither side has been heard by the other. Each fuels the disagreement by treating the other's feelings as unreal or irrelevant.

So long as the antagonists hear only facts, they are stuck with judging whether the facts are "true" and whether, therefore, they can agree and still hold on to their own integrity. This confusion between the words (facts) and the music (feelings) is the single biggest stumbling block to supporting others. Supporting can happen only if agreement is treated as a secondary matter, one to be held in abeyance, while we try to hear and understand what the other person is saying. In short, what's required is the skill of supporting the feelings of people with whom we disagree.

Consider this "instant replay" of the physician-administrator meeting—an event incidentally that actually took place after the group had been introduced to the concepts of supporting and confronting. The dialog, based on mutual supporting, takes a turn for the better.

Physician #1: We still see the plan as a threat to our practices.

Administrator #1: Well, that isn't what we intended. I recognize that it's a threat from your point of view, and that all of you are opposed to it. I think it *could* be a threat in the long run unless we work together to minimize the impact. Given the heat from the government, I don't see many choices.

Physician #1: Well, we know that you need to go in this direction and that you're doing the best you can with a bad situation. However, we want a voice in this. If you're willing to take our problems into account, I think we can work out a plan to achieve what you want.

The problem is unresolved. The substantive disagreements have still to be confronted. Yet the mood of the parties to work it out has changed dramatically.

Really Listening

Sometimes, the *intention* to support is evident from the start, yet people still end up behaving in ways exactly the opposite of what was intended. Consider this vignette, overheard in a factory.

Supervisor: I'm running late, If we don't finish this job by 5, we'll blow the contract. What'll I do?

Office manager (*who is also his friend*): Don't sweat it. Look at the job you did last time. With a record like yours they can't fire you for one mistake.

Supervisor: Well, that's easy for you to say. I am sweating it, and with a boss like mine you never know what he'll do.

Office manager: Ah, why don't you have a cup of coffee and calm down? It'll be all right.

The supervisor has asked his friend for help. Intending support, she fails him by denying his feelings ("don't sweat it") and providing a rationalization for not solving the problem ("a record like yours"). In short he is advised, as a solution, to stop feeling what he feels.

In fact, the foreman does have a good record and won't lose his job. In fact, even if the job isn't finished by five, the contract will not be blown. It is also a fact, though, that he's running late and believes catastrophe will ensue. Those are the facts that he considers important. He will not feel supported unless his friend validates his priorities by demonstrating that he is being taken seriously. A better response would have been:

Supervisor: I'm running late. If we don't finish this job by 5, we'll blow the contract. What'll I do?

Office manager: Yeah, I can see you're running late, and if the contract's blown, that could be serious. What's the best way I can help you?

The office manager shows that she accepts the supervisor's feelings. Instead of providing a nonsolution, she asks how to help. If the supervisor feels supported, he will be more open to influence, on the one hand, and more capable of discovering his own solution, on the other.

There are four things people often do, intending to support, that are not at all supportive:

1. Give unsolicited advice. "If I were you, I would. . . ."
2. Tell people they "shouldn't feel that way." Who says so? They do feel that way.
3. Minimize the problem. "Oh, that's not so bad. You should be glad you don't have *real* troubles. Let me tell you about *my* boss."
4. Accept the obligation to solve the problem—without being asked. "Well, the first thing you should do is get on the phone and. . . ."

There are also four actions that most people will see as supportive:

1. Repeat what you've heard. "Let's see if I understand you. You're saying that. . . ."
2. Put *both* facts and feelings into a statement about what has been said. "You're annoyed (feeling) with me because (fact) I haven't made the phone call yet."
3. Empathize. "I can see why you're angry in this situation. I would be too."
4. Ask the other person what, if anything, they want from you. "How can I help you with this?"

The last point is especially important. Frequently, people just want somebody to *hear* them. Simply listening often solves the problem. Offering advice, denying feelings, or proposing courses of action without being asked tells others they have *not* been heard.

Suppose You Don't Agree?

What happens when the other person is wrong in what he or she has said or directly contradicts a belief or course of action important to us?

Here we need a second skill that requires us to recognize differences. This was the stage toward which the physicians and administrators in our earlier example were moving, the point at which they would confront their disagreement.

When we ask managers what the word "confront" means to them, we consistently get back words loaded with negative feelings: challenge, fight, argue, defend, battle, force. These words are consistent with only one of several dictionary definitions, the one that means "to face in hostility and defiance." Rarely do managers provide another, equally valid connotation—to "face squarely." This is not the same thing as challenging, arguing, or fighting.

Learning to face a difference squarely is not always easy to do. Most people find they must give up the attitude ingrained since childhood that disagreement is "bad" and avoiding conflict is "good." Paradoxically, this attitude directly contradicts an equally powerful feeling that solving problems is "good" and indecisiveness "bad." This leads to two traps—avoiding conflict on the one hand and moving towards premature resolution on the other.

It might be helpful here to note that nonconfronters often fear the risks of genuine interaction—anger, rejection, tension, and so forth. They have a strong need to be "nice" all the time. Yet the risks of not confronting seem equally unappetizing—less power, reduced influence, lower performance, less likelihood of achieving goals.

The issue is not *whether* to confront, but rather *when* and *how* to confront skillfully. Conflict is inevitable, legitimate, and potentially useful in all important relationships.

To exploit fully the potential of conflict, however, we must also avoid rushing toward premature resolution. Conflict often starts innocently, with relatively simple differences, yet the drive to premature resolution can quickly escalate the conflict.

We now have an escalated misunderstanding—each party actively opposing the other's stand and refusing to accept the other's solution. One or the other party may hate conflict. In that case a guerrilla action—delay or denial—will probably ensue.

Exploring the Differences

What's called for early on is an exploration of the differences that lie between disagreement and misunderstanding. Confronting means making explicit the differences that exist between two individuals, and its success depends entirely on the ability of both parties to express their differences as strongly as possible.

There is a verbal clue that a conflict is about to escalate without sufficient exploration of differences. That clue is "but." It has no place in successful confronting.

Sales manager: I'm a little behind on first-quarter results, maybe 8 percent short of forecast. I know you said we need to be ahead of forecast at this point. I'm not sure how much. Anyway, that's the story.

Vice-president–sales: Well, I don't like it. You may be 8 percent behind, *but* you said eight weeks ago things were looking good. I'll never be able to explain this to my boss—he expects us to be ahead of forecast every quarter, and I expect you to be, too.

Sales manager: I didn't realize then that the new promotional displays would fall flat. Besides, marketing really let us down in sending out samples. *But* I wouldn't worry. We'll make it up in the second quarter.

Vice-president–sales: I want you to be ahead of forecast, no ands, ifs, or buts.

Sales manager: But I'm not ahead.

Vice-president–sales: Well, you better get ahead.

Here each party moves to cancel the other's feelings. The vice-president seeks to deny the reality of the worrisome 8 percent with a "but you said." The sales manager, in turn, has a "but" of his own. He wouldn't worry, even though the boss is obviously worried. Neither confronts the issues—the difference between goal and performance, the consequences for each party, the potential for resolution. It never develops that the sales manager sees the issue as a temporary slump easily overcome, nor that the vice-president may be in serious trouble with *his* boss unless he can make a convincing explanation. The parties have no resolution. The implied threat, "You better get ahead," suggests that warfare, open or underground, is where they're heading.

Imagine that each knew how important supporting the other person's position was to a productive resolution. The conversation might go something like this:

Sales manager: I'm a little behind on first-quarter results, maybe 8 percent short of forecast. I know you said we need to be ahead at this point.

Vice-president–sales: Well, I'm disappointed, and I guess you are, too. I'm glad you let me know. How did it happen?

Sales manager: The new promotional displays bombed out; and we were slow to get the samples out. I think we can make it up in the second quarter.

Vice-president–sales: Well, my boss isn't going to like it either. At the same time he has a right to know that's where we stand. I'm counting on you to catch up. Can you do it? Do you need any help?

Sales manager: I think we can do it. I realize your boss keeps the heat on. I'll do my best to avoid this the next time.

Here, both parties treat the differences—in this case, of expectations—as real. The slack sales are real, so is the vice-president's disappointment, so is the pressure from above. By acknowledging all this, the parties clarify the potential misunderstanding from the beginning. Instead of escalation, they move towards resolution.

Some of us confront more naturally than we support. For others it's just the reverse. To always confront and never support is to deny the needs of others. To always support and never confront is to deny your own needs. Without both skills, working with others will be much less successful than any of us would like. As we improve these skills we will put more energy into solving the problem and less into fighting to be heard.

Consulting Patterns of Successful Managers

MELVILLE HENSEY

Successful managers consult in their daily work with associates and staff. This consulting pattern is vital to their decision making and problem solving and the reason for their success. Yet it is little noticed or discussed.

Management literature makes little or no reference to it, except for Lawrence Miller's discussion of "decisions by command, consultation, or consensus" in *American Spirit* (Morrow, 1984). Managers themselves don't notice it, probably because they are more concerned with their search for other opinions, alternatives, or reactions and the problem at hand.

Nevertheless, when faced with problems or opportunities of a complex nature, wise managers turn to others for advice. They know they have too little useful information or that their knowledge, while considerable, is inconclusive. Then, again, others' interests, priorities, or sensitivities may be involved or the support of others to a course of action may be necessary but not forthcoming unless they are consulted. Most often these needs are simply *felt*. The managers intuitively move from a situation of confusion toward clarity.

Consulting Patterns

Successful managers seem to be continually gathering "data"—opinions, feelings, and ideas, as well as facts. Intense periods alternate with slow periods, but data gathering is a *major* activity.

Consulting patterns take two forms:

One-to-one conferences—perhaps in the corridor or by phone, casual (unplanned) contacts as well as formal meetings.

Group conferences—whether work meetings, for that or some other purpose, or social gatherings.

A manager's approach to consulting is individual. He or she may pose the problem/opportunity and ask for views and/or ideas or reactions to a specific plan; gather data in a round-about way of questioning; raise an issue, then ask for any thoughts about it; or give detailed background about a situation and/or describe an intended course of action, while more or less open to others' points or objections. Sometimes a variety of techniques is used, depending on the circumstances. The method isn't as important, though,

Reprinted from *Supervisory Management*, May 1986

as the fact that the manager recognizes the need to get and consider others' views, ideas, concerns, interests, and feelings before making a decision, planning, or acting in some way. Such managers stand out because of the resulting performance.

- A good-to-excellent bottom line in all parts of the economic cycle
- People who are developing new skills and taking on more responsibility
- New products, services, clients, and markets, even in "stable" businesses
- Repeat clients or customers for their services or products
- Special recognition in the form of promotions, awards, requests for talks or visits, and the like
- Performance reviews above average

Needless to say, for consulting to have such a positive impact on performance, a manager must truly listen.

Managers Who Don't

Less successful managers are much more likely to deal with complex problems or opportunities by relying on graphs, reports, and printouts of their own views or ideas. They may be persuaded by one person's (or group's) views or a particularly visible or emotional aspect of the issue. They may have a pet theory of their own or be willing to listen only to views with which they are comfortable.

Why don't more managers use consulting patterns, or use them often enough? From my own experiences as a manager and observations of other managers at many levels, I suspect the reasons to be:

- *Fear* of being seen as needing help or input
- *The need to be right*—"My way or no way"
- *Impatience*—needing to do something now, right or wrong
- *Unwillingness to take the time* to check something out (although not doing so may mean having to do it over)
- *Lack of experience* or technique—they just never discovered the usefulness of consulting

Clearly, this article is written for those managers in the last group. Try it. Consulting others on problems and opportunities is tangibly rewarding and personally satisfying (to all parties).

How to Tell Your Boss He's Wrong

DON MICHAEL McDONALD

All of us have faced situations in which the person to whom we report made an "unreasonable" request. How did we respond? How could we have better handled the situation? That's the question asked a group of managers from different organization levels and from profit and not-for-profit settings. Their experiences and responses may prove insightful the next time your boss is wrong.

Dilemma of the Thinking Subordinate

The central issue is authority. This is the ability to decide what others will do. Submission to authority is expected by most institutions, but the thinking subordinate will ask, "Don't I have the responsibility to speak up if I see something wrong?"

To that question, the answer is yes. Authority can be usurped not only by not obeying a directive but also by not equipping a boss for a good decision. You weaken your boss if you withhold alternatives or other information he or she needs for the best decisions. "My boss needs me to tell him what I see from my position," said one of the managers interviewed. "He can't know everything, and I may be closer to the problem. But I don't make his decisions for him or contradict his decisions."

By offering alternatives for a decision, you are not taking away your boss's right to make the decision. What if he or she doesn't do what you suggest? One top manager's reply to this is, "If you have no authority to make the decision, then you have no responsibility for the outcome." Your responsibility is information.

When to Disagree Upwardly

Even wise King Solomon implied that it was possible to disagree with him, but he wrote, "A wise heart knows the proper time and procedure." Disagreeing with one in authority cannot be done in the same way as with a subordinate.

As a boss, you can "direct" a subordinate, because you are in the position to decide the outcome. As a subordinate, you can inform or suggest proactively. "Proactively" is key here; you need to take the initiative before there is an obvious problem and while alternatives still abound.

Reprinted from *Management Solutions*, December 1988

While a patently rebellious subordinate is worse than useless, a proactive subordinate is far more valuable than one who blindly obeys. Even then, though, you need:

The right attitude. Attitude is all important," said one top manager. "I can't assume I'm right and he's wrong. Perhaps he knows something I don't know. For that reason, I always try to pose my concerns and suggestions in the form of a question." In other words, you let your boss say so if your idea is better.

"Even before I go in," continued this senior manager, "I need to mentally prepare to do whatever my boss decides." This manager doesn't intend to do battle with the boss, for, as the manager says, "he does not bear the sword for nothing."

One warning: You not only must have the right attitude, you must communicate the right attitude. When you say, "but," you don't want your boss to interpret "rebellion." You never say—you never even imply—that you are unwilling to do what the boss says. The best approach varies within each organization's culture, but the best approach always communicates cooperation.

To keep from coming across as defiant, you should consider your words in advance. Likewise, be careful about the setting you pick to confront your boss. You don't want to choose a setting that puts him or her in a bad light before peers or subordinates.

It also helps if you and your boss know each other well. If your boss "knows" you, he or she is less likely to misinterpret your words.

A mutual understanding of roles. The role of decision-maker is something you and your boss will constantly have to redefine with changes in skill, task, and mutual confidence. If you see a potential conflict in a coming decision, you should try to head if off with discussion. This article may even make a good basis for discussion. You can mark it up and show it to your boss. The suggestions of others may not work best in your case, but they are a starting point for exploration.

How to Disagree Upwardly

Telling your boss he's wrong can be risky even with the best of bosses, but sometimes it is better for both of you if you do. The question is, "How?" The most frequently used responses are:

- "But that isn't in my job description."
- "No, that won't work; I have a better idea."
- "That goes against my other boss's directives."
- "I won't do that. It's unethical."

Are there better ways of handling such situations? Here's what our group of managers say they did— and got results.

"That's not my job." It's better for both you and your organization if your boss doesn't think in terms of job descriptions. You want to encourage him or her to think in terms of purpose—what has to be achieved. Attention should focus on what should be done before it is placed on who should do it.

Let's assume that you disagree with your boss. One positive yet honest alternative is to say, "OK, I'll get on it. But you know, Bill does this kind of thing a lot in his job. He has already established the contacts and could probably get quicker results for you. Do you mind if I ask him to place these calls?" Here, an offer is made to take the work to the appropriate person. Perhaps, though, your position or work relationship makes that impractical. In such a situation, you might agree to the work, then suggest that your manager take the work to the more qualified or experienced person. Either way, your boss hears that someone else is better qualified to do the task, not that you are unwilling.

"That won't work; I have a better idea." This is close to throwing down the gauntlet. A better response is, "Help me to understand why we are going to do it this way." Notice that there is no implications that you will not do it your boss's way.

After your boss has shared with you his or her reasons, you can say, "If that's what you want, I'll do it, but may I suggest a way that could be faster (cheaper, more efficient, etc.)?"

A labor negotiator told me that she had once suggested an alternative approach to her boss, but he had continued with his original plan. Shortly thereafter, she was with her boss when he heard that his plan was failing. She leaned over and said, "I think you could still make the deal if we just change this part. . . . What do you think?" The change was made; the deal went through. Her second suggestion was actually her original suggestion, but she was wise enough not to say, "Why don't you just do what I said in the first place?"

"Once I presented an idea to a boss who didn't think it would work," recalled another manager. "A few days later, he came back with the same idea restated, acting like it was original." The subconscious had recorded what the conscious had rejected. The manager's response? "That's a great idea. I bet it works."

Sometimes you must choose between recognition and retaining your influence.

"That goes against my other boss." This is a stickier issue, but not an unusual one. It's not impossible for your boss's boss to give you a directive that contradicts your immediate boss's instructions. What do you do then?

One worker who faced this dilemma reported his frustration to his immediate boss after the fact. "He's higher in the organization than either of us. What else could I do but throw out what we had been so faithfully working on?"

His boss explained, "If you don't have the authority to say 'no,' then you don't have the authority to say 'yes' either. Your authority comes through the chain." Under the circumstances, the manager told his subordinate, his best response would have been to apologize for his inability to act and explain that he would review the matter before his immediate boss as quickly as possible.

An employee in another organization told a similar story with a different ending.

When asked to take on a key project, he told his boss's boss, "I'll do as you ask, but do you realize that John gave me this other project as a priority?"

"That's not as important" was the response. "We need to get on this right away."

"Sure, but would you please help me by putting your request in writing before I switch over to the other project?"

Note how here, again, the manager shows a willingness to proceed.

In both of these cases, it was impossible to bring both the boss's boss and immediate boss together. In most instances, the best answer is to get them into the same room or on the phone immediately. It is also wise to let the person requesting the change know that there is a conflict. If upper-level communication is not possible before you must comply, then you should insure that your immediate boss finds out as soon as possible thereafter. Remember, too, the conflict is not yours, no matter to which project or boss you feel most committed. You do not have the authority to choose, and as the saying goes, "you cannot serve two masters."

"No, that's unethical." Have you ever had a boss expect the unethical from you? It's not as infrequent an occurrence as we would all like to believe. To one extent or another, ethical differences exist in every organization.

A financial broker said, "If it's not a moral issue, I'm willing to do whatever is asked, but I won't— can't—compromise my ethics for anyone. If people know that, they won't ask."

"Everyone has an ethical code," said another manager with a variety of job experience. "It may or may not be written in the corporate handbook, but you can read it in the daily decision-making pattern."

In one job, this manager found lying to vendors to be the norm. Before he was ever confronted or compromised, he went to his boss. "I notice it is common practice here to tell vendors that payments are coming when they are not," he said. "I have a personal ethic that prevents me from doing that. I want you to know up front so you won't unknowingly put me into a position where I can't do what you want."

Notice that the manager neither required the boss to change his ethic nor apologized for his own. Conflicting ethics requires communication, not confrontation. You are not telling the boss what his or her ethics should be. Changing the boss is not your responsibility. You are just communicating your own limitations and why. In the case cited, the manager was able to continue at his job and had several friendly opportunities to discuss values with the boss thereafter.

Summing Up

Bosses make decisions but they cannot make good ones in an information vacuum. When you are in a position to see what your boss does not, communicate cooperation first, information second, and alternatives third. If possible, prepare in advance for disagreement, rehearsing appropriate words and building rapport with the boss. If his or her directives call for unreasonable sacrifice or compromise on your part, communicate your limitations as soon as possible. If you cannot comply with the final decisions, for ethical reasons or otherwise, you should look for another position for the sake of everyone involved.

Part X

PERFORMANCE APPRAISALS

Getting Ready for the Appraisal Interview

DAN H. NIX

One of your subordinates is due for a performance appraisal. Are you ready for the meeting? You may have all the documentation you'll need and you may have prepared all the forms you're required to use, but have you prepared yourself?

Giving performance appraisals is probably one of the least palatable aspects of a supervisor's job. Organizations provide their supervisors with evaluation instruments, forms, or guides to aid them, but most supervisors are still uncomfortable about this awkward and often ineffectual process.

When questioned about the difficulties encountered in the evaluation process, supervisors find it hard to explain why they feel uneasy about the appraisal. One problem may be that a great many of them have had little, if any, training in conducting an evaluation interview. And even those who have been exposed to appraisal dos and don'ts still feel uncomfortable about taking on the responsibility of judging another person—and what's worse, *discussing* their judgment with that individual. They worry about the effect that interview may have on future relations with the subordinate. This seems particularly to be a problem where the supervisor was promoted from within his or her work group and now is in the position of having to evaluate former peers.

Reprinted from *Supervisory Management,* July 1980

Feelings

How does one go about conducting an appraisal interview or, perhaps more importantly, how does one *prepare* to conduct such a meeting?

Much has been written about the need for open communication, the clear articulation of work goals and department objectives, and a positive climate during the interview. Equally important to the interview's success, however, is the supervisor's awareness of his or her own feelings about the session. After all, the evaluation process requires a two-way dialogue. The supervisor must be aware of how his or her feelings will affect the outcome of the interview. Those feelings stem from two concerns of the supervisor, namely, the past performance of the individual and the perceived impact—positive, neutral, or negative— that the interview might have on the supervisor/subordinate relationship. It is a rare individual who can evaluate and/or criticize another and not wonder what effect there will be on their future relationship.

In order to help supervisors put their feelings in the proper perspective, we have developed "Pre-Interview Gut-Level Scales." These scales can provide a supervisor with an understanding of his or her fears about the upcoming interview. Even more important, though, they are a planning tool that the supervisor can use to prepare for the session.

The scales are tied to a series of questions shown in Figure 1 that the interviewer must answer in his or her own mind prior to the actual interview. It is best to answer the questions about each subordinate before tackling your organization's standard appraisal form.

The first step is for the supervisor to answer each of the first four questions with the soon-to-be-appraised subordinate in mind. The questions must be answered, not necessarily in writing, but honestly, candidly, and with some serious thought. (Remember, the performance review is serious business; another person's career can depend on it.) The supervisor then complies with items five and six by approximating responses on the continua. The scales labeled A, B, C, and D in Figure 2 are next marked. The numbers are then transferred to the score profile shown in Figure 3. To develop the profile, straight lines are drawn connecting each score. The final step is the determination from the profile of the position the employee would occupy on the planning matrix in Figure 4.

Figure 1

Pre-Interview

First ask yourself questions one through four, then mark the scales in questions five and six.
1. How do I *really* feel about evaluating this person? (Gut-level reaction only!)
2. Why do I feel this way (either good or bad)?
3. What is the worst possible outcome of this evaluation interview? (Let your deepest fears decide this.)
4. What is the best possible outcome of this evaluation interview? (Be positive here.)
5. Indicate on the scale the likelihood of the occurrence of either number three or number four, whichever you feel is most likely.

Worst		Best
Possible	No Change	Possible

6. Indicate on the scale the overall performance rating you think you will assign this person.

| Unsatisfactory | Average | Outstanding |

Figure 2

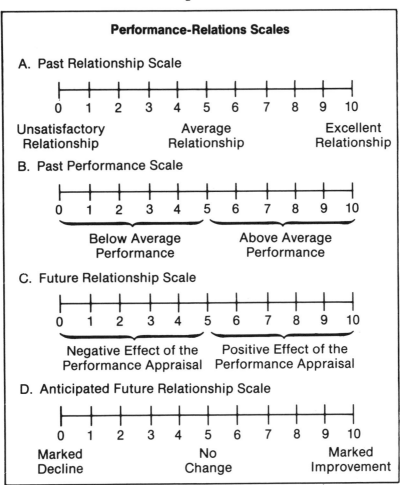

Performance-Relations Scales

A. Past Relationship Scale

0 1 2 3 4 5 6 7 8 9 10

Unsatisfactory   Average   Excellent
Relationship   Relationship   Relationship

B. Past Performance Scale

0 1 2 3 4 5 6 7 8 9 10

Below Average   Above Average
Performance   Performance

C. Future Relationship Scale

0 1 2 3 4 5 6 7 8 9 10

Negative Effect of the   Positive Effect of the
Performance Appraisal   Performance Appraisal

D. Anticipated Future Relationship Scale

0 1 2 3 4 5 6 7 8 9 10

Marked   No   Marked
Decline   Change   Improvement

Planning Matrix

The matrix contains nine boxes, each one signifying a different performance/relationship level. Identifying from the profile the position the employee will occupy on the planning matrix can help the supervisor plan the actual interview and enable him or her to determine developmental needs, the future focus and objectives of the supervisor/subordinate relationship, and the impact that the appraisal will have on performance.

Let's look at each of the boxes in the matrix to see how a supervisor should respond during the performance appraisal interview in each instance.

▪ *Position #1.* Low future relationship, low future performance. Of all the positions, this is obviously the least desirable. In this instance, the supervisor should plan on conveying concern about performance. The subordinate's shortcomings, dysfunctional behavior, lack of knowledge, and so forth need to be dealt with in an open, candid interview. Needless to say, this position requires the most planning and preparation on the part of the supervisor.

▪ *Position #2.* Low future relationship, average future performance. In this situation, the supervisor

Figure 3

Score Profile			

Past Performance Score	Past Relationship Score	Projected Relationship Score	Projected Performance Score
High 10	10	10	10
Average 5	5	5	5
Poor 0	0	0	0

should stress specifics about how performance can be improved and examine the reasons behind the negative relationship. Here, the supervisor must be concerned with his or her own relating skills and should take the lead in attempting to improve the relationship.

▪ *Position #3.* Low future relationship, high future performance. The concern here obviously should be with the supervisor/subordinate relationship. Performance may be high now, but a poor relationship can change that. The first steps in improving the relationship may need to be taken by the supervisor, and the appraisal interview is a good time to begin.

▪ *Position #4.* Average future relationship, low future performance. In this case, the supervisor's goal is to improve performance while maintaining or improving the relationship. This might be ap-

Figure 4

Planning Matrix

		Projected Future Performance		
		Low	Average	High
Projected Future Relationship	Low	1	2	3
	Average	4	5	6
	High	7	8	9

proached best from the performance side, discussing specifics about performance weaknesses accompanied by positives about the relationship.

• *Position #5.* Average future relationship, average future performance. This employee has the potential for going either way and must be encouraged in a positive manner so as to enhance both performance and relationship.

• *Position #6.* Average future relationship, high future performance. The employee shows much promise. In fact, he or she might have the potential to be a supervisor one day. In this instance, the manager needs to emphasize performance while attempting to nurture the relationship. Again, this nurturing is the responsibility of the supervisor.

• *Position #7.* High future relationship, low future performance. The supervisor has a good relationship with the subordinate, yet the subordinate demonstrates a low level of productivity. The supervisor and employee need to re-examine their roles, responsibilities, and relationship. The supervisor must take the lead in such a situation.

• *Position #8.* High future relationship, average future performance. This employee relates positively with the supervisor and does adequate work. The potential for improvement is a plus factor, and the supervisor should attempt to build on that while maintaining the high relationship.

• *Position #9.* High future relationship, high future performance. This is the ideal position. It is possible that this subordinate is a key employee, and he or she should be given appropriate recognition. This type of employee can contribute significantly to the achievement of the organization's objectives as well as to overall group cohesiveness.

Preparation Makes the Difference

The performance appraisal is indeed an often poorly executed supervisory responsibility. Recognizing the fact that preparation, planning, and thought are vital to the process is the first step to meaningful, productive evaluations. By following the steps outlined here, a supervisor can better prepare himself or herself to constructively discuss performance with the subordinate and improve their relationship. One interesting side benefit to the supervisor of the process is the opportunity to analyze objectively the information gathered to determine patterns in performance or relationships within the department. The supervisor may gain as much insight from this process about his or her management style as may be learned about how to conduct performance appraisal. At the very least, the supervisor will approach the session more securely. Coupling the "getting-ready" system with the organization's appraisal system the supervisor should find that he or she is better prepared and more comfortable about the task to be faced.

Let's Talk: Discussing Job Performance

EDWARD L. LEVINE

Millie Moderne, an up-and-coming manager of XYZ, Inc., has set up an appointment with one of her employees, Dudley DoWell, to conduct a job performance review. The meeting was set up two weeks before and will be held in the quiet of her office. As Millie waits for Dudley, she checks to see that she's done everything that personnel told her to do during a two-hour training session. The company is using a new performance appraisal system, and the form for rating job performances uses rating scales that have actual descriptions of good and poor job performance. Millie is checking to see that she has completed all the paperwork required when Dudley knocks and enters her office.

Dudley: Hi, Millie. I'm here for the performance review.

Millie: (Thinking: *Dudley looks as nervous as I feel. I hate these annual performance review discussions.*) Yes, thank you for coming, Dudley. Come on in and sit down. It's that time again. We've got to fill out the new company performance form, then I have to decide on how much of a raise to recommend for you this year based on your ratings.

Dudley: (Thinking: *I hope I get good ratings; I think I deserve them.*) O.K., I'm ready if you are.

Millie: You've probably heard about this new form. It's keyed to specific instances of good and poor job performance. On the basis of your performance over the past year, I've filled in each of the rating categories. As you can see, I've rated you on the high end of the scales for almost every category. What do you think about that?

Dudley: (Thinking: *Uh oh, here comes the bad news.*) I . . . uh . . . appreciate that.

Millie: However, in two of the categories—report writing and safety—I didn't think you were quite up to snuff. So I rated you a bit below the middle of the scale. You do agree with these ratings, don't you?

Dudley: (Thinking: *I really don't see how she got that.*) Oh . . . sure.

Millie: Dudley, I'll be recommending you for a 7 percent merit increase based on your performance, and I expect you to keep up the good work. I also want you to do your best to shore up these weak areas, O.K.?

Dudley: Well I'm not sure . . . (Thinking: *Gee, my reports are better than Joe's, and my safety record is better than Jane's, but they got higher ratings than I did.*) I'll try my best.

The author gratefully acknowledges the suggestions of H. H. Meyer and Jeffrey Jones, University of South Florida.

Reprinted from *Supervisory Management*, October 1980

The scene ends with Dudley leaving Millie's office looking very disappointed. One week later Millie receives a letter of resignation from Dudley saying that he has taken a job with XYZ's chief competitor.

What Went Wrong

Despite the brand new performance rating form and a well-meaning manager, the performance review was a disaster. Why? First and foremost, no real communication took place. Millie did most of the talking. Another problem was Millie's use of praise to soften the blow of her criticism. As Dudley himself recognized, all the praise did was to set him up for the poor ratings to come. Still another problem was that no clear, specific targets were set up for improvements in the problem areas. Dudley was left without any idea of how his reports could be improved or how he could improve his safety rating.

Although it did not go well, Millie's performance review with Dudley is at least as good as the typical review. Millie was given training. She set the performance review session up in advance, and she held it in private in the comfort of her office. Also, she used a job-related rating form, and she encouraged Dudley to do better in his weak areas. All these features are likely to be missing in many performance review meetings.

Although there are performance review programs that contain some of these features, I have yet to encounter an organizationwide performance appraisal program that is worthwhile. This is a rather sweeping statement, you may think, and you are probably reacting to it with disbelief. You are probably thinking that the statement could not possibly be applied to your own organization. You might point out that in your organization the files are full of properly completed performance rating forms, and everyone seems to be satisfied with the process.

I would respond by pointing out that practically everybody is rated above average or better. Most managers who have to make a decision about a promotion or a transfer ignore the forms prepared on the employee in question and discuss the person's performance with his or her supervisor to see how the individual *really* performs. (In fact, given the value of the forms as perceived by supervisors, if the organization's policy were changed so that completion of the rating forms were not required, the percentage of forms completed would drop drastically.) A careful review of the records will also show very little relationship between the performance ratings and salary increases. Finally, and most important, the annual performance review will have had virtually no impact on productivity, except perhaps for a short period right before it and right afterward.

These problems, along with those evident in Millie's meeting with Dudley, lead directly to a disappointing conclusion: Performance appraisal practices currently fail to enhance productivity, maintain a worker's organizational commitment, or even accomplish purely administrative objectives. For many organizations, performance appraisal programs not only fail to achieve these ends but, in fact, work against their achievement.

The Need for Communication

We can do without the kind of performance appraisal programs typically found in organizations today. Their costs far outweigh their benefits. At the same time, communication between a supervisor and a subordinate about job performance is critical.

This is a time of severe economic crisis. Inflation is running rampant, and a key antidote, workforce productivity, is declining rather than advancing. One study of employee theft and counterproductive behavior in retail stores, electronic manufacturing firms, and hospitals in the Minneapolis/St. Paul area shows that approximately 67 percent of the 5,000 workers questioned took excessively long lunch and coffee breaks. Approximately 17 percent reported that they purposely did slow or sloppy work; and over 25 percent took sick days when they were not ill. Research suggests that a substantial number of workers are becoming less satisfied with their jobs and more alienated from their work organizations.

Although one-to-one communication about performance between a supervisor and a subordinate cannot be expected by itself to alleviate these problems, such communication can certainly contribute to their solution.

Interestingly, the performance appraisal review is one of the most thoroughly researched topics in the personnel field. We currently possess sufficient knowledge to design such programs properly. The fact that we are not taking advantage of this knowledge is a mystery. Perhaps social scientists have not communicated the knowledge properly. Perhaps managers are too busy to listen. Perhaps organizations are too locked into traditional performance appraisal programs. Whatever the explanation, the mystery had better be cleared up quickly if business and government are to cope with the challenges that lie ahead in coming decades.

The sorry state of affairs I have portrayed certainly appears to suggest that offering more advice on performance review programs is merely whistling in the wind. However, the importance of the topic prompts me to forge ahead anyway.

For those of you who are not ready to take the steps necessary to improve your communication about job performance, I will offer a number of findings from the research on performance appraisal in the next section. You can stop reading there.

For those of you who are ready to make a greater commitment, I will go into more detail. However, you *committed* managers should be advised that you cannot learn how to communicate about job performance effectively merely by reading this or any other article or book. You need to take advantage of high-quality training programs, prepare for your communication sessions thoroughly, and be willing to engage in intense, extended communication sessions.

A Very Short Course on Performance Appraisal

The short list of dos and don'ts to follow should allow you to hold up your end of the conversation on performance appraisal at a cocktail party. You may even impress your personnel officer with your knowledge. In fact, if you apply these principles, your performance appraisal interviews may improve somewhat. However, I will not guarantee any substantial increases in productivity.

The Dos

1. Base your job performance rating on just that—job performance—not personality, appearance, or mannerisms.
2. Use rating scales based on a careful analysis of the job and also objective performance indicators, if available. This will ensure that your ratings can withstand a legal challenge.
3. Take advantage of your organization's training programs on how to conduct the yearly performance appraisal interview.
4. Make an appointment for the annual performance appraisal interview at least one week in advance.
5. At the interview itself, encourage your employee to participate in the discussion.
6. Be helpful, enthusiastic, and positive in your comments.
7. Try to help your employee solve any problems that stand in the way of excellent job performance.

The Don'ts

1. Don't criticize. Avoid criticism as much as possible during the annual performance appraisal interview.
2. Don't commit the two most frequent performance rating errors—the halo error and the leniency error. The halo error occurs when you come to an overall judgment about a subordinate's performance, then rate him or her the same on every scale in the rating form, without taking note of the person's strengths and weaknesses. The leniency error usually produces ratings that are higher than a worker deserves.

3. Don't dominate the appraisal interview. Encourage an employee to speak.
4. Don't be satisfied to tell a worker to do his or her best over the coming year. Instead, set specific targets for performance improvement, if needed.

Communicating About Job Performance: The Advanced Course

You committed managers who are reading this have no doubt noticed that I use the phrase communicating about job performance and not the terms "performance evaluation," "performance appraisal," or "performance rating." There is a good reason for this. If you really want to improve productivity, *you have to scrap the annual performance appraisal interview and the rating form that goes along with it.* Instead of ratings that come once a year, you should be communicating with your employee at least once every three months, or more if necessary, about job performance targets and how they can be achieved. You should be providing feedback on results, whenever appropriate and necessary. You should also be communicating whenever problems arise that your employee and you feel can be resolved by one-to-one discussion.

Some of you may be protesting that you need the rating form for your records, for promotion decisions, layoff decisions, or perhaps most important of all for annual salary increases. But H. H. Meyer, an expert in this area, has noted that performance review discussions cannot accomplish both these administrative needs and at the same time the requirements for heightened motivation to achieve improved productivity. As experience indicates, organizations cannot resolve performance problems with better rating forms. I cannot emphasize too much the point that performance improvement is *not a measurement* problem.

Performance Goals—The Foundation of Productivity

The first step in a job performance communications program is a meeting, or a series of meetings, between you and your subordinate to set performance targets. This, of course, is not new, but a standard part of such well-known managerial techniques as management by objectives. However, you may find some new slants in what I am recommending.

Anytime an employee is past the break-in period, you are ready to embark on a goal-setting conference. Your first task is to insure that your employee understands the significance of his or her job in relation to the entire work organization and your division. Here you are working to gain commitment to the organization and to overcome alienation. Most employees need to feel that they are contributing to a worthwhile enterprise; and, as the organization's primary representative to your subordinates, it is up to you to make this take place. Goals set in a vacuum may have some short-term benefits but will not overcome such consequences of alienation or dissatisfaction as turnover, accidents, and misuse of work time.

Once your employee is clear on how his or her job fits into the total organization, and how worthwhile the organization is in general, you are ready to begin discussing the full scope of the employee's job. This discussion must continue until you both have a clear understanding of all the functions, duties, and responsibilities contained in the job. You should be taking notes as this discussion proceeds. If the discussion is rather long and the job complicated, then you should stop here and get your notes typed before the next meeting.

Following your conference about job content, begin working together to set goals and objectives for each major job function. Job goals should be made as tangible as possible so that the employee may monitor his or her own progress if possible. Goals may be stated in terms of the level or quality of work desired, the amount or quantity of work desired, and the date by which a particular assignment should be completed. Goals may also be set on the basis of the work behaviors in which an employee should engage.

Generally, the more specific the goal is, the better. So, if you can formulate goals in terms of all four aspects—quality, quantity, target date, and the work behaviors by which goals are to be achieved—then your goals will be of high specificity. Sometimes the formulation of goals on the basis of all four aspects is impossible. Don't let this bother you. If goals can only be formulated on one or two aspects, let it go at that.

When you are setting goals, you should bear in mind that the goals should be difficult but attainable. They must also be accepted by your employee. A good deal of *mutual* discussion and negotiation is appropriate at this stage. What may facilitate the process is your assurance that the goals set will not be rigid and inflexible but will be subject to change as you both gain some experience with them. As part of your discussion of goals, you need to give consideration to decisions about which goals are more and less important. Also, you must *not* avoid discussion of goals that are long term in nature, say two or three years. One of the criticisms of goal setting has been that short-term results are emphasized sometimes at the cost of the long-term good of the organization. Your discussion of where the job fits into the overall organizational picture and your attention to long-term goals should help to offset this problem.

Another point deserves emphasis. I have indicated that goals may be set in terms of the work behaviors needed to achieve them. During the goal-setting process it is helpful to spend time discussing any confusion or lack of knowledge the employee may have about how to go about achieving the goals. You should also reassure your subordinate that you will be available to assist in the accomplishment of any and all goals.

If appropriate, you may wish to set goals in such special areas as safety, affirmative action, or work attendance. To reinforce your discussion about the organization, you might want to set some goals that are relevant to organizational needs. For example, one such goal might be to come up with at least one suggestion over the following three months to improve relationships between the employee's department and other units in the company.

Your goal setting concerned with job performance is now finished. However, the process cannot be considered complete until you have discussed goals for self-improvement with your employee. Such goals should be set for relatively long periods of time, say six months to one year. They should be set in such a fashion that they are obviously related to the interests and career aspirations of your subordinate. In many occupations where new knowledge is rapidly increasing or the technology is rapidly advancing, the setting of personal development goals with your subordinate is critical to avoid the problem of obsolescence.

At the conclusion of the entire goal-setting process, all the mutually agreed upon goals should be written out, and both you and your employees should have a copy.

Some of you rightfully may object to the idea of goal setting with employees who lack control over their jobs. For example, an employee tending a conveyor belt that moves at a fixed speed has little way of adjusting his or her behavior. Of course, goal setting in these circumstances will not be appropriate or worthwhile except in the area of self-development, probably on the employee's own time, to achieve career goals.

Reviewing Progress and Resetting Goals

A short time after your goal-setting discussions have been concluded, certainly no more than a month afterwards, you and your employee should get together again. Both of you should come to the meeting fully prepared to discuss progress toward goal achievement and the possible need to reset goals.

At the conference, you should begin by asking your employee to talk about any aspect of the goals and progress toward goal achievement that he or she wishes. Then you might launch a discussion about whether goals in any area should be reset, either higher or lower. Perhaps the job has changed so that a new goal or set of goals has to be established.

During the discussion you should *refrain from any criticism whatsoever.* Offer encouragement and praise for *real* progress only. Take notes at the meeting, and prepare a copy for your subordinate's inspection and approval. If you have differences of opinion as to what transpired at the meeting, get together again and resolve them.

The next meeting of this sort should be held whenever either you or your subordinate feels the need for it, but certainly no more than two months from the time of the initial review meeting. Regular meetings at three-month intervals, *and no more,* may be held thereafter. Many of these meetings may be short and uneventful, if few problems need solving. Each time, a written record of these meetings should be made. By the second or third review session you should be prepared to provide some additional reward other than verbal praise for the real accomplishments you are likely to see. The nature of this reward may vary from a bonus to a challenging new assignment, to a written commendation. The type of reward will, of course, depend on what you have at your command as a manager to give and your employee's most important needs. In no instance do you fill out any sort of rating form or scale under the procedure I have described.

During the review session it may become clear that your employee needs some on-the-job training or coaching from you. Or perhaps a formal training program in some skill area is necessary. You should take steps to provide the necessary training as soon as you can.

Impact on Job Satisfaction

Besides increasing productivity, goal setting should increase an employee's job satisfaction. This is because the goal setting will insure that your employee is clear on his or her role in the organization. Also, most of us enjoy situations in which we are performing well and in which we are challenged, and the goal-setting approach I described should achieve these ends as well. The rewards that you provide for real accomplishments, rewards which are based on the employee's needs, should also enhance job satisfaction.

Based on the fact that you are getting results and have established an excellent working relationship with your subordinate, I would bet that your job satisfaction would increase, too.

Is there any place left for an annual review discussion? I think so, but its role is quite a bit different in the communication-about-performance system I envision. The annual discussion would deal *only* with your employee's progress in self-development, along with possibilities for advancement in the organization. Again, both you and your employee should prepare carefully for this meeting. In particular, you should be concerned with gathering information about job openings and their requirements.

Administrative Requirements

With the procedure outlined, some administrative requirements will presumably be unmet. For example, there will be no prepared job performance forms for use in promotional or transfer decisions. But then the usual distorted and error-filled rating forms that are clogging personnel files are useless for such decisions. And the use of performance ratings for promotion and transfer decisions turns them into selection procedures and, as such, makes them subject to equal employment opportunity laws. If someone filed a complaint, it is unlikely that many such forms would be adjudged valid in a court of law.

Generally, supervisors who are making promotional or transfer decisions should conduct carefully structured interviews with the candidates and their supervisors that are designed to yield information on key attributes needed for success in the new job. This process would be supplemented by the use of professionally developed and validated examinations. Past performance ratings are virtually unnecessary for a selection procedure of this kind.

Still another administrative requirement that would presumably be unmet unless a yearly rating form was prepared is the skills inventory. This inventory is usually used in large organizations to describe the abilities, work experience, and other attributes of the organization's workers. The system I have described should create a far more detailed record of job performance and work experience gained by an individual worker than any of the rating forms with which I am acquainted.

Probably the most critical administrative requirement that you might be wondering about is the awarding of merit increases based on yearly performance ratings. Because the issue of pay is so complicated, and because there are so many differences from one situation to another, it is impossible to treat the issue here in detail. All I can offer now is the conclusion that a merit increase program that is based on a yearly performance appraisal is incompatible with, and would undermine, the system described. Should you be locked into a yearly merit increase system, you will at least have a very detailed goal-achievement record to fall back on. Merit increases would therefore reflect the entire year's results rather than the most recent results or the results that just happened to have stuck in your memory.

Likelihood for Change

All this may seem "pie in the sky" to you. Strangely, the characteristics of an organization that doom a performance review system to failure are the very same characteristics that require a program of formal supervisory ratings on a yearly basis in the first place. This means that the success of the goal setting and review system I have described may not happen unless basic changes occur in the organization itself. This may *not* be too much to expect because organizations will face increasing pressures to enhance productivity.

In the meantime, even though you may not be able completely to implement the type of system I have described, you might still attempt to go as far as you can to open communications with your subordinate about job performance. Use praise whenever possible and appropriate, and set challenging but attainable goals in the most important work performance areas. Job performance maintenance and improvement is a communication problem, not a measurement problem.

Learning to Level With Employees

CHERYL K. NEEDELL and GEORGE ALWON

Despite the recent popularity of assertiveness training courses, most managers are still ambivalent about telling an employee that they do not like what he or she is doing. It is the one concern that is consistently voiced by participants in management training programs. Many confuse assertiveness (the matter-of-fact verbalization of one's feelings) with aggression (attacking, loss of control, violence). But in fact, when aggression takes place, it is often because assertiveness has been avoided or because one was not skilled in effective confrontation.

How would you handle this situation? Barbara, a valued subordinate, has been arriving to work later and later over the past three months. This morning, you see her enter the office at 10:00 A.M., a full two hours late.

Would you feel inadequate or uncomfortable in dealing with Barbara? Would you be concerned that you will appear to be too aggressive or hostile, or that you will embarrass her? Would you have trouble getting psyched up to talk to her about her tardiness? Would you view confrontation as an obstacle to get over rather than as a challenge to meet?

Why We Resist

If your answer to each of these questions is "yes," it's understandable. Like almost everyone else, you were brought up to avoid confrontation at all costs. Do you remember your parents advising you, "If you don't have anything nice to say, don't say anything"? This established a standard that was reinforced by compliments for saying positive things. How often have you heard, "That Janie is so nice to be around—never a nasty word about anything"? Many of us were brought up with the philosophy that it is best not to make waves.

Second, we all have a need to be liked, respected, and accepted by our peers. We are afraid that if we talk about things that others do not like, they will not like *us*.

Third, many of us mistakenly take responsibility for other people's feelings. When a friend does not like something we say, we ask ourselves, "Did we hurt his or her feelings?" We also often consider other people's feelings more important than our own. We often forget about our own hurt feelings when we do not say anything.

Reprinted from *Supervisory Management*, January 1983

Fourth, our past plays a large part in a decision whether to confront someone in the present. If we had a bad experience because we either overreacted or were wishy-washy, we lose confidence in our ability to confront again. Or some past attempt may have been met with lack of support. For instance, did you once confront an employee for excessive absenteeism only to have your boss tell the worker not to worry about it?

Fifth, there is a fear of the negative consequences of one's actions—the "what if" syndrome: "what if . . . the situation gets worse instead of better; there are organizational repercussions and I lose my job; or the other person does something even worse to get back at me and I am blamed for the individual's behavior?"

Finally, wishful thinking and inertia allow us to procrastinate. We hope that the situation will improve on its own or we feel that this just isn't the "right" time. The longer we put the confrontation off, the more difficult it is to deal with. And the greater the chance that we will overreact and experience negative consequences when we eventually say something.

A Way Around Confrontation

In addition to our "natural" resistance to confrontation, our typical ways of meeting such challenges often compound the problem. Would you react to Barbara's tardiness in any of the following ways?

- *Silence.* "If I don't say anything, perhaps she will notice that I'm upset and will realize why."
- *Excuse.* "It's really not such a big thing and I hate to sound picky, but you really are arriving to work pretty late these days."
- *Sarcasm.* "Maybe you should ask Santa for a new alarm clock for Christmas."
- *Demands.* "Either you are on time tomorrow, or you are fired!"
- *Personal attack.* "You are a lazy, selfish person!"

These techniques produce results, but not necessarily the results we are looking for. Dr. Thomas Gordon, author of *Leader Effectiveness Training,* identifies three criteria for measuring the effectiveness of a confrontation. Gordon says a confrontation is successful when:

1. The other person's behavior changes in the manner desired,
2. The self-esteem of the other person is preserved, and
3. One's relationship with the other person remains intact.

How do the typical ways of confronting measure up to these criteria?

Silence and withdrawal do not increase the likelihood that the other person will change. Silence may also contribute to the problem as we build up feelings of resentment and anger because the other person has not changed.

Apologetic confrontations such as, "I hate to bring this up, but . . . ," often leave the other person confused as to how important this issue really is. The chance for a change in behavior is better than with silence, but not much.

With sarcasm, one is taking the chance that the other person will not understand what is being said beneath the humor. Do you *really* expect the person to change or are you kidding around? Sarcasm is often biting and can be easily interpreted as ridicule. The effects on self-esteem and the relationship depend on how the other person perceives the comment. This is impossible to predict. Often the person laughing the loudest is planning to retaliate.

Demands and personal attacks are the least likely to meet Dr. Gordon's three criteria. In both techniques, the implication is, "I know better than you." Short-term changes may occur in the other person's behavior, but what happens to self-esteem and to the relationship? This situation is ripe for sabotage. For example, Barbara may stay late to complete the report but will not verify the statistics.

Constructive Confrontation

The best relationships are built on open, direct, and honest communications. However, with confrontations, we need to remember that the goal of the "honest communication" is to achieve behavioral change without attacking the other personally or jeopardizing the relationship.

Constructive confrontation involves several elements:

1. An objective description of the undesirable behavior
2. Listening to the response
3. Identification of the effects
4. Description of future expectations
5. Commitment or agreement as to future behavior

As a supervisor, you should begin your confrontation by identifying the *behavior,* not the attitude, that is offensive to you. A behavior is something you can see, feel, touch, or hear. What exactly is the other person *doing* that you do not like? People are much less resistant to changing their behavior than to modifying an attitude or a value. Once the behavior is pinpointed, you want to convey this message in as an objective and a nonoffensive manner as possible. For example, "Barbara, I noticed you arriving at your desk today at 10:00, instead of the 8:00 starting time."

Identifying this discrepancy between the behavior and your expectations is often enough to motivate the other person to change. Usually the strong-arm approach is overkill in first-time situations. Remember, you are informing the other person of behavior that you do not appreciate, not nailing the person to the wall.

The confronted person may simply choose to agree to change, to apologize, or to present you with information that explains the behavior. For this reason, it is important to give the other person a chance to respond. After you communicate your own feelings, listen.

Helpful at this point is the process of active listening. Quite simply, it involves sending back to the other person a reflection of what was said. This may be done by restating the person's response, summarizing it, or mirroring it with a description of both the feelings and content of the message you perceived. This gives the individual the opportunity to clarify your interpretation of the message. It also allows you to convey empathy and a respect for the other person's right to feelings and thoughts that may be different from your own. If Barbara's response was, "You are always picking on me. Susan comes in late every day but you never say anything to her!" your reply might be, "You feel that you are being judged unfairly because you see others also coming in late and do not think that they have been spoken to."

To maximize a person's desire to change, you may want to explain how this unacceptable behavior affects *you* in a negative way. "When you are away from your desk, Barbara, it creates much more work for me since my time gets taken up answering your phone calls."

Describing the impact on you of the person's behavior is effective because of the universal need to be liked and respected. If you have developed a good relationship with Barbara, she will want to change because she likes you and does not want to cause additional problems for you. If she works for you, there will also be the need for approval since you control promotions, merit raises, work schedules, and the like.

In relationships with your employees, it is helpful to clarify your expectations. Communicating your expectations at the beginning of a relationship before problems arise is an effective way of minimizing the number of confrontations later on. But when you share your expectations, it is important to verify that the other person understands exactly what you want.

Preparing for Confrontation

In my experience, the anticipation of the confrontation meeting is at least as difficult for most people as the confrontation itself. For this reason, I coach people on adequate preparation.

Prepare yourself/maintain control of your emotions. Often when you get "hot under the collar," you say things that you later regret. The higher you allow your emotional temperature to rise, the hotter the other person is likely to get. Before your meeting is a good time to practice deep breathing or otherwise try to relax.

Rehearse what you will say. Determine beforehand what you hope to accomplish by the confrontation and decide what you want to say. Compare your planned message with Gordon's three criteria. Will your confrontation style preserve your relationship, protect the other's self-esteem, and increase the likelihood that the other person will change?

Monitor your voice tone, facial expressions, and body language. The words you choose may be neutral, but your nonverbal message could be deadly. The difference between aggression and assertion is usually *how* you say what you say. For example, standing with your hands on your hips or your finger wagging in front of Barbara's face will be perceived as aggressive, regardless of what you are saying.

Be prepared to listen. Expect the unexpected. People usually have strong reactions to a confrontation. The response may be tears, anger, apologies, or stony silence. A key to a successful discussion is your ability to hear what the other person has to say. Encourage the individual to express his or her feelings, whatever they are. This lays the groundwork for negotiation.

Showing empathy does not mean backing down. You may understand the difficulty of the other person's situation and still hold firm to your own standards.

Once you both understand each other's position, the discussion needs to focus on where you go from there.

At this point, you may choose to change your expectations, the other person may agree to change his or her behavior, or you may both agree to work toward finding a mutually acceptable solution. Whatever is agreed upon, it is essential that both parties are clear about what the next step will be. When you conclude the confrontation meeting, it is your responsibility to state clearly your understanding of what decision has been made and to obtain clarification from the other party.

Misunderstandings, different expectations, and differences of opinion are inevitable between two or more thinking people. The strongest relationships are those in which differences and conflicts are out in the open and dealt with: Confrontation is merely the initial step in identifying differences. A confrontation provides the confronted person with the opportunity to look at his or her behavior and decide whether or not to change. The principles for constructive confrontation are applicable in all interpersonal relationships but learning to confront effectively is a skill crucial to being a successful supervisor or manager.

Putting Their Performance in Writing

MICHAEL SMITH

Since it is not possible to remember every aspect of an employee's performance, it is essential for a manager to keep records (documentation). Managers may balk at spending the time needed to document or resist committing themselves. But these records serve as the basis for the fair and objective performance evaluations that employees expect, as well as the foundation for future feedback.

And, most important in this litigious environment, if an evaluation is questioned, documentation can support it. This is especially important when charges of discrimination are investigated.

Documentation should record and summarize subordinates' performance. Managers should not try to produce only positive or only negative documentation. An employee's performance should determine the content of the documentation.

Both positive and negative feedback can help motivate an employee to improve performance. When an employee hears that the work he or she is doing is noticed and appreciated, chances are good that the individual will work harder to achieve even better results. In the case of specific poor performance, the employee may be unaware of the problem. Documentation can help the manager explain precisely why what an employee is doing is a problem and give the person an opportunity to change. And pointing to specific incidents, a manager can avoid accusations of arbitrariness, prejudice, or scapegoating.

Guidelines

The following guidelines should be considered when preparing documentation:

- Do not rely on memory. Write things down soon after they happen.
- Document facts, not opinions.
- Record direct observations of actions and results. Include hearsay only in special circumstances.
- Do not include documentation that is not behavioral.
- Be consistent.

It is not enough to write opinions; for example, "Harry did a poor job on his assignment." That may be true but it's not a very useful thing to tell Harry. How would he or yourself, nine months from now,

Reprinted from *Management Solutions*, March 1987

Figure 1

Try Your Hand

Here's an opportunity to test your ability to distinguish between ineffective and effective documentation.

Choose the *better* documentation sample in each of the pairs below. These are not perfect examples, but one is better than the other.

1. A. Generally cluttered and confused paperwork; spends a great deal of time, including time at home, getting reports done.
    B. Needs improvement in organizing and planning work. Must find faster ways to get the job done. Has ability to improve in this area.
2. A. Has average abilities in oral communication. Needs to develop a technique for organizing ideas similar to that used in written communication. Knows the material but has difficulty getting it across in meetings.
    B. Fails to provide background information and introductions to oral presentations. This, combined with lengthy discussion of technical details in a recent presentation to nontechnical people, led to almost complete loss of audience attention.
3. A. Has shown no evidence of stress in the face of the pressures of the current assignment. Grasps important aspects of problems to be dealt with and gets the job done, no matter what comes up.
    B. Recently, the Blackstone project, for which he is responsible, was damaged by fire. His performance continued at usual high level; he organized activities well, and equipment was back on line the next day.
4. A. On two assignments for upper management, deadlines were missed due to time spent on lower priority work. On both occasions, the delay affected the schedules of other departments.
    B. Needs improvement in organizing and planning work. Must learn to plan for the effect his work activities have on other organizations.
5. A. Has difficulty communicating ideas effectively.
    B. Uses broad, general terms and omits critical information.
6. A. Changed long-standing reporting practice without checking effects on related practices in other departments.
    B. Failed to adequately consider the long-term consequences of decision.
7. A. When asked to administer a standardized training workshop, took the responsibility to first revise the training materials (which had been accepted in the past) to correct errors and inconsistencies.
    B. Strives to enlarge scope of responsibility. Is not satisfied with "just getting by."

---

know what the word "poor" referred to. "Harry submitted erroneous figures to the auditor" is a better record. Even better documentation would include a statement to the effect that "failing to doublecheck the numbers in order to meet the deadline" was the cause of the problem. In Figure 1, you are asked to choose the better documentation in each case. Figure 2 tells you the correct response.

In most cases, hearsay should not be included in documentation. However, managers often get reports about their subordinates' performance. When these reports confirm the managers' observations, there is no problem. But when these reports contradict the managers' observations or focus on behavior they haven't observed, managers may want to use this input as a guide for their own observations. They will want to look for behavior that confirms or denies the new information. There can be a risk in doing this, of course. The manager might be biased by the hearsay information. However, this risk is much less serious than the risk in accepting hearsay information without questioning it.

Managers will want to take note of another person's comments about a subordinate's performance when:

Figure 2

Answers to Exercise

1. *A* is best because it describes behavior. *B* is more evaluative, saying only that the person should be better. *B* implies performance problems but is not specific enough. *A* could be improved by indicating why the clutter, confusion, and time spent at home are problems.

    The phrase "including work at home" in *A* also needs to be clarified. Doing work at home might be indicative of an individual who is willing to extend himself or herself to do more work *or* it could be symptomatic of an inefficient use of time at work. The significance of this behavior should be stated rather than implied.

2. *B* is better documentation. It is very specific and shows what happened. *A* is evaluative and, again, only indicates the person should improve.

3. *B* is, again, the better documentation. It says what the person *did* and answers the "so what?" question—the equipment was back on line the next day. While the description in *A* may be true, "gets the job done" is not specific and it's unclear how not showing stress and grasping important aspects of problems constitute getting the job done.

4. *A* is better. *B* is just "should improve, should learn." Maybe the person should do these things, but *B* is not good documentation.

5. *B* is better. *A* is a judgmental statement. For *A* to be good documentation, it should be paired with *B*.

6. *A* is better than *B*, though not by much. *A* is behavioral, but it doesn't provide an answer to "so what?" *B* doesn't mean much without knowing what the consequences were.

7. *A* is the better documentation. *A* is specific and behavioral. In fact, *A* describes what *B* is trying to say.

- The subordinate is working on a project with or for others
- The subordinate works in another location or the job is designed so that the manager has only infrequent opportunities for observation
- The subordinate deals more or less independently with other departments or with people outside the firm
- The complaint is about an employee's behavior, not simple his or her attitude. For example, a person might say that the manager's subordinate is "lazy, introverted, and requires approval for anything he might accomplish." This does not constitute behavior documentation. A noteworthy comment might be, "George doesn't meet established deadlines; he doesn't make the phone calls necessary to get the job done unless he's prompted more than once; and he stops working until I personally review his work and tell him he's correct."

The documentation should be such that a third party reading the documentation should be able to agree with the manager's conclusions. The reader will have reached these conclusions by reading descriptions of the employee's behavior, not the manager's opinion of the employee.

Needless to say, managers should be consistent, documenting the performance of every subordinate, not just those who are performing unsatisfactorily. This way, they cannot be accused of inventing a case against any subordinate—something managers must be particularly cautious of, especially when "protected class" employees are involved.

Putting the Guidelines Into Practice

When to document. The sooner, the better. Documentation is like fish—unless it's prepared quickly, it goes "bad." The longer the delay, the less accurate the documentation.

How to document. There is no one best way to document. Approaches range from documenting in detail every instance of relevant job behavior to producing a single short paragraph summarizing a period of time.

Documenting everything is clearly unrealistic. Likewise, a paragraph describing a year of accomplishments is inadequate. A mix of two basic kinds of documentation is usually best.

Summary documentation is one and is a single note summarizing a series of observations over time. Single instance documentation is the other and involves documentation of single observations of behavior as they occur or at milestones in a long-term responsibility. Managers usually find that certain job situations lend themselves to ongoing documentation of single instances, while others are better documented on a summary basis. For example, summaries are most appropriate for behavior that occurs often and is intermingled with other work activities.

Summaries should be based on informal notes made as work behavior occurs.

Some managers kept notebooks or journals. Some make weekly summaries. Some make notes as convenient and review them periodically. Any way of collecting and consolidating information that works is acceptable.

What to document. Any job-related performance could be documented. But only significant behavior that affects or that may later affect the output of the job or the work of others needs to be documented by the supervisor.

Documenting performance is not an easy task. The most difficult aspect is describing behavior in specific terms. But effective documentation states as specifically as possible what the employee *did*. It also describes the circumstances surrounding the subordinate's behavior. The extent and significance of the behavior as compared to expected job performance should be clear. Extent is a "how much" measure. It specifies results achieved versus expectations. Significance is a "so what" measure and could include:

- Difficulty—not how hard it was for the employee to do the task but how hard it is to find someone capable of this achievement
- Supervision required
- Circumstances that helped or hindered achievement

How much to document. There is no simple answer. But a reasonable standard might be: enough documentation that a knowledgeable reader would understand and agree with the manager's evaluation.

Congruence

Supervisory documentation (written records of performance), communication (feedback, coaching, reviews, and so forth), and action (ratings, recommendations for raises, promotions, and termination) should all be congruent. The level of performance—satisfactory, unsatisfactory, or outstanding—should be evident. And the documentation, and the subsequent management action should fit together. Too often, managers wrongly document poor performance but talk with poor performers about only the positive aspects of their performance. Other managers make the mistake of talking with good performers about only the negative aspects of their performance.

Documenting Employee Performance

MICHAEL SMITH

A supervisor is conferring with the personnel manager, as follows:

Supervisor: I've had it with Harry; he isn't performing. I want to terminate him.
Personnel manager: Let me see your documentation. . . .
Supervisor: What documentation?

Could you be the supervisor in this conversation? It's common for personnel management to expect supervisors to know how to document performance. But, unless you have been exposed to a rather extensive appraisal process course, you probably have never learned how to keep track of performance.

Documentation is a skill needed by every supervising manager. Doing it well takes adherence to a reasonable standard and some practice. But once documenting performance becomes a habit, wasted time and some potentially uncomfortable situations can be avoided.

Uses of Documentation

Documentation serves many purposes. One of its most important uses is to show the reasoning that led to necessary, though unpleasant, decisions to terminate or discipline employees. However, it is just as important to document *good* performance. Written documentation can be a memory jogger for performance reviews, justification for moves, promotions, raises, or rebuttal to EEO complaints involving work performance.

You should not seek to produce either positive or negative documentation. What you do is document performance. The employee's performance determines what you write. And once written, you are able to talk from *facts,* not from memory. You are preparing "silent feedback." That is, silent until you talk with the person you are writing about. It is useless as a means of producing behavior change unless you talk with the employee about his or her performance and work with the individual to try to improve it.

Both positive and negative feedback can help a supervisor motivate an employee to improved performance. When an employee hears that the work he or she is doing is appreciated, chances are good that the individual will work harder to achieve even better results. In the case of the poor performer, he or she

Reprinted from *Supervisory Management,* September 1979

may be unaware of the problem. Accurate and unbiased documentation can help a supervisor explain precisely what an employee is doing wrong, thus giving him or her a chance to change. By pointing out performance in specific incidents, a supervisor cannot be accused of prejudice or simply placing blame. This is one of the major benefits of documentation.

It is not enough to give your opinion, or to write statements like "Harry did a poor job on his last assignment." Instead, you should say *why* Harry did a poor job—and what he could have done to have succeeded. The following can be used as guidelines in preparing documentation:

1. Be accurate.
2. Document facts, not opinions.
3. Note direct performance observations of actions and results. Do not include hearsay in your documentation.
4. Do not rely on your memory. Write things down soon after they happen.
5. Do not include documentation that is not behavioral.
6. Be consistent.

The last two guidelines could use some clarification. By behavioral, we do not mean psychological. What we do mean is that the documentation should describe an employee's behavior, not his or her attitude. For instance, you might write in an employee's file that he is "lazy, introverted, and requires approval for anything he might accomplish." This does not constitute behavioral documentation. Instead, you should write, "Harry doesn't meet established deadlines, he doesn't make the phone calls necessary to get the job done unless he's prompted more than once, and lastly, he stops working until I personally review his work and tell him he's correct." By documenting his actions (or his lack of action), a third party reading your documentation will undoubtedly reach the same conclusions that you have, but the reader will have reached them by reading your observations of the employee in question, not your opinion.

The sixth guideline—be consistent—means that it is important to document the performance of all of your subordinates—not just those who are performing unsatisfactorily. It's worth repeating here also the dictum that both positive and negative performance be documented. This way you cannot be accused of inventing a case against your employee, something you must be particularly cautious of, especially when minority or women employees are involved.

Besides ensuring that the written record is accurate, behavioral, and consistent, some other things must be considered, too. One is congruence.

Congruence

Congruence is expected of supervisory documentation (written records of performance), communication (feedback, coaching, reviews, and so on) and action (ratings, recommendations for raises, promotions, and terminations). Whether the performance is good, poor, or outstanding should be evident in the documentation, the communication, and subsequent management action.

Managers often write about poor performance but talk with a poor performer only about the good aspects of his or her performance, or with a good performer only about the poor aspects of performance. Neither of these situations is very helpful in the long run. It is quite important for your own credibility that you document, talk, and act based on your observations of performance. Usually an individual's performance will be composed of both positive and negative elements. If the total picture is negative, serious thought should be given to what should be done to help the person improve. With ongoing documentation the need for improvement will become apparent before the yearly appraisal session, and the employee may be able to improve before his or her appraisal is affected. If the total picture is positive, you want to make sure your subordinate gets the appropriate message—"You're doing well and continued performance at or above what you've been doing will continue or even improve your rating."

How Much Documentation?

How much documentation is enough? A useful "rule of thumb" would be to assume someone else at your level with appropriate experience was going to look at your documentation. He or she should be able to come to the same conclusion you did or should at least be able to say, "I can see how you concluded that." That's enough documentation.

Documentation, of course, can be overdone too. If you record page after page of minute details, you waste time and intimidate your subordinate. Only those aspects of performance that significantly contribute to or hamper the work effort are appropriate for documentation.

Try to use some discretion in deciding how much time to devote to documentation. If something unusual occurs, it is best to write it down as soon as possible, lest you forget. For everyday occurrences, a weekly or monthly summary of the employee's behavior should suffice.

Test Yourself

Documentation requires time and effort, but the factual base for decisions, ratings, and discussions that it provides makes it all worthwhile.

To see if you can identify accurate, behavioral, and consistent documentation, read the ABCs of

Figure 1

ABCs of Documentation	
Documentation Should Be:	*To Document Performance*
Accurate	Record *objective* facts concerning actual performance as they occur rather than from memory.
	Record only *job-related* behavior.
	Record *direct observations* rather than relying on "hearsay" reports from others.
Behavioral	Describe *specific behavior* rather than making evaluative statements or describing an individual's personality.
Consistent	Record both *positive and negative* behaviors rather than emphasizing either.
	Keep the same basic format and level of detail of documentation for *each* subordinate.
	Maintain documentation on all employees in a given work group. Periodically review the collective documentation to be sure that desired quantity, quality, and consistency are being maintained.

Figure 2

Test Yourself

Sample Documentation	A	B	C
	(yes, no, or not applicable)		

Documentation of a secretary's performance (the secretary serves three supervisors and five engineers):

1. Secretary made only two errors on the report. _____ _____ _____
2. Secretary was able to compile revised client list while maintaining usual production. _____ _____ _____
3. The standard of 90 percent of all correspondence with no typos met last month. _____ _____ _____
4. I've heard that secretary wastes time when making copies. _____ _____ _____
5. During the year the secretary was too nasty for her own good. _____ _____ _____

Documentation of an engineer:

6. Engineer prepared technical evaluation report on her own with little assistance. Report was concise, clear, and highlighted the impact of the new specification changes. Recommendations made were evaluated by the standards group, and most of them were implemented. _____ _____ _____
7. Engineer gave technical presentation to customer group, didn't control audience, visuals were poor, spoke in monotone voice. Didn't answer questions well. Supervisor had to take over meeting to "salvage it." _____ _____ _____
8. Engineer met following objective: to create scheduling procedure for project XYZ that was usable by purchasing, contract administration, and field construction people. This was done two months after starting the project. _____ _____ _____
9. Engineer's "know-it-all" attitude interferes with her work. _____ _____ _____

For a training specialist:

10. Seven of eight "students" have reported that trainer is abusive in class, cutting people off, not answering questions, and scolding students for being wrong. _____ _____ _____

For an accountant:

11. Accountant didn't cross check "124" report figures with "388" report. This resulted in

	A	B	C
	(yes, no, or not applicable)		
incorrect data being given to the general manager.	————	————	————

For a supervisor:

	A	B	C
12. Supervisor doesn't delegate properly.	————	————	————
13. Supervisor gives most assignments to one subordinate, thereby creating one overloaded subordinate and other subordinates with little to do.	————	————	————
14. Supervisor is an excellent leader.	————	————	————
15. Supervisor lacks proper knowledge of structural engineering to give guidance to engineers under his direction.	————	————	————
16. Supervisor documents performance of her subordinates following the ABC approach. She also conducts quarterly reviews of performance, and her subordinates "accept" her ratings.	————	————	————
17. Supervisor doesn't accept criticism well.	————	————	————

Documentation in Figure 1 and take the test in Figure 2. Note that Figure 2 contains three columns labeled A, B, and C. The A column stands for accurate; the B, for behavioral; and the C, for consistent—representing the three basic requirements for proper documentation of employee performance. Read the sample documentation and mark "yes, no, or not applicable" under each column. When you are finished, check your answers (see Figure 3 on page 334) to see how well you understand the principles of performance documentation.

Figure 3

Answers to Test Yourself

The issue of consistency cannot be addressed on any of these statements because there is not enough data. Consistency is a matter of documenting positive and negative performance over time. It also requires keeping the same basic format and level of documentation for all subordinates.

Accurate	Behavioral	Question	Rationale
Yes	Yes	1, 2, 3	This is an objective, factual, specific-behavior record.
No	No	4	This is hearsay—someone else's opinion that time is being wasted.
No	No	5	Trusting memory for a year's observation is not accurate; it might be job-related but definitely not behavioral. This statement is based on a subjective judgment and is poor documentation.
Yes	Yes	6, 7, 8	This is a very clear, specific behavioral description of what was accomplished.
No	No	9	It might be accurate, but it is worthless feedback to the engineer. It is definitely a personality description rather than a job-related behavior. How it interferes with work and just what a know-it-all attitude is are questions it raises.
Yes	Yes	10	Although hearsay, the job of a trainer is such that frequent observation isn't always possible so hearsay is okay here. This documentation is best used when substantiated by at least one classroom observation.
Yes	Yes	11	This is an objective, factual, specific-behavior record.
Yes	No	12	This documentation might be accurate but is not specific enough.
Yes	Yes	13	This is an objective, factual, specific-behavior record.
Yes	No	14	This might be true, but what does the statement mean and does it relate to department results?
Yes	Yes	15	This is a judgment, yes, but it is specific, factual, and clear.
Yes	Yes	16	This is objective, factual, specific behavior.
No	No	17	This might be true but few of us do accept criticism well. Documentation of this behavior needs to be more specific, and job relevance must be shown.

Five Steps to Making Performance Appraisal Writing Easier

SHELLEY KRANTZ

Do you dread having to write performance appraisals? Do you procrastinate? And, if you push yourself to write them, do you feel anxious that what you wrote was vague, inaccurate, or maybe even illegal?

Ring true? If so, you're not alone. Hundreds of supervisors in organizations throughout the country complain about writing performance appraisals. Most, in fact, suffer from a performance appraisal writer's block. Why is this so?

One answer has to do with the nature of the supervisory job and the nature of writing. Most supervisors are "action people." They are used to either getting the work done through others or doing the work themselves. The supervisory job moves quickly, is highly interactive, and very results-oriented. Writing, on the other hand, is not interactive. It usually does not move quickly, and one cannot always count on results. It's passive, not active; it's isolated, not people-involved. No wonder it's not easy for supervisors.

Any writing is difficult enough for the action-oriented supervisor. But when it comes to writing performance appraisals, the problems are multiplied. When you write a performance appraisal, you have additional, *legitimate* fears, such as:

"What I'm writing will be cast in stone. What if I change my mind? What if I misunderstand an employee—if I overlooked something vital in the appraisal? How can I be *sure* of my evaluation?"

"My writing is awful. I don't use proper grammar—I'm sure my punctuation is terrible! My own boss and perhaps his boss will be reviewing these—what if I misspell words? What will they think?"

"What if I say something illegal? I can't keep up with all these affirmative action laws and the dos and don'ts. What if I've unintentionally really messed up?"

"I can't remember all the back-up stuff. I really believe I know how to evaluate my people—but I've forgotten so many of the specifics. Will my appraisals be O.K. without them? Will I need to invent fillers?"

While each of these concerns is valid, they can be overcome. What's needed is skill building through practice. Writing, like any other skill, gets better, easier, and faster the more one does it. By using the following tips in writing performance appraisals, you will also find that the process can actually become more satisfying and productive.

Reprinted from *Supervisory Management,* December 1983

The Steps

Step #1—start smart. Ask yourself: How much time do I need to write these appraisals? How much time am I willing to spend? What are my time constraints? When do I really need to get started? When is the best time for me to write? Where's the best place for me to write? Is there anyone I can ask to look over my work or give me encouragement? What are the company's expectations and guidelines on what is to be written? Are there any exemplary samples of past appraisals that I can use as guides?

Know the answers to these questions before you begin. Make yourself a writing plan and stick to it.

Step #2—job notes. Record your thoughts anywhere—on napkins, scratch paper, or a tape recorder if you think of yourself as a talker rather than a writer. Carry a small pad around with you. Relying on your memory just won't do. Make it a habit to *record* those ideas that pop into your head when you least expect them.

Don't analyze or critique, *just write.* Keep a critical-incident file. Critical incidents are those events that make an employee stand out, either positively or negatively. What you need are specific examples of why you feel the way you do—what was or was not done, chronologically, to the minutest detail.

You can draw from your notes and critical-incident file the information you need to make your writing task easier. It's much easier this way than sitting down and staring at a blank piece of paper.

Step #3—organize. Gather together your notes, your company's performance appraisal form, your documentation, your critical-incident file, and your company's performance standards. Consolidate your notes according to what is to be written on the form. If your form has space for paragraph descriptions of employee performance, organize your notes first according to the performance factors being appraised. If further division of the material is necessary, divide it by simply looking for a logical beginning, middle, and end.

Find the method that works best for you. Don't worry that no one else uses your method of organization.*

Step #4—write. If you've completed the first three steps, the writing step should really be quite easy. Work from the organization that you created in step three. Don't ponder each word, just spill it out. Promise yourself that no one will see this first draft but you. When you write, be sure that you are as specific as possible in describing the performance.

To give you an idea of what "specificity" really means, here are a few phrases, taken from an actual appraisal that are *not specific.*

> . . . maintains good cost records . . . shows excellent results . . . demonstrates professional results . . . established an effective schedule.

What are "good cost records"? Are they organized? Neat? Systematic? What are "excellent results"? Are they accurate? Logical? What are "professional results"? How do they differ from excellent results? What is "an effective schedule"? Is it flexible, creative, consistent? See the problem?

It's remediable by using specific words and examples when you write a performance appraisal. To illustrate the point, think of one of your employees. Look at the words listed below and select one word that describes that employee's performance on the job. (Note that the words are both positive and negative.)

> ambiguous, apathetic, capable, clear thinking, careless, disorderly, efficient, helpful, hostile, inventive, organized, precise, thorough.

Now that you've selected one word that describes this employee's performance, build a sentence around the word. For example, for the key word *precise.*

*The following exercises are taken from *Win-Win Performance Appraisal: A Guide for the Manager* by Beverly Kaye and Shelley Krantz.

Sondra is precise in 90 percent of her secretarial work. She proofreads her work thoroughly and can be counted on to get the work out on schedule on a week-to-week basis.

Notice that the use of exact numbers helped the above example and made it more specific. Many supervisors try to avoid using exact numbers because they fear committing themselves on paper; they want to take a safe middle ground. This does nothing to maximize the potential effect a specific and exact performance appraisal can have.

Here are some other examples:

Instead of	*Why not use?*
Caused a significant loss	Caused a 53% loss
Has a good attendance record	Has a 96 percent attendance record
Sold a contract for a substantial amount	Sold a contract for $34 million

The more specific and exact the appraisal document is, the more helpful it will be to employees in formulating performance improvement plans. Being specific also protects you in the eyes of the law.

Step #5—edit. After you're written the performance appraisal, put it away for an hour or two, if you're pressed for time, or better yet for 24 hours. Give yourself a break. When you go back to the performance appraisal, your editing needs will be clearer to you. Just cross out any unnecessary words, cut the jargon, make sure that everything you have written is logical, specific, and easily understandable to anyone else who might read it. The test is to ask yourself: If another manager read this, would he or she be able to describe this employee's performance accurately?

The Payoff

By practicing the five-step process described here, you can take the fear out of appraisal writing, and *you will see a payoff.* In the beginning, it may take you a little longer to write an evaluation than you would like, but *consistent* practice and logical application of these five steps will make the performance appraisal writing task (indeed, all of your business writing tasks) less painful and more satisfying. More importantly, writing specific, logical, well-documented performance appraisals will go a long way toward maximizing the potential impact that appraisals can have on employee job performance.

Nonevaluative Approaches to Performance Appraisals

LES WALLACE

For the supervisor who deals predominantly with high-quality performers, the performance appraisal process is not a frightening one. But though every supervisor would prefer to work in this type of situation, most find themselves working with employees whose performance ranges from unacceptable to exceptional and therefore having to adjust their discussion appraisals to fit each employee. For the supervisor untrained in counseling on different kinds of performance problems, adjusting his or her approach to fit the needs of high-quality and lower-quality performers can be difficult—and in some cases, disturbing.

For example, during a conversation I had recently with one production supervisor, he bragged that he thoroughly enjoyed writing and discussing the performance evaluations of his 26 subordinates. But two weeks later this same supervisor was back on the phone, frantically asking for advice on how to handle a poor performer and complaining that this difficult appraisal was taking all the fun out of the process.

So this is the most common appraisal situation for supervisors: They have employees at all levels of performance—good, poor, and mediocre—and they have personnel forms and management strategies by the dozens to follow in carrying out the appraisals. But the biggest problem for supervisors is that employees react to the appraisal on a personal level, *not* on a professional one. And unfortunately many supervisors lack the communication skills to get the essential message of an appraisal across to the employee without causing bigger problems in the process. As Douglas McGregor pointed out some 20 years ago, problems with adequate performance appraisals revolve around "a normal dislike of criticizing a subordinate and perhaps having to argue about it and a lack of skill needed to handle the interview."

Questions for the Supervisor

Now that we have some idea of the problems supervisors face when they enter the appraisal arena, let us ask: What communicative approaches could a supervisor use to more clearly communicate to an employee what he or she must do to improve performance? At the same time, what approaches would help reduce employee hostility and defensiveness and also generate cooperation in working to improve performance?

Most suggestions that have been made for improving the appraisal process *deal more with the theory*

Reprinted from *Supervisory Management*, March 1978

of performance appraisal and the goals of a supportive exchange rather than with concrete skills and examples on how to achieve these goals. Whether one looks at the problem-solving interview, the participative approach to performance improvement, or the supportive-defensive climate contrasts, these are all theories suggesting a particular approach but omitting the specifics on how to put the approach into practice. As one personnel manager remarked to me recently, "Who could disagree with such ideas? I just want my supervisors to learn how to make these theories useful."

Consequently, I want to make some specific suggestions for the supervisors who have to face their subordinates eyeball-to-eyeball during performance appraisals. By utilizing such suggestions, a supervisor should be able to get much more mileage out of the performance interview and be able to approach counseling sessions with high, medium, or low performers with the same self-assured attitude.

Evaluative vs. Descriptive

First, what are the conditions in an interview that lead to employee defensiveness rather than to the more desired cooperation? Of course, we know that when a supervisor exhibits *evaluative*—that is, blame-putting—behavior, this will almost always elicit defensive behavior from an employee. But beyond this, the more personal, negative, and accusatory the evaluation by a supervisor is, the more hostile and defensive the employee will become.

The way to avoid evoking such defensive behavior is by using *descriptive* rather than evaluative approaches to the problem. By simply stating, in a nonpersonal way, that a problem exists and then describing that problem, the supervisor makes it possible for him and the employee to arrive at a joint decision—or even an employee-initiated decision—on how to resolve the problem. Some examples of both evaluative and descriptive comments that the supervisor might make in performance appraisals are as follows:

Evaluative	*Descriptive*
"You simply can't keep making these stupid mistakes."	"We're still having a problem reducing the number of scrap parts produced."
"Bob, you're tactless and undiplomatic."	"Some people interpret your candor as hostility."
"You're too belligerent when dealing with co-workers."	"Many employees perceive your attitude to be belligerent."
"The accident was your fault. You ignored the safety regulations on that project."	"This accident appears to involve some differences in interpreting the safety regulations."

Using descriptive, nonevaluative comments in the appraisal interview, the supervisor is signaling to the employee that he wants to analyze and discuss a problem, not look for an "easy out" or demean the employee. In such a way, the interview can then move on to the more constructive elements of the appraisal process.

The Threat of Control

Sometimes in a performance appraisal the supervisor will make the mistake of assuming a *control* communicative stance. This stance emphasizes the superior's power over the subordinate, and it reflects an error in the supervisor's thinking because, like most of us, employees don't like to feel dominated by another person and react defensively when they do.

Opposed to the control stance is *problem orientation,* which is a communicative approach designed to allay an employee's fear and increase his sense of personal control over whatever problems exist.

Problem orientation conveys a respect for the employee's ability to work on a problem and to formulate meaningful answers to the problem. Examples of these approaches that could be found in many performance appraisals are:

Control	*Problem Orientation*
"John, I'd like to see you doing X, Y, and Z over the next week."	"John, what sort of things might we do here?"
"I think the only answer is to move you over by Margaret on the line."	"One possibility is to have you move over by Margaret on the line. Is that likely to help?"
"I think my suggestions are clear, so why don't you get back to work?"	"Let's think about these possibilities and get back together next week, after you've thought about them."
"Arthur, you'd better tone down your criticism of co-workers."	"Arthur, this sensitivity among co-workers requires us all to try for a bit more diplomacy."
"You've got a problem here."	"We've got a problem here."
"I've decided what you must do to reduce mistakes."	"Have you thought about what we might do to reduce mistakes?"

Problem-oriented communication will generate more options for solving the problem by encouraging the employee to make suggestions and inducing a mutual concern for controlling the problem, *not* the person. Furthermore, problem orientation can also improve the appraisal discussion by aiding both parties in truly listening to what the other is saying, by encouraging both parties to offer suggestions, and by fostering a more open climate in which disagreement is not only tolerated but invited.

Neutrality and Empathy

Just as inimical to the appraisal process as control is a supervisor's *neutrality,* which is usually interpreted by the subordinate to be disinterest about the outcome's impact on the employee. Like the rest of us, employees tend to be more guarded and less communicative when their superior lacks real concern over their welfare. Ironically, supervisors who display such unconcern often are very interested in their employees, but they don't realize that some of their actions are interpreted by subordinates to be indicative of a neutral attitude.

Showing *empathy,* on the other hand, signals a clear concern for the employee and his situation. But to get this message across unequivocally, the supervisor must make an overt communication attempt—one that the employee cannot help but notice. Some examples of neutral and empathetic approaches are:

Neutrality	*Empathy*
"I really don't know what we can do about it."	"At this point I can't think of anything, but I know where we might look for help."
"Well, that's one way to look at it."	"I get the feeling you don't feel confident with our original plan."
"I didn't know that."	"I wasn't aware of that. Let me make sure I understand."
"Too bad, but we all go through that."	"I think I know how you're feeling. I can remember one experience I had that was similar. . . ."
"You could have something there, but let's get back to the real problem."	"I'm not certain I understand how that relates to this problem. Why don't you fill me in before we go on?"

Supervisors communicate empathy best when they listen well, when they follow up on suggestions, and when they inquire how employees feel about questions and solutions raised in the appraisal. Displaying a concerned sympathy about difficult problems will also signal an understanding attitude by the supervisor and encourage the employee's cooperation.

A Need for Equality

In any discussion between a superior and a subordinate—whether the distinction has been brought about by legal, financial, or emotional factors—if the superior uses communicative techniques that emphasize his *superiority,* this will correspondingly induce feelings of unworthiness in the subordinate. For example, the supervisor who keeps the subordinate at arm's length by stifling feedback and overtly rejecting his help only increases the employee's need to defend himself and prove his self-worth.

However, the supervisor who tries to reduce the distance between himself and his employees encourages the employees to feel they share a certain *equality* with the supervisor. This feeling can be aided by a supervisor showing concern for sharing information with the subordinates and gaining their input in solving problems. Some characteristic differences between superiority- and equality-evoking comments can be seen in these examples:

Superiority	*Equality*
"Bob, I've worked with this problem for ten years and ought to know what will work."	"This idea has worked before. Do you think it might work in this case?"
"Well, I don't think I need to give you all the background. Why don't we just do it this way for now?"	"Arthur, you might find some of the background information helpful, so let me fill you in a bit."
"The supervisory staff thought this policy through pretty thoroughly."	"We've only discussed this policy at the supervisors' meetings and I'm interested in your reactions and thoughts."
"Oh, the rationale should be of no interest to you people on the line."	"Let me go over the rationale with you. Some of you might find it helpful."
"Look, I'm being paid to make these decisions, not you."	"I'll have to make the final decision, Mary, but why don't you get your suggestions in to me right away?"

Of course, workers generally do not expect complete equality from their bosses, nor are they interested in sharing the supervisor's responsibility for decisions that are implemented. Instead, they appreciate a supervisor who shares information with them, seeks their feedback, and listens to their concerns. Such communicative approaches can easily be made part of the performance appraisal process, and the supervisor should see a more enthusiastic and less defensive attitude among employees as a result.

Who Has the Last Word?

Supervisors who emphasize *certainty* tend to phrase everything they say as if the last word had been said and a decision could never be changed. Such a dogmatic stance makes the employee feel that there is no need to offer new ideas or different solutions to the approach already outlined by the supervisor. This in turn leads to loss of morale and a feeling of powerlessness among employees.

But a supervisor who shows *provisionalism* demonstrates that he is willing to have his own ideas be challenged in order to arrive at the best possible solution to a problem. Communication that encourages analysis and investigation can restore enthusiasm and provide a challenge for employees that might otherwise not be there. Examples of certainty and provisionalism are:

Certainty	*Provisionalism*
"I know what the problem is, Tom. I don't think I need another opinion."	"I have a view of the problem, Tom, but I'd be interested in your perception."
"This is the way we're going to do things. Period."	"Let's try this for a couple of weeks, then we can reconsider, based on that experience."
"I've thought these suggestions through thoroughly, Mary, so let's not waste time arguing."	"I've tried to think these suggestions through pretty thoroughly, Mary. Can you see anything I may have left out?"

Let us add that a provisional approach does not deny the fact that decisions have to be made and policies adhered to. Instead, it suggests that decision making is an alterable process and that employee suggestions and creativity are important to and appreciated by management.

From Appraisal to Analysis

These examples of communicative approaches are all designed to help the supervisor reduce the defensiveness of employees, and as such they also share a common base: They emphasize a process of *analysis,* rather than *appraisal,* of employee problems. Of course, inherent in any analysis is some evaluation of past performance, but hopefully the employee will be led to approach this evaluation from a more participative and less defensive position. Instead of being told simply that he or she failed, the employee's help is enlisted to pinpoint problems and come up with answers to problems. An analytical process should emphasize the employee's personal worth and demonstrate the confidence that management has in the employee's ability to learn from and improve on past behavior.

Unfortunately, not all employees will be able to recognize and resolve their performance problems, no matter what supervisors do. But the supervisor who validates an employee's worth through supportive, nonevaluative communicative techniques will at least find that his suggestions to the employee on improving performance are received with less defensiveness and anger. Similarly, supervisors I have talked with report several other benefits that result from using nonevaluative communicative techniques, including:

- Improved creativity in solving problems, due to greater employee input
- Less supervisory reluctance to discuss employee performance problems
- A clearer understanding by the employee of why and how he or she needs to change work behavior
- The growth of a climate of cooperation, which increases individual and group motivation to achieve performance goals
- Greater employee self-reliance, which improves the individual's ability to diagnose problems and react quickly with less supervisory assistance

The supervisor who implements constructive, nonevaluative appraisal techniques becomes more of a leader and teacher to his or her employees and less of a disciplinarian. This also means that employees come to see the supervisor as more of a friend and helper who assists them when their own ideas and abilities run short and less of a management representative looking for a scapegoat on whom to blame poor performances. Of course, implementing such techniques does not essentially change the performance appraisal; a supervisor's suggestions and high performance goals remain part of the process. But constructive communicative techniques, when correctly used, should make the process a little less painful and intimidating for all concerned.

Using Appraisals to Set Objectives

BOB WOOTEN

Performance appraisals are generally used in evaluating employees for raises, promotions, demotions, and terminations. In recent years, some supervisors have raised questions about the effectiveness of current appraisal systems, all of which have certain inherent problems. Gathering information for an appraisal can be difficult, and many employees are suspicious of the way in which the information is to be used. Add to these problems the attitude of many supervisors that performance appraisals are too time-consuming and of little value, and it becomes clear why few appraisal interviews are successful in motivating employees to improved performance.

It is often overlooked that appraisal sessions can be an important part of management by objectives, which relies heavily on employee input. If managed properly, the appraisal session can be a time for the supervisor and employee to agree on their common objectives and establish standards based on an understanding of each other's point of view.

The March of Theory

In theory, a performance appraisal should be a positive experience, but in actual practice it often loses its motivating effect. This negative result can frequently be traced to the supervisor's manner in discussing the evaluation with the employee. An appraisal that offers no constructive suggestions for improvement, for example, may cause bad feelings that will hinder, not improve, an employee's performance.

Outdated performance appraisal procedures are still used by many modern business organizations. These procedures were developed to overcome the problem of subjectivity by supervisors by structuring the appraisal format, but in the process they sometimes seem to depersonalize the process. Some procedures in use since the Second World War, for instance, use a checklist format that focuses on such production factors as quality, quantity, and worker dependability. This style of evaluation treats the individual as a replaceable cog in a production machine in which the best cog receives the highest rating. In pursuit of objectivity, this approach aggravates employee fears of dehumanization by creating a framework in which the employee forfeits individuality to the job.

One of the most successful employee appraisal systems grew out of the concept of management by objectives (MBO). In the MBO method of appraisal, the employee assesses his or her job and then develops a self-appraisal that includes some specific short-term goals.

Reprinted from *Supervisory Management,* November 1981

Until now, the MBO style of appraisal has generally been used only with management-level personnel. Employee resistance to change, one of the most common barriers to organizational innovation, becomes more pronounced when a program like management by objectives is adopted. Employees become apprehensive about the establishment of new controls and react in a negative way.

This is not inevitable, however. If employees are introduced to change in a positive manner, as they can be in the participative MBO appraisal process, the organization can pick up a significant level of employee support.

Giving Employees a Stake in MBO

The value of an MBO program is based on two premises:

1. Individuals (employees) will support a goal or goals if they agree that the objectives are acceptable.
2. Individuals will support an objective if they expect to be personally successful in their efforts.

With these two points in mind, the value of conducting the performance appraisal with MBO should become more clear. The MBO process stresses two-way communication between management and employees, and this goes a long way toward reducing the subjectivity of the appraisal session at the same time that it gives the employee a sense of participation in setting the organization's objectives.

In theory and in practice, to maximize the benefits of the appraisal session to MBO, management must first maximize the employee's willingness to participate. The employee must be able to see himself or herself in a homogeneous relationship with the organization, and this is where the communication and evaluation (C&E) technique comes in as a pre-appraisal tool.

An evaluation should first of all confirm the employee's current job objectives. If employees are vague about their current duties, they may resent new goals if these must be accomplished in addition to the duties already outlined in the job description. The appraisal session can be used to harmonize their current objectives with organizational change and at the same time show employees how to align their personal goals with organizational objectives. The C&E technique prepares the employee for this session.

Preceding the MBO appraisal session, C&E encourages the employee to ask important questions about his or her career goals and their relation to the company's plans. The technique stimulates communication between supervisors and employees, which may later help to reduce friction between the two during the appraisal. Since the final appraisal is discussed during a postevaluation conference, the supervisor's role as judge is moderated, recasting him or her as an individual attempting to help subordinates perform at a more productive level.

Procedure—The Forms

The communication and evaluation forms used in the C&E process consist of three separate sections. The sections are designed to be completed by the employees, the employee's supervisor, and an impartial third party. After all forms are completed, the parties meet for a private, informal discussion.

Form A consists of three pages and should be completed by the person being evaluated. The first C&E page contains a minimal description of the employee—name, age, position, years of service, and educational background. The remainder of the form carries completion instructions, including a typical example of job objectives.

Page two of form A provides space for listing the employee's five most important job objectives (as he or she perceives them) in decreasing order of importance. Following each objective a rating box is provided. The employee checks the box that best describes his or her own performance. The classifications include: (1) very well, (2) better than most, (3) about as well as others, and (4) need to improve. These rather middle-of-the-road descriptions were chosen because people are generally hesitant to describe themselves as either exceptionally good or exceptionally bad.

The remaining categories on page two of form A serve as communication stimulators to be used during the informal evaluation conference. If the employee and supervisor disagree about the worker's perception of performance, the supporting remarks can be used as a basis for discussion. The last box, "I need help, let's talk about it," is for the employee who feels that some schooling or special attention is needed to meet one or more of the job objectives. Later, during the informal conference, an actual plan to help the employee realize personal objectives can be synthesized from this information.

The final page of form A may be informally labeled "the career development section." This portion of the C&E requests the employee to evaluate, in written form, his or her career goals. This allows the company to evaluate the employee's ambitions. More importantly, this section opens a door for career counseling. If an employee's anticipated short-range goals will not lead to reasonable long-range goals, he or she may need to make new decisions.

Form B has a format similar to form A except that it is completed by the employee's supervisor. Each job objective should be listed in descending order of importance, then supported by checking appropriate comments. The "I need help, let's talk about it" box has been replaced by two boxes titled, "Training will improve performance," and "Experience will improve performance." These two categories should serve to stimulate discussion during the appraisal conference. Also, close examination of each may point out obvious reasons for disparity between the supervisor's and the employee's evaluations. The final page has similar career development questions as found on form A, but on this page the supervisor attempts to estimate the worker's career opportunities. In addition, the supervisor is asked to identify the subordinate's strong points and weak points, which will also provide valuable insight into the employee's potential.

Form C is labeled a "disparity chart" and is completed by a third party. The disparity chart is used to compare job objectives as ranked by the employee and by the supervisor. The purpose of the disparity chart is to encourage communication between supervisor and employee during the appraisal conference later on.

Foundation for Objectives

Completion of the evaluation provides fertile ground for appraisals geared to management by objectives. The C&E concept does not ensure positive MBO results, but it informs both management and the employee about the existing state of employee development. It is upon this foundation that MBO will be carried out.

Telling Subordinates What to Do And How to Do It

JACK W. ENGLISH and JAY I. GOTTESMAN

"Tom, I guess you know Ned Wright is leaving, and we'd like one of your people to replace him. It will be a nice promotion. Who's your best performer?"

"Well, Bill, I'm not sure. . . ."

Sound familiar? How do you determine who is *your* best performer? Do you know how well each of the people in your department is performing? One way to know the answers to these questions is through the use of performance standards.

As a supervisor, it's your responsibility to direct and evaluate your subordinates' performance. Your employees need to know *what* you want them to do and *how* you want them to do it. Performance standards are one way of doing both—telling your subordinates what you want them to do *and* how you want it done.

Explaining the Job

There are some prerequisites to an employee-employer discussion of job standards. First, the subordinate should understand his or her role in the unit. How does he or she fit in? The answer to this question should be apparent from the employee's job description, but, unfortunately, it rarely tells the whole story. As a supervisor your first task, then, is to describe to the employee *what his or her major duties are*.

Next, you should discuss how these duties are to be carried out. For example, you might tell the employee that he or she is to interact with others *cooperatively* or be at his or her station *punctually*. You should also explain such important aspects of the job as quality controls, safety requirements, and company policies.

The entire conversation on job duties and how they are to be carried out should be *participative*. The employee should be involved to whatever extent possible in determining his or her own job responsibilities. If you allow the employee to participate, he or she will not only have a clearer understanding of what you want but also be more personally committed to achieving it.

After the employee understands his or her role in your unit, you should focus on the specific individ-

Reprinted from *Supervisory Management*, July 1979

ualized goals you would like your subordinate to achieve. Studies have shown that the *use of goals results in higher levels of employee productivity.*

Setting Effective Goals

To get the most mileage while working on individualized goals, these simple rules are suggested:

1. Set job-relevant goals. When you judge the employee's level of accomplishment against his or her goals, you will be judging the individual's performance. Goal accomplishment is a valid, job-related measure of employee effectiveness.

2. Make the goals specific. The employee will have a clear understanding of exactly what you want when his or her goals are specific. General goals such as "do your best" are helpful, but specific goals such as "I'd like to see the job completed this week" have proven to be more effective in motivating employees.

3. Make the goals difficult. The employee will produce more if the goals are difficult than he will if the goals are easy. Easy goals do not represent a challenge to the employee and do not provide satisfaction once they are met.

4. Make the goals reasonable. If the goals are too difficult, the employee may become discouraged and give up working toward them or use the difficult goals as an excuse for poor performance. The most effective goals are those that are both difficult *and* reasonable.

5. Let the employee participate in setting the goals. Employee participation in setting individualized goals leads to a clearer understanding of what is intended and how it is to be accomplished.

6. Get the employee to accept the goals. The employee is likely to perform better if he or she understands the goals and accepts them as *his or hers.*

7. Give the employee feedback. It's important for an employee to be evaluated *both* during an assignment and after completing it. Give the employee both positive and negative information about his or her performance in relation to established goals and do it as frequently as needed.

Other Criteria

While individualized goals satisfy the need to set employee standards, most of us use other types of standards as well. For example, we all have our own idea of the perfect employee.

In judging subordinates we are all tempted to use popular catch phrases that describe an individual's traits, motives, values, and interests. We then attempt to convert these to standards. For example, we often describe employees as "having a pleasant personality," "being cooperative," "willing to work," "extremely loyal," "very conscientious," "honest and ethical," and "well controlled." All of these and similar judgments are convenient standards, but they lack objectivity, are prone to personal bias, and are not demonstrably job-related. Employee performance standards based upon traits often aren't performance standards at all.

Another approach to standard setting is to focus on an employee's potential for performing on the job. In this case we judge what we *believe* to be the employee's capabilities and compare these with what we *believe* are required for good job performance. Saying an employee is "smart," "knows the job," "is a good problem solver," "has the required skills," "has a good track record," and so on is to judge potential. Like traits, judgments of potential are also subjective and prone to bias. Though potential may be more job-related than traits, in most cases we are not really sure just what the employee's potential is or how to measure it with respect to the requirements of the job.

Setting standards on an objective, rather than a subjective, basis is more desirable. And the best type of standard is based on job results.

Objective observations record that the employee "is always at the work bench (or desk) during work hours," "wears a safety helmet and glasses while in the work area," "is rarely absent from the job," "helps co-workers," "completes the job," and so forth. These are directly job-related and can be verified by the observations of *others* as well. They are therefore legitimate measures of job performance. But *the best type of standard is based on job results*. Results are even more objective than observations of behavior, are not subject to personal bias, and are obviously job-related.

In many cases, job results can be counted or measured: number of units completed, amount of scrap generated, number of rejects, number of calls handled, number of complaints satisfied, number of invoices processed, number of orders picked, number of sick days, and number of accidents. Job results are a tangible measure of an employee's accomplishments.

Two supervisors can judge the same employee and disagree completely on his performance if they use standards based on employee traits. They may be in better agreement if their standards are based on potential. They should be in close agreement if their standards are based on observations of behavior. But they are likely to be almost completely in agreement if they use standards based on results.

Benefits of Standards

If you use goals to direct your subordinates and results to evaluate them, your unit should perform at a high productivity level, for an employee will perform best when he or she knows the answers to the following questions:

1. What is expected of me?
2. How am I supposed to accomplish the work?
3. How will I be evaluated?

In addition, you will have less need to be defensive, apologetic, or uncertain in evaluating your subordinates. You will find it easier to document and defend such personnel decisions as raises, promotions, transfers, disciplinary actions, and terminations. Even if you are challenged under laws such as equal employment opportunity or mandatory retirement, the availability of data from well-designed employee performance standards puts you way ahead of the game.

Developing and applying good performance standards in evaluating employees is certainly a challenging task, but the rewards are well worth the effort.

MBO: Setting Objectives

C. R. DILLON

Management by objectives (MBO) is based on the belief that the future of a company can be improved by active intervention *now*. It is an approach to management designed to encourage initiative and prevent working at cross-purposes—or, indeed, for no purpose at all. It shifts emphasis from sterile procedures to accomplishing results.

For managers, the value of the process involved—setting objectives, implementing them, and measuring results achieved—lies as much in their participation in it as in the progress achieved. Participation stimulates the development of a deeper understanding of the business and its environment; it forces the systematic formation and evaluation of alternatives that would not otherwise be considered. It releases creativity that is often suppressed by routine activities and the need to respond to crises.

The first step is to set objectives—to make future commitments for the enterprise and the individual that are designed to achieve a certain set of results. This commitment includes the resources of people, money, facilities, and time.

Even though an organization's future is uncertain, it must act and react in ways that will improve its outlook. Organizations that are overly preoccupied with the present and past may leave their forward directions ill defined.

A decision to make improvements by implementing certain objectives should be the result of analysis and evaluation of the enterprise's needs. It begins by forecasting—by looking at what lies ahead in business and society and determining ways in which an organization can best use this future situation.

Such forecasts are vital in planning and establishing objectives for improvement. The strategy of managing by objectives uses these forecasts as a basis from which to determine alternative directions. One classification of forecasts is by time period—that is, long range and short range. Long-range and short-range forecasts should be written into all plans. George S. Odiorne suggests that four questions be answered in the process:

1. Where are we now?
2. If we didn't do anything differently, where would we be in one-five-ten years? Do we like those answers?
3. If not, then where would we like to be?
4. What are the optional courses open to us, and which one should we choose?

Reprinted from *Supervisory Management*, April 1976

If we realize where we are and perhaps how we arrived there, we might then see where we are trending toward and take action to avoid some of the undesirable conditions that lie ahead. No organization is inexorably headed on an unalterable course; it is entirely possible to set a new course.

Finding Organizational Objectives

Several approaches are available to help determine needed improvements that may serve as a basis of objective-setting. They are:

1. *The consensus method.* It relies on opinions held by a group, committee, or conference concerning the future course of an organization or a department. A highly subjective approach, it relies on both the experience and the intuition of participants. Although the individual contributions are biased and individualistic, the consensus approach combines and averages these contributions.

The pooling of experience and judgment, the ease and simplicity of making contributions, and the involvement of people who will ultimately set objectives all help provide a motivational climate in which objectives can be most easily reached. Disadvantages of the approach, which include reliance on opinions, lack of objective data, and nonnumeric averaging, must be weighed against these advantages.

2. *The problem-areas method.* The process starts with the identification of areas plagued with frequent, recurring problems that are difficult to solve. Use of this approach involves analysis of the kinds of problems involved, histories of these problems, problem trends, and probabilistic occurrences. This information is gathered from an examination of opinions, reactions, reports, and other data in the problem areas. Suggestions for improvements and solutions are solicited both from those who are part of the problems and from others who are merely related to the problems.

Enlisting the aid of people in the problem areas stimulates motivation to improve. It is senseless for any objective-setting program to plan future improvements without addressing itself to current problems.

3. *The maximize-opportunities method.* This approach focuses upon innovative opportunities, which may be systematically sought through brainstorming sessions. Improvement ideas may range from minor innovations that advance the organization by increments to breakthroughs that result in major progress. Idea seekers are encouraged to look outside the company for conditions or opportunities that, when acted upon, would make the best use of internal resources. Such an opportunity might be in the shape of a possible future market for an as-yet-undeveloped product.

4. *Numerical forecasting methods.* Numerical forecasting employs ratios, statistics, and mathematics to measure and project movements within a company with a reasonable degree of accuracy. Projection can reveal what troubles will exist, their magnitude, and deviations from known directions. These deviations from present directions will suggest new approaches and improvements a company can adopt.

Numerical methods tend to be more objective than nonnumerical ones and, when properly used, are reliable and useful for estimating trends and growth. But although the numerical description of critical relationships makes it easier to check results, numbers tend to oversimplify and at best should be regarded as indicators. Furthermore, numerical methods are based on assumptions that, if faulty, could throw an entire forecast off despite the precision of the method itself.

5. *The situation-action model method.* This method offers a way of finding objectives by using a verbal probability model. The structure contains several related steps—including (1) collecting effects from a situational analysis, (2) determining causes of situational effects, (3) finding alternatives to causes in the situation, and (4) choosing the best alternative.

By following these steps in the appropriate situation, the manager can use a situation-action model to find objectives for his organization.

Setting Objectives

Objective setting is a process, not an event. A formalized statement of objectives must be meaningful to those who are committed to its implementation.

The broad areas identified for potential improvements provide the basis for adopting and setting objectives. The setting process involves getting the management team together to commit resources through mutual agreement until a formal statement of objectives emerges.

Formal statements set forth commitments made by individuals, groups, departments, or the entire organization. Formal statements are written, communicated, supported by top management, and interlocked with those of other organizational groups; the whole organization is accountable for implementing the statements.

Setting an objective is a formal process committing the use of an organization's resources by those expected to deliver the results. It is based on the principle that if you want to get maximum results from people, you have to get them involved and accountable for those results.

Formulating meaningful statements of objectives takes thought and careful analysis. The intention behind each objective must be made clear in the formal statement, which should specify the action to be taken.

Objectives should be quantified to the greatest extent possible. The more concrete the information a manager can build into his objective statement, the more likely it is that he will be able to achieve agreement among others whose commitment he needs. Quantified objectives specify both the quantity of results expected and the time period in which they are to be achieved. One should use words that indicate how much; terms that can be proved or demonstrated; precise terms designating actions that can be controlled and measured; and terms that lend themselves to clarification through percentages, ratios, numbers, averages, index numbers, correlations, and standard deviations.

How Many Objectives?

The number of objectives to pursue during a particular period varies from company to company. The most suitable number of objectives for a particular company depends on the kind and number of improvements that must be made within a time period.

Every authority in the area has his own idea about the number of objectives to be selected for an individual. Some have suggested that no position should have more than two to five; others that six to ten should do the job adequately; and still others that eight objectives for each of five major functions are appropriate. The number of objectives to be set should naturally be based on the nature of the job to be accomplished, the criticality of the achievement, and the management level at which objectives are being set. (In other words, the higher the management level and the more critical the achievement, the fewer the objectives.)

Improvement forecasts are bound to yield several potentially attractive objectives with equal or near-equal appeal. The decision maker must select those that will give him the greatest return on his investments of time, money, and personnel. He may also, of course, wish to retain some longstanding objectives.

A useful guide for selecting objectives from a wide assortment of possibilities is to assign relative values and weights to alternative objectives. This usually requires arranging and weighting an assortment of objectives according to utility or payoff. A "payoff array" is simply a list of objectives ranked according to their expected value or payoff, from highest to lowest.

After objectives have been set throughout an organization, a network of objectives should result—one in which objectives are interlocked with each other. This interlocking must begin when objectives are being set.

Appraisal by Results

Many MBO efforts incorporate a system of appraisal by results—performance appraisal made in terms of progress in meeting objectives. Appraisal interviews are also occasions for setting new objectives—with superior and subordinate jointly setting them. The two decide jointly on ways in which performance can be improved, develop short-term and long-term improvement projects or objectives, and set ways in which performance can be measured.

This approach to performance appraisal focuses on results achieved by the subordinate rather than his personality or innate qualities. Plans for implementation are evolved and approved. When the implementation period is completed, the subordinate and supervisor evaluate what he has done and discuss his progress. The process is repeated for the next period with a set of new performance objectives for the individual. A comprehensive appraisal conference by superior and subordinate on results achieved forms the basis for setting new objectives for the next period. The process repeats itself through a cycle of performance review, objective setting, plan evolution, performance, performance appraisal, and setting of new objectives.

Thus the appraisal-by-results approach focuses on improvement of subordinates' performance. It provides employees with a means by which they can understand what is expected of them and how they should go about achieving it. Because of the superior-subordinate relationships involved, interlocking occurs naturally—in a management hierarchy, everyone is superior to some and subordinate to others.

Just as a superior must set objectives jointly with his subordinates, so must he set objectives jointly with his boss. Thus interlocking occurs throughout the levels of the organization. Sometimes, interlocking is achieved in group objective-setting sessions carried out at an organization's various levels.

MBO: Implementing Objectives and Measuring Progress

C. R. DILLON

Before proceeding to implement objectives or letting employees proceed with theirs, managers must double-check the availability of equipment, materials, facilities, skills, and any other resources needed to meet all objectives. Where there are problems, these should be solved or the objective revised before final commitment is made. This procedure, called validation of objectives, is used as a final step before commitment to ensure that the objectives selected meet organizational and individual needs; where they do, the chances of successful achievement are enhanced.

Such validation determines the confidence that an individual, department, or company may have in reaching objectives within the stated time limits. Risks, assumptions, and changing requirements are checked and analyzed to see where faults or failures can occur with implementation.

Commitment—Implementing Objectives

Once objectives are firmly set, those who set them are committed to perform according to expectations. Of course, objective statements can be reconsidered, renegotiated, and revised in light of new information and needs—but managers must convey through attitude and action that a set objective is a binding pledge or promise.

People at various levels in the organization whose effort and cooperation will be required must understand the anticipated results to be achieved and their own high accountability for delivering them. With this understanding, all those involved take on a commitment to work and strive as a team. Because of the timing and coordination required, the involvement and participation of large numbers of people tends to reinforce the permanent quality of commitments. This is all to the good, since objective-setting procedures are frequently so interrelated that a change in one area will cause an upset in other areas.

Implementing Objectives

Implementing objectives involves taking action to get things done—the practical effort necessary to carry out what is intended. The ability to get things done is the hallmark of a good manager. Where there

Reprinted from *Supervisory Management,* May 1976

is a good manager, of course, there are also employees who can get things done to meet objectives set.

Motivation is the term used to describe what a manager does to inspire and encourage subordinates to participate in objectives programs because they want to, not because they are driven to. It involves coaching—day-to-day, face-to-face urging, directing, and helping subordinates to reach and meet their commitments. It sometimes places a heavy demand on a manager's persuasive skills in getting agreement when there are differences or disputes.

Motivators are job conditions or factors that cause subordinates to act because they derive satisfaction from doing so. When these motivators relate to the work itself, they provide built-in incentives for the subordinate to complete work. Thus building motivators into objectives increases the drive to reach them.

"One Man's Meat . . ."

Of course, what motivates one subordinate may not motivate another—and the same goes for de-motivators. What is needed is a workable scheme for applying important motivators (more autonomy over the job, for one example) in combinations and proportions attractive to a given individual at a given time while avoiding demotivators (poor pay and poor working conditions, to name two). You may recognize in this scheme Frederick Herzberg's theory of motivation, based on satisfiers (things that motivate people to higher achievement) and dissatisfiers (things like poor pay that demotivate and must be straightened out before satisfiers can have an effect). Such a scheme should be planned and implemented on a schedule similar to production schedules, control schedules, and maintenance schedules. Because of individual variations, each motivational scheme or program should be custom-built.

It's important to realize that, over time, motivators can become demotivators. What was once a challenge may now inspire only boredom. For this reason, and because of individual differences, a person's motivational program must be reconsidered every time new objectives are set. Motivators must be built in and demotivators avoided in terms of company objectives and the needs of those expected to implement them.

Consideration of work plans, motivators, and demotivators is undertaken in light of employee needs to stimulate employee satisfaction through the achievement of objectives. This work of building in motivators and avoiding demotivators must be done before the dates for assessing an objective's progress are set.

Related Processes

In setting up a motivational program, several related processes must be undertaken:

1. Analyze objectives or task assignments in terms of their technical, financial, and human relations requirements.
2. Recognize that disparity may exist between company expectations and employee behavior.
3. After analyzing the "whys" of employee needs and behavior, work toward developing the skills to narrow the disparity.
4. Develop a list of potential motivators.
5. Select motivators on the basis of a "best fit" in achieving objectives.
6. Build motivators into statements of objectives.

Measuring Progress

Progress toward achieving objectives should be measured periodically, preferably at checkpoints or target dates established when objectives are set. This provides a measure of control over completion of the objective; that is, if an employee's progress report indicates a deviation of actual progress from targeted progress, corrective action can be taken to get the objective back on target in time to make its completion deadline.

Controlling is, in large part, follow-up. It helps ensure that targeted achievement is accomplished within defined standards. There may be many standards, but four are most essential:

1. Quantity (How much?)
2. Quality (How good?)
3. Time (When accomplished?)
4. Cost (What expense?)

The precise amount or level of these standards was, of course, stipulated when objectives were set. Comparing actual performance with predetermined standards and ascertaining any difference is vital to keeping implementation processes on course. Sometimes there is overshooting of the target, sometimes undershooting. It is the undershooting that becomes a matter for concern and correction.

An effective status-reporting system is one designed to keep all levels of management completely informed on the developments in and status of the implementation of objectives that affect them. Status reporting must be an integral part of an organization's total information flow, with emphasis on reporting in time for the decision making and adjustments required to make any corrections.

Accurate record keeping, follow-up reports, and status information on progress are needed in order to take the best possible corrective action at the best possible time with the appropriate employees. This means that status reporting must be frequent enough to permit fast corrective action when necessary. However, perfect progress should not be expected in any status reporting system. The most one can realistically aim for is a minimum number of deviations from plan, a minimum number of corrective actions, and fluctuations that remain within acceptable limits. A "down" in one measurement period must be compensated for by an "up" in a period closely following.

An Interlocking Control System

Ordinarily, an objectives control system is a total system in the sense that it embraces all aspects of company commitments and activities. It needs to be a total system to ensure that all subobjectives and programmed activities are synchronized and operating as intended. With this total view, higher management can review the manner in which each part is progressing in relation to the whole. For this reason, the objectives control system must be integrated and interlocked among levels.

All data, information, performance indicators, and progress measurements must be related and structured into this system. Within this overall system, of course, each manager will have his own objectives control system that gives him fingertip control of program and its progress. He can tailor-fit its structure to meet the needs of his group and section. However, he must be sure that it is compatible with that of the overall company.

When managers operate their objectives programs out of sight of their supervisors and other managers, an overview of the entire program is difficult to obtain. The larger the company practicing management by objectives, the greater its need for managers to be knowledgeable and effective in areas beyond their direct observation.

Since control is based on measurement of progress, it is necessary to adopt a basis of measurement that will disclose both qualitative and quantitative progress being made in relation to expected progress. It must be remembered that the basic purpose of MBO strategy is to accomplish results, to get things done. However impressive the activities programmed to reach key objectives, it is still results that justify them.

Ratios are frequently useful in expressing progress toward achieving results. (A common ratio is E/I, or expense in relation to income, where this is applicable. Another might be the number of widgets produced over the targeted number.) Ratios can be plotted on a graph, diagrammed on a control chart, or tabulated on a matrix—all of which convey at a glance the progress being made toward the accomplishment of objectives.

Ratios can also be used in ways that pinpoint group progress separately from that of other groups. A word of warning, however: ratios and percentages should be used with care because they can be deceptive; numbers often convey an accuracy and precision that does not exist. Handled carefully, however, ratios can be extremely useful tools.

Performance Appraisals

Used accurately, MBO offers a sound basis on which to review the performance of an individual manager or employee. The rater can use fairly concrete information—in terms of progress toward completion of objectives—as a basis for his appraisal. The person being rated participates in setting his or her performance requirements (objectives). The circumstances make for less subjectivity and a more impartial attitude toward the appraisal process generally.

The technique of MBO-based performance appraisals has significant advantages over many other appraisal methods currently used. For example:

1. *Appraisals are tied to on-the-job results.* Appraisal focuses on job requirements and work results rather than personality traits or general characteristics. Specified objectives are tied to results needed and expected by the company. Evaluation is tailored to an already well-structured situation. Objective-setting sharpens the definition of job clarification and responsibility and thus provides a framework for more accurate appraisals.

2. *Appraisals promote objectivity.* Supervisors are usually reluctant to cite deficiencies without outstanding evidence. The accumulation of accurate performance information during the MBO process helps the supervisor be more objective—and less timid—about confronting a subordinate with evidence of poor performance. His solid ground is built on information with which the employee is already acquainted.

3. *Appraisals allow for two-way feedback.* The appraisal is not a passive, one-way event. Both supervisor and subordinate have input in assessing job performance and setting new objectives. Such an approach improves communication and motivation.

4. *Appraisals encourage the pursuit of opportunities.* Appraisals do not have to follow past practices or procedures. Indeed, the objective-setting process is ideal for incorporating new opportunities or challenges. Because it is future-oriented, it encourages employee innovation.

5. *Appraisals encourage performance improvement.* Chief among the several purposes of appraisal is the stimulation of improvement in individual performance. Individual employee commitment to the achievement of objectives gives a built-in impetus to performance improvement.

Feedback as a Performance Management Technique

MICHAEL SMITH

Feedback is a critical part of the performance improvement and performance review process, benefiting both managers and subordinates. From a manager's perspective, it helps maintain or improve current employee performance. For employees, effective feedback answers the often unspoken question, "How am I doing?" The annual performance review with its accompanying documentation is feedback. That's true. But that feedback is often too late! In order to influence performance, feedback must be ongoing.

There are two basic types of feedback:

Maintenance feedback ("keep up the good work"), which recognizes good work, general competence, or exemplary performance.

Improvement feedback ("change is needed"), which calls attention to poor work, areas of incompetence, or problem behavior.

All "official" documentation (for example, comments written on appraisal forms) should be shared with the subordinate. But not all feedback needs to be this formal or written down. If a manager has a choice between "writing someone up" and talking to the person about performance, an adult-to-adult conversation is the better approach.

Ongoing Feedback

Almost any book on performance reviews or performance improvement will emphasize the importance of ongoing feedback. What is ongoing feedback? It's nothing more than performance-related discussions that convey "how am I doing" information to the employee.

It is wrong to save up feedback and once or twice a year dump it all on the subordinate. Done this way, feedback doesn't have the motivating and relationship-building influence it can otherwise have. Employees can't improve if they don't know a problem exists.

Ongoing feedback is an essential management tool. It may be hard for managers who moved up in an environment where they were told "no news is good news" and "I'll tell you if you do anything wrong" to accept, but ongoing feedback to subordinates is essential to building an effective work environment.

Reprinted from *Management Solutions,* April 1987

Giving constant attention to performance fosters a results orientation that will truly benefit the organization. This attention to performance takes two forms.

Formal reviews of performance as typified in the statement "Let's get together this afternoon. We'll discuss your work during the past three months, what's current, and plans for the immediate future."

Informal, almost off-hand reviews that may be more powerful in the long run by providing a constant reminder that performance matters. This reminder may come in the form of a statement like "I'm pleased to see that you've brought this project to a close under budget. That's quite an accomplishment! Is there something we can learn from your experience?" Or it may take the form of a question like "Did you proofread that memo before you gave it to me? No? In that case, take it back and proofread it. We've talked about this before and . . ."

Guidelines

1. *Feedback is most useful when it is specific and descriptive, not evaluative.* Effective feedback describes specifically what the person did rather than makes a judgment or broad generalization. For example, telling a subordinate that he is "bad mannered" may be an accurate statement, but it is inadequate feedback. The subordinate doesn't know what to change. A better way to convey the information would be, "You have interrupted three people in the last half hour."

Value judgments or generalizations only confuse the issue (for example, "You're lazy" instead of "You took twice as long as I expected to do that task"). Likewise, it is more useful to hear "You talked too much in the meeting" than to be described as "domineering."

Describing behavior in a specific way enhances the value of the feedback. And the feedback recipient is more inclined to listen and accept the information.

2. *Effective feedback is aimed at behavior under the employee's control.* Every action people take may be under their control, but some aspects of behavior are difficult, perhaps impossible, to change. Physical or personality characteristics are a good example. Most people will welcome or at least be willing to listen to feedback about writing style, presentation skills, and the like. But people resent feedback about, and have difficulty trying to change, a naturally hoarse voice, nervous tic, or personality trait. This is not to say that personality or attitude is not an appropriate subject for a manager's concern and feedback. It may be—but *only* if it affects the employee's work or the work of others. And when dealt with, the behavior should be discussed in terms of its effect on the work or work environment.

3. *Effective feedback is well-timed.* Receiving feedback about last month's behavior is like getting an insurance cancellation notice after an accident. Immediate feedback is best! Feedback should be delayed only to avoid embarrassing an employee in front of others or to get more information.

4. *Effective feedback is constructive.* The manager should be seen as helping, not as attacking. Toward that, the feedback should show the employee how performance could have been better. The manager describes "what happened," not "what should have happened," then explains how it could have been done differently.

Some employees will reject any feedback that disagrees with their own view of themselves, no matter what is said or how it is said. In such a case, a manager needs to be as specific and constructive as possible. The subordinate may still reject the feedback. But the manager will be sure the employee understands specifically what performance needs to be changed and how that performance could be improved.

Managers should avoid asking the question, "Why did you make such a mistake?" It will only cause subordinates to respond defensively. Employees who purposely make mistakes are saboteurs, and they should not be allowed to remain. Rather than ask, "Why did you screw up?" managers should ask, "What happened?" or "How do you think this could have been avoided?" or another problem solving, data gathering question.

5. *Effective feedback is appropriate to employees' needs/desires.* Every person has a unique set of needs and desires, and this is certainly true with respect to feedback. But too often managers treat all

employees alike in terms of feedback. To be effective, managers need to adjust the timing and content of their feedback to match the particular situation and the needs/preferences of the subordinate involved.

For example, some subordinates won't hear positive feedback unless it is repeated frequently or is in an exaggerated form. Others remember every negative thing that's ever been said to them, whether it was intended as negative feedback or not. Some employees prefer to receive frequent feedback. Usually, high performers want a lot of feedback and ask for it directly. Managers whose first response is to believe asking for feedback is a sign of weakness or an attempt by the subordinate to obtain "guarantees" of future positive appraisal treatment should consider the subordinate's pattern of past performance before giving feedback.

Finally, some subordinates would prefer the manager give no feedback.

Summarizing, the manager's responsibility for feedback can't be communicated in a simple formula. The timing and content of feedback must be tailored to best fit the situation that is at hand and the needs of the subordinate or subordinates involved.

Potential Pitfalls

If feedback is such a good way of learning about the effects of one's behavior, why do people resist? Managers may avoid giving feedback for any of the following reasons:

- They don't believe feedback is necessary; they say, " 'No news is good news' was enough for me."
- They believe they are not competent to judge others.
- They anticipate a negative reaction by the subordinate.
- They don't often give positive feedback.
- The want to avoid having the feedback "used against them in the annual performance review discussion and rating."

Employees avoid opportunities for feedback or do not listen to or accept feedback for these reasons:

- They don't trust the manager's motivation.
- The feedback is not clear.
- They don't respect the manager's judgment.
- The feedback doesn't agree with the subordinates' opinion.
- In the past they have felt they were betrayed by managers who only talked positively but rated negatively.

Accentuate the Positive?

Giving and receiving negative feedback is almost always difficult. Perhaps the best advice is, "Be free with both positive and negative feedback about performance." Managers should confront all situations requiring negative feedback to be sure employees are given every opportunity to improve.

It's helpful in such a situation, though, to start the performance discussion with positive comments. An employee is more likely to listen if the discussion begins on a positive note. However, praise should be relevant to the situation and shouldn't be given when it isn't warranted. Managers should not invent positive feedback. But in most cases, some aspects of performance will be worthy of positive feedback and appreciation.

A word of caution, however. Many managers adopt a routine of beginning performance discussions with positive comments, switching to negative feedback, and concluding with glowing words of appreciation. This "sandwich technique" sends a mixed message. Too often, it confuses subordinates or raises false hopes that performance problems are not *that* serious. Instead, whenever possible, significant "bad news" should be discussed separately to be sure the message and its importance are fully understood.

The timing and content of feedback should vary based on the significance of the employee's performance. Feedback should be like radio and television commercials that are intentionally louder to capture audience attention. Extremes of performance (positive or negative) need to be identified so subordinates realize how far from expected performance they are. And employees should be appropriately commended or encouraged to improve performance.

Positive Reinforcement

Many behavioral scientists have highlighted the power of positive reinforcement for maintaining and encouraging effective employee behavior. High expectations and positive reinforcement of achievement can dramatically affect productivity.

Paul Brown, in his book *Managing Behavior on the Job,* encourages managers to focus on achievement detection, rather than on error detection, as a method of fostering effective performance. He suggests that managers check their personal use of positive reinforcement by auditing their compliment/criticism ratio. Brown suggests that managers tally on an index card attempts to increase effective behavior by giving positive feedback (+), and decrease ineffective behavior by giving negative feedback (−). After keeping track for a few days, they should check the ratio. Typically, the amount of critical feedback given will far exceed the positive feedback given.

Managers who find they give more negative than positive feedback are often dissatisfied with their ability to influence subordinates' behavior. Accentuating the positive aspects of subordinates' performance will alter the ratio and increase their influence. This is not to suggest that they should accept or ignore poor performance—simply that a preponderance of positive feedback, balanced with negative feedback when it is truly warranted, yields optimum results.

Will Your Next Performance Appraisal Land You in Court?

THE EDITORS OF THE ALEXANDER HAMILTON INSTITUTE

Have you ever said anything like the following when you conducted a performance appraisal?

"Don't worry, Joe—as long as you do good work, you'll always have a job in this company. . . ."
"I know it's not a big raise, but for a young man, you're doing pretty well. . . ."
"If you do everything I say, there's no reason at all why you can't expect to be head of your department within a couple of years. . . ."
"Let's face it, Mike—you are getting on in years, so we thought you might want to take on a new and less stressful position over in . . ."

If you have, you and your company could be in for a big lawsuit—and you and your company could lose. Managers are increasingly being held accountable for what they say during performance appraisal sessions. Employees who feel that they haven't been given a fair shake by their bosses are going to court to fight back, and more times than not they are winning.

The 22-Year Veteran

To illustrate how easy it is for a manager to fall into this legal trap, let's consider the case of Harry, a 22-year veteran engineer for a household appliance firm. Over that time, his annual performance evaluations, while not perfect, were generally favorable. He received high praise for his technical performance and for the way he handled special projects, but he also was criticized for some shortcomings in his supervisory techniques. The appraisals also cited "a tendency to resist new ideas."

Those minor faults became major problems the day Harry was passed over for a promotion to manufacturing vice-president. Joe, the successful candidate—and Harry's new boss—had been hired the same day as Harry. And Harry bitterly resented his colleague's jump ahead.

Almost immediately there was a change in Harry's attitude. When Joe called a meeting to discuss

Reprinted from *Management Solutions,* July 1986

problems in the manufacturing operation, Harry refused to participate. There were no problems to be discussed, he maintained. Later, when another executive questioned a cost estimate from Harry's department, Harry stalked out of the meeting.

With these incidents to jog their memories, company executives began to remember earlier incidents in which Harry had displayed stubborn, intemperate behavior. It became obvious that his performance had been slipping for some time.

This was the background when Harry came due for his next evaluation.

The job of evaluating Harry fell uneasily on Joe. He peppered the evaluation form with comments like:

"Have talked to Harry several times about better incentive systems but no action."

"Little results in this area."

"Harry is difficult to work with. He is antagonistic toward others and must be pressured to face and complete projects."

Joe did not believe in showing the evaluation forms to his employees. He did, however, discuss his poor ratings with Harry. Joe told Harry that he would not receive a wage increase that year. Too many essential jobs were not being done. Joe also discussed the areas in which he felt Harry had fallen short.

By the time the interview was over, Joe felt sure he had made one thing clear: He was seriously unhappy with Harry's performance. "You have a lot of talent," he concluded. "We haven't decided what to do with you."

The Decision: Discharge

At about the same time, an outside consultant hired by Joe was reviewing the manufacturing division's performance. The final report included a comment that Harry "seems to lack initiative—seems burned out based on his performance."

The consultant recommended that the engineering division be reorganized. There was no place for Harry and he was discharged. At a meeting with Harry, Joe explained to him the reasons why he was being discharged. They included poor attitude, lack of cooperation, and lack of leadership. Harry had no visible reaction at the time, but he obviously did have one later. The company found itself facing an age discrimination suit.

The company had done nearly everything right, said the judge who heard the case. The company did have legitimate reasons to discharge Harry. "Burnout" can be such a reason if it leads to substandard performance. This can be true even if the problem stems from the employee's age and length of service. A personality conflict can also be grounds for discharge.

In any event, the judge ruled the company was within its rights to set performance standards for its management employees and to discharge Harry when he was not able to meet them.

However, the judge continued, the company had made one serious error: *No one had ever directly told Harry his job was in danger.*

Making the Options Clear

True, most employees probably would have gotten the message from the final performance appraisal, the judge acknowledged. Joe had gone over the specific criticisms in detail. He also denied Harry a raise. However, Joe had stumbled at the next step. By that time, he was seriously considering discharge. His only comment, though, was the ambiguous, "We haven't decided what to do with you."

"Put yourself in Harry's place," the judge suggested. He had been with the company for 22 years. For most of that time, his performance had been satisfactory. He had become accustomed to job security. It is possible, then, that even when his job was on the line, he could not recognize it. Vague comments just won't penetrate such an attitude. Harry should have received a clear, specific warning of what was at stake.

At least, the judge continued, the company should have paid closer attention to its own policies and traditions. They called for a specific final warning that a person's job is in danger and a chance for the person to improve before the company resorts to discharge.

This company fell into an easy trap. It had established a system of regular, effective performance appraisals. The system certainly identified Harry's developing problems. It provided the basis for an "improve, or else" ultimatum.

Even the best system, though, must be implemented properly. This is where Joe fell down. He never gave a clear, complete message to Harry.

In part, this could stem from a natural reaction. He had some very bad news for an old colleague. Joe might naturally try to soften the blow with an unclear comment.

That was understandable, but it still wasn't right. Joe did Harry no favor by avoiding the issue. He only made things more difficult later when the discharge became inevitable.

Saying What You Mean

Richard J. Simmons, a Los Angeles attorney who specializes in employee rights cases, sees this as a typical human problem of the appraisal process. The supervisor, naturally enough, doesn't want to be a "bad guy." So he or she tries to become a "good guy" instead. The supervisor may be vague about his or her conclusions, as Joe was, or rate all employees, no matter their performance, as no worse than "average." In the latter case, all the other ratings are inflated to match. A "good" employee is really only average, and anyone who actually is above average is rated as "outstanding."

Some time or other, Simmons warns, a "good" employee, who really is only an average employee, will drop to below-average performance. Ultimately, the only solution will be to terminate this person. Then in court, the supervisor will try to convince the jury that this employee had built up an established record of substantial performance. This testimony won't stand up well against a pile of appraisal documents that describe this employee as "good." Employees' lawyers like to project those documents on large screens, Simmons points out. It multiplies their impact.

Other legal experts also have cited this problem of rating inflation. The inflated ratings may be valid when you compare one employee with another under the same inflated scale. Yet no matter what you meant, "to the outside observer, 'good' means good."

Preventive Measures

The best prevention is to base the assessment on a fixed list of job-related performance characteristics. This focuses attention on each characteristic individually. This can help a reluctant critic give a more honest assessment of the employee's performance in each area.

To strengthen the review process, any evaluation of a supervisor's performance should include an assessment of how well that supervisor evaluates employees.

The Two-Sided Process

Simmons also points out that until recently, supervisors have seldom had to account for the way they conduct their appraisals. Only in the last few decades have the courts and administrative agencies required that they justify routine personnel actions. Until then, the appraisal was a one-sided process, conducted by and for the employer.

That old habit remains. Appraisal is still primarily a process in which the supervisor judges the employee. That power is easy to abuse. Even where the supervisor tries to give a fair and honest appraisal, an objecting individual who takes a large company to court is likely to find a sympathetic jury.

The solution to this problem is to make sure the appraisal is a two-way communication process. Encourage the employee to respond to your comments. If the employee disagrees with your assessment, provide room to include that response on the rating form.

Offering the employee a chance to object has a legal advantage, too. The employee who passes up this opportunity won't be in such a strong position should the matter go to court.

Continuing informal comments on an employee's performance are important, too. Don't give the employee a chance to claim that an unfavorable review came as a complete surprise.

Part XI

PLANNING AND CONTROL

Stepping Up to Supervision: Planning for Success

H. KENT BAKER and STEVAN R. HOLMBERG

Newly appointed supervisors fail for many reasons. But one of the most common is failure to develop sound, workable plans. As a person moves up from being an employee, with no management responsibilities, to the new role of supervisor, the time and attention that he or she must give to planning increase markedly. Not only is the individual now responsible for planning a new, enlarged set of activities, but also he or she must plan relative to the boss and subordinates.

Typically, fledgling supervisors take an extremely short-range, crisis-oriented approach to planning. They get caught up in performing activities, dealing with today's problems and survival. This approach might be acceptable in the short run, but over time small problems expand into much larger ones, and objectives and time schedules become even more difficult to meet. If things continue to go as they are— that is, if the supervisor continues not to plan—he or she is likely to spend every working minute on firefighting.

This is what happened to Don North.

In his relatively brief tenure as a supervisor, Don seemed to be constantly fighting fires. As soon as one was out, another arose. He never had enough time to look beyond the next day's potential crises. After a few weeks Don sensed a growing frustration from both his boss and employees. His superiors felt that he gave little attention to longer-range planning. Several of his workers complained about unclear job assignments, lack of schedules, and imprecise targets of performance.

Reprinted from *Supervisory Management*, November 1981

Why Plans Fail

Despite the importance of planning, even some experienced managers tend to overlook planning. They point to the high failure rate of their past plans to explain their current reluctance to spend even a few minutes in planning.

According to George Steiner, the reasons why plans fail can be divided into four categories:

1. Factors in getting started
2. A misunderstanding of what planning is
3. Problems in doing planning
4. Difficulties in using the plans once they are created

For instance, one reason that plans fail is that the supervisor assigns the responsibility of planning to a subordinate rather than doing the job himself or herself. This was one of the traps that Don fell into. By delegating planning, Don, in essence, abdicated all responsibility for planning on the assumption that someone else would now successfully fulfill that task. The subordinate did attempt to come up with some plans for the department, but Don was so involved in solving current problems that he had little time to review these. The fact that the subordinate also had many other job responsibilities further complicated the situation. Just like Don, the employee tended to get involved in solving day-to-day problems and found there was very little time left to devote to developing a plan for the department.

While Don North made an effort to get started in the planning process, he was not really convinced that planning was something that could be done at a departmental level. He saw planning as something reserved to middle managers, if not to top management. Managers higher in the organizational structure had the time and luxury to do planning; he did not, he thought. Don felt that his department and others' should be more involved in making things happen. Complex, formal, long-range planning, Don felt, was far beyond his capabilities and the capabilities of his area. What Don did not appreciate was the fact that plans *can* be developed in a way that is appropriate to the needs and resources of any organizational unit, no matter its size. A supervisor can start in planning at a relatively simple level and with a minimum of paper work. Basic plans can then be expanded and developed in more depth as greater experience with the planning process is gained.

Don also had problems in understanding exactly what was involved in planning. He failed to see that planning was an integral part of the management function.

Basically, planning involves deciding on objectives, then developing strategies to achieve those objectives. The resource implications of these strategies must also be developed, and finally an action plan (including an implementation schedule) should be sketched out. Once plans have been developed, a mechanism for evaluation and feedback must be built in to ensure that activities go according to plan.

In his conversations with colleagues, it became evident that Don had another basic misunderstanding about planning. Don believed that he could plan for one or two areas within his department and not for the rest. In fact, that was exactly the way that he had started to do planning with and through a subordinate. Because of this piecemeal approach, major scheduling and other problems began to develop.

Steps in Successful Planning

It would probably have helped Don if he had taken the time to identify what he wanted planning to do. *Planning the planning process* is literally the first step in developing successful plans for a department. The planning process itself consists of seven major steps:

1. Identify the major external factors.
2. Identify and evaluate the department's current situation.
3. Establish department objectives.

4. Determine product, service, or program output planning for the department.
5. Determine resource requirements.
6. Develop implementation plans.
7. Monitor and evaluate plans.

As noted, budgeting or financial planning (for example, determining financial resources) comes near the end of the planning process; it is not the starting point. While new supervisors may be much more comfortable going "right to the numbers," the earlier steps in the planning process are essential to creation of a successful plan.

1. Identify major external factors. A supervisor needs to think through the major factors outside of his or her department that will influence the ultimate success or failure of the department's activities. These factors may be internal to the organization at large or they may be external. Many of the factors outside of the organization itself will probably be focused on much more intensely in higher-level planning efforts. Still, they may be relevant for planning in a department like Don's. They might include evolving consumer needs, changes in government regulations, critical technological changes, changes in social attitudes and values, and changes in the competitive relationships of the firms in that industry.

The ultimate objectives in looking at external factors from a supervisor's perspective should be two-fold: (1) to develop a set of planning assumptions (which would then comprise the foundation upon which a supervisor could build his or her plans) and (2) to assess the opportunities and threats to the department after a thorough consideration of these external factors. Although this task might sound ominous, it need not be overly complex. Indeed, it can be done on two sheets of paper. On one sheet the supervisor identifies the planning assumptions and their potential impacts. He or she divides the second sheet into two parts, identifying opportunities on the left-hand side and listing threats on the right-hand side.

2. Identify and evaluate your department's current situation. In identifying and evaluating your department's current situation, supervisors would find it extremely useful to gain a historical perspective on how their departments have evolved. Identifying existing objectives, whether written or informal, offers a starting point. Undertaking an historical trend analysis of the basic output of their department is the second step. Determining resource composition over time provides additional perspective. The results of looking at the current as well as historical situation can be captured on three or four pages of paper.

On the basis of the first two steps, a supervisor is in a better position to assess his or her department's strengths and weaknesses. These strengths and weaknesses could be simply listed on one sheet of paper.

The supervisor is now ready for Step 3—specifying the major objectives of his department.

3. Establish department objectives. It is at this point that the supervisor establishes what he or she wants the department to accomplish and when those objectives should be achieved. Of course, determining one's own objectives and one's department's objectives is not an easy task. A supervisor has to balance his or her own objectives and the department's objectives with those of the boss and the organization. To the extent possible, these objectives should be built around quantitative and time-related information. In this way, the supervisor will be better able to measure and evaluate how well he or she is doing throughout the course of the year.

Only after objectives have been determined should the supervisor begin to consider the major service, program, or product output of his or her department.

4. Determine product, service, or program output planning. This step in the planning process involves developing a wide range of alternatives to achieve the previously identified objectives.

By the conclusion of Step 4 in the planning process, a supervisor should have identified major external factors, major historical data and the current department situation, the department's objectives, and a wide range of alternatives to achieve those objectives or outcome expectations. Consequently, all of the planning activities down to and including Step 4 identify what the manager wants to accomplish, why that is important, and generally some of the ways to accomplish those end results. The supervisor's next task is to determine how he or she will accomplish those results that involve resource planning.

5. Determine resource requirements and plans. Resource planning should involve consideration of four major categories of resources: people, organizational needs, physical facilities, and money. The objectives and the way the supervisor decides to achieve those objectives will largely dictate his or her human-resource needs over the upcoming year. Involved will be decisions not only about the number of people but also about their skill levels.

Once a supervisor has completed the human resource end of planning, he or she must then consider how to organize the department. The organizational format depends on human resource planning as well as on output. Three dimensions—product or service, human resources, and organization—determine plans for the physical facilities. Will the manager need more space than the department currently has? Will he or she need other major physical facilities within the next year? What other equipment will be needed to meet objectives over the next year? These questions must be answered in their proper sequence.

The last major element of resource planning is financial planning. Here, a supervisor would want to develop cost information on the alternative ways to achieve the objectives. These financial resource plans might include more than one set of budgets. In fact, a supervisor might develop one set of budgets under the most optimistic assumptions, then develop an alternative set of budgets under a pessimistic set of assumptions. In this way, he or she can focus on the upside opportunities as well as the downside risks for his or her department during the upcoming year or years.

6. Develop implementation plans. Implementation is critical. The implementation strategy should reflect the timing of various activities, how they are to be accomplished, and who is to be assigned the responsibility and the authority to undertake these tasks. A well-prepared implementation strategy will save time and prevent possible major errors in trying to accomplish the plans. The implementation plans will highlight interrelationships as well as interdependencies, will help sequence major activities and events essential to the accomplishment of the objectives, and establish essential benchmarks by which progress can be measured throughout the year.

7. Monitor and evaluate plans. To ensure that progress is being made toward implementation of the plans, a supervisor should consider developing a test to monitor and evaluate progress. Major activities identified in the implementation portion of the plan could be reviewed on a monthly or a quarterly basis, whichever is more appropriate. It is essential at this stage in the planning process for a supervisor to decide when he or she will review the plans and then to make a commitment to conduct a review on a periodic basis.

Participation

Having completed the seven steps in the planning process, a supervisor has a practical, usable, and workable plan for his or her department. In arriving at the content of the plan itself, the person should consider involving his or her boss and workers. Indeed, if planning is going to work, it is essential to involve both one's boss and one's subordinates in the entire process.

Don, for example, should have gone to his boss and tried to get input as well as participation in the planning process. His boss's expectations were one of the key variables in Don's plan for his department. If Don could have identified these expectations and incorporated them into his plans, the probability of success would have been greater.

Once Don had finished the plans for his department, he should have returned to his boss to obtain additional input. The result of these later discussions would be a consensus between Don and his boss concerning the objectives, best strategy, and resource demands or requirements for Don's department over the upcoming years.

Identifying and incorporating the expectations of one's boss in the early stages as well as throughout the planning process will not only add substantively to the content of the plans developed but also ensure that one's year-end evaluation is based on a common set of expectations. A more precise understanding between a supervisor and his or her boss will enhance the effectiveness of the plans and lead to positive reinforcement in the reward and evaluation process.

In addition to involving his or her boss in the planning process, a supervisor should involve employees at appropriate points in the process. They may have insights about the objectives, alternative ways to achieve them, and the realism of resource requirements. In addition, they may have input about critical factors or trends in the department's current situation. Furthermore, through involvement in the planning process, they will assume a greater identification with the resulting plans. Their commitment to the plans may be essential to the actual implementation.

Mission Planning at the Operational Level

ALFRED M. COKE

Planning raises a red flag in the minds of most managers. Perhaps yours, too. But it doesn't have to do so. Actually, planning can be a fulfilling managerial task if approached in a creative way.

What blocks us from accepting this is our past training and experience with the formal planning process. Many managers avoid planning because it involves thinking, the hardest work we do, and paperwork, the thing we all wish to avoid. In general, planning is viewed as a cumbersome task requiring precious time and effort and producing little results.

If resistance to mission planning is to be reduced, the mechanics must be rethought. A practical approach is shown in Figure 1. Here planning is simplified by dividing the process into two major parts and clarifying the steps in each part. This concept has proven efficient and reliable in practical applications in a variety of organizational settings.

The System

Organizational goals or objectives provide the middle manager with tasks. If the system is working correctly, corporate planners provide information to middle management about what the organization has to accomplish, when they wish it done, and what standards they expect. These tasks become the goals and objectives for middle management. The process is then repeated downward through first-line supervision to the workers who implement the tasks.

Middle managers must translate their goals into action plans so that work can be done. The first step in accomplishing this is to achieve clarity about the job to be done. The method recommended is the OMR (Outcomes, Methods, and Resources) model. The model reverses the usual thought process. Normally one begins by thinking in terms of available resources and how the job is to be done. Little or no real attention is given to what is to be accomplished. Most jobs are taken at face value, which usually creates problems as the work proceeds and the inadequacies of improper planning begin to show.

To prevent unnecessary delays or false starts, it's important to begin the planning process by thinking about outcomes. Specifically, you have to ask what you wish to achieve. You need to write specific objectives identifying the areas you wish to improve, alter, reduce, or maintain. The objectives should

Reprinted from *Supervisory Management,* May 1985

Figure 1

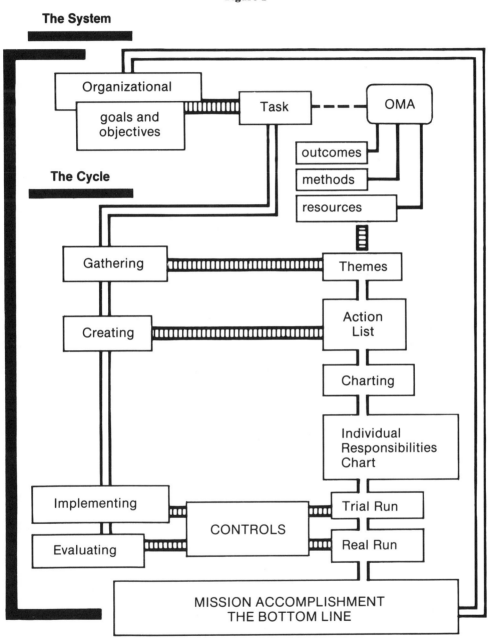

specify timeframes for achieving each task, the individuals responsible, and the standards of success. In writing an objective, keep in mind its impact on the organization.

Once clarity is reached about outcomes, the methods to achieve the end results should be considered. The force field analysis shown in Figure 2 is a powerful technique to understand influences in the system that help or hinder getting the job done.

Six questions should be answered to develop the analysis.

Figure 2
Force Field Analysis

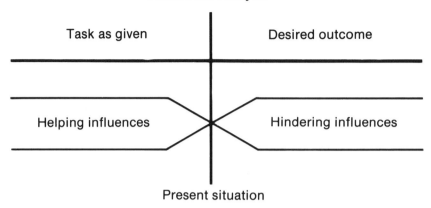

1. How should I do the task?
2. What obstacles keep me from doing the task to the required standards?
3. What factors help me in completing the task to the required standards?
4. How can I increase the helping influences and decrease the hindering influences?
5. What alternative methods are available?
6. What is the best possible method?

Answering these questions triggers a complete analysis of the task and identification of alternative methods that otherwise would not have been considered.

The last consideration in the OMR model is resources—that is, the materials used in accomplishing the task. Resources are either abundant or limited. In either case, criteria must be applied in the selection of the appropriate ones for the job at hand. Selection criteria include:

Costs. A particular resource should be considered in terms of how much it adds or subtracts from the bottom line. Some resources are nice to have but not worth their costs in terms of their contribution to the job.

Quality. Different parts of the job require different standards of materials. The idea is neither to skimp nor to overkill but rather to match the quality of the material to the requirement of the job.

Quantity. How much is needed of this resource? Planning in terms of quantity prevents overstocking of materials or shortages at critical points.

Accessibility of resources. Consideration should be given to the availability of needed items. Long delays due to delivery problems cannot be tolerated. Alternative sources should be identified during this step.

Time. Standards are directly linked to time. Different methods are required if higher standards must be met in a shorter time period.

Working through the OMR model is time consuming at the beginning but has a high payoff later in the planning process. The information generated provides a solid basis for understanding the details of the job at hand and the interrelationships and interdependencies of its various parts. This understanding arms you with the knowledge necessary to design the action plan.

Beginning the Process

You can use a simplified planning process consisting of four basic steps.

Information gathering is the first step and involves collecting all the information, known or not yet known, about the task. During the OMR process, a great deal of data was produced. The purpose of this step is to consolidate all the information into one body of knowledge.

Also, during the OMR process, you usually work alone to determine the outcomes, methods, and resources. This represents "homework" for the information-gathering step because the latter is the perfect place to bring together the management team to conduct the planning. If properly done, the old saying "Two heads are better than one" will hold true. From your previous work, the team will have a solid starting point.

Next, the team brainstorms or discusses the problem and all its related issues. The discussion should be freeflowing and unrestricted in scope, thereby generating many creative ideas. The ultimate purpose of the discussion is to develop central themes for the plan. These will emerge as the discussion encompasses the many aspects of the problem.

The Plan

The next step of the cycle involves *creation of the plan*. This produces three products. Developing these takes up a major portion of the planning time.

Two of these products, an action list and a flow chart, are created almost simultaneously. Themes are translated into actions to become the action list. Charting is the visual representation of the entire project.

To prepare an action list (see Figure 3), each action is recorded along with its due date, who is responsible for it, and who should be told that the action is completed. In preparing the list, actions should be placed in chronological order. If the resulting flow chart is to be computerized, the data must be in order before they can be fed into the computer.

The flow chart mirrors the project from its beginning to its end. A simple flow chart has three major components:

Figure 3

Action List Worksheet			
Action	Date Due	By Whom	Report to
1.			
2.			
3.			
4.			
5.			

1. *An action list.* The project is broken down into a series of actions based on the action list.
2. *A flow plan.* This consists of a diagram laying out the actions in the sequence in which they must be accomplished to complete the overall project. This layout also shows the interrelationships and interdependencies between the various actions that must be accomplished—that is, those actions that are dependent on the prior accomplishment of others are connected to those others.
3. *A time sequence.* This is a calendar depicting the start of each action, the time required for the action, and finally the end date of the action. It also displays the overall schedule for the project.

A simplified flow chart is shown in Figure 4. Two circles connected with a line represent the start of an action, the activity, and the end of the action.

The third step in creating the plan is formal assignment of individual responsibilities for the execution of the plan. This is a relatively easy task if the action list has been properly completed. The individual responsibilities chart resembles the action list in that it lists actions, due dates, and the like. The difference is that the action list includes all the steps in completing the project, while the individual responsibilities chart lists only the steps assigned to the person whose name appears at the top of the chart. An individual responsibility chart helps each member of the team see quickly and easily exactly what he or she is specifically responsible for.

The Need for Trial Runs

The third step in the planning cycle is *implementation of the plan.* Actually doing the project encompasses a practice session or trial run and the actual run.

If possible, rehearse the plan. Practice sessions point out the potential errors that even the best planners fail to see.

If the bugs are worked out during the practice session and everything is in place, execution of the actual task is relatively simple.

To insure that the task is running according to plan, *controls must be* implemented. This leads to the last step—*evaluating the plan.*

Evaluating the plan entails more than examination of the results. The question is how to control the flow of the plan to ensure the end products are achieved.

Control theory tells us that there are certain principles to be followed when establishing systems controls. Controls should be objective, clearly defining what is to be scrutinized. They should be flexible in execution. Slippage is likely to occur in almost all plans and consequently extra time should be built in as a safeguard. Controls should be cost-effective. You don't want to spend more on project checks than the project itself! And lastly, controls should be understandable to everyone using them or involved with the plan.

Controls also provide you with another payoff. If controls are established to point out exceptions,

Figure 4

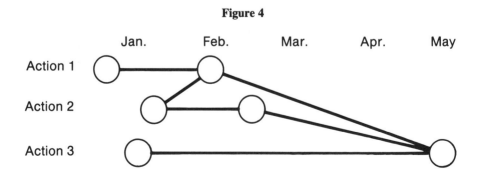

you are saved from dealing with the routine. Subordinates can deal with commonplace problems; your time is saved for problems that are exceptions to the plan.

In Conclusion

Mission planning can be accomplished in an orderly fashion by generating and processing a large amount of information through a cycle that is understandable to you as a working manager. The last thing needed at the operational level is another time consuming process added to an already busy day. The systematic planning cycle presented here is intended to solidify your thoughts on a process you may already be doing and to economize your efforts.

Taking the Strategic Planning Initiative

ALAN BRACHE

Setting strategy—a vision of the future direction of an organization—is the role of senior management, or so goes the prevailing wisdom. Only senior management is in control of external and internal factors that shape the organization's products and markets. Where does that leave middle managers? More often than not, they are left out of the formal process of setting strategy.

The belief that strategy should be the business of the top team and nobody else is as flawed as the belief that the strategy of a sports team is solely the business of the coach or manager. In both cases, the viability of the strategy depends upon input from others. As importantly, the effective implementation of that strategy is largely dependent upon others. No matter how well the strategic vision marries the internal ability to the external reality; no matter how incisively and creatively the strategy defines the products and services, the competitive advantage to be exploited, and the results to be achieved; no matter how practical, well reasoned, and downright appealing the strategy—the top management team cannot, by itself, transform that vision into victory in the marketplace any more than a head coach can transform a "winning strategy" into victory on the field or court without the scouts, other coaches, and players.

Those scouts, other coaches, and players are middle managers, whose role in strategy formulation and implementation is critical to success. For a strategy to succeed, middle managers need to provide the top team with information that will enable it to develop a winning strategy, understand and be committed to the strategy, understand their specific contribution to the effective implementation of the strategy, and assist the top team in monitoring the execution of the strategy.

It is top management's responsibility to bring middle managers into the strategic picture, but it often doesn't assume that responsibility. That leaves the middle managers with two alternatives—to sit back waiting and hoping to be involved, or to take the initiative, assuming a role in the strategic success of the organization. The following is a game plan for the middle manager who wants to pursue the proactive alternative.

Providing Strategic Information

Middle managers are generally closer to available information about the internal and external variables affecting the direction of the organization than the top team members are. Even if it is not requested, the proactive middle manager can provide top management with strategically useful information on prod-

Reprinted from *Management Solutions*, June 1986

uct performance, customer reactions/buying criteria, competitive activity, social/political/economic/regulatory/market trends (it's not only the market research people who have this information), and development of internal marketing/sales/research and development/production/distribution/management capabilities.

The quality of the strategic decision making in an organization is only as good as the quality and quantity of this kind of information. The strategic middle manager, sensitive to how the information that daily crosses his or her desk might be used by senior management in setting strategy, highlights those key facts and routes them upward. The manager operates much like the assistant coach who sees a weakness in the opponent's play or an underused strength on his or her team and informs the head coach.

Middle Managers in the Dark

In the ideal situation, the top management team communicates the appropriate parts of the strategy to middle managers. But in practice many often don't, even when they think they have. I recently conducted a session with a group of middle managers from a FORTUNE 100 company. I was told that the strategy had been thoroughly communicated and that the workshop should focus on building the strategy into the participants' jobs. I began the day with a "strategic I.Q." survey that asked questions like "Are you clear on the scope of your organization's products/services?" "Can you clearly define your organization's customer groups?" and "Do you know the organization's product-market priorities?" Less than one third of the group answered "yes." The senior management's communication was apparently less than "thorough."

The two most common reasons for top management's not communicating its strategy are a fear that the information will leak to the competition and a belief that middle managers don't have a "need to know." At first, the competition argument seems to make sense. If the strategy is not communicated to middle managers, the odds of its getting into the hands of the competition are lower. However, the probability of it ever being implemented is almost zero, so what's the value of secrecy? Secondly, an intelligent competitor can deduce most of an organization's strategy by simply observing its marketplace behaviors, such as product introductions and withdrawals, market entries and exits, pricing, advertising, facility construction, and hiring. While the top team should certainly establish safeguards against leaks of strategic information, the adverse consequences of leaks are usually less severe than the risks of not communicating the strategy internally.

The "need to know" justification for not communicating strategy implies that middle managers can make their day-to-day decisions in a vacuum. How can middle managers effectively make decisions regarding staffing, project priorities, budget allocation, pricing, equipment purchase, and customer service without the strategy as a context for that decision making? For example, a strategy based primarily on being the low-cost producer suggests different decisions in these areas than one based on superior product reliability, features, or availability.

Another difficulty arises when middle managers make decisions without knowing the strategic direction envisioned by top management. An unintended "counter strategy" is set up because the decisions middle managers make carry their own strategic significance. A sound strategic direction is set by top management but is never implemented thanks in part to this communication gap which cuts out middle managers—the real implementers of strategy.

Filling the Communication Gap

If the strategic decision makers do not recognize the importance of strategy communication, they can often be persuaded by a middle manager who says, "I could do my job more effectively if I knew more about the overall direction and priorities of the organization." If the top team purports to believe in communication but has not done an effective job, it is once again the responsibility of the middle manager to take the initiative and ask the questions that will enable him or her to understand the strategy. These questions include:

- What are the internal and external assumptions upon which the strategy is based?
- What are the values, principles, or fundamental beliefs that underlie the strategy?
- What is the competitive advantage upon which the strategy is based?
- What is the scope of products (and of services) offered?
- What is the relative emphasis on the various products and markets?
- What will represent our primary source of new business? new products? new markets?
- What capabilities are being developed to carry out this strategy?
- What is the plan for implementing the strategy?
- How is the success of the strategy being measured?

Once middle managers have these answers, which may come more from "reading the tea leaves" of organizational behavior than from senior managers, they have the rudder they need to effectively steer the boat they command (be it a freighter or a dinghy).

Setting Unit Strategy

The organizational unit the middle manager directs should have a strategy. This would answer some of the same fundamental questions as the overall strategy: Who is my unit's customer (externally or internally)? What are my unit's strategic priorities? What capabilities does my unit need? How will the strategic success of my unit be assessed? In addition, the unit should have a mission statement that specifically states its contribution to the overall strategy.

The long term effect of a unit strategy can be significant in shaping top management's strategic decision making. While the conventional wisdom holds that senior management "sets" the strategy in advance, in fact the CEO and his or her top lieutenants more often "select" a strategic direction from a few obvious alternatives that are working in the units. This is likely to increase with the recent interest in innovation and intrapreneurialism: companies are looking for ways to encourage innovation or at least avoid discouraging innovation.

Contributing to Strategy Implementation

Establishing a unit strategy is important but it is not enough. For a strategy to take hold, it should be woven even more tightly into the fabric of the organization by being incorporated into the jobs of the people who play a role in its implementation. Job descriptions, the standards or goals against which job performance is measured, and the reward system all ought to have a strategic, as well as an operational, dimension. For example, the ABC Company's strategy may indicate that a primary source of new business will be through the sale of new products to existing customers. In this organization, salesforce performance should be judged not only on the amount of revenue produced but on the percentage of revenue that is derived from new product sales: market researchers should be assessed on their ability to identify new product needs in existing products; product designers should be looked at in terms of their research into and development of new products that fill the identified needs, and so on. The middle managers who supervise these individuals should build the strategy into their jobs and reward strategic contributions.

Middle managers can make another contribution to the implementation of the strategy through their resource allocation decisions. Priorities for channeling budget, personnel, and equipment time should be consistent with the strategic direction. For example, one would expect ABC's market research manager to have more of his or her budget, staff, and computer time devoted to unearthing new needs in existing customers than to seeking opportunities to open new markets.

Many middle managers are responsible not only for allocating resources but also for acquiring and developing people. Once again, the types of skills that managers bring into and grow within their units should reflect the strategic priorities. The research and development manager in the ABC Company should be more concerned with acquiring and developing new product research capabilities than skills in refining existing products. While both sets of skills are important, the strategy sets clear priorities.

Finally, middle managers who have control over their structures should ensure that the workflow and reporting relationships support, or at the very least do not impede, the implementations of the strategy. For example, a strong product management structure in ABC may stand in the way of the introduction of products designed to meet new market needs.

Monitoring the Execution of the Strategy

When implementing a strategy, two questions are important. The first is, Are we implementing the strategy that we developed? Middle managers play a critical role in answering this question. They are usually in the best position to know if the strategy is being carried out. Internal factors such as resource allocation, development of capabilities, and product-market priorities indicate whether the strategy is becoming reality.

If a middle manager is not asked to provide the strategic decision makers with information in these areas, he or she should take the initiative and furnish it to those who can use it to ensure that the strategy is being implemented.

Equally important is the question, Is the strategy we developed the right strategy? Because an organization can implement the wrong strategy effectively, the middle manager's strategic responsibilities include providing data that will enable the top team to make any necessary adjustments to the strategic direction. Middle managers can help answer questions such as: Are the assumptions upon which the strategy is based (for example, that no new competitors will enter the market, that the need for the product is enduring, that the market will grow at X percent) still valid? Are revenue and profits meeting projections? Are the market share targets being met? How are current and potential customers reacting to strategic actions (for example, advertising focusing on a new competitive advantage)?

What's in It for the Middle Manager?

If an organization's top management team does not ask middle managers to make these strategic contributions, why should middle managers seize the initiative and take as many of these actions as possible?

1. Most significantly, if middle managers assume their strategic responsibilities, the development and implementation of the organization's strategy can only improve. If the strategy is more effective, the probability of better organizational results and a healthier climate increases dramatically. It is clearly in the middle manager's interest to work in a successful, healthy organization.

2. The top management team most likely has not carved out a strategic role for middle managers because it doesn't understand the potential of that role. The middle manager who educates his or her managers as to that potential and who is able to demonstrate its power is likely to be both noticed and rewarded.

3. At the very least, a clear understanding of the strategy will provide the middle manager with greater direction for his or her day-to-day operational decision making.

4. Being part of the strategic action is intrinsically enjoyable. The middle manager who plays a strategic role is more likely to see clearly the big picture and the importance of his or her function in the future success of the organization. Understanding the relationships and interdependencies among the many tiles that contribute to the overall mosaic enables the middle manager to reap the rewards of membership in an organization community.

For the First-Time Planner

DONALD O. JEWELL, GEORGE E. MANNERS, JR., and
SANDRA F. JEWELL

"When you fail to plan, you plan to fail." This is one of the few basic truths of management. But like many such tenets, too many managers ignore it. They and their work group fail to plot a course, blaming bad luck for their lack of success and attributing dumb luck to those who succeed.

Have you ever heard a manager described as intuitive? "Wally just seems to understand what's going on while others don't." Well, the fact of the matter is, Wally isn't intuitive or doesn't have second sight. It's just that he's done his homework. He's planned. He has considered the choices and adopted a course of action based on his evaluation. He's no more intuitive than those who stand by in wonder at his success.

Return on Invested Time

The outcome of planning is simply an increase in one's chances of succeeding. As a manager, you can still fail if you plan. Luck does play a role of sorts. You may also make a mistake. For instance, you may forget to properly communicate your plan to those who can make it work. But when you make an effort to plan, you increase the chance of achieving your goal.

Why?

- Planning forces you to think through what must happen if the goal is to be reached.
- Planning forces you to confront questions about the time and resources needed.
- Planning helps you expect problems and determine beforehand how they can be avoided.
- Planning gives you a way to involve others in working toward the goal.
- Planning helps you develop ways to measure your progress.

What Is a Plan?

You've probably heard others compare a plan to a roadmap. By that, they mean that the plan tells you and others how you intend to get where you need to be. It clearly states where you are going and why

Reprinted from *Supervisory Management,* July 1984

you want to be there. It should state where you are now and why you need to be someplace else, and it should clearly show the route you will take in getting from where you are to where you want to be. Possible problems along the route need to be identified so you can prepare and deal with them. Alternate routes also should be determined, just in case the main route is blocked unexpectedly.

You also need to figure out ahead of time what kind of resources and support you need to make a safe and successful trip. And to make sure you don't get where you think you need or want to be and wish you hadn't made the trip, you need to figure out what the trip will cost. You have to decide if the trip is really worth the effort.

By identifying key landmarks along the route, you can also make sure you are on the right path and that you are moving at the right speed.

As with road maps, a plan can be either general or detailed. How general or specific it needs to be depends on:

- The experience of those involved in the planning. If they've been there before, they needn't spend as much time planning.
- The difficulties of the plan
- The ability of those involved to follow plans

The following are a few rules that should help ensure the success of your plan:

- Be more specific than you think is needed.
- Get everyone involved in deciding which route is best and what problems may occur.
- Make sure everyone involved in preparing for the trip has a copy of the itinerary or plan.
- Don't lose sight of where you are trying to go. The plan is a means, not an end.

The Planning Process

Effective planning is simply a process of reasoning and thinking. To focus thinking, the following steps should be followed:

- Have an overall goal for the plan (quality improvement, plant maintenance, or the like).
- Collect information on what the current situation is and describe it in simple statements.
- Collect information about what the future may hold for your work group and describe it realistically.
- Identify the important threats that may prevent your group (or company) from achieving its goal.
- Identify the big opportunities.
- Try to identify *several* choices in dealing with threats and opportunities.
- Evaluate the advantages and disadvantages of each choice, including the resources required to make each one work.
- Identify the roadblocks to successful implementation of each.
- Develop an overall action plan that has the best chance of succeeding.
- Develop a contingency plan for dealing with the unexpected.
- Set specific objectives along the way as a means of determining whether the plan is on schedule.

Sounds simple, doesn't it? Yet the process requires a lot of attention. It can run aground for a variety of reasons.

One has to do with the system itself. Organizations often develop complicated systems for planning around these 11 points. The idea is to force managers who might otherwise not plan to follow the process. But too often managers instead become buried under layers of paperwork that end up collecting dust.

When those who plan don't involve those who will execute the plan, problems also arise. The manager who involves people, instead of simply data, in the planning process will likely have a more effective plan. There are two reasons why—quality and acceptance.

First, groups always produce higher-quality planning outcomes than a manager working alone, for groups can identify threats and opportunities that the manager on his or her own might miss.

Second, and more important, participation in the planning process increases acceptance of the plan by those who must make it work.

Another reason that plans fail is that the planner tries to look too far into the future. This can be just as bad as not planning at all. Although different levels within an organization require different planning time-frames, for the most part it's best not to look beyond a year as the basis for a realistic plan.

The most important factor in the success of the planning process is the plan itself. The quality of the plan can be evaluated by asking the following questions:

- Is it clear? Do people understand it?
- Does it agree with the values and purpose of the organization?
- Does the plan deal effectively with both the threats and opportunities identified?
- Does it identify the items of importance to the work group?
- To what extent are there specific, measurable goals and objectives?
- Is the plan a real basis for action?
- Does the overall plan contain contingencies in case of a serious internal or outside event?
- Does the plan include a way of obtaining feedback on its success?
- Is the plan flexible enough in case it needs to be changed?

Planning Begins "at Home"

Many managers blame their company for their inability to plan. Although you may work for an organization that lacks direction and doesn't reward or support planning, that shouldn't stop you from planning. Someone must deal with the uncertainty created for your work group.

Make no mistake about it; good planning pays off. It creates shared values; it creates direction; it creates work excitement; it increases one's ability to manage. And that's what you are paid for.

Goal Setting: How to Work Smarter

GARY SANTAVICCA and SANDRA F. JEWELL

Goal setting is an important part of the planning process, answering the question, "Where do we want to be?" Only after this question is asked and answered is it possible to answer the other key question in the process, "How will we get there?"

Goal setting is critical for effective planning, for perceptions about what is important may differ, and unless time is spent in discussing and mutually agreeing on a department's goals, time may be wasted on the wrong activities. Goals focus effort where it is needed most, helping a department "work smarter."

Well-written goals also enable us to check progress to see if we are on the right track. By comparing our results to the goals, we can determine how effective we have been and take the needed steps to improve.

Some Questions to Ask

To set useful goals, we need to consider the following:

1. What are the company's goals?
2. What demands will be made of the work group in the future?
3. What conditions will affect our work in the future?
4. What do we need to accomplish?
5. What desirable results can we identify?
6. What results should we look for along the way?

Goal setting involves looking into the future. Of course, we can't be sure what will happen. But we can make very good predictions based on what we know about the past and the present. Usually, our future is controlled by the plans of others: higher management, customers, suppliers, and government. So our forecasting task requires that we keep others' plans in mind when setting our own.

Often, one set of goals must be achieved in order for another set to be attained. For instance, production may have to produce X-plus widgets and have them in the stores if a single two-for plan of marketing is to succeed.

© 1984, The Mescon Group

Reprinted from *Supervisory Management,* September 1984

Also, the company has overall goals that establish the direction for each of its divisions. These divisions in turn have goals that determine the plans of the work groups within them. Suppose, for instance, a corporate goal was to increase production by 20 percent within 12 months. A divisional goal might be to reduce downtime due to equipment trouble, streamline operating procedures, and upgrade skills. On a departmental level, the goals might be as follows:

1. All group members will complete a one-half day course on trouble-shooting equipment problems by May 1.
2. Jim, Barbara, and Mike will study materials delivery and present recommendations for improvements by March 1.
3. At least two people will have the ability to operate each processing machine by October 1.

Participative Goal Setting

When the employees who will be asked to accomplish the goals participate in the goal setting process, the likelihood of the goals being reached is increased. Employees can offer information about their abilities and resources that will make the goals more realistic. Also, when employees help set goals, they better understand them. Then they can work more intelligently and creatively to meet them. Finally, since the employees themselves set the goals, they will be more supportive of them and try harder to meet them.

By involving his or her employees in setting or finalizing goals, a manager benefits in three ways:

1. The goals set will be based on the best information available.
2. The employees will understand how their work fits into the group and the company; this will add to their sense of job satisfaction, encouraging them to take more responsibility for achieving results.
3. The employees will learn about each other. This aids cooperation and coordination, particularly in team settings where members need to rely on one another to achieve the needed results.

The Basics of Good Goals

Effective goals have certain common characteristics:

1. They are specific. When there is no confusion about the desired result, the likelihood of its being achieved increases.
2. They are behavior- or performance-based. When a goal is clearly related to the actions needed to achieve it, it is also more attainable.
3. They are realistic. Goals that are considered unreachable usually result in plans that lack meaning and employees burned out from frustration.
4. They have target dates by which time they must be achieved. Open-ended goals are likely to be neglected because there is no sense of urgency associated with them.
5. They are clearly observable/measurable. If not, it's impossible to know if or how well they are being met.
6. They are continually reviewed and updated. As conditions change, results may need to change. Continual review allows one to keep goals and actions in line with changing conditions.

Goals that meet these criteria put the work group on a firm foundation for the next step in the planning process—developing action plans.

Some Simple Action Planning Tools

RICH TEWELL

Management at Farley & Richter needed to get some printed information out to some clients. The information was important, there was a great deal of it, and there wasn't much time available.

The company had its own print shop managed by Charlie Benson. When Charlie learned of the project, he swung into action. He pulled all jobs off the presses and yelled to Joe, one of his employees, to change the ink on press number 1 and Fred, another subordinate, to get all the yellow 20-pound paper from the storeroom. Within 30 minutes, the job was on the press.

Sounds like Charlie Benson is a hero, doesn't it? Well, consider the results.

Two other important jobs that had been on the presses and had been suddenly pulled off were delivered so late they were useless. They had almost been completed when Charlie ordered them stopped.

The yellow paper supply was quickly used up so the crisis job couldn't be finished on that color of paper. The job had to be started all over again with another paper stock. As a consequence, time and paper were wasted.

Joe and Fred became sullen and uncooperative because they hadn't been told what was going on. Things appeared to be confused to them, but they felt excluded and therefore refrained from doing more than they were told to do.

Sound familiar? Too often, a critical job becomes a disaster because the person in charge didn't plan before he (or she) acted. The argument given for that behavior is that planning would be too time consuming. But planning doesn't have to be complicated or require a lot of time. Think of the many action planning tools already around us.

- The clock on the wall that tells us how many hours of production time remain in a shift
- The calendar on a desk that tells us that we have to plan around summer vacation schedules
- The slip of paper in a pocket that reminds us of things we must accomplish before the week is up
- The telephone call to another department that produces a piece of information we need to use when it's time to submit a materials order
- The short meeting with a manager that reveals the need to schedule overtime for the next week

There are more formal planning techniques that are equally unobtrusive. And learning how to use them can substantially improve our ability to get our work done, whether it's a long-term project or a last-minute task.

Reprinted from *Supervisory Management*, August 1985

A Resources Checklist

The first step in planning involves taking stock of the resources we have and the resources we will need. These can be shown on a checklist with a single column for each. The difference is the resources we must procure, and those would be indicated in a third column so labeled. Resources are divided into four categories: people, money, time, and materials/equipment.

Seeing our needs on paper helps us change our thinking about them.

In considering the people we will need, we should ask ourselves, "Who has what skills?" "Who is available?" and most important "Who would broaden his or her experience by getting a piece of the assignment?" One mistake that managers make, particularly in handling a crisis, is to try to do most of the work themselves. They don't divide up the job, although doing so could contribute to the training and development of their people as well as save themselves hours of time and stress, perhaps even make the difference in bringing a project in on schedule, within cost, and at quality expectations.

Scheduling

Scheduling is the next step in action planning and entails deciding the times at which events will take place as well as their order, or when certain processes or procedures will start and end. Just as a resources checklist helps in the beginning to identify what we will need to get the work done, a list of the events and processes necessary to complete the task or otherwise reach our goal can help assure that no step in the process is forgotten or delayed.

For instance, Robin Myers, a training specialist, was asked to develop and present a short training session to a group of managers. Her list of steps included: Establish what people need to know at this time about the logic, develop a training outline, get a visual aids specialist started on preparing slides, reserve training room for the desired day and time, prepare presentation, follow up on preparation of visual aids, practice presentation, and deliver the training session.

After Robin prepared her list, she put dates by each time. It took her less than five minutes to do this, and it saved the day because it helped her to see that she would have to get the visual aids specialist started early if she wanted her slides on time. Robin's predecessor had always demanded visuals the day they were needed—and seldom got them—and always wondered why people seemed uncooperative when the heat was on.

There are two types of scheduling. The first is forward scheduling, where the schedule results in a projected completion date. The second is backward scheduling, where the completion date is given and one must figure out how to get the project done by then. Needless to say, of the two, the more preferable is forward scheduling.

As part of the scheduling process, the critical points for follow up should be set. Casually asking, "How is it going?" every once in a while may not be bad, but it doesn't assure that the plan is working.

Critical points in a plan are those at which important actions will be taken and a mistake or delay will be costly, or when a chain of events is set in motion that cannot easily be reversed. Robin considered preparation of visual aids to be critical so she included follow up on them as part of her schedule.

Contingencies

Contingency planning is preparing for a course of events that is other than what we want or expect. The entire field is based on the beliefs that something is always waiting to go wrong, what will go wrong will be what you least expect, and when it does it will hit harder than you thought possible.

Contingency planning is a skill that has saved careers. If we could predict the future, it wouldn't be necessary. Since we can't, we need to gather in a meeting the people who have practical experience with the project in hand, then ask each one to write down the most likely contingency. This should be done without any discussion. We want each person's honest opinion. Next, each person should share his or her answer with the group. This is followed by a discussion of the possibility mentioned. Afterwards, the group votes, selecting the most likely contingency to plan for.

The elaborateness of the contingency plan developed will depend on how likely the possibility is and how risky it will be *not* to have a back-up plan.

To illustrate how this would work, let's assume that a group is planning the installation over the weekend of an important piece of equipment. The installation has to be supervised by a technician who will have to fly in from another location. No one is available locally to handle the task.

As part of its contingency planning, the group calls other plants that have had a similar assignment and asks their managers what is most likely to go wrong. It learns that what is most likely to happen is that the technician will not show up. His flight will be canceled by bad weather, or he will be sent to solve an emergency problem elsewhere—both situations that the work group cannot prevent or control. So as part of the group's contingency plan, its supervisor calls the manufacturer and asks if another technician, preferably one from an area of the country where the weather is good, can be placed on standby in the event that the first technician cannot make it.

Sound logical? It is, but it is amazing how the logical escapes us when we are faced with an emergency—or even before that, as we start work on a project.

The Need to Communicate

The final tool in planning—and perhaps least recognized as such—is communication. Communication can help action planning by:

- Letting others know of changes that affect the plan
- Communicating progress and motivating others to continue giving their best
- Continually asking for ideas or feedback
- Negotiating over options
- Asking for information from people who have special knowledge or experience

Planning isn't a lonely, mental activity. Nor is it a highly complex task. We plan all day and perhaps don't even realize it. Consider the clock, the calendar, the telephone, the slip of paper in our pocket, and management meetings. The resources checklist, schedule list, and contingency plan are really no more complicated than these other action planning tools. And wouldn't using them make life a lot easier?

An Action Planning Process for All

WALDRON BERRY

One of the hottest topics for managers during the past few years has been planning—first operational planning, then long-range planning, and finally strategic planning. Most of the recent discussions have been aimed at upper-level managers; they have reached lower levels only in terms of "numbers to be made." The strategies peddled by well-known consulting firms have been accompanied by such buzz words as learning curve, portfolio matrix, dogs, stars, and cash cows. During the past recession, the strategies did not seem to be working well, and top corporate managers were asking why. The consultants replied that the strategies were all right; managers simply were not implementing them properly. They should have said that successful implementation requires effective action planning by managers at *all* levels in an organization. Although consultants can help by providing education and training, action planning must be done by line managers and operations people if it is to be successful.

The Planning Process

Action planning should not be overly formalized involving excessive paperwork, but it does need some structure, and it is tough, time-consuming work. In today's competitive, rapidly changing environment, a company will not be successful unless its managers at all levels know how to plan, how to teach their subordinates to plan, and how to monitor and follow through on plans. Every person in the company should know what he or she is to accomplish and how and when and with whose help it is to be done. There are many action planning processes; the following is typical of many and has a proven track record. There are seven steps:

1. Establish objectives.
2. Determine specific actions necessary to accomplish the objectives.
3. Delegate necessary authority, assign responsibilities, and coordinate role assignments.
4. Schedule required actions.
5. Allocate resources.
6. Communicate, coordinate, and revise if necessary.
7. Provide appropriate incentives.

Reprinted from *Supervisory Management,* April 1984

Let's look at these elements of an action planning process in more detail.

1. *Establish objectives.* A unit manager must establish what the unit is to accomplish in clear, measurable, time-bounded terms. The objective should be agreed upon by the manager and subordinate (frequently another manager). Although the subordinate should not determine the objectives (as was suggested when MBO was first popular), he or she should participate in the setting of objectives that he or she is expected to accomplish.

For there to be appropriate monitoring, standards should be set that measure performance effectiveness. This is the first step in the monitoring process. For example, the objective of a company producing television sets might be to produce, in a six-month period, 165 sets a day of which 75 percent must be console models. For this objective, standards related to unit costs, standard hours, flow time, number of rejects, and down time could be set. The action plan is the framework for the monitoring process, as will be shown later.

2. *Determine specific actions necessary to accomplish the objective.* After the objective has been agreed upon, the specific actions required to accomplish the objective must be determined by the unit manager. This might include in the case above receiving materials, sending the materials along a chassis assembly line according to a specific flow schedule, and assembling the chassis into cabinets. Each of these activities would become a separate objective with its own action steps and therefore would be an action plan for a subordinate. An effective action plan for an organization should consist of a coordinated and consistent group of means-end (activities-objective) chains. The activities may be as detailed as the manager desires; however, if the plans are too detailed, a paperwork avalanche will result, creating an unfavorable impression on organizational members. On the other hand, there must be enough structure to the action plans so that everyone knows what is expected, and implementation of the plan can be objectively evaluated, appropriate feedback provided to the persons responsible for accomplishment of the activities, and the necessary action taken.

3. *Delegate authority, assign responsibility, and coordinate role assignments.* This step of the process is not difficult if all the related activities are to be done by subordinates in an autonomous unit in one specific location. Unfortunately, such situations do not often exist. In the case of the company producing TV sets, the raw materials may come from a distant source over which the manager has little control, the assembly line employees involved in manufacturing the components may be union members and there may be limits to the responsibilities the manager may assign, and/or the cabinets may be manufactured at a separate facility owned by the company or possibly by another organization. In such situations, the unit manager has to work with others outside his or her responsibility, coordinating the different role assignments. The manager can't just delegate the work, telling someone to "do it and don't ask questions."

Having to depend on others for support is the norm in most companies. Often a manager, to get a project done, must persuade his or her colleagues to provide the necessary assistance. When they realize they will receive minimal credit for such help, they may be less than enthusiastic about offering it. The manager has to be prepared to overcome any reluctance. Everyone involved in the operation must know his or her role thoroughly and be willing to carry it out as effectively as possible.

4. *Schedule the activities.* In scheduling the activities of an action plan, both timing and sequences of events must be considered. For example, let's assume that the marketing manager at our TV manufacturer has an objective to increase annual sales by 15 percent and plans to accomplish this by reducing the price of the TV sets. Wholesalers and retailers must be notified and the rate of production increased if, as the marketing manager assumes, sales will increase with the reduction of price. Does it make any difference whether the price reduction is announced first and later the production rate is increased, or should it be the other way around? If it is correct that decreasing price will increase sales volume, then the production rate should be increased first so that an adequate inventory of television sets is available to meet increased demand. The reputation of the company would be damaged if a price decrease were announced and no sets were available when required by wholesalers and retailers. As noted in the preceding step, the marketing manager will need to coordinate the increased production rate with the production manager who is in another functional area and over whom the marketing manager has no authority.

The time required for adequate inventory buildup must also be determined before the price decrease is announced. The time necessary to publicize properly the price decrease must be considered too.

Both timing and sequence are important if the plan is to be effective.

5. *Allocate resources.* Resources must be allocated to the units and individuals to whom objectives and activities have been assigned. Problems may arise at this point if financial, human, or physical resources are not available. If shortages occur, it may be necessary to return to an earlier step and revise the action plan. For example, if the production manager does not have the personnel or the equipment to increase the production rate on TVs as requested by the marketing manager and the company will not provide additional assistance, then the marketing manager will have to change his or her plan. Perhaps sales can be increased by bringing out a new product that has been underdeveloped, in which case additional roles will have to be coordinated with other functional managers like engineering or research and development. Such rethinking of plans is not uncommon and occurs in the later stages of the planning process as more and more unit managers become involved.

6. *Communicate, coordinate, and revise.* Now, everyone who will contribute to the plan must be brought together. One unit manager may have primary responsibility for accomplishing the objective, another in a different functional area may have secondary responsibility, another must be consulted, still another must be notified, and finally a manager at a higher level must approve the plan. The roles of all must be communicated, coordinated, understood, and accepted by the managers involved. If problems arise, one of the accountable managers may have to revert to an earlier step in the action plan and revise the plan accordingly. If the problem is due to lack of resources, frequently a higher-level manager will be able to allocate the needed resources, thus avoiding the need to revert to an earlier step.

7. *Provide appropriate incentives.* Unfortunately, most action planning processes end with the previous step. The fact that there must be incentives to motivate managers and their subordinates to strive to accomplish personnel and organizational objectives is too often ignored by management. But the fact is, no planning process, however rational and complete, can be successful without both monetary and nonmonetary incentives to influence the behavior of managers and their subordinates. Incentives can be in the form of penalties as well as rewards, although rewards should be stressed. Besides monetary rewards, a good planning process requires such nonmonetary incentives as employee training and advancement opportunities. Praise and feedback are also effective behavioral incentives. A well-designed incentive system that rewards people equitably, based on how well measurable objectives have been achieved, is the final step in an action plan that will motivate employees to work together to achieve organizational goals.

The Monitoring Process

The action plan is the framework for the monitoring process. The very close relationship between action planning and monitoring cannot be emphasized too strongly. For each objective established, there are standards set and this is the first step in the monitoring process. As activities are accomplished, the second step of the monitoring process is completed by measuring the actual results and comparing them with the planned results or standards. The third step is to evaluate the causes for any deviation between planned and actual results and feed-back the evaluation data to the person responsible for accomplishing the task. It is important to understand that deviations can be positive as well as negative.

The final step is to take corrective action. The objectives may be changed or the plan may be changed. Thus the last step of the monitoring process may take one back to the first step of the planning process.

The planning-monitoring interrelationship is shown in Figure 1.

The causes for deviation from the plan are erroneous assumptions about economic factors, setting unrealistically high goals, or incomplete or inaccurate listing of required planning activities. The emphasis in monitoring should be on evaluating the cause of deviations, feeding the information back to the responsible people, and correcting the problems rather than trying to find someone to blame.

Over the past several years, the monitoring process, often called the control process, has acquired a

Figure 1

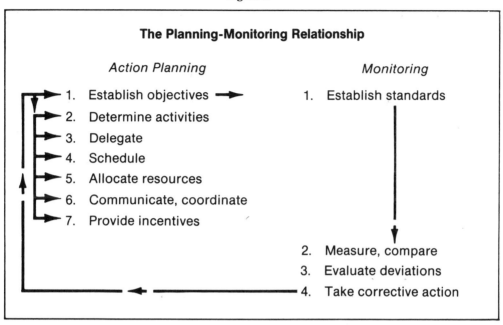

The Planning-Monitoring Relationship

Action Planning	Monitoring
1. Establish objectives ➤	1. Establish standards
2. Determine activities	
3. Delegate	
4. Schedule	
5. Allocate resources	
6. Communicate, coordinate	
7. Provide incentives	
	2. Measure, compare
	3. Evaluate deviations
	4. Take corrective action

bad reputation simply because the emphasis has been on fault finding and punishing people. The monitoring process *should* be a positive function and employees should not fear being evaluated; rather, they should look forward to the assistance that a good monitoring system provides.

Why Plan?

Establishing action planning in an organization will require some major changes in the thinking and behavior of managers and employees. People will strongly resist these changes unless they are properly prepared. Perhaps the best way to prepare them is to discuss the benefits of a company-wide planning-monitoring system. There are advantages for the organization, the manager, and the subordinate.

The organization. Organizational effectiveness is improved because the system focuses managerial effort toward congruent, results-oriented objectives. Coordination is more complete because work relationships among all levels of personnel as well as between peers in different functions are made clear. Communication is improved because congruent organizational and personal objectives establish a framework within which performance and progress can be discussed.

The manager. One of the manager's most important jobs is to train his or her subordinates. The planning process provides an excellent coaching framework for the manager because it establishes objectives for subordinates and generally outlines how the objectives are to be accomplished. Deviations can readily be determined by the manager, and assistance can be provided after evaluation of the situation. Manager-subordinate relations are strengthened because objectives are negotiated, performance is monitored, and feedback is given on a regular basis. The dialogue is helpful without being threatening. Finally, managers at all levels participate in the decision-making process.

The subordinate. Clear, measurable objectives are established; therefore, everyone knows what is expected. This also means that performance can be objectively measured on the basis of how well objectives have been accomplished and how effectively activities have been carried out. Feedback is also provided so a subordinate does not have to guess how well he or she is doing. It is a highly motivating situation because one is objectively measured and rewarded based on what one has accomplished.

Finally, as in the case of the manager, the subordinate has an opportunity to negotiate objectives and participate in the decision-making process.

Front Line Control

HARLAN R. JESSUP

The primary objective of your job as supervisor is to provide a service or produce a product of high quality, at minimum cost, and on time. You achieve this objective through people, and the costs you can control are primarily people costs.

However, because you may feel continuous pressure to complete the work and meet the schedule, you may overlook inefficient practices such as staffing your unit for peak loads until the labor-efficiency reports or headcount edicts finally catch up with you.

Front-line control, a process developed at General Electric, can prevent these problems because it gives you a daily focus on people costs that counterbalances the relentless and often single-minded pressure on output. It also makes it easier for you to formulate the daily objectives of your unit and develop a plan to meet them, communicate expectations to workers, check performance frequently against your plan, take corrective action before it's too late, and report interferences promptly.

Before describing how, let's discuss the seven principles of this approach and explain how they apply to you.

The Basic Principles

1. *Each work element must have a time standard or target that is current and reasonable.* While engineered standards are the best targets, today's good estimates are often far more believable than any standards from a dusty record book. The standard you use should reflect expected output from a qualified operator working at a normal pace without interruption. Though "performance allowances" may be necessary for scheduling or capacity planning, the standard you use must be designed to highlight interferences and not to hide them.

2. *Specific performance expectations for every job must be communicated to every worker.* Accepting these targets, even tacitly, amounts to a contract between you and your worker. So it's important that your worker understand what you expect, have a chance to agree or disagree, and know how you will measure his or her performance.

Reprinted from *Supervisory Management*, October 1985

3. *The unit must be staffed at the level needed to meet current output requirements.* Work expands to fill available time, and staffing at historical performance levels can only perpetuate inefficiencies. Therefore, if you staff your unit to meet the peak loads, you will surely be operating inefficiently in the slack periods.

4. *Every supervisor, at the beginning of every shift, must have a production plan that he or she can reasonably expect to meet.* The plan you develop must reflect scheduling priorities that are based on today's host lists and the master schedule requirements published a month ago. It must also reflect today's resource availability—the materials, tools, and people to do the job. If you can't meet the production schedule, you must prepare your best plan using current information, then feed back your plan to the scheduling unit.

For long-cycle and white-collar operations, the planning period may be a week rather than a shift, but the planning principle stands. You must work to an achievable plan, or you are planning for failure.

5. *At frequent intervals during the scheduled period (every hour or two in the shop, perhaps daily in the office), you must evaluate progress against the plan.* This means you must monitor output, either from every worker or just from key checkpoints. If you are not meeting the plan, you can make corrections before the end of the shift.

6. *Problems must be identified, addressed, and resolved.* You must document and classify lost time or variances from plan and see that a formal problem-solving procedure is in place so management can attend to the problems that arise.

7. *Every supervisor, every day, should be able to specify what his or her productivity is.* The labor efficiency report published a week from Thursday is irrelevant to the daily control of your shop. Only the daily indicator reflects your performance today. If you are asked, "How did you do yesterday?" instead of answering, "I met schedule," you should be able to say, for example, "I met schedule and I achieved 90 percent labor utilization."

Now that we've explained the principles of front-line control, let's look at the steps involved in implementing them.

Planning

The first thing you must do, planning, entails deciding what time values are appropriate for each work activity in your unit. If you have good time standards, or if you can apply percentage factors to your time standards to bring them up to date, you should use them. But if your time standards are nonexistent or hopelessly outdated, you should develop an estimate for each product family at each work station. Your target should not be based on what you have been getting from the work station but on what you should get if operating without interruption. To formulate your target, you should consider what constitutes a normal machine cycle with allowances for setups and material handling and what represents a good hour's production.

Next, you should develop a target table for each work station and include on your tables the common tasks that make up 80 percent of your operations. Incidental tasks or product varieties can often be grouped with the common tasks, or you can add them to your tables as the need occurs. But if you have a large variety of operations or products, you should select a limited number of key volume indicators—those operations or output measurements that are representative of the whole unit's output.

The Daily Schedule Control

The best format to use for your tables is the schedule control sheet.

For short-cycle operations you should use Figure 1. Under "work assignment" you can express your "target" in units per hour. Under "follow-up" you can document "actual" performance against "plan" at

Figure 1

Schedule Control
Short-Cycle Operations

Supervisor_____Area_____Date_____

Work Assignment					Follow-up								Report		
					Period 1		Period 2		Period 3		Period 4				
Name	Station	Job	Quantity	Target	Plan	Actual	Plan	Actual	Plan	Actual	Plan	Actual	Planned	Actual	% Productivity
										Totals					

regular intervals throughout the shift. And under "report" you can generate the productivity percent per worker by dividing the "actual" quantity produced for the day by the "planned" quantity. Finally, you can generate the productivity percent for all the workers on the shift combined by dividing the total "actual" quantities by the total "planned" quantities.

For long-cycle operations you should use Figure 2. Under "work assignment" you can express your "target" in hours per unit. Under "follow-up" you can document target "hours earned" against actual "hours worked" at regular intervals throughout the shift. And under "report" you can generate the productivity percent for each couple of workers by dividing the "hours earned" by the "hours worked." Finally, you can generate the productivity percent for all the workers on the shift by dividing the total "hours earned" by the total "hours worked."

On the back of the worksheets is a variance summary (see Figure 3) codifying the causes of lost time to highlight repetitive problems, explaining each problem, and listing immediate and future corrective actions.

Now let's look at how you could utilize the worksheets when you make each work assignment.

Recording Assignments

Before shift startup, you should fill out the first part of the schedule control. It might read like Figure 4 or Figure 5. Then you should make sure you communicate the specific assignments and your expectations to your workers. For Jones and Smith, you may do this by posting the target tables at the presses. For Black and White, you might say to them, "I want you to wire Unit 2 completely. Let me know how it goes during the day today because it should be ready for test by the end of the shift tomorrow."

Figure 2

Schedule Control
Long-Cycle Operations

Supervisor_____Area_____Date_____

Work Assignment				Follow-up								Report		
				Period 1		Period 2		Period 3		Period 4		Hours	Hours	%
Job	Names	Operation	Target	Hours Worked	Hours Earned	Hours Worked	Hours Earned	Hours Worked	Hours Earned	Hours Worked	Hours Earned	Worked	Planned	Productivity
											Totals			

Follow-up

Next, you should follow up on the workers' performance.

In the press room, for example, if after checking performance every hour you find that by noon Smith has produced the expected 200 parts, you should note 200 planned and 200 actual in the Period 4 "follow-up" column on the schedule control sheet (Figure 1) and comment to Smith, "Looks good!"

On the other hand, if you find that Jones has produced only 300 parts against the 400 planned, you should record the results in the Period 4 "follow-up" column (Figure 1) and ask him why. If it was a materials, equipment, or operator problem, you should record the lost time (one hour) and its cause on the variance report.

On the assembly floor, if everything goes according to plan, Black and White should be 25 percent through their wiring job at noon. If you find that they both lost an hour trying to find the engineer in order to get the latest revision of the wiring diagram, you should record six hours earned against eight hours worked in the Period 2 columns of the "follow-up" section (Figure 2). Then you should talk to Black and White to find out what caused the problem and to determine how to correct it. Did they act appropriately, or did they just put in a call and then sit and wait? Can they recover the time, or should you take other action? On the variance report, you should record the problem and document actions taken and future action needed.

At the end of the shift, you should enter the final data for each worker or pair of workers and talk to the operators about the day's performance. Then you should summarize the results for all of them combined and calculate the shift's productivity performance against plan. To cite two other examples: If you have a total of 20 operators, their performance might be recorded as 140 hours earned against 160 hours worked for a productivity factor of 88 percent. And if you have an assembly line with a total of ten

Figure 3

**Problem Identification
Variance Summary**

Supervisor_____Area_____Date_____

Work Station	Code	Hours Lost	Problem	Corrective Action	Action Complete (Y/N)

Variance Codes: A - Materials Quality   D - Design and Planning
B - Materials Availability   E - Operator
C - Tooling and Equipment   F - Other

operators, their performance might be recorded as 800 units produced against 1,000 units planned for a productivity factor of 80 percent.

Reporting

Once you have completed all the forms, you should discuss your unit's performance with your manager, making sure he or she understands what you are doing and what real problems need his or her attention. You can never win by concealing the real situation until the last day of the shipping period. But if you reveal a current problem, you will gain some understanding.

You should also track performance trends for yourself. Your day-to-day calculations won't mean much without a trend comparison, especially if you haven't had good measurements in the past. Tracking trends will help you to understand and communicate real performance gains. It will also help to reveal some of the chronic problems that look insignificant today but that will lead to significant lost opportunity if they persist.

Figure 4

Press Room Schedule Control

Name	Station	Job	Quantity	Target
J. Jones	Press #1	Part A	400	100/hr.
S. Smith	Press #2	Part B	200	50/hr.

Figure 5

Assembly Hour Schedule Control

Job	Names	Operation	Target
Unit 1 Assm.	B. Brown G. Green	Pipe complete	16 man-hrs.
Unit 2 Assm.	W. White B. Black	Wire complete	32 man-hrs.

The Bottom Line

As you can see thus far, front-line control can be a powerful tool to improve the performance of your unit. But to really improve productivity you must go one step further and increase the workload or reduce the workforce.

If more work is coming, you need to figure out how to do it without a proportionate increase in headcount. But if work levels are staying the same, you must reduce overtime, take advantage of attrition, and perhaps ask your boss to help transfer employees out of your unit.

Your new control procedures, your improved communication, and your problem-solving routines should give you confidence that you can do it. You might set yourself a goal of 10 percent or 15 percent more output per employee and take the necessary steps, painful as they may be, to achieve this goal in the next three months. If you succeed, you can congratulate yourself for a job well done.

Developing an Operational Plan for Better Performance Results

BOB POWERS

Quality performance depends on two premises. The first is that people will perform at desired levels if they are capable, have clearly defined job roles, know what is expected of them, have the tools to do the job, have the knowledge and skills to perform, receive feedback on how well they perform, and perceive and receive rewards for good performance. Together, these factors make up a *performance system*.

The second premise is that supervisors and managers can improve the performance of their employees by clearly defining and communicating an organizational purpose—what is important to members of the organization in carrying out their work, organizational aims and goals, responsibility for achieving aims and goals, and what constitutes successful accomplishment of the aims and goals.

These factors make up an *operational plan*.

An operational plan can unify employees of an organization, or members of a group, to work toward common goals. It is a systematically organized document that outlines the way a group intends to operate to achieve the goals and results identified.

Together, the operational plan and the performance system form the basis for both organizational and personal development. The two systems are a powerful means for focusing employees on attaining common goals and desired performance results. They are also clearly linked to and supported by one another. The value of even the best performance system is severely limited without a well-developed operational plan.

The Components of an Operational Plan

The operational plan consists of five components:

1. *The mission statement,* which defines an organization's or group's purpose or reason for existence
2. *Organizational or group values,* defining what is important to members of the organization in carrying out their mission
3. *Aims and goals,* which identify what the organization strives to achieve and reflect the direction an organization will take to achieve its mission

Reprinted from *Management Solutions*, September 1986

4. *Job roles,* indicating responsibility for achieving the group's goals
5. *Organizational objectives,* which define the intended accomplishments of the group or organization. They are measurable statements that define what constitutes successful progress toward and achievement of the aims and goals of the organization.

Each component of the operational plan stems from a statement of common purpose and links directly to another component. For example, the mission statement defines the common purpose of the group, while the aims and goals specify the direction the group will take to realize that mission. The job roles define responsibility for each aim and goal, while objectives identify the intended, measurable results of each aim and goal. Values link to all components and indicate what is important to the group in the way the other components are carried out.

Why an Operational Plan

A good operational plan can focus employees to achieve a common purpose; provide an organized, systematic approach to operating; establish an efficient means to monitor progress; and define success and reinforce successful action. Let's look at each of these potential benefits.

Focusing on a common purpose. Several years ago, I consulted with a large financial group that wanted to change the way the organization operated. It was up to 36 top managers to define the kind of organization they wanted to be. We brought the team together and asked each manager to define, in writing, the purpose of the organization. We ended up with 36 different answers. The managers defined the purpose of the organization in terms of their own jobs and nothing more.

When people lose sight of the real purpose of an organization, it is unlikely that the organization will fulfill that purpose. An operational plan can help to keep employees focused on the mission of the entire organization. If you'd like to find out whether your employees are working towards a common purpose, take ten minutes and try the Focus Test. Select, at random, a half dozen or so employees and ask each to take 60 seconds to write down the purpose of the organization. See whether the results indicate that your employees are focusing on one or many goals.

Organizing a plan for accomplishment. Have you ever had the feeling that "things are out of hand," that you are constantly reacting rather than being proactive? One of the most common complaints of managers is that they do not have the time to get organized. They are often so caught up with the day-to-day operations of the business that they cannot plan for long-term accomplishment. An operational plan can help by focusing attention on long-range goals.

Measuring progress. Tracking and monitoring progress can be an overwhelmingly time-consuming process. The operational plan is a useful tool for measuring progress and requires little, if any, filling out of forms and preparing of reports. Since every component of an operational plan springs from the mission statement, by monitoring attainment of the organizational objectives you will also be measuring progress toward the attainment of the mission statement. Quarterly reviews are an efficient means of gauging progress toward organizational objectives.

Defining success. If you don't know where you're going, you'll never know when you get there. An operational plan can tell you where that is.

I recently consulted with a work group that was considered very successful by the rest of the organization. Surprisingly, no one in the work group felt particularly successful. It turned out that even though the group regularly achieved successes, its members had no idea where they were headed and were consequently unable to perceive their achievements as successes. An operational plan forces you to identify where you are headed and lets you know when you get there.

Developing an Operational Plan

Operational plans should be developed annually and reviewed quarterly. The purpose of the quarterly review is to measure progress towards the attainment of objectives established in the plan.

The development of the plan begins with agreement on the mission statement. This forms the basis for the remaining components, which are generally developed in sequential order: values, aims and goals, job roles, and organizational objectives.

You should expect the development of your first operational plan to take anywhere from three to five days, depending on the size of your work team. Subsequent plans should take only two to three days.

Any number of people can be involved in the development of the operational plan. But more important than the number of people actually involved is the number of people who have had some input and consequently feel "ownership" of the plan. Even if only a few people worked on designing the plan itself, the entire work group can feel well represented by an operational plan that can help you to get what you set out to achieve.

Management Guidelines: Being in Control

GEORGE MILLER

Since the best of plans must deal with an uncertain future, a manager must have some means of adjusting his or her efforts to handle the unforeseen. This is the purpose of the control function. Whether the control mechanism is directed at job performance, the use of materials, or methods and procedures, its purpose is to verify that work is proceeding as planned and to allow adjustments to be made based on discovered variances. The basis of control is information in the hands of a responsible person and standards against which those data can be compared. The essence of control is action—no control has taken place unless the discovered variances have been dealt with.

There are two dangers in setting up controls: overcontrol and undercontrol. The following nine guidelines should help managers avoid these two extremes as well as aid them in setting up controls.

Guideline #1

The first guideline is: A manager increases his or her overall effectiveness by concentrating on significant variances from goals and standards.

It is easy for a manager to get involved in the details of activities and in the process overlook areas requiring immediate attention. That is why standards are so important. If a manager has determined in advance the timetable and the kinds of results that are wanted, he or she is more likely to take note when there are variances from the plan. Even with standards, though, there is the danger of a manager overlooking significant variances if he or she controls exclusively through personal inspection. So, a manager should set up a system of reporting designed to signal variances from plan and rely on this rather than upon on-the-spot observations to review operations.

What is advised here is control by exception. A manager has to be freed from detail work. So long as operations are proceeding according to plans, there is no reason for him or her to give time or attention to them except for morale-building or training purposes.

Application of the guideline. A manager should establish action steps for special projects and develop a system of reporting that alerts him or her to significant variances from the schedule. There should also

Reprinted from *Supervisory Management,* June 1981

be a course of action set up for all general activities and a reporting system that alerts the manager when key steps involved are not taken.

Guideline #2

The second guideline is: Time for control by exception is increased when standing decisions are established for recurring situations.

Much time is wasted when repetitive problems have to be redecided each time they arise. Organizationally, policies are developed to prevent this from happening and also to ensure uniform behavior in certain situations. But in individual work areas, supervisors and managers often waste much time redeciding repeat problems. This keeps them immersed in detail and reduces the time available to them for creative thinking and planning.

Application of the guideline. Each manager should consider where standing decisions (or policies) might be instituted within his or her operating area. Consideration should be given to such questions as overtime, vacations, purchasing practices, assignment of work, and machine maintenance. After arriving at these standing decisions, the manager should communicate them to staff, confining himself or herself to discussion of the "what" and "why" of situations wherever possible to avoid stifling individual initiative.

Since nothing in management is static, a manager should also periodically review his or her standing decisions to ensure that they are always applicable.

Guideline #3

The third guideline is: Employees tend to accept controls when they realize that they will make delegation of authority possible.

Paradoxically, the least freedom of action is present in those companies that have no automatic control systems. There, supervisors must depend entirely on personal inspection to determine how activities are proceeding. As a consequence, the observer's method of doing a job often tends to become the criterion for its performance, thus stifling initiative and reducing any challenge for the person doing the actual work. Where broad controls have been adopted, on the other hand, control is less personal and is results-oriented rather than prescriptive. So, tasks can be delegated, and employees can use their own initiative in getting them done.

Application of the guideline. Managers should explain the relationship between controls and delegation of authority to employment during coaching and training sessions. This might be a good time also to explain to subordinates how each one's goals fit into the overall organizational picture.

Guideline #4

The fourth guideline is: People tend to meet and exceed expectations when they have participated in their establishment.

Although the goals and standards engineered by an outside specialist may be technically correct, they tend to meet with resistance because the workers did not participate in their creation and feel no emotional or ego involvement in their attainment. Sometimes the resistance is subconscious. An employee will go through the motions but will not be motivated to meet or exceed the standards.

So, it is important to involve staff members, whenever feasible, in the setting of goals and standards by which their work will be judged. The key to getting things done through others is to get them to want to accomplish the desired result. Coercion builds no sense of commitment.

Application of the guideline. Managers should have their employees submit their recommendations for the standards by which work will be evaluated. This does not mean that the managers abdicate their responsibility for the final decision. Rather, they try to get their people to appreciate the needs of the overall enterprise and the part that their work plays in the process. Managers should respect workers' opinions and hear them out. If they disagree with their subordinates, they have the right to adjust upward the standards recommended. But managers also have the responsibility of explaining the reasons for the changes.

By participating in the goal-setting process, employees develop the ability to set high but realistic goals. And success in achieving these objectives encourages these individuals to extend themselves further.

If an employee continually sets goals that are too high, it may be because he or she is an incorrigible optimist out of touch with reality. If the person sets standards that are too low, it may be a clue to the fact that the employee is shielding himself or herself from the possibility of failure. The perceptive manager will be able to further appraise employees by the way they approach their part in the goal setting exercise.

Guideline #5

The fifth guideline is: Controls become practical and are even minimized when their potential benefits are compared to their costs.

Sometimes we get so enthusiastic about the clever "means" that we fail to compare the cost of these means against the benefits of the end results. For example, elaborate procedures are set up to save on office supplies when the cost of policing is more than the possible savings. We often see this kind of poor thinking. Indeed, companies sometimes spend thousands of dollars to save a few hundred or use tons of effort to accomplish ounces of results.

Application of the guideline. The desired end should constantly be kept in mind as we develop the means for accomplishing it. If the costs in terms of time and morale outweigh the potential benefits, the objective should be dropped or a simpler way of accomplishing it found.

In calculating the complete costs of control, quality, quantity, time, both direct and indirect costs, and psychological impact should be weighed carefully.

Guideline #6

The sixth guideline is: Control is most effective when established at strategic locations at the lowest level of the operating process and at each succeeding level where action is taking place.

All control is after the fact, effected through negative feedback. However, controls need not be post mortems useful only for future performance. If data regarding variances from targets are as soon as possible in the hands of the people doing the work and at the lowest level in the operating process, on-the-spot adjustments can be made.

Aiming the control effort at the lowest point in the process often can prevent an error from being carried through an entire operating cycle. Unfortunately, much control information is first sent to the higher levels of management. By the time the information has seeped down the line, the cycle is complete.

There is also a psychological benefit in following this guideline. When people are able to correct their own mistakes, they are saved from having to justify their actions. They can make adjustments when alerted to the variance and report the matter as a routine procedure.

Application of the guideline. Each manager and worker should be asked to think through the kinds of information they need to take corrective action in their work area. Everything within reason then should be done to provide them with this information. As a precaution, higher management should be informed about variances. But the first concern should be to get the information to the point where the actual work is being done.

Computers have made control data available at fantastic speed. However, employees and their supervisors must bear the responsibility for initiating the control reports they require.

Guideline #7

The seventh guideline is: Controls that encourage group pressure tend to be effective both in reducing supervisory involvement and achieving the desired end.

Members of a group are in the best position to police each other. Even where formal systems are not in effect, the group usually will exert pressure to bring in line a member who goofs off or abuses his or her privileges. When systems are set up that make the group aware of the behavior of its members, such self-control is encouraged. Say there is a rule that no more than two workers can be absent from the work site at the same time. It would be time consuming for a supervisor to try to police this requirement. Instead, a simple sign-out procedure could be used. Alternately, two special tags could be created. If both tags were in use, it would mean that two members of the group were absent. The group would police its members to see that the procedure was followed and that no individual took advantage of the group as a whole by abusing his or her rights in this area. The supervisor's involvement would be limited to control by exception or emergencies.

Application of the guideline. Each manager should determine where his or her own work group could control its members' actions in its own self-interest. Vacation schedules are one excellent example.

Guideline #8

The eighth guideline is: Control is facilitated when operating ratios are developed to signal variations from norms and objectives.

Facts and figures are fundamental in business, but raw data are of little value to a busy manager. They become meaningful only in comparison. It is important, therefore, for each manager to develop ratios and percentages to work with as control techniques.

The knowledge that a service station sells an average of 22,000 gallons of gasoline per month is of limited value. It is only when we compare gasoline sales to sales of oil, tires, and the like that the information becomes meaningful. Is a ratio of four gallons of oil for 1,000 gallons of gasoline in a predominantly residential area good, bad, or mediocre sales performance? Ratios of this nature are used all the time by businesses to gauge performance. However, other ratios specific to each job can be developed that are equally meaningful.

Application of the guideline. Each manager should think through the ratios that would be useful to him or her to evaluate operations and compare them to similar operations elsewhere. In developing these ratios, the manager may want to enlist the help of the accounting department or other specialists. Throughout this process, however, the manager should not lose track of his or her purpose: The reasons behind the figures are important, not the ratios themselves. Variances from norms should be used to channel the manager's efforts in getting at the real causes for fluctuations.

Guideline #9

The ninth guideline is: Controls become dynamic and progressive when standards and objectives are reviewed periodically so they reflect improved methods and changed circumstances.

When adopted, standards should represent the best thinking and experience of all involved. However, as we've said before, nothing in management is static. Situations change, and new methods and techniques are developed. If we do not change with them, we will never be in a competitive position to deal with the present and future. In setting up controls, a manager has to remember that he or she is dealing with the present while preparing for the future. While the individual can learn from the past, it should not be allowed to shackle him or her.

Application of the guideline. Periodically each manager should review the standards and objectives of his or her work group. At this time, both the supervisor and those reporting to him or her should identify all those factors that represent pertinent changes from the original premise on which the standards or objectives were established.

Standards should be reviewed at least annually.

Salary Budgeting:
How to Control Your Payroll

STANLEY B. HENRICI

As a supervisor there are some parts of your department you can control and some you can't. You would, of course, like to control the financial results. At the close of the year, more money should have come in than went out. But can you control that?

The "come in" part—revenue—is not entirely yours to command, and at first glance it may seem that you have more control over the "went out" part—expenses. But in both cases there are external forces at work—things you have to cope with rather than manage.

For these reasons it is essential that you keep a firm grip on those elements of your department that you *can* get hold of. One way, of course, is through budgeting. And one of the elements that you can control through budgeting is salary expense.

Reasons for Salary Budgeting

A salary budget is a forecast, made before the next fiscal year, of the salary expense that will be incurred for that year. With it you can:

- Hold the salary expenditure in line.
- Ensure equitable treatment of employees.
- Forecast cash flow.
- Plan business actions.
- Determine costs.

In formulating a salary budget, you may find it helpful to break the budget into two separate components. The first component is the number of people you have on staff. The simplest and most obvious approach is to prepare a list of the various positions in the department. However, if your objective is to reduce expenses—particularly overhead expenses, which often fall in the fixed category—you can go further than merely listing job titles. As an approach to cost reduction you can analyze the need for each salaried position.

Reprinted from *Supervisory Management,* October 1980

The second component of the salary budget is individual salaries. For each position listed, what level of pay will occur throughout the coming year? This, too, can be analyzed separately.

Constructing a reasonable salary budget is never easy, since you face many conflicting pressures. On the one hand, you have people sincerely interested in improving quality, sales volume, and all the other things for which they are directly accountable. To meet these objectives the supervisor needs an adequate force of employees. On the other hand, you have a financial imperative. Revenues must exceed outlays by X percent. Not three years from now, but in the year for which you are budgeting.

Reducing the salary payroll is never easy. It is an inescapable law of physics that where pressure exists, there is resistance to it. The resistance takes various forms. For example, supervisors may budget for unfilled positions; indefinite postponements in filling them provide a cushion against untoward events. And requests for budget reduction may be met by the virtuous excision of positions never filled, with associated claims of "savings."

There may be sufficient employees to provide for any conceivable spurt in workload or in absenteeism. There may even be plans for adding positions. These are customarily introduced in a confidential talk with the boss, beginning with the familiar disclaimer, "I am in no way interested in empire building, but. . . ." Then follows a reasoned explanation of how three more people are essential to handle increasingly onerous government requirements, to achieve operating economies, to attain quality control objectives, to sign on new accounts, or to realize fully the potential of the company computer.

All these measures may be perfectly legitimate. But, if in the course of salary budgeting the costs seem to be inching up to the high side, that list of budgeted positions deserves a close look. High salary expense may be due to too many salaries—which in turn reflect vague assignments, unnecessary work, poor supervision, confused workflow, rework, and other devourers of salaried man-hours.

Staffing Analysis

Organizations that are clearly expanding, noncompetitive, and well-funded characteristically have more "give" in their payroll than those that are fighting an uphill battle. If you are in the prosperous group, your salary budget may well be based on the existing number of people, plus whatever recruitment is foreseen for growth.

If, on the other hand, you are engaged in financial mountain climbing, you may wish to discover if an excess of salaried positions is one of the impediments holding you back.

Employers use several techniques for salary force regulation, some of which are described below. None of them is supereffective in all circumstances, but each can be of some value.

▪ *"Voluntary" reduction.* Supervisors are asked to carefully review staffing and eliminate unnecessary positions. This plea produces mixed results. Some supervisors go along; some dig in their heels. Many get upset and deny that they have superfluous positions.

▪ *"Stipulated" reduction.* Supervisors are told that there will be a moratorium on hiring or an across-the-board reduction of X percent in the number of salaried employees. In certain parts of the enterprise, however, either of these nonselective actions may do more harm than good.

▪ *Peak employment elimination.* Smoothing the peaks can help reduce salary commitments. Examination of the number of employees available may disclose that the company has geared its staffing to periodic spurts—special sales, custom orders, month-end closings, seasonal swings, emergencies, and the like. An alternative is to employ freelancers, consultants, service bureaus, or temporary employees for the crests and to staff permanently only for the average.

▪ *Overhead value analysis.* This is a technique for examining the functions of each position (and the time involved) in order to eliminate the least necessary functions and thereby reduce man-hours. Since the study involves the employees themselves, it can be both effective and disruptive.

▪ *Zero-base budgeting.* This extension of overhead value analysis relies on supervisory ranking of job functions in terms of essentiality or disposability. The idea is to sacrifice the least needed. The merits of this approach are those of cost reduction; the defects, if any, are the large amounts of time, paperwork, and review required along with the opportunities for "sandbagging" by judicious ranking of indispensable services last.

▪ *Organizational systems analysis.* If the two previous techniques may be called "micro," since they address individual positions, organizational systems analysis may be termed "macro," since it looks at the organization as a whole. The analysis involves a study of overall organizational objectives and the means employed to attain them. In doing so, it particularly considers the interplay of authority, accountability, and information flow among the parts of the company in order to discover functions that are duplicate, dead-ending, or obsolete as well as functions that are not currently being performed but should be. Because it is organization-oriented, the analysis differs from the more limited systems studies associated with accounting and data processing activities.

Salary Levels

To a certain extent, you can determine unilaterally how many people your budget payroll will cover. You have somewhat less freedom determining the salary levels that those people will receive. Several variables can affect salary levels and hence your budget.

The first of these are merit or progressive increases. Your budget must provide for these. If you have been giving merit or progressive increases to move employees up through the salary ranges, you are probably locked into this practice. It is expected as part of the unwritten understanding between you and your employees. Therefore, you have to provide for it in the budget.

At the same time you do have some control over the frequency and amount of these increases. Giving them early and large, with a fair amount of "superior" ratings, will bind your employees to you—at least until the next increase is due. Giving them late and small will cause some dissatisfaction but will probably not lead to a mass exodus. You can get away with scrimping now and then, but once you become identified as a low-paying employer you may experience a change in personnel.

Another factor affecting the general salary level is turnover. For example, if you have employees who will retire or resign in the coming year, to be replaced by newcomers, this change in mix will slightly lower the general salary level. Low-salary-range incumbents are stepping into the shoes of high-level ones. If you are contracting or expanding your salaried force, the change may affect the general salary level for which you are budgeting. Who will leave—the youngest employees or those highest in their ranges? Who will come in—novices or thoroughly experienced professionals who will be range-high? If you expect promotions to occur, or internal functions to be turned over to outside contractors, these changes may also affect your salary mix.

The timing of salary-level changes also influences the budget. Is a range adjustment increase given en masse, or is it parceled out over the year? Do merit and tenure increases cluster, because of past practices, in specific months? If they come near the beginning of the year, your total salary budget will be higher than if they are spread uniformly over the 12 months.

In addition to all the variables mentioned, special one-time circumstances usually foreseeable, must be taken into account. Organizational realignments, job reevaluation programs, spinoffs and acquisitions, policy revisions, and make-versus-buy decisions—all these can affect both the size of the salaried force and its salary level. Indirectly, changes in vacation, holidays, time off, and overtime pay provisions may have a bearing.

Detailed Budgeting

One common method of salary budgeting is to prepare a line-by-line, month-by-month forecast for the coming year. For this example, it is assumed that:

1. A general range adjustment increase of 6 percent will be given to all salaried employees in August.

2. The merit increase schedule is:

Outstanding	7 percent
Superior	5 percent
Satisfactory	3 percent

3. Smith, the machinist, may retire on June 1, to be replaced by Jones, who will receive a 10 percent promotional increase. Regardless of his decision, Smith will be entitled to one month's vacation in pay in the same month.
4. Jones will probably receive a 5 percent merit increase in October, if performing as expected as a machinist.
5. An additional clerk will be hired at the entry level on May 1. Thus the material needed for preparation of this budget consists of both factual data and estimates. The factual data are the names, positions, and present salaries of the various employees. The estimated data include:
   —Best guesses as to the amount of general increase that survey data will suggest for the August date
   —Likelihood of Smith's retiring on June 1 and being replaced by Jones
   —Need to hire a new clerk in May to prepare for the vacancy created by Jones's promotion
   —Timing and amount of merit increases for the various employees, based on informal opinion in advance of more exact information at appraisal time
   —January names and salaries, assuming the budget is prepared several months in advance

Laborious though this compilation may seem, it is fairly easy to perform, especially if each supervisor does it for the employees he or she directs. As a simplifying measure, a "satisfactory" rating may be assumed for all employees. Then an overall percentage can be added to the total to allow for the departmentwide dispersion of advanced ratings.

Some employers have found it convenient to run precalculated increases through their computer to produce budget schedules. The supervisor can then adjust the schedules for expected separations, transfers, or hires.

Problems and Risks

Beyond the pure headache of having to do budgets at all lie a few difficulties that can arise in planning budgets and following up. Most of these stem from the disparity between warm expectations at budget time and cold reality in the ensuing year.

• *Overoptimism.* Overoptimism on revenues may lead to overoptimism on the salary budget. Then if revenues do not meet the forecast, the manager is unable to cover all fixed overhead. If last-minute attempts at correction entail a reduction in predicted salary increases, he or she is in personnel trouble.

• *Ignoring guidelines.* The salary budget should agree with the guidelines for increases. If the budget is based on rough estimates of 5 percent increases and the guidelines for merit, tenure, and range adjustment increases provide for 8 percent, unexpected variances may pop up as the year progresses. Once again, corrective efforts may lead to inequities and grievances. Therefore, if the salary budget calls for stringencies, it is well to get revised guidelines in effect promptly so that outlays will not persist at a rate incompatible with budget objectives. Conversely, if the budget reliably portends prosperity, with an accompanying ability to support competitive salaries, the guidelines should be revised upward as necessary.

• *Padding.* It is not uncommon for some supervisors to budget for unfilled positions. These may be positions formerly filled and now temporarily vacant or new positions that the supervisor proposes to add to the payroll. Or they may be positions that the supervisor has no intention of filling but has listed as protection in case of a budgeting emergency. In all *three* cases, these empty slots should be carefully reviewed as possible sources of budget reduction.

▪ *Understaffing.* The opposite of padding is understaffing—failing to budget for the additional salaried personnel that will be needed for proposed expansions of operation. When budgeted increases in revenue are contingent on opening a new department, adding to supervisory, sales, and professional resources, or going to a second or third shift, the salary budget should certainly include the added obligations.

Often only top management has the overview needed to foresee such changes; department heads have a narrower outlook.

▪ *Publicity.* Unintended disclosure about the salary budget can lead to trouble. Budgets, to be sure, need some publicity. No one can work within a budget without knowing what the budget is. At the same time, salary budgets can be a sensitive issue. If it becomes generally known that the salary budget is predicated on workforce reductions or additions—that changes in the organization are an integral part of its assumptions—morale is bound to decline. Disclosure of the line-by-line budgeting of individual salaries can be especially troublesome. Employees infer that the budgeted increases—estimated though they may be—are locked-in certainties. For all these reasons, some firms find it advisable to keep the salary budget confidential and separate from other financial controls.

▪ *Incompleteness.* There are a number of ways in which a salary budget may be made to look smaller than it really is. This can lead to surprises later on if unplanned expenses drive net profit below the budgeted level. Accordingly, the salary budget should be carefully screened to make sure that it includes all possible expenses that act like salaries but that are typically called something else. Salaried overtime pay is a good example. If it is apt to occur, it should be included in the budget.

It should be understood that the salary budget is not an irrevocable commitment. It is a statement of expectations. How well you can live within it depends on a host of external circumstances, not the least of which is actual performance throughout the year in other, nonsalary segments of the total department budget.

Nine Steps to Cost Control

JAMES J. SEMRADEK, JR.

Every manager would like to find ways to cut costs in his or her department. Elaborate cost-reduction programs are often touted, but many fail because they lack one or more of the essential elements to be effective. Here, we'll discuss ten relatively simple steps that any manager can use to effectively implement an in-house cost-reduction program.

The first and most basic step necessary to implement such a program is to identify areas of high cost-reduction potential. This can be done by breaking down costs into major categories. If it costs ten dollars, for example, to manufacture a widget, break that cost down into its major categories: material, labor, and overhead.

Then divide each of these into logical categories. Material costs, for example, might be divided into purchased parts and manufactured parts. Then each of those categories should be broken down into *its* specific parts. These should be listed in descending order of their total cost (unit cost times yearly volume). Finally, the higher priced elements should be analyzed to see whether substituting materials, making modifications in the process, or manufacturing the parts in-house could yield a savings.

This same procedure should be repeated for the other major categories until all significant and readily apparent cost-reduction potential has been identified. The second major step is to list all the things that must be done to achieve a particular savings. If, for example, one of the identified areas of cost-reduction potential is to use a substitute material on a high-volume part, then you should list all the steps necessary to put the substitute material into use. This should be done as completely as possible for all potential cost-reduction areas. As you compile a list of the necessary steps to cut costs, you will also be discovering whether or not the idea is practical. If you begin to see all sorts of hidden costs and problems, you will have to revise your idea or look for other cost-reduction areas.

Measure Savings

Next you should develop a way to measure savings. This will help you determine the effectiveness of each cost-reduction idea. You can use any of several methods to measure savings: pounds per man-hour, cost per unit, cost per square foot, cost per income dollar, and so forth. Choose whatever measure is most appropriate under the circumstances. To make sure the cost-saving measure is used objectively,

Reprinted from *Supervisory Management*, April 1976

let the accounting department approve it and be responsible both for the calculation tracking and for the distribution of measured savings over a period of time.

The fourth step is to review—with key management personnel—the findings generated from the first three steps. It is important for higher management to understand the program completely and make a firm commitment to support it. Once the commitment has been obtained, you should try to involve higher management in the program. In some situations, providing a monthly update may be enough; in others, a key management person might play a very active part in implementing the program. If you aren't sure what level of management involvement is most appropriate in your company, discuss it with your boss.

Establish Implementation Committee

A formal implementation organization—perhaps an implementation action committee—should be established. This committee should include a chairperson who would be responsible for the overall implementation of the project, a key management-team member to provide the clout to break any "log jams" that arise, and as many others as necessary to implement specific segments of the program. The implementation action committee should provide program guidance, track implementation progress, and resolve implementation problems. The following ground rules should keep such a committee running smoothly:

1. The chairperson should be the one responsible for implementing the entire project.
2. A task list should be established to include all tasks required to implement the program, a person responsible for implementing each task, and a completion date for each task.
3. Meetings should be held weekly.
4. Each meeting should have an agenda.
5. No meeting should exceed one hour.
6. A secretary should be appointed and the minutes distributed immediately after each meeting.

These general rules may, of course, need to be modified to fit a particular situation.

Communicate the Program

The sixth step is to communicate the program to all who will be affected. It is critical that all personnel who will be affected in any way by the program become familiar with it. Although this step is extremely important, it is frequently overlooked. If you aren't sure whether a person or department will be affected by the program, it is best to include them in the program communication process, anyway.

The communication process can take many forms. You can schedule a small group meeting in which a short program presentation is made. This gives everyone who will be affected by the program the opportunity to ask questions on an informal basis. By holding these meetings before the program is implemented, you have an opportunity to point out possible problems to be avoided when the program is implemented.

The seventh step is the implementation process. This can be handled quite easily if the first six steps were carried out effectively. However, the implementation process can be very difficult or even impossible if any of the first six steps were overlooked or handled improperly. It is important to begin by implementing a portion of the project that can be achieved easily and to the satisfaction of all personnel. Successful implementation of the first element will demonstrate that tangible results are achievable and will gain support for the program.

Rarely can any plan be implemented without some revisions. So don't hesitate to revise as necessary. The important thing to remember during this eighth step is to communicate revisions to all who will be affected. If written procedures are involved, make sure that they are revised, updated, and communicated to everyone concerned.

Audit the Program's Progress

The ninth step is to periodically audit the program's progress. A meaningful and effective audit can be performed by identifying program "pulse points" and monitoring progress at these points. Distribute a copy of the audit report to key management personnel so that if action is required, the responsible manager will be aware of the need.

During the implementation phase of a major cost-reduction program, many changes are made within a relatively short period of time. Change involves people, and most of us generally resist change. The tenth step, therefore, is to be persistent—especially during the implementation process. Persistence is the final key to effective cost reduction.

Is Your Span of Control Right for You?

DONALD W. DRUMTRA

How many people can you supervise without losing control in your department and without diminishing your ability as a supervisor? How many people can you supervise and still have time to attain your own important objectives? In determining the answers to these questions, remember that just as the hand of man can span only a limited number of notes on the piano, the mind of man can span only a limited number of immediate supervisory contacts. The ability to answer these questions will help you to be a better supervisor and find your optimum span of control.

Your optimum span of control is the number of people that you can supervise and still function efficiently in your job. It is also your most efficient and effective span of control—the one that produces the greatest profit or has the least cost.

The meaning of the term *span of control,* which is about thirty-five years old, is still a subject of discussion among different scholars of management theory. The words themselves, however, have clear meanings: *Span* is the "full extent or reach of anything," and *control* is "the act or power of controlling, dominating, or commanding," according to one dictionary. Thus, the term *span of control* would appear to mean the full extent or reach of command of a supervisor. It signifies the number of personnel (assistants, secretaries, and all other subordinates) directly responsible to him. Span applies to the horizontal reach of the supervisor, and control applies to the direct superior-subordinate relationship.

The supervisor can usually exert some influence on the size of his span of control and his optimum span of control. Yet his influence on the span of control is probably greatest in small business where he is not required to comply with tables of organization, such as the ones that are operative in most governmental agencies. But wherever the supervisor works, there are several considerations that will determine his optimum span of control.

The Supervisor's Time

The first consideration that will determine the supervisor's optimum span of control is the time that he has available to supervise his subordinates. If a high-level supervisor must have nonsupervisory time for planning, coordinating with his peers, and just plain thinking—that time is not available for supervision.

Reprinted from *Supervisory Management,* August 1972

Similarly, the foreman has duties that, though not all of a planning and thinking nature, reduce the time he has available for supervision. He must keep records; make reports; attend meetings; confer with his superior, with staff people, and other department heads. All of this takes time.

Once a realistic determination of the time that must be spent in nonsupervisory work has been made, the time available for supervision can be easily determined. (Total time less nonsupervisory time yields supervisory time.) Once the time available for supervision is determined, then the physical limitation of the number of subordinates may be determined.

For example, if a supervisor has found that his time available for supervision is 20 hours per week, and the time that he must spend in discussion with each subordinate is four hours per week, then the total number of subordinates he may have is five ($20 \div 4 = 5$). If, on the other hand, the subordinates take only two hours each, the total number may be increased to ten ($10 = 20 \div 2$).

The application of this approach is not as easy as it may first appear, for although the average amount of time available for supervision per week may be determined without too much difficulty, the amount of time required for the supervision of each subordinate is considerably more difficult to determine. Various factors affect this time. By using various management techniques, such as holding discussions with more than one subordinate at a time, the supervisor could reduce the average weekly time for supervision of each subordinate to a very small amount.

Amount of Direction Required

One of the basic considerations for determining the time required to supervise each subordinate is the amount of direction that must be given him. This is dependent not only on the job, but on the subordinate's ability and motivation to do the job. It is easy to supervise a large number of subordinates who do routine jobs, but it is difficult to ensure that new jobs are done correctly. A group of subordinates whose jobs are repetitive would require little supervision once the job is learned.

This is often the case in such offices as the orders section of the Government Printing Office, where clerical personnel are required to take public orders and send out the appropriate document. Once the task is learned, there is little requirement for supervision. Assuming that there are 20 hours available for supervision per week and, say, 15 minutes for average supervision per employee per week (four employees per hour), a supervisor could easily supervise 80 routine jobs ($20 \times 4 = 80$).

The Nature of the Task

Though what is routine for one employee may not be routine for another with less ability, jobs may be made easier by several methods. One method is to divide the tasks into small units and assign a group of similar units to each employee. Such a method is used extensively in production-line factories. Another method is to keep employees in the same or similar jobs once a task is learned so the learning process will not have to be repeated. A third method is to issue clear instructions on how to do the job. Regardless of the method that is being used, it is clear that the more repetitive and routine subordinates' jobs are, the less time a manager will have to spend on supervision, the more subordinates he may effectively supervise, and the larger his span of control will be.

Closely coupled with the routinization of a task is its difficulty. As a job becomes more difficult, it becomes harder to describe in a written directive. The less direction that is provided the worker, the more originality he must use to accomplish the tasks assigned, and the more responsibility he must assume in using his own methods.

If all his subordinates were performing similar tasks, the supervisor would not have a complex job; but as job diversity and the differences between each subordinate's job increase, the supervisor must know more and more in order to supervise effectively.

The Supervisor's Knowledge

For the above reason, the more thoroughly a supervisor has to know the jobs of his people, the fewer subordinates he can effectively manage. In this case, a supervisor's optimum span of control is in inverse proportion to how well he must know the mechanics involved in each subordinate's job.

The traditional measure of a supervisor's ability to supervise has been his knowledge of the tasks of the people under him. Managers have always believed that the person who had the most detailed knowledge of all aspects of his department's operations was the person who could utilize the most subordinates. But this is most often not the case.

The foreman, who must be able to do all or most of the jobs that his subordinates are doing in order to keep their respect, can handle only a small number of workers. It is at higher levels, where the supervisor is required to know only the general nature of a specialist's job in order to supervise his work, that his span of control will increase. Depending upon the supervisor's total general knowledge of his subordinates' tasks and the unit's goals, a higher-level supervisor's optimum span will be larger because of the less detailed knowledge he must have of his subordinates' tasks.

Stability of Tasks

Another factor influencing the difficulty of supervising subordinates is the stability of their tasks, or how often their jobs change. If the subordinate's work involves constant change, as does the job of a soldier in the front line of a battlefield, the number of subordinates assigned to the supervisor will have to be reduced to allow effective supervision. In most businesses, which operate in a peacetime environment, this factor requires little consideration. But in an organization established for emergency situations—like the fire department, police department, and ambulance patrols—there will be smaller optimum spans of control than in regular industry because of the constant change of the work environment and the change in the details of a subordinate's tasks.

The Supervisor's Ability

Some management scholars believe that the physical and psychological capabilities of the supervisor, more than any other consideration, have the greatest effect on his optimum span of control. The supervisor's ability reflects how well he is able to get his people to accomplish the tasks that they have been assigned. The importance given this ability has increased as theories of management have progressed from the mechanical to the humanistic.

Included in this consideration of the supervisor's ability is his "span of attention." The emotional aspects of attention—the ability of the supervisor to deal with interruptions that occur when quite a variety of persons come to him for consultation, discussion, and decision—are important factors in determining his span-of-attention capability. It will be affected by how well he can work with and through his subordinates. And this becomes more and more important as one moves from the lower to the higher levels of an organization.

A supervisor who is used to and can work well with people will have a much wider optimum span of control than one who does not. Very little ability is required to enforce detailed policy if it is clearly and concisely written and available. But the ability to encourage greater output or to convince a subordinate not to make the same mistake again and again takes great skill in handling people.

The Supervisor's Attitude

The supervisor's attitudes or convictions determine what kind of manager he will be, and often may mask his actual ability. A supervisor who believes that efficient management necessarily calls for few subordinates—because he believes that human beings have a limited span of attention—will try to limit the number of subordinates he has. He will probably become frustrated if many problems are given to him simultaneously.

On the other hand, there is the high-level manager who cherishes the misleading image of the "efficient executive." He sees his value as a businessman measured by the number of people reporting to him directly. He likes the sense of power and self-importance generated by a queue on his doormat. Indeed, there may be a vast difference between the number of subordinates that a supervisor believes he should supervise and the actual number he does supervise or can supervise.

Relationships With Subordinates

Along with considering the influence of a supervisor's ability and attitude on his optimum span of control, he should also consider the influence of the relationship that he has with each of his subordinates. When the type of work requires that his subordinates coordinate with each other, then he may also have to give consideration to the relationship *among* his subordinates.

For instance, if a supervisor has a direct single relationship with each of his subordinates, then he will have three direct single relationships with three subordinates—one with each.

He can also have a direct relationship with each group of his subordinates and/or with one of his subordinates in the presence of other subordinates. Thus, a supervisor with three subordinates (A, B, and C) would have a minimum of four direct group relationships: with A and B, with B and C; with A and C; and with A, B, and C together. He would have a maximum of nine direct group relationships: with A with (or in the presence of) B; with A with C; with A with B and C; with B with A; with B with C; with B with A and C; with C with A; with C with B; and finally, with C with A and B. To top it all off, he must consider the direct cross-relationships that his subordinates have with each other.

The purpose of considering all these groups is that they help the supervisor coordinate his workers at the operative level. They also help solve the dilemma of the limited span of control, because when subordinates can be considered as a group, rather than as individuals, the span of control can become indefinitely extensible.

In jobs where all subordinates perform the same task, for instance, coordination may be handled in mass meetings where the supervisor discusses new policy and common problems with all or most of his subordinates simultaneously, and where subordinates may exchange information common to all through the question-and-answer type of discussion. This type of coordination takes very little of the supervisor's time per employee, and allows the supervisor to ignore many of the specific interrelationships among his subordinates.

If, however, the supervisor must discuss problems individually with each of his subordinates, and is dependent upon each subordinate's capability and inclination to interchange information with his peers, then the supervisor must be much more concerned with relationships among his subordinates. These considerations are essential for a supervisor to make a realistic appraisal of his span of control.

A Supervisor's Assistants

The final consideration that we should look at in determining a supervisor's span of control is the assistance that he is provided. His assistance comprises all the personal and staff assistants who are assigned to him.

The first assistant introduced into any organization is usually the secretary or clerk who is assigned to take care of the routine and administrative work of the supervisor in order to allow him more time to supervise and perform the other functions that his job requires. The normal secretary has little *de jure* authority over the supervisor's other subordinates and is not directly connected with the organization's objectives. For this reason, he or she is not counted in the supervisor's span-of-*action* control, which refers to the number of subordinates a supervisor has who carry out the actions required to achieve the overall goals of his unit. But the secretary is considered part of his span-of-*assistance* control, which refers to the number of subordinates a supervisor has who assist him in the supervision of his action subordinates or assist him in his administrative duties. But, if the secretary saves time for the supervisor, he or she can increase the supervisor's *optimum* span-of-action control.

Often, several personal assistants will be assigned to a supervisor, thus further increasing his span of administrative control. As the number of assistants increase, his optimum span-of-action control is also increased, because of the time that he will be able to save. There is a point of diminishing returns, however, where the addition of more assistants and the accompanying increase in span-of-assistance control will not change or even reduce the span-of-action control. This point is reached when the supervisor must devote a significant portion of his time to supervising his assistants.

The Staff Assistant

A personal assistant's duties will require formal work only with and through the supervisor, with little coordination with his other subordinates. If, however, the personal assistant were granted organizational authority and were required to coordinate his work with the supervisor's other workers, then the assistant would become a staff assistant.

The staff assistant has a more complex effect on the span of control than does the personal assistant. He or she may be assigned to many places in the organizational structure and provide help in as many areas. The staff assistant is counted in the manager's span-of-action control, because he or she directly contributes to the accomplishment of the organization's goals and provides assistance to the manager. In fact, such assistants can increase the supervisor's optimum span-of-action control by several subordinates.

Several staff assistants can be employed to provide assistance in separate areas under a supervisor's control. In the military, for instance, there is a group of staff officers called the general staff. Within the general staff organization, there is a great need for coordination among staff officers—so the military places an assistant called the chief of staff between the commander and the staff officers in order to assist them with the coordination.

If the chief of staff has direct responsibility for staff assistance and has the associated authority over the staff, then the commander's span of control will include only the chief of staff (and other subordinates) while the other officers will come under the chief of staff's span of control. If, on the other hand, the chief of staff's responsibilty is strictly one of coordination, then all the staff officers would count in the commander's span of control. In such an organization, a span of 20 is not uncommon.

A *de jure* line-and-staff organization may not be one in reality. This happens when the staff assistants assume authority over the line subordinates. In this case, the distinctions between span-of-line authority and span-of-staff authority become quite difficult to determine—and the determination of optimum span of control becomes very complex. But one thing is clear: Up to a certain point, the addition of personal and staff assistants increases both the span of action and the span of administrative control of the supervisor.

Part XII

PROBLEM SOLVING/ DECISION MAKING

Problem-Solving Techniques That Always Cause Problems

FREDERICK HAAS

During the past few years the business scene has undergone radical changes that require comparable adjustments in executive behavior. It seems that life has become one big headache for the executive, and creative problem solving is one ability that he or she cannot do without.

Some executives use their creativity in a way never imagined by the management textbooks, looking not for solutions but stalling tactics in dealing with problems. These executives do not want to play by the rules. They usually try to avoid stressful experiences at all costs. After all, they reason, why should one face the challenges of organizational life unnecessarily? Even when in Rome, why do as the Romans do?

For those individuals, I have chosen eight situations showing how to achieve success while avoiding the unpleasant necessity of making decisions and applying oneself to the job. I am pleased to report that the techniques described have been battle-tested under actual corporate conditions. You have probably seen them used.

Reprinted from *Supervisory Management*, September 1979

Situation #1

You have compiled a vast amount of unrelated information for a research project at great cost to the company. You know that some of it must be of value, yet you're unwilling or unable to sort it out. What do you do?

Solution. Simply reproduce all the data and mail them to as many people as you can, along with a request for comment on terms pertinent to their areas of expertise. You are certain to get something back more or less useful and, anyway, this gets you off the hook with your boss. When he or she asks for a progress report, you merely state that you haven't yet received feedback. Inasmuch as some of your addressees will probably throw the material away, you never will. Thus you stall indefinitely.

Situation #2

You have been asked to provide certain information that you either don't have, or have questions about. You are supposed to be an authority on this subject and cannot avoid responding. What do you do?

Solution. Fortunately, there are several ways to approach this problem.

First, write the material out in your usual indistinct, garbled, illegible style. If top management can interpret what you wrote and solve the problem, you're a hero. If it compounds the problem, you can claim that your report was misread.

Second, provide the information over the telephone, also using your best garbled manner. The results are the same as with the memo.

Third, provide the information but credit some other source. This is the least risky alternative, but you cannot be as big a hero merely by quoting another source.

Situation #3

You are blowing the deadline on your report, memo, or forecast. You need help.

Solution. The most common solution to this problem is to finish the project whenever you can and date it so that it appears to have made the deadline. You will claim, of course, that some irresponsible third party held it up.

For variety's sake, you can challenge the technical validity of the request for the report or claim you lost the request or never received it. You then ask for an extension on the deadline.

Still another possibility is to wait until the person requesting the project contacts you, then claim you sent your response and accuse that person of losing it. This forces the individual to ransack his or her files and gives you the additional time necessary to finish the work. You then send the individual a file copy bearing an earlier date, just to prove that you mailed out the original some time ago.

Situation #4

Your boss is out of town and you are acting in his or her place. This means that if the work goes well, the boss will be congratulated on making a good choice; if it goes poorly, you are the "fall guy." You have managed up to this point to avoid making a decision, but suddenly several members of the department come storming into your office with a problem and you are trapped. What do you do now?

Solution. This problem has only one acceptable solution. You cannot use your natural impulse to stall until the boss returns, since he or she may be gone a week. You must handle this situation exactly as the boss would. To start, you ask for all the details and reflect for a few moments. Then you bark out a firm decision. It doesn't matter which way you decide as long as you don't bother working too hard at it. Just be fast and firm. You bide your time and before anyone can act on your decision, you reverse it. You must do this in the same firm, decisive manner in which you made the original decision, stating that circumstances have altered conditions (whatever that means). The advantage of this technique is obvious. You are given credit for making two firm, executive-style decisions, and the organization hasn't moved one inch off dead center.

Situation #5

Due to the inevitable shuffling that always seems to be taking place in your company, you get a new boss. The boss calls a staff meeting and you get the unmistakable impression that he or she expects the staff (including you) to get the work done. You have managed to establish a comfortable situation in which there is plenty of time for social activity, personal errands, and some productive work at a leisurely pace, and you don't want to have it disturbed. What's your solution to the problem?

Solution. This one is a piece of cake for someone with your resourcefulness. You simply collect everything you have done for the last couple of years, have your secretary type up covering memos bearing today's date and requiring the new boss's signature, and present the stack to the boss as the week's output from your department. As you drop the stack on his or her desk, you casually inquire if he or she really intends to review all this paperwork every week. If the answer is no, you've got it made; if the answer is yes, you just wait a few days and get your transfer request out.

Situation #6

You are called upon to chair a meeting because you are the authority on the topic under discussion. Unfortunately, due to the pressing nature of other details (you have a new secretary), you have not kept informed on the topic. What can you do?

Solution. Convene the meeting and make some opening remarks. You must know something about the subject. If not, read something. Make a controversial statement in order to compel someone to challenge you. If necessary, reverse yourself. Once someone has taken up the challenge, retaliate, drawing other members into the melee. As soon as the meeting has fallen apart satisfactorily, adjourn it, stating that obviously nothing can be accomplished in such chaos. You then report to your superiors that these individuals simply are not able to get results.

Situation #7

Unfortunately, you are not making enough money to live in the style to which you think you should be accustomed. What can you do?

Solution. This one is so obvious I almost omitted it. It's laughably simple: You merely purchase the things you want on credit by puffing up your position and income as required to obtain the credit (companies usually do not release salary information). If the creditors begin to close in on you, remind them that they surely wouldn't want to do anything to injure the reputation of the company you work for. If they get nasty and threaten in writing to take legal action, take the letters to your boss and point out that the company can be spared embarrassment if your salary is boosted significantly.

Situation #8

On returning to your office you find a message asking you to call someone you are particularly eager to avoid because you do not have the information you promised him or her.

Solution. You determine when the individual will be out of his or her office and return the call, leaving your name and—this is important—an incorrect extension. This accomplishes two things. First, it gets you off the hook. After all, you returned the call; it's not your fault that he or she wasn't there. Second, it gives the individual a cold trail to follow in trying to find you.

A Final Word

I'm certain that these examples and suggestions haven't solved all the problems that managers will encounter, but that is not my intention. They are offered only as a guide to getting an individual's thinking into gear. If you want your boss to think that you're an old hand at solving difficult problems and tackling assignments while you're only applying cosmetic surgery to situations that require serious and thoughtful consideration, then consider these solutions. Otherwise, don't! Buckpassing and procrastination have always had their places in business—but of course, they have no place in the management style of a good supervisor.

How to Make Different Kinds of Decisions

PETER G. KIRBY

Management, to paraphrase several definitions, is the allocation of scarce human and physical resources in ways designed to achieve objectives. As a tool of management, decision making permits the best selection among alternatives for the efficient, effective allocation of limited human and other resources. These scarce resources, physical and human, are what we need to achieve results. Physical resources encompass such objects as buildings, supplies, and specific items that we need in order to serve our customers. Human resources, of course, are the people who make up the team—a team that, with our help and assistance, will achieve desired results for the organization. The decisions that managers make are the moving forces that accomplish goals and objectives through the proper utilization of scarce resources.

Decisions come in varying sizes, shapes, and complexities. Whether one person can teach another how to make decisions is questionable. As managers, however, we can certainly give people the opportunity to make decisions. It seems only fair that if we can't teach others how to make effective decisions, we must give them the opportunity to fail—without danger of retribution—in making decisions. Once decisions have been made, both good and bad, we can sit down with the person who made them to (1) categorize them and (2) examine the approach and process used in making them. In this way, we develop a coaching situation designed to help individual employees—particularly those with managerial promise—improve their future decisions.

The purpose of this article is to define the main types of decisions we make and develop a framework for categorizing them. Once we are able to categorize decisions, we have a method of (1) helping others evaluate their decisions, (2) discussing methods of improvement, and (3) reinforcing good practices.

Decision making is most often identified with problem situations. To start any discussion on decision making, one must arrive at the proper identification of the problem—being as specific as possible. Obviously, it is difficult to make a decision about something unless we understand the exact nature of the problem.

As managers, our responsibilities are (1) to know our objectives; (2) to be able to see variations among paths that lead to these objectives; (3) to be able to identify alternatives for correcting the deviations involved; and (4) to look at the implications of these alternatives before making the final decision. Once this process is complete, we then decide.

Reprinted from *Supervisory Management*, February 1977

Categories of Decisions

Let's start by defining the various types of decisions we make. Four major types of decisions are categorized as: (1) considered decisions, (2) operational decisions, (3) swallow-hard decisions, and (4) ten-second decisions. Although there are similarities among the categories, each has distinctive characteristics.

1. *Considered decisions.* Considered decisions have a major effect on the total operation time—time needed to gather and analyze facts and data before the final alternative is selected. A considered decision, for example, may involve the purchase of new equipment. Or it may involve an addition to or deletion from the company's products or services. It may be even more important: the redesign of an entire building or plant.

Considered decisions are not the kind we make every day; rather, they tend to be complicated and call for considerable reflection. In addition to a lot of personal thought, they require interaction with others, because the perceptions and ideas of other people often provide multiple alternatives that help in approaching the problem situation.

In seeking this kind of help, we ask associates for their opinions, we sound out their feelings, we identify what they know about the subject. We might turn to experienced people to find out how they feel or how they see the situation—or we might involve people with little or no experience in order to get a fresh point of view. Peter Drucker suggests that this kind of decision requires dissent. If you have a staff, they should be brought together and encouraged to poke holes in the alternatives. Such dissent often leads to the appropriate decision. In fact, the final decision that is made as a result of this interaction may have little or no relationship to the original alternatives.

Each alternative should be scrutinized in terms of its implementation problem. To get a lead on these, ask the following questions: "What are the possible reactions of the people who will be involved?" "Does this decision mean more people, fewer people, people with newer skills?" "How is it going to affect our customers?" "How is it going to affect our vendors; should they be involved?" It is not enough to look merely at the *internal* implications of considered decisions. At an early stage, the implications for those who are involved with the organization in one way or another must be dealt with.

Obviously, then, a considered decision requires time—time to find alternatives, to seek other opinions, to get dissent, to determine implementation problems. Incorporating these elements in a decision-making situation leads to appropriate decisions that can be implemented with minimum trouble and maximum probability of success.

2. *Operational decisions.* Operational decisions are those made practically every day. Some of these decisions, in fact, may be made at approximately the same time each day, and they may prevent problems as well as solve them.

Each day, for example, we must make decisions ensuring that we provide the services expected by our customers. Once made, these decisions are either implemented that day or are scheduled for implementation later—perhaps providing for the supplies needed to meet our needs tomorrow. Input for such decisions may come from several sources. In setting daily production levels for subordinates, for example, we consider historical data as well as our production needs. We also take inventories of our supplies and products. On the basis of such data we put in orders to provide for our projected needs.

From a management development point of view, operational decisions give subordinates an excellent opportunity to practice decision making. A subordinate, for instance, may draw up production needs. After these projections are verified and discussed between manager and subordinate, the decision is implemented. The same approach may be applied to taking inventories and ordering products or supplies. After review and discussion with the manager, subordinates can eventually make decisions by themselves. Periodic reviews and later discussions reinforce good decisions and reveal areas in which other directions might have been appropriate.

After several "practice" situations in which decisions are planned out and discussed before being implemented, the subordinate can be released to make the choices. When, for example, the decision concerns replacing an employee who called in sick for his scheduled shift, the subordinate can determine whether a replacement is needed and, if so, how one can be secured. The manager may then review the process to that point, allow the decision to be made, or correct and coach as necessary. Once the manager is confident of the subordinate's decisions in this area, he or she can delegate that responsibility.

Operational decisions are frequently characterized by consistency in timing. Some are made almost on schedule—often on a daily basis, such as decisions concerning production levels. They are vital to the smooth flow of daily business and have immediate as well as short-term impact. From a developmental standpoint, they provide good framework for "practicing" the decision-making process.

3. *Swallow-hard decisions.* Swallow-hard decisions are ones that are often personally uncomfortable to make because they may result in discomfort or uneasiness for subordinates or others. These can be generally classified as decisions impacting interpersonal relationships—that is, decisions affecting relationships among people in an organization. But although this kind of decision makes us feel uncomfortable, it is a kind of decision that is necessary—the kind that we, as managers, are paid to make.

Consider a decision on changing the way employees are scheduled. Say that a manager's boss looks at the schedule and decides that scheduling should be done in a different manner. Because of the subordinate manager's personal knowledge of the organization and its people, he may feel that this new approach would be disastrous to morale.

A swallow-hard decision is called for. As subordinate in the boss-subordinate relationship, the manager has the obligation to tell his boss that the new plan is not a good one. The manager also has the obligation to give specific reasons why the new schedule would be harmful. In this case it might be the loss of people because of scheduling problems, a lowering of morale, a lowering of service, or a lowering of product quality.

Once the supervisor has presented his position, along with back-up reasons, the manager has three alternatives. He can say: (1) "I see your position and we will not change the schedule" (perhaps a swallow-hard decision itself), or (2) "I see your position and I think we should modify my original idea and change the schedule in this manner," or (3) "I see your position, but we are going to do it my way."

If the boss opts for the third choice, then we again have a swallow-hard decision. The new swallow-hard decision is that, although the manager doesn't totally agree with the third choice, he has given his opinion and ideas, and they have been rejected. The manager now has the obligation to swallow hard and carry out the decision as outlined by his boss.

We see then that a swallow-hard decision is one that usually involves interpersonal relationships—one that causes discomfort for the person making the decision as well as for those affected by the decision. There is often an element of personal risk in these decisions—but despite this risk (or perhaps because of it), we are paid as managers to make swallow-hard decisions.

4. *Ten-second decisions.* Ten-second decisions are ones we make during daily operation. They are the decisions that bring our operation together, keep it ready for the customer, keep it alive and running well. The overriding factor in a ten-second decision is the pressure to make it quickly.

This is the kind of decision called for when employees request a day or an hour off—because they often must know immediately. Rarely do they say, "I need tomorrow off, but you don't have to give me your answer until I leave tonight." The urgency of such a decision places it in the ten-second category.

Ten-second decisions are significantly different from snap decisions. Snap decisions are those that come without *any* thought. As Peter Drucker would say, snap decisions come with rapid fire and hit many targets—but rarely solve the real problem.

Before we make a ten-second decision, we must first determine whether the situation really requires one. Basically, we are asking, "I know this person wants the answer now—but is the answer potentially of such consequence that I should delay answering the request?" Too many times the precedents we set—and the rules and guidelines we inherit—result from ten-second decisions that perhaps should have been considered or are operational decisions.

Second, if we do decide to make a ten-second decision, then we should determine the major objective of that decision. Before we leap in and "solve the problem," we should first determine what we are trying to accomplish with this ten-second decision. Before we try to do anything, we should know why we are trying to do it, what results we are trying to obtain, and how it will affect the total operation.

Third, once we have identified our objectives, we must determine what alternatives are available. Here are two questions to ask: "What are the different ways in which we can approach this ten-second decision?" "What are the various answers available for the different directions I can go in?" All decisions, we said earlier, are selections of alternatives involved in allocating our scarce resources, physical and human. That means there are many alternatives, many ways we can fit the resources together. That means there are different selections we can make concerning these scarce resources. We must give serious thought to the alternatives available before we jump in and make a choice.

Fourth, once we have considered alternatives, the last question concerns implications. That is, what could go wrong in the future if we pursue a given course of action? As we mentioned earlier, many precedents spring from decisions made "on the spot." To avoid unwanted precedents, we should ask the following questions: "What could possibly go wrong in the future if I grant this person this request?" "Will it set a precedent?" "How will it affect my operation later?"

Obviously, it takes more than ten seconds to seek out the above information—but it's not necessary to ponderously ask each and every question in each and every situation. We can, however, train ourselves to consider these four areas when responding to problem situations that require quick decisions. If we do this automatically, we can shift from making snap decisions to making sound ten-second decisions.

Application of Model

These four categories of decisions are handy ones in helping us make the decisions needed for the smooth operation of an organization. By periodically stopping and examining the decisions we make, then categorizing them as suggested, we may improve the batting average of our decisions. Such categories are also useful in developing potential managers by improving or reinforcing their decision-making abilities. Periodically, we can sit down with subordinates, categorize the decisions they have made over a specific period, look at the results in terms of objectives, and review with them what other alternatives might have been selected.

A Realistic Look at Decision Making

ROBARD Y. HUGHES

A great mystique has grown up around the act of making a decision. According to one way of thinking, the decision is all-important in business. A manager sits alone in an office, valiantly considering various alternative courses of action. After quickly absorbing a mountain of computer-produced information, the individual eliminates the least feasible of his or her options. At last, our executive chooses the one clear-cut plan that is best designed to achieve the set objectives. The manager communicates his or her decision; and at once a complex of human and inanimate machinery springs into action to carry it out.

This is a dramatic and attractive picture. The only trouble with it is that it lacks any connection with reality.

In fact, decision making is more likely to happen this way. A harried executive, with ten other matters on his or her mind and with a constantly ringing telephone, struggles to make sense out of some stacks of information that may or may not be relevant. Our real-life manager wishes to know more about the actual situation, so he or she talks with some subordinates, each of whom gives the executive a carefully censored, one-sided view of the situation, the objectives, and the means at hand. Finally, the manager makes a delaying, compromise "decision" that does not look very forthright or very incisive. And his or her operation struggles along pretty much the way it has been going.

The Reality

There are certain things that should be faced about the topic of decision making. Most business decisions are not hard-edged and clear-cut; they are slippery and amorphous. Because the information explosion confronts us with vast reams of data—and the infinite opportunity to collect more data—we often find ourselves inundated with facts to such an extent that we are unable to see any clear pattern that would help in making the decision. Indeed, the more unlimited the information-generating machinery becomes, the more dubious a guide it may be to the manager.

Reliance on colleagues and subordinates for facts is an equally shaky proposition. The higher a manager moves in the chain of command, the more isolated he or she is from the ways in which things actually work. When the manager asks people for information, they tell him or her what they want the person to hear or what they think the person wants to hear. Few subordinates—even those with the greatest desire to be objective—will go all-out to tell the boss anything that places themselves in an unflattering

Reprinted from *Supervisory Management*, January 1980

light. Policy-level executives are always lamenting the fact that those who report to them do not "tell it like it is." "Subordinates are unwilling to criticize and disagree." "They don't come forward with divergent and innovative ideas." "They fail to display 'guts.'" (One vice-president, taxed with this charge, answered, "I've got guts, but I don't want to see them all over the boardroom. I've got a job to hang onto.")

No matter how objectively an executive may react to bad news, and no matter how nice a person he or she may be, the power the individual possesses scares those in a reporting relationship. So the information our manager gets from this source is biased, incomplete, and sometimes even untruthful.

The Value of Hunches

When faced with a problem, most managers with any experience and insight form immediate impressions. They quickly generate hunches about what should be done. But we are urged nowadays to mistrust our hunches. To act on instinct is not scientific; it is flying by the seat of the pants. And so executives may sorrowfully turn their eyes away from the solution that occurred to them instantly, undertaking instead a long and torturous trek along the ramifications of the decision tree. They receive more and more bits of information. They wander farther and farther from the initial hunch. And in the end they make an "objective" decision based on incomplete and imperfectly understood data—a decision that is not nearly as good as the one they would have made if they had acted on the hunch.

A manager should not permit his or her healthy instincts to be "educated" out. We cannot make ourselves into computers that receive input through the eyes and ears, flash and whir, then emit printouts through the mouth. Human beings have certain advantages over computers. When a person has been working and managing in a field for some years, his or her "hunches" are more than just random flights of fancy. They may be instantaneous efforts by the brain to rifle through multitudinous files, pull out the pertinent experiences and ideas, collate them, and provide a faster answer. Hunches are the product of instinct, experience, perceptiveness, and intelligence. It would be foolhardy to act on a hunch without checking; but it is wasteful to totally ignore the "flash" answer from the brain when it is confronted with a problem.

Action!

Decisions are thought to be all-important. In truth, however, the objective "rightness" of a decision may not be nearly as important as the vigor with which it is implemented. A manager may go through an intense decision-making process. He or she may concentrate on the pure, unadulterated facts and may pursue the most logical and effective alternative with ruthless objectivity. Our manager may then make his or her decision and begin to implement the choice.

Nothing happens. The organization does not respond to the decision. The manager has learned that a decision may stand by itself as a beautiful piece of thinking, but if it is not accepted by those who are supposed to carry it out, it will not work. Sometimes the problem may lie in the way in which the decision is communicated. More often it is a matter of the subordinates not "buying" the course of action and giving it less-than-maximum support.

Since decisiveness is such a highly prized management trait, it is no wonder that there has arisen a numerical approach to rating managers that involves adding up the decisions made. Aggressive and ambitious executives set out early in their careers to show that they are "not afraid to make decisions." Not only do they make fast decisions when confronted with problems, they seem to go out of their way to find decisions to make. Harry Truman's most celebrated remark is "The buck stops here." Fine. But some managers are buck-grabbers. They want to make every decision. It is almost as if a willingness to let a decision ride were a confession of poor management ability.

Managers, by and large, make far too many decisions. Among the decisions they choose to make, there are numerous ones that should be made at lower levels. This is not just because subordinates should be trained in decision making and allowed to participate in the management process, although these are worthy objectives. Another, more practical reason is that these executives are more likely to be wrong on the *small* decisions, those that could be made at lower levels, than on the large ones. These managers have inevitably drifted away from the immediate workplace. Their feel for trends and people is often second-hand. Small developments in technology and methods have totally escaped them. So when these higher-level managers make decisions about things with which their subordinates are more intimately acquainted, they frequently go astray. And this is not good not only because it costs time and money but because it takes a large bite out of their credibility. If the boss makes a mistake about something this small, subordinates ask, how can he or she be right about the really big things?

Actually the boss is more apt to be right about the "really big things," because the factors involved in them are more closely attuned to recent experiences and thinking. But, unfortunately, the workers don't see that.

There are a lot of decisions that should be referred down the line. There are other decisions that shouldn't be made at all, at least not right away.

In certain quarters it is considered heresy to counsel delay in decision making. Speed is thought to be essential. The manager who says, "Let's wait a while," is dismissed as a procrastinator. It is the person who jumps in and decides *something*—even if it is wrong—who receives the kudos. Consider how often we hear a manager boast about a bum decision. "Yes," he says, "I blew it, but at least I had the guts to take a stand." The other person, the one who wanted to wait until the dust had settled, probably had a more constructive idea—but not as dramatic. His or her caution runs counter to the cult of action.

A manager should always ask himself or herself if it is necessary to make a decision at all and, if so, must the decision be made now. When a situation is falling apart rapidly, obviously something must be done fast. But there are also times when we can see looming clouds but cannot yet gauge whether they will thicken into a bad storm or ultimately blow over. Is a decision necessary then and there? One school of thought says "Yes." But is this right? Sometimes any decision made when a decision is not necessary—no matter how well-thought-out the decision may be—is harmful. In medicine there is a term "iatrogenic intervention." This is when you go to the doctor, and he makes you sicker. A few years ago the Giants pitcher Juan Marichal contracted a fungus infection and sought treatment. The infection would have kept him out of action. The penicillin treatment almost killed him. He missed most of the season. Marichal had a problem, all right; but he would have been a lot better off with delay and less decisive action.

Sometimes conditions correct themselves, and decisions are not needed. This is not an exciting approach to the subject. It is not dramatic. But it makes sense. When a decision carries a high-risk factor, and when the situation it is supposed to correct is not getting precipitously worse, it is often better to wait. I am not advocating the ducking of necessary decisions by applying the rationale that "more information" must be sought (it's always possible to seek more information). But it is undeniable that not every decision must be made rapidly and on the spot. Some of the biggest goofs in business history have resulted from some of the most firm-jawed decisive approaches.

Overreaction

We sometimes try to relieve the nagging pressure of deadlines and relatively minor inconveniences by taking large and unjustified chances. (Why else would a driver—delayed in a traffic jam—break free and do 50 in a 25-mile-an-hour zone?) Badgered by petty annoyances, we magnify the odds in our favor and minimize the risk of failure. Don't do it. And don't let your subordinates do it either. Specifically:

■ *Watch for signs of dangerous impatience or time-stress in yourself and your subordinates.* The individual who has been working for some time on a painstaking and intricate job may be getting impatient enough to do something rash. The worker who is laboring to complete a project against a rigid deadline may be about to cut some corners that will put the project in jeopardy. Let the workers know you understand the pressure they are under.

■ *Emphasize the cost of major mistakes.* There are some risks that are just too great to warrant running—no matter what the apparent odds against "something happening." The supervisor who runs a machine at too high a speed may be right when he says that chances are nothing will go wrong; but when the result of a breakdown will be a major calamity, the risk can never be justified.

■ *Give workers (or yourself) clear and simple cautions.* "Don't—under any circumstances—overload a machine." "Don't do anything that might rock the boat at a critical point in the negotiations."

■ *See if the strain can be eased.* If a project is becoming dangerously boring, can a change of pace be found? If a deadline is leading to excessive risk-taking, what will it cost in resources and money to provide help in meeting the deadline?

■ *Above all, realize that we all share the tendency to skate on thin ice sometimes.* Long experience, skill, and a previous record of reliability provide no guarantees against sudden and rash risk-taking. Under provocation, anyone may do it, including you. Knowing this, you are better prepared to spot the conditions under which it may happen and take steps to prevent it.

When you or a subordinate feels pressured, irritated, or impatient, watch out. This is the wrong time for a decision to be made.

Making a Decision

There are a variety of step-by-step decision-making plans recommended to executives. The particular one you follow is less important than your understanding of the steps in the process in which you are involved. Let's look at these eight steps to decision making.

1. *Define the problem.* State primary and secondary aims. Examine thoroughly the things to be accomplished. Make them broad and general.

2. *Redefine the problem in terms of specific objectives.* Translate the general aims into quantitative goals—in terms of time, dollars, units. Intersperse the main goals with subgoals.

3. *Ask how your own goals fit in with overall organizational goals.* For example, it would not be wise to give a heavy buildup to an area that the company will be phasing out. Conform your goals to the overall objective of the organization.

4. *Line up alternatives.* Judge them against your initial instinctive choice, if you have one. Consider all reasonable alternatives objectively. Look ahead to the foreseeable consequences of each alternative.

5. *Review resources.* Each alternative takes time, manpower, and money. How much do you have to apply? How much will you have six months from now? Make a detailed inventory of resources needed for each alternative and compare them with what you have and what you will have.

6. *List and evaluate the consequences that will ensue if the decision turns out to be incorrect.* Do this for each possible decision—including the decision to do nothing.

7. *Make an effort to presell the decision.* Don't kid subordinates about their participation in the decision, but talk with key people about the alternatives. Get relevant information and opinions, and try to draw out objections.

8. *Decide—and implement.* By word and action, let everyone know of your continuing commitment to the plan.

Decision making is not a mystical rite. It is an important part of executive practice but not necessarily the paramount function of a manager. Still, the manager who knows which decision to make—and realizes the limitations within which he or she makes them—will be a more effective manager.

Individual vs. Group Approaches
To Decision Making

JOHN J. SHERWOOD and FLORENCE M. HOYLMAN

A well-known joke belittling the effectiveness of groups says, "The camel is a horse designed by a committee." This statement reflects the attitude that groups often fail to use common sense in accomplishing their tasks. Nevertheless, from corporate boards of directors to fraternity membership committees, groups are used for problem solving and decision making by almost all organizations.

Although the use of groups is frequent and the dissatisfaction with the products of group efforts is widespread, managers often lack clear and explicit criteria by which to decide when to assign a problem to a group for solution and when to assign it to an individual. The purpose of this article is to provide such a straightforward set of criteria for determining whether a group or an individual is likely to produce better results on a given task. In addition, for those instances when the task is referred to a group, we offer some guidelines on how to manage the group for the most effective outcomes.

Choosing Between a Group and an Individual

There are five factors to consider whenever one is faced with deciding whether to assign a particular task to an individual or solution or to a group of people for their joint consideration: the nature of the task itself; the importance of general acceptance of, or commitment to, a solution for its implementation; the value placed on the quality of the decision; the competence, investment, and role in implementation of each person involved; and the anticipated operating effectiveness of the group, especially its leadership.

The nature of the problem or task. The nature of the task itself is the first and most important criterion for any manager to consider when deciding what to do with a problem. Research tells us that individuals are more effective than groups as idea generators and as creative problem solvers. In other words, individuals working separately are more creative than individuals working together in groups. (The one exception to this is when individuals get together for a brainstorming session. When brainstorming, a group becomes a collection of noninteracting individuals following an established procedure. Under these conditions, groups generate more ideas than individuals working alone.) Let's examine the best approach to several categories of tasks in terms of these research findings.

Reprinted from *Supervisory Management*, April 1978

One category is *creative tasks*. When the task calls for a creative solution—that is, a new alternative or a heretofore unconsidered option—an individual is a better choice than a group. For example, individuals do better than groups at creating or constructing an original crossword puzzle, designing a technical component, or writing a computer program. When seeking a creative outcome, one would do better to find an expert in the area of concern rather than to assemble a number of people.

Another category is *convergent or integrative tasks*. When the problem requires that various bits of information be brought together to produce a solution—such as developing a business strategy, evaluating a new product, or solving a crossword puzzle—groups can offer superior outcomes. The *proviso* here is, of course, that the group of people is capable of working together effectively. The operating effectiveness of the group is a key factor and will be discussed in detail below.

Next are *independent tasks*. Sometimes in our eagerness to establish more teamwork, persons whose jobs are for the most part independent of one another are encouraged to work as a team. When interaction with others is required to get the job done—because of the flow of the work process, the necessity to share information or skills, or other forms of task interdependency—then frequent or occasional work together as a group may be very useful. One way, however, to assure *un*satisfactory work-group meetings is to insist that people whose jobs are in the main independent of one another work together as a team. Effective managers understand which of their subordinates need to work together to get their jobs done and which do not.

Goal setting should also be considered. The lesson of management by objectives (MBO) is that persons should be involved in determining the goals that are designed to guide their behavior and against which they will be evaluated. When goal setting is done in relevant groupings of managers and their subordinates, more commitment to individual objectives can be expected. This discussion leads us to consider the question of commitment, which is the second factor to consider in deciding whether a particular matter is better suited for a group or an individual.

The importance of general acceptance of, or commitment to, a solution for its implementation. Research has shown that when people participate in the process of reaching a decision, they have more commitment to that decision—that is, they feel more ownership over the outcome. Therefore, they are likely to have a greater interest in it and to work harder to insure the satisfactory implementation of the outcome.

On the other hand, when an individual solves a problem or makes a decision, two tasks still remain for him or her. First, others must be persuaded that the particular outcome is the best or at least is a desirable course to follow. Second, others must agree to act on this decision and carry it out. The principle here is that participation in the decision-making process increases ownership of the outcome and, therefore, reduces the problems of surveillance, monitoring, and follow-up in its implementation.

Not all solutions to problems depend on the support of other people for effective implementation. Therefore, a manager needs to be aware of those issues requiring commitment by others in order for a solution to work and convene those people who will be critical to a solution's effective implementation. Clearly, all decisions are not so dependent on others that they should be addressed by group action. In some cases, a manager may be willing to make a decision he or she knows to be unpopular or to assign a problem to an individual expert for solution, with the knowledge that additional resources will need to be invested in monitoring its implementation.

The value placed on the quality of the decision. The best managers are aware when they are making trade-offs between the quality of the outcomes of a decision and the anticipated difficulties in seeing that the decision is carried out fully and in a timely manner.

If a manager is sufficiently concerned with distributing responsibility to ensure that a solution will be carried out completely and with dispatch, he or she may accept a solution of somewhat lower quality because it has widespread acceptance rather than insisting on a solution of somewhat higher quality that lacks acceptability to those persons on whom the manager must depend for its implementation.

The quality of a group product, in contrast to one produced by an individual expert in the field, varies depending on the competencies of group members and information available to them, plus how effectively they are able to work together as a group.

The characteristics of individual group members. When assembling a group of people to solve a problem or make a decision, a manager needs to consider each possible member of the group with three guidelines in mind: the expertise each individual will bring to the particular problem under consideration, the stake each person would have in the outcome, and the role each is likely to play in implementing any decision—that is, how dependent others will be on each member's support of the overall group solution. Keeping these factors in mind, it is obvious that managers will probably not wish to convene the same collection of individuals to address every issue.

There is an additional characteristic of the members of a group that deserves consideration, and this is how effectively they are able to work together. This is the fifth criterion to use in deciding whether to assign a problem to a group or to an individual: *The operating effectiveness of the group—especially its leadership.* A question that needs to be raised each time a new group is assembled is: How effective will this collection of people be in working together to produce a solution of merit? It may be a better choice to ask an individual to solve a problem or make a decision, rather than to call several people together who will have great difficulty in working effectively as a group.

The skills of the leader of the group are particularly important, because the leader can do more than any other person both to enhance and to block the effectiveness of group efforts. Key leadership issues are discussed below, along with a set of guidelines for productive work in groups.

In summary, the five variables that should be considered in deciding whether a group or an individual is the better locus for addressing a particular problem are: whether the task is creative or integrative in nature, how important acceptance of the decision or commitment to the solution is for implementation by those who must carry it out, the value placed on the quality of the decision and any trade-offs that appear to be necessary to assure acceptance, the competency and investment of each person involved and the role each person plays in implementing the decision, and, last, the anticipated operating effectiveness of the group, taking into account the critical role of the group leadership.

It is to the operating effectiveness of groups that we now turn our attention. First, we will consider what it is that groups have to offer—that is, the assets of groups. Then we will offer a discussion of the reasons why groups often fail to meet our expectations for performance—that is, the *liabilities* of groups. The final section of the paper deals with various considerations of leadership.

Assets of Groups

Greater total knowledge and information. Even where one person (for example, the boss or a technical expert) knows much more than anyone else, the limited and unique information of others can fill important gaps. There is simply more information, experience, and competencies in a group as a whole than in any one of its members. The issue, therefore, becomes how to make this expanded pool available and utilize it effectively.

Greater variety of approaches. Each person brings a somewhat different perspective to a problem, and these different ways of viewing the world can open avenues of consideration that are outside the awareness of any single individual. In addition, we all get into ruts in our thinking or into patterned ways of defining problems and approaching issues. Assembling a number of people expands the potential ways a particular problem can be approached.

Increased acceptance. When individuals have an active part in the decision-making process, each individual's ownership of the outcome is increased. The responsibility people feel for making the solution work is thereby enhanced. As we mentioned earlier, when an individual solves a problem, two additional problems remain: persuading others both to accept the solution and to carry it out.

Reduced communication problems. The implementation of a decision is likely to be smoother and to require less surveillance when people possess full knowledge of the goals and obstacles, the alternatives that were considered but rejected, and the facts, opinions, and projections leading to the decision that was made.

It is clear that a group has more firepower than an individual, and an assembly of people has an expanded potential for new perspectives and integrative solutions. How then can five or ten capable persons meet together to solve a problem or make a decision, only to leave the meeting frustrated and having made little progress or having developed outcomes that are acceptable to only a few of the principals? In answer to this and other questions, the following is a discussion of the important obstacles to effective group functioning:

Liabilities of Groups

Social pressures to conform. Sometimes majorities or powerful minorities—or even the boss—pressure people into going along with lower-quality decisions. In their desire to be good group members or to be accepted, people sometimes keep their disagreements to themselves or only voice them after the meeting to close associates.

Quick convergence. In a group there is frequently a tendency to seize quickly on a solution that seems to have support. The apparent acceptance of an idea can overshadow appropriate concerns for quality or accuracy. Agreement is often erroneously assumed to signal the correct or the best solution.

Furthermore, ideas of higher quality that are introduced late in a discussion may have little chance of real consideration. Research has shown that when groups are required to produce two solutions to every problem, the second solution is frequently the better of the two.

A dominant individual. Sometimes one person prevails because of status, activity level, verbal skills, or stubborn persistence—all of which may be unrelated to competence in the particular task facing the group. Since a leader is particularly likely to dominate a discussion, his or her skills at avoiding, and insights into, the consequences of excessive control are especially important.

Secondary goals or hidden agendas. Often individuals are working simultaneously on the assigned task and—covertly—on their own needs. Their hidden agendas may include personal pride, protection of one's position or department, desires for visibility or acceptance, or personality conflicts with others who are present. Some of these factors lead to attempts to "win the decision" rather than to find the best solution; other factors lead to moves for prominence, deference, and other responses.

Time constraints. Available time may restrict the group's potential. It simply takes more time for a group to make a decision than it does for a single individual. It also takes a good deal of time for a group to develop the skills and procedures required for effective work—that is, to capitalize on the assets mentioned earlier and to limit the liabilities inherent in any group effort.

Problems with disagreement. Issues are often sharpened, and therefore clarified, when there are differences or conflicts between members of a group in defining the problem, gaining preferred solutions, obtaining information, and establishing perspectives. However, because disagreement affects people differently, it may also block progress due to hard feelings between individuals. Some people experience disagreement as a cue to attack; others react to conflict and controversy by freezing or withdrawing.

When disagreement is well managed, new ideas and innovative solutions are often the outcomes. When differences between people are seen as sources of new information rather than as obstacles to be overcome, solutions tend to be more creative.

Premature discussion of solutions. Confusion and conflict occasionally arise over proposed solutions because there is not yet sufficient agreement or clarity concerning the problem to be addressed. Unwittingly, the different solutions are being offered to solve different problems. Both the quality and the acceptance of solutions increase when the seeking of solutions is delayed until both goals and potential obstacles are identified.

Identifying and mobilizing the resources of a group and overcoming the obstacles to effective group functioning are keys to a group's success. The quality of a group's decision obviously depends on whether the people with the best ideas or those with the worst ideas are more influential. The declaration, "Let's get all the facts on the table and then make a decision," is a naive wish, as the foregoing catalog of the liabilities of groups indicates. Getting all relevant information on the table and ensuring that it receives an appropriate hearing is a very difficult task. It is to this task of effective leadership that we now turn.

Effective Leadership

Once the decision has been made to assign a job to a group of people, the behavior of the group's leadership becomes critical to its success. It is important to recognize that the more the responsibility for leadership is shared by all members of a problem-solving group, the more productive and creative that group is likely to be—provided that this kind of behavior, where responsibilities are shared and group members take initiatives, does not threaten the formal leader (that is, the boss).

In problem-solving groups, effective leadership promotes the utilization of all members as relevant resources and insures open and accurate communication among them. It is important, therefore, to understand *the leadership dilemma:* The more power a leader has, the more positive the contributions he or she can make to a group's functioning and to its procedures. On the other hand, the more power a leader has, the more his or her own behavior can be a barrier to the free exchange of ideas.

For most groups, the best solutions come with a *strong* leader working with *strong* group members. In this situation, conflict and disagreement tend to be creative and all resources have opportunities to be fully utilized. Such a situation occurs when: There is a two-way communication, but two-way initiatives—and responsibilities for leadership activities are shared. This situation also assumes that the strength of subordinates, coupled with their assuming responsibilities for leadership functions, does not threaten the boss. As was said earlier, the boss can do more than anyone else to facilitate or block effective group functioning.

There are several things required from members of a problem-solving group in which leadership is conceived as a set of *functions* to be performed by anyone seeing the need, rather than as a *role* to be filled by the boss. These functions include encouraging broad participation by bringing others into the discussion and by protecting minority points of view, assuming responsibility for accurate communications between other group members, summarizing progress by pointing out where things stand at the moment, and questioning the appropriateness or the order of agenda items.

The more each of these requirements of effective leadership are shared and performed by all members of a problem-solving group, the more productive and creative that group is likely to be—provided this kind of behavior does not threaten the boss. It is the boss who can do more than anyone else to create both an unintentional "camel" as the group's product and to provoke the attitude among the membership that we have all experienced: "If I can only get through this meeting, then I can get some work done!" On the other hand, the boss can do the most to provide the conditions for effective group efforts.

In summary, some of the world's most productive and progressive organizations are managed by executive committees. Likewise, some of any organization's problems can best be handled by a committee or similar group of employees. This article is our attempt to provide some guidelines for when groups are a good choice for suggesting solutions to day-to-day problems in the life of a manager and some insights into how to make those groups function more effectively.

The Supervisor's Survival Guide: Involving Your Staff In the Decision-Making Process

KEN THOMPSON and ROBERT E. PITTS

A major problem in all organizations is a growing feeling of alienation among their employees. They feel like robots, that no one cares about them as human beings. They believe they could contribute their knowledge of the work to efforts to produce more at less cost, but nobody listens.

Such feelings lead to employee dissatisfaction within the organization, dissatisfaction that shows up in high absentee and turnover rates and low productivity rates. The employee feels that the organization simply doesn't consider any input into decision making except that from individuals in management who in some all-knowing manner make decisions about everything in great detail. Orders are passed down to the supervisor who is expected to carry them out through his or her subordinates. Little attention is given to subordinate input even at the first level of supervision. The attitude of supervisors seems to be, "They are paid to do their job. Let them do their work, and I will do the managing."

Organizations have attempted to overcome employee alienation by encouraging the exchange of information between supervisors and subordinates. With improved communications supervisors could better understand subordinates, and subordinates could begin to understand the organization's decision-making process and environment. Some organizations have attempted to go even farther, enriching jobs by actually involving the work group in decision making.

Unfortunately, many enrichment programs have done little either to increase employee satisfaction or productivity. It's been a matter generally of communication for communication's sake. Workers and supervisors have talked without purpose. Everyone knew that the organization was not going to seriously consider subordinate input. When workers were allowed to participate in decisions, the decisions were trivial, not concerning the essential aspects of the job environment.

Still, communication is important in the organization. In every work group, members frequently can make important contributions to how the job should be done and problems solved. Today's employee is better educated and better informed than ever before, and a good employee at any level may possess tremendous insight into how his particular job functions.

Communication is possible as well as desirable. Supervisors need to tap work-group input and to foster organizational satisfaction through improved communications at all levels. It's possible to accom-

Reprinted from *Supervisory Management,* April 1979

plish this twofold objective by using Goal-Directed Group Support (GDGS), a technique that involves the work group in decision making.

Before looking at this technique, let's look more closely at what's been done so far to increase employee job satisfaction.

The Human Relations Approach

The human relations approach to management was developed to allow the organization to better address the needs of the employee. Studies of employee needs had indicated that they were generally unhappy and dissatisfied with their work environment. A happy employee was equated with a productive employee, and supervisors were instructed to meet the needs of the employees to coax them into better performance. Organizations assumed a more indulgent role with the intent of making employees so happy that they would want to work. Communication for communication's sake was suggested, since groups that communicated well appeared to be happier than those that didn't. Managers began to consider employee job satisfaction as an important part of the work-environment equation. Little emphasis, however, was given performance when implementing this approach to management. No attempt was made to link satisfaction and performance. It was assumed that performance would increase if satisfaction first increased. But the end result was little improvement in either.

From the human relations approach, job enrichment evolved. It is an attempt to build into the job factors that tend to increase satisfaction and performance alike. In effect, the job is modified so that the individual's needs are fulfilled through the performance of the task. Equal importance is now given job performance and job satisfaction. Satisfaction is derived from the job itself and what the individual can or cannot do to reach the objectives of the task. If greater autonomy and decision-making ability are included with the task, greater satisfaction is thought to evolve. If the individual can see some direct benefit of reaching his objectives on the job—for example, personal gain or satisfying intrinsic needs—then greater satisfaction should occur with increased involvement within the organization and improved work performance.

The structuring of the job so that it meets these objectives is very easy to advocate but not easy to do. One particular technique to increase the effectiveness of the job structure and meet employee needs is participatory management. The supervisor is directed to share decision making with the employee and allow the individual the greatest degree of freedom possible to structure his or her own task. This approach can work, but more likely it fails. Decentralization of the decision making must be done with a great deal of skill. Too often problems arise with respect to the true scope of the decentralization process and the amount of authority given.

Problems With Group Decision Making

One key problem that may occur when group decision making is tried is that the supervisor will initially indicate that the group will have absolute decision-making authority. This posture is relatively difficult to maintain when the supervisor is not in control of some of the directives that will be passed down from the upper levels of the organization. A second problem results from a lack of trust. The members of a work group are told they will be given much more freedom in structuring their work environment and will be allowed to make many of the decisions previously made by management. Many of these experiments have failed because managements didn't really trust the workers' abilities to make the decisions. Employees quickly realize that they have not actually been given a greater degree of freedom to do their jobs, and satisfaction drops drastically.

To make group participation work, you must be willing to live with the decisions that come from the participants. Also, to make it work, you must never promise prerogatives that you cannot or are unwilling to relinquish to your subordinates. Rather, establish boundaries within which the group is free to make decisions. Provide guidance as to the options the group may consider. It is important to remember that it is your job as supervisor to provide leadership. Your group still needs and expects that. But you now establish guidelines rather than give specifics on how the work group should perform its tasks.

Group Decision Making—Making It Work!

To be truly effective as a means of reaching organizational objectives, work-group communication development needs to include a goal orientation. After all, the purpose of a work group is to combine the energies of several people so that output is more than what would be produced if the same individuals worked separately.

As a supervisor, you want to forge a communication system that encourages input for group goal attainment from all group members. Such an approach is a far cry from calls to simply get people talking; we want to focus their energies through Goal-Directed Group Support. This approach was developed for use in improving communications within work groups in organizations of all types. In essence the approach has five steps.

The steps of the GDGS program attempt to develop a means for the manager to assess group feelings toward particular problems. It should be stressed from its first use that the approach will only be a medium for input by the work group to aid in the decision-making process; it will not achieve total group control. A total democratic system is not feasible in most organizations because of their nature and the upper-level decision-making process.

Step no. 1: weekly or biweekly group meetings. An essential step in the process is the establishment of formal meetings to discuss progress and problems in the work environment. It is extremely important that there be constant communications and feedback within the work group and between the work group and the supervisor. These meetings can be brief, and they should be scheduled at sufficient intervals so that problems and frustrations are not allowed to build within the work group and prevent the manager and work team from accomplishing their mutual goals.

Step no. 2: at the meeting—a diagnostic problem-solving approach (DPS). Instead of the usual approach of finding fault when things are going wrong, the GDGS approach fosters a diagnostic approach to communications. The manager's role at the meeting is directed toward finding solutions to problems rather than attempting to assess blame. The supervisor must maintain a very low profile and encourage subordinate input into the resolution of problems. He or she should say, for example, "There has been an increase in the scrap rate in the past week. What do you think we can do to lower the rate?"

Often the first step is to better define the problem by identifying some of the reasons it is occurring. The discussion must *not* be accusatory but rather solution-oriented. The manager allows the work group to examine a general problem and single out specific areas in which to apply solutions to the problem. Work-group members often have special insights into a problem. They deal with the situation at the most basic level while the supervisor does not. For example, from the discussion on the high scrap rate, it might have been decided that the problem with scrap loss was caused by insufficient testing of the material before use. Without work-group input, it might have taken the supervisor a great deal of time and effort to isolate the core problem. Further, in his or her examination of the situation, the supervisor most likely would have dwelt on the possibility that the workers were simply not performing their job correctly.

Step no. 3: solution development. The group is next immersed in the task of resolving the problem. It is important for the manager to assume the role of a resource person rather than that of an active participant. The manager should try to limit himself or herself to pointing out how upper-level management may react to potential solutions. The supervisor should not monopolize the conversation or actively direct the discussion. If the work group gets the feeling that the decision has already been made, then the whole effort will have been in vain. In fact, in most cases, a feigned attempt at group inclusion in decision making is a greater disaster than no attempt. In the former, the manager is dishonest with his or her group; in the latter, at least the supervisor is forthright and not pretending to be democratic.

The supervisor should attempt to create an environment in which each group member feels free to participate. No idea should be rejected "out of hand." Group members should feel that what they suggest will be seriously considered and that the group's evaluations are highly valued.

It is very useful to write down each proposal and develop a list of solutions before any one idea is discussed at length. In this manner all possible ideas are presented by the group for its consideration. Encourage a wide range of ideas. Look for that new, unexpected idea that might mean a breakthrough in problem solution.

Once the list is of sufficient length, the next step is group discussion of the solutions. In this part of the process the supervisor should attempt to indicate his or her initial feelings on the subject, then open the discussion for comments with an open mind. A true discussion is desired—one in which the supervisor provides the managerial framework within which the merits of each proposed solution may be evaluated by the work group.

The supervisor should listen and learn how his or her employees evaluate each proposal and the environment in which it might be implemented. The objective of this stage of the GDGS is to analyze the proposed solutions from a work-group viewpoint with the goal of giving the members input into the decision making.

Step no. 4: discussion of the final solution. After the various proposals have been examined by the group, the supervisor must select the best solution. Hopefully, it will be one upon which the group has reached a consensus. The selection may or may not take place at the same meeting, depending upon the amount of additional information that may be needed. It is beneficial if the supervisor discusses the various proposals and indicates why they were or were not chosen. Thus the group may be able to understand the decision-making process; even if its solution was not chosen, it may understand why not.

The work-group members should understand that they are a part of the decision process but that final authority to approve the group's solutions must rest with the supervisor. That individual, however, must always consider consensus solutions carefully. Whenever possible, when such solutions fall within policy guidelines, they should be implemented. Employees will work harder and with real commitment when they are dealing with their solution, not something just handed down as a new order or procedure.

Step no. 5: feedback. Once a solution is decided upon and implemented, the supervisor should provide feedback as to the success of the solution and what sorts of problems were encountered in its implementation. While current management literature would indicate that allowing participation in decision making is one of the most effective ways of increasing performance and satisfaction, we would add that providing feedback is equally essential to maintaining a high level of interest in what is going on in the organization. Feedback not only on group performance, but also on other aspects of the internal and external environment that may affect the work group in the future, is important to the satisfaction of the work group with its job—and with your job of managing.

In summary, the GDGS system attempts to bring into focus the important contribution that the group can make in decision making. It is a systematic approach to foster group participation in problem solving. GDGS is more than just a communication tool; it is a carefully managed work-group activity that is directed toward problem solving. As such, it is an important supervisory skill for the supervisor with a work group that can no longer be expected to follow blindly and that wants to make important contributions in many areas formerly reserved exclusively for management.

Group Conflict

Besides fostering group participation in problem solving, Goal-Directed Group Support is an excellent tool for solving group conflict. By using GDGS, the supervisor does not get embroiled in the conflict; nor is he considered to be taking sides. Rather, with it, he works at resolving a conflict that is within the organization. This preserves the trust and personal commitment between work group and supervisor.

GDGS can also be a powerful tool for linking the supervisor and the work group into a single unit. The GDGS meeting can be a forum to explain the actions that you as a supervisor have taken to blunt negative decisions from the upper levels. Trust and personal allegiance are built through open communications. The technique makes the group aware that you as a supervisor are faced with constraints from above also; and while you may not always agree with top management, you, too, must abide by its decisions.

Diagnostic Communication Ability

Goal-Directed Group Support is most effective when the supervisor has increased his or her Diagnostic Communication Ability (DCA). This skill aids in developing a spirit of trust and personal allegiance between the work group and its supervisor. It is a process that produces a level of supervisory maturity that is relatively uncommon in most organizations. The approach is simple; but if used, it guarantees a positive reaction from the work group.

In essence, DCA attempts to foster the same sort of organizational commitment by the work group as GDGS. The DCA model is directed toward improving the morale and satisfaction of the work group while at the same time encouraging greater goal direction in the work environment. The benefits for the supervisor are improved departmental performance and a greater commitment by the workforce to its supervisor. The approach is directed at improving the process or manner in which a supervisor communicates with his or her workforce. The supervisor must direct his or her efforts toward solving problems in the organization rather than punishing people for creating the problems. The DCA communicates that attitude.

Each of the three steps in the DCA must be implemented for the others to have meaning.

Step no. 1: fact finding. The worst thing a supervisor can do is to react without knowing what the facts in a situation are. This is doubly true when the situation calls for some punitive action or "chewing out." The supervisor with good DCA will first find out the facts behind a particular incident before making a decision or taking action. Assumptions are dangerous.

A midwest plastics company was having difficulty with one of its employees. The employee did not perform well and often seemed to be antagonistic toward any form of corrective help from the supervisor. One day the supervisor saw several employees around the problem employee's work area. The supervisor immediately assumed that they were all "goofing off," and he yelled at them to get back to work. In reality the men were showing the problem employee how to better do his job.

Know what is going on before you act. Be sure of your facts. Don't commit yourself to actions that you will be sorry for in the future.

Step no. 2: diagnostic problem solving. The second step includes diagnosing the problem, then solving it in light of the diagnosis. Less emphasis is placed on fault finding and more on the resolution of the problem. With the information that was gathered in step one, the supervisor attempts to deal with the problem in a professional way. He or she searches for a just solution that will maintain the support and respect of his or her workforce. Consider the way a supervisor handled a loud, disruptive disagreement that occurred. The supervisor did not immediately punish each individual but rather attempted to determine what really happened. Then the supervisor got the individuals together to see what could be done about the problem. The approach during the meeting was not one of telling each of the men that he was wrong to argue but rather stressing how to solve the problem regardless of whose fault it was. (Remember, in diagnostic problem solving, the goal is to solve the problem, not find fault and punish people.) The problem was resolved, and the men subsequently became good friends. The supervisor maintained—and enhanced—the respect the group had for its leader.

Step no. 3: decisive action. After steps one and two are completed, you must act in a confident and decisive manner. Decide upon your course of action, then start the implementation process. In this way, the workforce will understand that you, as a supervisor, will get things done. Decisive action is especially necessary if the work group has had a part in the resolution of the problem. The group will be anxious to see if its solution is workable. It is very important that it see some form of action being taken. The responsiveness of the supervisor can never be discounted—it is important in the supervisor's maintaining effective relations with the work group and avoiding feelings of job alienation within its ranks.

Problems are not likely to go away. As a supervisor, a large part of your managerial responsibility is to make necessary judgments and then act. Well-planned, decisive action gets results and gains respect. Be a manager who does things to solve problems, not a manager who lets problems manage him.

Both Goal-Directed Group Support and Diagnostic Communication Ability can do much to improve the working climate for a work group and its supervisor. A supervisor should apply both of these tools in a systematic approach to solving problems. They are the foundation for a positive and enriching work climate. As a supervisor, how you act is as important as what you know. GDGS and DCA prescribe the ways that you should act to insure that you can deal effectively with your subordinates.

How to Make a Better Decision

DON CARUTH and BILL MIDDLEBROOK

First-line supervisors frequently tell us, "I don't need to worry about problem solving and decision making because my boss is there to tell me what to do whenever I need to know." Such a statement indicates a lack of understanding concerning management responsibilities, not only by the supervisor but also by his or her boss. All levels of supervision, from the front line to top management, confront and deal with problems requiring effective solution and decision making.

Problem solving and decision making are not the only activities of a supervisor, but they are extremely important ones. Much of a supervisor's success depends upon his or her ability to identify the causes of problems and develop workable solutions for resolving them. Before launching into an examination of these two activities, it might be well to define a few terms.

What is a problem? A problem is any question or matter involving doubt, uncertainty, or difficulty; it is a question posed for solution or discussion. Most of the time there is a tendency to regard problems in a negative context, to see each as a deviation from standard—something that needs correcting, an unpleasant mess that must be straightened out, or a disruption in normal operations. While it is true that a problem may be any or all of these things (and thus negative in tone), it is also true that a problem may have a positive side to it. How can a problem be positive? It can be so when it represents an *opportunity* to improve a situation, to alter a condition for the better, or to correct a deficiency.

What is decision making? Decision making is the process of selecting a course of action from among two or more alternatives. Put quite simply, it is the process of making up one's mind. As an activity, decision making does not occupy much of a supervisor's time. Very little time, in fact, may actually be spent in deciding upon a course of action; however, decision making is the riskiest part of a supervisor's job. Every time a supervisor makes a decision, he or she runs the *risk* that the opted solution may not work. Consequently, supervisors must pay careful attention to this particular management task.

What is problem solving? Problem solving is a general term that is used to refer to the *entire* process of analyzing situations and arriving at workable solutions. Frequently the terms "problem solving" and "decision making" are used interchangeably. From a technical standpoint, however, this is incorrect. Decision making is a *point* in the overall process—the point at which an alternative course of action is selected. Problem solving is concerned not only with this step but also with the other steps of analysis, implementation, evaluation, and so forth.

Reprinted from *Supervisory Management,* July 1981

Steps to Successful Problem Solving

Problem solutions may be arrived at in many different ways—sometimes by hit or miss, sometimes by just plain luck, or sometimes by the "blind hog" approach (even a blind hog, so the saying goes, finds an acorn now and then). *Consistent success* in problem solving is not likely to be the product of the foregoing approaches. Rather a *systematic, logical* approach should be used, not only for greater success, but also for greater consistency in analysis. The following rational, systematic approach has been found useful for handling supervisory problems:

1. Define or identify the problem.
2. Get the facts.
3. Interpret the facts.
4. Develop alternative solutions.
5. Select the best practical solution.
6. Implement the solution.
7. Evaluate the effectiveness of the solution.

Let's examine each of these steps in detail. During this process keep in mind that the procedure will work *no matter what the problem is*—whether it is job-related or a personal situation that needs resolution.

Define the problem. The most difficult step in problem solving and decision making is to identify the *real* problem. Frequently problem *effect* is mistaken for problem *cause:* The root cause is confused with the outward manifestation. Consider an example—employee turnover. Many supervisors view excessive turnover as a "problem" It is actually a *symptom* of an underlying difficulty, the visible result of such problems as poor supervision, boring work assignments, improper hiring criteria, and inadequate salaries. If turnover is identified as the problem, any actions taken toward solution will be dealing only with symptoms; the real cause may never be addressed and the problem may persist. In attempting to define the problem, a supervisor must look for the *root cause,* the *unexploited opportunity,* the gap between what is currently being done and what actually should be done.

Obviously problem definition requires care. A supervisor must resist the temptation to "shoot from the hip." All too often instant analysis turns out to be wrong. Careful thinking is required to isolate the real problem.

Once the problem has been identified, the supervisor should state it clearly so that all those people involved in its analysis and solution can understand it. The more carefully a problem has been defined, the better the chances that it can be effectively communicated to others. The old adage holds true: "If it isn't clear to you, it won't be clear to anyone else."

Problem identification can be facilitated if a supervisor is continually on the lookout for *emerging problems.* Most problems don't occur spontaneously—they usually foreshadow their coming. The manager who is alert can catch many problems in their *incipiency,* the stage where they are easiest to solve. To use two current management buzz-words, a supervisor should be "proactive" rather than "reactive" when it comes to problem identification.

Get the facts. The second step in problem solving is to gather all the factual information that will be needed to make a careful assessment of the situation. Sources of factual information include accounting records, drawings, specifications, procedures, regulations, reports, and actual observation of the situation. A frequently overlooked source of facts is the employee or group of employees involved in the problem situation. Being closest to the actual operation or process, employees often have ideas about what should be done to eliminate a problem. The wise supervisor will heed the suggestions of these individuals.

How many facts does a supervisor need to solve a problem? This is a question that can't be answered in the abstract. The situation determines how much information is required for problem resolution. One thing, however, is certain: A supervisor will never have all the facts. To wait for all the facts to come in before proceeding further is to suffer from "paralysis by analysis." A helpful approach is to look for the development of trends, the formation of patterns that indicate that information is starting to fall into place.

In gathering information for problem-solving purposes, a supervisor should be careful about discarding data because they may seem irrelevant. Getting the facts is, and should be, concerned with collection, not with evaluation.

Interpret the facts. This step actually begins as data are amassed. In the interpretation stage, facts are *fitted together;* their relationships to each other are considered. Probing questions are asked: What caused this to happen? Where does the responsibility for the breakdown lie? Has this ever happened before? Is it a human performance problem? Is it a design flaw? What is the potential magnitude of the problem if it remains uncorrected? The type of problem, obviously, will affect the kind of questions asked. The point a supervisor should remember about interpretation is to be "hard-nosed" in asking questions. Probe. Dig. Analyze. Finally the facts will begin to take shape. Often, the process of interpreting facts is similar to working a jigsaw puzzle: One starts with the edges and gradually fits piece to piece until a picture emerges.

A supervisor should keep in mind that *opinions, feelings, attitudes,* and *perceptions* can interfere with the interpretation of factual information. Facts can become colored by one's own experiences. If this happens, the facts will not be correctly interpreted.

Develop alternative solutions. The next step in problem solving is to come up with some alternative approaches to resolving the problem situation. The two most common sources of alternatives are a supervisor's own past experiences and the past experiences of others. Often there are more alternatives than first meet the eye. In this stage of the analysis, the objective is *generation* of alternatives, not analysis of their feasibility. Just because some alternative has never been tried in the past should not prevent a supervisor from suggesting it as a possible alternative in the current situation.

How many alternatives should be developed? Enough so that there is assurance that the full range of possibilities has been considered. In some cases, this may be three or four; in other cases, it may be as many as five or six. In large measure the type of problem and its complexity will suggest or influence the number of alternatives that need to be developed. There is, however, one alternative that should always be considered: to do nothing. A supervisor should always ask himself or herself, "What would happen if I did nothing? Would the condition improve? Deteriorate? Go away?" Perhaps no action may be required.

Select the best practical solution. This is the *decision-making phase* in the problem-solving process. Initially a "weeding out" approach is used; that is, all of the alternatives developed are scanned, and those that do not appear readily suitable are thrown out. The remainder are then more rigorously assessed.

Each of the alternatives evaluated should be analyzed in terms of its *direct* as well as *indirect* impact on the problem. *Tangible* factors are such items as costs, production rates, cash flow, delivery schedules, and rate of return. *Intangible* or qualitative factors include impact on employee morale, potential resistance to a new procedure, and effect on work group solidarity.

A supervisor must also be on the alert for any *unsought consequences* that an alternative might produce if implemented. For example, a reduction in force might be a simple way of reducing manufacturing costs. But if the productivity of remaining workers drops because of low morale resulting from the layoff of other workers, the solution may produce an even worse problem than the one it was supposed to cure.

Any benefit to be produced by the alternative solution must be carefully weighed against the costs associated with that solution. If the costs outweigh the benefits, the search for a suitable alternative must continue.

If one word about a problem solution should be emphasized, it is "practical." Whatever alternative is selected must be a *workable* solution. There are many examples of alleged solutions that didn't work as planned because managers forgot that one word. In the day-to-day world of organizational realities, *optimal solutions* may not be possible. Knowing this, the perceptive supervisor selects the solution that he or she knows is satisfactory and then works hard to see that it succeeds.

Implement the solution. Once an alternative has been selected, the next step is to put it into operation. The proposed solution should be implemented as expeditiously as possible to reap its full benefits and eliminate the problem it is intended to correct. However, those affected by the implementation of the solution must be notified, trained, and prepared. To implement a solution without adequate advance preparation of those involved is to court disaster. Communication is crucial. The solution will meet less resistance and will be more successful when everyone concerned knows why, how, when, where, what, and who will be affected by the implementation of the solution. Remember, it is not the change per se that upsets people; it is the way it is implemented.

Evaluate the effectiveness of the solution. Every implementation of a solution should be followed up to see if it is producing the results it was supposed to produce. Frequently the best solutions on paper don't work out as they are supposed to. Consequently, it is necessary to monitor the solution for a while to observe the effect that it is having. Questions that need to be asked about effectivenesses are: Is it doing what it is supposed to do? Are costs really lower? Has production actually increased? Are we now on delivery schedule? Have employees accepted it? In the event that the answer to these or similar questions is "no," then it is back to the drawing board. It may be necessary to select another alternative or to redefine the problem. In any event, another solution will have to be chosen if the one selected initially is not doing the job it was supposed to do.

Mistakes to Avoid

As Peter Drucker points out, decision making is not the *only* job of a supervisor, but it is the one with the greatest consequences associated with it. Thus it is essential that supervisors know what mistakes to avoid in problem solving and decision making. Some of the more common mistakes are:

The mistake of the unnecessary decision. Because decisions entail risk, it is important for a supervisor to know when to take a risk and when to let "sleeping dogs" lie. On occasion the nature of a problem will be such that no action should be taken; in such circumstances, a supervisor should decide not to decide in order to avoid taking unnecessary risks.

The mistake of fighting the recurring problem. Many supervisors fight battles with the same problems over and over. To do so is not only unnecessary but also inefficient. Recurring problems should be resolved through the development of policies, procedures, and standing plans rather than handled individually each time they arise.

The mistake of not evaluating benefits in terms of cost. Where benefits are not analyzed in terms of costs, the most sweeping, far-fetched kinds of decisions are likely to be made; grandiose schemes are apt to be implemented to solve simple problems. The end results must always be examined in the light of what costs—tangible as well as intangible—will be encountered in producing them.

The mistake of the delayed decision. Decisions, unlike wine or cheese, do not necessarily improve with age. Yet many supervisors procrastinate when it comes to making a decision. Speedy decisions— not snap decisions—are beneficial in at least two ways: First, a decision made in a timely fashion provides a manager with more time to correct a situation should his or her original decision turn out to be the wrong one; and second, making a decision quickly takes the problem from a supervisor's mind and allows him or her to go on to other problems. The decision is taken and the supervisor can move on to other concerns instead of agonizing over a course of action.

Problem solving and decision making? They are not the only jobs of a supervisor, but they are crucial tasks that must be carried out *effectively.* These tasks must be approached with care so that sound decisions and successful problem solving occur in the organization at every level of supervision.

The Positive Side of Unpopular Decisions

LES G. RADFORD

Remember how as children no one wanted to play the bad guy? When someone had to play the role, there was a tendency to play for sympathy. Adults in supervisory positions tend to behave similarly, especially when it comes to making hard decisions that might make them unpopular with their peers and subordinates. Yet work situations sometimes require supervisors to make unpopular decisions, and to do so in a way that won't create additional problems. In short, a supervisor has to be prepared to be unpopular—to *seem* to be the "bad guy" when the need arises.

The Penalties of Popularity

Supervisors who refuse to make unpopular decisions when needed undermine their own managerial role in several ways. In the first place, they jeopardize management's objectives. If, for example, assemblyline workers are allowed to grow lax in the area of quality control, the number of rejects will increase and the cost per accepted product will also increase. Who's to blame? The supervisor, because he or she allowed the situation to continue rather than enforce unpopular but necessary performance standards.

Such timidity can also threaten harmonious work relationships. Often, when an unpopular decision has to be made, a supervisor will play for sympathy, holding others responsible for the decision. But disassociating oneself from the decision making process can cause workers to become cynical about management's capabilities and disrespectful toward their company and its objectives. It also makes the supervisor appear more like a "yes-man" than a leader.

A supervisor who is characterized as soft because he or she never makes an unpopular decision, or takes responsibility for one, rarely gains the respect necessary to lead. For a businessperson in a leadership role, a lack of respect can mean that workers will not follow unless it suits them. That's not leadership; that's a potential disaster.

Developing the Positive

Sooner or later, a supervisor will encounter a situation that calls for a decision that will be unpopular among those whom it affects. Such a decision can easily be delivered in a brutal, insensitive, dictatorial

Reprinted from *Supervisory Management*, November 1982

manner, accentuating the negative in a way that could create further problems, which is the last thing a supervisor wants. Admittedly more difficult but by no means impossible to accomplish is the development of the positive side of a potentially unpopular decision. This can earn a supervisor long-term respect as a leader while correcting the problem that necessitated the decision.

Here's how you as a supervisor can develop the positive side. Before acting on a decision, evaluate it in terms of whether or not it will achieve the desired results. Examine its potential unpopularity. To whom would the decision be unpopular, if at all? And why might that happen?

For example, let's say you are put in charge of an assembly section that has not increased its productivity for over a year. Top management wants more output, so you investigate and find that most workers disregard the work rules, taking long lunch periods and coffee breaks and returning to work stations with refreshments in hand. In this case, any decision to tighten up the enforcement of company work rules will be unpopular with those who disregard them. How do you deal with this situation?

To prevent a decision from appearing arbitrary or as punishment, structure it. Structuring means that you do not simply announce your decision and expect it to be followed. A decision to tighten up work rules in the above example, for instance, could easily be viewed as arbitrary or as punishment unless it were preceded by a discussion of the problem with workers either individually or as a group. That way, you communicate your observations and conclusions, (namely, that productivity is affected by lax work rules), provide a limited forum for response, and offer (through advanced warning) an opportunity for workers to voluntarily comply with the rules. You may not even have to lay down the law.

Unpopular Change

Most but not all unpopular decisions involve change of some kind. Tightening work rules is a change from a lax policy to an enforced one. Decisions connected with technical innovations and their subsequent changes are often unpopular because they can be viewed as a threat to job security or to the accustomed way of doing things. Terminating an employee is a change that can be an unpopular one if the person has friends among fellow workers, or if the termination is viewed as ominous by those who fear they may be next.

To the extent that change is involved, you should try to have subordinates participate in the decision making process. You should also take measures to implement that change gradually whenever possible.

In making potentially unpopular changes, you must be open to alternatives so long as the desired results are achieved. For example, going back to the productivity problem owed to poor rule enforcement, you may have learned through discussions that the reason workers take long lunch periods and coffee breaks is because they have begun to feel fatigued earlier in the day. Why? Because one of the first things that the previous department head did as supervisor was to remove the speakers that piped in music. To him, music was a distraction and had nothing to do with eliminating mental fatigue, and he opposed any attempt to bring it back. Putting the merits of the argument aside, what you as the new supervisor have is an alternative worth considering.

Earning Respect

No matter how unpopular a decision may be, remember that it is *your* decision. Identify yourself with it and accept responsibility for it. The respect this will earn will outlive any temporary unpopularity.

Why Are People Indecisive?

W. A. DELANEY

One frequent complaint of senior executives is "my managers won't make decisions." Survey after survey have discovered that indecision is a major problem. It arrests or stops career advancement, yet those who suffer from it do very little about their affliction. Few managers would argue with the old saying, "No decision is the worst decision," yet this describes what many of them do, over and over again.

An Emotional Issue?

Why are some people indecisive? I don't really know, but here are some possible causes:

- Fear of the unknown
- Fear of making a wrong decision or a mistake
- Fear of acting on one's own
- Lack of "good judgment"
- Fear of taking responsibility or standing alone on an issue

These are emotional problems, and they can overwhelm the individuals so affected. Some of these people are not even aware that they are indecisive; others are aware of it but try to hide or suppress this fact from others. It is painful to observe this latter group when faced with a decision. Among the excuses I've heard are:

- "I wasn't sure what to do, so I decided to wait."
- "I need more information."
- "I'm not feeling well. I'm going home."

Then there are those managers who try to pass the decision-making buck:

- "I thought you were going to settle this."
- "That's not my job!"

Reprinted from *Supervisory Management*, December 1982

- "You're the boss. Don't ask me what I think; just tell me what to do."
- "Why is it up to me?"

Indecisive people can be quite creative in explaining away their indecisiveness. But then the problem isn't a matter of intellect; it's an emotional issue. Some indecisive people are very intelligent; they just don't like making decisions, and they won't make them.

I've seen managers go through several interviews with executives of a company in order to get a job, then waffle when the job was offered to them. Why? I don't know. One would assume that they wanted the positions; otherwise, why would they go through two or three interviews with the prospective employer?

Recently the son of a friend lost out on an excellent job opportunity. He had gone through several interviews at the company and verbally been offered the job and accepted. But when he was asked to meet with the head of the organization, he said that he wanted a few more days to think over his decision. The young man desperately wanted the position since the pay would enable his wife to give up her job and care for their young child. Later, he told me that he didn't know why he had asked for a delay in accepting the offer. In any case, he never received the written offer. When he called to ask why, he was told that the president of the firm felt that he was indecisive. He should have been prepared to say "yes" or "no." Instead, he waffled and lost out. His mother thinks that it was a terrible thing for the boss to do. She was shocked when I told her that I would have done the same thing had I been in the boss's position.

I have very strong feelings on the issue. If someone is chronically indecisive, they should face the fact, accept it, and learn to live with it. At work, they must seek and accept jobs that do not require any decision-making responsibilities or at best only involve decisions of a minor or insignificant nature. Even here, they may pause or be indecisive, but at least it won't cause any major problems. I have seen some managers stopped in their tracks over what color to order for new typewriters, where to hold the Christmas party, what food to serve, what color to order for the company softball team hats and jackets, and the like.

A Change in Perspective

Some people are indecisive by their nature; others are indecisive because of the situation in which they find themselves. For instance, decisive people become indecisive when promoted to a higher level or otherwise experience a change in the nature of their jobs. Why this happens is best explained by an example.

Consider a scientist who is very good at his job. For many years, he has done excellent work. Education and experience have taught him never to assume. You study, measure, compute, and recompute; you know where you are at all times. You never move ahead with any loose ends behind you. You move ahead one step at a time; if you are uncertain, you stop to investigate the situation. That's the scientific method.

Now let's assume this person becomes a manager. A decision is called for, but all the pertinent information never can be known. Our scientist may have to predict or guess about future events, then decide what to do. The problem may even change while he is trying to solve it. Among the decisions facing him now might be:

- "How high can we price the proposal and still win the bid?"
- "Shall we build the new plant? Why not just use overtime instead in the old plant?"
- "Charlie seems to be acting up again. He promised he wouldn't behave that way ever again, but this is his third warning. He's been with us for 20 years, but since his divorce he really has gone downhill. What shall I do about him?"
- "Shall we concentrate on that one big job or pass it by and go after several smaller jobs? The big one is very profitable, but I don't like having only a few customers. The little ones are more trouble

and less profitable, but then we aren't too dependent on any one client. We can't do both so which should we choose?"

In situations like these, the scientist-turned-manager may become indecisive. He doesn't know what to do since there is no right or wrong answer. What worked once in the past may never work again. Management is an art form, not a science. There are scientific management tools, but decision making isn't one of them. Decision making involves a human being using his or her judgment.

It is easy to see then why some previously very effective people can suddenly become fearful, indecisive, and ineffective when they are promoted from a job that depends on the scientific approach to a management position. The new job may not be one that suits their individual personality or training.

Moving from a position in which one had complete confidence or mastery of the situation into a new area where one is never sure about things is very difficult. Some people just can't make the adjustment. Fortunately, most can. For them, the period of indecision passes with time and some experience. If the former is a scientist, accountant, or someone who is decisive by nature, he or she will eventually start again to make decisions when the rules of the game are clear and decisions have to be made. If this person is intelligent and uses all the information available, it's likely that the decisions will be as good as any decisions can be.

Quality Decisions

One point worth mentioning: Decisiveness is not a function of intelligence, but intellect does influence the quality of decisions. Consider the kinds of decisions that might be made by someone who is unintelligent but decisive by nature. There are such people, although luckily they are rare. These people make decisions but they are not hampered or encumbered by the careful thought process that those with good judgment use before they make decisions. One of my firm's secretaries was like this. She was very young and very sure of herself. She would continually make snap decisions on her own and she would not stop, no matter how many times she was told to do so. It was in her nature. Before she left us, she did the following:

- She decided that she needed a new typewriter, so she ordered a new $1,300 machine on her own. The order was cancelled when the bill came in.
- She told company personnel to change the hours on their time cards and messed up the monthly payroll accounts.
- She decided that her boss was too busy to accept a call from the firm's biggest client, and she told the person to call back later. It was not a mistake; she knew who was calling.
- She refused to put an emergency call through to her boss. His son had been injured at school, and the principal was calling to ask if the child could be taken to a doctor. This decision was her last. It led to her demotion to the typing pool, and her resignation followed soon after.

Perhaps this young woman would still be with us if she had asked for help in making her decisions. That would have been the wise thing to do.

As a manager, I've found that it pays to ask for dissenting opinions and others' viewpoints before making a decision. And once the decision is made, a review or critique is a good thing, even if the decision proved to be a good one. The decision making process can always be improved upon.

The Bottom Line

When it comes to decision making, each of us has to decide for himself or herself. Some of us may love it. Others may take it as it comes. Those of us who avoid it like a plague perhaps should not be managers.

If you are a manager and have to make a decision, then make it. You will make mistakes as everyone does, but you can learn from these. No decision is worse than any decision you could make. If you let others decide for you, that's not good either. If they decide rightly on a regular basis, they should have your job and that fact will become known sooner or later to your boss. If you let others make your decisions for you and they turn out badly, then you'll gain nothing from the experience. You can't learn a thing from a mistake that someone else made on your behalf.

How to Generate New Ideas

DARRELL W. RAY and BARBARA L. WILEY

Ideas are the most powerful tool in any organization. Supervisors who encourage their employees to come up with ideas and who implement them will help their organizations to be much more productive.

Take the following example. At an electric motor manufacturing plant, a crew ran out of wax in which to dip armatures. In the past its supervisor, Brad, had shown an openness to new ideas from his subordinates so they frequently made suggestions about how to increase productivity. As a result, he was always ahead of quota. This time Brad was faced with having his full second shift sit idle while falling far behind quota. Then one of his employees asked, "Why couldn't we use the old wax? It doesn't get dirty, and all we do is throw it away."

It was a great idea and only required scraping out the vats and recycling the wax. The crew got through the shift with only an hour of downtime and actually exceeded its quota that evening. The net result was a savings of thousands of dollars in resources and productivity over the next few months.

Because Brad had shown a receptivity to new ideas, his employee felt free to make a suggestion. Had she decided it was dangerous to express ideas, she would not have used her initiative.

Having employees who can be counted on to contribute to problem solving has added to Brad's organizational prestige. A supervisor whose crew comes up with a new way to solve an old production problem is much more useful to the organization and therefore has more power than higher-level managers who are unable to generate and propagate ideas within their groups.

So what prevents ideas from being developed, shared, and freely used in the workplace? Why, for example, does a supervisor say in a staff meeting, "We have a real problem with the downtime on press No. 2; I'm open to any ideas on how we can do better preventive maintenance on it" only to have no one come up with a single idea? The reason is that the supervisor by his or her approach to problem solving and idea generation unintentionally discourages subordinates from coming up with ideas. The supervisor does this by being too protective of his or her own ideas.

Ideonarcissism

Supervisors who love their ideas simply because they produced them suffer from "ideonarcissism." Just as Narcissus in Greek mythology became entranced with his own good looks, supervisors can become

Reprinted from *Supervisory Management,* November 1985

convinced that they are the only ones who have good ideas. With such an attitude, they often are unable to get others to accept their ideas and they stifle the creative process in others.

If they do the latter to their employees, their employees' creativity may be channeled in less desirable directions.

Brad, our supervisor at the electric motor manufacturing plant, could have shown a lack of interest in employees' ideas by ignoring them or even by punishing employees whose ideas were contrary to his own. In that event, it is likely the employee in the story would have withheld her suggestion, thus wasting time and resources. If she felt that she had little personal power in her job and that her ideas were not listened to, she might have even found ways to waste the wax and to run out of it more often. As many firms have found, if creativity is not used productively, it may be used destructively.

Overcoming Ideonarcissism

There are three steps a supervisor can take to overcome ideonarcissism. First, the individual must recognize the egotism of thinking his or her idea is unique and the product of a wonderfully creative mind. We are all temporary repositories of ideas received from others. As Sir Isaac Newton put it, "If I have seen further, it is by standing upon the shoulders of giants."

Second, the supervisor must develop an antiroutine streak in employees that will serve as a fertile ground for growing and maturing ideas. The seeds of creativity wither rapidly in an overly routinized workplace, so the supervisor should try to eliminate rigid ways of doing things.

Third, if imitation is the highest form of flattery, then seeing one's ideas taken up by others is the greatest source of gratification to a person interested in generating and spreading good ideas. On the other hand, insisting that one's ideas be fully and properly credited is the least effective method of disseminating ideas. It breeds secretiveness, jealousy, and inhibits others from improving or changing them. Ideas are not born fully mature but need the opportunity to grow and take shape in the minds of others. And while releasing ownership can be painful at first, it paves the way for new sources of satisfaction as the supervisor's influence in the organization increases.

Seeking personal recognition and glory is counterproductive, and eventually it is seen as grandstanding or poor team playing. It is not the responsibility of the supervisor to create a perfect idea but to foster a receptive environment in which ideas can grow.

Becoming an Idea Generator

A supervisor can become an idea generator and wield influence throughout the organization without causing resistance or becoming a stumbling block to his or her own ideas. Here's how.

Idea vending. Many people are lazy and don't read widely in their fields. The idea vendor can become a valuable resource for them by maintaining files of potentially relevant articles on a wide variety of subjects then forwarding materials to them. The information should be offered without strings and without follow-up. Whether the recipient uses the material or not, idea vending builds strong work relationships because people become accustomed to getting good ideas from the idea generator.

Listening. The effective idea generator circulates throughout the unit or organization, listening to problems others are having. Then he or she goes to the files and pulls out articles relevant to what was heard.

Many times normal organizational resistance can prevent truly useful ideas from being accepted. The more controversial or threatening an idea, the greater the need for discreet idea generation. Here are a few suggestions:

Idea attribution. The idea generator should select someone who might benefit from an idea and reveal small pieces of the idea in a casual conversation. When the person picks up any of the pieces, the idea generator should immediately attribute that piece to the other person by saying, "You put a new twist on that; I like that idea." The next step is to support that person's idea in subtle ways at meetings or in conversations. Patience is the watchword, for good ideas may take months, even years, to grow.

Higher-order attribution. Key people in the field often come up with good ideas. The idea generator should find a key person's idea that resembles his or her own and propose the idea through that person's words. It could go something like this: "I heard Tom Hopkins, a nationally known sales trainer, speak on sales development last year and he emphasized the importance of follow-up after the sale. I wonder what ideas we could come up with to show clients we really are interested in them even after a sale?"

Targeting. If the idea generator is unable to communicate directly with the person who could benefit from an idea or who has the power to implement it, he or she should communicate the idea to one or two people who regularly meet with that person. This technique is especially useful in organizations that rigidly adhere to the chain of command. Once the idea has been communicated, the idea generator can subtly reinforce it in meetings and communications over a period of time.

The Supervisor's Dilemma

Besides spreading good ideas throughout the organization, the supervisor must know how to elicit them from subordinates. The question is, how can this be done without the supervisor giving up authority or intimidating employees?

The approaches just cited can be used, but there are others that are particularly effective for supervisors.

Individual project implementation. When assigning someone a major project, the supervisor should clearly identify the problem to be resolved, then tell the employee to think about it for two weeks and come back with ideas for resolving it. Both supervisor and subordinate should then discuss these and agree on what direction to take. It is important to clarify the boundaries of the problem but to remain open to new ways of defining and conceptualizing it. Supervisors who use this approach generally get many good ideas from their employees and a high level of commitment to the final decision.

Adverse impact strategy. It's hard to resist an idea whose time has come. But what most supervisors fail to recognize is that there's an art to making an idea's time come. Too often supervisors will identify a problem, discover a good solution, and bulldoze it through without regard to the culture of the workplace. It's important that new ideas or solutions be introduced in such a way as to create as few problems as possible.

One way is through the adverse impact strategy. The supervisor defines the problem to the staff and suggests that a solution may be needed in the near future. For example, the supervisor could say:

"I want you to think about what we will need to do to keep production running as long as possible and minimize downtime if we have to retool for the new type X model. I'm not sure when or even if we'll change over, but give it some thought as you work on the line these next few weeks."

During this time, the supervisor could occasionally mention the problem to people in casual conversation. At the next staff meeting the supervisor could outline a vague course of action and ask for staffers' ideas and feedback. At subsequent meetings, the supervisor could restate the course of action, incorporating new ideas generated by the group and asking for feedback. When sufficient time has elapsed, a decision could be implemented swiftly and without debate. This approach allows enough time for close examination of the problem, refinement of the solution, effective planning for implementation, and, most important, subordinates' psychological adjustment to the change.

Yes-man test. A supervisor could deliberately propose a poor idea; if subordinates accept it, that may indicate they are easily intimidated or dependent on authority. In such a case, the supervisor should help the group learn to judge ideas by what they're worth, not by who said them. If subordinates fail to objectively evaluate ideas, it means that supervisor has failed to communicate an openness to receiving objective feedback.

Unfortunately, the same problem could happen to supervisors. In one instance, a department head who was particularly eager to please the CEO went back to his unit and implemented the "bad" idea. The CEO learned of this only after a good deal of trouble began surfacing in another department that was adversely affected by the changes.

The idea-generating methods discussed in this article should be used with discretion and concern for the greater good of the organization and the people who work there.

Manipulating ideas without manipulating people is a task that requires a strong sense of values, excellent listening skills, and the systematic sacrifice of one's own need for immediate gratification. The supervisor who can do it will inevitably see his or her influence spread quietly and deeply throughout the organization.

If You Want Your Ideas Approved

D. KEITH DENTON

You may have an idea about how to improve productivity or to change procedures so that the work is done more efficiently. To get a chance to try the idea out, you will need support from others in your organization. This often takes more than logic or "right answers" on your side. Technical expertise is not enough. If you want to get your idea accepted and get others to cooperate, you need to focus on three things: image, human relations, and persuasion techniques.

Image

Convincing others of the merit of your idea starts with your own image. To a great extent, acceptance of your idea depends on what others think of you. For example, if they believe you are manipulative or "up to something," they will not trust you. Suggestions made will be ignored or attacked because who says it is more important than what he or she said. It may not be logical, but if we admire someone for any reason, we will often be more receptive and more easily persuaded by their ideas. Likewise, if we dislike someone because we think they are lazy, pompous, or condescending, we often hear what we expect, not what they said. Verbal, nonverbal, and written communications are all open to interpretation.

Given how image can help or hinder, it's important you become aware of your image. People identify with and respect someone who is fair, honest, and trustworthy. Respect can come partly from associating with respected people and organizations but it is mainly determined by actions. The key is to treat people as you would like to be treated. There are people who want freedom but do not give it to employees, who want a "piece of the action" but do not let others participate in decisions, who value honesty but feel justified in "stonewalling" others, who want to be treated fairly but sometimes appear to play favorites. If you fall into any of these categories, you need to work on your image. Don't assume yours cannot be improved. You can begin to improve your image by applying some basic relations techniques. In the process, you increase the likelihood of getting your ideas accepted.

Human Relations Techniques

Be a good listener. This is one way to enhance your image. Listeners are valued by all of us. Our best friends are often our friends because they listen to us. We know we can tell them something and they

Reprinted from *Management Solutions*, September 1986

will listen. They listen to both the *content* and the *feelings* about what we are saying. They understand what we mean.

We are not good listeners if we assume someone is going to say something uninteresting or unimportant or mentally criticize and attack the person talking. Unfortunately, we often make a point of becoming overstimulated and begin opposing instead of listening. Good listeners recognize that people do not always need advice, just someone to listen so they can air their feelings. Listeners who receive information without criticizing are valuable because they get a clear picture of that person's feelings.

Watch your language. Using *denotative* rather than *connotative* language is another human relations technique to practice. Connotative words are emotionally charged words that cause a reaction—for instance, "manipulate" or "stupid." Using words like these in conversation get a reaction but do not create a positive atmosphere for solving problems. Denotative language avoids value judgments. They are neutral words such as "manage," instead of "manipulate," or "train," instead of "brainwash." If you want to get ideas accepted, watch your language and focus on listening to the other person's point of view.

Openly share information. Your ideas will more easily be accepted if you openly share information. When you make information available about a decision or proposal, you begin the process of *displaying* trust, behavior that makes people more receptive.

Look for shades. Managers who successfully implement ideas recognize shades of differences and know the world is not black and white. They do not classify people as to whether they are with or against them. Instead, they try to seek common ground where agreement is possible. They know that classifying people as adversaries only produces a strong tendency to solidify opposition. So they make it a point to show that they are *willing to work with others* to find solutions. After all, usually the input of others does produce a better approach since more alternatives can be evaluated.

Be open-minded. In this process of exchanging ideas about the best approach or solutions, try to remain open-minded about your ideas and the ideas of others. While this is easy to say, it is very difficult to implement since it requires you to freely listen to others' criticisms.

Basically, the closed-minded or dogmatic person practices extremely selective perception and only sees what he or she wants to see. In the belief that he or she has the "truth," this person shuts out information that is the opposite of his or her personal viewpoint. Such a person does not have good human relations and will not obtain cooperation in implementing his or her ideas since anyone who disagrees will be perceived as an enemy. Open-minded people have empathy for others and are able to see and understand someone else's point of view or attitude. Because they are willing to adjust their perception of what the best method is of obtaining goals, they are more likely to gain.

Persuasive Techniques

The importance of using human relations techniques cannot be overstated, but they are not the final answer. In some cases, people will resent you because of who you are, not what you do. In other cases, you may be dealing with an extremely closed-minded person. This is why mastering persuasive techniques is essential if you are to successfully get your ideas and proposals approved. It gives you options in even the most caustic environment.

There are five steps for promoting the approval of some idea or project. But even before you start, you need to do some planning and strategizing. First, you must clearly understand in your own mind what you want to accomplish. You need to decide before meeting with the person whose approval you need exactly what will be the purpose of your discussion and in what specific areas you will need support or approval.

Only with this understanding can you:

1. Capture attention.
2. Help isolate a need for the idea or project.
3. Show how the proposal satisfies the need.

4. Help the other person visualize the benefits of accepting the idea.
5. Have others perform some action.

Getting someone's attention consists of more than simply asking if someone is listening. This could include making a statement about some recent incident that pertains to the topic. It might also include a quote from some respected member of the organization. A startling statement emphasizing a key point could serve the same purpose. A vivid illustration of some problem that could result from the neglect of your idea could also accomplish this first step.

Isolating some need that is important to the listener is the logical second step. A question like, "Have you ever been irritated at . . . ," or some similar rhetorical question, is one method of isolating such a need.

Needless to say, to isolate a need you must have some understanding of the person to whom you are talking and his or her personal or organizational goals.

Once the person agrees that some need exists, then your next step is to show how you can *satisfy* that need. This process allows a problem-solving format. You are presenting a problem, then showing how to solve that problem. During your discussion you will want to help the other person visualize how some condition will improve if your idea is accepted.

The following is a hypothetical case demonstrating the five-step process.

Danclover Corporation is a medium-sized company that has a policy of subcontracting items that are too specialized for its operation. Recently the company decided to subcontract the design and development of a prototype aluminum part. Carter-Reynolds, Inc. is one of the companies bidding for the contract. Its bid was lowest, but its method of manufacturing is different from what was envisioned by Danclover. The head of engineering has asked the person in charge of manufacturing, Carl O'Hagen, and the directors of personnel, quality control, and purchasing to review the proposal.

O'Hagen doesn't like the design submitted by Carter-Reynolds and prefers instead a more traditional design submitted by the two other bidders. The personnel and quality control directors have neutral feelings about the new design. But Mark Hannah who heads up purchasing likes the bid submitted by Carter-Reynolds for two reasons. For one, Carter-Reynolds has done subcontracting work in the past for the firm and has a good record. For another, the Carter-Reynolds design was several thousand dollars cheaper than the designs of its closest competitors. Based on this reasoning, even though Danclover knows its own in-house expert has not recommended the design, it is preparing to award the contract to Carter-Reynolds.

Unfortunately, within many companies this would be the end of the story. The in-house expert might believe that he has "done his job" by expressing a negative opinion about the design. Purchasing believes it is acting in a manner consistent with management's cost-conscious attitude. If the product does work, then nothing would come of the disagreement except that the manufacturing and purchasing departments would be at odds for awhile. However, if the design is faulty, then valuable time and thousands of dollars would unnecessarily have been spent by Danclover.

Rather than accept the situation as it is, Carl decides to discuss the difference of opinion with Mark. Specifically, he plans to win Mark's cooperation in rejecting the Carter-Reynolds proposal or at least fully explore the ramifications of the decision to use Carter-Reynolds. After listening to Mark's reasons for selecting Carter-Reynolds, Carl responds with a statement of opinion that opens up the following dialogue:

Carl: Mark, I am aware of our company's emphasis on cost-consciousness. However, there are other considerations besides the cost. (*opinion*)

Mark: Carl, you aren't going to give me that risky design stuff again, are you? I've already told you that I've heard that stuff before, and that there are other considerations besides just your opinion about the effectiveness of the design. (*opinion*)

Realizing that Mark is projecting a defensive posture, Carl decides to use a more persuasive approach. He also knows he has to guard against becoming defensive himself.

Carl: O.K., Mark, but just listen a minute. As you sign these contracts, have you ever noticed how many of them do not involve major design innovations? (*attention step*) I was looking over my records and found that about 95 percent of our contracts are involved with projects that do not involve radical or unusual designs. (*fact*)

Mark: You're missing the point. If we're to be a market leader, we want to use the most innovative technology that we can. I think Carter-Reynolds has a lot of experience in this area, and that is why I am recommending the firm. (*opinion*)

Carl: O.K., we disagree on the value of the design, but let me ask you a question. Just for the sake of discussion, suppose that these new parts are unsatisfactory. Furthermore, suppose that the method of manufacture is not capable of producing parts within the tolerances that we need. Have you thought what will happen then? (*need step*)

Mark: Well, in that unlikely event, we will have to find another method of manufacture.

Carl: Who would be responsible for the initial tooling cost involved in building the unsuccessful prototype? (*need step and appeal to cost consciousness*)

Mark: Well . . . uh . . . Carter-Reynolds would, of course.

Carl: Why?

Mark: Because we were buying a product it couldn't deliver.

Carl: But we approved the design. The firm showed us the design that it was going to use and a purchase order was issued. The purchase order to begin the tooling process is a legal contract, isn't it? (*need step and appeal to professional reputation*)

Mark: Uh . . . yes. But we are concerned with the specific design. We are basing our faith in Carter-Reynolds. If the firm can't deliver, then it will have to absorb the cost. (*opinion*)

At this point, Carl has recognized an area where potential misunderstanding might exist and decides to try to clear up the confusion.

Carl: Are you sure that Carter-Reynolds understands its obligations? As an engineer, I would assume that Danclover was buying the process and not just an end product. If I were Carter-Reynolds, and the part failed, I would expect Danclover to pay. (*need step and appeal to reasoning ability*)

Mark: Hmm. . . .

Carl: I believe I see a solution to the problem. If you still want to try out the design, then I think that we could get a legal contract having Carter-Reynolds accept responsibility for a design failure. (*satisfaction step*)

Mark: Yeah, that's a possibility.

Carl: Imagine how you would feel if something goes wrong and you are able to walk into the boss's office and show him that agreement. (*visualization step*)

Mark: Yes, that would certainly help. Well, listen, Carl, I'm going to check this out, and I'll get back with you.

Carl hasn't won fully but by seeking a cooperative atmosphere, he has at least helped to get a more thorough review of the situation. In the process he has gained additional influence and respect in the eyes of someone that could pay off next time he needs support for an idea or a project.

The above illustration shows only one way that persuasion can be used to create a cooperative attitude. In many cases you have a specific project or task that must be completed. Whenever you encounter resistance to your project, these techniques could be used to increase the probability of success.

Summary

The end result of a confident and competent image, coupled with good human relations skills, is cooperation and support for your ideas. If you make a habit of mapping out plans for solving your problems, instead of randomly attacking a situation, then that probability is further increased. While discussions rarely go exactly according to plans, such an approach can be useful. If you have an objective clearly in mind, research the background surrounding the unwanted condition, and identify persuasive arguments, then you will be more successful at getting your ideas and proposals accepted.

How to Nourish the Creative Employee

DONALD W. MYERS

The best supervisor is not necessarily the one who tries singlehandedly to come up with solutions to organizational problems. A more important quality is the ability to channel employee ideas into the mainstream of the organization. To do that requires an understanding of the care and feeding of the creative employee.

The following quiz is a test of your capacity as a supervisor for managing creativity. It is divided into four parts: the human elements of creativity, the impact of the organizational environment, the effect of management philosophy, and the cultural aspects of creativity. Be honest with yourself in answering the questions, and try not to look at the answers before giving your opinion. Answer each question as true or false. The correct answers are explained beneath each question.

The Human Aspects of Creativity

1. Creativity and personal growth are interrelated.

TRUE. When employees are treated as adults who can creatively contribute to the success of the organization, they mature as human beings. An environment conducive to creativity is a prerequisite for self-fulfillment since creativity is in the main a personal expression of one's self. The individual releases creative energies that provide personal fulfillment and satisfaction, which according to Abraham Maslow is an indication of a "healthy personality."

2. Employee creativity is the result of planned management action.

FALSE. Creativity will exist independent of management's actions. Management's role is to direct the creative behavior. As an example, one researcher found that where work methods were strictly prescribed, employees engaged in a variety of creative activities, including different types of games, purposeless antics, and singing. In this case, the creative behavior that was used to counter job monotony was harmless. Creativity can, however, have more harmful manifestations, including clever methods to restrict output—even sabotage. It is the nature of the frustrated employee to either withdraw by engaging in day-dreaming and absenteeism, or to exhibit aggressive behavior in overt violations of organizational rules.

3. There is no proven correlation between creativity and employee performance.

Reprinted from *Supervisory Management,* February 1981

FALSE. Many managers feel that creativity has a detrimental effect upon productivity. They believe that employees who are thinking about ideas are wasting time that should be spent producing. But research conducted by myself and others shows a statistically significant correlation between employee creativity and job performance. Creative employees seem to have a zealous regard for long hours and difficult work.

4. Creative problem-solving is a function of the left hemisphere of the brain.

FALSE. The right half of the brain controls the creative thought process used in solving problems. It is also the source of thought in initiating new programs and analyzing contingencies. The left half of the brain controls logic and decision making based on the routine and familiar. While right hemispheric thought leads to new hypotheses, it is the left side that verifies and rationally analyzes those hypotheses. Studies have shown that in the proper environment people can be induced to utilize the right half of their brain and thus develop their creative abilities.

5. Supervisors could be aided considerably if only there were some means of measuring creativity.

FALSE. There is already a considerable body of research regarding the measurement of creativity. The problem is putting those findings to work.

The Organization

6. Opportunities for employee creativity are limited in most organizations.

TRUE. The opportunities for creative expression are limited because organizations have not encouraged employees to tackle the myriad problems that every organization faces. Intel Vice-Chairman Robert N. Noyce, for one, believes that one of the reasons Japan is winning the competitive industrial battle with the United States is that U.S. manufacturers discourage innovation.

7. Extrinsic rewards like cash and praise are needed to arouse the creative abilities in employees.

TRUE. While intrinsic rewards are important, they cannot be the sole basis for encouraging creativity. Researchers have found that extrinsic reward systems have a significant impact on employees' creativity. The energies employees expend in creative efforts are a function of their desire for a particular reward and their expectation of receiving it. Employees value recognition in the form of money and praise (extrinsic rewards), as well as in the form of meaningful work assignments (intrinsic rewards) that allow them the freedom to choose methods and procedures in accomplishing tasks.

8. One of the principal deficiencies of the scientific management of Frederick W. Taylor is that it ignores the contribution of employee creativity.

FALSE. Taylor was perhaps the first person in management to recognize the creative efforts of employees to cooperatively reduce productive energies. The confusion about Taylor stems from the fact that he advocated scientifically determined methods of work. Consequently, he is criticized for having been insensitive to the human aspects of work and in favor of a more task-oriented approach to management. While some of the criticism may be valid, it cannot be said that he was unmindful of the effects of employee creativity on efficiency.

9. Creativity is an individual process that involves four stages of ideation—preparation, incubation, illumination, and verification.

FALSE. Elton Mayo, writing on the Hawthorne studies, noted that positive group creativity could be obtained by asking for group solutions to problems and by consulting the group about proposed changes. He also found that group involvement assured commitment to the accomplishment of goals.

10. Inflexible organizations prevent employees from exhibiting their creative talents.

FALSE. Inflexible organizations require employees to be more creative in adapting. Gordon Allport has said that creativity is fundamental in personal adaptation to organizational life. The problem for management is the direction of creativity. Many arbitration cases testify to elaborate disciplinary procedures designed to coerce employee compliance to inflexible rules and procedures.

Management Philosophy

11. The creative potential of employees is limited.

FALSE. Your answer to this question reflects your philosophy of management. Douglas McGregor says that Theory X managers would answer true while Theory Y managers would say false, believing that creativity, like other human characteristics, is distributed in varying degrees among people. One of the paramount demands upon managers in the 1980s is to tap the creative potential in employees.

12. Creativity can be developed in employees.

FALSE. While the answer to this one may seem tricky, the concept is not. Employees develop their creative talents, not management. Organizations can aid employees in their development of latent creative abilities, however, by providing an encouraging work environment. The proper atmosphere consists of a management philosophy that recognizes the value of creativity and nourishes ideas with job descriptions that are not tightly constraining, a reward system that is fair, and supervisors who communicate with employees.

13. Suggestion programs are necessary to ensure constructive creativity.

FALSE. While suggestion programs can be excellent for channeling creative energies, they do not guarantee constructive commitment. Systems like suggestion programs can promote employee creativity only if management demonstrates its willingness to recognize the importance of creative ideas. While both the system and the philosophy are important, the latter is more significant because it establishes the rationale for a system's existence. Mary Parker Follett said that people are not going to think creatively unless there is a reason for them to do so.

14. The objective of employee creativity is to obtain ideas that increase the efficiency of the organization.

FALSE. More benefits (or at least as many) result from the by-products of employee creativity than from the direct application of ideas. In my research, I have found that safety, for instance, can be improved when employees and managers are asked to focus their creative energies on finding ways to reduce accidents. A by-product is a heightened safety-consciousness among employees in their daily work. When employees are challenged to think creatively about their work, they seek to know more about their jobs and in the process become more competent and efficient. This self-development aspect of creativity is continuous as employees attempt to gain increasing amounts of knowledge to improve existing skills. This cyclical development can also promote adult personality development. Certainly the organization benefits from the direct application of ideas, but it profits to an even greater degree from the maturative process in which employees seek greater responsibility, become self-regulated, and develop as people.

15. The immediate supervisor determines the quality and quantity of employee creativity.

FALSE. Top management, through its organizational objectives, determines the quality of employee creativity. Supervisors only reflect the concerns of top management.

The Cultural Aspects

16. Creativity and intelligence are related.

FALSE. In a study I conducted, there was no evidence of a difference in creativity between 100 mentally retarded employees and 100 non-retarded employees engaged in the same work and employed in the same organization. Other studies have also failed to indicate a correlation between intelligence and creativity.

17. Creative employees are usually long-haired types who are constantly dreaming up impractical schemes.

FALSE. There may be creative employees who fit that description but for the most part there's no point in trying to identify creative people by their physical features, personal attire, and so forth. The best way to tell is to ask employees for solutions to problems. Familiarity with workers will make their abilities clear enough—provided the organization really wants ideas, treats employees fairly, and gives them adequate recognition for their initiative.

18. Employees usually have little interest in using their creative abilities to help the organization.

TRUE. Researchers have noted that employees usually have little inclination to be constructively creative in their jobs. One of the principal reasons for this is the cultural pressure for conformity. Regimentation begins early in life at school and continues through the work career. During that time expressions of creativity are too often subjected to criticism and even ridicule. Not enough effort is made to stimulate and recognize creativity through intrinsic (meaningful work, opportunity for personal growth, and the like) rewards and extrinsic (money and praise) rewards. The result is inertia and apathy.

19. Research and development is the most appropriate function for creative employees.

FALSE. All organizational functions are appropriate for employee creativity. While there is a tendency to view research and development as the principal—even the sole—domain for creativity, experience has shown that for businesses to remain competitive, employee creativity is needed at all levels and in all functions. The most appropriate place for its use is where the need is greatest.

20. Managers do not appreciate the importance of employee creativity in organizational efficiency.

FALSE. Most modern-day managers realize that creativity is important. The problem is that they don't know what to do about it. As one manager said in a seminar I recently conducted, "I know all about creativity—you should hear the excuses I get from employees who show up late for work on Monday mornings." That's the negative side of creativity. Unfortunately, the positive side is not nearly so evident because employees are often frustrated in their creative efforts.

Part XIII

TIME MANAGEMENT

Building a Professional Image: Dealing With Time Problems

H. KENT BAKER and PHILIP I. MORGAN

John Thomas doesn't plan his day or set priorities. Instead, he drifts from one task to another, delays big or important jobs, and misses deadlines. He can't say "no," so he takes on more work than he's able to handle. Although he has capable staffers, John rarely delegates because he lacks confidence in them and prefers to do the job himself. Sometimes he feels overwhelmed and frustrated because there simply isn't enough time to get everything done.

John is in a time trap. He thinks, "If only I had more time, I'd be able to get out from under this mess." But John's problem isn't a lack of time. Rather, it is his use of his time. He needs to work smarter, not harder.

A supervisor's image may be tarnished or enhanced by how he or she deals with time. John's haphazard approach to managing time contributes to not only an impression of inefficiency and ineffectiveness but also a poor self-image.

An important step in building a professional image is developing a time management strategy. Good time management doesn't happen by accident; it requires a conscientious effort. Devising a personalized time management strategy begins by answering three questions:

1. Where does my time go?
2. Where should my time go?
3. How can I use my time better?

Reprinted from *Supervisory Management*, October 1985

Where Does My Time Go?

Time management problems often stem from poor work habits. Unfortunately, some supervisors are unaware that their habits are a major cause of their time problems. Habits become so ingrained that they are not questioned. For example, John probably isn't aware of some of the things that he is doing—not scheduling, procrastinating, changing priorities, and missing deadlines. Without this awareness, he won't have any idea that he needs to modify his work habits and patterns.

What about you? Are you aware of how you spend your time?

There are several techniques for determining this. The most elaborate and accurate method is the time log. This involves recording your activities every 15 to 20 minutes over several days to have a sufficient number of observations for analysis. You then summarize and analyze the things you do to determine how you can make better use of your time.

In analyzing your time log, you need to ask yourself:

- What are the major activities or events that cause me to use my time ineffectively?
- Which of these tasks can be performed only by me?
- What activities can be delegated, better controlled, or eliminated?

Answering these questions helps you analyze where your time goes and will suggest areas for improvement. For example, you may discover that many of your timewasters are under your control. Thus, the key to managing your time problems may rest directly with you. If you are a part of the problem, you can become a part of the solution.

A time log has the advantage of providing a complete and accurate record of how you spend your time. But it isn't the only way you can determine this. If your job makes such recordkeeping difficult, for example, you might seek feedback from others about your work habits. Select people whom you can trust to be candid. You can facilitate this by giving them your own assessment of your work habits and asking them to comment. Remember, though, for this approach to work, you must be able to accept constructive criticism without becoming defensive.

Where Should My Time Go?

Time is often wasted because of a lack of direction or focus on the job. For example, John Thomas becomes easily sidetracked and wastes time because he does not plan his day or set priorities. John should determine what he really wants to accomplish and then allocate specific blocks of time to these tasks. Instead, he shifts from one task to another, racing to put out fire after fire rather than complete specific goals or objectives.

John claims he is too busy to plan, but one can always take the time to plan. Planning may require a few minutes of thought, commitment, and effort. However, the few minutes devoted to planning a day or a week's activities can help avoid continuous crises. Time spent planning is not time wasted but time invested. Planning can actually help to get more done in less time with better results.

Your planning should start with a determination of what you really want to accomplish. This requires setting short- and long-range goals. These goals should be written up, reviewed frequently, and be as specific and measurable as possible.

Operationalize your goals by using a daily "to do" list. To transform seeming chaos into a list of manageable activities, identify on a piece of paper those tasks that require attention, cross off those items as they are completed adding new items as needed, and rewrite the list for the next day. To prevent the list from becoming too long or cumbersome, concentrate on the important tasks and avoid listing routine chores.

Determining the activities to be performed is only one aspect of time planning. Another is to arrange the items according to their priority. Obviously, not all items on a "to do" list are equally important. Those of greater importance should be distinguished from those of lesser value, thus allowing you to concentrate on completing those tasks with the highest priority and greatest value the first thing in the morning. Low priority tasks can be saved until later in the day. There are two good reasons for doing this. First, you may find it easier to work on more difficult tasks when your energy level is high than when it is low. Second, completing the high priority tasks early provides a sense of accomplishment and eliminates the stress associated with putting off important tasks.

How Can I Use My Time Better?

Once you have determined where your time goes and where it should go, you are ready to apply some appropriate time management principles. A warning is in order before you begin. Principles of time management should be individualized to meet your specific situation, that is, these principles don't apply equally to everyone. Your challenge is to select from the common sense guidelines those that best fit your special circumstances and integrate them into your own personalized time management strategy.

Let's consider John Thomas once again and some of the things that he—and you—might do to gain better control of available time.

1. *Develop good time habits.* John's time problems stem from bad time habits. Apparently he is motivated to do the job but just doesn't know how to do it in an efficient and effective manner. John needs to break old habits and develop new ones. He should target one or two habits for change and begin working on them immediately.

For example, John doesn't have a prioritized plan for his day. So it will help him to develop a daily "to do" list. To make sure the new habit sticks, he should launch the new habit as strongly as possible. Old habits are often difficult to break, and determination is needed to establish new ways of doing things. Hence, he needs to set up a routine that contrasts sharply with his old way of doing things. Second, he shouldn't let an exception occur until the new habit is firmly established. Allowing exceptions simply prolongs the development of the new habit. Third, he should act immediately on his resolution. He shouldn't allow himself to procrastinate.

2. *Schedule the day.* John also drifts from one task to another with little thought. This bad time habit can be overcome through proper scheduling, including blocking out part of the day or week for major projects.

In blocking out time for priority items, John should consider the constraints and special conditions of his job. There may be certain times of the day when he should be available to others. Designating such time to work on priority items would probably be inappropriate.

He should also match his work with his body cycle. There may be times when he works best, such as early in the morning. Such times should be blocked out for working on priority items because he is likely to be most productive then. The end of the day should be reserved for working on lower priority items that require less mental or physical effort.

Effective scheduling requires flexibility in order to accommodate unexpected events. Some uncommitted or slack time is needed to handle unforeseen crises, interruptions, and even opportunities. A schedule that fills every available moment and leaves no room for unplanned events will probably be self-defeating. So it is important not to overschedule.

Another scheduling suggestion is to consolidate similar tasks. This would minimize interruptions and allow John to concentrate on the work at hand. For example, instead of making calls throughout the day, John might group and make outgoing calls at specific times. Frequent callers can also be informed when the best time to reach him is.

3. *Stop procrastinating.* John has a tendency to delay big or important jobs and thus misses deadlines. In other words, he is a procrastinator.

There is nothing wrong with putting things off as long as the right things are procrastinated. In fact, an important principle of time management is to do the important things first and delay the less important things. But some managers are indiscriminate in what they put off doing.

Before John can do anything about his problem of procrastination, he must first determine the reason for it. For example, people often do the things they enjoy first and procrastinate on the tasks they dislike. Procrastination may also stem from such causes as fear, boredom, laziness, or the feeling that the task is overwhelming.

Let's assume that John typically works on smaller tasks with the idea of working up to bigger ones. What often happens is that the tough jobs simply don't get done because too much time is spent doing unimportant ones. The solution is to reverse the process. John should start on the important tasks immediately, if at all possible, and then work his way down his list of priorities.

If the reason for procrastination is boredom, then attacking the boring job when his energy level is highest may be the answer. Getting it out of the way can also provide a feeling of relief and eliminate the anxiety associated with having to face it later.

Sometimes a task is put off because it seems overwhelming. Such tasks can be handled in several ways. One is to divide and conquer; that is, divide the large task into small parts and begin with an easy part just to get started. By completing parts of the project, the project becomes less overwhelming. Also, many managers find an unfinished project more of a motivator than an unstarted one.

Another approach to easing the task of starting a major project is to get more information. Often gathering data about the task provides a better idea of how to approach it and may even stimulate interest. Some supervisors are fearful of starting a project because they really do not know much about it. Information can allay fears by placing a project in its proper perspective.

Other steps toward overcoming procrastination are to work with someone else, make a commitment to others, set a time limit for each job, and reward oneself for the task completed. Regardless of the method used to stop procrastination, it is generally better to do anything that will help move the task along than to procrastinate.

4. *Learn to say "no."* John has another time management problem—he can't say "no." Perhaps he doesn't want to hurt someone's feelings or just wants to be cooperative. He is willing to assume another assignment or someone else's work when asked. Consequently, he has more to do than time to do it. Both his personal performance and mental health suffer because he feels overwhelmed and frustrated.

This is a frequent problem of supervisors. How about you? Occasionally, you may not have any choice but to say "yes." But even when a choice is available, do you still hedge and accept a responsibility you neither want nor have time to perform?

If that is a problem with you, the next time, before agreeing to something that you don't want to do, think about the consequences. For example, if you are in the midst of an important project and someone drops in and says, "Can I see you for a minute?" don't drop what you are doing just to take care of the person's problem unless it is truly urgent. If the matter is not important, propose an alternative. Say, for instance, "I won't be able to discuss that with you now because I have a deadline, but I can stop by your office in an hour."

Saying "no" requires some courage and tact but it is one of the quickest ways of staying on track and avoiding excessive commitments.

5. *Delegate whenever possible.* A final time problem John has is his failure to delegate.

Lack of delegation can be an enormous timewaster. By failing to delegate, a supervisor reduces his or her effectiveness as well as fails to develop staffers. John's failure to delegate stems from his lack of confidence in his employees. Consequently, he ends up taking on many jobs that appropriately should be assigned to others. Hence, he finds himself running out of time while those who report to him run out of work.

If you think the only way to get something done right is to do it yourself, then you may be overwhelmed with work. Try to break the "do-it-yourself" habit. Time devoted to training and motivating people to do tasks that you habitually perform will reduce your day-to-day burdens and enrich the work of others.

Conclusion

Time is one of our most valuable resources, but too many people are like John Thomas, taking a haphazard approach to managing it. Consequently, their image is tarnished and they fail to achieve their full potential. How do you compare with John Thomas? Ironically, it takes time to learn how to use time effectively, but the practice of good time management principles is an investment that could pay handsome rewards for you—a positive professional image.

Time Management:
Making Every Minute Count

LARRY G. McDOUGLE

Time is one of those words in the English language with which everyone is familiar but is often hard put to define. Although the concept of time is universal, each person has his or her own particular definition.

The supervisor sees time as the pivotal factor to be reckoned with in getting done his or her own job and the jobs of his or her subordinates. Good time management is one of the characteristics of good supervision, and there are a number of points that every supervisor should know and remember when trying to make the most of the most valuable resource available to him or her.

They are that:

■ *Time is money.* This adage is as true as it is old. Supervisors must realize that it is as valid for their own time as it is for their employees. Lateness in getting a project completed or a decision made can result in a substantial decline in profits for an organization.

■ *Time is irreversible.* The standard dictionary definition of time underscores the fact that it cannot be reclaimed. Hence, lost time represents a major source of waste for any organization.

■ *Time is equal for all.* Although people are not born with equal abilities or opportunities, they have the same 24 hours a day, seven days a week, 52 weeks a year, and so on, available to them. The issue then becomes one of how that time is managed.

■ *Time can be maximized.* Those who have time to get their work done and who also have time to enjoy non-work-related activities have learned the difference between quality and quantity. They make every minute count.

■ *Time can be wasted.* Of all the resources available to mankind, time is the most mismanaged. The list of contributing factors is almost endless. Ironically, many of the modern-day technological advances that make our lives much more productive and comfortable are also the major time grabbers. Examples include the computer, copy machine, and the ubiquitous telephone.

Time Wasters

As a supervisor, you know how important it is to effectively utilize every minute of your time and your subordinates. Nothing undermines this effort at productivity so much as engaging in meaningless

Reprinted from *Supervisory Management*, August 1979

activities. You have to develop work habits that eliminate this unnecessary waste of time. Typical time wasters include:

■ *Interruptions.* Whether caused by telephone, visitors, or employees monopolizing a supervisor's time, interruptions can be devastating to work output if not properly managed.

■ *Meetings.* Meetings are an ingenious device for simultaneously wasting the time of more than one person. Make meetings count! Never call a meeting if the same objective can be accomplished by memo, telephone, or a personal visit, or if the purpose is nothing more than the dissemination of information.

■ *Inability to say "no."* Perhaps the most successful way to prevent yourself from wasting time is by saying "no." There is an old saying that if you want a job done, look for someone who is already busy. Although there is a measure of truth to this, there comes a time when an individual has to protect his or her time from exploitation. There is a limit as to how much any one person can do.

■ *Filing.* Particular attention must be paid to what is filed. Thanks (or no thanks) to the copy machine, paper can now be generated in staggering amounts. More than half of it should probably be disposed of immediately. If you are uncertain about the importance of a given piece of correspondence, consider using this technique: Place it on the corner of your desk near the waste basket; if a follow-up doesn't appear within 30 days, throw it away. It obviously wasn't very important.

■ *Unfinished business.* A great deal of time is wasted by people who have good intentions when they begin an assignment but never get around to completing it. Managers of baseball teams have become prematurely gray from games lost because a batter failed to score the runner on third base at the end of an inning. The rules in baseball don't allow for partial runs. Neither do the rules for effective management.

Supervisory follow-through can play an important role in making sure a job gets done. As supervisor, you should establish a deadline for the completion of a task, insist on progress reports, and praise an employee for a job well done. The last is a sure-fire guarantee that the next assignment will be performed even better.

■ *Indecisiveness.* Effective supervisors are not afraid to make decisions, even those decisions that may bring controversy. Indecision wastes time and money and destroys employee morale. How many times have you heard managers and other supervisors say to one another, "I really don't care what they do as long as they do something."

Perhaps even more counterproductive than the supervisor who can't decide is the one who keeps changing his or her mind. Most people are reluctant to follow someone who can't decide where he or she is going.

Techniques for Managing Time

To help you control your time, consider the use of the following:

■ *The desk calendar.* Most supervisors are aware that the calendar can be used for scheduling meetings and appointments, but it can also be used effectively for noting deadlines, due dates for reports, and items requiring supervisory follow-through. It is helpful to schedule tasks and appointments in advance, thus avoiding the unenviable position of needing to be in more than one place or to do more than one thing at the same time.

■ *To-be-done sheets.* A very effective approach for managing time is to carry a notebook containing a list of daily or weekly activities that have to be completed. As tasks are accomplished they can be crossed off; others are added as they come to mind. This technique can be especially valuable as a reminder on correspondence to be addressed, phone calls to be made or returned, information to be obtained, and people to see.

■ *Planning sheets.* The planning sheet acts as a reference guide to completed activities and those that are pending. It can help the supervisor zero in on how much time is required and should be allocated to complete a given task.

■ *Reflection.* Periodically, supervisors should take time out to reflect on how office matters are progressing. Your use of time needs to be continuously reviewed, analyzed, and evaluated. Taking time to think can be a profitable exercise for every supervisor. In fact, it may be better than jogging.

The Ten Commandments of Good Management

Now that we've discussed good time management practices and ways you can develop them, let's look at what I consider to be must-dos of good management that relate to good time management. Remember that part of effective supervision is the efficient use of time. Adhering to these "ten commandments" will help you improve your use of time and, as a result, your style of supervision.

1. *Thou shalt have no other clocks before thee.* Excessive clock watching may be symptomatic of deep-rooted personnel problems that a supervisor cannot afford to ignore. Chances are that the employee who continually checks the time is not satisfied with his or her job and, as a consequence, is unmotivated and unproductive. A college professor I know had a group of students who spent more time watching the clock than paying attention to what was being said in class. One day they discovered a sign beside the clock. It read, "Time is passing. . . . Are you?" Your effectiveness as a supervisor will be challenged when your subordinates fail to perform.

2. *Thou shalt not kill time.* Hockey is a sport in which a team's ability to kill time during its opponent's power play is highly valued. Few businesses, however, can survive for long when they possess an overabundance of paid time killers. Employees who do this are actually wasting their most valuable resource, and a supervisor who is concerned about the welfare of his or her employees and the organization should not tolerate it for too long.

3. *Honor thy secretary and staff.* A good secretary is worth his or her weight in gold. Too many supervisors don't know how to make proper use of one. An informed secretary can eliminate interruptions by screening telephone calls and visitors and sorting correspondence from junk mail. Likewise, a staff that is properly utilized can make a supervisor look good and enhance his or her chances for promotion.

4. *Thou shalt not steal another person's time.* Every organization seems to employ people who apparently don't have enough work to keep themselves busy and as a result float from office to office and disturb those who do. They are not only stealing time from the company; they are also stealing precious time from their co-workers. The economic implications are sobering.

5. *Thou shalt not bear false witness about the use of time.* There are many employees who are less than truthful about the use of their time. It is probably one of the reasons time clocks were invented. As individuals progress upward in the management hierarchy, their amount of discretionary time increases and with it an increased requirement for self-accountability.

6. *Thou shalt not eat lunch alone.* Taking one hour for lunch each day adds up to the equivalent of more than six full weeks of work per year. There isn't a supervisor in the world who couldn't accomplish a great deal given six weeks.

Lunch hours are necessary but they should not be wasted. This is not to say that all lunch hours have to be business-related. Nor does it deny the importance of private time for meditation and reflection. But lunchtime represents a marvelous opportunity for making contacts, getting to know co-workers better, and making yourself known to higher-level managers. Supervisors who take advantage of this time are bettering their chances of recognition and promotion.

7. *Thou shalt take thy vacation.* Every organization has a few workaholic supervisors who think they are so indispensable that they can't afford to take a vacation. Some of them even convince themselves that refusal to take a vacation is a mark of dedication. Nothing could be further from the truth. People need to periodically get away from the job, no matter how satisfying or rewarding it may be.

8. *Thou shalt not procrastinate.* Most people are naturally inclined to put off doing anything that is unpleasant, but the simplest advice is the best advice—do it and be done with it.

9. *Thou shalt not be afraid of work.* The world is full of supervisors who lack effectiveness because they lack confidence in themselves. They dread the thought of making a presentation before a group because they fear embarrassment or rejection, and they are afraid to take on a new assignment because

they "don't know enough about it." People who experience these types of fears should remember one thing: There is no substitute for being prepared. A supervisor who does his or her homework will seldom have cause to be embarrassed or afraid.

10. *Thou shalt not covet another's time.* How often are the following expressions heard? "How do they find time to do everything?" "I wish I had time to do some of the things that they are doing. There just aren't enough hours in the day." People who covet someone else's time have not learned how to use their own—and never will unless they are willing to work at it.

Some Ideas to Consider

Most supervisors are familiar with Douglas McGregor's Theory X-Theory Y styles of management. According to these theories, an individual's supervisory style reflects how he or she views human nature. The Theory X manager assumes that people are basically lazy and attempt to avoid work at all costs. The Theory Y supervisor believes that people are willing to do a day's work for a day's pay. No attempt will be made here to debate the relative merits of either approach, but the supervisor should realize that the inherent view he or she has with regard to employee motivation will have direct implications on the effective use of his or her time and that of subordinates. It will be reflected in such areas as the closeness of supervision, degree of delegation, and involvement in decision making.

Subordinates have a right to know what is expected of them. The supervisor must make a conscious effort to establish and communicate goals and objectives to the employee, and those who understand the objectives of the organization stand a better chance of being committed to them. Commitment is the key word. An organization with committed people is not likely to have a time-management problem.

Theories have their rightful place, but there is no substitute for common sense when it comes to management of time and people. Common sense is an expression much like time in that people recognize it but have trouble defining it. There is no doubt that common sense is a highly desirable quality in any supervisor. It will manifest itself in a number of ways. For example, the effective supervisor recognizes that all people do not work continuously at the same speed. Individuals experience fatigue, encounter family problems, suffer unavoidable delays on the job, and have legitimate absences from work. Although a certain measure of uniformity is both desirable and necessary, the supervisor must be prepared to show flexibility when the situation demands it.

Supervisors who manage their time successfully have mastered the art of filtering out the few important from the many trivial on-the-job activities. The good supervisor is one who is not a victim of time but its master and helps his or her subordinates to achieve mastery as well. Remember that your objective is not to get the most out of your subordinates, but rather the best.

Do You Have to Suffer From All Those Interruptions?

MERRILL E. DOUGLASS

Have you ever thought about how often you are interrupted in the course of your work day? Would you say twice an hour? Maybe three or four times an hour? Could it be as much as eight to ten times an hour? Actually, if you work in an office, you will be interrupted about every six to nine minutes on average. That means from six to ten interruptions every hour. Over the course of the day, you could easily be involved with dozens of interruptions.

Although you face a huge stream of interruptions daily, you probably haven't done much more than complain about it. You simply assume that it is a part of the job and there is nothing that *can* be done about it. That is partly true, and partly false. Interruptions are part of your job, but that doesn't mean you have to accept the way they are occurring now.

Sometimes it is your attitude about interruptions that needs adjusting. You need to prioritize your activities to see that your time is being focused on the right things, then accept responsibility for controlling interruptions in your work. Admittedly, some interruptions you can't control. But there are others you can. For example, you can't control when someone calls you, but you can control whether or not to take the call. You may not be able to prevent people popping into your office, but perhaps you can influence how long they stay.

A Matter of Control

Control often begins with an assumption. If you think there is nothing you can do, you are probably right. But if you believe there is some way you can change the situation, you will keep looking and experimenting until you find a better way.

For instance, for telephone interruptions, here are several things that might help:

- Have your secretary screen incoming calls and offer to help callers on any routine matters.
- Establish quiet hours during which you accept only emergency calls. Have someone take messages so you can return calls later.

Reprinted from *Management Solutions*, July 1987

- Tell people who call you regularly when you prefer to receive calls. Most people will cooperate and try to call at the preferred times, especially if they realize the chances are much better of actually getting you at that time.
- Get through the social "small talk" as quickly as possible. Get right to the point and stay there.
- Bring calls to a prompt close.
- Tell long-winded callers that you have a pressing appointment or deadline.

On the other hand, perhaps most of your interruptions are drop-in visitors. If so, here are several ideas that might help you control those interruptions:

- Close your door for some quiet time. Regular quiet time will allow you to concentrate on tasks and accomplish a great deal in a short time.
- Encourage the use of appointments rather than unscheduled visits.
- Go to the other person's office if he or she must see you; you'll have more control of when to leave.
- Stand up when someone comes in, and remain standing while you talk. Things never last as long when you are standing.
- Meet visitors outside your office. Hold stand-up conferences in hallways, reception areas, conference rooms.
- Rearrange your furniture so you are not facing the traffic flow. If you can avoid eye-contact with people passing by, you will block many casual interruptions.
- Have your staff members save up several items and go over them all at one time. Do this yourself, too. If everyone would simply bunch things together, the interruption problem would be cut in half immediately.
- Be candid when someone asks, "Got a minute?" Learn to say "no." Be quick to take time for critical issues, but slow to respond to trivial issues. Practice saying no, and learn to recognize when no is the appropriate answer.

The key word is "appropriate." Interruptions are the biggest timewaster listed by most people. Because of this, there is a tendency to consider all interruptions as negative. But interruptions can also be very positive. One manager recently told me that a customer's visit is never an interruption. What he meant is that he considers customers as very important. You might think about your own interruptions. You will probably find that it is the negative ones that frustrate you most. If you could reduce the negative ones, you would be way ahead.

A Problem-Solving Approach

It also helps to think of negative interruptions as problems. Step one in problem solving is to identify or define the problem. To do that, you need facts. But if you are like most of us, you are reluctant to collect data. Instead, you will look for a quick fix, an easy solution to an impossible condition.

For example, I recently received a call from my friend, Charlie, who owns a business. "What's the problem, Charlie?" "The telephone is driving me crazy." "How many calls do you get every day?" "Lots of 'em." "I see. And exactly who calls you?" "Everyone." "Well, what do they call about?" "Everything." "What do you want from me?" "Don't you have a couple of quick ideas that will solve my telephone problem?"

That is where most of us are. We get lots of everything from everybody—the fuzzy mess. And we want to solve it all with a quick gimmick.

Interruptions aren't neat. They are all jumbled up and stacked on top of one another. They are not the crisp, clean kind of problem you love to tackle—they really are a fuzzy mess, and most of us prefer to leave a fuzzy mess alone.

Seem absurd? We hear it all the time. Most of us want a quick fix for a general problem. We never realize that "general" problems aren't solvable. We can only solve specific problems.

Consequently, if you face a lot of interruptions in your job the best thing you could do is to record them all for several days. When do they occur? Are they telephone calls or drop-in visits? How long do they last? Who is involved? What is it about? How important was it? An interruption log is easy to keep and will provide you an amazing insight into your job.

When you complete your interruption log, study the data. Look for patterns. For instance, you will probably notice that a few people interrupt you often—far more than average. They should be bunching things together for you. Or you may find that many different people call you about the same things. Perhaps you need to reexamine how information can be disseminated better. Some interruption patterns will reveal weaknesses in your training procedures. You may see that you socialize far more than you realize. Whatever the patterns you find, you will be able to break your interruptions into definable problems and tackle them one at a time.

Few people attempt a really serious approach to interruptions. They "don't have time" to find the source of their problems. Often, they simply assume a cause or look for a scapegoat. It is simpler to pass quick judgments than to define the problem, analyze the facts, and develop good solutions.

Do Unto Others . . .

In our seminars, discussions about interruptions usually reveal another interesting point. Most people see interruptions as something other people do to them. They seldom consider what they do to others. Think about it. When someone mentions interruptions, what image immediately comes to your mind? Isn't it mostly of other people interrupting you? Only rarely do people mention that they are also big interrupters. But we all interrupt. It is not just *them,* it is also *me.* If you and I began to improve the way we interrupt others, perhaps they'd start reciprocating. One last point: Whatever you do, be firm with time but gracious with people. It never pays to be rude. While it may offer a short-term gain, the long-term penalties are too high. What is more, it isn't even necessary. There is almost always a way to resolve interruption problems graciously and leave others feeling good about themselves . . . and good about you, too.

The "Deadline" Syndrome

ARTHUR G. SHARP

Andersonville was an infamous Confederate prison camp during the American Civil War. Thirteen thousand Union prisoners died there—many of them because of "deadlines."

The prison guards established a protective boundary, called the "deadline," between themselves and the captives. The guards warned the prisoners not to cross the line. To do so meant death. Nevertheless, many of the prisoners did go over—and died. Some crossed on purpose, others went by mistake. Whatever the reason, the results were tragic.

While today adherence to deadlines is no longer a matter of live or death, it can have a critical effect on an individual's chances for advancement, particularly those of someone like a supervisor, who is responsible for quality jobs completed on schedule.

The Use and Abuse of Deadlines

The use of deadlines can add a valuable management control, but they more often hurt than help. This is just what happened to Phil, the manager of a corporate personnel department.

Phil's boss, Ted, told him that he wanted a particular job completed and on his desk in two weeks. Phil explained that it was not possible. There were too many other people involved in getting the job done. Ted, however, gave him a classic executive answer: "I don't care. My boss wants it done. How you get it done is your problem. I expect it on my desk in two weeks!"

Phil found himself forced to give his subordinates less time to get the job done. He knew they would be unhappy—but he had no choice.

"You're kidding!" one of his subordinates gasped. "Do you realize that we have to coordinate tasks with typists, outside vendors, and a few other people outside our department? They don't care about our deadline; they have enough trouble with their own. We won't get the job done in a month—let alone two weeks!"

"We have to do it," Phil replied. "We have a deadline."

The group tried hard, but despite its efforts, the job was not completed on time. Ted was upset with Phil's inability to meet the deadline, and Phil, in turn, passed the displeasure on to his subordinates. Ironically, none of the individuals involved was totally responsible for the failure. The real culprit was the deadline, one of the most misused weapons in management's arsenal of techniques.

Supervisors fall into four basic groups in their approach to setting deadlines:

Reprinted from *Supervisory Management*, October 1979

1. Those who set unrealistic, impossible-to-meet deadlines.
2. Those who set deadlines that, loosely translated, mean "Whenever you get around to it—even never, if you don't feel like doing the job."
3. Those who don't set deadlines at all.
4. Those who set realistic, attainable deadlines.

The members of the first group create special problems for themselves. Because they do not first consult their subordinates, or consider the myriad details that must be taken care of before the job is completed, they lose control over the job and place undue pressure on their workers, who then take shortcuts to finish the job. Frequently the finished product is inferior, and the deadline is not met anyhow. This practice is inefficient, unproductive—and also too common.

Loose deadlines, or no deadlines at all, can be just as risky as unrealistic ones. A supervisor who assigns subordinates to jobs and tells them to complete them "whenever you get around to it" is inviting trouble. Individuals who are given this vague direction are prone to give such jobs low priority. Often, in cases like this, the supervisor suddenly demands that the jobs be done immediately, and the individuals who have put off the assignments are faced with unexpected pressure and react the same as those who are given unrealistic deadlines. Again, the jobs may be finished but not as thoroughly as they would have been if the subordinates had known beforehand precisely when they were due.

The Right Approach

The most effective supervisors are those who set realistic, attainable deadlines. They carefully consider what is necessary to do a job, anticipate problems, and arrive at dates that are satisfactory to everyone working toward the goal. They do not commit themselves or their subordinates to any date until they have thoroughly evaluated an assignment.

In setting deadlines, supervisors should follow these four simple rules:

1. Allow some flexibility in establishing deadlines.
2. Consult the people who are going to do the work.
3. Anticipate problems.
4. Monitor the progress of a job.

Let's look at each of these four rules more closely. The value of the first should be obvious. Allowing some flexibility in setting deadlines compensates for unexpected problems that might impede progress.

Deadlines should be set based on the scope, importance, and complexity of each job. Under no circumstances should a supervisor set purely arbitrary deadlines. Many supervisors, in an effort to please their superiors, do not consider all of the factors involved in setting realistic deadlines—to their detriment. They will assure their superiors that they can complete a job by the prescribed date just to placate them, knowing full well that it is impossible. But while ambitious estimates may impress upper-level management at first, any delays in completing a job or failing to meet a deadline ultimately destroy the supervisor's credibility. To avoid this, supervisors should honestly estimate how much time is required to complete an assignment and allow sufficient time to do the job properly. In the long run, realistic estimates are accepted by upper-level management, who are usually willing to negotiate deadlines for legitimate reasons.

The Subordinate's Role

Some supervisors feel that they bear the entire responsibility for setting deadlines. This is a typical managerial fallacy. The more complex a job, the more essential it is that supervisors ask for time estimates from their people. When a particular task requires several people coordinating various activities, it becomes mandatory that more than one person be consulted. For simple jobs, supervisors should make their own estimates. In any case, supervisors would do well to make it a habit of asking their subordinates for an estimate of time they feel is necessary to complete their jobs. This serves the following purposes:

- It enables supervisors to involve their workers in the decision-making process.
- It gives the workers a feeling of participation and value.
- It compels everyone involved in the project to consider honestly the essential time factor.

In Cases of Emergency

The third and first rules for setting deadlines go hand in hand.

No matter how carefully supervisors plan, they cannot foresee everything that can go wrong with an assignment. Predicting problems is only a guessing game, at best. The important thing the supervisor must realize is that something can go amiss, and he or she should allow for setbacks when establishing a deadline.

The expectation of problems leads to our fourth rule, which is to monitor the progress of the job.

Supervisors who handle a job from beginning to end know if they will meet their deadline or not. If problems do develop, they are generally able to solve them without changing the due date. Of course, major problems can necessitate adjusting a deadline. This is of little consequence to supervisors who set dates realistically in the first place. For them, the deadline is a practical, invaluable management technique. They use it properly to help themselves establish reputations for reliability and credibility—and as a tool for success.

Getting Organized

ROSALIND GOLD

A crowded desk may be convincing evidence that you have a lot of work to do—or that you're totally inefficient! In either case, though, it is a signal that it is time to get organized.

Professionals apply the lean-storage principle to eliminate office clutter: They visually divide a workspace and keep the most accessible areas leanest, the least accessible areas most crowded.

Figure 1 shows the application of the lean-storage principle to some bookshelves. The very top and bottom shelves, the hardest to reach, hold notebooks and other books seldom used. Shelf #2 contains materials used fairly often—notice the extra space that makes it very easy to remove and replace items. Shelves #3 and #4—the most accessible—are nearly empty, providing a manager with plenty of space to temporarily store papers and keep important items handy.

Every working space can be improved by the lean-storage principle—shelves, files, credenzas, even a desk drawer.

But What About All the . . . ?

The next step is to clear your desktop for action. That means you'll need filing space for the items that are there now. Because your desk drawer is so convenient, you'll want to keep it lean. Reserve it for the work that you're currently handling. Having those papers close at hand lets you retrieve information instantly and—equally important—lets you put papers away fast, so your desk stays neat. Paperwork to which you refer less frequently belongs in a personal file cabinet or in the department's regular filing system.

Here are four ways to make personal filing easier:

1. Don't try to organize files logically. Instead, organize them to match the way you think. For easiest retrieval, use file names that correspond to the words on your daily to-do list. For instance, if you write "Finish the Lancaster Project" on your to-do list, name the file folder "Lancaster." You'll automatically remember where you put the Lancaster papers. (Incidentally, when the Lancaster project is finished, transfer the folder to a more remote place. Why use prime storage space for past history?)

Reprinted from *Supervisory Management*, February 1983

Figure 1

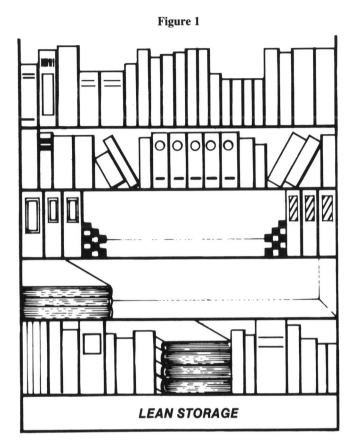

LEAN STORAGE

2. Stuff the file folders with as many papers as fit. This advice runs contrary to conventional teaching, but it makes good sense: There is less chance of misfiling, and there are fewer folders to handle when you retrieve or put papers away.

3. For that special document—the one that you always seem to need but can never find—set aside a special folder.

4. Miscellaneous items—those notorious desk clutterers—can be handled with three special files: An "ideas" file for the notes you write yourself; a "self-development" file for course brochures and self-development plans that a manager needs; and a "someday" file for any papers that you might need someday and are reluctant to part with.

Mastering the In-Basket

Keep your workspace free from clutter by setting aside a special place for the incoming mail. One manager I know calls this mail station "central receiving." Actually, it's a brown wooden box on top of his credenza and he stores everything there that flows in during the day.

Unless you receive mail that demands instant attention, you're better off setting aside one hour a day to go through the in-basket. This habit prevents incoming mail from distracting you while you're busy with other matters and keeps your desk top clear so that you can work more efficiently.

When you're ready to process the mail, sort it into three piles—material to discard, material to route, and material to keep. Throw the discard pile out. Send the route pile immediately on its way. Papers that you don't feel confident about discarding or routing—but that don't require immediate action—belong in the "someday" file for later reference.

The remaining mail can then be sorted into three file folders, color-coded for easy identification. "A" priority mail might go into a red file folder to be answered today, "B" priority mail into a blue file folder to be handled tomorrow, and "C" priority mail into a yellow file folder to be handled at the end of the week.

This sorting process should take only five or ten minutes, which leaves fifty minutes to respond to all the mail in the red file folder, (if extra time permits, you can begin to handle what you can in the blue folder.) A time limit is essential: having a deadline prevents you from proceeding too casually.

By Friday, of course, the blue and yellow folders will be full, so set aside some extra time that day to process the mail in them. That way, when you leave for the weekend, you will enjoy the pleasure of knowing that all the mail folders are empty. For most managers, that freedom alone makes the self-discipline worthwhile. Consider these benefits, too: Expediting the mail is an excellent way to sharpen your decision-making abilities. Concentrating on the red folder daily ensures that you spend your time where it counts the most. The majority of work that crosses a manager's desk does not warrant the amount of quality attention that top priorities, by definition, require. So it makes sense for you to handle less important mail at your convenience and at one sitting so they don't use up more of your time than they really deserve.

Your Secret Weapon

There's one more step to getting organized—maintaining a master control book, a looseleaf binder that holds the plans, notes, checklists, and other information to which you refer constantly. Not only does it guarantee that your essential operating information is always handy, it reinforces your memory—just flip to the appropriate page when you need to check a detail. (Note to procrastinators: Tough assignments go faster when you have notes, checklists, and models to get you started.)

To create your own master control book, get a three-ring binder with five section dividers. In time, you can customize the book to suit your own needs, but for starters here's a plan that has worked for hundreds of managers.

Section 1: today. In this part of the master control book, keep your daily to-do lists and any relevant notes.

Section 2: followup. Here you should put 12 assignment logs like the one shown in Figure 2. Set up one log for each calendar month to keep tabs on all known commitments coming due.

Section 3: task plans. A task plan is a description of work to be done. Set up one page for every important task you receive. When an assignment is explained, jot down notes on the task plan. Each time you get more information, fill in more details. By the time you are actually ready to begin working on the assignment, you should have most of the background information that you will need to make a strong start.

Section 4: checklists. This section contains equipment control checklists, filing procedures, budget preparation checklists—you name it. If you don't have such checklists, consider developing them gradually. When delegating, they are indispensable. How often have you said, "I can do it faster myself"? Explaining a task to someone is very time consuming. But checklists cut down on this time, give your employees a procedure to follow (which helps reduce errors), and gives you a vehicle for monitoring work in progress.

Section 5: guide letters. Managers spend hours to produce written communications that are direct, readable, and persuasive. Why reinvent the wheel? Make yourself an extra copy of the best correspondence that you receive, and file it in Section 5. The next time that you are stuck for a good way to start a letter or a practical report format, get some instant help.

Figure 2

Assignment Log						
Date Assigned	Assignment	Estimated Completion Time	Deadline Date	Extended to	Date Delivered	Remarks

© 1981 Rosalind Gold, The Time Management Workshop

Finally . . .

One last note about getting organized: As long as you are alive and your personality is growing, any organizational system you select will have a life cycle. This means that periodically you will find yourself getting disorganized. Times like these often coincide with times when you get a new sense of yourself. An entirely new system is needed, one that more accurately reflects the person you have become. So take another look at your messy desk. It may indicate you've reached a new stage of growth in your career.

Are You Caught in a Web of "Administrivia"?

JACK A. HILL

Trivial concerns like who sits where and who provides telephone coverage during lunch capture employee attention, often shifting it away from organizational to personal goals. As employees react out of proportion to perceived pressures from others, organizational objectives seem to lose their importance. The situation could be ignored over the short term except that over the long term these little things called "trivia," left unattended, will fester and grow. Figure 1 diagrams some nonrational ways of approaching trivia.

Trivia's Effect on the Mind

One of the unfortunate aspects of trivia is its not-so-trivial costs. Dealing with it costs energy, time, and money. Energy is expended that can be translated into lost time—and time is money. Productivity problems occur as employees talk with fellow workers about the irritation, taking longer than normal to perform a job, and fantasize about getting even.

Conditions that some managers consider trivial and believe exact unwarranted intrusions into their time and other resources are seen as necessary use of their talents by their employees. It is a matter of perception.

Usually some common areas of agreement exist as shown in Figure 2.

B's perception of trivia includes areas T-1 and T-2, while A's perception of trivia focuses on areas T-2 and T-3. Both A and B agree that area T-2 is a time-wasting imposition of their respective energies. However, A can't understand why B doesn't see the importance of the situation in area T-1, and of course B wonders why A is frittering away time taking care of the unimportant matter in area T-1 when the problem T-3 deserves attention.

Trivia is not trivial to the people who have a stake in its outcome. This includes not only those directly involved but others who become involved when asked to "take my side." The effects of some trivial situations move through organizations in a network-like manner. Neither formal lines of communication nor people's feelings are respected.

Reprinted from *Supervisory Management*, September 1983

Figure 1
Trivia's Non-Program

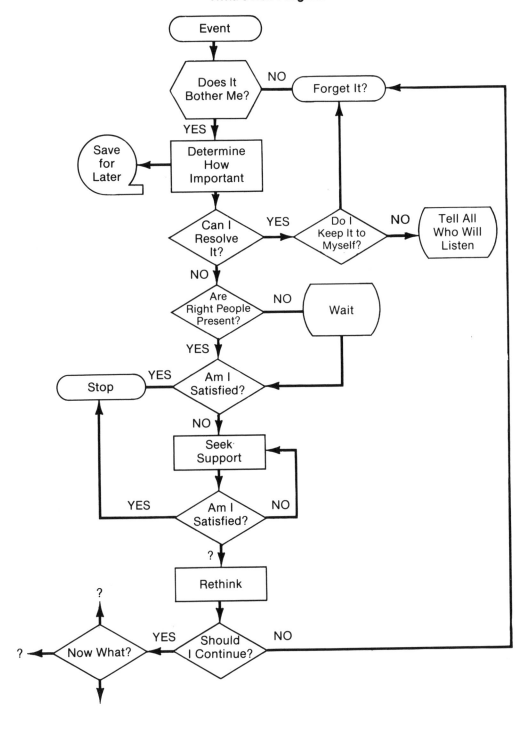

Figure 2
Trivia: Differences in Perception

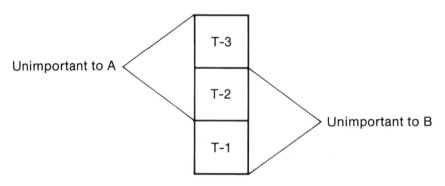

Trivia Tangles Objectives

Managers know how plans can go awry because a trivial matter was thrust forward for immediate attention. Personal problems take priority over organizational concerns as "administrivia" situations spread beyond the parties involved. The cause celebre needs its champions, followers, even camp followers who for the sake of friendship offer support. Given sufficient incendiary conditions, uninvolvement may be impossible. In effect, the person with the problem says, "If you're not with me, you're against me."

In any event, organizational serenity is difficult to achieve these days. There are too many ways for trivia to triumph. The technology of the workplace provides ample opportunities. On top of that people have proprietary feelings about their work, workplace, and so forth that can trigger emotional outbursts that seem uncalled for to objective observers.

Temperamental outbursts can occur as people argue about who answers the telephone; who sits where; who took the paper cutter, stapler, or paper punch; or whether someone should be called Miss or Mrs. instead of Ms.

Trivia, somewhat like accidents, arises from a proportioned mixture of three factors: time, place, and a triggering event. The time for trivia to blossom is any time. The place is any place. The trigger can be anything. The circumstances that could act as trigger won't be ignored because of such things as friendships, position in the organization, sex, or age. Good friends, for instance, may be more tolerant of each other's behavior, but when the time, place, and one's feelings combine into a critical mass, there will be an emotional explosion.

Time. The startup and end of the workday provide a setting for trivial circumstances to grow and become irritants.

People come to their jobs ready to work and become exasperated when, for instance, they can't find tools and supplies where they left them. Since it looks bad for them to be away from their work stations searching for something, they defensively try to place the blame for their idleness. One word leads to another.

The end of work and start of the lunch period also spawn conditions for trivia. People don't like to be late meeting friends or getting to a bus stop or car pool. Ill-timed requests to start a new task or redo something create discontent that can linger a long time.

Place. The human desire for possession makes space an important factor in the trivia equation.

- A long-service employee witnesses a less senior employee getting new tools, a desk, a better work station, and so forth and becomes angry and complains to co-workers and superiors about the injustices.

- An employee assigned to work in a congested area is annoyed when a colleague is given better working conditions.
- A worker is asked to perform a dirty job after being with a company four years. "I've paid my dues," she thinks to herself. "Why doesn't my supervisor give the task to the new hire?"
- Employees become enraged when they learn that others are being hired for similar work but at a higher wage because of "market conditions."

Most days contain events that given the right circumstances—like an unemptied wastebasket when all others have been emptied—can trigger an emotional outburst.

It is difficult for a manager to control place in order to prevent trivia because circumstances affect perceptions. The "right" place can become the "wrong" place under different conditions.

Triggering event. An individual's personality with its attendant values and attitudes influences what will trigger the emotional outburst or reaction that to others appears out of proportion—trivia. For the most part, the level of emotional maturity under the pressure of the circumstances determines whether a trigger will be pulled.

Behavior patterns determine how people will react. These can be divided into three categories: childish, adolescent, and adult. Children have a need for attention and may seize on anything convenient if it suits their purposes: a kick, a shove, an outburst, or any other attention-getter will be used. Adolescents need reinforcement for their fragile egos. The work situation provides them with many opportunities for showing off and otherwise proving themselves. The adult tends to be more philosophical and can shrug off many irritants. But given the right circumstances even the mature person can display childish or adolescent behavior patterns.

Let's look at two incidents to see how small matters can expand to consume inordinate amounts of time.

In the first one, in an air conditioned office staffed by nine persons, there was a portable fan used exclusively by an obese secretary. A clerk, also obese, coveted the fan—especially on days when the air conditioning wasn't sufficient. The clerk asked the supervisor to permit him to share the fan, and the supervisor agreed to the request.

The secretary learned of the change when the fan was not in its customary place. When she demanded it back, she was told about the new arrangement. The supervisor overheard the exchange and confirmed it. In a moment of anger, the secretary jerked the electric cord, causing the wires to part at the plug and sparks to flash.

People took sides over the issue. The secretary was unapproachable and even refused to take the fan back permanently when the clerk agreed to give it up if it meant so much. Her pride had been hurt.

After several weeks' effort to reconcile matters, the supervisor arranged a transfer for the secretary who never missed an opportunity to complain about what had happened. Unrelenting sarcasm from the secretary proved too much for the supervisor.

The fan incident could be rewritten to include the many kinds of company equipment over which there are squabbles. In this situation, however, the fan's importance became blurred by feelings of pride and spite.

The second situation concerns a pair of scissors issued by the management of a retail store. The scissors were entrusted to a clerk, Mildred, who was responsible for them during working hours and asked to keep them in her locker over night.

One day, Mildred was asked to cashier for an absent co-worker. In her haste to ready the cash register, she left her scissors on the cutting table where other employees used them. Because of misuse, they were nicked and otherwise dulled. At the end of the day, Mildred left for home never thinking about the scissors.

When she opened her locker the next day, she remembered about them. In a panic, she looked all over the store. When she asked her co-workers, they told her the manager had them.

In the manager's office, Mildred was reproached for her carelessness. Returning to her work station, she accused her co-workers of misusing the scissors and not telling her about them. Much of that day and several days thereafter Mildred spent placing guilt elsewhere.

Daily events like these provide ample opportunity for the small problems to develop that consume an inordinate amount of time in their resolution. A situation taken in stride one day becomes explosive another. The person receiving the brunt of a blow wonders, "What got into her?" Or, "What's bugging him?"

Intrusions of trivia into the workplace seem to be a way of life. But that's only natural since people spend a large portion of their lives there. Work becomes a place where they can fulfill many of their psychological needs. Although employers try to satisfy their workers, they can't provide all the conditions needed to make them happy (or even less unhappy). As a result, there are occasional creaks and groans that interrupt work routine and steal time away from productive activity.

Taming Trivia

What can managers do?

Certainly an effort should be made to deal with the irritation. When it is, the person with the problem usually feels better. The manager delivering the appreciated action also feels good. Organizations taking care of trivial problems are seen as caring.

Of course, these situations have to be dealt with quickly, inexpensively, and in ways that have long-lasting and valuable benefits. Trivia are time traps that can cause a manager to set aside important work and devote time and attention to little things with little return. Too much trivia are somewhat like having a "inbasket," and "outbasket," and a "back again" basket. The back-again situations cause *activities* to be mistaken for *results*.

Dealing with trivia takes up time so people with the authority to act have to weigh each demand against its cost in terms of other activities. An overall management philosophy dealing with the culture of the workplace can help cage the disruptive kinds of trivia that rarely develop. The remaining trivia is susceptible to immediate responses that can generally be taken without disturbing productivity.

Slaying the Paper Dragon

J. W. GILSDORF

Excessive paperwork threatens to block or smother the optimum flow of useful information in many departments. No matter how important the information, readers' eyes can and frequently do glaze over due to the sheer volume of paper that passes over the desk. Supervisors need a smooth and economical flow of necessary information, and a number of things can be done to help them and their paperbound organizations achieve that flow.

The most important thing an organization as a whole can do is to set a policy. An attitude favoring economical, timely, clear, simple communication should pervade the organization from the top down, and the executives' and upper-level managers' example should provide a guide and motivation for everyone else.

Reducing Paperwork Generally

In a large organization, much communication finds its way to paper unnecessarily. The problem worsens the larger an organization becomes, as more people depend on the written word for communication, and more people are needed to process the papers and to keep records on the increased number of people and papers.

Some of that paper must exist. But making papers is a habit, and managers should question their paper-producing habits.

Information is often produced (and copied and stored) just because it always has been. Here is an example. To make sure a given economy in materials is working, a manager is asked to record for a month a nonsignificant variance in the color of a small plastic toy in production. At the end of the month-long check, the manager is not asked to stop collecting the data. His boss forgot to mention it. Two years later the color variance report is still being prepared and filed. Its usefulness ended 23 months earlier. But the manager hasn't thought to question its value.

Information is often produced (and copied and stored) just because it can be. Electronic data processing, in particular, can give managers many interesting versions, permutations, and statistical treatments of information. But such plenty can result in too much of a good thing. Recall the story of the sorcerer's apprentice who made the broom bring water but didn't know how to make it stop. Similarly, some departments are drowning in printout. Management and the computer support staff should establish

Reprinted from *Supervisory Management*, April 1983

exactly what information is needed and in what form. Fortunately, the communication gap between managers and data processing support will diminish as a healthy trend grows: the trend for managers to be more computer-savvy and for computers to accept natural-language programming.

Much information, especially in large organizations, is produced routinely, and at low levels in the organization. Almost every employee keeps records of some sort. If departmental or organizational policy ensures that low-level paper-handlers are told *why* they are making or processing a given paper, they will be able to spot any possible way of improving, shortening, or perhaps even eliminating the paper. All people in an organization should be encouraged to feel pride in efficient communication.

On Listening

One of the most effective things a supervisor can do to control paperwork is to teach himself or herself and employees to listen. Indeed, at every level of the company, from CEO to file clerk, the habit of effective listening should be ingrained. If it is not, everyone who lacks it should receive training in it—no exceptions.

Sometimes people put things down on paper because they despair of getting the receiver's attention in any other way. Barriers to effective listening abound: distractions, emotions, preconceived ideas, inability to pick out main points, self-seeking, poor language skills, overload, idiosyncrasies. Good listeners overcome these obstacles. Poor listeners can be taught to do so. Everyone can be a good listener.

Unless a communicator can rely on another's willingness and ability to listen, he or she may seek safety by putting the message on paper—hence, the need for supervisors and managers at all levels to learn to listen. If a person with a message has already tried to communicate the matter orally and not been listened to, the written message amounts to duplication of effort and waste of time. The cost to efficiency and productivity is clear. What may not be immediately clear is the additional cost in morale. Not to be listened to is demotivating and destructive of self-esteem. Improvement of listening, then, besides reducing the paperwork problem, is likely to pay off in increased satisfaction.

Memos—Crucial Conservation Questions

Many managers dictate nearly all their internal communications, have them typewritten, keep copies of them on file, and send copies of them to anyone they think might be interested. These paper-makers should question their habits. Message-senders should ask: *"Does this message have to be sent?"* Some people's anxiety attacks result in a flurry of memos from their office. Some problems actually do go away if nothing is done. Sometimes the solution to a problem is action, not a memo. Sometimes the proposed recipient of a sender's advice will solve the problem himself or herself without getting a memo.

"Does the message have to be written?" A telephone call takes less time than a written message. More use might be made of interoffice telephone recording devices than is done at present. No one particularly warms to them, but they are efficient, and the caller can be sure that the message is transmitted exactly as he or she wants it (as is not the case if the person must go through a receptionist).

"Does a secretary have to type it?" If a message-sender can operate a keyboard, only one person's time, not two persons', needs to be spent.

"Does the message have to be typewritten at all?" If not, more time and money can be saved. Most writers of business communications jot notes before dictating or typing. If it would take only minimally longer to handwrite the message, the dictation and typewriting steps fall out, and two people's time can be spent more productively doing something else. And a legible handwritten message is fine for most internal purposes. Sometimes an answer to a letter or a memo can be jotted on the bottom of the same document and routed quickly back to the sender. If a copy must be kept NCR (No Carbon Required) paper is a great boon. Many organizations even use preprinted forms on NCR paper with space for an original message and an answer.

"Is a record needed?" Sometimes it is. Many times it is not. If a record must be kept, it should be filed in useful form according to a system that permits easy retrieval. A poor retrieval system will generate more paper; if the information cannot be located, it has to be rederived. In addition, files should be reviewed and purged systematically and sensibly, at given intervals. Conceivably, everything might be useful sometime. But an organization cannot store everything.

"Do all these recipients need to get a copy?" Most writers are rational about copying. However, some writers send copies of memos to a long list of recipients who may or may not be interested. A sender's motives may be laudable (for instance, courtesy or a genuine wish to inform) or self-serving (say, self-protection or self-aggrandizement). Whatever the motive, each sheet of paper takes the time of at least one person in the recipient's office, and several people's time if the message has to be delivered, opened, date-stamped, filed, and otherwise processed. The information should be worth the time it consumes, or the copy should not be sent.

Message-receivers can help, too. They should ask, "Do I need to receive this piece of paper?" Sometimes the receiver of a report or memo—or more usually, a copy of a report or memo—finds himself or herself glancing over a piece (or stack) of paper and pitching it into the wastebasket. If this happens very often, the receiver should check to see what list he or she is on and politely tell the sender that the information is not useful and not to send it any more.

One other thought. Sometimes the lack of a given paper will cause a problem. An occasional wrong judgment is inevitable. The question to ask is, "How much did that mistake cost, compared to what it would have cost to make or keep enough paper to prevent all possible mistakes?" If the company's policy on paperwork conservation is working correctly, mistakes will be few. The paper that is needed will be there, and the bales of paper that are not needed will not be there clogging the works.

Conciseness

If after considering these questions a supervisor still believes that a written message is in order, then conciseness should be the key. Let's look at three kinds of written messages and how they should be handled.

Memos. Trying to keep to a one-page limit, with exceptions only in rare instances, is best. The human mind is a summarizing machine, constantly processing and reducing input into manageable, usable information. A business writer's mind can be trained and encouraged to put this condensing habit to use on the job, transmitting only what the business reader will find useful.

The misguided motives that make people produce quantities of long wordy memos and letters should be discouraged. Some people write copious memos because they feel important doing so. Others are fearful of not being "covered" unless every aspect is down on paper with four copies on file. Others do not feel comfortable communicating orally.

Some hints that lead to brevity in writing style are:

1. Use short active-voice sentences.
2. Write as you would (carefully) speak.
3. Cultivate an atmosphere of trust and respect in the organization, so that no one needs to spend time and words on formalities.
4. Discourage bureaucratese or whatever name that empty, windy style is called in the organization.
5. Prefer short words to long ones, concrete words to abstract ones, specific words to general ones, familiar words to unfamiliar ones, and nouns and verbs to adjectives and adverbs.
6. Don't repeat. Write so that sentence rhythm and emphasis patterns signal what is important.
7. Write with the reader's needs, not the writer's, in mind.

A habitual offender, at whatever level in the organization, should spend one lunch-hour with a thin, low-priced paperback called *Revising Business Prose,* by Richard A. Lanham (New York: Scribner, 1981).

Reports. These are time-eaters for writer and reader. To save some preparation time, the person writing the report should ask the authorizer, "What use will be made of this report?"

Sometimes, too, a superior does not think through his or her request for a report. As Trevor J. Bentley (in *Information, Communication, and the Paperwork Explosion*) has observed, a manager asking for a report might mean any of these: " 'Send me a report. . . .' 'Go away. I'm not interested. . . .' 'Go find something to do.' " Even if a superior is a serious and thoughtful person who does not lightly ask for reports, asking this superior, "What use?" is still a good idea. When the report-writer knows exactly what information is needed and why, he or she can write a report that fills the need, and omit all the rest. In short, the person can fulfill his or her purpose as an intelligent summarizer. A writer who does not ask or is not told why a report is needed is doomed to guess, to make the report be all things to all readers. That purpose leads to length and to vagueness—to minimally useful, but long paperwork.

Modified-Sentence-Outline-Report. For some kinds of reports, a writer can achieve conciseness by a particular format, one that is gaining favor in business and government. That format is the modified sentence outline, or MSO format. The modified sentence outline is a standard sentence outline, expanded only so much as is necessary to communicate the needed information. The writer who is asked to report in MSO format knows he or she is to produce a report that *looks like an outline* and that the pressure is on to condense.

The MSO has a brief, paragraph-style introduction and conclusion. The body of the report—the sentence outline—can use Roman numerals and capital letters or some other standard form of outline notation, or it can omit these symbols if the writer prefers the appearance given by the use of outline indention alone.

The main modification of the conventional sentence outline is that any heading or subheading may run to two sentences if needed, or, at most, three.

MSO format is not applicable to all reports. Obviously, very complex reports, or reports that must depend on subtlety or persuasiveness for their success, will not make their best impression in MSO form. The writer and/or authorizer of the report can judge whether MSO format fits a given reporting task. If it does, the resulting report can be a treat to read—brief, clear, organized, rapidly read, easy to refer back to.

Computer Technology

Thus far, we have talked about traditional kinds of communication. Developments in communication technology also point to several ways in which paperwork can be reduced and time saved. Most of them involve the computer. Let's look briefly at these.

Electronic mail and message systems. Installing executive work stations will save some of the highest-priced time in the organization. The equipment is costly, but its cost is dropping and its usefulness rising at the same time worker salaries are increasing. Its use will cut time spent communicating and will also cut paperwork.

The manager's multi-function work station is generally a complex electronics set-up tied into many other information/communication devices. With this equipment the manager can often bypass the secretary, bypass any paper-producing step, and acquire information that once took days, many people, and a lot of paper to get. Today a manager's information system can create or re-create text, process it, store it and retrieve it, and communicate it remotely by a variety of means—none of which needs to produce paper unless the user wishes it.

The keyboard and phone give the user access to the computer and to a variety of other systems. On the communicating word processor (CWP) the user can type in a rough draft, manipulate the text, add to, delete from, route, and send the message. The user can dictate and store messages for secretarial staff to prepare and send by conventional means. Manager and secretary need not be free at the same time.

The work station can be used to compose and revise a message of any length, and to send it to one recipient or to a list of people. The recipient need not be there to receive messages; messages can be stored and accessed when the recipient is available to do so. This capability can end missed telephone calls, and the string of written memos they cause, for good.

The receiver of the stored messages needs a password or other special signal to get into his or her electronic mailbox. If security is exceptionally critical, the person can have encryption capability and verification of delivery.

Many of the electronic mail and message functions can be built into a portable terminal. A person can dictate and store messages, or enter new data while out in the field, and then contact the firm's home system by way of an ordinary telephone, transmit the messages and data, and receive information back. None of these steps would need to involve paper. The portables are getting smaller, lighter, and smarter. A common size fits easily under a plane seat.

Voice mail and voice compression. There are voice message systems (voice mail) that can digitize the human voice and then store, deliver, forward, and distribute the signal as the originator commands. If the called person is out of the office or tied up, the signal goes to that person's "electronic in-basket." The called person dials up the voice-message mailbox when he or she is free to do so. Then the digitized messages are reconverted into the voices of the senders.

Some experimentation is proceeding with voice compression, a specialized form of data compression that speeds the voice without raising the pitch Donald-Duck fashion. People can listen and comprehend about four times as fast as most people speak, and public speaking—as at conferences or meetings—is sometimes especially slow. If part of a voice teleconference, for example, is stored while the manager has to do other things, the manager can listen time-efficiently later to what was missed. The same would be true of sundry stored phone messages that come in while the manager is out.

Micrographs. Even necessary records can engulf a modern organization unless great care is taken in storage. A solution to the records-storage problem for an increasing number of firms is microstorage. Records are stored on roll film, microfiche, updatable microfiche, or aperture card. The records are indexed so that they can be retrieved, either manually, mechanically, or electronically (CAR, an abbreviation frequently seen, stands for Computer-Assisted Retrieval), and can be read or printed on a reader or reader/printer as needed.

Microforms can be created directly from data, without a paper step, by use of COM (Computer-Output Micrographics). Whether data, text, or graph, the information is stored in digitized form. The user can code the format in which he or she wants the information, and run the coded information from the computer through the COM recorder to create the microform.

Information Manager Position

In large, complex organizations, the development of an information manager position at a fairly high level in the firm has become a natural step. That person may have moved up from data processing, word processing/office management, or telecommunications staff, and designs simple, usable systems for information flow and storage.

The concept of information management does not work if it is treated as an afterthought. First, management discusses and agrees on policies for information management. The information manager can then design programs and procedures for appropriate flow and storage, and, in conjunction with appropriate departments, give training to all personnel who need it. The planning must be organization-wide, not department-by-department, and long-range, not ad hoc.

Policies, and training in their implementation, become especially important as the organization depends more and more heavily on electronic means of generating, moving, storing, and retrieving information. The new technology typically encounters some resistance when it is introduced. If training is provided at once, and if the information manager's department operates as a long-term resource for new users of the electronic communication equipment, resistance will be much less, and high morale and productivity will result from the change to the electronic office.

In addition, the information manager can monitor the organization for backlogs, duplication of information, routine forms and formats in need of streamlining, communicators in need of training, and many other information-flow problems. Attention given to these blocks will help information flow contribute to productivity.

Adding It Up

No manager can afford to let paperwork interfere with personal or departmental productivity. Indeed, set as an organizational goal, efficiency in communication cuts down the cost of operations. Training money spent improving workers' writing, speaking, and listening skills will pay off, and the whole organization, top-down, will subscribe to and practice conciseness and economy in communicating.

Top management needs to set policy, then see that it is carried out. Necessary paperwork systems need to be devised, periodically reviewed and coordinated with changing needs. Habitual producers of long and copious paper need to learn how to control their habit. People need to be told the *why* of communications so that they can shape their messages economically. The more often communication can go directly and informally from sender to receiver, rather than through office support personnel and inefficient delivery systems, the more economical that communication can be.

Information storage and retrieval systems should be logical, simple, and understood by all users; and a document should not be filed simply because it *can* be filed. If cost-benefit analysis prompts the purchase of electronic work-stations, efficient use must be made of them once they are installed. People newly introduced to sophisticated electronic communication equipment are often so intrigued by it that their enthusiasm leads to indiscriminate use. The company's needs must dictate what information is generated by the equipment.

As a company becomes larger, and a greater number of people require greater amounts of information flow to coordinate their efforts, the organization will probably need information-management staff; in turn, these staff need the strong support of line management. The result, toward which everyone should work, is clear, concise, accurate information, ready when needed.

Putting Your Files in Order

STEVEN BUCKMAN

One problem that nearly every manager encounters at some point is a difficulty in handling information. The increased use of computers with their sophisticated data bases will do a great deal to reduce this problem. However, for the time being, many managers must continue to use the same systems that have been used for the last half century: paper files and folders.

Often, the "system" used varies widely from office to office and in many cases there may be only one person in the office who has any idea how to find a particular scrap of paper. The most widely used system is the alphabet. Material may be filed according to the first letter of the company involved, or perhaps the individual involved, or the state, or some other criterion. Obviously this tends to create some confusion in an office where more than one person might need access to files.

The Messed Up Files

Let's look at a case in point involving a sales representative for a small textile company. Usually, when Al Miller requires the file for one of his clients, his secretary gets it for him.

Over several weeks Al had fallen behind in some of his sales reports so he decided to work one Saturday to get caught up. One of the projects he wanted to work on was the quarterly report that his supervisor required he file for each salesperson working for him. In order to do this, he had to review the activity of all the major accounts.

On Saturday, he arrived bright and early and began to gather all of the information that he would need: sales budgets, personnel records, and so forth. As he went to the files. Al thought to himself how strange it was, since his secretary was always the one to get files for him. As he opened the first drawer, his bemusement began to turn to bewilderment. He discovered that the accounts were not filed by the name of the sales representative handling the account as he thought they would be. "Well, perhaps by the name of the company," he thought. "That may make things a little more difficult since now I will have to pick out each one by referring to another list."

When Al began his search, he discovered he still had not broken the now seemingly unbreakable cipher of the filing system. In fact the more he looked at the files, the more they seemed to be in disarray.

Reprinted from *Supervisory Management,* October 1983

After several more attempts, he gave up and went home. He couldn't believe that the young man he recently hired could have such a problem keeping the files in order.

Monday morning arrived and Al promptly called Jim into his office. "I came into the office early Saturday morning to get caught up on some work and I couldn't find any of the information I needed. How could you have messed up the files so much in just four weeks? When Jane worked for me, she was always able to get whatever I needed quickly."

"Mr. Miller, I'm using the same system that Jane used. At first it seemed a little confusing to me, too, but I soon got used to it."

"Well, what's the big secret? How can I find what I am looking for?"

"Jane suggested that we file all accounts by the name of the city in which the office is located. She said that she first started the system to help her with your mailing lists."

Al thought to himself, "That was over three years ago when we worked on that special sales effort." Then and there he decided that he would work with Jim in developing a better file system.

Obviously, there are many problems with the way information is filed in Al Miller's office. While this may be an overdramatic example, everyone has felt at some time like Al, not knowing where something is yet knowing that it must be somewhere.

The Backbone of the System

The best file system is one that is developed around its users' job responsibilities. Most managers have a variety of functions to perform, and the file system used ought to reflect this fact. The system also should be easily communicated to someone unfamiliar with it. For example, the system should be straightforward enough to allow one's boss to come in and find something in the files that he or she might need.

The way to create such a system is first to review exactly what functional areas one is responsible for. These broad categories may serve as headings for the file system. Most good file systems are developed using a number system. Thus, for Al Miller, we might have

1000 Budgeting
2000 Marketing and advertising programs
3000 Account files
4000 Personnel

and so on. If Al had responsibilities in other areas such as risk management or employee benefits, they would also be included as major headings.

Once Al had listed all these headings, he might want to begin to break each one down even further. So:

1000 Budgeting
    1100 Sales budget
        1110 Sales budgets, Eastern division
            1110.0182 Sales budget, 1st qtr-1982
            1110.0282 Sales budget, 2nd qtr-1982
            1110.0382 Sales budget, 3rd qtr-1982
        1120 Sales budgets, South division
            1120.0182 Sales budget, 1st qtr-1982
            1120.0282 Sales budget, 2nd qtr-1982
    1200 Personnel budgets
        1210 Personnel budgets, Eastern division
            1210.0182 Personnel budget, 1st qtr-1982
            1210.0282 Personnel budget, 1st qtr-1982

Some of the advantages of this type of file system are:

- Each major heading can be broken down to at least four increasingly restrictive subheadings.
- All information coming into or going out of the office can be assigned a file number.
- The system can be easily communicated to anyone who requires access to the files.
- A directory can be made available to anyone who requires one and updates are easily included.
- It is relatively easy to cross-reference the system.

Working With the System

In practice the system would work like this: All information that is to be filed is assigned a file number. In many cases, it may be easier for a manager to assign the numbers by glancing at a readily available file directory at his or her desk. When information is needed from the file, anyone can go to the file directory and locate the file by skimming through the headings. Since all files are in numerical order, locating a folder should never be a problem.

When information comes in that does not easily fit into one of the files in current use, all a manager needs do is create a new file number, fit it into the existing number system where it is appropriate, and make a note of it in the file directory. Every two or three months, the file directory should be retyped and redistributed as required.

In developing your own system, you may want to consider assigning a file number to all outgoing correspondence and sending a copy of all correspondence to the appropriate file.

A good, useful filing system takes some time to develop. During the start-up when all the files need to be reviewed, it may be particularly time consuming. But there is nothing like the joy of knowing *exactly* where to find that one small piece of paper that is going to answer the question of the day.

In the near future, we may all sit in front of computer terminals and type in our requests for information. Until then, this is a good alternative.

Making the Most Effective Use of Secretarial Help

J. HOWARD JACKSON and IRIS W. JOHNSON

Secretaries continue to be the most misused resources in business despite the impact a cooperative relationship between manager and secretary would have on office productivity. While some employees who carry the title of secretary seem to be content not to go beyond the job description, many find having to do little more than clerical detail work frustrating. Management's failure to realize that this vital link in the organization's communication network cannot be replaced by a computer and its flagrant disregard for secretaries' professionalism further make it difficult to attract bright, enthusiastic young people to the profession. They believe that being a secretary is little more than being a servant.

With the advent of office automation—especially word processing—much of the drudgery associated with the secretarial position has been eliminated. New technology has freed secretaries to do more creative tasks and become more assistants than clerks. They are certainly aptly placed to be of invaluable service to the manager. In many cases, they are the first to hear of important policy changes, customer and client problems, new competition, and company scandal.

Most secretaries find a busy office a challenge yet too often have long days with nothing to do. If executives who are inundated with work have the luxury of a competent secretary, they can increase their productivity. All it takes is practicing the following suggestions to build a more effective relationship:

Sincere Appreciation

1. *Recognize good work.* "Thank you, you did a good job," never becomes trite when it is said sincerely. Verbal recognition costs nothing, and it is repaid many times over in extra effort, improved morale, improved client relationships, and greater employee productivity. Employees who are sincerely appreciated often do nice things without being asked. So managers should get in the habit of giving sincere praise when it is earned.

2. *Be available.* A manager needs to set aside some time for support staff. Secretaries complain that their executives have time for clients, co-workers, family, and friends but often spend only a fleeting moment with them. Misinformation and conflict are inevitable when the only instructions given by a busy executive are on the way to a meeting or to catch a plane. The executive who makes the most effective

Reprinted from *Management Solutions,* January 1988

use of a secretary/assistant will set aside some time each day or at least three times a week to check calendars, dictate correspondence, delegate tasks, and discuss priorities. Occasionally, it helps to discuss the secretary's career goals, professional interests, and advancement opportunities, and to exercise mutual give-and-take on office problems—personal, procedural, and policy-related barriers to productivity on both sides of the desk.

3. *Maintain confidentiality.* Every manager has the right to expect his or her secretary to keep certain matters confidential. The secretary has the same right. A manager shouldn't tell others about his or her secretary's faults; rather, the manager should tell the secretary. If a secretary shares personal problems, such as a pending divorce, a manager should keep the confidence. A good team relationship between manager and secretary is built on a strong foundation of trust.

Broaden Job Responsibilities

4. *Delegate creative as well as routine tasks.* Routine office procedures—filing, keyboarding, proofreading, copying, and recordkeeping—are a part of the secretarial job. Secretaries accept this when they accept the job; however, the old adage "Variety is the spice of life" is as true of the secretary's work as it is of the teacher's, the advertising executive's, or the company president's. One of the best ways to enrich a secretary's job is to delegate responsibility for a project that requires initiative and creativity. Planning a company conference, designing a letterhead or form, restructuring the filing system, and composing letters are all examples of creative tasks. One word of caution: A manager should delegate but not abdicate; that is, he or she shouldn't assign a task to the secretary for which he or she has neither the authority nor the ability to carry out. A manager needs to start slowly, not overwhelming the employee with a gigantic task, then walking away. After delegating, the manager should check, encourage and help out. The project should be a team effort, with planning done well in advance and target dates discussed frequently. Most important, credit should be given the secretary for his or her contribution to the project.

5. *Learn the difference between service and servitude.* Secretaries, when asked whether they resent making coffee and watering plants, invariably reply, "It depends upon the boss." Therein lies the answer to most productivity problems or to the lack of them in any office. Managers who demand or expect a cup of coffee, transportation at 6 a.m. to the airport via the secretary's personal car, and delivery of the spouse's watch at the jeweler's during lunch hour can expect resentment—and rightfully so. On the other hand, the manager who remembers his or her secretary's birthday, expresses an interest in the well-being of the secretary and the secretary's family, occasionally brings a souvenir from a trip, and assists the secretary in achieving personal and professional goals will find these kindnesses are returned.

A Positive, Cheerful Mood

6. *Control temper, tongue, and mood.* Only a recluse can afford the luxury of moods. If you work with others, you can display only one mood—a positive cheerful one.

Frank, two-way communication in a controlled climate of respect will develop a better relationship with any support personnel. There should be no screams, no public put downs. Criticism should be in private.

Certainly, a manager shouldn't patronize support staff by calling someone "my boy," or "my girl," "honey," "dear," or "the clerical help."

7. *Include support staff in decisions that affect their work.* When word processors, microcomputers, copiers, and telecommunications equipment became popular in the mid-'70s and early '80s, millions of dollars were spent to install these labor-saving devices. Frequently, decisions concerning configurations, brands, supplies and so forth were made without consulting the people who would ultimately operate the equipment. The equipment was purchased and installed and employees, with two days of training consisting of little more than a vendor's manual, were expected to produce error-free correspondence and

reports in less time than before. In many cases, the results were traumatic for the executive and the support personnel who operated the equipment.

Many of the problems could have been reduced if support personnel had been included in the decisions. They would then have bought into the change. They would have been more challenged to learn about operations of the equipment and would likely have been productive in a shorter time. They could have helped managers avoid paying for features that were not needed and could have recommended those that would have been helpful. By asking for the support staff's advice and opinion, management would really have been consulting the experts—for it is at this level that the real test of new equipment and new systems takes place.

8. *Recognize that there is a life outside the office.* Most employees reserve their evenings and weekends for essential chores, such as shopping and laundry, and for hobbies, family, friends, and enough recreation to get a fresh start on the next week. Unexpected rush jobs that require overtime disrupt this. Most secretaries do not mind giving an extra hour or two at the end of the day or even on Saturday morning when a genuine emergency occurs. Such a sacrifice, however, is resented if it is the result of poor planning or procrastination on the part of the manager. Infringing upon an employee's personal time, whether it is for typing an overdue report or meeting a client at the airport after hours, is one of the best ways to dampen a secretary's enthusiasm, kill morale, and ultimately lose a good employee. A wise executive overcomes the need for overtime assistance by setting priorities and letting the secretary keep him or her on target.

9. *Keep the secretary informed.* A sense of "being in on what's happening in the organization" gives a secretary confidence and a feeling of being a part of the team. Aside from a boost to morale, such knowledge enables the secretary to answer questions intelligently, make wise commitments, and avoid sounding foolish when a client or top officer asks the whereabouts of the executive.

The last should be emphasized. Many executives leave their offices without telling their secretary— or anybody else—where they are going and if or when they will return. In such cases, it is difficult for the secretary to answer questions and maintain an image of executive and secretarial efficiency. Making a habit of telling a secretary where one is going, if and when one will return, and how to handle any situation that might be pending is one that can work for the benefit of both executive and secretary.

"I'd Like You to Meet . . ."

10. *Acquaint the secretary with the "Who's Who" list.* When important customers, clients, family, and colleagues call in person, they should be introduced to the secretary. This helps the secretary put names with faces and to protect the executive's time. If there are people the manager prefers not to see or to see for only a short time (the colleague who, with a little encouragement, will stay all morning, for example), the manager should work out a system with his or her secretary to minimize such interruptions.

Being ignored when important visitors call on the employer is a common complaint of support personnel in many offices. After all, introducing strangers to office personnel is common courtesy. This is especially true when it is the secretary who must arrange lodging, transportation, appointments, refreshments, and travel reimbursements.

11. *Be flexible.* A manager should allow support staff to attend conferences and seminars. But more important he or she should encourage application of the ideas that come from attendance. Ways to update procedures, forms, language, supplies, and equipment should be discussed and good ideas implemented and evaluated. An atmosphere should exist where no serious idea is too large or too small to be considered.

Another area for flexibility involves human relations. A manager should assist the secretary and other support staff in handling different people and situations. Many clients, customers, and staff will vent their wrath upon a defenseless secretary. A manager should prevent such abuse by backing the secretary in a crisis. Additionally, the manager should identify procedures for handling future cases in his or her absence.

12. *Train support personnel then trust them.* Whether it's a first secretary or someone else's secretary who comes with the managerial job, this rule should be followed. A manager should consider what is essential to his or her team's productivity then, in conference with the secretary, discuss expectations, ask if they seem realistic, and clarify any that seem hazy or questionable. Outlined should be the secretary's responsibilities for handling mail, making travel arrangements, correcting grammar, spelling, punctuation—some employers recognize the secretary's expertise here; others allow no deviation from what is dictated. In other words, the parameters for initiative should be set. The secretary then should be trusted to perform without constant checking. It is traumatic for a secretary to be told to use the latest letter formats then be reprimanded for using a new non-sexist salutation in a letter to a corporation.

13. *Remember the role the secretary plays in depicting your organization.* An employee's lack of pride in the job is reflected when a high-ranking company official calls and is told by the secretary, "I don't know where she is; they never tell me anything," or when given an important document to type, the secretary retypes obvious errors and mails the document without calling them to the manager's attention. Such blatant disregard for the image of the company also paints for the public a portrait of a disorganized executive who does not have the best interests of the firm at heart. To build a team, it is essential to remember that there is no more powerful force than a secretary who is competent and who has a "can do" attitude, and manager who is secure enough to maximize the potential of this key support person.

Part XIV

TRAINING

Unlocking Employee Potential: Developing Skills

CRAIG ERIC SCHNEIER, DAVID MacCOY, and SEYMOUR BURCHMAN

Most companies look to unlock employee potential through training. Indeed, an estimated $4 billion is spent annually on company training programs. But in truth, the formal classroom training in large companies has been found to do very little to develop the skills needed to gain competitive advantage. Formal training programs are not the sole answer to unlocking employee potential. Actually, managers involved in regular face-to-face contact with employees are in a better position to assist employees in making real contributions.

Many managers do not recognize this. They expect formal training programs to do the job, but on-the-job training (OJT) is often the least costly and most effective strategy for contributing to the skill development of employees.

Exceptional managers have found ways to influence employees *on-the-job*. With an in-depth knowledge of company strategy and operations, and the capability to help people learn, they unlock employee potential using several *informal* methods. The following four are the key to unlocking potential by developing skills:

1. Identifying skill deficiencies and development opportunities
2. Making good performance better
3. Overcoming skill deficits
4. Preparing for the future

Reprinted from *Management Solutions*, February 1988

Identifying Skill Deficiencies and Development Opportunities

Solving performance problems begins with clarifying the root problem. If people are *able* to perform but are unwilling, rewards are a problem. If people are *willing* to perform but are unable to do so, skill development is required. If ability is the problem, managers with effective skills can address this by:

Training—adding new skill or knowledge and helping to apply it
Coaching—clarifying expectations, uncovering problems, and providing feedback
Counseling—empathizing; helping to respond to setbacks, and encouraging and advising
Mentoring—developing a relationship to transfer skill and knowledge, "sponsoring" a more junior person, and acting as a "model" of effective behavior

Line management training, coaching, counseling, and mentoring skills are viewed as critical for success at many of the best companies. Specifying the relationship between company operations and employee performance and potential must be a priority of all managers. Managers have several available methods to assess how their unit or the company stands with respect to the strengths and weaknesses of its talent base, but one of the best resources is the performance appraisal. This is a key source for information on potential talent, as well as skill deficiencies in the workforce. Indeed, there is no substitute for input from employees—actively listening to their problems and designing solutions together. Managers who routinely include subordinates in planning and decision making will obtain this information easily. The key is creation of an environment in which the development of skills and personal growth are fostered and openly encouraged.

Following several years during which the reject level was significantly above the industry norm, a large Canadian footwear manufacturer developed an approach to identify skill deficiencies and opportunities in order to develop employees in the sewing and cutting lines. The manager met biweekly with line supervisors to discuss staff performance summaries and key operational indicators (that is, rejects and waste). Within one month, supervisors and the manager developed a greater awareness of skill deficiencies and were able to dedicate time to working with employees in a variety of useful ways (for example, asking employees to model specific, effective behaviors in order to build skills). Eventually, the most skilled employees were recruited to assist in the training process as role models. Ongoing scrutiny of performance data helped the manager identify production areas that needed special attention. As a result, productivity skyrocketed.

Making Good Performance Better

One of the most satisfying tasks of a manager is to work with capable employees to make their good performance even better. Two ways of enhancing performance are coaching and serving as a mentor.

The "coach" advises and encourages the development of superior skills to given feedback on performance, acting as a role model, and helping the individual practice specific skills. Creating a climate for strong two-way communication makes coaching activities particularly effective, as a service manager at a highly respected health care organization found out. She assigned a group of top performers to a company task force responsible for developing policies and procedures necessary for the introduction of new services. She coached the task force on conducting negotiations with customer organizations using simulated negotiation meetings and role playing. Each participant practiced negotiation skills and received feedback on performance. Each member became more successful in launching services with customer organizations. Several have identified new, innovative opportunities for the organization that have improved both services and profits. The manager was thus able to offer new challenges to current top performers. They received recognition, and their overall worth to the company was enhanced.

Serving as a mentor involves an experienced person sharing accumulated wisdom about the performance and knowledge of company practices. Mentoring is often informal, although some companies assign mentors. Benefits of mentoring include: reducing the orientation time for new employees; sensitizing new people to the values and practices of the company and transferring these values to them; providing a mechanism to share wisdom, knowledge, and effective practices; preparing key performers for promotion; and providing attention for individuals with special concerns (for example, an executive from a foreign subsidiary transferred to the U.S.).

To be an effective mentor, a manager must have the basic skill to support interpersonal relationships, as well as an interest in coaching, counseling, and career planning.

Overcoming Skill Deficits

Managers can assist employees to overcome skill deficits and address problem performance by counseling and, in some cases, arranging for employees to rotate jobs in order to develop new knowledge and skill.

Counseling can correct problem performance, thereby helping people whose productivity may have slipped or who may be going through a period where performance is not up to company standards. Counseling is an ongoing process of monitoring performance, identifying problems, and determining steps to correct these problems. Counseling is often combined with coaching and can be done formally or informally. It is used to encourage an individual and correct weaknesses before a crisis emerges. Counseling helps managers and subordinates clarify expectations and uncover hidden strengths.

A manager of administration with a large pharmaceutical company, for example, observed a highly valued supervisor's involvement in a growing number of conflicts with the sales division. Complaints from regional sales managers increased to the point where some action had to be taken. The manager initiated a counseling process with the supervisor to address the issue. Performance problems were identified and expectations were clarified. The manager also coached the supervisor on how to conduct himself in future interactions with sales personnel. The counseling process helped identify that the supervisor required additional computer training in order to keep up with the demands of the job. Counseling and encouragement helped the manager to unlock this supervisor's potential. Within two months, complaints from the sales manager stopped, and positive reports were received.

Brief tours of duty in various positions in an organization, a form of job rotation, can develop knowledge, skills, and attitudes and also unlock employee potential. A standard procedure at such companies as General Electric and General Foods, job rotation prepares key employees for new roles. It can be a powerful tool for overcoming skill deficits if the employee is given assignments for specific time periods in work areas that offer skill-building opportunities and provide broader understanding of the company's strategies and objectives.

Preparing for the Future

Managers can also assist in unlocking employee potential by looking at the future requirements of key jobs and taking steps to ensure that employees with the requisite skills will be available. There is no doubt that assessing performance problems and performance capabilities as well as coaching, mentoring, counseling, and job rotation, can help prepare for the future. However, the selection of skilled and talented people and career planning are perhaps even more powerful tools at the manager's disposal.

Managers can assist in the selection process at a strategic level by identifying criteria for the selection of employees. A failure of line managers is abdicating to staff units the process of developing selection criteria. These managers may benefit from technical assistance of staff units that may be in a position to forecast the additional talent required to meet new challenges. However, they have the "hands-on" role in selecting the "right" people. This is a talent that managers must develop in order to avoid costly recruiting errors.

Besides this, managers with detailed knowledge of plans and strategies for growth must transmit this information in various ways to their employees to assist them with career planning. As with all of the tools for unlocking employee potential explained here, no special systems or paperwork is required to help plan for careers. Managers can simply inquire about subordinates' interests and preferences and, knowing the direction of the organization and their unit, can help their employees plan their careers. Plans to help add skills and experience in the short and long term can be developed and implemented. Effective managers know where their people are and where they are going. Matching individual skills and interests to organization needs is a hallmark of the effective manager as a skill developer.

Getting Started

In order to unlock employee potential by developing skills, managers themselves must have the fundamental skill and the interest to help establish a climate for growth and high performance. The key skills and interests include:

1. The *commitment* to take the time to understand the current and emerging requirements of the company and its people
2. A good *sense of company and unit strategic direction* and an ability to translate this into *performance expectations* for groups and individuals
3. A *genuine interest* in the employee as an individual company performer
4. The ability to be an *active listener* who can hear, interpret, clarify, and understand the employee's viewpoint
5. The ability to give *clear, candid feedback* on performance that will assist in bringing about improvements
6. The willingness to *reinforce* and *encourage* good and improving performance
7. The *flexibility* to help develop the variety of effective plans and activities necessary to unlock the potential of each individual subordinate

Many managers have been successful in increasing value and reducing costs by unlocking employee potential through development of skills. By coaching, mentoring, role modeling, counseling, and varying job assignments, they have found ways to reinforce the strategic direction of the company and enhancing the value of human resources to develop a sustainable competitive advantage.

Tapping a Hidden Resource

LINDA J. SEGALL

I'll bet you have a friend who owns a $500 microwave oven and only uses it to warm leftovers. Or maybe you know someone who has invested in an IBM personal computer and only turns it on to balance his checkbook once a month. Or perhaps you have a brother-in-law who has purchased a professional-quality, fully-programmable 35 mm camera, complete with a zoom lens, fast shutter, and automatic film advance—and only takes it out to snap the annual family Christmas pictures.

We all know people who have expensive "toys" that they let sit idle on a shelf simply because they *don't know how to take advantage* of what these resources can do; they never learned how to use them.

There's a good possibility you may have a rich but underutilized resource in your company. That resource is your human resources development (HRD) specialist (aka training manager, internal consultant, or organization development specialist). Like the microwave oven, personal computer, and programmable camera, the HRD specialist has the potential for making your (supervisory) life more satisfying. But, also like any other resource, you must learn when and how to use it. That means recognizing situations in which this staff support specialist can help you become a more successful supervisor.

In the Event . . .

Over the years, you have learned to link situations in your work day with appropriate support staff. Consider these examples:

- If an employee files a grievance, or there is need to take disciplinary action, you call the labor relations specialist for advice.
- When you discover a safety hazard created by faulty machine design, you call the mechanical engineer to correct it.
- If an employee falls and pulls a muscle in his leg, you call the medical department.
- If a worker wants to know why an additional deduction was taken out of her paycheck, you telephone the payroll administrator to look into it.
- If there is a question about insurance payments, you ask the benefits manager for clarification.

Reprinted from *Supervisory Management*, March 1986

In these instances, the situation itself clearly flags an appropriate support person for you to contact. But when do you call the HRD specialist? What, in fact, is an HRD-type situation?

An HRD situation is one in which the specialist can integrate his or her responsibilities with yours to help you create a more effective organization. These responsibilities might include the following, depending on the organization:

- Identifying training needs
- Providing appropriate in-house training programs
- Coordinating external training and educational opportunities
- Consulting with management on human resources issues
- Increasing organizational effectiveness through appropriate interventions

HRD-Type Situations

It may not be clear what these accountability phrases mean in terms of your work environment. To better understand how the HRD specialist complements your supervisory role, let's look at some HRD-type situations.

Situation #1: cross-training. Your manager has decided that all personnel in your department should be cross-trained in order to increase productivity levels. You believe this will be an unpopular move but agree to do the cross-training.

In this situation, the HRD specialist can help you *identify the kind of training* that needs to be done by isolating with you the critical skills used and tasks performed in each job affected by the cross-training.

Additionally, he or she can review with you an effective on-the-job training approach and coach you and your designated instructors (that is *provide appropriate in-house training*) in effective instructor's techniques.

The HRD specialist may also recommend approaches that involve your employees in the design and scheduling of the training in order to minimize the adverse effects caused by a change of procedure. In this way, the individual would be *serving as a consultant.*

Situation #2: non-productive meetings. With the growing emphasis on employee involvement, your manager expects you to hold group problem-solving meetings with your workforce. You've tried this several times, but the results have been nonproductive: Your employees either "cut up" and disrupt the meetings, or more often they "clam up" and refuse to participate.

There can be many reasons for the failure of your meetings. Your HRD representative can observe you in action to ascertain the trouble. Based on his or her observations, he or she might recommend *training* in group leadership skills for yourself or in group problem-solving for your employees (according to *needs identified*), or he or she might propose a formal *intervention,* such as teambuilding, to develop a group "buy-in" for improved departmental effectiveness.

Situation #3: outside training opportunities. One of your weekly reports requires several hours to complete because of the amount of information to be compiled. You recognize that a personal computer could reduce the time spent on this one report, and could also be used to increase departmental productivity in other areas too, but you don't know where to get training.

The HRD specialist is knowledgeable about outside training and educational opportunities, and he or she can arrange for your enrollment (that is, *coordinate outside training opportunities*) in a class that most closely meets your individual needs.

Situation #4: the marginal employee. With one exception, all your employees are well motivated and highly productive. The exception's performance has been unsatisfactory for some time, and you've talked with her on several occasions with little results. Her work improves only briefly following counseling. You've discussed the situation with your boss, but he's left it entirely in your lap. You are at a loss about what to do.

The HRD specialist's role in such a situation is as a *consultant*. He or she can encourage you to ventilate your frustrations and then help you explore possible causes of the employee's marginal performance and ways to get her to meet performance standards. The HRD specialist can even "role play" a counseling session with you to coach you on the use of these insights into the employee's problems.

In other words, the HRD specialist is a good sounding-board for discussing personnel problems.

Situation #5: setting goals. The company is very concerned about improving productivity, and management is now requiring all supervisors to set yearly goals. This is the first time in 15 years as a supervisor that you have been asked to do this, and you are at a loss. After all, your work is routine production. You don't determine what or how much to produce. What kinds of goals can you set?

Goal setting can be exasperating to someone who has never done it before. Your HRD specialist can help you look at your departmental organization in a new light and set direction on things within your control like quality of product, scrap generation, or downtime. This goal setting can help you to *improve* your *organizational effectiveness*.

Situation #6: interdepartmental conflict. Although yours is an operating department (the "bread and butter" of the plant), the maintenance department seems to ignore your requests for assistance. Sometimes your operators must wait hours before a machine is repaired. That results in unscheduled overtime and subsequent increased production costs. It seems that maintenance doesn't understand your priorities. You would like to have a meeting with appropriate maintenance and production personnel to work out the problem but you're afraid such a meeting would deteriorate into a shouting match.

Such a situation can benefit from involvement of the HRD specialist. As a neutral party, he or she can bring together the two departments and facilitate a problem-solving session to establish a common understanding of priorities.

Even if one of the departments decides not to participate in a mutual problem-solving session, the HRD specialist can still help by facilitating a problem-solving session with the willing department. During the session, the participants would examine things they themselves could do to make the situation more tolerable. Either way, third-party facilitation, an effective *intervention*, encourages organizational growth.

There are few flags that go up to announce "This situation calls for the HRD specialist," but each time you call him or her, you will gain experience in knowing when to call the next time. You will find that the HRD specialist is an accessible, versatile person who can help you increase your effectiveness in any situation involving your employees, yourself, or your department. As you call upon him or her, the result will be a full utilization of a valuable company resource, and—more important—successive achievements in your own supervisory management.

The Supervisor's Role in a Training Needs Analysis

LAURA K. FLEMING and ANN M. APKING

Does your work group suffer from poor performance or high turnover? If so, your firm may decide to conduct a training needs analysis. A consultant will visit the organization to analyze the personnel problem in order to develop a training program to correct it. The needs analysis can also be used to determine whether a performance problem stems from a training deficiency or some other issue. Since the success of the analysis depends on the consultant's getting complete and accurate information, it is important for you to be familiar with the needs analysis process.

Preparation for the Needs Analysis

The consultant will have to thoroughly assess the environmental conditions in which the organization operates, including the political, economic, social, and technological factors. This means that you must prepare for the needs analysis. You will have to identify the long- and short-term goals of your organization, locate staffing charts, and outline any changes that have occurred in the organizational culture.

Your next step should be to supply the consultant with background information: Who identified the problem? What are the company's expectations of the work groups? Who might support or hinder the needs analysis in the group? What information systems exist? What training materials are being used now and what were used previously? The consultant will also want to evaluate job descriptions, performance appraisals, and work samples. It will also help to identify the experts in the group who can serve as information resources, and to prepare a list of outstanding, average, and low performers.

Finally, you'll have to prepare your employees for the needs analysis. Discussing the upcoming analysis with your work group will build support for the effort and emphasize the importance of developing an effective training program. It will also focus attention on the positive outcomes of such an analysis.

Reprinted from *Supervisory Management,* May 1986

The Needs Analysis Process

In order to fully assist a training consultant, you should know what a needs analysis involves. There are seven steps the consultant will follow in completing a training needs analysis:

1. *Defining objectives.* This involves identifying the goals and the scope of the needs analysis, as well as the competencies and shortcomings in the organization. The consultant will specify the knowledge, behaviors, incentives, and motives of the target group, in addition to the information and tools at its disposal.

2. *Identifying data.* The consultant will then examine the data that you have collected prior to his or her arrival: attitude surveys, job descriptions, performance appraisals, work samples, and the like.

3. *Selecting a method for gathering data.* The needs analysis will require additional information. Some of the possible techniques for acquiring these data are interviews, observations, surveys, and reviews of written resources.

4. *Gathering data.* The selected method will then be modified to suit your organization—for example, the consultant may conduct interviews individually rather than in groups.

5. *Analyzing and verifying data.* Once the data have been gathered, the consultant will identify the problem as either a training deficiency or a performance problem. He or she will also determine the scope of the problem, its cost to the organization, and the priorities that management should adopt in eliminating the problem.

6. *Preparing the final report.* The consultant will then select the most appropriate solution. It should be cost-effective and consistent with organizational policies.

7. *Making the presentation.* The final report will be put into written form and presented to management. The consultant will then explain his or her findings and justify the recommended solutions.

Trust Your Judgment

It is in your best interests to work closely with the consultant to ensure the completeness and accuracy of the needs analysis. But you should not hesitate to evaluate for yourself whether the techniques and rationales used by the consultant are sound. You may wish to ask the following questions: What is the consultant's reason for selecting specific data collection tools? Who will be interviewed during the needs analysis and why? What is the schedule for completing the data gathering? Will the information collected remain confidential?

It is also your responsibility to review the data collected by the consultant, to identify technical errors in the documentation, and to verify the content to be included in the final report.

Summary

By becoming familiar with the needs analysis process, you can work more closely and knowledgeably with a training consultant. In this way, the consultant will be able to uncover aspects of a problem that would have taken him or her much longer to discover unassisted, and you will be able to significantly contribute to the productivity of your work group through the development of an effective training program.

Keeping Account of Employees' Skills

HARRY A. WASHING and KURT W. BOVEINGTON

Managing professionals is a real challenge for today's supervisors. This is true in all fields but especially in data processing whose professionals enjoy a great deal of job mobility. Indeed, DP professionals have a different view of career advancement from other employees. DP professionals are like other specialists in that they are proud of their skills and experience and want to increase their expertise. To minimize the turnover of professionals, supervisors must challenge and satisfy their needs. This involves a joint effort between supervisors and employees.

One possible strategy is to develop a skills-functions model. This model can contain a variety of personnel information as well as information regarding the various positions of and the skills required by professionals. Its use can help supervisors make better use of their professionals, who will in turn benefit by enjoying greater job satisfaction.

Although the description that follows is related to the model's use in a DP organization, and the model itself was developed with that in mind, its application is broader; a model can be developed for other kinds of jobs as well.

Development and Design of the Model

A typical skills inventory can maintain an unlimited amount of information on each employee. In addition to biographical data, employment history, appraisal ratings, career goals, and training sessions attended, information on the specific skills and/or experience of each employee can be a component of the skills inventory.

The skills-functions model is ultimately derived from the work unit's mission, the jobs to be performed, and the skills required to effectively perform those jobs. Even in a typical DP organization or unit, the jobs could be numerous and the skills detailed and endless. The skills, however, can be logically consolidated into groups such as functional analysis and design, technical analysis and design, application programming and coding, systems programming and coding, data base administration, computer operating, procedures writing, technical writing, and administrative management.

Once this is done, the next step is to determine where and how the skill groups are used, with what tools, and in what ways. This involves identifying all applications, hardware, software and operating systems, languages, and any other significant characteristics of the environment. Again, if such a list

Reprinted from *Supervisory Management*, May 1986

results in too much detail or overlap exists among the functions, then these functions may be grouped together in a manner that still meets the needs of management. Figure 1 shows some possible organizational functions.

The final step in this process is to link the skill groups with the organizational functions. Not all functions match with every skill group. Thus, the combinations of skill groups with relevant organizational functions result in linkages that reflect the particular DP organization or unit. Each relevant skill-function combination can be arranged in a matrix model and used as a basis for tracking individual employees' career goals. (See Figure 2.)

Various codes could be adopted to refer to different levels of proficiency. The model could then be adjusted to indicate the degree of proficiency attained, the degree of proficiency desirable, and to indicate those functions not applicable for certain skill-function linkages. In addition, codes or identification symbols for the various skill groups and functions could be adopted and linked with the various DP positions. All of this information can be readily portrayed directly on the model.

A supervisor who is familiar with the skills-functions model and the respective codes and the career paths available can more effectively and constructively perform his or her human resource functions.

Using the Model

There are many uses for such a model. It can be used for human resource planning, management and employee development, promotions, transfers, job rotations, internal recruiting and consulting, and career counseling. Obviously, the uses of the model depend upon the needs of the organization.

The model can serve as a mechanism to grade or chart each individual employee in terms of the skill-function linkages. By loading these linkages into an automated system, the skills and experiences of each employee can be easily maintained and compared with the linkages reflected in the model. This can ensure that employees possess the necessary skills prior to being promoted to higher-level positions.

In addition to facilitating promotions, the model can also direct job transfers and rotations and other development activities. With a detailed account of each employee, management can determine which employees are lacking specific skills and the best way to deal with the deficiencies. Through proper transfers, rotations, and development, management can assure itself of a pool of employees proficient at the skills that meet the organization's needs.

Figure 1

Organizational Functions	
Applications	Hardware
Accounts Receivable	IBM
Accounts Payable	Digital
General Ledger	IBM PC
Order and Billing	
Inventory Control	
Personnel and Payroll	
Software and Operating Systems	Languages
OS/DOS	IDMS
CICS	Cobol
DMSII	Basic
Unix	PL/1

Figure 2

A Skills-Function Model

ORGANIZATIONAL FUNCTIONS / DATA PROCESSING SKILL GROUPS	APPLICATIONS						HARDWARE			SOFTWARE AND OPERATING SYSTEMS				LANGUAGES			
	Accounts Receivable	Accounts Payable	General Ledger	Order & Billing	Inventory Control	Personnel & Payroll	IBM	Digital	IBM PC	OS/DOS	CICS	DMSII	Unix	IDMS	Cobol	Basic	PL/1
Functional Anal. & Des.																	
Technical Anal. & Des.																	
Application Prog. & Cond.																	
Systems Prog. & Cond.																	
Data Base Admin.																	
Computer Operating																	
Procedures Writing																	
Technical Writing																	
Administrative Management																	

Another use of the model is to assist management in matching employee skills with current or future job demands. For some assignments, a supervisor may be looking for the "right individual with the right qualifications." By tapping into the model, a supervisor may be able to more effectively match an employee with the job in question.

Career counseling can also benefit from the use of the model. A skills-functions model like that portrayed contains very useful information for supervisors and employees alike and can serve as a communication vehicle during the counseling session. For instance, employees may want to inquire about the availability of applications, hardware, software, or languages in terms of their career goals, or they may merely have some questions concerning the various DP positions. They may also want to communicate their feelings about certain skill groups. This can lead to a constructive dialogue between supervisor and employee and this in turn can reveal the need for additional training in a specific skill group or function.

Human resource planning is still another area that could benefit from such a model. Once the number of people and skills required are determined, one can examine the current baseline as reflected in the skills-functions model for the DP organization or unit. The resulting gap between the estimated demand for human resources and current supply may indicate the need to upgrade the supply. This can be accomplished through external recruiting, transfers, rotations, specialized training and development, or promotions.

Maintenance of the Model

The collection and maintenance of detailed data on all employees require continual attention. This information can be maintained manually, although an automated system would ease the updating, sorting, and retrieval functions. Input to the system can be done through a CRT screen or an input document that reflects the model in terms of skill groups and functions. In large organizations, the information can be maintained "on-line" through a local area network. However, with many CRT stations having access to sensitive information, proper security and tight controls are needed.

In addition, a number of policies and procedures should be developed regarding the use of the skills-functions model in such areas as job descriptions, promotions, transfers, job rotations, employee training and development, career counseling, and internal consulting. The nature of these policies will depend upon organizational priorities, such as developing human resources or hiring them.

Also vital are policies governing input, updating, sorting, and retrieval as well as the type and nature of information maintained on each employee. Since much of this information can be quite sensitive, a policy should be developed that assures consistency and integrity regarding the type of information maintained, how it is to be used, and by whom.

Because of the dynamic environment of segments of the DP industry, the model must be constantly updated: Hardware, software, and languages can become obsolete over time and new technologies may take their place. One strategy might be to form a committee that would meet on a regular basis. This committee would review the current set of organizational functions in light of environmental forces and make recommendations concerning additions or deletions to the model and suggest some policy changes.

Conclusion

The skills-functions model is one tool for strengthening the human resource functions within any organization or unit. Although it was designed for a DP organization, with different skill groups and for other organizational functions it may be used for other job categories with the same positive results. By keeping an account of each employees' skills in relation to a normative state as reflected in the model, management can more effectively match skills with job demands. In addition, employees will gain a feeling of self-determination in terms of their own careers, which will assure that personal as well as organizational goals are fulfilled.

Helping Employees Make the Transition From Classroom to Workplace

RONALD L. DETRICK

Educators and managers often find themselves facing off over the subject of technical and vocational school graduates making a smooth transition from the classroom to the workplace. One thing they agree on is this: A communication gap exists.

Frequently those in business and industry complain that technical and vocational schools just aren't turning out the right kinds of graduates. Maybe they don't have the right skills. Maybe they don't even have proficiency in the basic skills. Too often, these complaints—which may be valid—never develop beyond the griping stage, for vocational and technical schools, particularly public systems, seem unapproachable.

But perhaps this feeling does technical education a disservice. While much has been written about the need for educators to help transform students into employees, little has been said about the managers' role in this process, and they have a very real stake in the matter.

Early Involvement

The ease with which graduates of vocational training institutes enter the job market and become productive employees has a direct bearing on the profitability of their company. Human resources are the key to the successful running of any organization, and it makes good business sense to give personnel the attention they deserve.

It makes even better business sense to give them that attention early—by taking a more active role in the education process that is shaping them into potential employees. In that way everyone benefits. The educational institution is helped to improve its services; the student graduates are better prepared for the job market; and the businessperson will gain a more qualified new employee whose personal growth and expansion will more likely be able to parallel that of the company.

Bridging the Gap

What can employers and managers do? Following are eight basic steps to ensure that both you and your new employees benefit from the full use of their potential:

Reprinted from *Supervisory Management*, October 1983

1. *Investigate local vocational education systems.* Take the time to find out what's happening with vocational education in your area. You may find that private vocational schools—educational systems run by people who speak the languages of both business and education—are able to bridge the communication gap.

The level of sophistication today, in curricula and equipment, will probably surprise you. In any case, you will be better informed to voice opinions or complaints. (It's well known that everybody is an "expert" in education—they've either gone to school or known someone who has.)

2. *Communicate with educators regularly.* Work with local vocational schools instead of against them. Let them know your current needs and what your business anticipates a few years down the road. If you hire their graduates, give them a progress report—let them know what skills have been useful and which haven't been up to par.

3. *Match the skills of graduates to your needs.* Make an effort to identify your company's needs and then look for graduates with the skills required. Many businesspeople say to educators, "Just give us someone who can read and write and has a good attitude—we can teach them the rest." While it's true that having basic skills and a positive work ethic is important, there is more to it than that—would you hire a hard-working secretary who can read and write but can't type or file?

On the other hand, it is relatively simple to hire graduates trained, for example, to do word processing on an IBM model and teach them to operate a Wang.

On the Job

4. *Make an effort to understand the graduate.* Employment is like a marriage: To be successful, both parties have to be happy. You're looking for dependable, productive workers. The graduates are looking for secure, fulfilling work. Don't forget that many may be undergoing their first real job interview; it can be a frightening and humbling experience. After determining their skill levels, let them know what's expected of them, but do it with empathy.

5. *Develop an orientation program for new employees.* It isn't enough to show new employees to their desks and wish them good luck. Such a hit-or-miss approach to orientation is unfair to the employee, co-workers, and the firm itself. Speed up productivity by giving graduates an introduction to the work environment and a clear explanation of their duties. A formal orientation program can reduce anxiety and facilitate assimilation.

6. *Anticipate on-going training needs.* You can expect and should demand a standard level of skills from graduates you hire. What you cannot expect is that they will never again need training. A good employee will want to grow and expand capabilities; learning should be a never-ending process.

7. *Establish assessment and evaulation procedures.* From the first day on the job, new graduates are being assessed. Have they been taught the right skills for the job? Are they capable in those skills? Are they interested in doing a good job? These questions will be asked, and it is best if they are answered in an orderly manner. If your firm has none, set up procedures for formal evaluation and use them.

8. *Examine your policies on staff development and organizational development.* There are two areas of development for all companies: increasing the productivity of the individual and increasing the productivity of the organization. The best results are achieved when these two factors are in unison. An employee who is experiencing self-satisfaction and also contributing to the goals and objectives of the company represents the best of all possibilities.

In conclusion, it is apparent that employers and managers can take positive action to communicate with vocational schools and increase the productivity of the graduates they hire. Working with vocational schools to improve the education of potential employees might be compared to the scouting procedures used in professional sports. The pro teams know it is in their best interests to check out—*early*—star players in schools that have winning reputations. It's a gameplan that can work equally well in the business world.

Becoming a Mentor:
Are the Risks Worth the Rewards?

THEODORE J. HALATIN and ROSE E. KNOTTS

The concept of mentoring has received considerable attention recently, most of it focused on the rewards and the attractiveness of the relationship for the manager. Little space has been given to the possible dangers in a mentor-protégé relationship.

Although the association between mentor and protégé is normally amicable and mutually beneficial, the potential for an unsatisfactory relationship exists. It is expedient, therefore, for a manager to be aware of such vulnerabilities before becoming a mentor or encouraging employees to become protégés.

Vulnerabilities

There are numerous overt and covert potential hazards of mentorship:

Employee jealousy. Jealousy, resentment, and malevolent factions may surface in an organization when a manager develops a mentor-protégé relationship with an employee if other employees perceive themselves as being at a disadvantage in receiving recognition, assistance, or rewards. Retaliations from these employees can result in the form of punitive groups or systems that ridicule and condemn the mentor, the protégé, and the relationship. In extreme situations, this "kangaroo court" could possibly exert undue pressures to the extent that the manager becomes ineffective.

Time demands. The mentor relationship can place restrictive time constraints on the already overworked and busy manager. Because of on-the-job or away-from-the-job time that must be spent developing the protégé, the mentor must be willing to postpone or delegate many tasks as well as extend the work day to complete necessary responsibilities.

Emotional involvement. The potential for emotional involvement is great as the mentor shares in the protégé's successes and failures. Situations may necessitate a spirit of cooperation with a third party who has not been supportive or has created problems for the protégé. If the mentor's interaction with the third party is based on emotions rather than rationality, adverse feedback may affect not only the mentor and the protégé but the organization.

Sexual involvement. When the mentor and protégé are of opposite sexes, the possibility of sexual

Reprinted from *Supervisory Management,* February 1982

involvement (rumored or real) may surface. Or the reactions of a jealous spouse could lead to an unpalatable domestic situation that could disrupt the harmony of the organization or department.

Image attractiveness. A mentor or protégé may feel compelled to be pretentious in an attempt to impress the other. While this stems from a motivation to solicit respect, information that might be important to the other might be disguised. Open and honest communication is necessary to prevent this type of deceptiveness.

Overdependency. Overdependency can inhibit the goals of the relationship as well as the protégé by making the person a puppet who cannot function without someone to pull the strings. Ordinarily it is the protégé who is guilty of excessive dependency on the mentor, but it is possible for the situation to be reversed. In such cases the mentor is reacting to encouragement from the protégé.

Prohibitive domain. There are areas of involvement that are off limits to the mentor/manager. Unbiased decisions in everyday situations must be made so that the mentor will not be accused of interfering in an area where he or she has no authority or legitimate right.

Blackmail. Professional and personal information shared with the other in a mentoring situation could be used for the purpose of blackmail. Before sharing confidential information with the protégé, the mentor should consider the potential for a hazardous or an embarrassing situation if an attempt is ever made to blackmail the manager.

Embarrassment. Personal or professional failures by either the mentor or the protégé may be a source of embarrassment to the other. Whether or not a failure was directly caused by the protégé, the stigma usually exists and may spill over onto the mentor.

Loyalty. Although the major purpose of a mentoring relationship is some sort of reciprocal exchange, some people use the situation as a temporary stepping stone. In such cases, loyalty to the mentor is discarded as soon as his or her support is no longer needed for career advancement. Not only can this have a demoralizing effect on the abused manager, but it can also create inhibitions and reservations about serving again as a mentor.

Combat the Dangers

The manager considering becoming a mentor can avoid many of the dangers and increase the chances for a successful mentor relationship by prudent analysis of the potential outcomes.

First, the manager should look at what he or she expects to get out of the relationship. What are the intrinsic and extrinsic benefits to the mentor—the person who is investing a great deal of energy and time in the development of another? In other words, what are the opportunity costs to the mentor?

The next step should be to evaluate the protégé. Does this person have the qualities necessary for success? Are those involved in the relationship compatible? Will the protégé meet expectations?

The final phase involves an analysis of the situation. Is the timing appropriate? Will the protégé accept the guidance of the mentor? Will the relationship achieve the ends sought?

A mentor relationship can provide benefits to the manager, the protégé, and the organization; but alertness to the development of a problem situation is important. The manager has the responsibility for seeing that the concept is developed properly and that accountability for the outcome is assumed.

Making the Manager a Better Trainer

LESLIE A. BRYAN, JR.

What one word best describes how first-line supervisors are evaluated? How about *performance?* Performance is, of course, a function of many things, perhaps the most important of which is how effectively the supervisor gets things accomplished through others. Training is an important part of this. Indeed, it is possible to say that a supervisor's performance evaluation is closely linked to his or her ability as a trainer of others.

Training for most supervisors is a continuous, never-ending responsibility. A supervisor must deal not only with new employees having no skills but with old employees having obsolete skills, transferred employees having different skills, and present employees having poor or undeveloped skills. But the payoff for the time spent in training is high. A supervisor can loosen his or her supervision, the performance of the department will improve, operational problems will decrease, and respect for the supervisor will increase. The trainee, too, benefits. For the trainee, it means increased job performance and satisfaction, freedom from close supervision, increased personal growth and development, and improved morale, confidence, and self-esteem. The organization gains from increased productivity and decreased operational problems. In fact, everyone is a winner when supervisors are effective trainers.

My experience as a training consultant to a midwestern public utility has taught me that the initial reaction of supervisors when asked if they do any training is, "People come to us already trained by our training department." This may be true. In many cases supervisors do not personally do the training. But a 1981 American Society of Training and Development survey yielded these percentages to the question, "How do supervisors train their employees?"

- Ninety percent have them work alongside an experienced employee.
- Fifty-seven percent personally do the training.
- Forty-two percent use the company's training department.
- Twenty-seven percent use outside training.
- Five percent provide no training.

No matter what the previous training may have been, even the most proficient employee is seldom ready to step into a job and begin operating as a team member.

Reprinted from *Supervisory Management,* April 1984

The Orientation

Training starts with the employee orientation. The first day on any new job, there is usually some confusion. Even such seemingly simple questions as, "Where do I eat lunch," "Can I or can't I leave my work area without permission," and "How do I answer the phone," need to be answered.

Typically during orientation supervisors cover work rules, the department organization, and introductions to co-workers; however, often overlooked is something even more important in the long run—pride in the organization and a feeling of the importance of the work to be done. Human relations experts say that employees will work harder if they can relate their efforts to the final product. There are a number of ways supervisors can do this. In a service organization, for example, a supervisor could build pride in his or her new recruits by sharing with them letters of appreciation from customers or stories demonstrating the value of the services provided.

The value of the equipment that the new hire will handle can also be used to demonstrate the importance of the individual's work. Whether it is a $1,500 typewriter or a multimillion dollar aircraft, dollars impress people. Company slogans and mottos can accomplish the same purpose. General Electric's "Progress is our most important product," and DuPont's "Better things for better living through chemistry," are used not only to sell products but to encourage and motivate employees.

If an orientation is effective, a new employee should know that he or she is not just a security badge number but a unique human being, valuable and important to the organization.

Informal Training

After the orientation, the supervisor must focus his or her training efforts on the continuous demands of in-service training. This takes two forms: formal and informal. Let's look at the informal first.

Most supervisors do more informal training than they realize. This training takes four forms.

If learning is defined as changing the way people think or behave by changing knowledge levels, skills, or attitude, then the very presence of the supervisor can serve as a training experience. In essence, the supervisor's presence causes a conditioned response. The sound of his or her footsteps or the buzz of the intercom affect the employee's performance in the same way that a bell made Pavlov's dog hungry.

B. F. Skinner noted that one trains people by the use of operant conditioning, that is, the way one reinforces behavior. By praising, punishing, or ignoring the actions of those who work for them, supervisors are in fact training them.

Another frequently used method of informal training, especially on the job, is observation and example. The danger in relying on this method of training is that the trainee may observe the wrong example or may observe a good example but not understand the reasons behind what is being done. A journeyman electrician once related his experience. He was never given any formal instruction about insulating himself when disconnecting electrical cables, just told to "watch ol' Joe" who had been doing it for years. The apprentice observed that the old timer never insulated himself prior to touching the cables, but he did stand on one leg while making the disconnection. When the trainee attempted to disconnect the cables, he also stood on one leg. He did not take the proper grounding and insulation precautions and received a severe electrical shock. He later discovered a significant difference between the old timer and himself—"ol' Joe" had a wooden leg.

Finally, employees are trained by the use of the SOS method, the sink or swim or trial and error approach. This is obviously not the best training method for any new employee and certainly not for someone who will operate expensive or dangerous equipment.

A Planned Approach

Training, to be successful, must be planned and guided, not an informal, "catch as catch can" experience. Supervisors involved in skill training should practice these eight steps:

1. *Pre-evaluate*. Although not perfectly applicable to skill training, an understanding of Bloom's hierarchy of the Cognitive Domain is useful when considering the pre-training proficiency levels of students, according to *Approaches to Training and Development* (Addison-Wesley, 1978). Suppose a supervisor's task is to teach Ohm's Law to apprentice electricians. It would be important for the manager/trainer to know the electricians' level of knowledge prior to starting the training. Consider the following hierarchy of knowledge level:

- *Awareness*. They have heard of Ohm's Law.
- *Knowledge*. They know that Ohm's Law is represented by the formula E = IR, but that's about all they do know.
- *Comprehension*. They have an understanding of the components E, I, and R.
- *Application*. They can use the formula, even if it is only to plug in the numbers and do the computation.
- *Analysis*. They understand the law and the theory behind it and are able to use both to solve problems.
- *Evaluation*. They are able to prove the law.

One colleague, in teaching skills, has observed four skill levels and wryly labeled them:

- *Unconsciously incompetent*. The trainee does not realize that he or she is not competent. This is obviously a dangerous level, for the person is prone to move levers and throw switches to see what will happen.
- *Consciously incompetent*. The trainee realizes his or her incompetency and is, one hopes, ready to learn.
- *Consciously competent*. The trainee can do the skill with thought and effort or perhaps with a checklist.
- *Unconsciously competent*. The trainee has thoroughly mastered the skill and does the task unconsciously. This person is the most highly qualified but also can be dangerously complacent.

Despite the humorous side of these labels, they should make clear the need for a trainer to evaluate knowledge or skill level before beginning instruction and to begin instruction at the appropriate level.

2. *Plan*. Two important functions necessary but often overlooked in the planning stage of skill instruction are job analysis and objective setting.

Since trainers almost invariably come from the highly skilled and perhaps unconsciously competent, they should always do some job analysis to ensure that they include all the necessary skill tasks in their training plans. A skill to be taught should be broken down into its smallest parts or tasks so it can be understood by the student. Supervisors who are at the unconsciously competent skill level may be surprised at how many steps they would have neglected to explain had they not done this exercise. For example, in my seminars we do a job breakdown of the tasks necessary to teach my 15 year old daughter how to fill a car with gas at a self-service gas station. Few realize beforehand that there are 20 to 25 steps in that process.

How detailed the job breakdown is depends on the skill level of the trainee, supporting the importance of the pre-evaluation in successful task training. According to Martin M. Broadwell (*The Supervisor and On-the-Job Training*, Addison-Wesley, 1975), the interaction of job analysis and pre-evaluation can be represented by the equation: job requirements or standards minus trainee evaluation or job performance equals training requirements.

A second element of the planning stage is objective setting. Lesson planning should support the desired change in the way the trainee thinks or acts. What knowledge is the trainee expected to gain? What skill is he or she expected to develop? What change in attitude or behavior is desired? In the *College Teaching Workshop Study Guide for Designing Instruction*, the ACE method's usefulness in developing lesson objectives is discussed. The ACE method asks, What should the trainee accomplish under what conditions (memory, open book, checklist), and how will the learning be evaluated?

Objectives should not only be used to help develop the lesson plan but be shared with students before the training to help them focus on what is important.

3. *Prepare.* Students are in the training session for all sorts of reasons. They may be there to get out of work, to socialize, or just because the boss told them to be there. The purpose of this stage in the training process is to motivate the employee to learn by finding a positive way to answer the question, "What's in it for me?"

4 & 5. *Presentation and performance.* As Martin Broadwell points out, the presentation and performance stages are best viewed as a three-step process:

Step 1. In the first step, the instructor explains and demonstrates each task or stage on the job. An instructor, for instance, would explain and then demonstrate each step of the turn-on process of a machine. In the course of the explanation, he or she would emphasize key points, particularly safety matters.

Step 2. The instructor performs the operation while the student explains. In the second step, the instructor operates the machine or does the task while the student talks him or her through it.

Step 3. Now the student has a hands-on chance to demonstrate the skill.

An instructor shouldn't stop after the first step in the process on the assumption that the training is finished. Often, after a demonstration, an instructor will ask, "You understand? Have you got it now?" It is human nature for the student, not wanting to appear stupid, to nod his or her head, only to botch up the operation when on his or her own.

Visual aids can also be used to help the learning process. Les Donaldson and Edward E. Scannel, authors of *Human Resource Development, The New Trainer's Guide* (Addison-Wesley, 1979), state that about 83 percent of all we learn is learned through sight.

6. *Practice.* The learning process is designed to bring about a relatively permanent change in the way one thinks or behaves. To accomplish its objective, one has to overlearn—develop the ability to transfer the learning from the classroom to the real world of the workplace. The only way to do this is through practice. The trainee must feel comfortable enough with the new skills that he or she will not revert to old, pre-training habits in emergencies.

7. *Performance evaluation.* At the end of the instruction, the trainer should be prepared to answer two questions: Does the student meet the objectives that were established in the planning stage? How good a job did the manager do as an instructor? Both are vital questions.

8. *Follow up.* The use of new skills is strongly influenced by the attitudes of the boss and peer group. When the trainee is told, "I know that is what you were taught but we do it this way here," it's unlikely that he or she will make use of the newly acquired skills. Behavior learned in the classroom will seldom be carried over into the job unless it is already used there and those who use it are rewarded for doing so. Given the time pressure of the workplace, supervisors often reward wrong behavior and punish right behavior. This, of course, is particularly dangerous in terms of safety because it encourages unsafe shortcuts.

In Conclusion

Training by numbers—that is, simply following the eight steps of *skill training* described—does not guarantee a successful training experience. Just as the first-line supervisor as disciplinarian has to be an amateur psychologist, so too the supervisor as trainer has to be a semi-professional educational psychologist. From my experience as a trainer and educator of trainers, I have found the following laws and principles of learning psychology to be useful in increasing the effectiveness of the training.

1. *The Law of Readiness.* No one learns without motivation; trainees must want to learn.
2. *The Law of Intensity.* Training must use the senses, and the more the better.
3. *The Law of Receptivity.* Trainees are affected by environmental and emotional factors and by

external pressures and commitments. Training is most successful when these stresses are reduced as much as possible.

4. *The Law of Association.* Past experiences and the experiences of other trainees should be a part of the training experience.

5. *The Law of Primacy and Recency.* People remember best the ideas and concepts that are discussed first and last and have the most difficulty remembering what came in between.

6. *The Law of Relevancy.* A person learns more quickly and the learning is lasting when it has immediate meaning to the person.

7. *The Law of Exercise.* We learn best by doing.

8. *The Law of Effect.* Trainees need successes to reinforce the instruction.

9. *The Law of Differences.* People have different speeds at which they learn. Trainers should be aware of this and should use the faster learners to help the slow ones.

10. *The Law of the Learning and Forgetting Curves.* Learning and unlearning is a continuous process.

That's why it is so important to review and practice what has been taught.

I take no credit for the originality of these principles. They can be found in a number of books in various forms and under different labels (see *Human Resource Development, The New Trainer's Guide and Management of Training Programs*). But I do vouch for their value in any training effort and their efficacy when used in conjunction with the eight steps of skills training.

What to Do When Your Employees Plateau

JOHN N. BARTUNEK

Most individuals reach their level of highest employment long before they can retire. It's not unusual for a department to have one or two members who are bored with their current jobs and have no chance for upward mobility. Some employees will accept this situation, maintaining or improving their current level of performance. But others—usually high-achievers—refuse to accept the fact that they have plateaued. They become discontented. Over time their morale and productivity decline.

This is not a new problem but it is a bigger one than in the past. Plateauing has taken on increased importance as employees in the 30 to 40 year old range (the so-called "baby boomers") increasingly compete for a fixed number of available positions. But the sheer numbers of employees is not the only factor causing an increase in career plateauing. The relative state of the economy together with the increased competition from foreign firms have contributed to career plateauing through layoffs, mergers, and cutbacks in staff. Walter Kiechel wrote in the May 3, 1982 issue of *Fortune,* "Most baby-boomers have already had to adjust their expectations downward, finding for example that a college degree doesn't guarantee you an interesting job, or any job at all for that matter."

As firms analyze their organizational structure and eliminate, combine, or leave open various positions, employees are experiencing less movement and longer durations in current positions. In firms that have been hard hit by the past recession, departments may be smaller and may be staffed by individuals who previously were in managerial positions.

From an organizational viewpoint, plateauing is an issue that will have to be addressed in the near future, since the employee discontent it causes may ultimately affect the bottom line. Departmentally, there are steps that individual managers with plateaued subordinates can take to help these individuals. The solution lies in a special counseling and developmental effort. As I mentioned, plateaued employees fall into two categories. There are those who are not out to "break the records" but perform competently. Their life priorities are different from the high-achievers who expect unlimited career growth and now find that growth stalled. These individuals, the "high achievers," Louis E. Davis wrote in the August 1981 issue of *Administrative Management,* have a desire for ". . . self-control, self-development, (and) meaningful work. . . ." They need to be helped to realize and accept the situation and explore alternative career options. These high-achievers need individual professional growth attention and recognition that their work is useful, needed, and important. This is not to say that the competent employees do not need some

Reprinted from *Supervisory Management,* July 1984

high-achiever type of counseling. But for the most part they require counseling and training that reflect their aspirations, which have been scaled down through experience and personal interests.

Negative Sanctions

If the plateaued employee's performance has dropped severely and the individual's discontent is affecting not only his or her productivity but the productivity of the department as a whole, a manager may have no other alternative but to use negative sanctions. In essence, the supervisor says, "If you don't get your act together, you're fired!" The hope is that the employee will conform to the supervisor's expectations because the individual knows what will happen if he or she doesn't. But it's not enough with negative sanctions to redirect stress about job content to stress about keeping the job. The cause of the stress needs to be acknowledged and neutralized and the employee's behavior turned around. To do that the manager needs to meet with the plateaued subordinate and discuss the problem and its effect on the behavior of co-workers within the organizational unit. The expectations of management should be stated; there should be no room left for misunderstandings about what was said. Penalties about which the employee knows in advance should be imposed with increasing severity if no change in behavior occurs. If after a period of time it becomes apparent that no change is likely, then termination proceedings should be considered.

This process is successful only if feedback is continuous. Improvements in behavior need to be acknowledged and reinforced. Otherwise, negative sanctions will only further alienate the plateaued employee.

Performance Counseling

In most instances, the problems with a plateaued employee needn't reach a level where disciplinary action is the only likely solution. If a supervisor intervenes early enough, the problem may be remedied with positive counseling through the use of performance appraisals. The process is viewed as a problem-solving opportunity and not a fault-finding journey. As with negative sanctions, the cause of the problem needs to be acknowledged and its effect on the employee's performance identified and discussed. There should be two-way communication, with the supervisor soliciting and listening to the employee's self-evaluation and ideas for solving the problem and improving his or her performance.

The employee's participation in this process allows him or her to assume greater responsibility for the outcome and should increase his or her desire to improve performance. Since the meeting involves an exchange of communications, the final conclusions reached should be stated explicitly and in writing to see that both supervisor and employee are in agreement.

Even after the employee has committed himself or herself to the agreement, the performance appraisal/counseling process is not complete. Checkpoints or other measurement criteria need to be established so that both parties can evaluate the employee's progress. It must be emphasized that the counseling is not a one-time deal. Especially when dealing with the plateaued employee, counseling should be a continuing series of meetings designed to develop the employee. These meetings are based on the premise that the employee "has the ultimate responsibility for development improvement," as Randall Brett and Alan J. Fredian noted in the December 1981 issue of *Personnel Administrator.*

The review process should be constructive, with both parties meeting periodically to review performance based on earlier agreed-on expectations. As difficult as it may be, there should be no review of performance based on expectations not discussed earlier or incorporated into the written performance appraisal document. If the employee is to be held responsible for additional tasks or chooses to assume additional responsibility for an area, an agreement should be reached and incorporated into the appraisal document with appropriate yardsticks to measure performance.

Retraining Options

As part of the performance counseling, a manager may want to introduce the idea of retraining. Both outside programs and in-house workshops help the plateaued employee develop new skills that may lead to a new career opportunity. The unspoken organizational expectation is that the employee who has benefitted by these programs (especially if tuition-assistance was provided) will utilize the skills in a position within the firm.

Regardless of the extent of financial aid provided by the firm, the initiative to register and complete an outside course (or obtain a degree or certification) should rest with the employee. As with negative sanctions or the appraisal process itself, the employee's commitment makes the difference between a successful and an unsuccessful development effort.

This is not the case with an in-house training program. With it the company assumes the responsibility and takes the initiative in retraining the employee. In-house training is also more specialized than outside courses and is usually directed to the specific needs of the organization. For the plateaued employee, it offers a change of pace and an opportunity to acquire new skills without a major investment of time and money.

It's important that on-the-job training not be seen as busy-work or worthless or as something that is required for the company as a whole. When such perceptions occur, the "I don't care" attitude of the plateaued employee will be reinforced. To keep this from happening, the employee should be given the opportunity to select the training that best contributes to his or her immediate and future goals and those of the organization.

Plateauing can cause individual and organizationwide alienation and frustration and contribute to a counterproductive working climate. Failure to acknowledge the problem of plateauing will not cause it to disappear. Actually, acknowledgment is the first step toward resolution of the situation. Through discussion of the situation, the employee is made aware of his or her worth to the organization. and how the organization and employee can together satisfy each other's goals. Plateauing may be inevitable, for it exists in virtually all organizations and affects both good and bad performers. But if both employee and manager address the situation through counseling and training, career plateauing does not have to be the end of a person's career with an organization. Rather, it can be the start of a productive and rejuvenated career.

Contributors

George Alwon is associated with Leadership Consultants, Chapel Hill, North Carolina.

Ann M. Apking is affiliated with Creative Universal, Inc.

George W. Ayers is Assistant Administrator for Professional Services at Brynn Marr Hospital, Jacksonville, North Carolina.

Mark S. Bacon is with Bacon & Company, Cerritos, California.

H. Kent Baker, Ph.D., is Professor of Finance, Kogod College of Business Administration, The American University.

Barry J. Baroni, MBA, J.D., LL.M., is Professor of Labor Law and Arbitration at the University of New Orleans and a consultant and practicing labor arbitrator. He is a member of the Washington, D.C., and Louisiana Bars and was previously employed as Deputy Assistant General Counsel in the General Counsel's Office of the National Labor Relations Board in Washington, D.C.

John N. Bartunek serves as Instructor, Western Illinois University.

Robert R. Bell, Ph.D., is Chairman of the Department of Business Management, Tennessee Technological University.

Waldron Berry, Ph.D., is Associate Professor of Management, College of Business Administration, University of Central Florida.

Kurt W. Boveington is associated with NCR Corporation.

Alan Brache is the President of Product Development for Kepner Tregoe, Inc.

Darrel R. Brown, Ph.D., is Professor of Management, School of Business, Virginia Commonwealth University.

Leslie A. Bryan, Jr., Ph.D., is Assistant Professor of Supervision, Purdue University.

Steven Buckman is Personnel Manager, Insalaco's Supermarkets, Pittston, Pennsylvania.

Anthony J. Buonocore is President of "The Learning Edge," a consulting group located in Mendham, New Jersey.

Seymour Burchman is Senior Consultant and National Director of Executive Compensation Practice at Sibson & Company, Inc.

William G. Callarman is in the Department of Management at the College of Business Administration at the University of Central Florida.

Don Caruth, Ph.D., SPHR, is Associate Professor of Management at the College of Business and Technology, East Texas State University.

Robert Chasnoff is affiliated with Kean College of New Jersey, Union, New Jersey.

Alfred M. Coke, Ph.D., is Senior Consultant, Synergistic Systems, Denham Springs, Louisiana.

Jerry Conrath is an independent consultant, part-time college instructor, and writer on management and education issues. He is the author of *Our Other Youth*.

Contributors' affiliations are those at the time of original publication.

Mary F. Cook is Personnel Director, Rocky Mountain Energy Company.

Laurence P. Corbett is a partner of Corbett & Kane, an Oakland, California–based law firm.

James H. Corey, Jr., is Director of Human Resources, Quick Chek Food Stores.

Robert F. DeGise is Consultant, Promotion Services, Industrial Division, Caterpillar Tractor Company.

W. A. Delaney is President, Analysis & Computer Systems, Inc.

D. Keith Denton, Ph.D., is Associate Professor of Management in Southwest Missouri State University's Department of Management.

Ronald L. Detrick, Ed.D., is Vice President of Education, Centers Division, National Education Corporation.

Elizabeth Dickerson is President of Corporate Dynamics, a management consulting firm located in Hinsdale, Illinois.

C. R. Dillon is Corporate Manager, Administrative Directives Systems, McDonnell Douglas Corporation, St. Louis, Missouri.

Curtis E. Dobbs is Management Services Supervisor, Ernst & Ernst, Dallas, Texas.

Merrill E. Douglass heads up the Time Management Center located in Grandville, Michigan.

Donald W. Drumtra serves as Captain in the United States Air Force.

Jack W. English, Ph.D., is Human Resource Consultant, Mobil Oil Corporation.

Laura K. Fleming is affiliated with Creative Universal, Inc.

Joseph M. Fox is Chairman of Software A&E, Inc. He formerly served as Vice President of IBM's Federal Systems Division. His interest in executive development led to his book *Executive Qualities*.

William H. Franklin, Jr., Ph.D., is Professor of Business Administration, College of Business Administration, Georgia State University.

J. W. Gilsdorf is with the College of Business Administration, Department of Administrative Services, Arizona State University.

Myron Glassman is Professor in the College of Business and Public Administration at Old Dominion University.

Rosalind Gold is Management Development Consultant at Gold Consulting in New York City.

Ronald H. Gorman is Associate Professor of Management, The American University.

Jay I. Gottesman, Ph.D., is Manager, Industrial Services Center for Management of Organizational Resources, Stevens Institute of Technology.

Frederick Haas is Associate Professor of Management, Virginia Commonwealth University.

Theodore J. Halatin, Ph.D., is Professor of Management, School of Business, Southwest Texas State University.

Carol Hannah is Director of Training, Manpower Temporary Services.

Stanley B. Henrici is former General Manager, Organizational Systems, Heinz, U.S.A.

Melville Hensey is affiliated with Hensey Associates, management consulting engineers in Cincinnati, Ohio.

Jack A. Hill, Ph.D., is Professor and Chairman, Management and Organizational Behavior Program, College of Business Administration, University of Nebraska at Omaha.

Charles J. Hobson is affiliated with Indiana University-Northwest.

John J. Hobson is affiliated with Troy State University.

Robert B. Hobson is affiliated with the Hopkinsville, Kentucky Community Mental Health Center.

Andrew K. Hoh is Assistant Professor of Management, Creighton University.

A. T. Hollingsworth is Professor of Management, University of South Carolina.

John Hollwitz is Assistant Professor of English and Speech, Creighton University.

Stevan R. Holmberg, DBA, is affiliated with Kogod College of Business Administration, The American University.

Florence M. Hoylman is affiliated with Organizational Consultants, Inc., West Lafayette, Indiana.

Robard Y. Hughes is Professor of Management and Marketing, California State University.

J. Howard Jackson is in the Department of Management at VCU School of Business.

Harlan R. Jessup is associated with General Electric.

Donald O. Jewell, Ph.D., is affiliated with The Mescon Group, organization design consultants located in Atlanta, Georgia.

Sandra F. Jewell, Ph.D., is affiliated with The Mescon Group, organization design consultants located in Atlanta, Georgia.

Iris W. Johnson is in the Department of Management at VCU School of Business.

H. B. Karp, Ph.D., is an organizational psychologist who heads the consulting firm Personal Growth Systems, located in Virginia Beach, Virginia. He is the author of *Personal Power: An Unorthodox Guide to Success.*

J. Bernard Keys, Ph.D., is Assistant Dean and Director of MBA Studies, Tennessee Technological University.

Corwin P. King, Ph.D., is in the Department of Communication at Central Washington University.

Peter G. Kirby is Manager, Management Development, Red Lobster Inns of America, Inc., Orlando, Florida.

William Kirkwood, Ph.D., is Assistant Professor of Leadership Communication at East Tennessee State University.

Brian H. Kleiner, Ph.D., is Assistant Professor of Management, California State University-Fullerton.

Rose E. Knotts, Ph.D., is Associate Professor of Management, Arkansas State University.

Barbara Knudson-Fields is Principal of Human Development Consulting in Boise, Idaho.

Shelley Krantz is affiliated with Shelley Krantz and Associates, Studio City, California.

Edward L. Levine is Associate Professor of Industrial/Organizational Psychology, University of South Florida.

David MacCoy is Senior Consultant at Sibson & Company, Inc.

Roger B. Madsen is a Boise, Idaho, attorney specializing in employment law.

George E. Manners, Jr., Ph.D., is affiliated with The Mescon Group, organization design consultants located in Atlanta, Georgia.

C. James Maselko is Senior Vice President, Block Petrella Weisbord.

Eric Matthiesen is Associate Professor of English and Speech, Creighton University.

R. Bruce McAfee is Professor in the College of Business and Public Administration at Old Dominion University.

William W. McCartney is in the Department of Management at the College of Business Administration at the University of Central Florida.

Don Michael McDonald is a management trainer and consultant located in San Bernardino, California.

Larry G. McDougle is Director, Division of General and Technical Studies, Indiana University at Kokomo.

Bruce E. McEwan, D.B.A., CPCU, ARM, is Adjunct Professor, College of Business Administration, University of Hawaii at Manoa.

V. Dallas Merrell, Ph.D., is a management consultant.

Anthony M. Micolo is Vice President of Human Resources, The Dime Savings Bank of New York.

Bill Middlebrook, Ph.D., is Vice President, Caruth Management Consultants, Inc.

George Miller is affiliated with George Miller Associates.

Gordon P. Miller is President of Decision Training Systems, a management consulting firm located in Orbord, New Hampshire.

Philip I. Morgan, Ph.D., is a management consultant located in Arlington, Virginia.

Mary Walsh Mossop is an organizational consultant located in Washington, D.C.

Peter Muniz is affiliated with Peter Muniz & Associates, Somerset, New Jersey.

Donald W. Myers is Associate Professor of Management, School of Business Administration, Winthrop College.

James L. Nave is Administrator, Roane State Community College, Oak Ridge, Tennessee.

Cheryl K. Needell is Director, Leadership Consultants, Belle Mead, New Jersey.

Oliver L. Niehouse is President, Oliver L. Niehouse and Associates, Inc.

Dan H. Nix is Director, Center for Management Development, J. Sargeant Reynolds Community College.

J. Alan Ofner is President of Managing Change, Inc., located in Great Neck, New York.

Jack J. Phillips is Manager, Administration at Vulcan Materials Company.

Robert E. Pitts, Ph.D., is Assistant Professor of Marketing, College of Business Administration, University of Notre Dame.

Bob Powers is Senior Partner in the international consultancy, the Vanguard Group.

D. W. Prah is affiliated with Gallahue & Prah Relocation Consultants, Naperville, Illinois.

Trezzie A. Pressley, Ph.D., APD, is Professor and Head of Marketing and Management, East Texas State University.

Marcia Ann Pulich, Ph.D., is Associate Professor at the College of Business and Economics at the University of Wisconsin-Whitewater.

Les G. Radford is Management Consultant, Oliver L. Niehouse & Associates, Inc.

Abdul Rahman A. Al-Jafary, Ph.D., is Assistant Professor, College of Industrial Management, University of Petroleum & Minerals, Dhahran, Saudi Arabia.

Darrell W. Ray, Ed.D., is Director of Staff Development, State Youth Center, Atchison, Kansas.

John K. Ross is Assistant Professor of Management, School of Business, Southwest Texas State University.

Roberta Royal holds a master of science degree in nursing.

Bruce D. Sanders, Ph.D., is a consulting psychologist.

Gary Santavicca is affiliated with the Signa-ACORN Employee Assistance Program.

Craig Eric Schneier is Managing Principal and National Director of Human Resources and Organization at Sibson & Company, Inc.

Gary Schuman, Ph.D., is a consulting psychologist and Principal of Performance Management Corporation, an Alexandria, Virginia–based firm specializing in performance planning, career development, team building, sales training, employee motivation, and interpersonal communication.

Linda J. Segall is Human Resources Administrator, Training & Development, Aluminum Company of America.

Joseph Seltzer, Ph.D., is Associate Professor and Head of the Management Department at LaSalle University, Philadelphia, Pennsylvania.

James J. Semradek, Jr., is Associate, A. T. Kearney, Inc., Chicago, Illinois.

Arthur G. Sharp is a freelance writer from Rocky Hill, Connecticut.

Andrew Sherwood is Chairman of The Goodrich & Sherwood Company, the nation's largest full-service human resources management consulting firm.

John J. Sherwood is Professor of Organizational Psychology and Administrative Sciences, Purdue University.

Harvey H. Shore is Associate Professor of Industrial Administration, University of Connecticut.

Donald B. Simmons is a member of the Department of Speech Communications, Asbury College.

Michael Smith is Manager, Human Resource Development, Research-Cottrell.

Peg Snyder is President of The Snyder Consulting Group, a firm of organization development specialists based in Madison, Wisconsin. She is also a director and senior consultant of The Center for Managerial Growth and Development, headquartered in Washington, D.C.

L. Marshall Stellfox is Executive Vice President, The Goodrich & Sherwood Company.

John M. Stormes is Communications and Training Consultant, National Educational Media, Inc., Encino, California.

James B. Stull, Ph.D., is Professor at the School of Business, San Jose State University.

Rich Tewell is affiliated with The Mescon Group, organization design consultants located in Atlanta, Georgia.

Phyllis Thomas, Ph.D., is affiliated with Middle Tennessee State University, Murfreesboro, Tennessee.

Ken Thompson, Ph.D., is Assistant Professor of Management, College of Business Administration, University of Notre Dame.

Jean W. Vining, Ed.D., is Associate Professor of Office Administration, University of New Orleans.

Les Wallace is Assistant Professor, Department of Speech and Theatre Arts, Colorado State University.

Richard J. Walsh, Ph.D., is Director of Staff Development, American Appraisal Associates, Inc., Milwaukee, Wisconsin.

Harry A. Washing is with the School of Business Administration at The University of Dayton.

Marvin R. Weisbord is Senior Vice President, Block Petrella Weisbord.

Lars-Erik Wiberg is a consultant, specializing in career and organization planning, in Boston, Massachusetts.

Barbara L. Wiley is Team Manager, Gaines Food., Inc., Topeka, Kansas.

Janice Wilson, Ph.D., is Assistant Professor of Leadership Communication at East Tennessee State University.

Bob Wooten, Ph.D., is a member of the Management-Marketing-Finance Department, Lemar University.

Augusta C. Yrle, Ed.D., is Assistant Professor of Office Administration, University of New Orleans.

Donald G. Zauderer is Director of the Institute for Human Resource Development at The American University, Washington, D.C. Zauderer's research, teaching, and consultancy have focused on leadership development in private and public sector organizations.

Index